EXCELLENCE IN ELECTRICAL

ADDISON-WESLEY ⚛ THE SIGN

AND COMPUTER ENGINEERING

EXCELLENCE IN ELECTRICAL

ADDISON-WESLEY ⚛ THE SIGN

AND COMPUTER ENGINEERING

EXCELLENCE IN ELECTRICAL

ADDISON-WESLEY ⚛ THE SIGN

AND COMPUTER ENGINEERING

EXCELLENCE IN ELECTRICAL

ADDISON-WESLEY ⚛ THE SIGN

AND COMPUTER ENGINEERING

EXCELLENCE IN ELECTRICAL

ADDISON-WESLEY ⚛ THE SIGN

AND COMPUTER ENGINEERING

EXCELLENCE IN ELECTRICAL

ADDISON-WESLEY ⚛ THE SIGN

AND COMPUTER ENGINEERING

EXCELLENCE IN ELECTRICAL

ADDISON-WESLEY ⚛ THE SIGN

AND COMPUTER ENGINEERING

EXCELLENCE IN ELECTRICAL

ADDISON-WESLEY ⚛ THE SIGN

AND COMPUTER ENGINEERING

DIGITAL
IMAGE
PROCESSING
Second Edition

DIGITAL IMAGE PROCESSING

Second Edition

Rafael C. Gonzalez

Electrical Engineering Department
University of Tennessee
Knoxville
and
Perceptics Corporation
Knoxville, Tennessee

Paul Wintz

Consultant

ADDISON-WESLEY PUBLISHING COMPANY

Reading, Massachusetts · Menlo Park, California
Don Mills, Ontario · Wokingham, England
Amsterdam · Sydney · Singapore · Tokyo
Madrid · Bogotá · Santiago · San Juan

Library of Congress Cataloging-in-Publication Data

Gonzalez, Rafael C.
  Digital image processing.

  Bibliography: p.
  Includes index.
  1. Image processing—Digital techniques.   I. Wintz,
Paul A.   II. Title.
TA1632.G66   1987   621.36′7   86-28759
ISBN 0-201-11026-1

Reprinted with corrections November, 1987

FGHIJ-MA-898

To Connie, Ralph,
and Robert

PREFACE

Interest in digital image processing techniques dates back to the early 1920s when digitized pictures of world news events were first transmitted by submarine cable between New York and London. Applications of digital image processing concepts, however, did not become widespread until the middle 1960s, when third-generation digital computers began to offer the speed and storage capabilities required for practical implementation of image processing algorithms. Since then, this area has experienced vigorous growth, having been a subject of interdisciplinary study and research in such fields as engineering, computer science, information science, statistics, physics, chemistry, biology, and medicine. The results of these efforts have established the value of image processing techniques in a variety of problems ranging from restoration and enhancement of space-probe pictures to processing of fingerprints for commercial transactions. The continued rapid growth of this field has prompted us to prepare a second edition of *Digital Image Processing,* which contains extensive revisions and new material not found in the original text.

As in the first edition, the principal objectives of this book are to provide an introduction to basic concepts and techniques for digital image processing and to lay a foundation that can be used as the basis for further study and research in this field. To achieve these objectives, we have focused attention on material that we feel is fundamental and where the scope of application is not limited to specialized problems.

In this edition, the original material has been augmented by 49 new sections, 86 new figures, and over 100 new references. Problems have been included at the end of every chapter and an instructor's manual containing problem solutions and course recommendations is now available from the publisher. The mathematical level of the book continues to be well within the grasp of senior college students in a technical discipline, such as engineering or computer science, that requires introductory preparation in mathematical analysis, matrix theory, probability, and computer programming.

A brief overview of the new material is as follows. Chapter 2 has been extended to include additional discussions on geometric relationships between pixels, and a new section has been added that deals with arithmetic and logic operations via mask processing. We included this material because it has been increasingly used in hardware image processors during the past five years. We have also added a new section on imaging geometry that covers topics ranging from image translation, scaling, and rotation to perspective transformations, camera modeling, and stereo imaging. Chapter 3 has been expanded to include the Hough transform, a method that has become quite popular in recent years for feature extraction and characterization. Chapter 4 has been revised extensively and includes new sections on local enhancement techniques and the development of a method for generating spatial convolution masks from filters specified in the frequency domain. This latter material is also applicable to image restoration; an appropriate development of the method for this purpose has been included in Chapter 5. We have also added to that chapter a new section dealing with geometric transformations for image warping. This material, in conjunction with the new material in Chapter 2 dealing with perspective transformations, provides a comprehensive set of tools for altering the geometrical appearance of an image. The material in Chapter 6 has been revised, and references dealing with recent reviews of data compression techniques have been added. The original Chapter 7 dealing with segmentation and description has been totally rewritten, resulting in two separate chapters. The new Chapter 7 deals only with segmentation and covers material ranging from adaptive thresholding to the use of object motion in segmentation. Chapter 8 deals with representation and description and covers new material on topics such as boundary descriptors, skeletonizing techniques, textural descriptors, and descriptions of similarity.

It has been our experience that one of the principal features that attracts students to a course in image processing is the opportunity to implement and to test with real data the concepts and algorithms developed in the classroom. The ideal environment for this is provided by an image processing system that includes an image digitizer, a general-purpose computer, and image display equipment. The appendices to this book provide an alternative route for instruction when such a system is not available. Appendix A contains FORTRAN subroutines for displaying gray-tone images on an ordinary lineprinter, and Appendix B contains a set of coded images suitable for experimenting with the methods discussed in the text. This material can be utilized in conjunction with almost any general-purpose computer, thus allowing the reader to gain experience with image processing techniques through algorithm implementation and visual display of the results.

Digital Image Processing is one of three related books published by Addison-Wesley. The first of these, *Pattern Recognition Principles* (Tou and Gonzalez, 1974) describes deterministic, statistical, and syntactic pattern recognition concepts. This latter topic is treated in greater depth in *Syntactic Pattern Recognition: An Introduction* (Gonzalez and Thomason, 1978), which can be used by itself or as a supplement to *Pattern Recognition Principles*. The objective of these books is to provide a unified, introductory treatment of pattern recognition and image processing concepts with emphasis on fundamentals and consistency of notation.

R.C.G.
P.W.

ACKNOWLEDGMENTS

We are indebted to a number of individuals who, either through discussions or by providing the facilities for our work, have contributed to the preparation of this book. In particular, we wish to extend our appreciation to W.L. Green, W.T. Snyder, R.E. Woods, D. Brzakovic, J.H. Abel, E.L. Hall, J.M. Googe, F.N. Peebles, R.C. Kryter, M.T. Borelli, C.T. Huggins, M.G. Thomason, W.R. Wade, D.W. Bouldin, and W. Frei.

As is true with most projects carried out in a university environment, our students over the past few years have significantly influenced not only our thinking, but also the topics and material included in the text. The following individuals have worked with us in various aspects of digital image processing during the course of their graduate work at the University of Tennessee and at Purdue University: M. Abidi, C. Hayden, M. Goldston, D. Cate, R. Eason, A. Perez, J. Herrera, Z. Bell, F. Contrera, R. Salinas, J.D. Birdwell, B.A. Fittes, J.M. Harris, M.E. Casey, A. Miller, T.G. Saba, Po Chen, J. Duan, J. Essman, J. Gattis, J. Gupta, A. Habibi, C. Proctor, P. Ready, M. Tasto, W. Wilder, L. Wilkins, and T. Wallace.

We also wish to thank R.G. Gruber, G.S. Sodowski, and G.W. Roulette for their editorial assistance, G.C. Guerrant and R.E. Wright for the art work, and Michelle Bethel, Vicki Bohanan, Diana Scott, Mary Bearden, and Margaret Barbour for their excellent typing of the manuscript.

In addition, we express our appreciation to the Lockheed Missiles and Space Co., Westinghouse, Martin Marietta, the U.S. Customs Office, Texas Instruments, the U.S. Army, the National Science Foundation, the Center for Instrumentation and Control at the University of Tennessee, NORDA, the National Aeronautics and Space Administration, the Office of Naval Research, the Oak Ridge National Laboratory, and the Defense Advanced Research Projects Agency for their sponsorship of our research activities in image processing and pattern recognition.

Special thanks go to Tom Robbins of Addison-Wesley for his commitment to this book, to Laura Skinger for managing the project, and to Sherry Berg who did an excellent job supervising production.

Finally, we wish to acknowledge the individuals and organizations cited in the captions of numerous figures throughout the book for their permission to use that material.

CONTENTS

Chapter 6   IMAGE ENCODING

DIGITAL
IMAGE
PROCESSING
Second Edition

CHAPTER 1

INTRODUCTION

One picture is worth more than ten
thousand words.
Anonymous

1.1 BACKGROUND

Interest in digital image processing methods stems from two principal application areas: improvement of pictorial information for human interpretation, and processing of scene data for autonomous machine perception. One of the first applications of image processing techniques in the first category was in improving digitized newspaper pictures sent by submarine cable between London and New York. Introduction of the Bartlane cable picture transmission system in the early 1920s reduced the time required to transport a picture across the Atlantic from more than a week to less than three hours. Pictures were coded for cable transmission and then reconstructed at the receiving end by specialized printing equipment. Figure 1.1 was transmitted in this way and reproduced on a telegraph printer fitted with type faces simulating a halftone pattern.

Some of the initial problems in improving the visual quality of these early digital pictures were related to the selection of printing procedures and the distribution of brightness levels. The printing method used to obtain Fig. 1.1 was abandoned toward the end of 1921 in favor of a technique based on photographic reproduction made from tapes perforated at the telegraph receiving terminal. Figure 1.2 shows an image obtained using this method. The improvements over Fig. 1.1 are evident, both in tonal quality and in resolution.

The early Bartlane systems were capable of coding images in 5 distinct brightness levels. This capability was increased to 15 levels in 1929. Figure 1.3 is indicative of the type of image that could be obtained using the 15-tone equipment. During this period, the reproduction process was also improved considerably by the introduc-

Figure 1.1 A digital picture produced in 1921 from a coded tape by a telegraph printer with special type faces. (From McFarlane [1972].)

tion of a system for developing a film plate via light beams that were modulated by the coded picture tape.

Although improvements on processing methods for transmitted digital pictures continued to be made over the next 35 years, it took the combined advents of large-scale digital computers and the space program to bring into focus the potentials of image processing concepts. Work on using computer techniques for improving images from a space probe began at the Jet Propulsion Laboratory (Pasadena, Calif.) in 1964, when pictures of the moon transmitted by Ranger 7 were processed by a computer to correct various types of image distortion inherent in the on-board television camera. These techniques served as the basis for improved methods used in the enhancement and restoration of images from such familiar programs as the Surveyor missions to the moon, the Mariner series of flyby missions to Mars, and the Apollo manned flights to the moon.

From 1964 until this writing, the field of image processing has experienced vigorous growth. In addition to applications in the space program, digital image processing techniques are used today in a variety of problems that, although often unrelated, share a common need for methods capable of enhancing pictorial information for human interpretation and analysis. In medicine, for instance, physicians are assisted by computer procedures that enhance the contrast or code the intensity levels into color for easier interpretation of x-rays and other biomedical images. The same or similar techniques are used by geographers in studying pollution patterns from aerial and satellite imagery. Image enhancement and restoration procedures

Figure 1.2 A digital picture made from a tape punched after the signals had crossed the Atlantic twice. Some errors are visible. (From McFarlane [1972].)

Figure 1.3 Unretouched cable picture of Generals Pershing and Foch, transmitted by 15-tone equipment from London to New York. (From McFarlane [1972].)

have been used to process degraded images depicting unrecoverable objects or experimental results too expensive to duplicate. There have been instances in archeology, for example, where blurred pictures that were the only available records of rare artifacts lost or damaged after being photographed, have been successfully restored by image processing methods. In physics and related fields, images of experiments in such areas as high-energy plasmas and electron microscopy are routinely enhanced by computer techniques. Similar successful applications of image processing concepts can be found in astronomy, biology, nuclear medicine, law enforcement, defense, and industrial applications.

Some typical examples of the results obtainable with digital image processing techniques are shown in Fig. 1.4. The original images are shown on the left and the corresponding computer-processed images on the right. Figure 1.4(a) is a picture of the Martian surface that was corrupted by interference during transmission to Earth by a space probe. The interference, which in this case appears as a set of vertical, structured lines, can be almost completely removed by computer processing, as shown in Fig. 1.4(b). Figures 1.4(c) and (d) illustrate the considerable improvement that can be made on an x-ray image by contrast and edge enhancement. The image shown in Fig. 1.4(e) was blurred by uniform motion during exposure, and the image shown in Fig. 1.4(f) resulted after application of a deblurring algorithm. These illustrations are typical of those discussed in detail in Chapters 4 and 5.

The foregoing examples have in common the fact that processing results are intended for human interpretation. The second major area of application of digital image processing techniques mentioned at the beginning of this section is in problems dealing with machine perception. In this case, interest is focused on procedures for

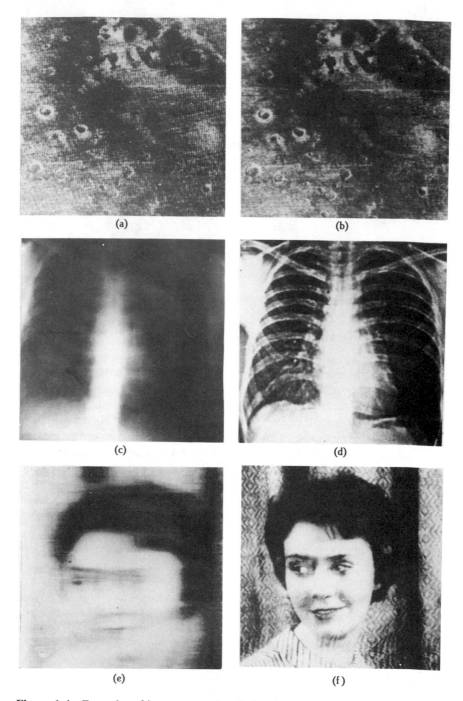

(a)

(b)

(c)

(d)

(e)

(f)

Figure 1.4 Examples of image processing. Left column: original digital images. Right column: images after processing.

extracting from an image information in a form suitable for computer processing. Often, this information bears little resemblance to visual features used by humans in interpreting the content of an image. Examples of the type of information used in machine perception are statistical moments, Fourier transform coefficients, and multidimensional distance measures.

Typical problems in machine perception that routinely employ image processing techniques are automatic character recognition, industrial robots for product assembly and inspection, military recognizance, automatic processing of fingerprints, screening of x-rays and blood samples, and machine processing of aerial and satellite imagery for weather prediction and crop assessment.

1.2 DIGITAL IMAGE REPRESENTATION

As used in this book, the term *monochrome image* or simply *image*, refers to a two-dimensional light intensity function $f(x, y)$, where x and y denote spatial coordinates and the value of f at any point (x, y) is proportional to the brightness (or *gray level*) of the image at that point. An example illustrating the axis convention used throughout the following chapters is shown in Fig. 1.5. It is sometimes useful

Figure 1.5 Axis convention used for digital image representation.

to view an image function in perspective with the third axis being brightness. If Fig. 1.5 were viewed in this way it would appear as a series of active peaks in regions with numerous changes in brightness levels and smoother regions or plateaus where the brightness levels varied little or were constant. If we follow the convention of assigning proportionately higher values to brighter areas, the height of the components in the plot would be proportional to the corresponding brightness in the image.

A *digital image* is an image $f(x, y)$ that has been discretized both in spatial coordinates and in brightness. We may consider a digital image as a matrix whose row and column indices identify a point in the image and the corresponding matrix element value identifies the gray level at that point. The elements of such a digital array are called *image elements, picture elements, pixels,* or *pels,* with the last two names being commonly used abbreviations of "picture elements."

Although the size of a digital image varies with the application, it will become evident in the following chapters that there are numerous advantages to selecting square arrays with sizes and number of gray levels that are integer powers of 2. For example, a typical size comparable in quality to a monochrome TV image is a 512×512 array with 128 gray levels.

With the exception of a discussion in Chapter 4 of pseudo-color techniques for image enhancement, all the images considered in this book are digital monochrome images of the form described above. Thus we will not be concerned with topics in three-dimensional scene analysis nor with optical techniques for image processing.

1.3   ELEMENTS OF A DIGITAL IMAGE PROCESSING SYSTEM

The components of a basic, general-purpose digital image processing system are shown in Fig. 1.6. The operation of each block in Fig. 1.6 is explained briefly below.

1.3.1   Image Processors

A digital image processor is the heart of any image processing system. An image processor consists of a set of hardware modules that perform four basic functions: image acquisition, storage, low-level (fast) processing, and display. Typically, the image acquisition module has a TV signal as the input (see Section 1.3.2) and converts this signal into digital form, both spatially and in amplitude (see Section 2.3). Most modern image processors are capable of digitizing a TV image in one frame-time (i.e., 1/30th of a second). For this reason, the image acquisition module is often referred to as a *frame grabber*.

The storage module, often called a *frame buffer*, is a memory capable of storing an entire digital image. Usually, several such modules are incorporated in an image processor. The single most distinguishing characteristic of an image storage module is that the contents of the memory can be loaded or read at TV rates (on the order of 30 images per second). This feature allows the image acquisition module to

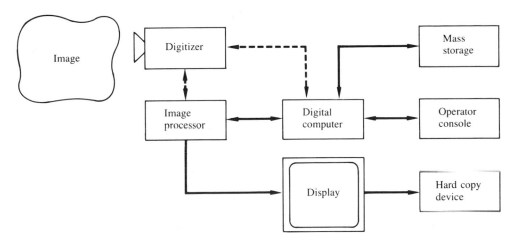

Figure 1.6   Elements of a digital image processing system. The dashed lines indicate that typically only one of the two connections is made.

deposit a complete image into storage as fast as it is being grabbed. Conversely, the memory can be addressed at TV rates by a display module, which outputs the image to a TV monitor, as discussed in Section 1.3.5. Other memory-addressing modes allow virtually instantaneous image *zoom*, as well as *scroll* (vertical shifts) and *pan* (horizontal shifts).

The processing module performs low-level functions such as arithmetic and logic operations. Thus this module is often called an *Arithmetic-Logic Unit* (ALU). It is a specialized hardware device designed specifically to gain speed by processing pixels in parallel. The function of the display module is to read an image memory, convert the stored digital information into an analog video signal, and output this signal to a TV monitor or other video device. Typical additional hardware display options include gray-level transformation functions and graphics, as well as alphanumeric overlays.

1.3.2 Digitizers

A digitizer converts an image into a numerical representation suitable for input into a digital computer. Among the most commonly used input devices are microdensitometers, flying spot scanners, image dissectors, vidicon cameras, and photosensitive solid-state arrays. The first two devices require that the image to be digitized be in the form of a transparency (e.g., a film negative) or photograph. Image dissectors, vidicon cameras, and solid-state arrays can accept images recorded in this manner, but they have the additional advantage of being able to digitize natural images that have sufficient light intensity to excite the detector.

In microdensitometers the transparency or photograph is mounted on a flat bed or wrapped around a drum. Scanning is accomplished by focusing a beam of light on the image and translating the bed or rotating the drum in relation to the beam. In the case of transparencies the beam passes through the film; in photographs it is reflected from the surface of the image. In both cases the beam is focused on a photodetector and the gray level at any point in the image is recorded by the detector based on the intensity of the beam. A digital image is obtained by allowing only discrete values of intensity and position in the output. Although microdensitometers are slow devices, they are capable of high degrees of position accuracy due to the essentially continuous nature of the mechanical translation used in the digitization process.

Flying spot scanners also operate on the principle of focusing a transmitted or reflected source beam on a photodetector. In this case, however, the image is stationary and the light source is a cathode-ray tube (CRT) in which a beam of electrons, deflected by electromagnets, impinges on a fluorescent phosphor surface. The beam thereby produces a spot of light that moves in a scanning pattern on the face of the tube. The fact that the beam is moved electronically allows high scanning speeds. Flying spot scanners are also ideally suited for applications in which it is desirable to control the beam scanning pattern externally (e.g., in tracing the boundaries of objects in an image). This flexibility is afforded by the fact that the position of the electron beam is quickly and easily established by external voltage signals applied to the electromagnets.

In image dissectors and vidicon cameras the image is focused directly on the surface of a photosensitive tube whose response is proportional to the incident light pattern. Dissector operation is based on the principle of electronic emission, where the image incident on the photosensitive surface produces an electron beam whose cross section is roughly the same as the geometry of the tube surface. Image pickup is accomplished by using electromagnets to deflect the entire beam past a pinhole located in the back of the dissector tube. The pinhole lets through only a small cross section of the beam and thus "looks" at one point in the image at a time. Since photoemissive materials are very inefficient, the time that the pinhole has to look at the point source in order to collect enough electrons tends to make image dissectors rather slow digitizers. Most devices integrate the emission of each input point over a specified time interval before yielding a signal that is proportional to the brightness of the point. This integration capability is beneficial in terms of noise reduction, thus making image dissectors attractive in applications where high signal-to-noise ratios are required. As in flying spot scanners, control of the scanning pattern in image dissectors is easily varied by external voltage signals applied to the electromagnets.

The operation of vidicon cameras is based on the principle of photoconductivity. An image focused on the tube surface produces a pattern of varying conductivity that matches the distribution of brightness in the optical image. An independent, finely focused electron beam scans the rear surface of the photoconductive target, and, by charge neutralization, this beam creates a potential difference that produces on a collector a signal proportional to the input brightness pattern. A digital image is obtained by quantizing this signal, as well as the corresponding position of the scanning beam.

Solid-state arrays are composed of discrete silicon imaging elements, called *photosites*, that have a voltage output proportional to the intensity of the incident light. Solid-state arrays are organized in one of two principal geometrical arrangements: *line scan sensors* and *area sensors*. A line scan sensor consists of a row of photosites and produces a two-dimensional image by relative motion between the scene and the detector. An area sensor is composed of a matrix of photosites and is therefore capable of capturing an image in the same manner as, say, a vidicon tube.

Vidicon and area sensors are typically packaged as TV cameras. Image digitization is achieved by feeding the output of the camera into the image acquisition module, as discussed in the previous section. Although TV cameras are in general less accurate than the systems discussed above, they have numerous advantages that in many applications outweigh their relative lack of precision. Vidicon systems, for example, are among the most inexpensive digitizers in the market. They also have the distinct advantage that the image being digitized can be viewed in its entirety on a TV monitor. This capability, not available in any of the systems discussed above, is ideal for general-purpose applications.

1.3.3 Digital Computers

Although, as mentioned in Section 1.3.1, an image processor may be equipped with internal processing capabilities, the level of this processing is rather low in sophistication. Thus one usually finds that image processors are interfaced to a general-purpose computer, which provides versatility as well as ease of programming. Computer systems used for image processing range from microprocessor devices to large computer systems capable of performing computationally intensive functions on large image arrays. The principal parameters influencing the structure of a computer for image processing are the intended application and the required data throughput. For dedicated applications (which normally dictate low cost) a well-equipped microcomputer or minicomputer will often be sufficient. If the application involves extensive program development or is characterized by significant data throughputs, a mainframe computer would most likely be required. In this case, a computer with virtual memory addressing capabilities has significant advantages. Virtual addressing makes disk peripheral storage available to the user as if it were main memory. This feature, which is transparent to the user, is of crucial importance because digital images utilize large amounts of memory during processing. The alternative to virtual addressing is a set of user-supplied complex routines whose only function is to swap image segments in and out of peripheral storage during processing.

1.3.4   Storage Devices

A digital image consisting of 512 × 512 pixels, each of which is quantized into eight bits, requires 0.25 megabytes of storage. Thus providing adequate bulk storage facilities is one of the most important aspects in the design of a general-purpose image processing system. The three principal storage media used in this type of work are magnetic disks, magnetic tapes, and optical disks. Magnetic disks with a capacity of 700 megabytes or more are common. A 700-megabyte disk would hold on the order of 2800 images of the size mentioned above. High-density magnetic tapes (6400 bytes per inch) can store one such image in approximately four feet of tape. Optical disks, which are based on laser writing and reading technology, have recently become commercially available. The storage capacity of a single optical disk platter can approach 4 gigabytes, which translates into approximately 16,000 images per disk.

1.3.5   Display and Recording Devices

Monochrome and color television monitors are the principal display devices used in modern image processing systems. Monitors are driven by the output(s) of the image display module in the image processor, as discussed in Section 1.3.1. These signals can also be fed into an image recording device whose function is to produce a hard copy (slides, photographs, and transparencies) of the image being viewed on the monitor screen. Other display media include CRTs and printing devices.

In CRT systems the horizontal and vertical positions of each element in the image array are converted into voltages that are used to deflect the CRT's electron beam, thus providing the two-dimensional drive necessary to produce an output image. At each deflection point, the intensity of the beam is modulated by using a voltage that is proportional to the value of the corresponding point in the numerical array, varying from zero intensity outputs for points whose numerical value corresponds to black, to maximum intensity for white points. The resulting variable-intensity light pattern is recorded by a photographic camera focused on the face of the cathode-ray tube. Some systems employ a long-persistence phosphor tube, which also allows viewing of the entire image after the scanning process is completed. Although images recorded by a photographic process can be of excellent quality, the same images generally appear of poor tonality when shown to an observer on a long-persistence CRT because of limitations in the human visual system when responding to this type of display.

Printing image display devices are useful primarily for low-resolution image processing work. One simple approach for generating gray-tone images directly on paper is to use the overstrike capability of a standard line printer. The gray level of any point in the printout can be controlled by the number and density of the characters overprinted at that point. By properly selecting the character set it is possible to achieve reasonably good gray-level distributions with a simple computer program and relatively few characters. An example of this approach is given in

Appendix A. Other common means of recording an image directly on paper include laser printers, heat-sensitive paper devices, and ink-spray systems.

1.4   ORGANIZATION OF THE BOOK

Techniques for image processing may be divided into four principal categories: (1) image digitization; (2) image enhancement and restoration; (3) image encoding; and (4) image segmentation, representation, and description. The material in the following chapters is organized in essentially the same order as these problem areas.

As discussed in Sections 1.2 and 1.3, the digitization problem is one of converting continuous brightness and spatial coordinates into discrete components. A preliminary discussion of digitization and its effect on image quality is given in Chapter 2, while a more theoretical treatment of the sampling process is developed in Chapter 3. Digitization considerations are a natural extension of the main theme of these two chapters, which is the introduction of concepts and mathematical tools used throughout the rest of the book.

Enhancement and restoration techniques deal with the improvement of a given image for human or machine perception. Image enhancement is the topic of Chapter 4, while image restoration methods are covered in Chapter 5. Image encoding procedures, discussed in Chapter 6, are used to reduce the number of bits in a digital image. The encoding process often plays a central role in image processing for the purpose of minimizing storage or transmission requirements. Segmentation techniques are considered in Chapter 7. Segmentation is the process that subdivides an image into its constituent regions or objects. Chapter 8 deals with representation and description, which are important processes in the implementation of autonomous image processing and analysis systems.

Two appendices are included at the end of the book. Appendix A contains a set of FORTRAN routines for displaying images on an ordinary line printer. Appendix B contains a set of coded digital images, which together with the routines in Appendix A, can be used to test with pictorial data the methods developed in the book.

REFERENCES

The references cited below are of a general nature and cover the spectrum of available image processing techniques and their applications. References given at the end of later chapters are keyed to specific topics discussed in the text. All references are cited by author, book, or journal name followed by the year of publication. The bibliography at the end of the book is organized in the same way and contains all pertinent information for each reference.

Some of the major journals that publish articles on image processing and related topics include: *Computer Vision, Graphics, and Image Processing, IEEE Transactions on Systems, Man and Cybernetics, IEEE Transactions on Pattern Analysis and Machine Intelligence, Pattern Recognition, IEEE Transactions on Medical Imaging, Journal of the Optical Society of America, IEEE Transactions on Information Theory, IEEE Transactions on Communications, IEEE Transac-*

tions on Acoustics, Speech and Signal Processing, Proceedings of the IEEE, and issues of the *IEEE Transactions on Computers* prior to 1980.

Other image processing books of interest include Andrews [1970], Pratt [1978], Castleman [1979], Hall [1979], and Rosenfeld and Kak [1982]. The literature on pattern recognition often contains articles related to image processing. The books by Duda and Hart [1973], Tou and Gonzalez [1974], Pavlidis [1977], Gonzalez and Thomason [1978], and Fu [1982] contain a guide to the literature on pattern recognition and related topics.

CHAPTER 2

DIGITAL IMAGE FUNDAMENTALS

Those who wish to succeed must ask the right preliminary questions.
Aristotle

The purpose of this chapter is to introduce the reader to a number of image concepts and to develop some of the notation that will be used throughout the book. The first section is a brief summary of the mechanics of the human visual system, including image formation in the eye and its capabilities for brightness adaptation and discrimination. Section 2.2 presents an image model based on the illumination–reflection phenomenon, which gives rise to most images perceived in our normal visual activities. The concepts of uniform image sampling and gray-level quantization are introduced in Section 2.3. Section 2.4 deals with relationships between pixels, such as connectivity and distance measures, which will be used extensively throughout the book. Section 2.5 contains a detailed discussion of imaging geometry and related topics. Finally, Section 2.6 contains an introduction to photographic film and some of its most important characteristics in terms of recording image processing results.

2.1 ELEMENTS OF VISUAL PERCEPTION

Since the ultimate goal of many of the techniques discussed in the following chapters is to aid the observer in interpreting the content of an image, it is important before proceeding to develop a basic understanding of the visual-perception process. The following discussion is a brief account of the human visual mechanism, with particular emphasis on concepts that will serve as a foundation to much of the material presented in later chapters.

2.1.1   Structure of the Human Eye

A horizontal cross section of the human eye is shown in Fig. 2.1. The eye is nearly spherical in form with an average diameter of approximately 20 mm. It is enclosed by three membranes: the *cornea* and *sclera* outer cover, the *choroid,* and the *retina.* The cornea is a tough, transparent tissue that covers the anterior surface of the eye. The sclera is continuous with the cornea; it is an opaque membrane that encloses the remainder of the optic globe.

   The choroid lies directly below the sclera. This membrane contains a network of blood vessels that serve as the major source of nutrition to the eye. The choroid coat is heavily pigmented and hence helps to reduce the amount of extraneous

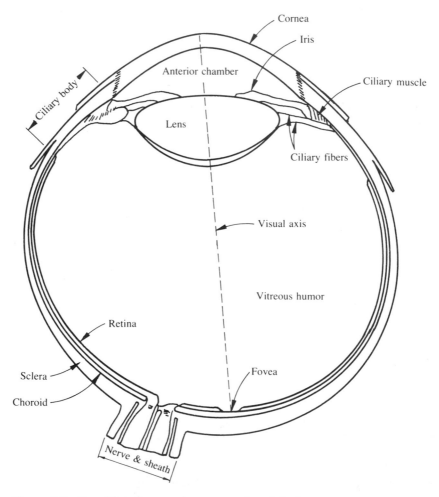

Figure 2.1   Simplified diagram of a cross section of the human eye.

light entering the eye and the backscatter within the optical globe. At its anterior extreme, the choroid is divided into the *ciliary body* and the *iris diaphragm*. The latter contracts or expands to control the amount of light that is permitted to enter the eye. The central opening of the iris (the *pupil*) is variable in diameter from approximately 2 mm up to 8 mm. The front of the iris contains the visible pigment of the eye, whereas the back contains a black pigment.

The innermost membrane of the eye is the retina, which lines the inside of the wall's entire posterior portion. When the eye is properly focused, light from an object outside the eye is imaged on the retina. Pattern vision is afforded by the distribution of discrete light receptors over the surface of the retina. There are two classes of receptors: *cones* and *rods*. The cones in each eye number between 6 and 7 million. They are located primarily in the central portion of the retina, called the *fovea*, and are highly sensitive to color. Humans can resolve fine details with these cones largely because each one is connected to its own nerve end. Muscles controlling the eye rotate the eyeball until the image of an object of interest falls on the fovea. Cone vision is known as *photopic* or bright-light vision.

The number of rods is much larger, being on the order of 75 to 150 million distributed over the retinal surface. The larger area of distribution and the fact that several rods are connected to a single nerve end reduce the amount of detail discernible by these receptors. Rods serve to give a general, overall picture of the field of view. They are not involved in color vision and are sensitive to low levels of illumination. For example, objects that appear brightly colored in daylight, when seen by moonlight appear as colorless forms because only the rods are stimulated. This is known as *scotopic* or dim-light vision.

The *lens* is made up of concentric layers of fibrous cells and is suspended by fibers that attach to the ciliary body. It contains 60 to 70 percent water, about 6 percent fat, and more protein than any other tissue in the eye. The lens is colored by a slightly yellow pigmentation that increases with age. It absorbs approximately 8 percent of the visible light spectrum, with relatively higher absorption at shorter wavelengths. Both infrared and ultraviolet light are absorbed appreciably by proteins within the lens structure and, in excessive amounts, can cause damage to the eye.

2.1.2 Image Formation in the Eye

The principal difference between the lens of the eye and an ordinary optical lens is that the former is flexible. As illustrated in Fig. 2.1, the radius of curvature of the anterior surface of the lens is greater than the radius of its posterior surface. The shape of the lens is controlled by the tension in the fibers of the ciliary body. To focus on distant objects, the controlling muscles cause the lens to be relatively flattened. Similarly, these muscles allow the lens to become thicker in order to focus on objects near the eye.

The distance between the focal center of the lens and the retina varies from approximately 17 mm down to about 14 mm, as the refractive power of the lens increases from its minimum to its maximum. When the eye is focused on an object farther than about 3 m away, the lens exhibits its lowest refractive power, and when focused on a very near object it is most strongly refractive. With this information, it is easy to calculate the size of the retinal image of any object. In Fig. 2.2, for example, the observer is looking at a tree 15 m high at a distance of 100 m. Letting x be the size of the retinal image in millimeters, we have from the geometry of Fig. 2.2 that $15/100 = x/17$ or $x = 2.55$ mm. As indicated in the previous section, the retinal image is reflected primarily in the area of the fovea. Perception then takes place by the relative excitation of light receptors, which transform radiant energy into electrical impulses that are ultimately decoded by the brain.

2.1.3 Brightness Adaptation and Discrimination

Since digital images are displayed as a discrete set of brightness points, the ability of the eye to discriminate between different brightness levels is an important consideration in presenting image processing results.

The range of light intensity levels to which the human visual system can adapt is enormous, being on the order of 10^{10} from the scotopic threshold to the glare limit. There is also considerable experimental evidence that indicates that subjective brightness (i.e., brightness as perceived by the human visual system) is a logarithmic function of the light intensity incident on the eye. This characteristic is illustrated in Fig. 2.3, which is a plot of light intensity versus subjective brightness. The long solid curve represents the range of intensities to which the visual system can adapt. In photopic vision alone, the range is about 10^6. The transition from scotopic to photopic vision is gradual over the approximate range from 0.001 to 0.1 millilambert (-3 to -1 mL in the log scale), as illustrated by the double branches of the adaptation curve in this range.

The key point in interpreting the impressive dynamic range depicted in Fig. 2.3 is that the visual system can by no means operate over such a range *simultaneously*. Rather, it accomplishes this large variation by changes in its overall sensitivity, a

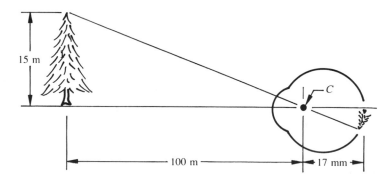

Figure 2.2 Optical representation of the eye looking at a tree. Point C is the optical center of the lens.

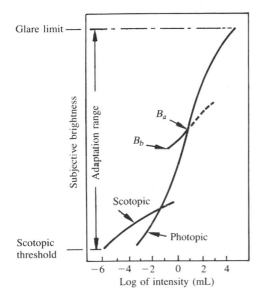

Figure 2.3 Range of subjective brightness sensations showing a particular adaptation level.

phenomenon known as *brightness adaptation*. The total range of intensity levels it can discriminate simultaneously is rather small when compared with the total adaptation range. For any given set of conditions, the current sensitivity level of the visual system is called the *brightness-adaptation level*, which may correspond, for example, to brightness B_a in Fig. 2.3. The short intersecting curve represents the range of subjective brightness that the eye can perceive when adapted to this level. It is noted that this range is rather restricted, having a level B_b at and below which all stimuli are perceived as indistinguishable blacks. The upper (dashed) portion of the curve is not actually restricted but, if extended too far, loses its meaning because much higher intensities would simply raise the adaptation level to a higher value than B_a.

The contrast sensitivity of the eye can be measured by exposing an observer to a uniform field of light of brightness B, with a sharp-edged circular target in the center, of brightness $B + \Delta B$, as shown in Fig. 2.4(a). ΔB is increased from zero until it is just noticeable. The just-noticeable difference ΔB is measured as a function of B. The quantity $\Delta B/B$ is called the Weber ratio and is nearly constant at about 2 percent over a very wide range of brightness levels, as shown in Fig. 2.4(b). This phenomenon has given rise to the idea that the human eye has a much wider dynamic range than manmade imaging systems. However, this does not correspond to any ordinary seeing situation and more-applicable results are obtained by using the pattern of Fig. 2.5(a). $\Delta B/B$ is again measured, but now B_0, the surrounding (adapting) brightness, is a parameter. The results are shown in Fig. 2.5(b). The dynamic range is about 2.2 log units centered about the adapting brightness, which is compara-

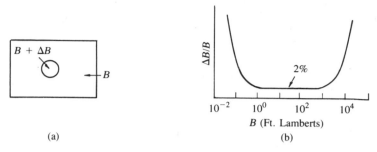

(a)   (b)

Figure 2.4   Contrast sensitivity with a constant background.

ble to what can be achieved with electronic imaging systems if they are correctly
adjusted for the background brightness. The ease and rapidity with which the eye
adapts itself—differently on different parts of the retina—is really the remarkable
characteristic, rather than its overall dynamic range. What is meant by a dynamic
range of 2.2 log units is that $\Delta B/B$ remains relatively constant in this range. As B
becomes more and more different from the adapting brightness B_0, the appearance
also changes. Thus a brightness about 1.5 log units higher or lower than B_0 appears
white or black, respectively. If the central target is set at a constant level while B_0
is varied over a wide range, the target appears to change from completely white to
completely black.

In the case of a complex image, the visual system does not adapt to a single
intensity level. Instead, it adapts to an average level that depends on the properties
of the image. As the eye roams about the scene, the instantaneous adaptation level
fluctuates about this average. For any point or small area in the image, the Weber
ratio is generally much larger than that obtained in an experimental environment
because of the lack of sharply defined boundaries and intensity variations in the

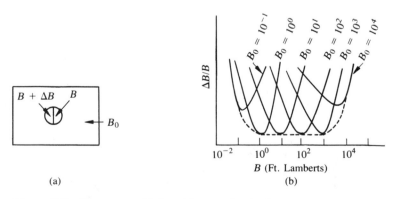

(a)   (b)

Figure 2.5   Contrast sensitivity with a varying background.

background. The result is that the eye can detect only in the neighborhood of one or two dozen intensity levels at any one point in a complex image. This does not mean, however, that an image need only be displayed in two dozen intensity levels to achieve satisfactory visual results. The above narrow discrimination range "tracks" the adaptation level as the latter changes in order to accommodate different intensity levels following eye movements about the scene. This allows a much larger range of *overall* intensity discrimination. To obtain displays that will appear reasonably smooth to the eye for a large class of image types, a range of over 100 intensity levels is generally required. This point will be considered in further detail in Section 2.3.

The brightness of a region, as perceived by the eye, depends on factors other than simply the light radiating from that region. In terms of image processing applications, one of the most interesting phenomena related to brightness perception is that the response of the human visual system tends to "overshoot" around the boundary of regions of different intensity. The result of this overshoot is to make areas of constant intensity appear as if they had varying brightness. In Fig. 2.6(a), for example, the image shown was created by varying the intensity according to the intensity profile shown below the photograph. Although the intensity variation is perfectly smooth, the eye perceives a brighter stripe in the region marked B and a darker stripe in the region marked D. These stripes are called *Mach bands*, after Ernst Mach who first described them in 1865. A more striking example of the Mach-band effect is shown in Fig. 2.6(b). As indicated by the intensity profile, each band in the photograph was created by using a constant intensity. To the eye, however, the brightness pattern in the image appears strongly scalloped, particularly around the boundaries.

2.2 AN IMAGE MODEL

As used in this book, the term *image* refers to a two-dimensional light-intensity function, denoted by $f(x, y)$, where the value or amplitude of f at spatial coordinates (x, y) gives the intensity (brightness) of the image at that point. Since light is a form of energy, $f(x, y)$ must be nonzero and finite, that is,

$$0 < f(x, y) < \infty. \tag{2.2-1}$$

The images we perceive in our everyday visual activities normally consist of light reflected from objects. The basic nature of $f(x, y)$ may be considered as being characterized by two components. One component is the amount of source light incident on the scene being viewed, while the other is the amount of light reflected by the objects in the scene. These components are appropriately called the *illumination* and *reflectance components*, and are denoted by $i(x, y)$ and $r(x, y)$, respectively. The functions $i(x, y)$ and $r(x, y)$ combine as a product to form $f(x, y)$:

$$f(x, y) = i(x, y)r(x, y), \tag{2.2-2}$$

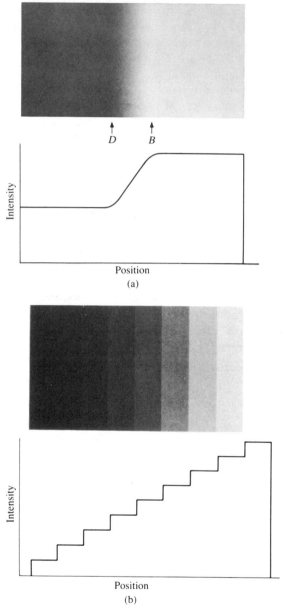

Figure 2.6   Examples of the Mach-band effect. (From Cornsweet [1970].)

where

$$0 < i(x, y) < \infty \tag{2.2-3}$$

and

$$0 < r(x, y) < 1. \tag{2.2-4}$$

Equation (2.2-4) indicates the fact that reflectance is bounded by 0 (total absorption) and 1 (total reflectance). The nature of $i(x, y)$ is determined by the light source, while $r(x, y)$ is determined by the characteristics of the objects in a scene.

The values given in Eqs. (2.2-3) and (2.2-4) are theoretical bounds. The following *average* numerical figures illustrate some typical ranges of $i(x, y)$. On a clear day, the sun may produce in excess of 9000 foot-candles of illumination on the surface of the earth. This figure decreases to less than 1000 foot-candles on a cloudy day. On a clear evening, a full moon yields about 0.01 foot-candle of illumination. The typical illumination level in a commercial office is about 100 foot-candles. Similarly, the following are some typical values of $r(x, y)$: 0.01 for black velvet, 0.65 for stainless steel, 0.80 for flat-white wall paint, 0.90 for silver-plated metal, and 0.93 for snow.

Throughout this book, the intensity of a monochrome image f at coordinates (x, y) will be called the *gray level* (l) of the image at that point. From Eqs. (2.2-2) through (2.2-4), it is evident that l lies in the range

$$L_{min} \leq l \leq L_{max}. \tag{2.2-5}$$

In theory, the only requirement on L_{min} is that it be positive, and on L_{max} that it be finite. In practice, $L_{min} = i_{min} r_{min}$ and $L_{max} = i_{max} r_{max}$. Using the above values of illumination and reflectance as a guideline, one may expect the values $L_{min} \approx 0.005$ and $L_{max} \approx 100$ for indoor image processing applications.

The interval $[L_{min}, L_{max}]$ is called the *gray scale*. It is common practice to shift this interval numerically to the interval $[0, L]$, where $l = 0$ is considered black and $l = L$ is considered white in the scale. All intermediate values are shades of gray varying continuously from black to white.

2.3 SAMPLING AND QUANTIZATION

2.3.1 Uniform Sampling and Quantization

In order to be in a form suitable for computer processing, an image function $f(x, y)$ must be digitized both spatially and in amplitude. Digitization of the spatial coordinates (x, y) will be referred to as *image sampling*, while amplitude digitization will be called *gray level quantization*.

Suppose that a continuous image $f(x, y)$ is approximated by equally spaced samples arranged in the form of an $N \times N$ array[†] as shown in Eq. (2.3-1), where

---

[†] Digitization of an image need not be limited to square arrays. However, following discussions will often be simplified by the adoption of this convention.

each element of the array is a discrete quantity:

$$
f(x, y) \approx
\begin{bmatrix}
f(0, 0) & f(0, 1) & \cdots & f(0, N-1) \\
f(1, 0) & f(1, 1) & \cdots & f(1, N-1) \\
\cdot & & & \\
\cdot & & & \\
\cdot & & & \\
f(N-1, 0) & f(N-1, 1) & \cdots & f(N-1, N-1)
\end{bmatrix}
\tag{2.3-1}
$$

The right side of this equation represents what is commonly called a *digital image*, while each element of the array is referred to as an *image element, picture element, pixel,* or *pel,* as indicated in Section 1.2. The terms "image" and "pixels" will be used throughout the following discussions to denote a digital image and its elements.

The above digitization process requires that a decision be made on a value for N as well as on the number of discrete gray levels allowed for each pixel. It is common practice in digital image processing to let these quantities be integer powers of two; that is,

$$
N = 2^n
\tag{2.3-2}
$$

and

$$
G = 2^m,
\tag{2.3-3}
$$

where G denotes the number of gray levels. It is assumed in this section that the discrete levels are equally spaced between 0 and L in the gray scale. Using Eqs. (2.3-2) and (2.3-3) the number, b, of bits required to store a digitized image is given by

$$
b = N \times N \times m.
\tag{2.3-4}
$$

Table 2.1   Number of Storage Bits for Various Values of N and m

N \ m	1	2	3	4	5	6	7	8
32	1,024	2,048	3,072	4,096	5,120	6,144	7,168	8,192
64	4,096	8,192	12,288	16,384	20,480	24,576	28,672	32,768
128	16,384	32,768	49,152	65,536	81,920	98,304	114,688	131,072
256	65,536	131,072	196,608	262,144	327,680	393,216	458,752	524,288
512	262,144	524,288	786,432	1,048,576	1,310,720	1,572,864	1,835,008	2,097,152

Table 2.2 Number of 8-bit Bytes of Storage for Various Values of N and m

N \ m	1	2	3	4	5	6	7	8
32	128	256	512	512	1,024	1,024	1,024	1,024
64	512	1,024	2,048	2,048	4,096	4,096	4,096	4,096
128	2,048	4,096	8,192	8,192	16,384	16,384	16,384	16,384
256	8,192	16,384	32,768	32,768	65,536	65,536	65,536	65,536
512	32,768	65,536	131,072	131,072	262,144	262,144	262,144	262,144

For example, a 128 × 128 image with 64 gray levels requires 98,304 bits of storage. Table 2.1 summarizes values of b for some typical ranges of N and m. Table 2.2 gives the corresponding number of 8-bit bytes. Generally, it is not practical from a programming point of view to fill a byte completely if this implies a pixel overlap from one byte to the next. Thus the figures in Table 2.2 represent the minimum number of bytes needed for each value of N and m when no overlap is allowed. For example, if $m = 5$, it is assumed that only one pixel is stored in a byte, even though this leaves three unused bits in the byte.

Since Eq. (2.3-1) is an approximation to a continuous image, a reasonable question to ask at this point is how many samples and gray levels are required for a good approximation. The *resolution* (i.e., the degree of discernible detail) of an image is strongly dependent on both N and m. The more these parameters are increased, the closer the digitized array will approximate the original image. However, Eq. (2.3-4) clearly points out the unfortunate fact that storage and, consequently, processing requirements increase rapidly as a function of N and m.

In view of the above comments, it is of interest to consider the effect that variations in N and m have on image quality. As might be suspected, a "good" image is difficult to define because quality requirements vary according to application. Figure 2.7 shows the effect of reducing the sampling-grid size on an image. Figure 2.7(a) is a 512 × 512, 256-level image showing Astronaut Buzz Aldrin during the first moon landing (note the reflection of Neil Armstrong on the face plate). Figures 2.7(b) through (f) show the same image, but with $N = 256, 128, 64, 32,$ and 16. In all cases the maximum number of allowed gray levels was kept at 256. Since the display area used for each image was the same (i.e., 512 × 512 display points), pixels in the lower-resolution images were duplicated in order to fill the entire display field. This produced a checkerboard effect, which is particularly noticeable in the low-resolution images. It is noted that the 256 × 256 image is reasonably close to Fig. 2.7(a), but image quality deteriorated rapidly for the other values of N.

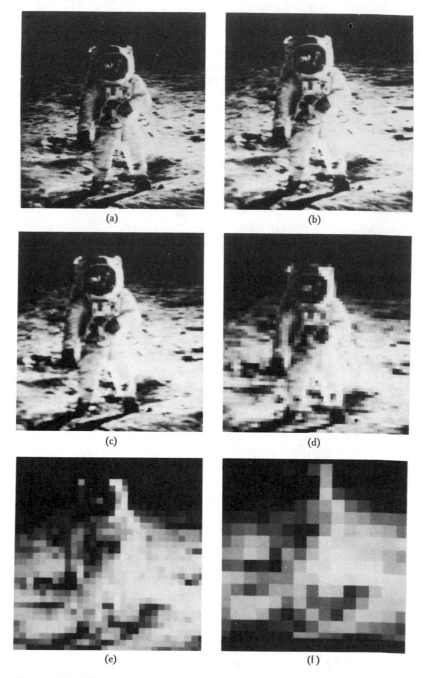

Figure 2.7 Effects of reducing sampling-grid size.

Figure 2.8 illustrates the effects produced by reducing the number of bits used to represent the gray levels in an image. Figure 2.8(a) is a picture of a subject digitized using a 512 × 512 array and 256 levels [$m = 8$ in Eq. (2.3-3)]. Figures 2.8(b) through (h) were obtained by reducing the number of bits from $m = 7$ to $m = 1$, respectively, while keeping the digitizing grid at 512 × 512. The 256-, 128-, and 64-level images are of acceptable quality. The 32-level image, however, has some mild "false contouring" in the smooth background area above the subject's right shoulder. This effect is considerably more pronounced in the image displayed in 16 levels, and increases sharply for the remaining images.

The number of samples and gray levels required to produce a faithful reproduction of an original image depends on the image itself. As a basis for comparison, the requirements to obtain a quality comparable to that of monochrome TV pictures over a wide range of image types are on the order of 512 × 512 pixels with 128 gray levels. As a rule, a minimum system for general image processing work should be able to display 256 × 256 pixels with 64 gray levels.

The above results illustrate the effects produced on image quality by varying N and m independently. However, these results only partially answer the question posed earlier since nothing has yet been said about the relation between these parameters. Huang [1965] considered this problem in an attempt to quantify experimentally the effects on image quality produced by varying N and m. The experiment consisted of a set of subjective tests. Three of the images used are shown in Fig. 2.9 on page 28. The woman's face is representative of an image with relatively little detail; the picture of the cameraman contains an intermediate amount of detail; and the crowd picture contains, by comparison, a large amount of detail information.

Sets of these three images were generated by varying N and m and observers were then asked to rank them according to their subjective quality. The results are summarized in Fig. 2.10 (page 29) in the form of *isopreference curves* in the N-m plane. Each point in this plane represents an image with values of N and m equal to the coordinates of that point. An isopreference curve is one in which the points represent images of equal subjective quality.

The isopreference curves of Fig. 2.10 are arranged, from left to right, in order of increasing subjective quality. These results suggest several empirical conclusions: (1) As expected, the quality of the images tends to increase as N and m are increased. There were a few cases in which, for fixed N, the quality improved by decreasing m. This is most likely due to the fact that a decrease in m generally increases the apparent contrast of an image. (2) The curves tend to become more vertical as the detail in the image increases. This suggests that for images with a large amount of detail only a few gray levels are needed. For example, it is noted in Fig. 2.10(c) that, for $N = 64$ or 128, image quality is not improved by an increase in m. This is not true for the curves in the other two figures. (3) The isopreference curves depart markedly from the curves of constant b, which are shown dotted in Fig. 2.10.

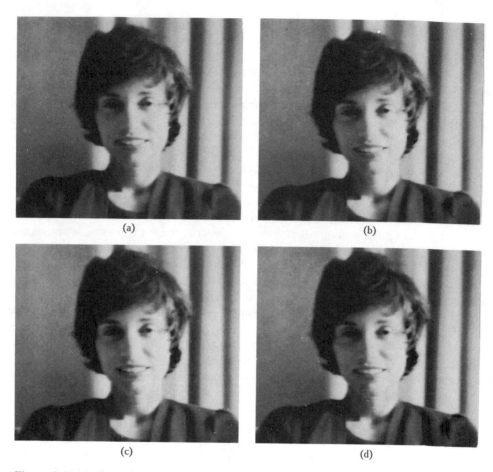

Figure 2.8   A 512 × 512 image displayed in 256, 128, 64, 32, 16, 8, 4, and 2 levels, respectively.

2.3.2   Nonuniform Sampling and Quantization

For a fixed value of N, it is possible in many cases to improve the appearance of an image by using an adaptive scheme where the sampling process depends on the characteristics of the image. In general, fine sampling is required in the neighborhood of sharp gray-level transitions, while coarse sampling may be employed in relatively smooth regions. Consider, for example, a simple image consisting of a face superimposed on a uniform background. Clearly, the background carries little detail information and can be quite adequately represented by coarse sampling. The face, on the other hand, contains considerably more detail. If the additional samples not used in the background are used in this region of the image the overall result will tend to improve, particularly if N is small. In distributing the samples, greater sample

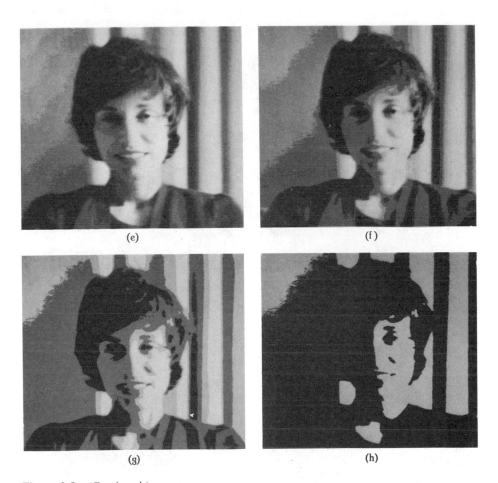

(e)   (f)

(g)   (h)

Figure 2.8 (Continued.)

concentration should be used in gray-level transition boundaries, such as the boundary between the face and the background in the preceding example.

It is important to note that the necessity of having to identify boundaries, even if only on a rough basis, is a definite drawback of the nonuniform sampling approach. Also, it should be kept in mind that this method is not practical for images containing relatively small uniform regions. For instance, nonuniform sampling would be difficult to justify for an image of a dense crowd of people.

When the number of gray levels must be kept small, it is usually desirable to use unequally spaced levels in the quantization process. A method similar to the nonuniform sampling technique discussed above may be used for the distribution of gray levels in an image. However, since the eye is relatively poor at estimating shades of gray near abrupt level changes, the approach in this case is to use few

Figure 2.9   Test images used in evaluating subjective image quality. (From Huang [1965].)

gray levels in the neighborhood of boundaries. The remaining levels can then be used in regions where gray-level variations are smooth, thus avoiding or reducing the false contours that often appear in these regions if they are too coarsely quantized.

This method is subject to the same observations made above regarding boundary detection and detail content. An alternative technique that is particularly attractive for distributing gray levels consists of computing the frequency of occurrence of all allowed levels. If gray levels in a certain range occur frequently, while others occur rarely, the quantization levels are finely spaced in this range and coarsely spaced outside of it. This method is sometimes called *tapered quantization*.

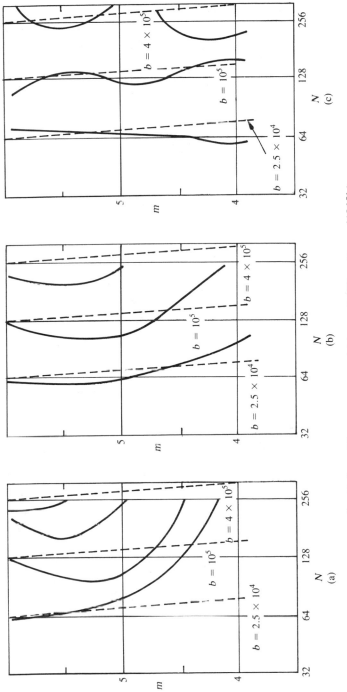

Figure 2.10 Isopreference curves for (a) face, (b) cameraman, and (c) crowd. (From Huang [1965].)

2.4   SOME BASIC RELATIONSHIPS BETWEEN PIXELS

In this section we consider several primitive, but important relationships between pixels in a digital image. As in the previous sections, an image will be denoted by $f(x, y)$. When referring to a particular pixel, we will use lowercase letters, such as p and q. A subset of pixels of $f(x, y)$ will be denoted by S.

2.4.1   Neighbors of a Pixel

A pixel p at coordinates (x, y) has four *horizontal* and *vertical* neighbors whose coordinates are given by

$$(x + 1, y), (x - 1, y), (x, y + 1), (x, y - 1).$$

This set of pixels, called the 4-*neighbors* of p, will be denoted by $N_4(p)$. It is noted that each of these pixels is a unit distance from (x, y) and also that some of the neighbors of p will be outside the digital image if (x, y) is on the border of the image.

The four *diagonal* neighbors of p have coordinates

$$(x + 1, y + 1), (x + 1, y - 1), (x - 1, y + 1), (x - 1, y - 1)$$

and will be denoted $N_D(p)$. These points, together with the 4-neighbors defined above, are called the 8-*neighbors* of p, denoted $N_8(p)$. As before, some of the points in $N_D(p)$ and $N_8(p)$ will be outside the image if (x, y) is on the border of the image.

2.4.2   Connectivity

Connectivity between pixels is an important concept used in establishing boundaries of objects and components of regions in an image. To establish whether two pixels are connected we must determine if they are adjacent in some sense (e.g., if they are 4-neighbors) and if their gray levels satisfy a specified criterion of similarity (e.g., if they are equal). For instance, in a binary image with values 0 and 1, two pixels may be 4-neighbors, but they are not said to be connected unless they have the same value.

Let V be the set of gray-level values used to define connectivity; for example, if only connectivity of pixels with intensities of 59, 60, and 61 is important, then $V = \{59, 60, 61\}$. We consider three types of connectivity:

(a) 4-*connectivity*. Two pixels p and q with values from V are 4-connected if q is in the set $N_4(p)$.

(b) 8-*connectivity*. Two pixels p and q with values from V are 8-connected if q is in the set $N_8(p)$.

(c) m-*connectivity* (mixed connectivity). Two pixels p and q with values from V are m-connected if

  (i) q is in $N_4(p)$, or

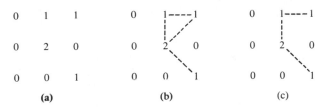

Figure 2.11   (a) Arrangement of pixels. (b) 8-neighbors of
the pixel labeled "2." (c) m-neighbors of the same pixel.
The dashed lines are paths between that pixel and its neighbors.

(ii) q is in $N_D(p)$ and the set $N_4(p) \cap N_4(q)$ is empty. (This is the set of pixels
that are 4-neighbors of both p and q and whose values are from V.)

Mixed connectivity is a modification of 8-connectivity and is introduced to
eliminate the multiple path connections (see below) that often arise when 8-connectiv-
ity is used. For example, consider the pixel arrangement shown in Fig. 2.11(a).
Assuming $V = \{1, 2\}$, the paths between 8-neighbors of the pixel with value 2 are
shown by dashed lines in Fig. 2.11(b). It is important to note the ambiguity in
path connections that results from allowing 8-connectivity. This ambiguity is removed
by using m-connectivity, as shown in Fig. 2.11(c).

A pixel p is *adjacent* to a pixel q if they are connected. We may define 4-, 8-,
or m-adjacency, depending on the type of connectivity specified. Two image subsets
S_1 and S_2 are adjacent if some pixel in S_1 is adjacent to some pixel in S_2.

A *path* from pixel p with coordinates (x, y) to pixel q with coordinates (s, t) is
a sequence of distinct pixels with coordinates

$$(x_0, y_0), (x_1, y_1), \ldots, (x_n, y_n),$$

where $(x_0, y_0) = (x, y)$ and $(x_n, y_n) = (s, t)$, (x_i, y_i) is adjacent to (x_{i-1}, y_{i-1}),
$1 \leq i \leq n$, and n is the *length* of the path. We may define 4-, 8-, or m-paths,
depending on the type of adjacency used.

If p and q are pixels of an image subset S then p is *connected* to q in S if
there is a path from p to q consisting entirely of pixels in S. For any pixel p in S,
the set of pixels in S that are connected to p is called a *connected component* of S.
It then follows that any two pixels of a connected component are connected to
each other, and that distinct connected components are disjoint.

2.4.3   Distance Measures

Given pixels p, q, and z, with coordinates (x, y), (s, t), and (u, v) respectively,
we call D a *distance function* or *metric* if

(a) $D(p, q) \geq 0$ $(D(p, q) = 0$ iff $p = q)$,

(b) $D(p, q) = D(q, p)$,

(c) $D(p, z) \leqslant D(p, q) + D(q, z)$.

The *Euclidean distance* between p and q is defined as

$$D_e(p, q) = [(x - s)^2 + (y - t)^2]^{1/2}. \qquad (2.4-1)$$

For this distance measure, the pixels having a distance less than or equal to some value r from (x, y) are the points contained in a disk of radius r centered at (x, y).

The D_4 *distance* (also called *city-block distance*) between p and q is defined as

$$D_4(p, q) = |x - s| + |y - t|. \qquad (2.4-2)$$

In this case the pixels having a D_4 distance from (x, y) less than or equal to some value r form a diamond centered at (x, y). For example, the pixels with D_4 distance $\leqslant 2$ from (x, y) (the center point) form the following contours of constant distance:

$$
\begin{array}{ccccc}
 & & 2 & & \\
 & 2 & 1 & 2 & \\
2 & 1 & 0 & 1 & 2 \\
 & 2 & 1 & 2 & \\
 & & 2 & & \\
\end{array}
$$

It is noted that the pixels with $D_4 = 1$ are the 4-neighbors of (x, y).

The D_8 *distance* (also called *chessboard distance*) between p and q is defined as

$$D_8(p, q) = \max(|x - s|, |y - t|). \qquad (2.4-3)$$

In this case the pixels with D_8 distance from (x, y) less than or equal to some value r form a square centered at (x, y). For example, the pixels with D_8 distance $\leqslant 2$ from (x, y) (the center point) form the following contours of constant distance:

$$
\begin{array}{ccccc}
2 & 2 & 2 & 2 & 2 \\
2 & 1 & 1 & 1 & 2 \\
2 & 1 & 0 & 1 & 2 \\
2 & 1 & 1 & 1 & 2 \\
2 & 2 & 2 & 2 & 2 \\
\end{array}
$$

It is noted that the pixels with $D_8 = 1$ are the 8-neighbors of (x, y).

It is also of interest to note that the D_4 distance between two points p and q is equal to the length of the shortest 4-path between these two points. Similar comments apply to the D_8 distance. In fact, we can consider both the D_4 and D_8 distances between p and q regardless of whether or not a connected path exists between them, since the definition of these distances involve only the coordinates of these points. When dealing with m-connectivity, however, the value of the distance (length of the path) between two pixels depends on the values of the pixels along the path as well as their neighbors. For instance, consider the following arrangement of pixels, where it is assumed that p, p_2, and p_4 have a value of 1 and p_1 and p_3 have a value of 0 or 1:

$$p_3 \quad p_4$$
$$p_1 \quad p_2$$
$$p$$

If we only allow connectivity of pixels valued 1, and p_1 and p_3 are 0, the m distance between p and p_4 is 2. If either p_1 or p_3 is 1, the distance is 3. If both p_1 and p_3 are 1, the distance is 4.

2.4.4 Arithmetic/Logic Operations

Arithmetic and logic operations between pixels are used extensively in most branches of image processing. The arithmetic operations between two pixels p and q are denoted as follows:

$$\text{Addition:} \quad p + q$$
$$\text{Subtraction:} \quad p - q$$
$$\text{Multiplication:} \quad p * q \text{ (also, } pq \text{ and } p \times q)$$
$$\text{Division:} \quad p \div q$$

Often, one of the pixels is a constant operand, as in the multiplication of an image by a constant.

The principal logic operations used in image processing are AND, OR, and COMPLEMENT, denoted by

$$\text{AND:} \quad p\text{AND}q \text{ (also, } p \cdot q)$$
$$\text{OR:} \quad p\text{OR}q \text{ (also, } p + q)$$
$$\text{COMPLEMENT:} \quad \text{NOT}q \text{ (also, } \bar{q})$$

It is well known that these operations are *functionally complete* in the sense that they can be combined to form any other logic operation. We also note that logic operations apply only to binary images, while the arithmetic operations apply to multivalued pixels.

The operations described above are used for image processing in basically two ways: on a pixel-by-pixel basis, or in neighborhood-oriented operations. For example, the addition of two images is accomplished on a pixel-by-pixel basis. Neighborhood processing is typically formulated in the context of so-called *mask operations* (the terms *template, window,* and *filter* are also often used to denote a mask). The idea behind mask operations is to let the value assigned to a pixel be a function of it and its neighbors. For instance, consider the subimage area shown in Fig. 2.12(a), and suppose that we wish to replace the value of e by the average value of the

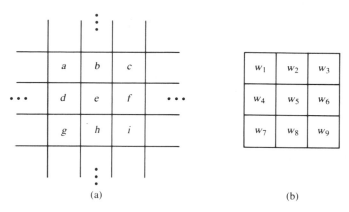

Figure 2.12 (a) Sub-area of an image showing pixel values.
(b) A 3 × 3 mask with general coefficients.

pixels in a 3 × 3 region centered at *e*. This entails performing an arithmetic operation
of the form

$$p = \frac{1}{9}\left(a + b + c + d + e + f + g + h + i\right)$$

and assigning to *e* the value of *p*.

With reference to the mask shown in Fig. 2.12(b), we may view the above
operation in more general terms by centering the mask at *e*, multiplying each pixel
under the mask by the corresponding coefficient, and adding the results; that is,

$$p = w_1 a + w_2 b + w_3 c + w_4 d + w_5 e + w_6 f + w_7 g + w_8 h + w_9 i. \quad (2.4\text{-}4)$$

If we let $w_i = 1/9$, $i = 1, 2, \ldots, 9$, this operation yields the same result as the
averaging procedure just discussed.

As will be seen in subsequent chapters, Eq. (2.4-4) is used widely in image
processing. By properly selecting the coefficients and applying the mask at each
pixel position in an image, it is possible to perform a variety of useful image
operations, such as noise reduction, region thinning, and feature detection. It is
noted, however, that applying a mask at each pixel location in an image is a computationally expensive task. For example, applying a 3 × 3 mask to a 512 × 512
image requires nine multiplications and eight additions at each pixel location, for a
total of 2,359,296 multiplications and 2,097,152 additions.

As indicated in Section 1.3.1, most modern image processors are equipped
with an Arithmetic-Logic Unit (ALU), whose function is to perform arithmetic and
logic operations in parallel, typically at video-frame rates. For U.S. standard video,
an ALU can perform an arithmetic or logic operation between two 512 × 512
images in 1/30th of a second. (This time interval is often called one *frame* or
one *frame time*.) Given the importance of mask operations in image processing, it

is of interest to consider in some detail how to use an ALU to accelerate mask processing. For the purpose of illustration, we consider the 3×3 mask shown in Fig. 2.12(b) and the implementation given in Eq. (2.4-4). However, the method is easily extendible to an $n \times m$ mask and other arithmetic or logic operations.

The algorithm given here requires two image frame buffers with the capability to scroll and pan by one pixel location (see Section 1.3.1). Let frame buffer A contain the image to which the mask is to be applied. At the end of the process, B will contain the result of the operation. The reader is reminded that ALU operations are performed on all pixels in one frame time, while all buffer shifts are performed virtually instantaneously. It is assumed that all shifts are by one pixel. Letting $B = A$ initially, and using a dash to indicate no operation, we proceed as follows:

Operations on A	Operations on B
—	Multiply by w_5
Shift right	—
—	Add w_4*A
Shift down	—
—	Add w_1*A
Shift left	—
—	Add w_2*A
Shift left	—
—	Add w_3*A
Shift up	—
—	Add w_6*A
Shift up	—
—	Add w_9*A
Shift right	—
—	Add w_8*A
Shift right	—
—	Add w_7*A
Shift left	—
Shift down	—

The last two shifts are required because at the end of the last operation on B the images are in a position equivalent to having the mask with its w_7 coefficient over the e position. The two shifts correct this misalignment.

The key to understanding the foregoing procedure is to examine what happens in a single pixel of B by considering how a mask would have to be shifted in order to produce the result of Eq. (2.4-4) in that location. The first operation on B produces w_5 multiplied by the pixel value at that location. Calling that location e, we have $w_5 e$ after this operation. The first shift to the right brings neighbor d (see

Fig. 2.12(a)) over that location. The next operation multiplies d by w_4 and adds the result to the location of the first step. So at this point we have $w_4d + w_5e$ at the location in question. The next shift on A and ALU operation on B produce $w_1a + w_4d + w_5e$ at that location, and so on. Since the operations are done in parallel for all locations in B, the procedure just explained takes place simultaneously at the other locations in that image. In most ALUs, the operation of multiplying an image by a constant (i.e., w_i*A) followed by an ADD is done in one frame time. Thus the ALU implementation of Eq. (2.4-4) for an entire image takes on the order of nine frame times (9/30th of a second). For an $n \times m$ mask it would take on the order of nm frame times.

2.5   IMAGING GEOMETRY

In the following discussion we consider several important transformations used in imaging, derive a camera model, and treat the stereo imaging problem in some detail.

2.5.1   Some Basic Transformations

The material in this section deals with the development of a unified representation for problems such as image rotation, scaling, and translation. All transformations are expressed in a three-dimensional (3D) Cartesian coordinate system in which a point has coordinates denoted by (X, Y, Z). In cases involving two-dimensional images, we will adhere to our previous convention of using the lowercase representation (x, y) to denote the coordinates of a pixel. It is common terminology to refer to (X, Y, Z) as the *world coordinates* of a point.

Translation
Suppose that we wish to translate a point with coordinates (X, Y, Z) to a new location by using displacements (X_0, Y_0, Z_0). The translation is easily accomplished by using the following equations:

$$X^* = X + X_0$$
$$Y^* = Y + Y_0 \qquad (2.5\text{-}1)$$
$$Z^* = Z + Z_0$$

where (X^*, Y^*, Z^*) are the coordinates of the new point. Equation (2.5-1) may be expressed in matrix form by writing

$$\begin{bmatrix} X^* \\ Y^* \\ Z^* \end{bmatrix} = \begin{bmatrix} 1 & 0 & 0 & X_0 \\ 0 & 1 & 0 & Y_0 \\ 0 & 0 & 1 & Z_0 \end{bmatrix} \begin{bmatrix} X \\ Y \\ Z \\ 1 \end{bmatrix} \qquad (2.5\text{-}2)$$

As indicated later in this section, it is often useful to concatenate several transformations to produce a composite result, such as translation, followed by scaling and then rotation. The notational representation of this process is simplified considerably by using square matrices. With this in mind, we may write Eq. (2.5-2) in the following form:

$$
\begin{bmatrix} X^* \\ Y^* \\ Z^* \\ 1 \end{bmatrix} = \begin{bmatrix} 1 & 0 & 0 & X_0 \\ 0 & 1 & 0 & Y_0 \\ 0 & 0 & 1 & Z_0 \\ 0 & 0 & 0 & 1 \end{bmatrix} \begin{bmatrix} X \\ Y \\ Z \\ 1 \end{bmatrix}
\tag{2.5-3}
$$

In terms of the values of X^*, Y^*, and Z^*, Eqs. (2.5-2) and (2.5-3) are equivalent. Throughout this section, we will use the unified matrix representation

$$
\mathbf{v}^* = \mathbf{A}\mathbf{v},
\tag{2.5-4}
$$

where $\mathbf{A}$ is a 4×4 transformation matrix, $\mathbf{v}$ is the column vector containing the original coordinates,

$$
\mathbf{v} = \begin{bmatrix} X \\ Y \\ Z \\ 1 \end{bmatrix}
\tag{2.5-5}
$$

and $\mathbf{v}^*$ is a column vector whose components are the transformed coordinates

$$
\mathbf{v}^* = \begin{bmatrix} X^* \\ Y^* \\ Z^* \\ 1 \end{bmatrix}
\tag{2.5-6}
$$

Using this notation, the matrix used for translation is given by

$$
\mathbf{T} = \begin{bmatrix} 1 & 0 & 0 & X_0 \\ 0 & 1 & 0 & Y_0 \\ 0 & 0 & 1 & Z_0 \\ 0 & 0 & 0 & 1 \end{bmatrix}
\tag{2.5-7}
$$

and the translation process is accomplished by using Eq. (2.5-4), so that $\mathbf{v}^* = \mathbf{T}\mathbf{v}$.

Scaling

Scaling by factors S_x, S_y, and S_z along the X, Y, and Z axes is given by the transformation matrix

$$
\mathbf{S} = \begin{bmatrix} S_x & 0 & 0 & 0 \\ 0 & S_y & 0 & 0 \\ 0 & 0 & S_z & 0 \\ 0 & 0 & 0 & 1 \end{bmatrix}
$$

(2.5-8)

Rotation

The transformations used for three-dimensional rotation are inherently more complex than the transformations discussed thus far. The simplest form of these transformations is for rotation of a point about the coordinate axes. To rotate a given point about an arbitrary point in space requires three transformations: the first translates the arbitrary point to the origin, the second performs the rotation, and the third translates the point back to its original position.

With reference to Fig. 2.13, rotation of a point about the Z coordinate axis by an angle θ is achieved by using the transformation

$$
\mathbf{R}_\theta = \begin{bmatrix} \cos \theta & \sin \theta & 0 & 0 \\ -\sin \theta & \cos \theta & 0 & 0 \\ 0 & 0 & 1 & 0 \\ 0 & 0 & 0 & 1 \end{bmatrix}
$$

(2.5-9)

The rotation angle θ is measured clockwise when looking at the origin from a point on the $+Z$ axis. It is noted that this transformation affects only the values of X and Y coordinates.

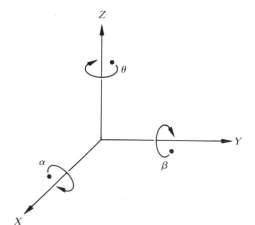

Figure 2.13   Rotation of a point about each of the coordinate axes. Angles are measured clockwise when looking along the rotation axis toward the origin.

Rotation of a point about the X axis by an angle α is performed by using the transformation

$$\mathbf{R}_\alpha = \begin{bmatrix} 1 & 0 & 0 & 0 \\ 0 & \cos\alpha & \sin\alpha & 0 \\ 0 & -\sin\alpha & \cos\alpha & 0 \\ 0 & 0 & 0 & 1 \end{bmatrix} \tag{2.5-10}$$

Finally, rotation of a point about the Y axis by an angle β is achieved by using the transformation

$$\mathbf{R}_\beta = \begin{bmatrix} \cos\beta & 0 & -\sin\beta & 0 \\ 0 & 1 & 0 & 0 \\ \sin\beta & 0 & \cos\beta & 0 \\ 0 & 0 & 0 & 1 \end{bmatrix} \tag{2.5-11}$$

Concatenation and inverse transformations
The application of several transformations can be represented by a single 4×4 transformation matrix. For example, translation, scaling, and rotation about the Z axis of a point $\mathbf{v}$ is given by

$$\mathbf{v}^* = \mathbf{R}_\theta(\mathbf{S}(\mathbf{T}\mathbf{v})) \\ = \mathbf{A}\mathbf{v}, \tag{2.5-12}$$

where $\mathbf{A}$ is the 4×4 matrix $\mathbf{A} = \mathbf{R}_\theta\mathbf{S}\mathbf{T}$. It is important to note that these matrices generally do not commute, so the order of application is important.

Although our discussion thus far has been limited to transformations of a single point, the same ideas extend to transforming a set of m points simultaneously by using a single transformation. With reference to Eq. (2.5-5), let $\mathbf{v}_1, \mathbf{v}_2, \ldots, \mathbf{v}_m$ represent the coordinates of m points. If we form a $4 \times m$ matrix $\mathbf{V}$ whose columns are these column vectors, then the simultaneous transformation of all these points by a 4×4 transformation matrix $\mathbf{A}$ is given by

$$\mathbf{V}^* = \mathbf{A}\mathbf{V}. \tag{2.5-13}$$

The resulting matrix $\mathbf{V}^*$ is $4 \times m$. Its ith column, $\mathbf{v}_i^*$, contains the coordinates of the transformed point corresponding to $\mathbf{v}_i$.

Before leaving this section, we point out that many of the transformations discussed above have inverse matrices that perform the opposite transformation and can be obtained by inspection. For example, the inverse translation matrix is

$$\mathbf{T}^{-1} = \begin{bmatrix} 1 & 0 & 0 & -X_0 \\ 0 & 1 & 0 & -Y_0 \\ 0 & 0 & 1 & -Z_0 \\ 0 & 0 & 0 & 1 \end{bmatrix} \tag{2.5-14}$$

Similarly, the inverse rotation matrix $\mathbf{R}_\theta^{-1}$ is given by

$$\mathbf{R}_\theta^{-1} = \begin{bmatrix} \cos(-\theta) & \sin(-\theta) & 0 & 0 \\ -\sin(-\theta) & \cos(-\theta) & 0 & 0 \\ 0 & 0 & 1 & 0 \\ 0 & 0 & 0 & 1 \end{bmatrix} \qquad (2.5\text{-}15)$$

The inverses of more-complex transformation matrices are usually obtained by numerical techniques.

2.5.2   Perspective Transformations

A perspective transformation (also called an imaging transformation) projects 3D points onto a plane. Perspective transformations play a central role in image processing because they provide an approximation to the manner in which an image is formed by viewing a three-dimensional world. These transformations are fundamentally different from those discussed in the previous section because they are nonlinear in that they involve division by coordinate values.

A model of the image formation process is shown in Fig. 2.14. We define the camera coordinate system (x, y, z) as having the image plane coincident with the xy plane and the optical axis (established by the center of the lens) along the z axis. Thus the center of the image plane is at the origin, and the center of the lens is at coordinates $(0, 0, \lambda)$. If the camera is in focus for distant objects, λ is the *focal length* of the lens. In this section, it is assumed that the camera coordinate system is aligned with the world coordinate system (X, Y, Z). This restriction will be removed in the following section.

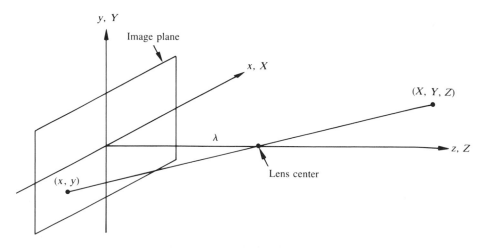

Figure 2.14   Basic model of the imaging process. The camera coordinate system (x, y, z) is aligned with the world coordinate system (X, Y, Z).

Let (X, Y, Z) be the world coordinates of any point in a 3D scene, as shown in Fig. 2.14. It will be assumed throughout the following discussion that $Z > \lambda$, that is, all points of interest lie in front of the lens. What we wish to do first is obtain a relationship that gives the coordinates (x, y) of the projection of the point (X, Y, Z) onto the image plane. This is easily accomplished by the use of similar triangles. With reference to Fig. 2.14, it follows that

$$\frac{x}{\lambda} = -\frac{X}{Z - \lambda} \tag{2.5-16}$$

$$= \frac{X}{\lambda - Z}$$

and

$$\frac{y}{\lambda} = -\frac{Y}{Z - \lambda} \tag{2.5-17}$$

$$= \frac{Y}{\lambda - Z},$$

where the negative signs in front of X and Y indicate that image points are actually inverted, as can be seen from the geometry of Fig. 2.14.

The image-plane coordinates of the projected 3D point follow directly from Eqs. (2.5-16) and (2.5-17):

$$x = \frac{\lambda X}{\lambda - Z} \tag{2.5-18}$$

and

$$y = \frac{\lambda Y}{\lambda - Z}. \tag{2.5-19}$$

It is important to note that these equations are nonlinear because they involve division by the variable Z. Although we could use them directly as shown above, it is often convenient to express these equations in linear matrix form as we did in the previous section for rotation, translation, and scaling. This can be accomplished easily by using homogeneous coordinates.

The homogeneous coordinates of a point with Cartesian coordinates (X, Y, Z) are defined as (kX, kY, kZ, k), where k is an arbitrary, nonzero constant. Clearly, conversion of homogeneous coordinates back to Cartesian coordinates is accomplished by dividing the first three homogeneous coordinates by the fourth. A point in the Cartesian world coordinate system may be expressed in vector form as

$$\mathbf{w} = \begin{bmatrix} X \\ Y \\ Z \end{bmatrix} \tag{2.5-20}$$

and its homogeneous counterpart is given by

$$\mathbf{w}_h = \begin{bmatrix} kX \\ kY \\ kZ \\ k \end{bmatrix} \tag{2.5-21}$$

If we define the *perspective transformation matrix*

$$\mathbf{P} = \begin{bmatrix} 1 & 0 & 0 & 0 \\ 0 & 1 & 0 & 0 \\ 0 & 0 & 1 & 0 \\ 0 & 0 & -\dfrac{1}{\lambda} & 1 \end{bmatrix} \tag{2.5-22}$$

then the product $\mathbf{Pw}_h$ yields a vector that we shall denote by $\mathbf{c}_h$:

$$\begin{aligned}
\mathbf{c}_h &= \mathbf{Pw}_h \\[4pt]
&= \begin{bmatrix} 1 & 0 & 0 & 0 \\ 0 & 1 & 0 & 0 \\ 0 & 0 & 1 & 0 \\ 0 & 0 & -\dfrac{1}{\lambda} & 1 \end{bmatrix} \begin{bmatrix} kX \\ kY \\ kZ \\ k \end{bmatrix} \\[4pt]
&= \begin{bmatrix} kX \\ kY \\ kZ \\ \dfrac{-kZ + k}{\lambda} \end{bmatrix}
\end{aligned} \tag{2.5-23}$$

The elements of $\mathbf{c}_h$ are the camera coordinates in homogeneous form. As indicated above, these coordinates can be converted to Cartesian form by dividing each of the first three components of $\mathbf{c}_h$ by the fourth. Thus the Cartesian coordinates of any point in the camera coordinate system are given in vector form by

$$\mathbf{c} = \begin{bmatrix} x \\ y \\ z \end{bmatrix} = \begin{bmatrix} \dfrac{\lambda X}{\lambda - Z} \\[6pt] \dfrac{\lambda Y}{\lambda - Z} \\[6pt] \dfrac{\lambda Z}{\lambda - Z} \end{bmatrix} \tag{2.5-24}$$

The first two components of **c** are the (x, y) coordinates in the image plane of a projected 3D point (X, Y, Z), as shown earlier in Eqs. (2.5-18) and (2.5-19). The third component is of no interest to us in terms of the model in Fig. 2.14. As will be seen below, this component acts as a free variable in the inverse perspective transformation.

The inverse perspective transformation maps an image point back into 3D. Thus from Eq. (2.5-23),

$$\mathbf{w}_h = \mathbf{P}^{-1}\mathbf{c}_h, \tag{2.5-25}$$

where $\mathbf{P}^{-1}$ is easily found to be

$$\mathbf{P}^{-1} = \begin{bmatrix} 1 & 0 & 0 & 0 \\ 0 & 1 & 0 & 0 \\ 0 & 0 & 1 & 0 \\ 0 & 0 & \dfrac{1}{\lambda} & 1 \end{bmatrix} \tag{2.5-26}$$

Suppose that a given image point has coordinates $(x_0, y_0, 0)$, where the 0 in the z location simply indicates the fact that the image plane is located at $z = 0$. This point may be expressed in homogeneous vector form as

$$\mathbf{c}_h = \begin{bmatrix} kx_0 \\ ky_0 \\ 0 \\ k \end{bmatrix} \tag{2.5-27}$$

Application of Eq. (2.5-25) then yields the homogeneous world coordinate vector

$$\mathbf{w}_h = \begin{bmatrix} kx_0 \\ ky_0 \\ 0 \\ k \end{bmatrix} \tag{2.5-28}$$

or, in Cartesian coordinates,

$$\mathbf{w} = \begin{bmatrix} X \\ Y \\ Z \end{bmatrix} = \begin{bmatrix} x_0 \\ y_0 \\ 0 \end{bmatrix} \tag{2.5-29}$$

This is obviously not what one would expect since it gives $Z = 0$ for *any* 3D point. The problem here is caused by the fact that mapping a 3D scene onto the image plane is a many-to-one transformation. The image point (x_0, y_0) corresponds to the set of collinear 3D points that lie on the line that passes through $(x_0, y_0, 0)$ and $(0, 0, \lambda)$. The equations of this line in the world coordinate system are obtained from Eqs. (2.5-18) and (2.5-19); that is,

$$X = \frac{x_0}{\lambda}(\lambda - Z) \tag{2.5-30}$$

and

$$Y = \frac{y_0}{\lambda}(\lambda - Z). \tag{2.5-31}$$

These equations show that unless we know something about the 3D point that generated a given image point (for example, its Z coordinate), we cannot completely recover the 3D point from its image. This observation, which certainly is not unexpected, can be used to formulate the inverse perspective transformation by using the z component of $\mathbf{c}_h$ as a free variable, instead of 0. Thus letting

$$\mathbf{c}_h = \begin{bmatrix} kx_0 \\ ky_0 \\ kz \\ k \end{bmatrix} \tag{2.5-32}$$

we now have from Eq. (2.5-25) that

$$\mathbf{w}_h = \begin{bmatrix} kx_0 \\ ky_0 \\ kz \\ \dfrac{kz + k}{\lambda} \end{bmatrix} \tag{2.5-33}$$

which, upon conversion to Cartesian coordinates yields

$$\mathbf{w} = \begin{bmatrix} X \\ Y \\ Z \end{bmatrix} = \begin{bmatrix} \dfrac{\lambda x_0}{\lambda + z} \\ \dfrac{\lambda y_0}{\lambda + z} \\ \dfrac{\lambda z}{\lambda + z} \end{bmatrix} \tag{2.5-34}$$

In other words, treating z as a free variable yields the equations

$$X = \frac{\lambda x_0}{\lambda + z}$$

$$Y = \frac{\lambda y_0}{\lambda + z} \tag{2.5-35}$$

$$Z = \frac{\lambda z}{\lambda + z}$$

Solving for z in terms of Z in the last equation and substituting in the first two expressions yields

$$X = \frac{x_0}{\lambda} (\lambda - Z) \tag{2.5-36}$$

$$Y = \frac{y_0}{\lambda} (\lambda - Z), \tag{2.5-37}$$

which agrees with the above observation that recovering a 3D point from its image by means of the inverse perspective transformation requires knowledge of at least one of the world coordinates of the point. This problem will be addressed again in Section 2.5.5.

2.5.3   Camera Model

Equations (2.5-23) and (2.5-24) characterize the formation of an image via the projection of 3D points onto an image plane. These two equations thus constitute a basic mathematical model of an imaging camera. This model is based on the assumption that the camera and world coordinate systems are coincident. In this section we consider a more general problem in which the two coordinate systems are allowed to be separate. However, the basic objective of obtaining the image-plane coordinates of any given world point remains the same.

The situation is depicted in Fig. 2.15, which shows a world coordinate system (X, Y, Z) used to locate both the camera and 3D points (denoted by $\mathbf{w}$). This figure also shows the camera coordinate system (x, y, z) and image points (denoted by $\mathbf{c}$). It is assumed that the camera is mounted on a gimbal, which allows pan through an angle θ and tilt through an angle α. In this discussion, pan is defined as the angle between the x and X axes, and tilt as the angle between the z and Z axes. The offset of the center of the gimbal from the origin of the world coordinate system is denoted by vector $\mathbf{w}_0$, and the offset of the center of the imaging plane with respect to the gimbal center is denoted by a vector $\mathbf{r}$, with components (r_1, r_2, r_3).

The concepts developed in the last two sections provide all the necessary tools to derive a camera model based on the geometrical arrangement of Fig. 2.15. The approach is to bring the camera and world coordinate systems into alignment by applying a set of transformations. After this has been accomplished, we simply apply the perspective transformation given in Eq. (2.5-22) to obtain the image-plane coordinates of any given world point. In other words, we first reduce the problem to the geometrical arrangement shown in Fig. 2.14 before applying the perspective transformation.

Suppose that, initially, the camera was in *normal position,* in the sense that the gimbal center and origin of the image plane were at the origin of the world coordinate system, and all axes were aligned. Starting from normal position, the geometrical arrangement of Fig. 2.15 can be achieved in a number of ways. We

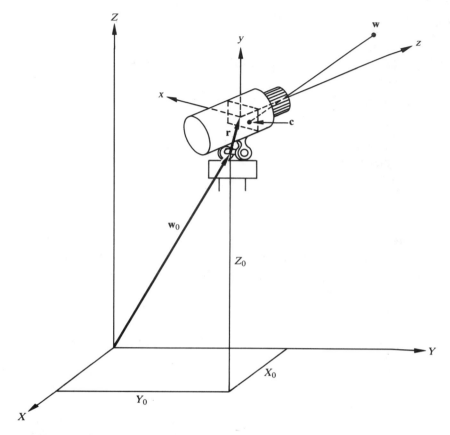

Figure 2.15 Imaging geometry with two coordinate systems. (From Fu, Gonzalez, and Lee [1987].)

assume the following sequence of steps: (1) displacement of the gimbal center from the origin, (2) pan of the x axis, (3) tilt of the z axis, and (4) displacement of the image plane with respect to the gimbal center.

Obviously, the sequence of mechanical steps just discussed does not affect the world points, since the set of points seen by the camera after it was moved from normal position is quite different. However, we can achieve normal position again simply by applying exactly the same sequence of steps to all world points. Since a camera in normal position satisfies the arrangement of Fig. 2.14 for application of the perspective transformation, our problem is thus reduced to applying to every world point a set of transformations that correspond to the steps given above.

Translation of the origin of the world coordinate system to the location of the gimbal center is accomplished by using the transformation matrix given in the following equation:

$$\mathbf{G} = \begin{bmatrix} 1 & 0 & 0 & -X_0 \\ 0 & 1 & 0 & -Y_0 \\ 0 & 0 & 1 & -Z_0 \\ 0 & 0 & 0 & 1 \end{bmatrix}$$

(2.5-38)

In other words, a homogeneous world point w_h that was at coordinates (X_0, Y_0, Z_0) is at the origin of the new coordinate system after the transformation $\mathbf{G}w_h$.

As indicated earlier, the pan angle is measured between the x and X axes. In normal position, these two axes are aligned. In order to pan the x axis through the desired angle, we simply rotate it by θ. The rotation is with respect to the z axis and is accomplished by using the transformation matrix $\mathbf{R}_\theta$ given in Eq. (2.5-9). In other words, application of this matrix to all points (including the point $\mathbf{G}w_h$) effectively rotates the x axis to the desired location. When using Eq. (2.5-9), it is important to keep clearly in mind the convention established in Fig. 2.13. That is, angles are considered positive when points are rotated clockwise, which implies a counterclockwise rotation of the camera about the z axis. The unrotated (0°) position corresponds to the case when the x and X axes are aligned.

At this point in the development the z and Z axes are still aligned. Since tilt is the angle between these two axes, we tilt the camera an angle α by rotating the z axis by α. The rotation is with respect to the x axis and is accomplished by applying the transformation matrix $\mathbf{R}_\alpha$ given in Eq. (2.5-10) to all points (including the point $\mathbf{R}_\theta\mathbf{G}w_h$). As above, a counterclockwise rotation of the camera implies positive angles, and the 0° mark is when the z and Z axes are aligned.[†]

According to the discussion in Section 2.5.4, the two rotation matrices can be concatenated into a single matrix, $\mathbf{R} = \mathbf{R}_\alpha \mathbf{R}_\theta$. It then follows from Eqs. (2.5-9) and (2.5-10) that

$$\mathbf{R} = \begin{bmatrix} \cos\theta & \sin\theta & 0 & 0 \\ -\sin\theta\cos\alpha & \cos\theta\cos\alpha & \sin\alpha & 0 \\ \sin\theta\sin\alpha & -\cos\theta\sin\alpha & \cos\alpha & 0 \\ 0 & 0 & 0 & 1 \end{bmatrix}$$

(2.5-39)

Finally, displacement of the origin of the image plane by vector $\mathbf{r}$ is achieved by the transformation matrix

$$\mathbf{C} = \begin{bmatrix} 1 & 0 & 0 & -r_1 \\ 0 & 1 & 0 & -r_2 \\ 0 & 0 & 1 & -r_3 \\ 0 & 0 & 0 & 1 \end{bmatrix}$$

(2.5-40)

[†] A useful way to visualize these transformations is to construct an axis system (e.g., with pipe cleaners), label the axes x, y, and z, and perform the rotations manually, one axis at a time.

Thus by applying to $\mathbf{w}_h$ the series of transformations $\mathbf{CRGw}_h$, we have brought the world and camera coordinate systems into coincidence. The image-plane coordinates of a point $\mathbf{w}_h$ are finally obtained by using Eq. (2.5-23). In other words, a homogeneous world point that is being viewed by a camera satisfying the geometrical arrangement shown in Fig. 2.15 has the following homogeneous representation in the camera coordinate system:

$$\mathbf{c}_h = \mathbf{PCRGw}_h. \tag{2.5-41}$$

This equation represents a perspective transformation involving two coordinate systems.

As indicated in the previous section, we obtain the Cartesian coordinates (x, y) of the imaged point by dividing the first and second components of $\mathbf{c}_h$ by the fourth. Expanding Eq. (2.5-41) and converting to Cartesian coordinates yields

$$x = \lambda \frac{(X - X_0)\cos\theta + (Y - Y_0)\sin\theta - r_1}{-(X - X_0)\sin\theta\,\sin\alpha + (Y - Y_0)\cos\theta\,\sin\alpha - (Z - Z_0)\cos\alpha + r_3 + \lambda} \tag{2.5-42}$$

and

$$y = \lambda \frac{-(X - X_0)\sin\theta\cos\alpha + (Y - Y_0)\cos\theta\cos\alpha + (Z - Z_0)\sin\alpha - r_2}{-(X - X_0)\sin\theta\,\sin\alpha + (Y - Y_0)\cos\theta\,\sin\alpha - (Z - Z_0)\cos\alpha + r_3 + \lambda} \tag{2.5-43}$$

which are the image coordinates of a point $\mathbf{w}$ whose world coordinates are (X, Y, Z). It is noted that these equations reduce to Eqs. (2.5-18) and (2.5-19) when $X_0 = Y_0 = Z_0 = 0$, $r_1 = r_2 = r_3 = 0$, and $\alpha = \theta = 0°$.

Example: As an illustration of the concepts just discussed, suppose that we wish to find the image coordinates of the corner of the block shown in Fig. 2.16. The camera is offset from the origin and is viewing the scene with a pan of 135° and a tilt of 135°. We will follow the convention established above that transformation angles are positive when the camera rotates in a counterclockwise manner as seen when viewing the origin along the axis of rotation.

Let us examine in detail the steps required to move the camera from normal position to the geometry shown in Fig. 2.16. The camera is shown in normal position in Fig. 2.17(a) and displaced from the origin in Fig. 2.17(b). It is important to note that, after this step, the world coordinate axes are used only to establish angle references. That is, after displacement of the world coordinate origin, all rotations take place about the new (camera) axes. Figure 2.17(c) shows a view along the z axis of the camera to establish pan. In this case the rotation of the camera about the z axis is counterclockwise, so world points are rotated about this axis in the opposite direction, which makes θ a positive angle. Figure 2.17(d) shows a view, after pan, along the x axis of the camera to establish tilt. The rotation about this axis is counterclockwise, which makes α a positive angle. The world coordinate

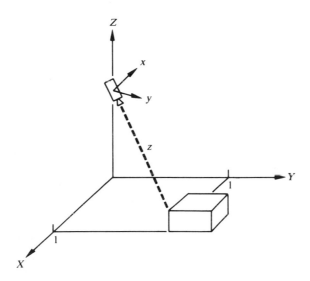

Figure 2.16 Camera viewing a 3D scene. (From Fu, Gonzalez, and Lee [1987].)

axes are shown dashed in the latter two figures to emphasize the fact that their only use is to establish the zero reference for the pan and tilt angles. We do not show in this figure the final step of displacing the image plane from the center of the gimbal.

The following parameter values apply to this problem:

$$X_0 = 0 \text{ m}$$

$$Y_0 = 0 \text{ m}$$

$$Z_0 = 1 \text{ m}$$

$$\alpha = 135°$$

$$\theta = 135°$$

$$r_1 = 0.03 \text{ m}$$

$$r_2 = r_3 = 0.02 \text{ m}$$

$$\lambda = 35 \text{ mm} = 0.035 \text{ m}$$

The corner in question is at coordinates $(X, Y, Z) = (1, 1, 0.2)$.

To compute the image coordinates of the block corner we simply substitute the above parameter values into Eqs. (2.5-42) and (2.5-43); that is,

$$x = \lambda \frac{-0.03}{-1.53 + \lambda}.$$

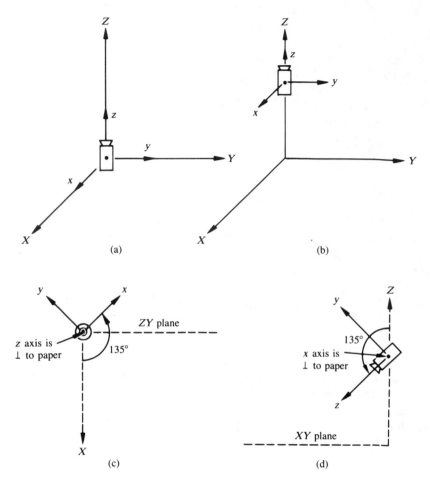

Figure 2.17 (a) Camera in normal position. (b) Gimbal center displaced from origin. (c) Observer view of rotation about z axis to determine pan angle. (d) Observer view of rotation about x axis for tilt. (From Fu, Gonzalez, and Lee [1987].)

Similarly,

$$y = \lambda \frac{-0.42}{-1.53 + \lambda}.$$

Substituting $\lambda = 0.035$ yields the image coordinates

$$x = 0.0007 \text{ m}$$

and

$$y = 0.009 \text{ m.}$$

We note that these coordinates are well within a 1×1 in. $(0.025 \times 0.025$ m) imaging plane. If, for example, we had used a lens with a 200-mm focal length, it is easily verified from the above results that the corner of the block would have been imaged outside the boundary of a plane with these dimensions (i.e., it would have been outside the effective field of view of the camera).

Finally, we point out that all coordinates obtained via the use of Eqs. (2.5-42) and (2.5-43) are with respect to the center of the image plane. A change of coordinates would be required to use the convention established earlier that the origin of an image is at its top left corner. □

2.5.4 Camera Calibration

In the previous section we obtained explicit equations for the image coordinates, (x, y), of a world point $\mathbf{w}$. As shown in Eqs. (2.5-42) and (2.5-43), implementation of these equations requires knowledge of the focal length, offsets, and angles of pan and tilt. While these parameters could be measured directly, it is often more convenient (e.g., when the camera moves frequently) to determine one or more of the parameters using the camera itself as a measuring device. This requires a set of image points whose world coordinates are known, and the computational procedure used to obtain the camera parameters using these known points is often referred to as *camera calibration*.

With reference to Eq. (2.5-41), let $\mathbf{A} = \mathbf{PCRG}$. The elements of $\mathbf{A}$ contain all the camera parameters, and we know from Eq. (2.5-41) that $\mathbf{c}_h = \mathbf{Aw}_h$. Letting $k = 1$ in the homogeneous representation, we may write

$$\begin{bmatrix} c_{h1} \\ c_{h2} \\ c_{h3} \\ c_{h4} \end{bmatrix} = \begin{bmatrix} a_{11} & a_{12} & a_{13} & a_{14} \\ a_{21} & a_{22} & a_{23} & a_{24} \\ a_{31} & a_{32} & a_{33} & a_{34} \\ a_{41} & a_{42} & a_{43} & a_{44} \end{bmatrix} \begin{bmatrix} X \\ Y \\ Z \\ 1 \end{bmatrix} \qquad (2.5\text{-}44)$$

From the discussion in the previous two sections we know that the camera coordinates in Cartesian form are given by

$$x = c_{h1}/c_{h4} \qquad (2.5\text{-}45)$$

and

$$y = c_{h2}/c_{h4}. \qquad (2.5\text{-}46)$$

Substituting $c_{h1} = xc_{h4}$ and $c_{h2} = yc_{h4}$ in Eq. (2.5-44) and expanding the matrix product yields

$$xc_{h4} = a_{11}X + a_{12}Y + a_{13}Z + a_{14}$$
$$yc_{h4} = a_{21}X + a_{22}Y + a_{23}Z + a_{24} \qquad (2.5\text{-}47)$$
$$c_{h4} = a_{41}X + a_{42}Y + a_{43}Z + a_{44},$$

where expansion of c_{h3} has been ignored because it is related to z.

Substitution of c_{h4} in the first two equations of (2.5-47) yields two equations with 12 unknown coefficients:

$$a_{11}X + a_{12}Y + a_{13}Z - a_{41}xX - a_{42}xY - a_{43}xZ - a_{44}x + a_{14} = 0 \qquad (2.5\text{-}48)$$

$$a_{21}X + a_{22}Y + a_{23}Z - a_{41}yX - a_{42}yY - a_{43}yZ - a_{44}y + a_{24} = 0 \qquad (2.5\text{-}49)$$

The calibration procedure then consists of (1) obtaining $m \geq 6$ world points (there are *two* equations) with known coordinates (X_i, Y_i, Z_i), $i = 1, 2, \ldots, m$, (2) imaging these points with the camera in a given position to obtain the corresponding image points (x_i, y_i), $i = 1, 2, \ldots, m$, and (3) using these results in Eqs. (2.5-48) and (2.5-49) to solve for the unknown coefficients. There are many numerical techniques for finding an optimal solution to a linear system of equations such as the one given by these equations (see, for example, Noble [1969]).

2.5.5   Stereo Imaging

It was noted in Section 2.5.2 that mapping a 3D scene onto an image plane is a many-to-one transformation. That is, an image point does not uniquely determine the location of a corresponding world point. It is shown in this section that the missing *depth* information can be obtained by using stereoscopic (*stereo* for short) imaging techniques.

As shown in Fig. 2.18, stereo imaging involves obtaining two separate image views of an object of interest (a single world point **w** in our present discussion). The distance between the centers of the two lenses is called the *baseline,* and the

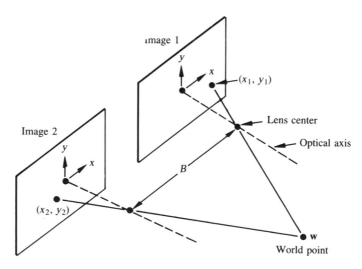

Figure 2.18   Model of the stereo imaging process. (From Fu, Gonzalez, and Lee [1987].)

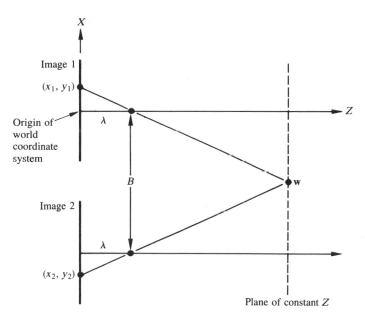

Figure 2.19 Top view of Fig. 2.18 with the first camera brought into coincidence with the world coordinate system. (From Fu, Gonzalez, and Lee [1987].)

objective is to find the coordinates (X, Y, Z) of the point w given its image points (x_1, y_1) and (x_2, y_2). It is assumed that the cameras are identical and that the coordinate systems of both cameras are perfectly aligned, differing only in the location of their origins, a condition usually met in practice. Recall our convention that, after the camera and world coordinate systems have been brought into coincidence, the xy plane of the image is aligned with the XY plane of the world coordinate system. Then, under the above assumption, the Z coordinate of w is exactly the same for both camera coordinate systems.

Suppose that we bring the first camera into coincidence with the world coordinate system, as shown in Fig. 2.19. Then, from Eq. (2.5-30), w lies on the line with (partial) coordinates

$$X_1 = \frac{x_1}{\lambda}(\lambda - Z_1),\tag{2.5-50}$$

where the subscripts on X and Z indicate that the first camera was moved to the origin of the world coordinate system, with the second camera and w following, but keeping the relative arrangement shown in Fig. 2.18. If, instead, the second camera had been brought to the origin of the world coordinate system, then we would have that **w** lies on the line with (partial) coordinates

$$X_2 = \frac{x_2}{\lambda} (\lambda - Z_2).$$
(2.5-51)

However, due to the separation between cameras and the fact that the Z coordinate of **w** is the same for both camera coordinate systems, it follows that

$$X_2 = X_1 + B$$
(2.5-52)

and

$$Z_2 = Z_1 = Z,$$
(2.5-53)

where, as indicated above, B is the baseline distance.

Substitution of Eqs. (2.5-52) and (2.5-53) into Eq. (2.5-50) and (2.5-51) results in the following equations:

$$X_1 = \frac{x_1}{\lambda} (\lambda - Z)$$
(2.5-54)

and

$$X_1 + B = \frac{x_2}{\lambda} (\lambda - Z).$$
(2.5-55)

Subtracting Eq. (2.5-54) from (2.5-55) and solving for Z yields the expression

$$Z = \lambda - \frac{\lambda B}{x_2 - x_1},$$
(2.5-56)

which indicates that if the difference between the corresponding image coordinates x_2 and x_1 can be determined, and the baseline and focal length are known, calculating the Z coordinate of **w** is a simple matter. The X and Y world coordinates then follow directly from Eqs. (2.5-30) and (2.5-31) using either (x_1, y_1) or (x_2, y_2).

The most difficult task in using Eq. (2.5-56) to obtain Z is to actually find two corresponding points in different images of the same scene. Since these points are generally in the same vicinity, a frequently used approach is to select a point within a small region in one of the image views and then attempt to find the best matching region in the other view by using correlation techniques, as discussed in Chapter 8. When the scene contains distinct features, such as prominent corners, a feature-matching approach will generally yield a faster solution for establishing correspondence.

Before leaving this discussion, we point out that the calibration procedure developed in the previous section is directly applicable to stereo imaging by simply treating the cameras independently.

2.6 PHOTOGRAPHIC FILM

Photographic film is an important element of image processing systems. It is often used as the medium where input images are recorded, and it is by far the most popular medium for recording output results. For these reasons, we conclude this chapter with a discussion of some basic properties of monochrome photographic film and their relation to image processing applications.

2.6.1 Film Structure and Exposure

A cross section of a typical photographic film as it would appear under magnification is shown in Fig. 2.20. It consists of the following layers and components: (1) a supercoat of gelatin used for protection against scratches and abrasion marks; (2) an emulsion layer consisting of minute silver halide crystals; (3) a substrate layer, which promotes adhesion of the emulsion to the film base; (4) the film base or support, made of cellulose triacetate or a related polymer; and (5) a backing layer to prevent curling.

When the film is exposed to light, the silver halide grains absorb optical energy and undergo a complex physical change. The grains that have absorbed a sufficient amount of energy contain tiny patches of metallic silver, called *development centers*. When the exposed film is developed, the existence of a single development center in a silver halide grain can precipitate the change of the entire grain to metallic silver. The grains that do not contain development centers do not undergo such a change. After development, the film is "fixed" by chemical removal of the remaining silver halide grains. The more light that reaches a given area of the film, the more silver halide is rendered developable and the denser the silver deposit that is formed there. Since the silver grains are largely opaque at optical frequencies, an image of gray tones is obtained where the brightness levels are reversed, thus producing the familiar film negative.

The process is repeated to obtain a positive picture. The negative is projected onto a sensitive paper carrying a silver halide emulsion similar to that used for the

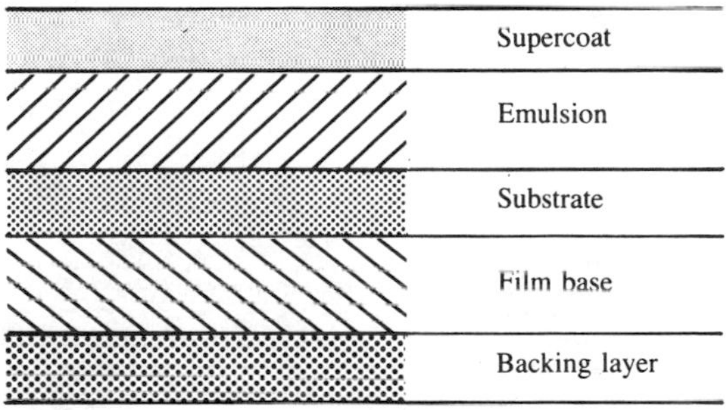

	Supercoat
	Emulsion
	Substrate
	Film base
	Backing layer

Figure 2.20 Structure of modern black-and-white film.

film. Exposure by a light source yields a latent image of the negative. After development, the paper bears a positive silver image. Enlargement of the negative is controlled by the choice of light source and size of positive paper used.

2.6.2 Film Characteristics

Of practical interest to the photographer are contrast, speed, graininess, and resolving power. An understanding of the effect of these parameters is particularly important in specialized applications such as photographing the results obtained in an image processing system.

Contrast

High-contrast films reproduce tone differences in the subject as large density differences in the photograph; low-contrast films translate tone differences as small density differences. The exposure E to which a film is subjected is defined as *energy per unit area* at each point on the photosensitive area. Exposure depends on the incident intensity I and the duration of the exposure T. These quantities are related by the expression

$$E = IT. \qquad (2.6\text{-}1)$$

The most widely used description of the photosensitive properties of photographic film is a plot of the density of the silver deposit on a film versus the logarithm of E. These curves are called characteristic curves, D-log-E curves (density vs. log exposure), and H & D curves (after Hurter and Driffield, who developed the method). Figure 2.21 shows a typical H & D curve for a photographic negative. When the

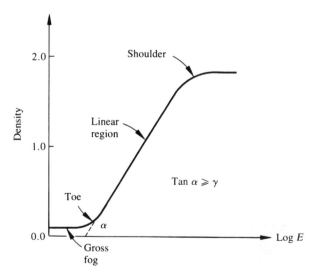

Figure 2.21   A typical H & D curve.

exposure is below a certain level, the density is independent of exposure and equal to a minimum value called the *gross fog*. In the *toe* of the curve, density begins to increase with increasing exposure. There follows a region of the curve in which density is linearly proportional to logarithmic exposure. The slope of this linear region is referred to as the film *gamma* (γ). Finally, the curve saturates in a region called the *shoulder*, and again there is no change in density with increasing exposure. The value of γ is a measure of film contrast: the steeper the slope, the higher the contrast rendered. General-purpose films of medium contrast have gammas in the range 0.7 to 1.0. High-contrast films have gammas on the order of 1.5 to 10. As a rule, films with relatively low gammas are used for continuous-tone reproduction; high-contrast films are used for copying line originals and other specialized purposes.

Speed
The speed of a film determines how much light is needed to produce a given amount of silver on development. The lower the speed, the longer the film must be exposed to record a given image. The most widely used standard of speed is the ASA scale. This scale is arithmetic, with the speed number directly proportional to the sensitivity of the film. A film of ASA 200 is twice as fast (and for a given subject requires half as much exposure) as a film of ASA 100. Some speed scales, such as the DIN system used in Europe, are logarithmic. Every increase of three in the DIN speed number doubles the actual speed. An ASA 50 film is equivalent to a DIN 18, an ASA 100 to a DIN 21, and so on.

General-purpose films for outdoor and some indoor photography have speeds between ASA 80 and ASA 160; fine-grain films for maximum image definition between ASA 20 and ASA 64; high-speed films for poor light and indoor photography between ASA 200 and ASA 500; and ultraspeed films for very low light levels from ASA 650 and up.

Graininess
The image derived from the silver halide crystals is discontinuous in structure. This gives an appearance of graininess in big enlargements. The effect is most prominent in fast films, which have comparatively large crystals; slower, fine-grain emulsions are therefore preferable in applications where fine detail is desired or where enlargement of the negatives is necessary.

Resolving power
The fineness of detail that a film can resolve depends not only on its graininess, but also on the light-scattering properties of the emulsion and on the contrast with which the film reproduces fine detail. Fine-grain films with thin emulsions yield the highest resolving power.

2.6.3   Diaphragm and Shutter Settings
Regardless of the type of film used, proper camera settings are essential in obtaining acceptable pictures. The principal settings are the lens diaphragm and shutter speed.

In the lens diaphragm, a series of leaves increase or decrease the size of the opening to control the amount of light passing through the lens to the film. The diaphragm control ring is calibrated with a scale of so-called f-numbers or stop numbers in a series such as: 1.4, 2, 2.8, 4, 5.6, 8, 11, 16, 22, and 32. The f-numbers are inversely proportional to the amount of light admitted. In the above series, each setting admits twice as much light as the next higher f-number (thus giving twice as much exposure), and half as much light as the next lower value. Shutter speed settings on present-day cameras also follow a standard double-or-half sequence. Typical speeds are 1, $\frac{1}{2}$, $\frac{1}{4}$, $\frac{1}{8}$, $\frac{1}{15}$, $\frac{1}{30}$, $\frac{1}{60}$, $\frac{1}{125}$, $\frac{1}{250}$, $\frac{1}{500}$, and $\frac{1}{1000}$ sec. The faster the shutter speed, the shorter the exposure time obtained.

The diaphragm and shutter control the amount of light reaching the film by adjusting the light intensity and the time during which it acts. Different aperture–shutter speed combinations can thus yield the same exposure. For example, diaphragm $f/2.8$ with $\frac{1}{250}$ sec, $f/4$ with $\frac{1}{125}$ sec, and $f/5.6$ with $\frac{1}{60}$ sec, all yield the same exposure. It should be noted, however, that the combination chosen for these two settings is not independent of the conditions under which a picture is taken. For example, when photographing a scene where depth of focus is of interest, the f-stop should be selected as high as possible to give the lens a "pin-hole" characteristic. For a given film, this requirement limits the range of shutter speeds that yield adequate exposures. In other applications, the shutter speed is the essential consideration. An example with image processing implications is the problem of photographing a television screen. In this case, the shutter speed must be set below the refreshing rate of the TV set ($\frac{1}{30}$ sec per frame) or trace back information that is too fast for the human eye to see will be recorded on the film. Typically, $\frac{1}{8}$ sec is adequate, although slower speeds are often used. Many of the images in this book, for example, were photographed at $\frac{1}{4}$ sec with Kodak Panatomic-X fine-grain film (ASA 32). The diaphragm settings were determined by using an exposure meter to measure the light intensity of each image.

2.7 CONCLUDING REMARKS

The material in this chapter is primarily background information for subsequent discussions. Our treatment of the human visual system, although brief, should give the reader a basic idea of the capabilities of the eye in perceiving pictorial information. Similarly, the image model developed in Section 2.2 is used in Chapter 4 as the basis for an image enhancement technique called *homomorphic filtering*.

The sampling ideas introduced in Section 2.3 are considered again in Section 3.3.9 after the necessary mathematical tools for a deeper analytical study of this problem are developed. Sampling and quantization considerations also play a central role in Chapter 6 in the context of image encoding applications, where the problem is one of compressing the large quantities of data that result from image digitization.

The material in Section 2.4 is basic to the understanding of numerous image processing techniques discussed in the following chapters. The imaging geometry concepts developed in Section 2.5 play an important role in situations where three-dimensional scene information must be correlated with images acquired by a camera and subsequently processed by a computer.

REFERENCES

The material presented in Sections 2.1.1 and 2.1.2 is based primarily on the books by Cornsweet [1970] and by Graham [1965]. Additional reading for Section 2.1.3 may be found in Sheppard [1968]; Sheppard, Stratton, and Gazley [1969]; and Stevens [1951]. The image model presented in Section 2.2 has been investigated by Oppenheim, Schafer, and Stockham [1968] in connection with image enhancement applications. References for the illumination and reflectance values used in that section are Moon [1961] and the *IES Lighting Handbook* [1972]. Some of the material presented in Section 2.3 is based on the work of Huang [1965]. The papers by Scoville [1965] and by Gaven, Tavitian, and Harabedian [1970] are also of interest. Additional reading for the material in Section 2.4 may be found in Toriwaki et al. [1979] and in Rosenfeld and Kak [1982]. Section 2.5 is from the book by Fu, Gonzalez, and Lee [1987]. References for Section 2.6 are Mees [1966], Perrin [1960], Nelson [1971], and *Kodak Plates and Films for Scientific Photography* [1973].

PROBLEMS

2.1 Suppose that a flat area with center at (x_0, y_0) is illuminated by a light source with intensity distribution

$$i(x, y) = Ke^{-[(x-x_0)^2+(y-y_0)^2]}.$$

If the reflectance characteristic of the area is

$$r(x, y) = 10(x - x_0) + 10(y - y_0) + 20.$$

What is the value of K that would yield an image intensity of 100 at (x_0, y_0)?

2.2 Assume that the area in Problem 2.1 now has a constant reflectance of 1, and let $K = 255$. If the resulting image is digitized with n bits of intensity resolution, and the eye can detect an abrupt change of eight shades of intensity between adjacent pixels, what is the value of n that will cause visible false contouring?

2.3 Sketch what the image in Problem 2.2 would look like for $n = 2$.

2.4 A common measure of transmission for digital data is the *baud rate,* defined as the number of bits transmitted per second. Generally, transmission is accomplished in packets consisting of a start bit, a byte (8 bits) of information, and a stop bit. Using this approach, answer the following:
  a) How many minutes would it take to transmit a 512×512 image with 256 gray levels at 300 baud?
  b) What would the time be at 9600 baud?
  c) Repeat (a) and (b) for a 1024×1024 image with 256 gray levels.

2.5 a) Show that the D_4 distance between two points p and q is equal to the shortest 4-path between these points.
  b) Is this path unique?

2.6 Consider the image segment shown below.
   a) Let $V = \{0, 1\}$ and compute the D_4, D_8, and D_m distances between p and q.
   b) Repeat for $V = \{1, 2\}$.

$$
\begin{array}{cccc}
3 & 1 & 2 & 1(q) \\
2 & 2 & 0 & 2 \\
1 & 2 & 1 & 1 \\
(p)1 & 0 & 1 & 2
\end{array}
$$

2.7 Consider the two image subsets S_1 and S_2 shown below. Given that $V = \{1\}$, determine if S_1 and S_2 are (a) 4-connected, (b) 8-connected, (c) m-connected.

$$
\begin{array}{ccccccccccc}
 & S_1 & & & & & S_2 & & & & \\
0 & 0 & 0 & 0 & 0 & 0 & 0 & 1 & 1 & 0 \\
1 & 0 & 0 & 1 & 0 & 0 & 1 & 0 & 0 & 1 \\
1 & 0 & 0 & 1 & 0 & 1 & 1 & 0 & 0 & 0 \\
0 & 0 & 1 & 1 & 1 & 0 & 0 & 0 & 0 & 0 \\
0 & 0 & 1 & 1 & 1 & 0 & 0 & 1 & 1 & 1
\end{array}
$$

2.8 a) Give the transformation matrix used to rotate an *image* by 45° in the clockwise direction.
   b) How would this transformation be used to achieve the desired image rotation?
   c) Use the matrix obtained in (a) to rotate the image point $(x, y) = (1, 0)$.

2.9 Determine if the world point with coordinates $(1/2, 1/2, \sqrt{2}/2)$ is on the optical axis of a camera located at $(0, 0, \sqrt{2})$, panned 135°, and tilted 135°. Assume a 50-mm lens and let $r_1 = r_2 = r_3 = 0$.

2.10 Start with Eq. (2.5-41) and derive Eqs. (2.5-42) and (2.5-43).

2.11 Modify the ALU procedure given in Section 2.4.4 to replace each pixel in an image by the average of its 4-neighbors. Do not include the pixel itself in the computation of the average.

2.12 The 3 ×·3 mask shown below is frequently used to compute the derivative in the x direction at each point in an image.

$$
\begin{array}{ccc}
-1 & -2 & -1 \\
0 & 0 & 0 \\
1 & 2 & 1
\end{array}
$$

Give an ALU procedure used to implement this operation.

CHAPTER 3

IMAGE TRANSFORMS

And be not conformed to this world:
but be ye transformed by the renewing
of your mind . . .
Romans 12:2

The material in this chapter deals primarily with the development of two-dimensional transforms and their properties. Transform theory has played a key role in image processing for a number of years, and it continues to be a topic of interest in theoretical as well as applied work in this field. Two-dimensional transforms are used in the following chapters for image enhancement, restoration, encoding, and description.

Although other transforms are discussed in some detail in this chapter, emphasis is placed on the Fourier transform because of its wide range of applications in image processing problems. The Fourier transform of one and two continuous variables is introduced in Section 3.1. These concepts are then expressed in discrete form in Section 3.2. Several important properties of the two-dimensional Fourier transform are developed and illustrated in Section 3.3. This section is followed by the development of a fast Fourier transform algorithm which can be used to reduce the number of calculations to a fraction of that required to implement the discrete Fourier transform by direct methods. Section 3.5 deals with the development of the Walsh, Hadamard, and Discrete Cosine transforms, and Section 3.6 introduces the Hotelling transform. Finally, Section 3.7 deals with the development of the Hough transform and some of its applications.

3.1 INTRODUCTION TO THE FOURIER TRANSFORM

Let $f(x)$ be a continuous function of a real variable x. The *Fourier transform* of $f(x)$, denoted by $\mathfrak{F}\{f(x)\}$, is defined by the equation

$$\Im\{f(x)\} = F(u) = \int_{-\infty}^{\infty} f(x) \exp[-j2\pi ux] \, dx, \tag{3.1-1}$$

where $j = \sqrt{-1}$.

Given $F(u)$, $f(x)$ can be obtained by using the *inverse Fourier transform*

$$\Im^{-1}\{F(u)\} = f(x)$$

$$= \int_{-\infty}^{\infty} F(u) \exp[j2\pi ux] \, du. \tag{3.1-2}$$

Equations (3.1-1) and (3.1-2), which are called the *Fourier transform pair*, can be shown to exist if $f(x)$ is continuous and integrable and $F(u)$ is integrable. These conditions are almost always satisfied in practice.

We will be concerned throughout this book with functions $f(x)$ that are real. The Fourier transform of a real function, however, is generally complex; that is,

$$F(u) = R(u) + jI(u), \tag{3.1-3}$$

where $R(u)$ and $I(u)$ are, respectively, the real and imaginary components of $F(u)$. It is often convenient to express Eq. (3.1-3) in exponential form:

$$F(u) = |F(u)|e^{j\phi(u)}, \tag{3.1-4}$$

where

$$|F(u)| = [R^2(u) + I^2(u)]^{1/2} \tag{3.1-5}$$

and

$$\phi(u) = \tan^{-1}\left[\frac{I(u)}{R(u)}\right]. \tag{3.1-6}$$

The magnitude function $|F(u)|$ is called the *Fourier spectrum* of $f(x)$, and $\phi(u)$ its *phase angle*. The square of the spectrum,

$$P(u) = |F(u)|^2$$

$$= R^2(u) + I^2(u) \tag{3.1-7}$$

is commonly referred to as the *power spectrum* of $f(x)$. The term *spectral density* is also commonly used to denote the power spectrum.

The variable u appearing in the Fourier transform is often called the *frequency variable*. This name arises from the fact that, using Euler's formula, the exponential term, $\exp[-j2\pi ux]$, may be expressed in the form:

$$\exp[-j2\pi ux] = \cos 2\pi ux - j \sin 2\pi ux. \tag{3.1-8}$$

If we interpret the integral in Eq. (3.1-1) as a limit-summation of discrete terms, it is evident that $F(u)$ is composed of an infinite sum of sine and cosine terms, and that each value of u determines the *frequency* of its corresponding sine–cosine pair.

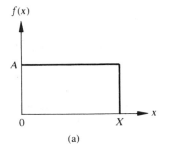

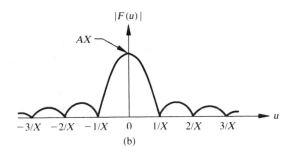

Figure 3.1   A simple function and its Fourier spectrum.

Example: Consider the simple function shown in Fig. 3.1(a). Its Fourier transform is obtained from Eq. (3.1-1) as follows:

$$F(u) = \int_{-\infty}^{\infty} f(x) \exp[-j2\pi ux]\, dx$$

$$= \int_{0}^{X} A \exp[-j2\pi ux]\, dx$$

$$= \frac{-A}{j2\pi u}\,[e^{-j2\pi ux}]_0^X = \frac{-A}{j2\pi u}\,[e^{-j2\pi uX} - 1]$$

$$= \frac{A}{j2\pi u}\,[e^{j\pi uX} - e^{-j\pi uX}]e^{-j\pi uX}$$

$$= \frac{A}{\pi u}\, \sin(\pi uX)\, e^{-j\pi uX},$$

which is a complex function. The Fourier spectrum is given by

$$|F(u)| = \left|\frac{A}{\pi u}\right|\, |\sin(\pi uX)|\, |e^{-j\pi uX}|$$

$$= AX \left|\frac{\sin(\pi uX)}{(\pi uX)}\right|.$$

A plot of $|F(u)|$ is shown in Fig. 3.1(b).   ☐

The Fourier transform can be easily extended to a function $f(x, y)$ of two variables. If $f(x, y)$ is continuous and integrable, and $F(u, v)$ is integrable, we have that the following Fourier transform pair exists:

$$\mathcal{F}\{f(x, y)\} = F(u, v) = \int\int_{-\infty}^{\infty} f(x, y) \exp[-j2\pi(ux + vy)]\, dx\, dy \qquad (3.1\text{-}9)$$

and

$$\mathfrak{F}^{-1}\{F(u, v)\} = f(x, y) = \int\!\!\int_{-\infty}^{\infty} F(u, v) \exp[j2\pi(ux + vy)] \, du \, dv, \quad (3.1\text{-}10)$$

where u and v are the frequency variables.

As in the one-dimensional case, the Fourier spectrum, phase, and power spectrum are, respectively, given by the relations:

$$|F(u, v)| = [R^2(u, v) + I^2(u, v)]^{1/2} \qquad (3.1\text{-}11)$$

$$\phi(u, v) = \tan^{-1}\left[\frac{I(u, v)}{R(u, v)}\right] \qquad (3.1\text{-}12)$$

and

$$P(u, v) = |F(u, v)|^2 = R^2(u, v) + I^2(u, v). \qquad (3.1\text{-}13)$$

Example: The Fourier transform of the function shown in Fig. 3.2(a) is given by

$$F(u, v) = \int\!\!\int_{-\infty}^{\infty} f(x, y) \exp[-j2\pi(ux + vy)] \, dx \, dy$$

$$= A \int_0^X \exp[-j2\pi ux] \, dx \int_0^Y \exp[-j2\pi vy] \, dy$$

$$= A \left[\frac{e^{-j2\pi ux}}{-j2\pi u}\right]_0^X \left[\frac{e^{-j2\pi vy}}{-j2\pi v}\right]_0^Y$$

$$= \frac{A}{-j2\pi u} [e^{-j2\pi uX} - 1] \frac{1}{-j2\pi v} [e^{-j2\pi vY} - 1]$$

$$= AXY \left[\frac{\sin(\pi uX) \, e^{-j\pi uX}}{(\pi uX)}\right] \left[\frac{\sin(\pi vY) \, e^{-j\pi vY}}{(\pi vY)}\right].$$

The spectrum is given by

$$|F(u, v)| = AXY \left|\frac{\sin(\pi uX)}{(\pi uX)}\right| \left|\frac{\sin(\pi vY)}{(\pi vY)}\right|.$$

A plot of this function is shown in Fig. 3.2(b) in three-dimensional perspective. Figure 3.2(c) shows the spectrum as an intensity function, where brightness is proportional to the amplitude of $|F(u, v)|$. Other examples of two-dimensional functions and their spectra are shown in Fig. 3.3. In this case, both $f(x, y)$ and $|F(u, v)|$ are shown as images. □

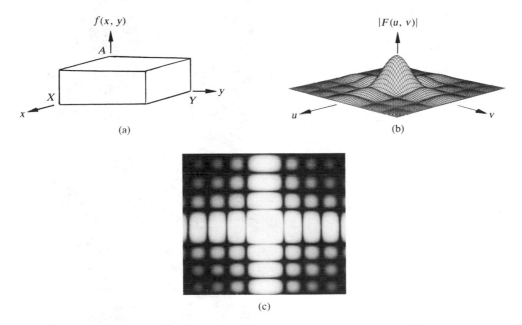

Figure 3.2 (a) A two-dimensional function, (b) its Fourier spectrum, and (c) the spectrum displayed as an intensity function.

3.2 THE DISCRETE FOURIER TRANSFORM

Suppose that a continuous function $f(x)$ is discretized into a sequence $\{f(x_0), f(x_0 + \Delta x), f(x_0 + 2\Delta x), \ldots, f(x_0 + [N - 1]\Delta x)\}$ by taking N samples Δx units apart, as shown in Fig. 3.4. It will be convenient in subsequent developments to use x as either a discrete or continuous variable, depending on the context of the discussion. We may do this by defining

$$f(x) = f(x_0 + x\,\Delta x), \qquad (3.2-1)$$

where x now assumes the discrete values $0, 1, 2, \ldots, N - 1$. In other words, the sequence $\{f(0), f(1), f(2), \ldots, f(N - 1)\}$ will be used to denote *any* N uniformly spaced samples from a corresponding continuous function.

With the above notation in mind, we have that the *discrete* Fourier transform pair that applies to sampled functions is given by[†]

$$F(u) = \frac{1}{N} \sum_{x=0}^{N-1} f(x) \exp[-j2\pi ux/N] \qquad (3.2-2)$$

[†] A proof of these results is outside the scope of this discussion. Proofs relating the continuous and discrete Fourier transforms can be found in Blackman and Tukey [1958]; Cooley, Lewis, and Welch [1967]; and Brigham [1974].

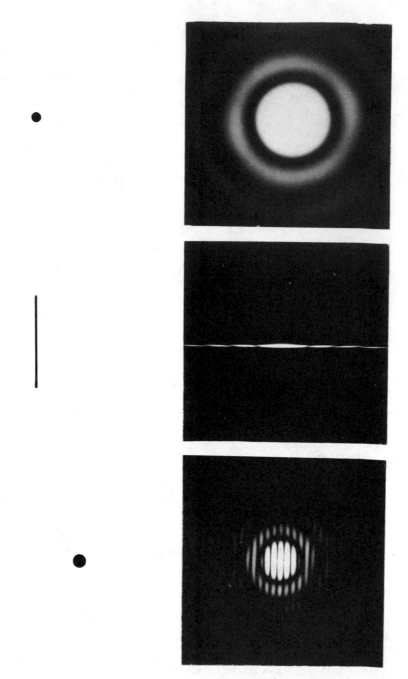

Figure 3.3   Some two-dimensional functions and their Fourier spectra.

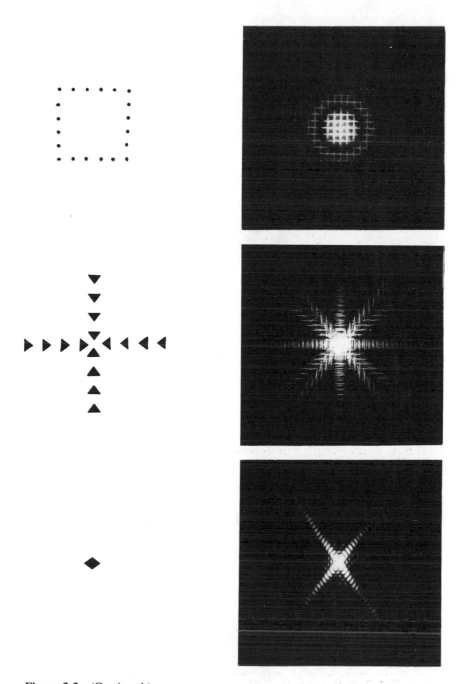

Figure 3.3 (Continued.)

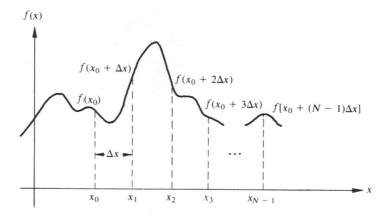

Figure 3.4 Sampling a continuous function.

for $u = 0, 1, 2, \ldots, N - 1$, and

$$f(x) = \sum_{u=0}^{N-1} F(u) \exp[j2\pi ux/N] \qquad (3.2\text{-}3)$$

for $x = 0, 1, 2, \ldots, N - 1$.

The values $u = 0, 1, 2, \ldots, N - 1$ in the discrete Fourier transform given in Eq. (3.2-2) correspond to samples of the continuous transform at values $0, \Delta u, 2\Delta u, \ldots, (N - 1)\Delta u$. In other words, we are letting $F(u)$ represent $F(u\Delta u)$. This notation is similar to that used for the discrete $f(x)$, with the exception that the samples of $F(u)$ start at the origin of the frequency axis. It can be shown that Δu and Δx are related by the expression

$$\Delta u = \frac{1}{N \, \Delta x}. \qquad (3.2\text{-}4)$$

In the two-variable case the discrete Fourier transform pair is given by the equations

$$F(u, v) = \frac{1}{MN} \sum_{x=0}^{M-1} \sum_{y=0}^{N-1} f(x, y) \exp[-j2\pi(ux/M + vy/N)] \qquad (3.2\text{-}5)$$

for $u = 0, 1, 2, \ldots, M - 1, v = 0, 1, 2, \ldots, N - 1$, and

$$f(x, y) = \sum_{u=0}^{M-1} \sum_{v=0}^{N-1} F(u, v) \exp[j2\pi(ux/M + vy/N)] \qquad (3.2\text{-}6)$$

for $x = 0, 1, 2, \ldots, M - 1$ and $y = 0, 1, 2, \ldots, N - 1$.

Sampling of a continuous function is now in a two-dimensional grid with divisions of width Δx and Δy in the x and y axis, respectively. As in the one-dimensional case, the discrete function $f(x, y)$ represents samples of the function $f(x_0 + x\Delta x,$ $y_0 + y\Delta y)$ for $x = 0, 1, 2, \ldots, M - 1$ and $y = 0, 1, 2, \ldots, N - 1$. Similar comments hold for $F(u, v)$. The sampling increments in the spatial and frequency domains are related by

$$\Delta u = \frac{1}{M\Delta x} \tag{3.2-7}$$

and

$$\Delta v = \frac{1}{N\Delta y}. \tag{3.2-8}$$

When images are sampled in a square array we have that $M = N$ and

$$F(u, v) = \frac{1}{N} \sum_{x=0}^{N-1} \sum_{y=0}^{N-1} f(x, y) \exp[-j2\pi(ux + vy)/N] \tag{3.2-9}$$

for $u, v = 0, 1, 2, \ldots, N - 1$, and

$$f(x, y) = \frac{1}{N} \sum_{u=0}^{N-1} \sum_{v=0}^{N-1} F(u, v) \exp[j2\pi(ux + vy)/N] \tag{3.2-10}$$

for $x, y = 0, 1, 2, \ldots, N - 1$. Note that in this case we have included a $1/N$ term in both expressions. Since $F(u, v)$ and $f(x, y)$ are a Fourier transform pair, the grouping of these constant multiplicative terms is arbitrary. In practice, images are typically digitized in square arrays, so we will be mostly concerned with the Fourier transform pair given in Eqs. (3.2-9) and (3.2-10). The formulation given in Eqs. (3.2-5) and (3.2-6) will be used from time to time in situations where it is important to stress generality of the image size.

The Fourier spectrum, phase, and energy spectrum of one- and two-dimensional discrete functions are also given by Eqs. (3.1-5) through (3.1-7) and Eqs. (3.1-11) through (3.1-13), respectively. The only difference is that the independent variables are discrete.

Unlike the continuous case, we need not be concerned about the existence of the discrete Fourier transform since both $F(u)$ and $F(u, v)$ always exist in the discrete case. In the one-dimensional case, for example, this can be shown by direct substitution of Eq. (3.2-3) into Eq. (3.2-2):

$$F(u) = \frac{1}{N} \sum_{x=0}^{N-1} \left[\sum_{r=0}^{N-1} F(r) \exp[j2\pi rx/N] \exp[\ j2\pi ux/N] \right]$$

$$= \frac{1}{N} \sum_{r=0}^{N-1} F(r) \left[\sum_{x=0}^{N-1} \exp[j2\pi rx/N] \exp[-j2\pi ux/N] \right] \tag{3.2-11}$$

$$= F(u).$$

Identity (3.2-11) follows from the orthogonality condition

$$\sum_{x=0}^{N-1} \exp[j2\pi rx/N] \exp[-j2\pi ux/N] = \begin{cases} N & \text{if } r = u, \\ 0 & \text{otherwise.} \end{cases} \tag{3.2-12}$$

Note that a change of variable from u to r was made in Eq. (3.2-2) to clarify the notation.

Substitution of Eq. (3.2-2) into Eq. (3.2-3) would also yield an identity on $f(x)$, thus indicating that the Fourier transform pair given by these equations always exists. A similar argument holds for the discrete, two-dimensional Fourier transform pair.

Example: As an illustration of Eqs. (3.2-2) and (3.2-3), consider the function shown in Fig. 3.5(a). If this function is sampled at the argument values $x_0 = 0.5$, $x_1 = 0.75$, $x_2 = 1.0$, and $x_3 = 1.25$, and if the argument is redefined as discussed above, we obtain the discrete function shown in Fig. 3.5(b).

Application of Eq. (3.2-2) to the resulting four samples yields the following sequence of steps:

$$F(0) = \frac{1}{4} \sum_{x=0}^{3} f(x) \exp[0]$$
$$= \frac{1}{4}[f(0) + f(1) + f(2) + f(3)]$$
$$= \frac{1}{4}[2 + 3 + 4 + 4]$$
$$= 3.25.$$

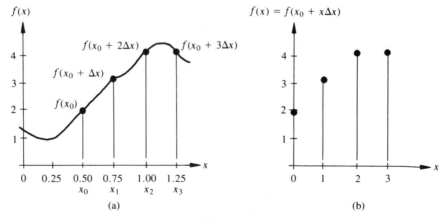

Figure 3.5 A simple function and samples in the x domain. In (a) x is a continuous variable; in (b) x is discrete.

$$F(1) = \frac{1}{4} \sum_{x=0}^{3} f(x) \exp[-j2\pi x/4]$$

$$= \frac{1}{4} [2e^0 + 3e^{-j\pi/2} + 4e^{-j\pi} + 4e^{-j3\pi/2}]$$

$$= \frac{1}{4} [-2 + j],$$

where the last step follows from Euler's formula. Continuing with this procedure, we obtain

$$F(2) = \frac{1}{4} \sum_{x=0}^{3} f(x) \exp[-j4\pi x/4]$$

$$= \frac{1}{4} [2e^0 + 3e^{-j\pi} + 4e^{-j2\pi} + 4e^{-j3\pi}]$$

$$= -\frac{1}{4} [1 + j0]$$

and

$$F(3) = \frac{1}{4} \sum_{x=0}^{3} f(x) \exp[-j6\pi x/4]$$

$$= \frac{1}{4} [2e^0 + 3e^{-j3\pi/2} + 4e^{-j3\pi} + 4e^{-j9\pi/2}]$$

$$= -\frac{1}{4} [2 + j].$$

It is noted that all values of $f(x)$ contribute to each of the four terms of the discrete Fourier transform. Conversely, all terms of the transform contribute in forming the inverse transform via Eq. (3.2-3). The procedure for obtaining the inverse is analogous to the one described above for computing $F(u)$.

The Fourier spectrum is obtained from the magnitude of each of the transform terms; that is,

$$|F(0)| = 3.25,$$
$$|F(1)| = [(2/4)^2 + (1/4)^2]^{1/2} = \sqrt{5}/4,$$
$$|F(2)| = [(1/4)^2 + (0/4)^2]^{1/2} = 1/4,$$

and

$$|F(3)| = [(2/4)^2 + (1/4)^2]^{1/2} = \sqrt{5}/4. \qquad \square$$

3.3 SOME PROPERTIES OF THE TWO-DIMENSIONAL FOURIER TRANSFORM

Attention is focused in this section on properties of the Fourier transform that will be of value in subsequent discussions. Although our primary interest is in two-dimensional, discrete transforms, the underlying concepts of some of these properties are much easier to grasp if they are presented first in their one-dimensional, continuous form.

Since several of the topics considered in this section are illustrated by images and their Fourier spectra displayed as intensity functions, some comments concerning these displays are in order before beginning a discussion of Fourier transform properties. Many image spectra decrease rather rapidly as a function of increasing frequency and therefore their high-frequency terms have a tendency to become obscured when displayed in image form. A useful processing technique that compensates for this difficulty consists of displaying the function

$$D(u, v) = \log(1 + |F(u, v)|) \qquad (3.3\text{-}1)$$

instead of $|F(u, v)|$. Use of this equation preserves the zero values in the frequency plane since $D(u, v) = 0$ when $|F(u, v)| = 0$. It is also noted that $D(u, v)$ is a nonnegative function.

As an illustration of the properties of the preceding logarithmic transformation, consider the Fourier spectra shown in Fig. 3.6. Part (a) of this figure is the spectrum of a pulse of unit width and height (see Fig. 3.1). Figure 3.6(b) shows the effect of using Eq. (3.3-1) and rescaling the results to the amplitude interval [0, 1]. It is noted that, although the peak value is still 1, the amplitude of the side lobes has increased slightly. The effect is more pronounced in Figs. 3.6(c)' and (d), where the maximum amplitude of $|F(u)|$ is assumed to be 20 instead of 1. In Fig. 3.6(d), which was rescaled after taking the log, the ratio of the central peak to the peak of any of the side lobes is much smaller than the corresponding ratio in Fig. 3.6(b). If one considers the amplitude of these functions as being proportional to intensity, it is evident that the side lobes of Fig. 3.6(d) would be more visible than those in Fig. 3.6(b).

The degree of amplitude equalization achieved by using Eq. (3.3-1) depends on the relative magnitude of the function $|F(u, v)|$, as illustrated in Fig. 3.6. In the one-dimensional case, the behavior of the ratio of the maximum to some minimum (nonzero) value of $F(u)$ as a function of amplitude can be examined by using the relation

$$R = \frac{\log(1 + KF_{max})}{\log(1 + KF_{min})}, \qquad (3.3\text{-}2)$$

where K is a scale factor.

Suppose, for example, that we consider the ratio of $F_{max} = 1.0$ to the peak of the first side lobe in Fig. 3.6(a). In this case, $F_{min} = 0.2$ and $F_{max}/F_{min} = 5.0$. In

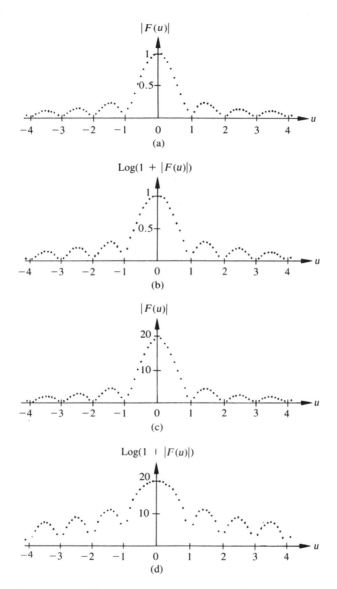

Figure 3.6 Effect of the log operation on a Fourier spectrum.

Fig. 3.6(b), on the other hand, use of the log operation yields the ratio $\log(1 + F_{max})/\log(1 + F_{min}) = 3.8$. Figure 3.6(c) is the same as Fig. 3.6(a), with the exception that all values have been multiplied by a scale factor of 20. Since the scale factor is the same for all values, the ratio F_{max}/F_{min} is again equal to 5.0. When the log is taken, however, we have the ratio $\log(1 + 20\,F_{max})/\log(1 + 20$

F_{min}) = 1.9, which is substantially smaller. The general behavior of R as a function of K is illustrated in Fig. 3.7 for the above values of F_{max} and F_{min}. It is noted that the ratio decreases rather quickly at first, but it levels off for values of K greater than about 40.

Use of Eq. (3.3-1) in a two-dimensional display of the spectrum greatly facilitates visual interpretation of the Fourier transform. An example of this is given in Fig. 3.8, which shows a picture of the planet Saturn, its normal spectrum, and the spectrum processed by adding 1 to $|F(u, v)|$, taking the log, and rescaling the values to the same gray scale used in displaying $|F(u, v)|$. By equalizing the range of values in the spectrum, use of the log operation clearly brings out low-level information that, if shown simply as $|F(u, v)|$, is beyond the dynamic range of the display system. Most Fourier spectra shown in image form throughout this book were processed using Eq. (3.3-1).

3.3.1 Separability

The discrete Fourier transform pair given in Eqs. (3.2-9) and (3.2-10) can be expressed in the separable forms

$$F(u, v) = \frac{1}{N} \sum_{x=0}^{N-1} \exp[-j2\pi ux/N] \sum_{y=0}^{N-1} f(x, y) \exp[-j2\pi vy/N] \qquad (3.3\text{-}3)$$

for $u, v = 0, 1, \ldots , N - 1$, and

$$f(x, y) = \frac{1}{N} \sum_{u=0}^{N-1} \exp[j2\pi ux/N] \sum_{v=0}^{N-1} F(u, v) \exp[j2\pi vy/N] \qquad (3.3\text{-}4)$$

for $x, y = 0, 1, \ldots , N - 1$.

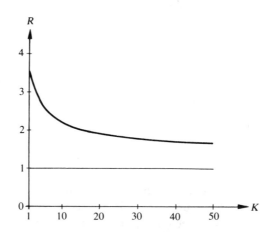

Figure 3.7   Behavior of Eq. (3.3–2) as a function of K for $F_{max} = 1.0$ and $F_{min} = 0.2$.

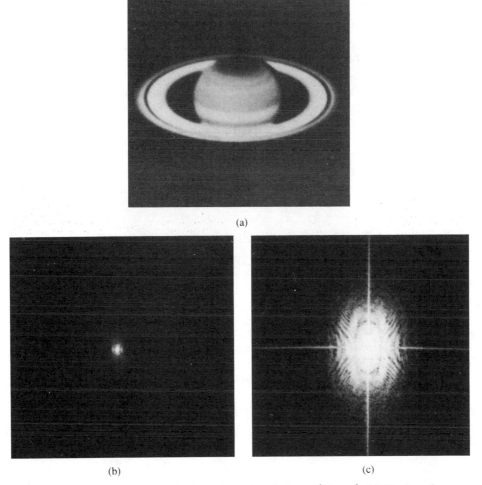

Figure 3.8 (a) A picture of the planet Saturn. (b) Display of $|F(u, v)|$. (c) Display of $\log(1 + |F(u, v)|)$.

For our purposes, the principal advantage of the separability property is that $F(u, v)$ or $f(x, y)$ can be obtained in two steps by successive applications of the one-dimensional Fourier transform or its inverse. This becomes evident if Eq. (3.3-3) is expressed in the form

$$F(u, v) = \frac{1}{N} \sum_{x=0}^{N-1} F(x, v) \exp[-j2\pi ux/N], \tag{3.3-5}$$

where

$$F(x, v) = N\left[\frac{1}{N}\sum_{y=0}^{N-1} f(x, y)\exp[-j2\pi vy/N]\right]. \tag{3.3-6}$$

For *each* value of x, the expression inside the brackets is a one-dimensional transform with frequency values $v = 0, 1, \ldots, N - 1$. Therefore the two-dimensional function $F(x, v)$ is obtained by taking a transform along *each* row of $f(x, y)$ and multiplying the result by N. The desired result, $F(u, v)$, is then obtained by taking a transform along each column of $F(x, v)$, as indicated by Eq. (3.3-5). The procedure is summarized in Fig. 3.9. It should be noted that the same results would be obtained by first taking transforms along the columns of $f(x, y)$ and then along the rows of the result. This is easily shown by reversing the order of the summations of Eq. (3.3-3). Identical comments hold for the implementation of Eq. (3.3-4).

3.3.2 Translation

The translation properties of the Fourier transform pair are given by

$$f(x,y)\exp[j2\pi(u_0x + v_0y)/N] \Leftrightarrow F(u - u_0, v - v_0) \tag{3.3-7a}$$

and

$$f(x - x_0, y - y_0) \Leftrightarrow F(u, v)\exp[-j2\pi(ux_0 + vy_0)/N], \tag{3.3-7b}$$

where the double arrow is used to indicate the correspondence between a function and its Fourier transform (and vice versa), as given in Eqs. (3.1-9) and (3.1-10) or Eqs. (3.2-9) and (3.2-10).

Equation (3.3-7a) shows that multiplying $f(x, y)$ by the indicated exponential term and taking the transform of the product results in a shift of the origin of the frequency plane to the point (u_0, v_0). Similarly, multiplying $F(u, v)$ by the exponential term shown and taking the inverse transform moves the origin of the spatial plane to (x_0, y_0).

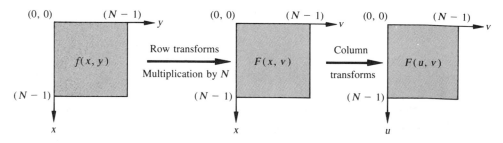

Figure 3.9   Computation of the two-dimensional Fourier transform as a series of one-dimensional transforms.

In this and the next chapter we will make considerable use of Eq. (3.3-7a), with $u_0 = v_0 = N/2$. In this case it follows that

$$\exp[j2\pi(u_0 x + v_0 y)/N] = e^{j\pi(x+y)}$$
$$= (-1)^{x+y}$$

and

$$f(x, y)(-1)^{x+y} \Leftrightarrow F(u - N/2, v - N/2). \tag{3.3-8}$$

Thus the origin of the Fourier transform of $f(x, y)$ can be moved to the center of its corresponding $N \times N$ frequency square simply by multiplying $f(x, y)$ by $(-1)^{x+y}$. In the one-variable case this reduces to multiplication of $f(x)$ by the term $(-1)^x$.

It is interesting to note from Eq. (3.3-7b) that a shift in $f(x, y)$ does not affect the magnitude of its Fourier transform, since

$$|F(u, v) \exp[-j2\pi(ux_0 + vy_0)/N]| = |F(u, v)|. \tag{3.3-9}$$

This should be kept in mind since visual examination of the transform is usually limited to a display of its magnitude.

3.3.3 Periodicity and Conjugate Symmetry

The discrete Fourier transform and its inverse are *periodic* with period $N;$ that is,

$$F(u, v) = F(u + N, v) = F(u, v + N) = F(u + N, v + N). \tag{3.3-10}$$

The validity of this property can be demonstrated by direct substitution of the variables of $(u + N)$ and $(v + N)$ in Eq. (3.2-9). Although Eq. (3.3-10) points out that $F(u, v)$ repeats itself for an infinite number of values of u and v, only the N values of each variable in any one period are required to obtain $f(x, y)$ from $F(u, v)$. In other words, only one period of the transform is necessary to completely specify $F(u, v)$ in the frequency domain. Similar comments hold for $f(x, y)$ in the spatial domain.

If $f(x, y)$ is real, the Fourier transform also exhibits conjugate symmetry since, in this case,

$$F(u, v) = F^*(-u, -v) \tag{3.3-11}$$

or, more interestingly,

$$|F(u, v)| = |F(-u, -v)|. \tag{3.3-12}$$

As mentioned earlier, it is often of interest to display the magnitude of the Fourier transform for interpretation purposes. In order to examine the implications of Eqs. (3.3-10) and (3.3-12) on a display of the transform magnitude, let us first consider the one-variable case, where

$$F(u) = F(u + N)$$

and

$$|F(u)| = |F(-u)|.$$

The periodicity property indicates that $F(u)$ has a period of length N, and the symmetry property shows that the magnitude of the transform is centered about the origin, as shown in Fig. 3.10(a). It is evident from this figure and the above comments that the magnitudes of the transform values from $([N/2] + 1)$ to $(N - 1)$ are images of the values in the half period on the left side of the origin. Since the discrete Fourier transform has been formulated for values of u in the interval $[0, N - 1]$, we see that the result of this formulation yields two back to back half periods in this interval. To display one full period, all that is necessary is to move the origin of the transform to the point $u = N/2$, as shown in Fig. 3.10(b). This is easily accomplished by multiplying $f(x)$ by $(-1)^x$ prior to taking the transform, as indicated earlier.

The same observations hold for the magnitude of the two-dimensional Fourier transform, with the exception that the results are considerably more difficult to interpret if the origin of the transform is not shifted to the frequency point $(N/2, N/2)$. This is shown in Figs. 3.11(b) and (c), where the latter figure was obtained by using the centering property of expression (3.3-8).

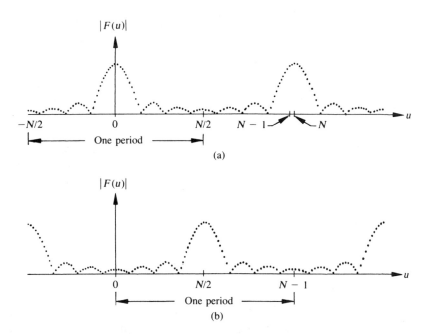

Figure 3.10   Illustration of the periodicity properties of the Fourier transform. (a) Fourier spectrum showing back-to-back half periods in the interval $[0, N - 1]$. (b) Shifted spectrum showing a full period in the same interval.

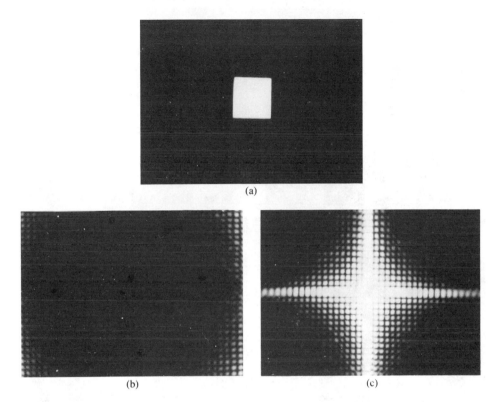

Figure 3.11 (a) A simple image. (b) Fourier spectrum without shifting. (c) Fourier spectrum shifted to the center of the frequency square.

3.3.4   Rotation

If we introduce the polar coordinates

$$x = r \cos \theta \qquad y = r \sin \theta \qquad u = \omega \cos \phi \qquad v = \omega \sin \phi$$

then $f(x, y)$ and $F(u, v)$ become $f(r, \theta)$ and $F(\omega, \phi)$, respectively. It can be shown by direct substitution in either the continuous or discrete Fourier transform pair that

$$f(r, \theta + \theta_0) \Leftrightarrow F(\omega, \phi + \theta_0). \tag{3.3-13}$$

In other words, if $f(x, y)$ is rotated by an angle θ_0, then $F(u, v)$ is rotated by the same angle. Similarly, rotating $F(u, v)$ causes $f(x, y)$ to be rotated by the same angle. This property is illustrated in Fig. 3.12.

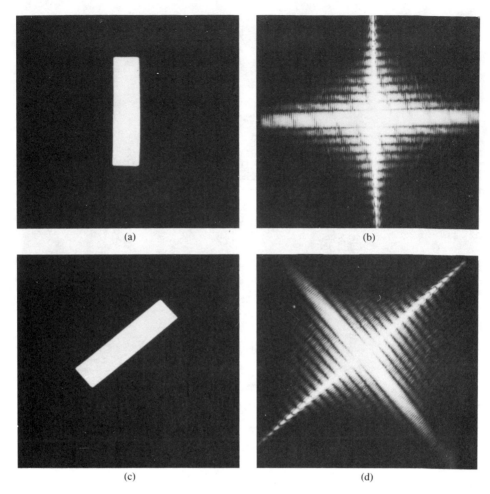

Figure 3.12 Rotational properties of the Fourier transform. (a) A simple image. (b) Spectrum. (c) Rotated image. (d) Resulting spectrum.

3.3.5   Distributivity and Scaling

It follows directly from the definition of the continuous or discrete transform pair that

$$\mathfrak{F}\{f_1(x, y) + f_2(x, y)\} = \mathfrak{F}\{f_1(x, y)\} + \mathfrak{F}\{f_2(x, y)\} \tag{3.3-14}$$

and, in general, that

$$\mathfrak{F}\{f_1(x, y) \cdot f_2(x, y)\} \neq \mathfrak{F}\{f_1(x, y)\} \cdot \mathfrak{F}\{f_2(x, y)\}. \tag{3.3-15}$$

In other words, the Fourier transform and its inverse are distributive over addition, but not over multiplication.

It is also easy to show that for two scalars a and b,

$$af(x, y) \Leftrightarrow aF(u, v) \qquad (3.3\text{-}16)$$

and

$$f(ax, by) \Leftrightarrow \frac{1}{|ab|} F(u/a, v/b). \qquad (3.3\text{-}17)$$

3.3.6 Average Value

A widely used definition of the average value of a two-dimensional discrete function is given by the expression

$$\bar{f}(x, y) = \frac{1}{N^2} \sum_{x=0}^{N-1} \sum_{y=0}^{N-1} f(x, y). \qquad (3.3\text{-}18)$$

Substitution of $u = v = 0$ in Eq. (3.2-9) yields

$$F(0, 0) = \frac{1}{N} \sum_{x=0}^{N-1} \sum_{y=0}^{N-1} f(x, y). \qquad (3.3\text{-}19)$$

Therefore we see that $\bar{f}(x, y)$ is related to the Fourier transform of $f(x, y)$ by the equation

$$\bar{f}(x, y) = \frac{1}{N} F(0, 0). \qquad (3.3\text{-}20)$$

3.3.7 Laplacian

The Laplacian of a two-variable function $f(x, y)$ is defined as

$$\nabla^2 f(x, y) = \frac{\partial^2 f}{\partial x^2} + \frac{\partial^2 f}{\partial y^2}. \qquad (3.3\text{-}21)$$

It follows from the definition of the two-dimensional Fourier transform that

$$\mathfrak{F}\{\nabla^2 f(x, y)\} \Leftrightarrow -(2\pi)^2 (u^2 + v^2) F(u, v). \qquad (3.3\text{-}22)$$

The Laplacian operator is useful for outlining edges in an image.

3.3.8 Convolution and Correlation

In this section we consider two Fourier transform relationships that constitute a basic link between the spatial and frequency domains. These relationships, called convolution and correlation, are of fundamental importance in developing a firm understanding of image processing techniques based on the Fourier transform. In order to clarify the concepts involved, we begin the discussion by considering convolution in one dimension and with continuous arguments. The development is then extended to the discrete case and, finally, to the two-dimensional continuous and discrete cases. The same format is followed in developing the concept of correlation.

Convolution

The convolution of two functions $f(x)$ and $g(x)$, denoted by $f(x)*g(x)$, is defined by the integral

$$f(x)*g(x) = \int_{-\infty}^{\infty} f(\alpha)g(x - \alpha)\, d\alpha, \tag{3.3-23}$$

where α is a dummy variable of integration. Since the mechanics of the convolution integral are not particularly easy to visualize, let us illustrate graphically the use of Eq. (3.3-23) by two simple examples.

Example: The first example demonstrates convolution of the functions $f(x)$ and $g(x)$ shown in Figs. 3.13(a) and (b), respectively. Before carrying out the integration, it is necessary to form the function $g(x - \alpha)$. This is shown in two steps in Figs. 3.13(c) and (d). It is noted that this operation is simply one of folding $g(\alpha)$ about the origin to give $g(-\alpha)$ and then displacing this function by x. Then, for any given value of x, we multiply $f(\alpha)$ by the corresponding $g(x - \alpha)$ and integrate the product from $-\infty$ to ∞. The product of $f(\alpha)$ and $g(x - \alpha)$ is the shaded portion of Fig. 3.13(e). This figure is valid for $0 \leq x \leq 1$. Since the product is 0 for values of α outside the interval $[0, x]$, we find that $f(x)*g(x) = x/2$, which is simply the area of the shaded region in Fig. 3.13(e). For x in the interval $[1, 2]$ we use Fig. 3.13(f). In this case, $f(x)*g(x) = (1 - x/2)$. Thus by noting that $f(\alpha)g(x - \alpha)$ is zero for values of x outside the interval $[0, 2]$, we have

$$f(x)*g(x) = \begin{cases} x/2 & 0 \leq x \leq 1 \\ 1 - x/2 & 1 \leq x \leq 2 \\ 0 & \text{elsewhere} \end{cases}$$

The result is shown in Fig. 3.13(g).   □

One aspect of Eq. (3.3-23), which will be of use later in this section, involves the convolution of a function $f(x)$ with the impulse function $\delta(x - x_0)$, which is defined by the relation

$$\int_{-\infty}^{\infty} f(x)\, \delta(x - x_0)\, dx = f(x_0). \tag{3.3-24}$$

The function $\delta(x - x_0)$ may be viewed as having an area of unity in an infinitesimal neighborhood about x_0 and being 0 everywhere else; that is,

$$\int_{-\infty}^{\infty} \delta(x - x_0)\, dx = \int_{x_0^-}^{x_0^+} \delta(x - x_0)\, dx = 1. \tag{3.3-25}$$

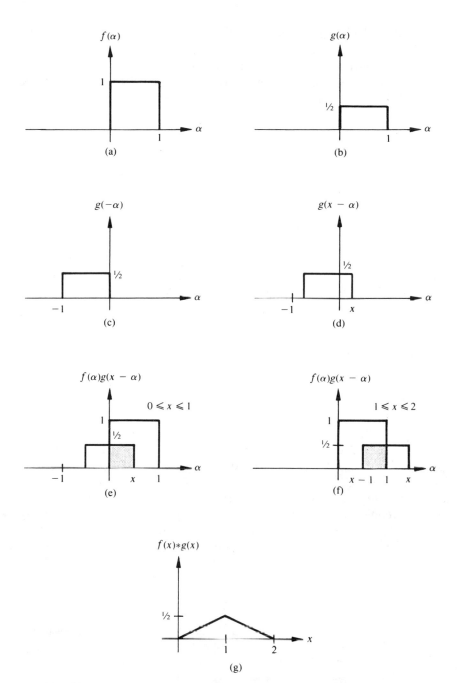

Figure 3.13 Graphical illustration of convolution. The shaded areas indicate regions where the product is not zero.

For most purposes we can say that $\delta(x - x_0)$ is located at $x = x_0$, and that the *strength* of the impulse is determined by the value of $f(x)$ at $x = x_0$. For instance, if $f(x) = A$, we have that $A\delta(x - x_0)$ is an impulse of strength A located at $x = x_0$. It is common practice to represent impulses graphically by an arrow located at x_0 and with height equal to the impulse strength. Figure 3.14 shows this representation for $A\delta(x - x_0)$.

Example: As a second illustration of the use of Eq. (3.3-23), suppose that the function $f(x)$ shown in Fig. 3.15(a) is convolved with the function $g(x) = \delta(x + T) + \delta(x) + \delta(x - T)$ shown in Fig. 3.15(b). By folding $g(x)$, sliding it past $f(x)$, and making use of Eqs. (3.3-23) and (3.3-24), we obtain the result shown in Fig. 3.15(c). It is noted that convolution in this case amounts merely to "copying" $f(x)$ at the location of each impulse. ☐

The importance of convolution in frequency-domain analysis lies in the fact that $f(x)*g(x)$ and $F(u)G(u)$ constitute a Fourier transform pair. In other words, if $f(x)$ has the Fourier transform $F(u)$ and $g(x)$ has the Fourier transform $G(u)$, then $f(x)*g(x)$ has the Fourier transform $F(u)G(u)$. This result, formally stated as

$$f(x)*g(x) \Leftrightarrow F(u)G(u) \qquad (3.3\text{-}26)$$

indicates that convolution in the x-domain can also be obtained by taking the inverse Fourier transform of the product $F(u)G(u)$. An analogous result is that convolution in the frequency domain reduces to multiplication in the x domain; that is

$$f(x)g(x) \Leftrightarrow F(u)*G(u). \qquad (3.3\text{-}27)$$

These two results are commonly referred to as the *convolution theorem*.

Suppose that instead of being continuous, $f(x)$ and $g(x)$ are discretized into sampled arrays of size A and B, respectively: $\{f(0), f(1), f(2), \ldots , f(A - 1)\}$, and $\{g(0), g(1), g(2), \ldots , g(B - 1)\}$. As pointed out in Section 3.3.3, the discrete Fourier transform and its inverse are periodic functions. In order to formulate a discrete convolution theorem that is consistent with this periodicity property, we may assume that the discrete functions $f(x)$ and $g(x)$ are periodic with some period M. The resulting convolution will then be periodic with the same period. The problem

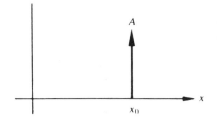

Figure 3.14   Graphical representation of $A\delta(x - x_0)$.

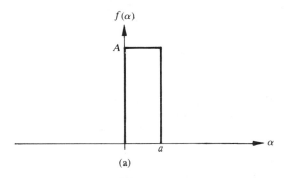

(a)

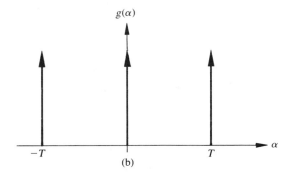

(b)

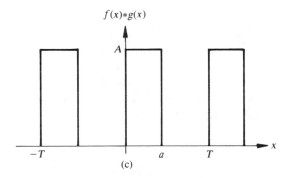

(c)

Figure 3.15   Convolution involving impulse functions.

is how to select a value for M. It can be shown (Brigham [1974]) that unless we choose

$$M \geqslant A + B - 1 \qquad (3.3\text{-}28)$$

the individual periods of the convolution will overlap; this overlap is commonly referred to as *wraparound error*. If $M = A + B - 1$, the periods will be adjacent; if $M > A + B - 1$, the periods will be spaced apart, with the degree of separation being equal to the difference between M and $A + B - 1$. Since the assumed period must be greater than either A or B, the length of the sampled sequences must be increased so that both are of length M. This can be done by appending zeros to the given samples to form the following *extended* sequences:

$$f_e(x) = \begin{cases} f(x) & 0 \leqslant x \leqslant A - 1 \\ 0 & A \leqslant x \leqslant M - 1 \end{cases}$$

and

$$g_e(x) = \begin{cases} g(x) & 0 \leqslant x \leqslant B - 1 \\ 0 & B \leqslant x \leqslant M - 1 \end{cases}$$

Based on this, we define the discrete convolution of $f_e(x)$ and $g_e(x)$ by the expression

$$f_e(x)*g_e(x) = \sum_{m=0}^{M-1} f_e(m)g_e(x - m) \qquad (3.3\text{-}29)$$

for $x = 0, 1, 2, \ldots, M - 1$. The convolution function is a discrete, periodic array of length M, with the values $x = 0, 1, 2, \ldots, M - 1$ describing a full period of $f_e(x)*g_e(x)$.

The mechanics of discrete convolution are basically the same as for continuous convolution. The only differences are that displacements take place in discrete increments corresponding to the separation between samples, and that integration is replaced by a summation. Similarly, Eqs. (3.3-26) and (3.3-27) also hold in the discrete case where, to avoid wraparound error, we use $f_e(x)$ and its transform. The discrete variables x and u assume values in the range $0, 1, 2, \ldots, M - 1$.

Example: The preceding considerations are illustrated graphically in Fig. 3.16 for continuous and discrete convolution. The diagrams for the discrete case show A samples for both $f(x)$ and $g(x)$ in the interval $[0, 1]$, as well as an assumed period of $M = A + B - 1 = 2A - 1$.

Note that the convolution function is periodic and that, since $M = 2A - 1$, the periods are adjacent. Choosing $M > 2A - 1$ would have produced a larger separation between these periods. It is also important to note that a period is completely described by M samples.　　　　　　　　　　　　　　　　　□

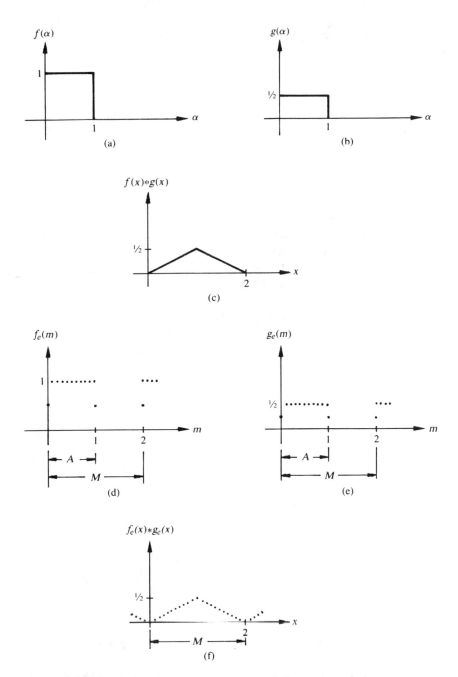

Figure 3.16   Comparison between continuous and discrete convolution.

Two-dimensional convolution is analogous in form to Eq. (3.3-23). Thus for two functions $f(x, y)$ and $g(x, y)$, we have

$$f(x, y)*g(x, y) = \int\int_{-\infty}^{\infty} f(\alpha, \beta)g(x - \alpha, y - \beta) \, d\alpha \, d\beta. \qquad (3.3-30)$$

The convolution theorem in two dimensions, then, is given by the relations

$$f(x, y)*g(x, y) \Leftrightarrow F(u, v)G(u, v) \qquad (3.3-31)$$

and

$$f(x, y)g(x, y) \Leftrightarrow F(u, v)*G(u, v). \qquad (3.3-32)$$

Equation (3.3-30) is more difficult to illustrate graphically than Eq. (3.3-23). Figure 3.17 shows the basic folding, displacement, and multiplication operations required for two-dimensional convolution. The result of varying the displacement variables, x and y, would be a two-dimensional convolution surface with a shape dependent on the nature of the functions involved in the process.

The two-dimensional, discrete convolution is formulated by letting $f(x, y)$ and $g(x, y)$ be discrete arrays of size $A \times B$ and $C \times D$, respectively. As in the one-dimensional case, these arrays must be assumed periodic with some period M and N in the x and y directions, respectively. Wraparound error in the individual convolution periods is avoided by choosing

$$M \geqslant A + C - 1 \qquad (3.3-33)$$

and

$$N \geqslant B + D - 1. \qquad (3.3-34)$$

The periodic sequences are formed by extending $f(x, y)$ and $g(x, y)$ as follows:

$$f_e(x, y) = \begin{cases} f(x, y) & 0 \leqslant x \leqslant A - 1 \quad \text{and} \quad 0 \leqslant y \leqslant B - 1 \\ 0 & A \leqslant x \leqslant M - 1 \quad \text{or} \quad B \leqslant y \leqslant N - 1 \end{cases}$$

and

$$g_e(x, y) = \begin{cases} g(x, y) & 0 \leqslant x \leqslant C - 1 \quad \text{and} \quad 0 \leqslant y \leqslant D - 1 \\ 0 & C \leqslant x \leqslant M - 1 \quad \text{or} \quad D \leqslant y \leqslant N - 1 \end{cases}$$

The two-dimensional convolution of $f_e(x, y)$ and $g_e(x, y)$ is given by the relation

$$f_e(x, y)*g_e(x, y) = \sum_{m=0}^{M-1}\sum_{n=0}^{N-1} f_e(m, n)g_e(x - m, y - n) \qquad (3.3-35)$$

for $x = 0, 1, 2, \ldots, M - 1$ and $y = 0, 1, 2, \ldots, N - 1$. The $M \times N$ array given by this equation is one period of the discrete, two-dimensional convolution. If M and N are chosen according to Eqs. (3.3-33) and (3.3-34), this array is guaranteed

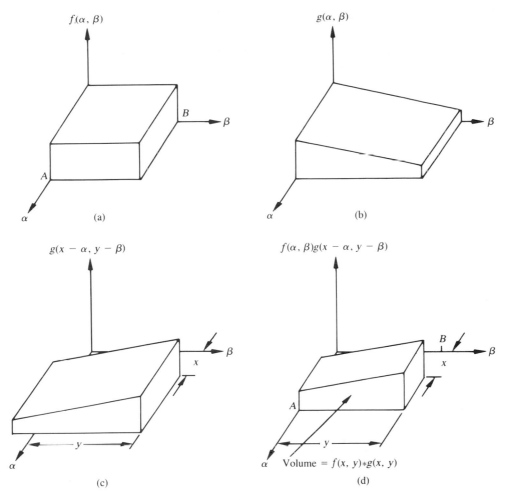

Figure 3.17 Illustration of the folding, displacement, and multiplication steps needed to perform two-dimensional convolution.

to be free of interference from other adjacent periods. As in the one-dimensional case, the continuous convolution theorem given in Eqs. (3.3-31) and (3.3-32) also applies to the discrete case with $u = 0, 1, 2, \ldots, M - 1$ and $v = 0, 1, 2, \ldots, N - 1$. All computations involve the extended functions $f_e(x, y)$ and $g_e(x, y)$.

The theoretical power of the convolution theorem will become evident in Section 3.3.9 when we discuss the sampling theorem. From a practical point of view, it is often more efficient to compute the discrete convolution in the frequency domain instead of using Eq. (3.3-35) directly. The procedure is to compute the Fourier transforms of $f_e(x, y)$ and $g_e(x, y)$ by using a fast Fourier transform (FFT) algorithm (see Section 3.4). The two transforms are then multiplied and the inverse Fourier transform of the product will yield the convolution function. A comparison by Brigham [1974] shows that, for one-dimensional arrays, the FFT approach is faster if the number of points is greater than 32. Although this figure is dependent on the particular machine and algorithms used, it is well below the number of points in a row or column of a typical image.

Correlation

The correlation† of two continuous functions $f(x)$ and $g(x)$, denoted by $f(x)\circ g(x)$, is defined by the relation

$$f(x)\circ g(x) = \int_{-\infty}^{\infty} f^*(\alpha)g(x + \alpha)\, d\alpha, \tag{3.3-36}$$

where * is the complex conjugate. The forms of Eqs. (3.3-36) and (3.3-23) are similar, the only difference being that the function $g(x)$ is not folded about the origin. Thus to perform correlation we simply slide $g(x)$ by $f(x)$ and integrate the product from $-\infty$ to ∞ for each value of displacement x. The procedure is illustrated in Fig. 3.18, which should be compared with Fig. 3.13.

The discrete equivalent of Eq. (3.3-36) is defined as

$$f_e(x)\circ g_e(x) = \sum_{m=0}^{M-1} f_e^*(m)g_e(x + m) \tag{3.3-37}$$

for $x = 0, 1, 2, \ldots, M - 1$. The comments made earlier regarding $f_e(x)$ and $g_e(x)$, the assumed periodicity of these functions, and the choice of values for M, also apply to Eq. (3.3-37).

Similar expressions hold for two dimensions. Thus if $f(x, y)$ and $g(x, y)$ are functions of continuous variables, their correlation is defined as

$$f(x, y)\circ g(x, y) = \int\!\!\int_{-\infty}^{\infty} f^*(\alpha, \beta)g(x + \alpha, y + \beta)\, d\alpha d\beta. \tag{3.3-38}$$

For the discrete case we have

$$f_e(x, y)\circ g_e(x, y) = \sum_{m=0}^{M-1}\sum_{n=0}^{N-1} f_e^*(m, n)g_e(x + m, y + n) \tag{3.3-39}$$

for $x = 0, 1, 2, \ldots, M - 1$ and $y = 0, 1, 2, \ldots, N - 1$. As in the case of discrete convolution, $f_e(x, y)$ and $g_e(x, y)$ are extended functions, and M and N are chosen according to Eqs. (3.3-33) and (3.3-34) in order to avoid wraparound error in the periods of the correlation function.

---

† If $f(x)$ and $g(x)$ are the same function, Eq. (3.3-36) is usually called the *autocorrelation* function; if $f(x)$ and $g(x)$ are different, the term *cross-correlation* is normally used.

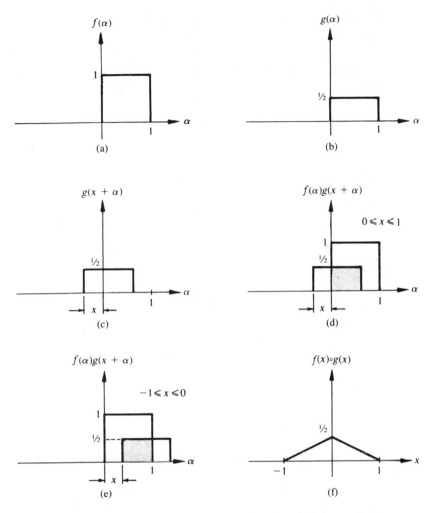

Figure 3.18   Graphical illustration of correlation. The shaded areas indicate regions where the product is not zero.

It can be shown for both the continuous and discrete cases that the following *correlation theorem* holds:

$$f(x, y) \circ g(x, y) \Leftrightarrow F^*(u, v)G(u, v) \tag{3.3-40}$$

and

$$f^*(x, y)g(x, y) \Leftrightarrow F(u, v) \circ G(u, v). \tag{3.3-41}$$

It is understood that, when interpreted for discrete variables, all functions are assumed to be extended and periodic.

One of the principal applications of correlation in image processing is in the area of *template* or *prototype matching,* where the problem is to find the closest match between a given unknown image and a set of images of known origin. One approach to this problem is to compute the correlation between the unknown and each of the known images. The closest match can then be found by selecting the image that yields the correlation function with the largest value. Since the resultant correlations are two-dimensional functions, this involves searching for the largest amplitude of each function. As in the case of discrete convolution, the computation of $f_e(x, y) \circ g_e(x, y)$ is often more efficiently carried out in the frequency domain using an FFT algorithm to obtain the forward and inverse transforms.

When comparing the results of discrete versus continuous convolution or correlation, it should be noted that the way we have defined the discrete cases amounts to evaluation of the continuous forms by rectangular integration. Thus if one wishes to compare discrete and continuous results on an absolute basis, Eqs. (3.3-29) and (3.3-37) should be multiplied by Δx, and Eqs. (3.3-35) and (3.3-39) by $\Delta x \Delta y$, where Δx and Δy are the separations between samples, as defined in Section 3.2. In Fig. 3.16, for example, the continuous and discrete convolution functions have the same amplitude because the discrete result was multiplied by Δx. When one is only computing and evaluating the discrete forms, however, the inclusion of these scale factors is a matter of preference. It is also important to note that all convolution and correlation expressions hold if $f(x)$ and $g(x)$, along with their corresponding transforms, are interchanged. This is also true if the functions are two dimensional.

3.3.9   Sampling

The basic idea of image sampling was introduced in Section 2.3 on an intuitive basis. The Fourier transform and the convolution theorem provide the tools for a deeper analytical study of this problem. In particular, we are interested in looking at the question of how many samples should be taken so that no information is lost in the sampling process. Expressed differently, the problem is one of establishing under what sampling conditions a continuous image can be fully recovered from a set of sampled values. We begin the analysis with the one-dimensional case.

One-dimensional functions

Consider the function shown in Fig. 3.19(a), which is assumed to extend from $-\infty$ to ∞, and suppose that the Fourier transform of $f(x)$ vanishes for values of u outside the interval $[-W, W]$. The transform might appear as shown in Fig. 3.19(b).[†] A function whose transform has this property for any finite value of W is called a *band-limited* function.

[†] Recall that the Fourier transform is a complex function. For simplicity, in the following graphical illustrations we show only the magnitude of the transforms. The ordinate axis, however, will be labeled with $F(u)$, $G(u)$, etc., to indicate that the concepts involved are valid for the complete transform, and not just its magnitude.

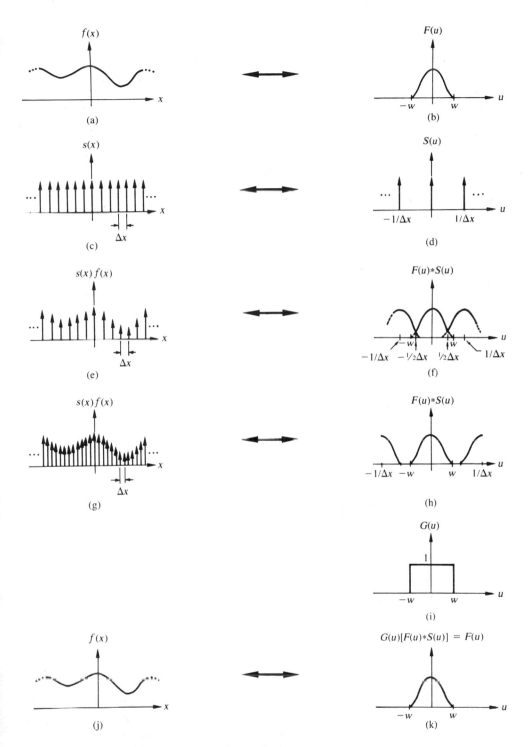

Figure 3.19 Graphical development of sampling concepts.

To obtain a sampled version of $f(x)$, we simply multiply this function by a sampling function $s(x)$, which consists of a train of impulses Δx units apart, as shown in Fig. 3.19(c). Since, by the convolution theorem, multiplication in the x domain is equivalent to convolution in the frequency domain, we obtain the Fourier transform shown in Fig. 3.19(f) for the product $s(x)f(x)$. It is noted that the transform is periodic with period $1/\Delta x$, and that the individual repetitions of $F(u)$ can overlap. In the first period, for example, the center of the overlapped region will occur at $u = 1/2\Delta x$ if the quantity $1/2\Delta x$ is less than W. Therefore to avoid this problem we select the sampling interval Δx so that $1/2\Delta x \geqslant W$, or

$$\Delta x \leqslant \frac{1}{2W}. \tag{3.3-42}$$

The result of decreasing Δx is shown in Figs. 3.19(g) and (h). The net effect is to separate the periods so that no overlap occurs. The importance of this operation lies in the fact that if one multiplies the transform of Fig. 3.19(h) by the function

$$G(u) = \begin{cases} 1 & -W \leqslant u \leqslant W \\ 0 & \text{elsewhere} \end{cases} \tag{3.3-43}$$

it becomes possible to isolate $F(u)$ completely, as shown in Fig. 3.19(k). The inverse Fourier transform then yields the original *continuous* function $f(x)$. The fact that a band-limited function can be recovered completely from samples whose spacing satisfies Eq. (3.3-42) is known as the *Whittaker–Shannon sampling theorem*.

It is important to keep in mind that all the frequency-domain information of a band-limited function is contained in the interval $[-W, W]$. If Eq. (3.3-42) is not satisfied, however, the transform in this interval is corrupted by contributions from adjacent periods. This phenomenon, frequently referred to as *aliasing*, precludes complete recovery of an undersampled function.

The foregoing results apply to functions that are of unlimited duration in the x domain. Since this implies an infinite sampling interval, it is of interest to examine the practical case where a function is sampled only over a finite region. This situation is shown graphically in Fig. 3.20. Parts (a) through (f) are the same as in Fig. 3.19, with the exception that the separation between samples is assumed to satisfy the sampling theorem so that no aliasing is present. A finite sampling interval $[0, X]$ can be represented mathematically by multiplying the sampled result shown in Fig. 3.20(e) by the function

$$h(x) = \begin{cases} 1 & 0 \leqslant x \leqslant X \\ 0 & \text{elsewhere} \end{cases} \tag{3.3-44}$$

This function, often called a *window*, and its Fourier transform are shown in Fig. 3.20(g) and (h), respectively. The results of multiplication are illustrated in Fig. 3.20(i) and (j). It is important to note that the final frequency domain result is obtained by convolving the function $S(u)*F(u)$ with $H(u)$, which is the Fourier

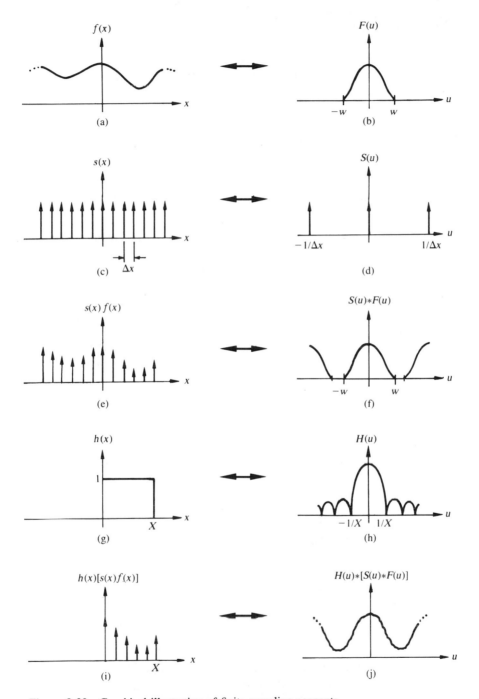

Figure 3.20   Graphical illustration of finite-sampling concepts.

transform of the window function $h(x)$. Since $H(u)$ has frequency components that extend to infinity, the convolution of these functions introduces a distortion in the frequency-domain representation of a function that has been sampled and limited to a finite region by $h(x)$, as shown in Fig. 3.20(j). Thus even if the separation between samples satisfies the sampling theorem, it is generally impossible to recover completely a function that has been sampled only in a finite region of the x domain. This fact can be appreciated by noting that it becomes impossible under these conditions to isolate the original Fourier transform. The only exception to this is when $f(x)$ is band-limited and periodic with a period equal to X. In this case it can be shown that the corruptions due to $H(u)$ cancel out, thus allowing complete recovery of $f(x)$ if the sampling theorem is satisfied. It is important to note that the recovered function still extends from $-\infty$ to ∞ and is *not* zero outside the range in which $h(x)$ is zero. These considerations lead us to the important conclusion that no function $f(x)$ of finite duration can be band limited. Conversely, a function that is band limited must extend from $-\infty$ to ∞ in the x domain. This is an important practical result because it establishes a fundamental limitation in our treatment of digital functions.

Before leaving the discussion of one-dimensional functions, it is of interest to use the above results to give an alternate reason for the periodicity of the discrete Fourier transform. We begin by noting that, thus far, all results in the frequency domain have been of a continuous nature. To obtain a discrete Fourier transform, we simply "sample" the continuous transform with a train of impulses that are Δu units apart. The situation is depicted in Fig. 3.21, where use has been made of Figs. 3.20(i) and (j). The notation $f(x)$ and $F(u)$ is used in Fig. 3.21 to facilitate comparison with the discussion in Section 3.2. It should be kept in mind, however, that Figs. 3.21(a) and (b) are assumed to be the result of the sequence of operations shown in Fig. 3.20.

As previously pointed out, sampling can be represented by multiplying the impulse train and the function of interest. In this case, we multiply $F(u)$ by $S(u)$ and obtain the result shown in Fig. 3.21(f). The equivalent operation in the x domain is convolution, which yields the function shown in Fig. 3.21(e). This function is periodic with period $1/\Delta u$. If N samples of $f(x)$ and $F(u)$ are taken and the spacings between samples are selected so that a period in each domain is covered by N uniformly spaced samples, we have that $N\Delta x = X$ in the x domain and $N\Delta u = 1/\Delta x$ in the frequency domain. The latter equation follows from the fact that the Fourier transform of a sampled function is periodic with period $1/\Delta x$, as shown earlier. It follows from this equation that

$$\Delta u = \frac{1}{N\Delta x}$$

(3.3-45)

which agrees with Eq. (3.2-4). Choosing this spacing yields the function in Fig. 3.21(e), which is periodic with period $1/\Delta u$. From Eq. (3.3-45) we have that $1/\Delta u = N\Delta x = X$, which is the overall sampling interval in Fig. 3.21(a).

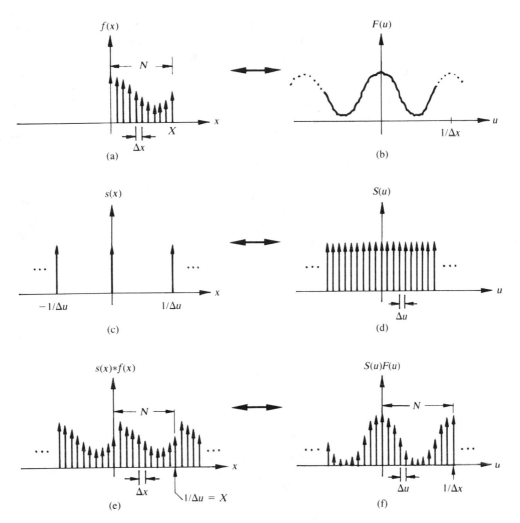

Figure 3.21 Graphical illustration of the discrete Fourier transform.

Two-dimensional functions

The sampling concepts developed above are, after some modifications in notation, directly applicable to two dimensional functions. The sampling process for these functions can be formulated mathematically by making use of the two-dimensional impulse function $\delta(x, y)$ which we define as follows:

$$\int\!\!\!\int_{-\infty}^{\infty} f(x, y)\delta(x - x_0, y - y_0)\, dx\, dy = f(x_0, y_0). \qquad (3.3\text{-}46)$$

The interpretation of Eq. (3.3-46) is analogous to that given in connection with Eqs. (3.3-24) and (3.3-25). A two-dimensional sampling function consisting of a train of impulses separated Δx units in the x direction and Δy units in the y direction is shown in Fig. 3.22.

Given a function $f(x, y)$, where x and y are continuous, a sampled function is obtained by forming the product $s(x, y)f(x, y)$. The equivalent operation in the frequency domain is convolution of $S(u, v)$ and $F(u, v)$, where $S(u, v)$ is a train of impulses with separation $1/\Delta x$ and $1/\Delta y$ in the u and v directions, respectively. If $f(x, y)$ is band limited (i.e., its Fourier transform vanishes outside some finite region R) the result of convolving $S(u, v)$ and $F(u, v)$ might look like the case shown in Fig. 3.23. It is noted that the function shown is periodic in two dimensions.

Let $2W_u$ and $2W_v$ represent the widths in the u and v directions, respectively, of the smallest rectangle that completely encloses the region R. Then, from Fig. 3.23, if $1/\Delta x > 2W_u$ and $1/\Delta y > 2W_v$ (i.e., there is no aliasing), one of the periods can be recovered completely if we multiply $S(u, v)*F(u, v)$ by the function

$$G(u, v) = \begin{cases} 1 & (u, v) \text{ inside one of the} \\ & \text{rectangles enclosing } R \\ 0 & \text{elsewhere} \end{cases} \qquad (3.3\text{-}47)$$

The inverse Fourier transform of $G(u, v)[S(u, v)*F(u, v)]$ yields $f(x, y)$.

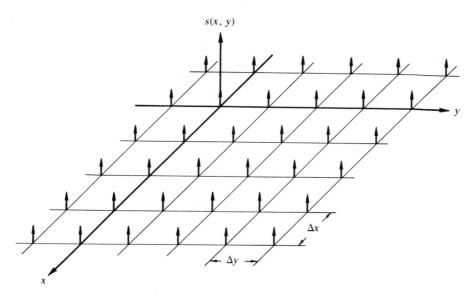

Figure 3.22 A two-dimensional sampling function.

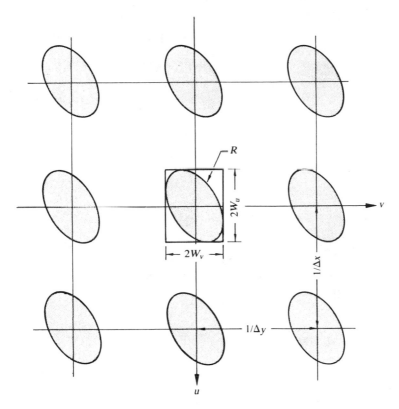

Figure 3.23 Frequency-domain representation of a sampled two-dimensional, band-limited function.

The foregoing considerations lead us to a form of the two-dimensional sampling theorem, which states that a band-limited function $f(x, y)$ can be recovered completely from samples whose separation is given by

$$\Delta x \leqslant \frac{1}{2W_u} \tag{3.3-48a}$$

and

$$\Delta y \leqslant \frac{1}{2W_v}. \tag{3.3-48b}$$

When $f(x, y)$ is spatially limited by using a two-dimensional window $h(x, y)$ analogous to the function $h(x)$ used in Fig. 3.20, we again have the problem that the transform of the sampled function is distorted by the convolution of $H(u, v)$ and $S(u, v) * F(u, v)$. This distortion, which is due to the spatially limited nature of digital images, precludes complete recovery of $f(x, y)$ from its samples. As in the one-dimensional case, periodic functions are an exception, but images satisfying this condition are rarely found in practice.

An argument similar to the one developed for the one-dimensional case can be carried out to show how periodicity arises in the two-dimensional, discrete Fourier transform. For an $N \times N$ image, this analysis would also yield the following results:

$$\Delta u = \frac{1}{N\Delta x} \qquad (3.3\text{-}49a)$$

and

$$\Delta v = \frac{1}{N\Delta y}. \qquad (3.3\text{-}49b)$$

These relationships between the sample separations guarantee that a complete (two-dimensional) period will be covered by $N \times N$ uniformly spaced values in both the spatial and frequency domains.

3.4   THE FAST FOURIER TRANSFORM

The number of complex multiplications and additions required to implement Eq. (3.2-2) is proportional to N^2. This can be seen easily by noting that, for each of the N values of u, expansion of the summation sign requires N complex multiplications of $f(x)$ by $\exp[-j2\pi ux/N]$ and $(N - 1)$ additions of the results. The terms of $\exp[-j2\pi ux/N]$ can be computed once and stored in a table for all subsequent applications. For this reason, the multiplication of u by x in these terms is usually not considered a direct part of the implementation.

In this section it is shown that, by properly decomposing Eq. (3.2-2), the number of multiply and add operations can be made proportional to $N \log_2 N$. The decomposition procedure is called the *fast Fourier transform* (FFT) *algorithm*. The reduction in proportionality from N^2 to $N \log_2 N$ multiply/add operations represents a significant saving in computational effort, as shown by the figures in Table 3.1. It is evident from this table that the FFT approach offers a considerable computational advantage over a direct implementation of the Fourier transform, particularly when N is relatively large. For example, a direct implementation of the transform for $N = 8192$ requires on the order of three quarters of an hour on a machine such as an IBM 7094. By contrast, the same job can be done on this machine in about 5 seconds using an FFT algorithm.

Attention is focused below on the development of an FFT algorithm of one variable. As pointed out in Section 3.3.1, a two-dimensional Fourier transform can be readily computed by a series of applications of the one-dimensional transform.

Table 3.1   A Comparison of N^2 versus $N \log_2 N$ for Various Values of N

N	N^2 (Direct FT)	$N \log_2 N$ (FFT)	Computational Advantage ($N/\log_2 N$)
2	4	2	2.00
4	16	8	2.00
8	64	24	2.67
16	256	64	4.00
32	1,024	160	6.40
64	4,096	384	10.67
128	16,384	896	18.29
256	65,536	2,048	32.00
512	262,144	4,608	56.89
1024	1,048,576	10,240	102.40
2048	4,194,304	22,528	186.18
4096	16,777,216	49,152	341.33
8192	67,108,864	106,496	630.15

3.4.1   FFT Algorithm

The FFT algorithm developed in this section is based on the so-called "successive doubling" method. It will be convenient in the following discussion to express Eq. (3.2-2) in the form

$$F(u) = \frac{1}{N} \sum_{x=0}^{N-1} f(x) W_N^{ux}, \qquad (3.4\text{-}1)$$

where

$$W_N = \exp[-j2\pi/N], \qquad (3.4\text{-}2)$$

and N is assumed to be of the form

$$N = 2^n, \qquad (3.4\text{-}3)$$

where n is a positive integer. Based on this, N can be expressed as

$$N = 2M, \qquad (3.4\text{-}4)$$

where M is also a positive integer. Substitution of Eq. (3.4-4) into Eq. (3.4-1) yields

$$F(u) = \frac{1}{2M} \sum_{x=0}^{2M-1} f(x) W_{2M}^{ux}$$
$$= \frac{1}{2} \left\{ \frac{1}{M} \sum_{x=0}^{M-1} f(2x) W_{2M}^{u(2x)} + \frac{1}{M} \sum_{x=0}^{M-1} f(2x+1) W_{2M}^{u(2x+1)} \right\}. \qquad (3.4\text{-}5)$$

Since, from Eq. (3.4-2), $W_{2M}^{2ux} = W_{M}^{ux}$, Eq. (3.4-5) may be expressed in the form

$$F(u) = \frac{1}{2}\left\{\frac{1}{M}\sum_{x=0}^{M-1} f(2x)W_{M}^{ux} + \frac{1}{M}\sum_{x=0}^{M-1} f(2x + 1)W_{M}^{ux}W_{2M}^{u}\right\}. \tag{3.4-6}$$

If we define

$$F_{\text{even}}(u) = \frac{1}{M}\sum_{x=0}^{M-1} f(2x)W_{M}^{ux} \tag{3.4-7}$$

for $u = 0, 1, 2, \ldots, M - 1$, and

$$F_{\text{odd}}(u) = \frac{1}{M}\sum_{x=0}^{M-1} f(2x + 1)W_{M}^{ux} \tag{3.4-8}$$

for $u = 0, 1, 2, \ldots, M - 1$, Eq. (3.4-6) then becomes

$$F(u) = \frac{1}{2}\{F_{\text{even}}(u) + F_{\text{odd}}(u)W_{2M}^{u}\}. \tag{3.4-9}$$

Also, since $W_{M}^{u+M} = W_{M}^{u}$ and $W_{2M}^{u+M} = -W_{2M}^{u}$, it follows from Eqs. (3.4-7) through (3.4-9) that

$$F(u + M) = \frac{1}{2}\{F_{\text{even}}(u) - F_{\text{odd}}(u)W_{2M}^{u}\}. \tag{3.4-10}$$

Careful analysis of Eqs. (3.4-7) through (3.4-10) reveals some interesting properties of these expressions. It is noted that an N-point transform can be computed by dividing the original expression into two parts, as indicated in Eqs. (3.4-9) and (3.4-10). Computation of the first half of $F(u)$ requires the evaluation of the two $(N/2)$-point transforms given in Eqs. (3.4-7) and (3.4-8). The resulting values of $F_{\text{even}}(u)$ and $F_{\text{odd}}(u)$ are then substituted into Eq. (3.4-9) to obtain $F(u)$ for $u = 0, 1, 2, \ldots, (N/2 - 1)$. The other half then follows directly from Eq. (3.4-10) without additional transform evaluations.

In order to examine the computational implications of the above procedure, let $m(n)$ and $a(n)$ represent the number of complex multiplications and additions, respectively, required to implement this method. As before, the number of samples is equal to 2^n, where n is a positive integer. Suppose first that $n = 1$. A two-point transform requires the evaluation of $F(0)$; then $F(1)$ follows from Eq. (3.4-10). To obtain $F(0)$, we must first compute $F_{\text{even}}(0)$ and $F_{\text{odd}}(0)$. In this case $M = 1$ and Eqs. (3.4-7) and (3.4-8) are one-point transforms. Since the Fourier transform of a single point is the sample itself, however, no multiplications or additions are required to obtain $F_{\text{even}}(0)$ and $F_{\text{odd}}(0)$. One multiplication of $F_{\text{odd}}(0)$ by W_{2}^{0} and one addition yield $F(0)$ from Eq. (3.4-9). $F(1)$ then follows from Eq. (3.4-10) with one more addition (we consider subtraction to be the same as addition). Since $F_{\text{odd}}(0)W_{2}^{0}$

was already computed, we have that the total number of operations required for a two-point transform consists of $m(1) = 1$ multiplication and $a(1) = 2$ additions.

The next allowed value for n is 2. According to the above development, a four-point transform can be divided into two parts. The first half of $F(u)$ requires evaluation of two, two-point transforms, as given in Eqs. (3.4-7) and (3.4-8) for $M = 2$. Since a two-point transform requires $m(1)$ multiplications and $a(1)$ additions, it is evident that evaluation of these two equations requires a total of $2m(1)$ multiplications and $2a(1)$ additions. Two further multiplications and additions are necessary to obtain $F(0)$ and $F(1)$ from Eq. (3.4-9). Since $F_{odd}(u)W_{2M}^u$ was already computed for $u = \{0, 1\}$, we find that two more additions give $F(2)$ and $F(3)$. The total is then $m(2) = 2m(1) + 2$ and $a(2) = 2a(1) + 4$.

When n is equal to 3, we consider two four-point transforms in the evaluation of $F_{even}(u)$ and $F_{odd}(u)$. These require $2m(2)$ multiplications and $2a(2)$ additions. Four more multiplications and eight more additions yield the complete transform. The total is then $m(3) = 2m(2) + 4$ and $a(3) = 2a(2) + 8$.

By continuing this argument one would find that, for any positive integer value of n, the number of multiplications and additions required to implement the FFT is given by the recursive expressions

$$m(n) = 2m(n - 1) + 2^{n-1} \quad n \geqslant 1 \tag{3.4-11}$$

and

$$a(n) = 2a(n - 1) + 2^n \quad n \geqslant 1, \tag{3.4-12}$$

where $m(0) = 0$ and $a(0) = 0$, since the transform of a single point does not require any additions or multiplications.

Implementation of Eqs. (3.4-7) through (3.4-10) constitutes the successive-doubling FFT algorithm. This name arises from the fact that a two-point transform is computed from two one-point transforms, a four-point transform from two two-point transforms, and so on, for any N that is equal to an integer power of 2.

3.4.2 Number of Operations

In this section it is shown by induction that the number of complex multiplications and additions required to implement the above FFT algorithm is given by

$$
\begin{aligned}
m(n) &= \frac{1}{2} 2^n \log_2 2^n \\
&= \frac{1}{2} N \log_2 N \\
&= \frac{1}{2} Nn \quad n \geqslant 1
\end{aligned}
\tag{3.4-13}
$$

and

$$a(n) = 2^n \log_2 2^n$$
$$= N \log_2 N \qquad (3.4\text{-}14)$$
$$= Nn \quad n \geqslant 1,$$

respectively.

First, it is necessary to prove that Eqs. (3.4-13) and (3.4-14) hold for $n = 1$. It was already shown that

$$m(1) = \tfrac{1}{2}(2)(1) = 1$$

and

$$a(1) = (2)(1) = 2.$$

Next, it is assumed that the expressions hold for n. It is then required to prove that they are also true for $n + 1$.

From Eq. (3.4-11) it follows that

$$m(n + 1) = 2m(n) + 2^n.$$

Substituting Eq. (3.4-13), which is assumed to be valid for n, yields

$$m(n + 1) = 2(\tfrac{1}{2}Nn) + 2^n$$
$$= 2(\tfrac{1}{2}2^n n) + 2^n$$
$$= 2^n(n + 1)$$
$$= \tfrac{1}{2}2^{n+1}(n + 1).$$

Equation (3.4-13) is therefore valid for all positive integer values of n.

From Eq. (3.4-12), we have

$$a(n + 1) = 2a(n) + 2^{n+1}.$$

Substitution of Eq. (3.4-14) for $a(n)$ yields

$$a(n + 1) = 2Nn + 2^{n+1}$$
$$= 2(2^n n) + 2^{n+1}$$
$$= 2^{n+1}(n + 1).$$

This completes the proof.

3.4.3 The Inverse FFT

Thus far, little has been said concerning the inverse Fourier transform. It turns out that any algorithm for implementing the discrete forward transform can also be used (with minor modifications in the input) to compute the inverse. To see this, let us consider Eqs. (3.2-2) and (3.2-3), which are repeated below:

$$F(u) = \frac{1}{N} \sum_{x=0}^{N-1} f(x) \exp[-j2\pi ux/N] \qquad (3.4\text{-}15)$$

and

$$f(x) = \sum_{u=0}^{N-1} F(u) \exp[j2\pi ux/N].$$ (3.4-16)

Taking the complex conjugate of Eq. (3.4-16) and dividing both sides by N yields

$$\frac{1}{N} f^*(x) = \frac{1}{N} \sum_{u=0}^{N-1} F^*(u) \exp[-j2\pi ux/N].$$ (3.4-17)

By comparing this result with Eq. (3.4-15) we see that the right side of Eq. (3.4-17) is in the form of the forward Fourier transform. Thus if we input $F^*(u)$ into an algorithm designed to compute the forward transform, the result will be the quantity $f^*(x)/N$. Taking the complex conjugate and multiplying by N yields the desired inverse $f(x)$.

For two-dimensional square arrays we take the complex conjugate of Eq. (3.2-10), that is,

$$f^*(x, y) = \frac{1}{N} \sum_{u=0}^{N-1} \sum_{v=0}^{N-1} F^*(u, v) \exp[-j2\pi(ux + vy)/N],$$ (3.4-18)

which we see is in the form of the two-dimensional forward transform given in Eq. (3.2-9). It therefore follows that if we input $F^*(u, v)$ into an algorithm designed to compute the forward transform, the result will be $f^*(x, y)$. By taking the complex conjugate of this result we obtain $f(x, y)$. In the case where $f(x)$ or $f(x, y)$ is real, the complex conjugate operation is unnecessary since $f(x) = f^*(x)$ and $f(x, y) = f^*(x, y)$ for real functions.

The fact that the two-dimensional transform is usually computed by successive passes of the one-dimensional transform is a frequent source of confusion when using the above technique to obtain the inverse. The reader should keep in mind the procedure outlined in Section 3.3.1 and avoid being misled by Eq. (3.4-17). In other words, when using a one-dimensional algorithm to compute the two-dimensional inverse, the method is not to compute the complex conjugate after each row or column is processed. Instead, the function $F^*(u, v)$ is treated as if it were $f(x, y)$ in the forward, two-dimensional transform procedure summarized in Fig. 3.9. The complex conjugate of the result (if necessary) will yield the proper inverse, $f(x, y)$.

3.4.4   Implementation

A computer implementation of the FFT algorithm developed in Section 3.4.1 is straightforward. The principal point to keep in mind is that the input data must be arranged in the order required for successive applications of Eqs. (3.4-7) and (3.4-8). The ordering procedure can be illustrated by a simple example. Suppose that we wish to use the successive doubling algorithm to compute the FFT of an eight-point function $\{f(0), f(1), \ldots , f(7)\}$. Equation (3.4-7) uses the samples with even arguments, $\{f(0), f(2), f(4), f(6)\}$, and Eq. (3.4-8) uses the samples with odd arguments, $\{f(1), f(3), f(5), f(7)\}$. However, each four-point transform is computed as two two-point transforms. This also requires the use of Eqs. (3.4-7) and (3.4-8). Thus to compute the FFT of the first set above, we must divide it into its even part $\{f(0), f(4)\}$ and odd part $\{f(2), f(6)\}$. Similarly, the second set is subdivided into $\{f(1), f(5)\}$ for Eq. (3.4-7) and $\{f(3), f(7)\}$ for Eq. (3.4-8). No further rearrangement is required since each two-element set is considered as having one even and one odd element. Combining these results, we have that the input array must be expressed in the form $\{f(0), f(4), f(2), f(6), f(1), f(5), f(3), f(7)\}$. The successive-doubling algorithm operates on this array in the manner shown in Fig. 3.24. At the first level of computation are four two-point transforms involving $\{f(0), f(4)\}$, $\{f(2), f(6)\}$, $\{f(1), f(5)\}$, and $\{f(3), f(7)\}$. The next level uses these results to form two four-point transforms, and the last level uses these two results to produce the desired transform.

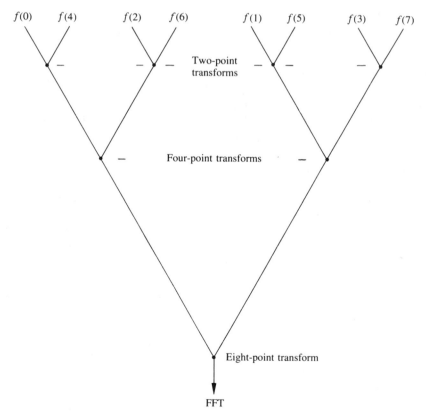

Figure 3.24 Ordered input array and its use in the successive-doubling method.

Fortunately, the general procedure for reordering an input array follows a simple *bit-reversal* rule. If we let x represent any valid argument value in $f(x)$, then the corresponding argument in the reordered array is given by expressing x in binary and reversing the bits. For example, if $N = 2^3$, the seventh element in the original array, $f(6)$, becomes the fourth element in the reordered array since $6 = 110_2$ becomes $011_2 = 3$ when the bits are reversed. It is noted that this is a left-to-right reversal of the binary number and should not be confused with the binary complement. The procedure is summarized in Table 3.2 for $N = 8$. If the reordered array is used in computing the FFT, the answer will be the elements of the Fourier transform in the correct order. Conversely, it can be shown that if the array is used in its natural order, the answer will be bit-reversed. Identical comments hold for computing the inverse transform.

A FORTRAN subroutine for computing the FFT by the successive-doubling method is shown in Fig. 3.25. The parameters in the subroutine argument are as follows. On input, F is an array whose transform is desired and LN is equal to n. On output, the array F contains the Fourier transform. It is noted that F is a complex array so that if the input is a real function the imaginary part of F must be set to zero before calling the subroutine.

The first part of the program, including the "DO 3" loop, performs reordering of the input data. The second part, including the "DO 5" loop, does the successive-doubling calculations. The "DO 6" loop divides the results by N. It has been estimated that, for $N = 1024$, this simple program is only about 12% less efficient than a more optimally written FORTRAN program that uses a table for storing values of W_{2M}^u.

Equations (3.3-3) through (3.3-6), along with Figs. 3.9 and 3.25, provide the necessary information for implementing the two-dimensional, forward FFT. The same concepts are applicable to the inverse transform by using the complex conjugate

Table 3.2 Example of Bit Reversal and Reordering of Array for Input into FFT Algorithm

Original Argument			Original Array	Bit-reversed Argument			Reordered Array
0	0	0	$f(0)$	0	0	0	$f(0)$
0	0	1	$f(1)$	1	0	0	$f(4)$
0	1	0	$f(2)$	0	1	0	$f(2)$
0	1	1	$f(3)$	1	1	0	$f(6)$
1	0	0	$f(4)$	0	0	1	$f(1)$
1	0	1	$f(5)$	1	0	1	$f(5)$
1	1	0	$f(6)$	0	1	1	$f(3)$
1	1	1	$f(7)$	1	1	1	$f(7)$

```
SUBROUTINE FFT(F,LN)
COMPLEX F(1024),U,W,T,CMPLX
PI=3.141593
N=2**LN
NV2=N/2
NM1=N-1
J=1
DO 3 I=1,NM1
     IF(I.GE.J) GO TO 1
     T=F(J)
     F(J)=F(I)
     F(I)=T
1    K=NV2
2    IF(K.GE.J) GO TO 3
     J=J-K
     K=K/2
     GO TO 2
3    J=J+K
DO 5 L=1,LN
     LE=2**L
     LE1=LE/2
     U=(1.0,0.0)
     W=CMPLX(COS(PI/LE1),-SIN(PI/LE1))
     DO 5 J=1,LE1
          DO 4 I=J,N,LE
               IP=I+LE1
               T=F(IP)*U
               F(IP)=F(I)-T
4              F(I)=F(I)+T
5         U=U*W
DO 6 I=1,N
6    F(I)=F(I)/FLOAT(N)
RETURN
END
```

Figure 3.25   A FORTRAN implementation of the succesive-doubling FFT algorithm. (Adapted from Cooley *et al.* [1969].)

of the Fourier transform as the input to the FFT subroutine, as indicated in Section 3.4.3.

It should be noted before leaving this section that it is possible to formulate the FFT using other integer bases greater than two. In fact, a base-three formulation requires slightly fewer operations than any other base (Cooley, Lewis, and Welch [1969]), but its disadvantage in terms of programming makes it an unattractive choice. A base-four is equal to a base-two implementation in terms of required operations, and all other bases are less efficient, requiring a progressively larger number of operations. Fast Fourier transform algorithms are usually formulated in a base-two format because it is easier to implement in assembly language.

3.5   OTHER SEPARABLE IMAGE TRANSFORMS

The one-dimensional, discrete Fourier transform is one of a class of important transforms that can be expressed in terms of the general relation

$$T(u) = \sum_{x=0}^{N-1} f(x)g(x, u), \tag{3.5-1}$$

where $T(u)$ is the transform of $f(x)$, $g(x, u)$ is the *forward transformation kernel*, and u assumes values in the range $0, 1, \ldots, N - 1$. Similarly, the inverse transform is given by the relation

$$f(x) = \sum_{u=0}^{N-1} T(u)h(x, u), \tag{3.5-2}$$

where $h(x, u)$ is the *inverse transformation kernel* and x assumes values in the range $0, 1, \ldots, N - 1$. The nature of a transform is determined by the properties of its transformation kernel.

For two-dimensional square arrays the forward and inverse transforms are given by the equations

$$T(u, v) = \sum_{x=0}^{N-1} \sum_{y=0}^{N-1} f(x, y)g(x, y, u, v) \tag{3.5-3}$$

and

$$f(x, y) = \sum_{u=0}^{N-1} \sum_{v=0}^{N-1} T(u, v)h(x, y, u, v), \tag{3.5-4}$$

where, as above, $g(x, y, u, v)$ and $h(x, y, u, v)$ are called the *forward* and *inverse transformation kernels*, respectively.

The forward kernel is said to be *separable* if

$$g(x, y, u, v) = g_1(x, u)g_2(y, v). \tag{3.5-5}$$

In addition, the kernel is *symmetric* if g_1 is functionally equal to g_2. In this case, Eq. (3.5-5) can be expressed in the form

$$g(x, y, u, v) = g_1(x, u)g_1(y, v). \tag{3.5-6}$$

Identical comments hold for the inverse kernel if $g(x, y, u, v)$ is replaced by $h(x, y, u, v)$ in Eqs. (3.5-5) and (3.5-6).

The two-dimensional Fourier transform is a special case of Eq. (3.5-3). It has the kernel

$$g(x, y, u, v) = \frac{1}{N} \exp[-j2\pi(ux + vy)/N],$$

which is separable and symmetric since

$$g(x, y, u, v) = g_1(x, u)g_1(y, v)$$

$$= \frac{1}{\sqrt{N}} \exp[-j2\pi ux/N] \frac{1}{\sqrt{N}} \exp[-j2\pi vy/N]. \qquad (3.5\text{-}7)$$

It is easily shown that the inverse Fourier kernel is also separable and symmetric.

A transform with a separable kernel can be computed in two steps, each requiring a one-dimensional transform. First, the one-dimensional transform is taken along each row of $f(x, y)$, yielding

$$T(x, v) = \sum_{y=0}^{N-1} f(x, y)g_2(y, v) \qquad (3.5\text{-}8)$$

for $x, v = 0, 1, 2, \ldots, N - 1$. Next, the one-dimensional transform is taken along each column of $T(x, v)$; this results in the expression

$$T(u, v) = \sum_{x=0}^{N-1} T(x, v)g_1(x, u) \qquad (3.5\text{-}9)$$

for $u, v = 0, 1, 2, \ldots, N - 1$. It is noted that this procedure agrees with the method given in Section 3.3.1 for the Fourier transform. The same final results are obtained if the transform is taken first along each column of $f(x, y)$ to obtain $T(y, u)$ and then along each row of the latter function to obtain $T(u, v)$. Similar comments hold for the inverse transform if $h(x, y, u, v)$ is separable.

If the kernel $g(x, y, u, v)$ is separable and symmetric, Eq. (3.5-3) can also be expressed in the following matrix form:

$$\mathbf{T} = \mathbf{AFA}, \qquad (3.5\text{-}10)$$

where $\mathbf{F}$ is the $N \times N$ image matrix, $\mathbf{A}$ is an $N \times N$ symmetric transformation matrix with elements $a_{ij} = g_1 (i, j)$, and $\mathbf{T}$ is the resulting $N \times N$ transform for values of u and v in the range $0, 1, 2, \ldots, N - 1$.

To obtain the inverse transform we premultiply and postmultiply Eq. (3.5-10) by an inverse transformation matrix $\mathbf{B}$. This operation yields the expression

$$\mathbf{BTB} = \mathbf{BAFAB}. \qquad (3.5\text{-}11)$$

If $\mathbf{B} = \mathbf{A}^{-1}$, it then follows that

$$\mathbf{F} = \mathbf{BTB}, \qquad (3.5\text{-}12)$$

which indicates that the digital image $\mathbf{F}$ can be recovered completely from its transform. If $\mathbf{B}$ is not equal to $\mathbf{A}^{-1}$, then use of Eq. (3.5-11) yields an approximation to $\mathbf{F}$, given by the relation

$$\hat{\mathbf{F}} = \mathbf{BAFAB}. \tag{3.5-13}$$

A number of transforms, including the Fourier, Walsh, Hadamard, and Discrete Cosine transforms, can be expressed in the forms of Eqs. (3.5-10) and (3.5-12). An important property of the resulting transformation matrices is that they can be decomposed into products of matrices with fewer nonzero entries than the original matrix. This result, first formulated by Good [1958] for the Fourier transform, reduces redundancy and, consequently, the number of operations required to implement a two-dimensional transform. The degree of reduction is equivalent to that achieved by an FFT algorithm, being on the order of $N \log_2 N$ multiply/add operations for each row or column of an $N \times N$ image. Although attention is focused in this book on computational procedures based on successive applications of one-dimensional algorithms to obtain the forward and inverse transforms of an image, it should be kept in mind that equivalent computational results can be obtained via a matrix formulation of the problem. The interested reader should consult the book by Andrews [1970] for additional details on this topic.

3.5.1 Walsh Transform

When $N = 2^n$, the discrete Walsh transform of a function $f(x)$, denoted by $W(u)$, is obtained by substituting the kernel

$$g(x, u) = \frac{1}{N} \prod_{i=0}^{n-1} (-1)^{b_i(x)b_{n-1-i}(u)} \tag{3.5-14}$$

into Eq. (3.5-1). In other words,

$$W(u) = \frac{1}{N} \sum_{x=0}^{N-1} f(x) \prod_{i=0}^{n-1} (-1)^{b_i(x)b_{n-1-i}(u)}, \tag{3.5-15}$$

where $b_k(z)$ is the kth bit in the binary representation of z. For example, if $n = 3$ and $z = 6$ (110 in binary), we have that $b_0(z) = 0$, $b_1(z) = 1$, and $b_2(z) = 1$.

The values of $g(x, u)$, excluding the $1/N$ constant term, are listed in Table 3.3 for $N = 8$. The array formed by the Walsh transformation kernel is a symmetric matrix whose rows and columns are orthogonal. These properties, which hold in general, lead to an inverse kernel that is identical to the forward kernel, except for a constant multiplicative factor of $1/N$; that is,

$$h(x, u) = \prod_{i=0}^{n-1} (-1)^{b_i(x)b_{n-1-i}(u)}. \tag{3.5-16}$$

Table 3.3   Values of the Walsh Transformation Kernel
for $N = 8$

u \ x	0	1	2	3	4	5	6	7
0	+	+	+	+	+	+	+	+
1	+	+	+	+	−	−	−	−
2	+	+	−	−	+	+	−	−
3	+	+	−	−	−	−	+	+
4	+	−	+	−	+	−	+	−
5	+	−	+	−	−	+	−	+
6	+	−	−	+	+	−	−	+
7	+	−	−	+	−	+	+	−

Thus the inverse Walsh transform is given by

$$f(x) = \sum_{u=0}^{N-1} W(u) \prod_{i=0}^{n-1} (-1)^{b_i(x)b_{n-1-i}(u)} \tag{3.5-17}$$

It is noted that, unlike the Fourier transform, which is based on trigonometric terms, the Walsh transform consists of a series expansion of basis functions whose values are $+1$ or -1.

The validity of Eq. (3.5-17) is easily established by substituting Eq. (3.5-15) for $W(u)$ and making use of the orthogonality condition mentioned above. It is also of interest to note from Eqs. (3.5-15) and (3.5-17) that the forward and inverse Walsh transforms differ only by the $1/N$ term. Thus any algorithm for computing the forward transform can be used directly to obtain the inverse transform simply by multiplying the result of the algorithm by N.

The two-dimensional forward and inverse Walsh kernels are given by the relations

$$g(x, y, u, v) = \frac{1}{N} \prod_{i=0}^{n-1} (-1)^{[b_i(x)b_{n-1-i}(u) + b_i(y)b_{n-1-i}(v)]} \tag{3.5-18}$$

and

$$h(x, y, u, v) = \frac{1}{N} \prod_{i=0}^{n-1} (-1)^{[b_i(x)b_{n-1-i}(u) + b_i(y)b_{n-1-i}(v)]}. \tag{3.5-19}$$

Although it is just as valid to group both $1/N$ terms in front of $g(x, y, u, v)$ or $h(x, y, u, v)$, the forms given in Eqs. (3.5-18) and (3.5-19) are preferable in image processing applications, where there is equal interest in taking the forward and inverse transforms. Since the formulation given in these equations yields identical kernels, it follows from Eqs. (3.5-3) and (3.5-4) that the forward and inverse Walsh transforms are also equal in form; that is,

$$W(u, v) = \frac{1}{N} \sum_{x=0}^{N-1} \sum_{y=0}^{N-1} f(x, y) \prod_{i=0}^{n-1} (-1)^{[b_i(x)b_{n-1-i}(u) + b_i(y)b_{n-1-i}(v)]} \tag{3.5-20}$$

and

$$f(x, y) = \frac{1}{N} \sum_{u=0}^{N-1} \sum_{v=0}^{N-1} W(u, v) \prod_{i=0}^{n-1} (-1)^{[b_i(x)b_{n-1-i}(u)+b_i(y)b_{n-1-i}(v)]}.\quad (3.5\text{-}21)$$

Thus any algorithm used to compute the two-dimensional forward Walsh transform can also be used without modification to compute the inverse transform.

The Walsh transform kernels are separable and symmetric since

$$
\begin{aligned}
g(x, y, u,v) &= g_1(x, u)\, g_1(y, v)\\
&= h_1(x, u)\, h_1(y, v)\\
&= \left[\frac{1}{\sqrt{N}} \prod_{i=0}^{n-1} (-1)^{b_i(x)b_{n-1-i}(u)}\right]\left[\frac{1}{\sqrt{N}} \prod_{i=0}^{n-1} (-1)^{b_i(y)b_{n-1-i}(v)}\right].
\end{aligned}
$$
$$(3.5\text{-}22)$$

It therefore follows that $W(u, v)$ and its inverse can be computed by successive applications of the one-dimensional Walsh transform given in Eq. (3.5-15). The procedure followed in the computation is the same as the one given in Section 3.3.1 and Fig. 3.9 for the Fourier transform.

The Walsh transform can be computed by a fast algorithm identical in form to the successive-doubling method given in Section 3.4.1 for the FFT. The only difference is that all exponential terms W_N are set equal to one in the case of the fast Walsh transform (FWT).[†] Equations (3.4-9) and (3.4-10), which are the basic relations leading to the FFT, then become

$$W(u) = \tfrac{1}{2}\{W_{\text{even}}(u) + W_{\text{odd}}(u)\} \quad (3.5\text{-}23)$$

and

$$W(u + M) = \tfrac{1}{2}\{W_{\text{even}}(u) - W_{\text{odd}}(u)\}, \quad (3.5\text{-}24)$$

where $M = N/2$, $u = 0, 1, \ldots, M - 1$, and $W(u)$ denotes the one-dimensional Walsh transform. Rather than giving a general proof of this result, let us illustrate the use of Eq. (3.5-15) and the validity of Eqs. (3.5-23) and (3.5-24) by means of a simple example. Further details on this subject may be found in Shanks [1969].

Example: If $N = 4$, use of Eq. (3.5-15) results in the following sequence of steps:

$$
\begin{aligned}
W(0) &= \frac{1}{4} \sum_{x=0}^{3} \left[f(x) \prod_{i=0}^{1} (-1)^{b_i(x)b_{1-i}(0)}\right]\\
&= \frac{1}{4}[f(0) + f(1) + f(2) + f(3)]
\end{aligned}
$$

[†] The use of W in this section to denote the Walsh transform should not be confused with our use of the same symbol in Section 3.4.1 to denote exponential terms.

$$W(1) = \frac{1}{4} \sum_{x=0}^{3} f(x) \prod_{i=0}^{1} (-1)^{b_i(x)b_{1-i}(1)} \Bigg]$$

$$= \frac{1}{4} [f(0) + f(1) - f(2) - f(3)]$$

$$W(2) = \frac{1}{4} \sum_{x=0}^{3} \left[f(x) \prod_{i=0}^{1} (-1)^{b_i(x)b_{1-i}(2)} \right]$$

$$= \frac{1}{4} [f(0) - f(1) + f(2) - f(3)]$$

$$W(3) = \frac{1}{4} \sum_{x=0}^{3} \left[f(x) \prod_{i=0}^{1} (-1)^{b_i(x)b_{1-i}(3)} \right]$$

$$= \frac{1}{4} [f(0) - f(1) - f(2) + f(3)]$$

In order to show the validity of Eqs. (3.5-23) and (3.5-24) we subdivide these results into two groups; that is,

$$W_{even}(0) = \tfrac{1}{2}[f(0) + f(2)] \quad W_{odd}(0) = \tfrac{1}{2}[f(1) + f(3)]$$
$$W_{even}(1) = \tfrac{1}{2}[f(0) - f(2)] \quad W_{odd}(1) = \tfrac{1}{2}[f(1) - f(3)]$$

From Eq. (3.5-23), we have

$$W(0) = \tfrac{1}{2}[W_{even}(0) + W_{odd}(0)]$$
$$= \tfrac{1}{4}[f(0) + f(1) + f(2) + f(3)]$$

and

$$W(1) = \tfrac{1}{2}[W_{even}(1) + W_{odd}(1)]$$
$$= \tfrac{1}{4}[f(0) + f(1) - f(2) - f(3)].$$

The next two terms are computed from these results using Eq. (3.5-24):

$$W(2) = \tfrac{1}{2}[W_{even}(0) - W_{odd}(0)]$$
$$= \tfrac{1}{4}[f(0) - f(1) + f(2) - f(3)]$$

and

$$W(3) = \tfrac{1}{2}[W_{even}(1) - W_{odd}(1)]$$
$$= \tfrac{1}{4}[f(0) - f(1) - f(2) + f(3)].$$

Thus computation of $W(u)$ by Eq. (3.5-15) or by Eqs. (3.5-23) and (3.5-24) yields identical results. ☐

As indicated above, an algorithm used to compute the FFT by the successive-doubling method can be easily modified for computing a fast Walsh transform simply by setting all trigonometric terms equal to 1. Figure 3.26 illustrates the required modifications for the FFT program given in Fig. 3.25. It is noted that the Walsh transform is real, thus requiring less computer storage for a given problem than the Fourier transform, which is generally complex.

3.5.2 Hadamard Transform

One of several known formulations for the one-dimensional, forward Hadamard kernel is given by the relation

$$g(x, u) = \frac{1}{N}(-1)^{\sum_{i=0}^{n-1} b_i(x)b_i(u)} \tag{3.5-25}$$

where the summation in the exponent is performed in modulo 2 arithmetic and, as in Eq. (3.5-14), $b_k(z)$ is the kth bit in the binary representation of z. Substitution

```
      SUBROUTINE FWT(F,LN)
      REAL F(1024),T
      N=2**LN
      NV2=N/2
      NM1=N-1
      J=1
      DO 3 I=1,NM1
         IF(I.GE.J) GO TO 1
         T=F(J)
         F(J)=F(I)
         F(I)=T
1        K=NV2
2        IF(K.GE.J) GO TO 3
         J=J-K
         K=K/2
         GO TO 2
3        J=J+K
      DO 5 L=1,LN
         LE=2**L
         LE1=LE/2
         DO 5 J=1,LE1
            DO 4 I=J,N,LE
               IP=I+LE1
               T=F(IP)
               F(IP)=F(I)-T
4              F(I)=F(I)+T
5           CONTINUE
      DO 6 I=1,N
6        F(I)=F(I)/FLOAT(N)
      RETURN
      END
```

Figure 3.26 Modification of the successive-doubling FFT algorithm for computing the fast Walsh transform.

of Eq. (3.5-25) into Eq. (3.5-1) yields the following expression for the one-dimensional Hadamard transform:

$$H(u) = \frac{1}{N} \sum_{x=0}^{N-1} f(x)(-1)^{\sum_{i=0}^{n-1} b_i(x)b_i(u)}$$

(3.5-26)

where $N = 2^n$, and u assumes values in the range $0, 1, 2, \ldots, N - 1$.

As in the case of the Walsh transform, the Hadamard kernel forms a matrix whose rows and columns are orthogonal. This condition again leads to an inverse kernel that, except for the $1/N$ term, is equal to the forward Hadamard kernel; that is,

$$h(x, u) = (-1)^{\sum_{i=0}^{n-1} b_i(x)b_i(u)}$$

(3.5-27)

Substitution of this kernel into Eq. (3.5-2) yields the following expression for the inverse Hadamard transform:

$$f(x) = \sum_{u=0}^{N-1} H(u)(-1)^{\sum_{i=0}^{n-1} b_i(x)b_i(u)}$$

(3.5-28)

for $x = 0, 1, 2, \ldots, N - 1$.

The two-dimensional kernels are similarly given by the relations

$$g(x, y, u, v) = \frac{1}{N}(-1)^{\sum_{i=0}^{n-1} [b_i(x)b_i(u)+b_i(y)b_i(v)]}$$

(3.5-29)

and

$$h(x, y, u, v) = \frac{1}{N}(-1)^{\sum_{i=0}^{n-1} [b_i(x)b_i(u)+b_i(y)b_i(v)]}$$

(3.5-30)

where the summation in the exponent is again carried out in modulo 2 arithmetic. It is noted that, as in the case of the Walsh transform, the two dimensional Hadamard kernels are identical.

Substitution of Eqs. (3.5-29) and (3.5-30) into Eqs. (3.5-3) and (3.5-4) yields the following two-dimensional Hadamard transform pair:

$$H(u, v) = \frac{1}{N} \sum_{x=0}^{N-1}\sum_{y=0}^{N-1} f(x, y)(-1)^{\sum_{i=0}^{n-1} [b_i(x)b_i(u)+b_i(y)b_i(v)]}$$

(3.5-31)

and

$$f(x, y) = \frac{1}{N} \sum_{u=0}^{N-1}\sum_{v=0}^{N-1} H(u, v)(-1)^{\sum_{i=0}^{n-1} [b_i(x)b_i(u)+b_i(y)b_i(v)]}$$

(3.5-32)

Since the forward and inverse transforms are identical, an algorithm used for computing $H(u, v)$ can be used without modification to obtain $f(x, y)$, and vice versa. It can also be shown by keeping in mind the modulo 2 summation that the Hadamard kernels are separable and symmetric. It therefore follows that

$$g(x,y,u,v) = g_1(x,u)g_1(y,v)$$
$$= h_1(x,u)h_1(y,v)$$
$$= \left[\frac{1}{\sqrt{N}}(-1)^{\sum_{i=0}^{n-1} b_i(x)b_i(u)}\right]\left[\frac{1}{\sqrt{N}}(-1)^{\sum_{i=0}^{n-1} b_i(y)b_i(v)}\right]. \tag{3.5-33}$$

With the exception of the $1/\sqrt{N}$ term, g_1 and h_1 are identical to Eq. (3.5-25). It is also noted that, since the two-dimensional Hadamard kernels are separable, the two-dimensional transform pair can be obtained by successive applications of any one-dimensional Hadamard transform algorithm.

The matrix of values produced by the one-dimensional Hadamard kernel given in Eq. (3.5-25) is shown in Table 3.4 for $N = 8$, where the constant $1/N$ term has been omitted for simplicity. It is noted that, although the entries in this table are the same as for the Walsh transform, the order of the rows and columns is different. In fact, when $N = 2^n$, this is the only difference between these two transforms. When N is not equal to an integer power of 2, the difference is more important. While the Walsh transform can be formulated for any positive integer value of N, existence of the Hadamard transform for values of N other than integer powers of 2 has been shown only up to $N = 200$.

Since most of the applications of transforms in image processing are based on $N = 2^n$ samples per row or column of an image, the use (and terminology) of the Walsh and Hadamard transforms is intermixed in the image processing literature, where the term Walsh–Hadamard transform is often used to denote either transform.

Two important features that might influence the choice of one of these transforms over the other are worth noting. As indicated in Section 3.5.2, the formulation

Table 3.4   Values of the Hadamard Transformation Kernel for $N = 8$

u \ x	0	1	2	3	4	5	6	7
0	+	+	+	+	+	+	+	+
1	+	−	+	−	+	−	+	−
2	+	+	−	−	+	+	−	−
3	+	−	−	+	+	−	−	+
4	+	+	+	+	−	−	−	−
5	+	−	+	−	−	+	−	+
6	+	+	−	−	−	−	+	+
7	+	−	−	+	−	+	+	−

given in Eq. (3.5-15) has the advantage that it can be expressed directly in a successive-doubling format. This allows computation of the FWT by a straightforward modification of the FFT algorithm developed in Section 3.4.1. Further modifications of doubling format. This allows computation of the FWT by a straightforward modification of the F FT algorithm developed in Section 3.4.1. Further modifications of this algorithm would be required to compute the fast Hadamard transform (FHT) to take into account the difference in ordering. An alternative approach is to use the FWT algorithm of Fig. 3.24 and then reorder the results to obtain the Hadamard transform.

Although the Hadamard ordering has disadvantages in terms of a successive-doubling implementation, it leads to a simple recursive relationship for the generation of the transformation matrices needed to implement Eqs. (3.5-10) and (3.5-12). The Hadamard matrix of lowest order (i.e., $N = 2$) is given by

$$\mathbf{H}_2 = \begin{bmatrix} 1 & 1 \\ 1 & -1 \end{bmatrix} \tag{3.5-34}$$

Then, letting $\mathbf{H}_N$ represent the matrix of order N, the recursive relationship is given by the expression

$$\mathbf{H}_{2N} = \begin{bmatrix} \mathbf{H}_N & \mathbf{H}_N \\ \mathbf{H}_N & -\mathbf{H}_N \end{bmatrix} \tag{3.5-35}$$

where $\mathbf{H}_{2N}$ is the Hadamard matrix of order $2N$, and it is assumed that $N = 2^n$.

The transformation matrix for use in Eq. (3.5-10) is obtained by normalizing the corresponding Hadamard matrix by the square root of the matrix order. Thus in the $N \times N$ case, these two matrices are related by the equation

$$\mathbf{A} = \frac{1}{\sqrt{N}} \mathbf{H}_N. \tag{3.5-36}$$

The expressions for the inverse Hadamard matrix are identical to Eqs. (3.5-34) through (3.5-36).

Example: Use of Eq. (3.5-34) and (3.5-35) leads to the following Hadamard matrices of order four and eight:

$$\mathbf{H}_4 = \begin{bmatrix} \mathbf{H}_2 & \mathbf{H}_2 \\ \mathbf{H}_2 & -\mathbf{H}_2 \end{bmatrix}$$

$$= \begin{bmatrix} + & + & + & + \\ + & - & + & - \\ + & + & - & - \\ + & - & - & + \end{bmatrix}$$

and

$$\mathbf{H}_8 = \begin{bmatrix} \mathbf{H}_4 & \mathbf{H}_4 \\ \mathbf{H}_4 & -\mathbf{H}_4 \end{bmatrix}$$

$$= \begin{bmatrix} + & + & + & + & + & + & + & + \\ + & - & + & - & + & - & + & - \\ + & + & - & - & + & + & - & - \\ + & - & - & + & + & - & - & + \\ + & + & + & + & - & - & - & - \\ + & - & + & - & - & + & - & + \\ + & + & - & - & - & - & + & + \\ + & - & - & + & - & + & + & - \end{bmatrix}$$

where $+$ and $-$ indicate $+1$ and -1, respectively.

As shown in Eqs. (3.5-25) and (3.5-33), $g(x, u)$ and $g_1(x, u)$ differ only by a constant multiplier term. Since $a_{ij} = g_1(i, j)$, it follows that the entries in the $\mathbf{A}$ matrix have the same form as the expansion of $g(x, u)$. This is easily seen, for example, by comparing Table 3.4 and the expression for $\mathbf{A} = \dfrac{1}{\sqrt{8}} \mathbf{H}_8$.   □

The number of sign changes along a column of the Hadamard matrix is often called the *sequency* of that column.[†] Since the elements of this matrix are derived from the kernel values, the sequency concept applies to the expansion of $g_1(x, u)$ for $x, u = 0, 1, \ldots, N - 1$. For instance, the sequencies of the eight columns of $\mathbf{H}_8$ and Table 3.4 are 0, 7, 3, 4, 1, 6, 2, and 5.

It is often of interest to express the Hadamard kernels so that the sequency increases as a function of increasing u. This formulation is analogous to the Fourier transform, where frequency also increases as a function of increasing u. The one-dimensional Hadamard kernel that achieves this particular ordering is given by the relation

$$g(x, u) = \frac{1}{N} (-1)^{\sum\limits_{i=0}^{n-1} b_i(x)p_i(u)} \tag{3.5-37}$$

where

$$\begin{aligned} p_0(u) &= b_{n-1}(u), \\ p_1(u) &= b_{n-1}(u) + b_{n-2}(u), \\ p_2(u) &= b_{n-2}(u) + b_{n-3}(u), \\ &\quad \vdots \\ p_{n-1}(u) &= b_1(u) + b_0(u). \end{aligned} \tag{3.5-38}$$

[†] As in the case of the Fourier transform, where u is a frequency variable, the concept of sequency is normally restricted to this variable. Thus the association of sequency with the columns of the Hadamard matrix is based on the assumption that the columns vary as a function of u and the rows as a function of x. This convention is used in Table 3.4.

As before, the summations in Eqs. (3.5-37) and (3.5-38) are performed in modulo 2 arithmetic. The expansion of Eq. (3.5-37) is shown in Table 3.5 for $N = 8$, where the constant multiplier term has been omitted for simplicity and the $+$ and $-$ entries indicate $+1$ and -1, respectively. It is noted that the columns and, by symmetry, the rows of this table are in order of increasing sequency.

The inverse, ordered Hadamard kernel is given by the expression

$$h(x, u) = (-1)^{\sum_{i=0}^{n-1} b_i(x)p_i(u)} \tag{3.5-39}$$

where $p_i(u)$ is computed using Eq. (3.5-38). Substitution of the forward and inverse kernels into Eqs. (3.5-1) and (3.5-2) yields the following ordered Hadamard transform pair:

$$H(u) = \frac{1}{N} \sum_{x=0}^{N-1} f(x)(-1)^{\sum_{i=0}^{n-1} b_i(x)p_i(u)} \tag{3.5-40}$$

and

$$f(x) = \sum_{u=0}^{N-1} H(u)(-1)^{\sum_{i=0}^{n-1} b_i(x)p_i(u)} \tag{3.5-41}$$

As in the unordered case, the two-dimensional kernels are separable and identical; they are given by the relations

$$g(x,y,u,v) = h(x,y,u,v)$$

$$= \frac{1}{N}(-1)^{\sum_{i=0}^{n-1} [b_i(x)p_i(u)+b_i(y)p_i(v)]} \tag{3.5-42}$$

Substitution of these kernels into Eqs. (3.5-3) and (3.5-4) yields the following two-dimensional, ordered Hadamard transform pair:

$$H(u, v) = \frac{1}{N} \sum_{x=0}^{N-1}\sum_{y=0}^{N-1} f(x,y)(-1)^{\sum_{i=0}^{n-1} [b_i(x)p_i(u)+b_i(y)p_i(v)]} \tag{3.5-43}$$

Table 3.5   Values of the Ordered Hadamard Kernel for $N = 8$

u \ x	0	1	2	3	4	5	6	7
0	+	+	+	+	+	+	+	+
1	+	+	+	+	−	−	−	−
2	+	+	−	−	−	−	+	+
3	+	+	−	−	+	+	−	−
4	+	−	−	+	+	−	−	+
5	+	−	−	+	−	+	+	−
6	+	−	+	−	−	+	−	+
7	+	−	+	−	+	−	+	−

and

$$f(x, y) = \frac{1}{N} \sum_{u=0}^{N-1} \sum_{v=0}^{N-1} H(u, v)(-1)^{\sum_{i=0}^{n-1} [b_i(x)p_i(u)+b_i(y)p_i(v)]} \qquad (3.5\text{-}44)$$

3.5.3 Discrete Cosine Transform

The forward kernel of the one-dimensional, Discrete Cosine transform (DCT) is given by the relations

$$g(x, 0) = \frac{1}{\sqrt{N}} \qquad (3.5\text{-}45\text{a})$$

$$g(x, u) = \sqrt{\frac{2}{N}} \cos \frac{(2x + 1)u\pi}{2N} \qquad (3.5\text{-}45\text{b})$$

for $x = 0, 1, \ldots , N - 1$ and $u = 1, 2, \ldots , N - 1$. Substitution of these expressions into Eq. (3.5-1) yields

$$C(0) = \frac{1}{\sqrt{N}} \sum_{x=0}^{N-1} f(x) \qquad (3.5\text{-}46\text{a})$$

$$C(u) = \sqrt{\frac{2}{N}} \sum_{x=0}^{N-1} f(x) \cos \frac{(2x + 1)u\pi}{2N}, \qquad (3.5\text{-}46\text{b})$$

where $C(u)$, $u = 0, 1, 2, \ldots , N - 1$, is the DCT of $f(x)$.

The inverse kernel is of the same form as in Eq. (3.5-45), and the inverse DCT is defined by the equation

$$f(x) = \frac{1}{\sqrt{N}} C(0) + \sqrt{\frac{2}{N}} \sum_{u=1}^{N-1} C(u) \cos \frac{(2x + 1)u\pi}{2N} \qquad (3.5\text{-}47)$$

for $x = 0, 1, 2, \ldots , N - 1$.

The two-dimensional forward DCT kernel is defined as

$$g(x, y, 0, 0) = \frac{1}{N} \qquad (3.5\text{-}48\text{a})$$

$$g(x, y, u, v) = \frac{1}{2N^3} [\cos(2x + 1)u\pi][\cos(2y + 1)v\pi] \qquad (3.5\text{-}48\text{b})$$

for $x, y = 0, 1, \ldots , N - 1$, and $u, v = 1, 2, \ldots , N - 1$. The inverse kernel is also of this form. Thus it follows from Eqs. (3.5-3) and (3.5-4) that the two-dimensional DCT pair is given by the expressions

$$C(0, 0) = \frac{1}{N} \sum_{x=0}^{N-1} \sum_{y=0}^{N-1} f(x, y) \qquad (3.5\text{-}49\text{a})$$

$$C(u, v) = \frac{1}{2N^3} \sum_{x=0}^{N-1}\sum_{y=0}^{N-1} f(x, y)[\cos(2x + 1)u\pi][\cos(2y + 1)v\pi]$$

(3.5-49b)

for $u, v = 1, 2, \ldots , N - 1$, and

$$f(x, y) = \frac{1}{N} C(0, 0)$$

$$+ \frac{1}{2N^3} \sum_{u=1}^{N-1}\sum_{v=1}^{N-1} C(u, v)[\cos(2x + 1)u\pi][\cos(2y + 1)v\pi]$$

(3.5-50)

for $x, y = 0, 1, \ldots , N - 1$.

By comparing Eqs. (3.5-45) and (3.5-48) we note that DCT transformation kernels are separable, so that the two-dimensional forward or inverse transform can be computed by successive applications of a one-dimensional DCT algorithm. In fact, an interesting property of the DCT is that it can be obtained directly from an FFT algorithm. This can be seen by expressing Eq. (3.5-46) in the equivalent form

$$C(0) = \frac{1}{\sqrt{N}} \sum_{x=0}^{N-1} f(x)$$

(3.5-51a)

and

$$C(u) = \sqrt{\frac{2}{N}} \operatorname{Re}\left\{\left[\exp\left(\frac{-j\pi u}{2N}\right)\right] \sum_{x=0}^{2N-1} f(x) \exp\left(\frac{-j\pi ux}{N}\right)\right\}$$

(3.5-51b)

where $u = 1, 2, \ldots , N - 1$; $f(x) = 0$ for $x = N, N + 1, \ldots , 2N - 1$; and Re $\{\cdot\}$ denotes the real part of the term enclosed. The summation term is recognized as a $2N$-point discrete Fourier transform. Similarly, a $2N$-point inverse FFT can be used to obtain $f(x)$ from $C(u)$.

3.6   THE HOTELLING TRANSFORM

Unlike the transforms discussed previously, the *Hotelling transform*[†] developed in this section is based on statistical properties of an image. The principal uses of this transform are in data compression and rotation applications.

As an introduction to the problem, suppose that an $N \times N$ image $f(x, y)$ is transmitted M times over some communication channel. Since any physical channel is subject to random disturbances, the set of received images, $\{f_1(x, y), f_2(x, y), \ldots f_M(x, y)\}$, will in general represent a statistical ensemble whose properties are

---

[†] This transform is also commonly referred to as the *eigenvector, principal component,* or *discrete Karhunen–Loève transform.*

determined by the channel characteristics and the nature of the disturbance. An example of such an ensemble is the set of images of the same scene transmitted by a space probe. In this case, the images are corrupted by atmospheric disturbances and electrical noise in the transmitter and receiver.

3.6.1 Formulation

Each sample image $f_i(x, y)$ can be expressed in the form of an N^2-dimensional vector x_i as follows:

$$\mathbf{x}_i = \begin{bmatrix} x_{i1} \\ x_{i2} \\ \vdots \\ x_{ij} \\ \vdots \\ x_{iN^2} \end{bmatrix} \tag{3.6-1}$$

where x_{ij} denotes the jth component of vector $\mathbf{x}_i$. One way to construct such a vector is to let the first N components of $\mathbf{x}_i$ be formed from the first row of $f_i(x, y)$ [i.e., $x_{i1} = f(0, 0)$, $x_{i2} = f(0, 1)$, . . . , $x_{iN} = f(0, N - 1)$]; the second set of N components from the second row; and so on. Another way is to use the columns of $f(x, y)$ instead of the rows. Of course, other representations are possible, but these two are the ones used most often.

The covariance matrix of the $\mathbf{x}$ vectors is defined as

$$\mathbf{C_x} = E\{(\mathbf{x} - \mathbf{m_x})(\mathbf{x} - \mathbf{m_x})'\}, \tag{3.6-2}$$

where

$$\mathbf{m_x} = E\{\mathbf{x}\} \tag{3.6-3}$$

is the mean vector, E is the expected value, and the prime (') indicates transposition. Equations (3.6-2) and (3.6-3) can be approximated from the samples by using the relations

$$\mathbf{m_x} \cong \frac{1}{M} \sum_{i=1}^{M} \mathbf{x}_i \tag{3.6-4}$$

and

$$\mathbf{C_x} \cong \frac{1}{M} \sum_{i=1}^{M} (\mathbf{x}_i - \mathbf{m_x})(\mathbf{x}_i - \mathbf{m_x})' \tag{3.6-5a}$$

or, equivalently,

$$\mathbf{C_x} \cong \frac{1}{M} \left[\sum_{i=1}^{M} \mathbf{x}_i \mathbf{x}_i' \right] - \mathbf{m_x} \mathbf{m_x}'. \tag{3.6-5b}$$

The mean vector is of dimensionality N^2 and $\mathbf{C_x}$ is an $N^2 \times N^2$ matrix.

Let e_i and λ_i, $i = 1, 2, \ldots, N^2$, be the eigenvectors and corresponding eigenvalues of C_x. It is assumed for convenience in notation that the eigenvalues have been arranged in decreasing order so that $\lambda_1 \geq \lambda_2 \geq \cdots \geq \lambda_{N^2}$. A transformation matrix whose rows are the eigenvectors of C_x is given by

$$A = \begin{bmatrix} e_{11} & e_{12} \cdots e_{1N^2} \\ e_{21} & e_{22} \cdots e_{2N^2} \\ \vdots & \\ e_{N^2 1} & e_{N^2 2} \cdots e_{N^2 N^2} \end{bmatrix} \tag{3.6-6}$$

where e_{ij} is the jth component of the ith eigenvector. The Hotelling transform then consists simply of multiplying a centralized image vector, $(x - m_x)$, by A to obtain a new image vector y; that is,

$$y = A(x - m_x). \tag{3.6-7}$$

Equation (3.6-7) has several important properties. Let us first examine the covariance matrix of the y vectors. This matrix is given by

$$C_y = E\{(y - m_y)(y - m_y)'\}, \tag{3.6-8}$$

where m_y is equal to the zero vector 0 as can be shown directly from Eqs. (3.6-3) and (3.6-7):

$$\begin{aligned} m_y &= E\{y\} \\ &= E\{A(x - m_x)\} \\ &= AE\{x\} - Am_x \\ &= 0. \end{aligned} \tag{3.6-9}$$

Substitution of Eqs. (3.6-7) and (3.6-9) into Eq. (3.6-8) yields the following expressions for C_y in terms of C_x:

$$\begin{aligned} C_y &= E\{(Ax - Am_x)(Ax - Am_x)'\} \\ &= E\{A(x - m_x)(x - m_x)'A'\} \\ &= AE\{(x - m_x)(x - m_x)'\}A' \\ &= AC_xA', \end{aligned} \tag{3.6-10}$$

where the last step follows from the definition of C_x given in Eq. (3.6-2).

It can be shown (Lawley and Maxwell [1963]) that C_y is a diagonal matrix with elements equal to the eigenvalues of C_x; that is,

$$C_y = \begin{bmatrix} \lambda_1 & & & 0 \\ & \lambda_2 & & \\ & & \ddots & \\ 0 & & & \lambda_{N^2} \end{bmatrix} \tag{3.6-11}$$

The importance of this property is that, since the terms off the main diagonal are 0, the elements of **y** are *uncorrelated*. In addition, each eigenvalue λ_i is equal to the variance of the *i*th element of **y** along eigenvector $\mathbf{e}_i$.

Another property, which will be shown in Chapter 6 to be useful for image coding, deals with the reconstruction of **x** from **y**. Since $\mathbf{C}_x$ is a real, symmetric matrix it is always possible to find a set of orthonormal eigenvectors (Noble [1969]). It therefore follows that $\mathbf{A}^{-1} = \mathbf{A}'$ and **x** can be reconstructed from **y** by using the relation

$$\mathbf{x} = \mathbf{A}'\mathbf{y} + \mathbf{m}_x. \tag{3.6-12}$$

Suppose, however, that instead of using all the eigenvectors of $\mathbf{C}_x$, we form **A** from the *K* eigenvectors corresponding to the largest eigenvalues. The **y** vectors will then be *K*-dimensional and the reconstruction given by Eq. (3.6-12) will no longer be exact. Let

$$\hat{\mathbf{x}} = \mathbf{A}'_K\mathbf{y} + \mathbf{m}_x \tag{3.6-13}$$

represent the approximation to **x** obtained with a transformation matrix $\mathbf{A}_K$ composed of the first *K* eigenvectors of $\mathbf{C}_x$. It can be shown that the mean square error *R* between **x** and $\hat{\mathbf{x}}$ is given by the expression

$$R = \sum_{j=1}^{N^2} \lambda_j - \sum_{j=1}^{K} \lambda_j \tag{3.6-14a}$$

$$= \sum_{j=K+1}^{N^2} \lambda_j. \tag{3.6-14b}$$

From Eq. (3.6-14a) we see that the error is zero if $K = N^2$ (i.e., if all the eigenvectors are used in the transformation). Since the λ_j's decrease monotonically, either form of Eq. (3.6-14) shows that the error is minimized by selecting the eigenvectors associated with the largest eigenvalues. Thus the Hotelling transform is optimal in the least-square-error sense.

The development of the Hotelling transform given above is quite different from the general approach presented in Section 3.5. The reason for this is that the Hotelling transformation matrix is not separable, thus precluding the use of Eq. (3.5-10). However, although this matrix is not separable, a fast algorithm based on using FFTs to obtain the Hotelling transform has been developed by Jain [1975].

3.6.2 Application to Image Rotation

One of the basic concepts underlying the derivation of the Hotelling transform is that the choice of basis vectors (i.e., rows of **A**) is made such that these vectors point in the direction of maximum variance of the data, subject to the constraint that all vectors be mutually orthogonal and the transformed components be uncorrelated. These requirements lead to the solution stated above that the bases are the eigenvectors of the covariance matrix. The required orientation of the eigenvectors leads to the optimal properties of the Hotelling transform since, when fewer than N^2 vectors are used in $\mathbf{A}$, the basis vectors selected correspond to the direction of largest variance in the data.

These properties can be used to advantage in image rotation. Let us consider the problem where an object has been extracted from an image and it is desired to rotate the object so that it is aligned in some standard or invariant direction. Many objects of interest in image processing applications (particularly man-made objects) can be easily standardized by performing a rotation that aligns the coordinate axes with the axes of maximum variance of the pixels in the object.

Consider the coordinate system with the x_1 and x_2 axes shown in Fig. 3.27. If new coordinates are chosen, with a different orientation but the same origin as the original system, then we shall say that there has been a rotation of axes in the plane. Let θ be the angle of rotation from the positive half of the x_1 axis to the positive half of the y_1 axis. It then follows from elementary trigonometry that the new and old axes are related by the equations

$$y_1 = x_1 \cos \theta + x_2 \sin \theta$$
$$y_2 = -x_1 \sin \theta + x_2 \cos \theta \qquad (3.6\text{-}15)$$

or

$$\begin{bmatrix} y_1 \\ y_2 \end{bmatrix} = \begin{bmatrix} \cos \theta & \sin \theta \\ -\sin \theta & \cos \theta \end{bmatrix} \begin{bmatrix} x_1 \\ x_2 \end{bmatrix} \qquad (3.6\text{-}16)$$

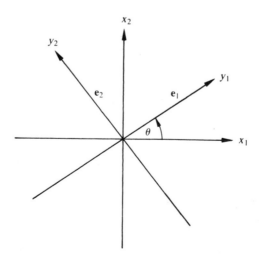

Figure 3.27   Rotation of coordinate system.

The original coordinates of each pixel in the object can be interpreted as two-dimensional random variables with mean

$$\mathbf{m_x} \cong \frac{1}{P} \sum_{i=1}^{P} \mathbf{x}_i \tag{3.6-17}$$

and covariance matrix

$$\mathbf{C_x} \cong \frac{1}{P} \left[\sum_{i=1}^{P} \mathbf{x}_i \mathbf{x}_i' \right] - \mathbf{m_x} \mathbf{m_x'}, \tag{3.6-18}$$

where P is the number of pixels in the object to be rotated and $\mathbf{x}_i$ is the vector composed of the coordinates of the ith pixel. It is noted that $\mathbf{m_x}$ is a two-dimensional vector and $\mathbf{C_x}$ a 2×2 matrix.

Since the eigenvectors of $\mathbf{C_x}$ point in the directions of maximum variance (subject to the constraint that they be orthogonal), a logical choice is to select the new coordinate system so that it will be aligned with these eigenvectors.

If we let the y_1 and y_2 axes be aligned with the *normalized* eigenvectors $\mathbf{e}_1$ and $\mathbf{e}_2$, it then follows from Fig. 3.27 that $\cos \theta = e_{11}$, $\sin \theta = e_{12}$, $-\sin \theta = e_{21}$, and $\cos \theta = e_{22}$, where e_{11} and e_{21} are the projections of $\mathbf{e}_1$ and $\mathbf{e}_2$ along the x_1 axis, and e_{12} and e_{22} are the projections of these two vectors along the x_2 axis. The rotation from the original coordinate system to this new system is then given by the relation.

$$\begin{bmatrix} y_1 \\ y_2 \end{bmatrix} = \begin{bmatrix} e_{11} & e_{12} \\ e_{21} & e_{22} \end{bmatrix} \begin{bmatrix} x_1 \\ x_2 \end{bmatrix} \tag{3.6-19}$$

which is seen to be in the familiar form $\mathbf{y} = \mathbf{Ax}$, where

$$\mathbf{A} = \begin{bmatrix} e_{11} & e_{12} \\ e_{21} & e_{22} \end{bmatrix} \tag{3.6-20a}$$

$$= \begin{bmatrix} \cos \theta & \sin \theta \\ -\sin \theta & \cos \theta \end{bmatrix} \tag{3.6-20b}$$

It is noted that Eq. (3.6-19) is analogous to a two-dimensional Hotelling transform where the mean has not been subtracted from the original vectors. Subtraction of the mean vector simply centralizes the object so that its center of gravity is at the origin of the new coordinate system. In this case, the transformation assumes the form $\mathbf{y} = \mathbf{A}(\mathbf{x} - \mathbf{m_x})$.

Interpretation of Eq. (3.6-19) is different in another respect from our earlier discussion of the Hotelling transform, where each vector was formed from pixels in an entire image. In the present application, we are concerned with the *coordinates* of pixels in a *single* image, and the ensemble of vectors used to arrive at the transformation matrix is derived from an object in the image.

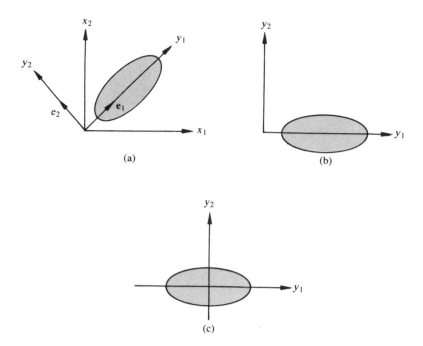

Figure 3.28 Rotation of a two-dimensional object. (a) Original data scatter showing direction of unit eigenvectors. (b) Data rotated by using the transformation $y = Ax$. (c) Data rotated and centralized by using the transformation $y = A(x - m_x)$.

The rotation–translation procedure is summarized in Fig. 3.28. Part (a) of this figure shows a simple object and the y_1 and y_2 axes chosen in the direction of their normalized eigenvectors. Figure 3.28(b) shows the object in the new coordinate system. Finally, Fig. 3.28(c) shows the result of rotation after the mean was subtracted from the data.

It is important to note that, if e_1 and e_2 are valid eigenvectors, the pairs $(e_1, -e_2)$, $(-e_1, e_2)$, and $(-e_1, -e_2)$ are also valid. Since the foregoing rotation procedure is based on a right-handed coordinate system, the choice of direction of the eigenvectors must be taken into account. Failure to do so can produce rotated results which are reflected about the origin in one or both of the new axes. Figure 3.29 illustrates the results of rotation for all possible directions of the eigenvectors;[†] the rotation in each case was obtained by aligning the y_1 axis with e_1, which is the eigenvector associated with the largest variance. Note ·that Fig. 3.29(a) shows the expected results. Figure 3.29(b) is based on a left-handed coordinate system and yields data

---

[†] Since the eigenvectors of the covariance matrix point in the directions of maximum variance, the only possible deviation of each vector is a change in sign.

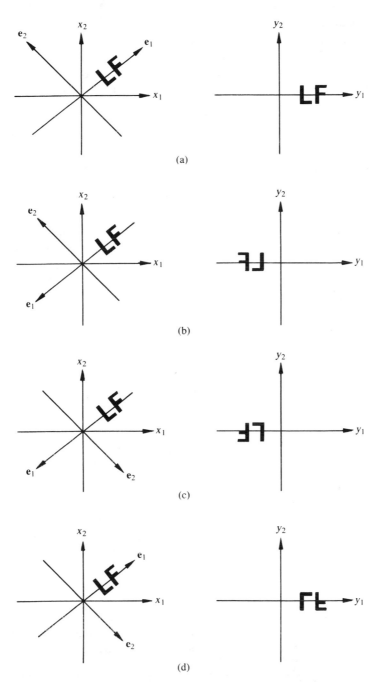

Figure 3.29   Example of possible directions of eigenvectors and corresponding rotation results.

that are reflected about the origin in the y_1 axis. Figure 3.29(c) is based on a right-handed system, but it also shows reflection about both axes. Actually this result is not incorrect; it merely points out the fact that it is not uncommon in practice to obtain the negative of the expected eigenvectors from a computational algorithm. Reversing the direction of both vectors would yield the same result as in Fig. 3.29(a). Finally, Fig. 3.29(d) again shows the reflection due to an improper coordinate system. It is noted that a right-handed system may or may not yield reflected results, but that a left-handed system will always be accompanied by this problem. In practice, the most common approach is to use a right-handed system and make provisions to handle both possible orientations of $\mathbf{e}_1$ and $\mathbf{e}_2$ in this system.

3.7   THE HOUGH TRANSFORM

Unlike the transforms discussed thus far, the concepts presented in this section deal with the detection of specific structural relationships between pixels in an image. As an introduction to this problem, suppose that given n points in an image we wish to find subsets of these points that lie on straight lines.[†] One possible solution is to first find all lines determined by every pair of points and then find all subsets of points that are close to particular lines. The problem with this procedure is that it involves finding $n(n - 1)/2 \sim n^2$ lines and then performing $(n)(n(n - 1))/2 \sim n^3$ comparisons of every point to all lines. This is computationally prohibitive in all but the most trivial applications.

This problem may be viewed in a different way using an approach proposed by Hough [1962] and commonly referred to as the *Hough transform*. Consider a point (x_i, y_i) and the general equation of a straight line in slope–intercept form, $y_i = ax_i + b$. There is an infinite number of lines that pass through (x_i, y_i), but they all satisfy the equation $y_i = ax_i + b$ for varying values of a and b. However, if we write this equation as $b = -x_i a + y_i$, and consider the ab plane (also called *parameter space*), then we have the equation of a *single* line for a fixed pair (x_i, y_i). Furthermore, a second point (x_j, y_j) will also have a line in parameter space associated with it, and this line will intersect the line associated with (x_i, y_i) at (a', b'), where a' is the slope and b' the intercept of the line containing both (x_i, y_i) and (x_j, y_j) in the xy plane. In fact, all points contained on this line will have lines in parameter space that intersect at (a', b'). These concepts are illustrated in Fig. 3.30.

The computational attractiveness of the Hough transform arises from subdividing the parameter space into so-called *accumulator cells*, as illustrated in Fig. 3.31, where (a_{max}, a_{min}) and (b_{max}, b_{min}) are the expected ranges of slope and intercept values. The cell at coordinates (i, j), with accumulator value $A(i, j)$, corresponds to the square associated with parameter space coordinates (a_i, b_j). Initially, these

---

[†] Typically, the points in question have been identified as being unique in some way, such as being edge pixels with intensities that exceed a given threshold value.

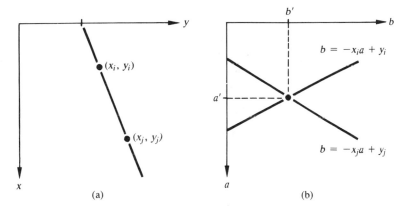

Figure 3.30   (a) xy plane. (b) Parameter space.

cells are set to zero. Then, for every point (x_k, y_k) in the image plane, we let the parameter a equal each of the allowed subdivision values on the a axis and solve for the corresponding b using the equation $b = -x_k a + y_k$. The resulting b's are then rounded off to the nearest allowed value in the b axis. If a choice of a_p results in solution b_q, we let $A(p, q) = A(p, q) + 1$. At the end of this procedure, a value of M in $A(i, j)$ corresponds to M points in the xy plane lying on the line $y = a_i x + b_j$. The accuracy of the collinearity of these points is established by the number of subdivisions in the ab plane.

It is noted that if we subdivide the a axis into K increments, then for every point (x_k, y_k) we obtain K values of b corresponding to the K possible values of a. Since there are n image points, this involves nK computations. Thus the procedure just discussed is *linear* in n, and the product nK does not approach the number of

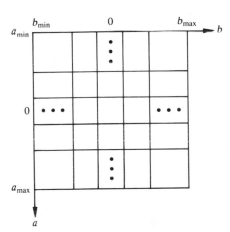

Figure 3.31   Quantization of the parameter plane for use in the Hough transform.

computations discussed at the beginning of this section unless K approaches or exceeds n.

A problem with using the equation $y = ax + b$ to represent a line is that both the slope and intercept approach infinity as the line approaches a vertical position. One way around this difficulty is to use the normal representation of a line, given by

$$x \cos \theta + y \sin \theta = \rho. \qquad (3.7\text{-}1)$$

The meaning of the parameters used in Eq. (3.7-1) is illustrated in Fig. 3.32(a). The use of this representation in constructing a table of accumulators is identical to the method discussed above for the slope–intercept representation. Instead of straight lines, however, we now have as loci sinusoidal curves in the $\rho\theta$ plane. As before, M collinear points lying on a line $x \cos \theta_j + y \sin \theta_j = \rho_i$ will yield M sinusoidal curves that intersect at (ρ_i, θ_j) in the parameter space. When we use the method of incrementing θ and solving for the corresponding ρ, the procedure will yield M entries in accumulator $A(i, j)$ associated with the cell determined by (ρ_i, θ_j). The subdivision of the parameter space is illustrated in Fig. 3.32(b).

The range of angle θ is $\pm 90°$, measured with respect to the x axis. Thus with reference to Fig. 3.32(a), a horizontal line has $\theta = 0°$, with ρ being equal to the positive x intercept. Similarly, a vertical line has $\theta = 90°$, with ρ being equal to the positive y intercept, or $\theta = -90°$, with ρ being equal to the negative y intercept.

Example: An illustration of the Hough transform based on Eq. (3.7-1) is shown in Fig. 3.33. Part (a) of this figure shows an image with five labeled points. The mapping of each of these points into the $\rho\theta$ plane is shown in Fig. 3.33(b). The

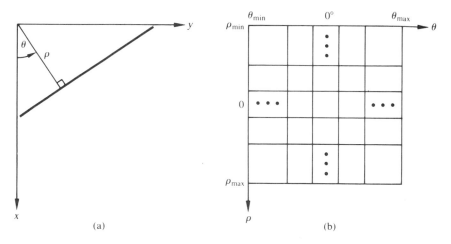

(a)   (b)

Figure 3.32   (a) Normal representation of a line. (b) Quantization of the $\rho\theta$ plane into cells.

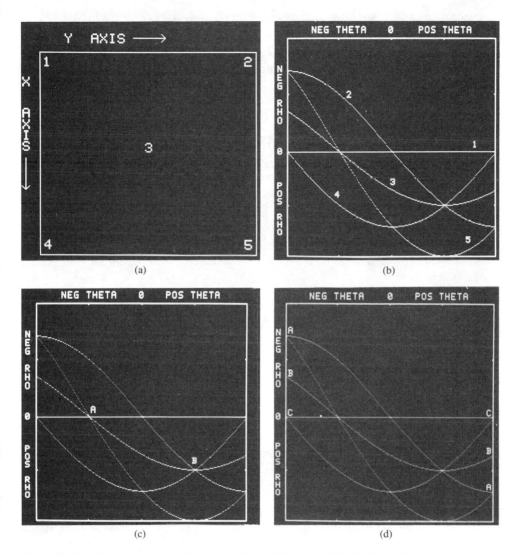

Figure 3.33 Illustration of the Hough transform. (Courtesy of D. R. Cate, Texas Instruments, Inc.)

range of θ values is $\pm 90°$ and the range of the ρ axis is $\pm \sqrt{2}\,D$, where D is the distance between corners in the image. Unlike the transform based on using the slope–intercept, each of these curves has a different sinusoidal shape. (The horizontal line resulting from the mapping of point 1 is a special case of a sinusoid with zero amplitude.) It is noted that, since a point at each extreme of the image was mapped, the Hough transform of any other point in the image would lie between the limits shown in Fig. 3.33(b).

The collinearity detection property of the Hough transform is illustrated in Fig. 3.33(c). Point A denotes the intersection of the curves corresponding to points 1, 3, and 5 in the xy image plane. The location of point A indicates that these three points lie on a straight line passing through the origin ($\rho = 0$) and oriented at $-45°$. Similarly, the curves intersecting at point B in the parameter space indicate that points 2, 3, and 4 lie on a straight line oriented at $45°$, and whose distance from the origin is one half the diagonal distance from the origin of the image to the opposite corner.

Finally, Fig. 3.33(d) indicates the fact that the Hough transform exhibits a reflective adjacency relationship at the right and left edges of the parameter space. This property, shown by the points marked A, B, and C in Fig. 3.33(d), is due to the manner in which θ and ρ change sign at the $\pm90°$ boundaries.   □

Although our attention has been focused thus far on straight lines, the Hough transform is applicable to any function of the form $g(\mathbf{x}, \mathbf{c}) = 0$, where $\mathbf{x}$ is a vector of coordinates and $\mathbf{c}$ is a vector of coefficients. For example, the points lying on the circle

$$(x - c_1)^2 + (y - c_2)^2 = c_3^2 \qquad (3.7\text{-}2)$$

can be detected by using the approach discussed above. The basic difference is that we now have three parameters (c_1, c_2, and c_3), which results in a three-dimensional parameter space with cubelike cells and accumulators of the form $A(i, j, k)$. The procedure is to increment c_1 and c_2, solve for the c_3 that satisfies Eq. (3.7-2), and update the accumulator corresponding to the cell associated with the triplet (c_1, c_2, c_3). Clearly, the complexity of the Hough transform is strongly dependent on the number of coordinates and coefficients in a given functional representation.

Before leaving this section, we point out that further generalizations of the Hough transform to detect curves with no simple analytic representations are possible. These concepts, which are extensions of the material presented above, are treated in detail by Ballard [1981].

3.8 CONCLUDING REMARKS

The principal purpose of this chapter has been to present a theoretical foundation of image transforms and their properties. Within this framework, the essential points necessary for a basic understanding of these concepts have been developed and illustrated.

The emphasis placed on the Fourier transform reflects its wide scope of application in image processing problems. The material on the fast Fourier transform is of particular importance because of its computational implications. The separability, centralization, and convolution properties of the Fourier transform will also be used extensively in the following chapters.

Transform theory has played a central role in the development of image processing as a formal discipline, as will be evident in subsequent discussions. In the next chapters, we consider some uses of the Fourier transform for image enhancement and restoration. Further discussions of the Walsh–Hadamard, discrete cosine, and Hotelling transforms is deferred until Chapter 6, where use is made of these transforms for image encoding.

The Hough transform has become increasingly popular in the past few years as a tool for image processing, computer vision, and scene understanding. Use will be made of this transform in Chapter 7 in connection with boundary-oriented segmentation techniques.

REFERENCES

Our treatment of the Fourier transform is of an introductory nature. The classic texts by Titchmarsh [1948] and Papoulis [1962] offer a comprehensive theoretical treatment of the continuous Fourier transform and its properties. The reader will have little difficulty finding additional references in this area. Most engineering circuits and communications books offer a variety of developments and explanations of the Fourier transform. The books by Van Valkenburg [1955], Carlson [1968], and Thomas [1969] are representative.

The derivation of the discrete Fourier transform from its continuous form is also covered extensively in the literature. Three good references on this topic are Blackman and Tukey [1958], Cooley, Lewis, and Welch [1967], and Brigham [1974]. The first and last references are particularly suited for introductory reading.

Formulation of the fast Fourier transform is often credited to Cooley and Tukey [1965]. The FFT, however, has an interesting history worth sketching here. In response to the Cooley–Tukey paper, Rudnick [1966] reported that he was using a similar technique, whose number of operations was also proportional to $N \log_2 N$, and which was based on a method published by Danielson and Lanczos [1942]. These authors, in turn, referenced Runge [1903, 1905] as the source of their technique. The latter two papers, together with the lecture notes of Runge and König [1939], contain the essential computational advantages of present FFT algorithms. Similar techniques were also published by Yates [1937], Stumpff [1939], Good [1958], and Thomas [1963]. A paper by Cooley, Lewis, and Welch [1967a] presents a historical summary and an interesting comparison of results prior to the 1965 Cooley–Tukey paper.

The FFT algorithm presented in this chapter is by no means a unique formulation. For example, the so-called Sande–Tukey algorithm (Gentleman and Sande [1966]) is based on an alternative decomposition of the input data. The book by Brigham [1974] contains a comprehensive discussion of this algorithm as well as numerous other formulations of the FFT including procedures for bases other than 2.

Although our attention has been focused exclusively on digital techniques, the reader should be aware that two-dimensional Fourier transforms can also be obtained by optical methods. The books by Papoulis [1968], Goodman [1968], and Hech and Zajac [1975] span the theoretical and applied aspects of optics and optical transforms at an introductory level.

Further reading in the matrix formulation of image transforms can be found in the book by Andrews [1970], which also develops the concept of matrix decomposition and discusses other image transforms in addition to the ones covered in this chapter. The papers by Good [1958], Gentleman [1968], and Kahaner [1970] are also of interest.

The original paper on the Walsh transform (Walsh [1923]) is worth reading from a historical point of view. Additional references on the transform are Fine [1949, 1950], Hammond and Johnson [1962], Henderson [1964], Shanks [1969], and Andrews [1970].

Further reading on the Hadamard transform can be found in the original paper by Hadamard [1893], and in Williamson [1944], Whelchel [1968], and Andrews [1970]. Two interesting notes dealing with the search for Hadamard matrices based on other than integer powers of 2 are Baumert [1962], and Golomb [1963]. The concept of sequency appears to have been introduced by Harmuth [1968]. References for the discrete cosine transform are Ahmed *et al.* [1974] and Ahmed and Rao [1975]. The latter reference also contains an extensive discussion of other orthogonal transforms.

Hotelling [1933] was the first to derive and publish the transformation that transforms discrete variables into uncorrelated coefficients. He referred to this technique as *the method of principal components*. His paper gives considerable insight into the method and is worth reading. Hotelling's transformation was rediscovered by Kramer and Mathews [1956] and Huang and Schultheiss [1963]. See Lawley and Maxwell [1963] for a general discussion of this topic.

The analogous transformation for transforming continuous data into a set of uncorrelated coefficients was discovered by Karhunen [1947] and Loève [1948] and is called the *Karhunen–Loève expansion*. See Selin [1965] for an excellent discussion. The result that the Karhunen–Loève expansion minimizes the mean-square truncation error was first published by Koschman [1954] and rediscovered by Brown [1960].

The Hough transform was first proposed by P. V. C. Hough [1962] in a U.S. patent, and later popularized by Duda and Hart [1972]. A generalization of the Hough transform for detecting arbitrary shapes has been proposed by Ballard [1981]. The Hough transform has found applicability in areas such as biomedical image processing (Kimme *et al.* [1975], Wechsler and Slansky [1977]), scene understanding (O'Gorman and Clowes [1976], Dudani and Luk [1977]), target tracking (Falconer [1977]), object inspection (Dyer [1983]), and character recognition (Kushnir *et al.* [1985]). Methods for reducing computational complexity have been investigated by Merlin and Farber [1975], and Davis [1982].

PROBLEMS

3.1 **a)** Starting with Eq. (3.1-9), show that the Fourier transform of the two-dimensional sinusoidal function $n(x, y) = A \sin(u_0 x + v_0 y)$ is $N(u, v) = -jA/2[\delta(u - u_0/2\pi, v - v_0/2\pi) - \delta(u + u_0/2\pi, v + v_0/2\pi)]$.

  b) Obtain the spectrum of $N(u, v)$.

3.2 A real function $f(x)$ can be decomposed as the sum of an even function and an odd function.

  a) Show that $f_{even}(x) = \frac{1}{2}[f(x) + f(-x)]$ and $f_{odd}(x) = \frac{1}{2}[f(x) - f(-x)]$.

  b) Show that $\mathfrak{F}[f_{even}(x)] = \text{Re}\{\mathfrak{F}[f(x)]\}$ and $\mathfrak{F}[f_{odd}(x)] = j\text{Im}\{\mathfrak{F}[f(x)]\}$.

3.3 Show that the Fourier transform of the autocorrelation function of $f(x)$ is the power spectrum (spectral density) $|F(u)|^2$.

3.4 Show the validity of Eqs. (3.3-7a) and (3.3-7b).

3.5 Obtain the Fourier transforms of (a) $df(x)/dx$, (b) $[\partial f(x, y)/\partial x + \partial f(x, y)/\partial y]$, and (c) $[\partial^2 f(x, y)/\partial x^2 + \partial^2 f(x, y)/\partial y^2]$. Assume that x and y are continuous variables.

3.6 Show that the discrete Fourier transform and its inverse are periodic functions. For simplicity, assume one-dimensional functions.

3.7 Show that the Fourier transform of the convolution of two functions is the product of their Fourier transforms. For simplicity, assume functions of one variable.

3.8 As indicated in Section 3.4.2, it takes $N \log_2 N$ additions and $\frac{1}{2}N \log_2 N$ multiplications to compute the FFT of N points. How many additions and multiplications would it take to compute the two-dimensional FFT of an $N \times N$ image?

3.9 With reference to the discussion in Section 3.4.1, show that

a) $W_{2M}^{2ux} = W_M^{ux}$,

b) $W_M^{u+M} = W_M^{u}$,

c) $W_{2M}^{u+M} = -W_{2M}^{u}$.

3.10 Numerous available FFT computer programs are restricted to one-dimensional, *real* data inputs. (a) Show how such an algorithm could be used to compute the FFT of one dimensional *complex* data. (b) What would be the procedure for using such an algorithm to compute the two-dimensional FFT of an image whose pixels are real numbers?

3.11 With reference to Table 3.2, how would you order a 16-point array for use with a successive-doubling FFT algorithm?

3.12 Show that Eqs. (3.5-15) and (3.5-17) constitute a transform pair (i.e., they are inverses of each other).

3.13 For a set of images of size 64×64, assume that the covariance matrix given in Eq. (3.6-11) turns out to be the identity matrix. What would be the mean square error between the original images and images reconstructed using Eq. (3.6-13) with only half of the original eigenvectors?

3.14 a) Explain why the Hough mapping of point 1 in Fig. 3.33(b) is a straight line.

b) Is this the only point that would produce this result?

c) Explain the reflective adjacency relationship illustrated in Fig. 3.33(d).

3.15 a) Develop a general procedure for obtaining the normal representation of a line given its slope-intercept equation $y = ax + b$.

b) Find the normal representation of the line $y = -2x + 1$.

CHAPTER 4

IMAGE ENHANCEMENT

*It makes all the difference whether one sees
darkness through the light or brightness
through the shadows.*
David Lindsay

The principal objective of enhancement techniques is to process a given image so that the result is more suitable than the original image for a specific application. The word ''specific'' is important because it establishes at the outset that the techniques discussed in this chapter are very much problem-oriented. Thus, for example, a method that is quite useful for enhancing x-ray images may not necessarily be the best approach for enhancing pictures of Mars transmitted by a space probe.

The approaches discussed in this chapter may be divided into two broad categories: frequency-domain methods and spatial-domain methods. Processing techniques in the first category are based on modifying the Fourier transform of an image. The spatial domain, on the other hand, refers to the image plane itself, and approaches in this category are based on direct manipulation of the pixels in an image.

The basic methodology underlying the material developed in this chapter is presented in Section 4.1. Section 4.2 deals with image enhancement by histogram-modification techniques. Sections 4.3 and 4.4 contain a number of approaches for image smoothing and sharpening, respectively. This discussion is followed in Section 4.5 by an enhancement technique based on the illumination-reflectance model introduced in Section 2.2. In Section 4.6 we develop a technique for generating small spatial masks from a filter function specified in the frequency domain. Finally, Section 4.7 contains an introduction to color fundamentals, as well as several applications of pseudo-color concepts to image enhancement.

4.1 BACKGROUND

The image-enhancement methods presented in this chapter are based on either *spatial-* or *frequency-domain* techniques. The purpose of this section is to develop the fundamental ideas underlying and relating these two approaches.

4.1.1 Spatial-Domain Methods

The term *spatial domain* refers to the aggregate of pixels composing an image, and spatial-domain methods are procedures that operate directly on these pixels. Image-processing functions in the spatial domain may be expressed as

$$g(x, y) = T[f(x, y)], \tag{4.1-1}$$

where $f(x, y)$ is the input image, $g(x, y)$ is the processed image, and T is an operator on f, defined over some neighborhood of (x, y). It is also possible to let T operate on a *set* of input images, such as performing the pixel-by-pixel sum of K images for noise reduction, as discussed in Section 4.3.4.

The principal approach used in defining a neighborhood about (x, y) is to use a square or rectangular subimage area centered at (x, y), as shown in Fig. 4.1. The center of the subimage is moved from pixel to pixel starting, say, at the top left corner, and applying the operator at each location (x, y) to yield the value of g at that location. Although other neighborhood shapes, such as a circle, are sometimes used, square arrays are by far the most predominant because of their ease of implementation.

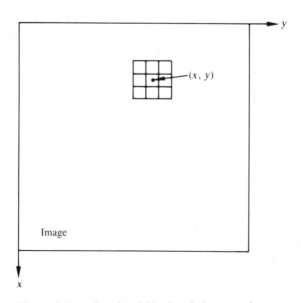

Figure 4.1 A 3 × 3 neighborhood about a point (x, y) in an image.

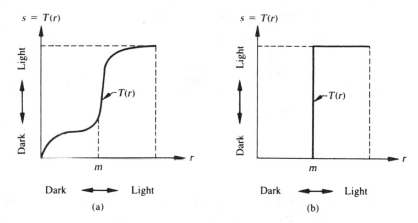

Figure 4.2   Gray-level transformation functions for contrast enhancement.

The simplest form of T is when the neighborhood is 1×1. In this case, g depends only on the value of f at (x, y) and T becomes a gray-level *transformation* (also called *mapping*) *function* of the form

$$s = T(r), \qquad (4.1\text{-}2)$$

where, for simplicity in notation, we use r and s as variables that denote the gray level of $f(x, y)$ and $g(x, y)$ at any point (x, y). As an illustration, if $T(r)$ has the form shown in Fig. 4.2(a), the effect of this transformation is to produce an image of higher contrast than the original by darkening the levels below a value m and brightening the levels above m in the original pixel spectrum. In this technique, known as *contrast stretching*, the levels of r below m are compressed by the transformation function into a narrow range of s toward the dark end of the spectrum; the opposite effect takes place for values of r above m. In the limiting case shown in Fig. 4.2(b), $T(r)$ produces a two-level (i.e., binary) image. As shown in the following sections, some fairly simple, yet powerful, processing approaches can be formulated using gray-level transformations.

Larger neighborhoods allow a variety of processing functions that, as will be seen in subsequent chapters, go beyond just image enhancement. Regardless of the specific application, however, the general approach is to let the values of f in a predefined neighborhood of (x, y) determine the value of g at those coordinates. One of the principal approaches in this formulation is based on the use of so-called *masks* (also referred to as *templates, windows,* or *filters*). Basically, a mask is a small (e.g., 3×3) two-dimensional array, such as the one shown in Fig. 4.1, whose coefficients are chosen to detect a given property in an image. As an introduction to this concept, suppose that we have an image of constant intensity that contains widely isolated points whose intensities are different from the background. These points can be detected by using the mask shown in Fig. 4.3. The procedure is as

-1	-1	-1
-1	8	-1
-1	-1	-1

Figure 4.3 A mask for detecting isolated points different from a constant background.

follows: The center of the mask (labeled 8) is moved around the image, as indicated in Fig. 4.1. At each pixel position in the image, we multiply every pixel that is contained within the mask area by the corresponding mask coefficient; that is, the pixel in the center of the mask is multiplied by 8, while its 8-neighbors are multiplied by -1. The results of these nine multiplications are then summed. If all the pixels within the mask area have the same value (constant background), the sum will be zero. If, on the other hand, the center of the mask is located at one of the isolated points, the sum will be different from zero. If the isolated point is in an off-center position the sum will also be different from zero, but the magnitude of the response will be weaker. These weaker responses can be eliminated by comparing the sum against a threshold.

As shown in Fig. 4.4, if we let w_1, w_2, . . . , w_9 represent mask coefficients and consider the 8-neighbors of (x, y), we may generalize the preceding discussion

w_1 $(x - 1, y - 1)$	w_2 $(x - 1, y)$	w_3 $(x - 1, y + 1)$
w_4 $(x, y - 1)$	w_5 (x, y)	w_6 $(x, y + 1)$
w_7 $(x + 1, y - 1)$	w_8 $(x + 1, y)$	w_9 $(x + 1, y + 1)$

Figure 4.4 A general 3×3 mask showing coefficients and corresponding image pixel locations.

as performing the following operation:

$$
\begin{aligned}
T[f(x, y)] = w_1 f(x-1, y-1) &+ w_2 f(x-1, y) \\
&+ w_3 f(x-1, y+1) + w_4 f(x, y-1) \\
&+ w_5 f(x, y) + w_6 f(x, y+1) + w_7 f(x+1, y-1) \\
&+ w_8 f(x+1, y) + w_9 f(x+1, y+1)
\end{aligned}
\tag{4.1-3}
$$

on a 3×3 neighborhood of (x, y). Larger masks are formed in a similar manner.

It is noted in Eq. (4.1-3) that changing the coefficients changes the function of the mask. For instance, if we select $w_i = 1/9$, $i = 1, 2, \ldots 9$, and let $g(x, y) = T[f(x, y)]$, then the values of g at (x, y) will be the average gray level of the pixel at (x, y) and its 8-neighbors. As indicated above, masks have a number of uses besides image enhancement. Some of these uses include image restoration, object segmentation, and computing the skeleton of a binary region.

4.1.2 Frequency-Domain Methods

The foundation of frequency-domain techniques is the convolution theorem. Let $g(x, y)$ be an image formed by the convolution of an image $f(x, y)$ and a position-invariant operator $h(x, y)$,[†] that is,

$$
g(x, y) = h(x, y) * f(x, y).
\tag{4.1-4}
$$

Then, from the convolution theorem (Section 3.3.8), we have that the following frequency-domain relation holds:

$$
G(u, v) = H(u, v) F(u, v),
\tag{4.1-5}
$$

where G, H, and F are the Fourier transforms of g, h, and f, respectively. The transform $H(u, v)$ is sometimes called the *transfer function* of the process.

It is shown later in this chapter that numerous image-enhancement problems can be expressed in the form of Eq (4.1-5). In a typical image-enhancement application, $f(x, y)$ is given and the goal, after computation of $F(u, v)$, is to select $H(u, v)$ so that the desired image, given by,

$$
g(x, y) = \mathfrak{F}^{-1}[H(u, v) F(u, v)]
\tag{4.1-6}
$$

exhibits some highlighted feature of $f(x, y)$. For instance, edges in $f(x, y)$ can be accentuated by using a function $H(u, v)$ that emphasizes the high-frequency components of $F(u, v)$.

It is worth noting that Eq. (4.1-4) describes a spatial process that is analogous to the use of the masks discussed in the previous section. In fact, the discrete convolution expression given in Eq. (3.3-35) is basically a mathematical representation of the mechanics involved in implementing the mask-shifting process explained in

---

[†] A position-invariant operator is one whose result depends only on the value of $f(x, y)$ at a given point in the image and not on the position of the point. Position invariance is an implicit requirement in the definition of the convolution integrals given in Eqs. (3.3-23) and (3.3-30).

Fig. 4.1. For this reason, the spatial masks discussed in the previous section are often called *convolution masks*. The key point to keep in mind, however, is that the convolution theorem requires that $H(u, v)$ and $h(x, y)$ be of the same size. Thus if $H(u, v)$ is, for example, of size 512×512, then Eq. (4.1-4) gives an equivalent spatial result only if $h(x, y)$ is of this size. As indicated in Section 3.3.8, a discrete convolution with large arrays is more efficiently carried out in the frequency domain via the fast Fourier transform (FFT). In Section 4.6 we develop a method for obtaining small spatial convolution masks that *approximate* a given $H(u, v)$ in a least-square-error sense and can thus be used for spatial processing. Finally, we point out that, as indicated in Section 3.3.8, discrete convolution is characterized by wraparound error unless the functions are assumed to be periodic with periods chosen according to Eqs. (3.3-33) and (3.3-34). In an image, wraparound error manifests itself as a distortion around the edges. In practice, however, this error is often not objectionable, even when the images are not extended using the procedure given in Section 3.3.8. The results given later in this chapter, for example, were obtained by direct FFT computations on the given images without extension.

Although it may already be obvious, let us emphasize before leaving this section that there is no general theory of image enhancement. When an image is processed for visual interpretation, the viewer is the ultimate judge of how well a particular method works. Visual evaluation of image quality is a highly subjective process, thus making the definition of a "good image" an elusive standard by which to compare algorithm performance. When the problem is one of processing images for machine perception, the evaluation task is somewhat easier. If, for example, one were dealing with a character-recognition application, the best image-processing method would be the one yielding the best machine-recognition results. It is noteworthy, however, that even in situations where a clear-cut criterion of performance can be imposed on the problem, one usually is still faced with a certain amount of trial and error before being able to settle on a particular image-processing approach.

4.2   IMAGE ENHANCEMENT BY HISTOGRAM-MODIFICATION TECHNIQUES

A histogram of gray-level content provides a global description of the appearance of an image. The methods discussed in this section achieve enhancement by modifying the histogram of a given image in a specified manner. The type and degree of enhancement obtained depends on the nature of the specified histogram.

4.2.1   Foundation

Let the variable r represent the gray level of the pixels in the image to be enhanced. For simplicity, it will be assumed in the following discussion that the pixel values have been normalized so that they lie in the range

$$0 \leq r \leq 1, \tag{4.2-1}$$

with $r = 0$ representing black and $r = 1$ representing white in the gray scale.

For any r in the interval $[0, 1]$, attention will be focused on transformations of the form

$$s = T(r), \qquad\qquad (4.2\text{-}2)$$

which produce a level s for every pixel value r in the original image. It is assumed that the transformation function given in Eq. (4.2-2) satisfies the conditions:

(a) $T(r)$ is single-valued and monotonically increasing in the interval $0 \leqslant r \leqslant 1$, and

(b) $0 \leqslant T(r) \leqslant 1$ for $0 \leqslant r \leqslant 1$.

Condition (a) preserves the order from black to white in the gray scale, while condition (b) guarantees a mapping that is consistent with the allowed range of pixel values. A transformation function satisfying these conditions is illustrated in Fig. 4.5.

The inverse transformation from s back to r will be denoted by

$$r = T^{-1}(s) \qquad 0 \leqslant s \leqslant 1, \qquad\qquad (4.2\text{-}3)$$

where it is assumed that $T^{-1}(s)$ also satisfies conditions (a) and (b) with respect to the variable s.

The gray levels in an image are random quantities in the interval $[0, 1]$. Assuming for a moment that they are continuous variables, the original and transformed gray levels can be characterized by their probability density functions $p_r(r)$ and $p_s(s)$, respectively. A great deal can be said about the general characteristics of an image

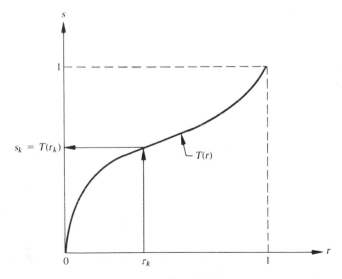

Figure 4.5   A gray-level transformation function.

from the density function of its gray levels. For example, an image whose gray levels have a density function like the one shown in Fig. 4.6(a) would have fairly dark characteristics since the majority of its levels are concentrated in the dark region of the gray scale. An image whose gray levels have a density function like the one shown in Fig. 4.6(b), on the other hand, would have predominant light tones since the majority of its pixels are light gray.

It follows from elementary probability theory that if $p_r(r)$ and $T(r)$ are known, and $T^{-1}(s)$ satisfies condition (a), then the probability density function of the transformed gray levels is given by the relation

$$p_s(s) = \left[p_r(r) \frac{dr}{ds} \right]_{r=T^{-1}(s)} \tag{4.2-4}$$

The following enhancement techniques are based on modifying the appearance of an image by controlling the probability density function of its gray levels via the transformation function $T(r)$.

4.2.2 Histogram Equalization

Consider the transformation function

$$s = T(r) = \int_0^r p_r(w)\, dw \qquad 0 \le r \le 1, \tag{4.2-5}$$

where w is a dummy variable of integration. The rightmost side of Eq. (4.2-5) is recognized as the cumulative distribution function (CDF) of r. The two conditions set forth in the previous section are satisfied by this transformation function since the CDF increases monotonically from 0 to 1 as a function of r.

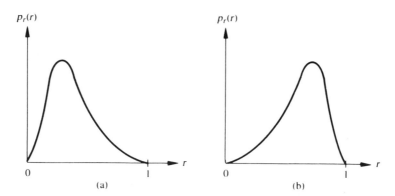

Figure 4.6   Gray-level probability density functions of (a) a "dark" image, and (b) a "light" image.

From Eq. (4.2-5) the derivative of s with respect to r is given by

$$\frac{ds}{dr} = p_r(r). \tag{4.2-6}$$

Substituting dr/ds into Eq. (4.2-4) yields

$$
\begin{aligned}
p_s(s) &= \left[p_r(r) \frac{1}{p_r(r)} \right]_{r=T^{-1}(s)} \\
&= [1]_{r=T^{-1}(s)} \\
&= 1 \qquad 0 \leq s \leq 1,
\end{aligned}
\tag{4.2-7}
$$

which is a uniform density in the interval of definition of the transformed variable s. It is noted that this result is independent of the inverse transformation function. This is important because it is not always easy to obtain $T^{-1}(s)$ analytically.

The foregoing development indicates that using a transformation function equal to the cumulative distribution of r produces an image whose gray levels have a uniform density. In terms of enhancement, this implies an increase in the dynamic range of the pixels, which, as will be seen below, can have a considerable effect in the appearance of an image.

Example: Before proceeding with a discussion of discrete variables, let us consider a simple illustration of the use of Eqs. (4.2-4) and (4.2-5). Assume that the levels r have the probability density function shown in Fig. 4.7(a). In this case $p_r(r)$ is given by

$$
p_r(r) = \begin{cases} -2r + 2 & 0 \leq r \leq 1 \\ 0 & \text{elsewhere.} \end{cases}
$$

Substitution of this expression in Eq. (4.2-5) yields the transformation function

$$
\begin{aligned}
s - T(r) &= \int_0^r (-2w + 2)\, dw \\
&= -r^2 + 2r.
\end{aligned}
$$

Although we only need $T(r)$ for histogram equalization, it will be instructive to show that the resulting density $p_s(s)$ is in fact uniform since this requires that $T^{-1}(s)$ be obtained. In practice this step is not required because Eq. (4.2-7) is independent of the inverse transformation function. Solving for r in terms of s yields

$$r = T^{-1}(s) = 1 \pm \sqrt{1 - s}.$$

Since r lies in the interval [0, 1], only the solution

$$r = T^{-1}(s) = 1 - \sqrt{1 - s}$$

is valid.

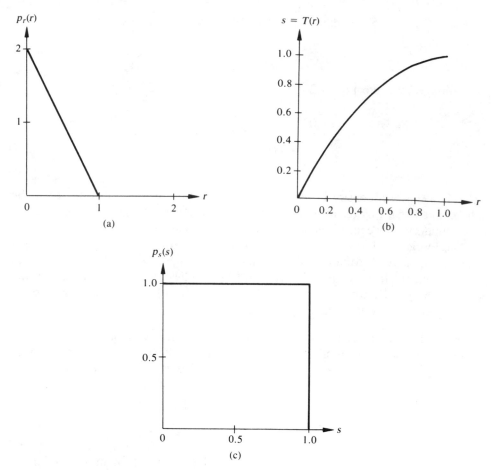

Figure 4.7 Illustration of the uniform-density transformation method. (a) Original probability density function. (b) Transformation function. (c) Resulting uniform density.

The probability density function of s is obtained by substituting the above results into Eq. (4.2-4):

$$p_s(s) = \left[p_r(r) \frac{dr}{ds} \right]_{r=T^{-1}(s)}$$

$$= \left[(-2r + 2) \frac{dr}{ds} \right]_{r=1-\sqrt{1-s}}$$

$$= \left[(2\sqrt{1-s}) \frac{d}{ds} (1 - \sqrt{1-s}) \right]$$

$$= 1 \qquad 0 \leqslant s \leqslant 1,$$

which is a uniform density in the desired range. The transformation function $T(r)$ is shown in Fig. 4.7(b), and $p_s(s)$ is shown in Fig. 4.7(c).   ☐

In order to be useful for digital image processing, the concepts developed above must be formulated in discrete form. For gray levels that assume discrete values, we deal with probabilities given by the relation

$$p_r(r_k) = \frac{n_k}{n} \qquad \begin{array}{l} 0 \leqslant r_k \leqslant 1 \\ k = 0, 1, \ldots, L - 1, \end{array} \qquad (4.2\text{-}8)$$

where L is the number of levels, $p_r(r_k)$ is the probability of the kth gray level, n_k is the number of times this level appears in the image, and n is the total number of pixels in the image. A plot of $p_r(r_k)$ versus r_k is usually called a *histogram,* and the technique used for obtaining a uniform histogram is known as *histogram equalization* or *histogram linearization.*

The discrete form of Eq. (4.2-5) is given by the relation

$$s_k = T(r_k) = \sum_{j=0}^{k} \frac{n_j}{n}$$

$$= \sum_{j=0}^{k} p_r(r_j) \qquad \begin{array}{l} 0 \leqslant r_k \leqslant 1 \\ k = 0, 1, \ldots, L - 1. \end{array} \qquad (4.2\text{-}9)$$

The inverse transformation is denoted by

$$r_k = T^{-1}(s_k) \qquad 0 \leqslant s_k \leqslant 1,$$

where both $T(r_k)$ and $T^{-1}(s_k)$ are assumed to satisfy conditions (a) and (b) stated in the previous section. It is noted that the transformation function $T(r_k)$ can be computed directly from the image in question by using Eq. (4.2-9). Although the inverse function $T^{-1}(s_k)$ is not used in histogram equalization, it plays a central role in the method discussed in the next section.

Example: Suppose that a 64 × 64, 8-level image has the gray-level distribution shown in Table 4.1. The histogram of these gray levels is shown in Fig. 4.8(a).

Table 4.1

r_k	n_k	$p_r(r_k) = n_k/n$
$r_0 = 0$	790	0.19
$r_1 = 1/7$	1023	0.25
$r_2 = 2/7$	850	0.21
$r_3 = 3/7$	656	0.16
$r_4 = 4/7$	329	0.08
$r_5 = 5/7$	245	0.06
$r_6 = 6/7$	122	0.03
$r_7 = 1$	81	0.02

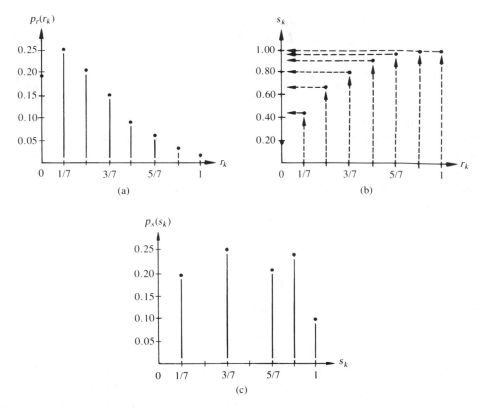

Figure 4.8 Illustration of the histogram-equalization method. (a) Original histogram. (b) Transformation function. (c) Equalized histogram.

The transformation function is obtained by using Eq. (4.2-9). For instance,

$$s_0 = T(r_0) = \sum_{j=0}^{0} p_r(r_j)$$

$$= p_r(r_0)$$

$$= 0.19.$$

Similarly,

$$s_1 = T(r_1) = \sum_{j=0}^{1} p_r(r_j)$$

$$= p_r(r_0) + p_r(r_1)$$

$$= 0.44$$

and

$$s_2 = 0.65 \qquad s_5 = 0.95$$
$$s_3 = 0.81 \qquad s_6 = 0.98$$
$$s_4 = 0.89 \qquad s_7 = 1.00.$$

The transformation function has the form shown in Fig. 4.8(b).

Since only eight equally spaced levels are allowed in this case, each of the transformed values must be assigned to its closest valid level. Thus we have

$$s_0 \cong 1/7 \qquad s_4 \cong 6/7$$
$$s_1 \cong 3/7 \qquad s_5 \cong 1$$
$$s_2 \cong 5/7 \qquad s_6 \cong 1$$
$$s_3 \cong 6/7 \qquad s_7 \cong 1.$$

It is noted that there are only five distinct histogram-equalized gray levels. Redefining the notation to take this into account yields the levels

$$s_0 = 1/7 \qquad s_3 = 6/7$$
$$s_1 = 3/7 \qquad s_4 = 1.$$
$$s_2 = 5/7$$

Since $r_0 = 0$ was mapped to $s_0 = 1/7$, there are 790 transformed pixels with this new value. Also, there are 1023 pixels with value $s_1 = 3/7$ and 850 pixels with value $s_2 = 5/7$. However, since both levels r_3 and r_4 were mapped to $s_3 = 6/7$, there are now $656 + 329 = 985$ pixels with this new value. Similarly, there are $245 + 122 + 81 = 448$ pixels with value $s_4 = 1$. Dividing these numbers by $n = 4096$ yields the histogram shown in Fig. 4.8(c). Since a histogram is an approximation to a probability density function, perfectly flat results are seldom obtained when working with discrete levels. □

Example: As a practical illustration of histogram equalization consider the image shown in Fig. 4.9(a) containing a picture of a dollar, which, due to a heavy shadow, is barely visible. The narrow range of values occupied by the pixels of this image is evident in the histogram shown in Fig. 4.9(b). The equalized histogram is shown in Fig. 4.9(c) and the processed image in Fig. 4.9(d). While the equalized histogram is, as expected, not perfectly flat throughout the full range of gray levels, considerable improvement over the original image was achieved by the spreading effect of the histogram-equalization technique. Although the final result is not an ideal picture, one should keep in mind the poor quality of the original. □

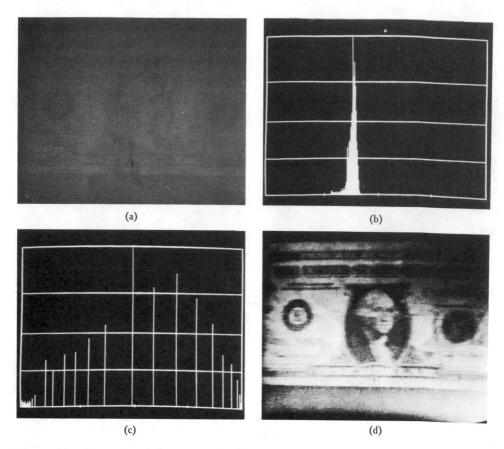

(a)   (b)

(c)   (d)

Figure 4.9   Illustration of the histogram-equalization approach. (a) Original image. (b) Original histogram. (c) Equalized histogram. (d) Enhanced image.

4.2.3   Direct Histogram Specification

Although the method discussed in the previous section is quite useful, it does not lend itself to interactive image-enhancement applications because the capabilities of this method are limited to the generation of only one result—an approximation to a uniform histogram.

It is sometimes desirable to be able to specify interactively particular histograms capable of highlighting certain gray-level ranges in an image. To see how this can be accomplished, let us return for a moment to continuous gray levels, and let $p_r(r)$ and $p_z(z)$ be the original and desired probability density functions, respectively. Suppose that a given image is first histogram equalized using Eq. (4.2-5); that is

$$s = T(r) = \int_0^r p_r(w) \, dw. \qquad (4.2\text{-}10)$$

If the desired image were available, its levels could also be equalized by using the transformation function

$$v = G(z) = \int_0^z p_z(w)\, dw. \qquad (4.2\text{-}11)$$

The inverse process, $z = G^{-1}(v)$, would then yield the desired levels back. This, of course, is a hypothetical formulation since the z levels are precisely what we are trying to obtain. It is noted, however, that $p_s(s)$ and $p_v(v)$ would be identical uniform densities since the final result of Eq. (4.2-5) is independent of the density inside the integral. Thus if instead of using v in the inverse process we use the uniform levels s obtained from the original image, the resulting levels, $z = G^{-1}(s)$, would have the desired probability density function. Assuming that $G^{-1}(s)$ is single-valued, the procedure can be summarized as follows:

(1) Equalize the levels of the original image using Eq. (4.2-5).
(2) Specify the desired density function and obtain the transformation function $G(z)$ using Eq. (4.2-11).
(3) Apply the inverse transformation function, $z = G^{-1}(s)$, to the levels obtained in Step (1).

This procedure yields a processed version of the original image, where the new gray levels are characterized by the specified density $p_z(z)$.

Although the method of histogram specification involves two transformation functions, $T(r)$ followed by $G^{-1}(s)$, it is a simple matter to combine both enhancement steps into one function that will yield the desired levels starting with the original pixels. From the above discussion, we have that

$$z = G^{-1}(s). \qquad (4.2\text{-}12)$$

Substitution of Eq. (4.2-5) in Eq. (4.2-12) results in the combined transformation function

$$z = G^{-1}[T(r)], \qquad (4.2\text{-}13)$$

which relates r to z. It is noted that, when $G^{-1}[T(r)] = T(r)$, this expression reduces to histogram equalization.

The implication of Eq. (4.2-13) is simply that an image need not be histogram-equalized explicitly. All that is required is that $T(r)$ be determined and combined with the inverse transformation function G^{-1}. The real problem in using the preceding method for continuous variables lies in obtaining the inverse function analytically. In the discrete case this problem is circumvented by the fact that the number of distinct gray levels is usually relatively small and it becomes feasible to calculate and store a mapping for each possible pixel value. The discrete formulation of the histogram-specification technique parallels Eqs. (4.2-8) and (4.2-9), as illustrated by the following example.

Example: Consider the 64 × 64, 8-level image values used in the second example given in Section 4.2.2. The histogram of this image is shown again in Fig. 4.10(a) for easy reference. It is desired to transform this histogram so that it will have the shape shown in Fig. 4.10(b). The values of the specified histogram are listed in Table 4.2.

The first step in the procedure is to obtain the histogram-equalization mappings. This was done in Section 4.2.2 with the results shown in Table 4.3. Next, we compute the transformation function using Eq. (4.2-9):

$$v_k = G(z_k) = \sum_{j=0}^{k} p_z(z_j).$$

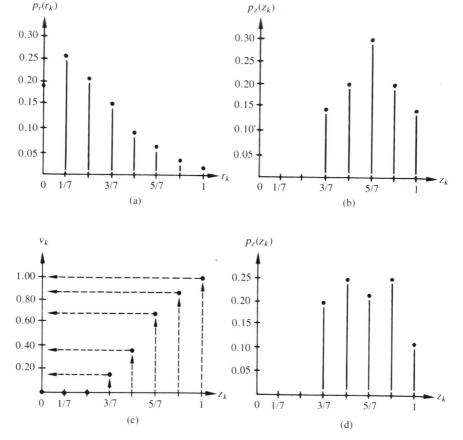

(a)

(b)

(c)

(d)

Figure 4.10   Illustration of the histogram-specification method. (a) Original histogram. (b) Specified histogram. (c) Transformation function. (d) Resulting histogram.

Table 4.2

z_k	$p_z(z_k)$
$z_0 = 0$	0.00
$z_1 = 1/7$	0.00
$z_2 = 2/7$	0.00
$z_3 = 3/7$	0.15
$z_4 = 4/7$	0.20
$z_5 = 5/7$	0.30
$z_6 = 6/7$	0.20
$z_7 = 1$	0.15

This yields the values

$$v_0 = G(z_0) = 0.00 \qquad v_4 = G(z_4) = 0.35$$
$$v_1 = G(z_1) = 0.00 \qquad v_5 = G(z_5) = 0.65$$
$$v_2 = G(z_2) = 0.00 \qquad v_6 = G(z_6) = 0.85$$
$$v_3 = G(z_3) = 0.15 \qquad v_7 = G(z_7) = 1.00.$$

The transformation function is shown in Fig. 4.10(c).

To obtain the z levels we apply the inverse of the G transformation obtained above to the histogram-equalized levels s_k. Since we are dealing with discrete values, an approximation must usually be made in the inverse mapping. For example, the closest match to $s_0 = 1/7 \approx 0.14$ is $G(z_3) = 0.15$ or, using the inverse, G^{-1} $(0.15) = z_3$. Thus s_0 is mapped to the level z_3. Using this procedure yields the following mappings:

$$s_0 = 1/7 \rightarrow z_3 = 3/7 \qquad s_3 = 6/7 \rightarrow z_6 = 6/7$$
$$s_1 = 3/7 \rightarrow z_4 = 4/7 \qquad s_4 = 1 \quad \rightarrow z_7 = 1.$$
$$s_2 = 5/7 \rightarrow z_5 = 5/7$$

Table 4.3

$r_j \rightarrow s_k$	n_k	$p_s(s_k)$
$r_0 \rightarrow s_0 = 1/7$	790	0.19
$r_1 \rightarrow s_1 = 3/7$	1023	0.25
$r_2 \rightarrow s_2 = 5/7$	850	0.21
$r_3, r_4 \rightarrow s_3 = 6/7$	985	0.24
$r_5, r_6, r_7 \rightarrow s_4 = 1$	448	0.11

Table 4.4

z_k	n_k	$p_z(z_k)$
$z_0 = 0$	0	0.00
$z_1 = 1/7$	0	0.00
$z_2 = 2/7$	0	0.00
$z_3 = 3/7$	790	0.19
$z_4 = 4/7$	1023	0.25
$z_5 = 5/7$	850	0.21
$z_6 = 6/7$	985	0.24
$z_7 = 1$	448	0.11

As indicated in Eq. (4.2-13), these results can be combined with those of histogram equalization to yield the following direct mappings:

$$r_0 = 0 \quad \rightarrow z_3 = 3/7 \qquad r_4 = 4/7 \rightarrow z_6 = 6/7$$
$$r_1 = 1/7 \rightarrow z_4 = 4/7 \qquad r_5 = 5/7 \rightarrow z_7 = 1$$
$$r_2 = 2/7 \rightarrow z_5 = 5/7 \qquad r_6 = 6/7 \rightarrow z_7 = 1$$
$$r_3 = 3/7 \rightarrow z_6 = 6/7 \qquad r_7 = 1 \quad \rightarrow z_7 = 1.$$

Redistributing the pixels according to these mappings and dividing by $n = 4096$ results in the histogram shown in Fig. 4.10(d). The values are listed in Table 4.4.

Note that, although each of the specified levels was filled, the resulting histogram is not particularly close to the desired shape. As in the case of histogram equalization, this error is due to the fact that the transformation is guaranteed to yield exact results only in the continuous case. As the number of levels decreases, the error between the specified and resulting histograms tends to increase. As will be seen below, however, very useful enhancement results can be obtained even with an approximation to a desired histogram. □

In practice, the inverse transformation from s to z is often not single-valued. This situation arises when there are unfilled levels in the specified histogram (which makes the CDF remain constant over the unfilled intervals), or in the process of rounding off $G^{-1}(s)$ to the nearest allowable level, as was done in the above example. Generally, the easiest solution to this problem is to assign the levels in such a way as to match the given histogram as closely as possible.

The principal difficulty in applying the histogram specification method to image enhancement lies in being able to construct a meaningful histogram. Two solutions to this problem are as follows. The first is to specify a particular probability density function (i.e., Gaussian, Rayleigh, log-normal, etc.) and then form a histogram by digitizing the given function. The second approach consists of specifying a histogram shape by means of a graphic device (like an interactive screen or drawing tablet) whose output is fed into the processor executing the histogram specification algorithm.

Example: As a practical illustration of the direct histogram-specification approach, consider Fig. 4.11(a), which shows a semi-dark room viewed from a doorway. Figure 4.11(b) shows the histogram-equalized image, and Fig. 4.11(c) is the result of interactive histogram specification. The histograms are shown in Fig. 4.11(d), which includes, from bottom to top, the original, equalized, specified, and resulting histograms.

Note that histogram equalization produced an image whose contrast was somewhat high, while the result shown in Fig. 4.11(c) has a much more balanced appearance.

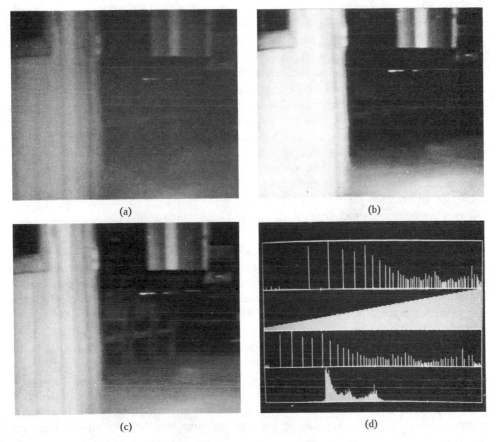

Figure 4.11   Illustration of the histogram-specification method. (a) Original image. (b) Histogram-equalized image. (c) Image enhanced by histogram specification. (d) Histograms.

Because of its flexibility, the direct-specification method can often yield results that are superior to histogram equalization.   □

4.2.4   Local Enhancement

The methods discussed in the previous two sections are global, in the sense that pixels are modified by a transformation function based on the gray-level distribution over an entire image. While this global approach is suitable for overall enhancement, it is often necessary to enhance details over small areas. Since the number of pixels in these areas may have negligible influence on the computation of a global transformation, the use of this type of transformation will not necessarily guarantee the desired local enhancement. The solution is to devise transformation functions that are based on the gray-level distribution, or other properties, in the neighborhood of every pixel in a given image.

The histogram-processing techniques developed in the last two sections are easily adaptable to local enhancement. The procedure is to define an $n \times m$ neighborhood and move the center of this area from pixel to pixel. At each location, we compute the histogram of the $n \times m$ points in the neighborhood and obtain either a histogram-equalization or histogram-specification transformation function. This function is finally used to map the level of the pixel centered in the neighborhood. The center of the $n \times m$ region is then moved to an adjacent pixel location and the procedure is repeated. Since only one new row or column of the neighborhood changes during a pixel-to-pixel translation of the region, it is possible to update the histogram obtained in the previous location with the new data introduced at each motion step. This approach has obvious advantages over repeatedly computing the histogram over all $n \times m$ pixels every time the region is moved one pixel location. Another approach often used to reduce computation is to employ non-overlapping regions, but this will usually produce an undesirable checkerboard effect.

Example: An illustration of local histogram equalization with the neighborhood moved from pixel to pixel is shown in Fig. 4.12. Part (a) of this figure shows an image that has been slightly blurred to reduce its noise content (see Section 4.3.1). Figure 4.12(b) shows the result of global histogram equalization. As is often the case when this technique is applied to smooth, noisy areas, Fig. 4.12(b) shows considerable enhancement of the noise, with a slight increase in contrast. Note, however, that no new structural details were brought out by this method. On the other hand, local histogram equalization using a neighborhood of size 7×7 revealed the presence of small squares inside the larger dark squares. The small squares were too close in gray level and their size too small to influence global histogram equalization in any significant way. It is also of interest to note the finer noise texture in Fig. 4.12(c), a result of local processing in relatively small neighborhoods.   □

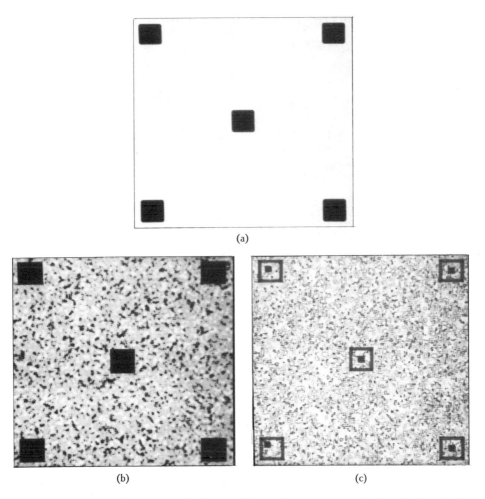

(a)

(b)   (c)

Figure 4.12   (a) Original image. (b) Result of global histogram equalization. (c) Result of local histogram equalization using a 7 × 7 neighborhood about each pixel. (From Fu, Gonzalez, and Lee [1987].)

Before leaving this section we point out that, instead of using histograms, one could base local enhancement on other properties of the pixel intensities in a neighborhood. The intensity mean and variance (or standard deviation) are two such properties frequently used because of their relevance to the appearance of an image. That is, the mean is a measure of average brightness and the variance is a measure of contrast.

A typical local transformation based on these concepts maps the intensity of an input image $f(x, y)$ into a new image $g(x, y)$ by performing the following transformation at each pixel location (x, y):

$$g(x, y) = A(x, y) \cdot [f(x, y) - m(x, y)] + m(x, y), \qquad (4.2\text{-}14)$$

where

$$A(x, y) = k \frac{M}{\sigma(x, y)} \qquad 0 < k < 1. \qquad (4.2\text{-}15)$$

In this formulation $m(x, y)$ and $\sigma(x, y)$ are the gray-level mean and standard deviation computed in a neighborhood centered at (x, y), M is the global mean of $f(x, y)$, and k is a constant in the range indicated above.

It is important to note that A, m, and σ are variable quantities that depend on a predefined neighborhood of (x, y). Application of the local gain factor $A(x, y)$ to the difference between $f(x, y)$ and the local mean amplifies local variations. Since $A(x, y)$ is inversely proportional to the standard deviation of the intensity, areas with low contrast receive larger gain. The mean is added back in Eq. (4.2-14) to restore the average intensity level of the image in the local region. In practice, it is often desirable to add back a fraction of the local mean and to restrict the variations of $A(x, y)$ between two limits (A_{min}, A_{max}) in order to balance large excursions of intensity in isolated regions.

Example: The preceding enhancement approach has been implemented in hardware by Narendra and Fitch [1981], and has the capability of processing images in real time (i.e., at 30 image frames/sec). An example of the capabilities of the technique using a local region on the order of 15×15 pixels is shown in Fig. 4.13. Note the enhancement of detail at the boundary between two regions of different overall gray levels and the rendition of gray-level details in each of the regions. □

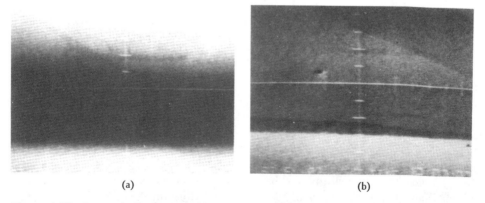

(a)   (b)

Figure 4.13   Images before and after local enhancement. (From Narendra and Fitch [1981].)

4.3   IMAGE SMOOTHING

Smoothing operations are used primarily for diminishing spurious effects that may be present in a digital image as a result of a poor sampling system or transmission channel. In this section we consider smoothing techniques in both the spatial and frequency domains.

4.3.1   Neighborhood Averaging

Neighborhood averaging is a straightforward spatial-domain technique for image smoothing. Given an $N \times N$ image $f(x, y)$, the procedure is to generate a smoothed image $g(x, y)$ whose gray level at every point (x, y) is obtained by averaging the gray-level values of the pixels of f contained in a predefined neighborhood of (x, y). In other words, the smoothed image is obtained by using the relation

$$g(x, y) = \frac{1}{M} \sum_{(n, m) \in S} f(n, m) \qquad (4.3\text{-}1)$$

for $x, y = 0, 1, \ldots, N - 1$. S is the set of coordinates of points in the neighborhood of the point (x, y), including (x, y) itself, and M is the total number of points in the neighborhood. If a 3×3 neighborhood is used, we note by comparing Eqs. (4.3-1) and (4.1-3) that the former equation is a special case of the latter with $w_i = 1/9$. Of course, we are not limited to square neighborhoods in Eq. (4.3-1), but these are by far the neighborhoods used most frequently due to ease of implementation.

Example: Figure 4.14 illustrates the smoothing effect produced by neighborhood averaging. Figure 4.14(a) is a simple four-level image corrupted by noise. Figures 4.14(b) through (f) are the results of processing the noisy image with neighborhoods of size $n \times n$, with $n = 3, 5, 9, 15$, and 31, respectively. It is noted that the degree of blurring is strongly proportional to the size of the neighborhood used. □

For a given neighborhood, the blurring effect produced by neighborhood averaging can be reduced by using a thresholding procedure; that is, instead of using Eq. (4.3-1), we form $g(x, y)$ according to the following criterion:

$$g(x, y) = \begin{cases} \dfrac{1}{M} \displaystyle\sum_{(m, n) \in S} f(m, n) & \text{if } \left| f(x, y) - \dfrac{1}{M} \displaystyle\sum_{(m, n) \in S} f(m, n) \right| < T \\[2ex] f(x, y) & \text{otherwise,} \end{cases} \qquad (4.3\text{-}2)$$

where T is a specified nonnegative threshold. The motivation behind this approach is to reduce blurring by leaving unchanged regions of an image with large (compared to T) variations in gray level. Generally, we expect these variations to correspond to edges, so using Eq. (4.3-2) will reduce the amount of edge blurring. Other regions of the image are processed as before.

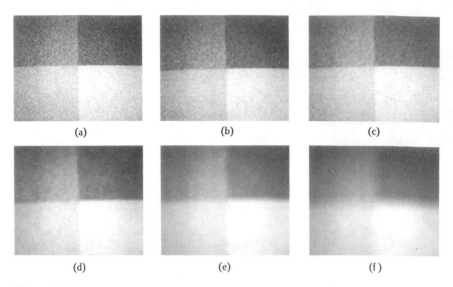

Figure 4.14 Example of neighborhood averaging. (a) Noisy image. (b) through (f), image processed using Eq. (4.3-1) with neighborhoods of size $n \times n$ with $n = 3, 5, 9, 15$, and 31, respectively.

Example: Figure 4.15 shows the result of processing the image of Fig. 4.14(a) with Eq. (4.3-2). A 9×9 neighborhood and $T = 10$ were used in this case. We note by comparing this result with Fig. 4.14(d) that, although equivalent smoothing was achieved by use of a threshold, the boundaries between the four squares are much sharper in Fig. 4.15. □

4.3.2 Median Filtering

One of the principal difficulties of the method discussed in the previous section is that it blurs edges and other sharp details. Although this problem can be somewhat circumvented by using a threshold, choosing the threshold value generally involves considerable trial and error. An alternative approach is to use *median filters,* in which we replace the gray level of each pixel by the median of the gray levels in a neighborhood of that pixel, instead of by the average. This method is particularly effective when the noise pattern consists of strong, spikelike components, and where the characteristic to be preserved is edge sharpness.

Recall that the median m of a set of values is such that half of the values in the set are less than m and half are greater than m. In order to perform median filtering in a neighborhood of a pixel we first sort the values of the pixel and its neighbors, determine the median, and assign this value to the pixel. For example, in a 3×3 neighborhood the median is the 5th largest value, in a 5×5 neighborhood the 13th largest value, and so on. When several values in a neighborhood are the

Figure 4.15 Smoothed image obtained by processing Fig. 4.14(a) with Eq. (4.3-2), using a 9 × 9 neighborhood and $T = 10$. Compare with Fig. 4.14(d).

same, we group all equal values as follows: Suppose that a 3 × 3 neighborhood has values (10, 20, 20, 20, 15, 20, 20, 25, 100). These values are sorted as (10, 15, 20, 20, 20, 20, 20, 25, 100), which results in a median of 20. A little thought will reveal that the principal function of median filtering is to force points with very distinct intensities to be more like their neighbors, thus actually eliminating intensity spikes that appear isolated in the area of the filter mask.

Example: Figure 4.16(a) shows an original image, and Fig. 4.16(b) shows the same image but with approximately 20% of the pixels corrupted by "impulse noise." The result of neighborhood averaging over a 5 × 5 area in shown in Fig. 4.16(c) and the result of a 5 × 5 median filter is shown in Fig. 4.16(d). The superiority of the median filter over neighborhood averaging needs no explanation. The bright dots remaining in Fig. 4.16(d) resulted from a large concentration of noise at those points, thus biasing the median calculation. Two or more passes with a median filter would eliminate these points.   ☐

4.3.3 Lowpass Filtering

Edges and other sharp transitions (such as noise) in the gray levels of an image contribute heavily to the high-frequency content of its Fourier transform. It therefore follows that blurring can be achieved via the frequency domain by attenuating a specified range of high frequency components in the transform of a given image.

From Eq. (4.1-5) we have the relation

$$G(u, v) = H(u, v)F(u, v), \tag{4.3-3}$$

where $F(u, v)$ is the transform of the image we wish to smooth. The problem is to select a function $H(u, v)$ that yields $G(u, v)$ by attenuating the high-frequency compo-

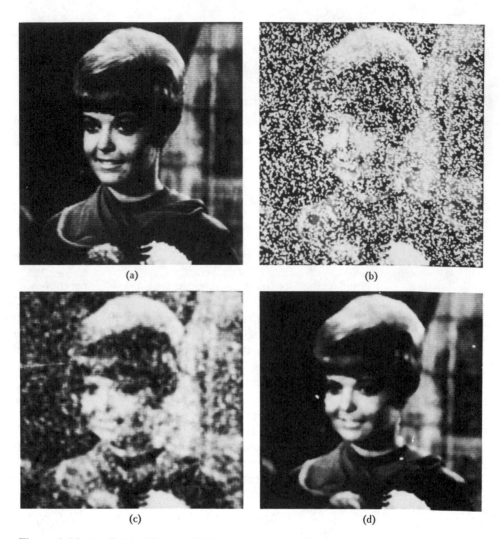

Figure 4.16   (a) Original image. (b) Image corrupted by impulse noise. (c) Result of 5 × 5 neighborhood averaging. (d) Result of 5 × 5 median filtering. (Courtesy of Martin Connor, Texas Instruments, Inc., Lewisville, Tex.)

nents of $F(u, v)$. The inverse transform of $G(u, v)$ will then yield the desired smoothed image $g(x, y)$. Since high-frequency components are "filtered out," and information in the low-frequency range is "passed" without attenuation, this method is commonly referred to as *lowpass filtering*. The function $H(u, v)$ is referred to in this context as a *filter transfer function*. Several low-pass-filtering approaches are discussed in the following paragraphs. In all cases, the filters are functions that affect corresponding real and imaginary components of the Fourier transform in exactly the same manner.

Such filters are referred to as *zero-phase-shift filters* because they do not alter the phase of the transform.

Ideal filter

A two-dimensional ideal lowpass filter (ILPF) is one whose transfer function satisfies the relation

$$H(u, v) = \begin{cases} 1 & \text{if } D(u, v) \leq D_0 \\ 0 & \text{if } D(u, v) > D_0, \end{cases} \tag{4.3-4}$$

where D_0 is a specified nonnegative quantity, and $D(u, v)$ is the distance from point (u, v) to the origin of the frequency plane; that is,

$$D(u, v) = (u^2 + v^2)^{1/2}. \tag{4.3-5}$$

A three-dimensional perspective plot of $H(u, v)$ versus u and v is shown in Fig. 4.17(a). The name *ideal* filter arises from the fact that all frequencies inside a circle of radius D_0 are passed with no attenuation, while all frequencies outside this circle are completely attenuated.

The lowpass filters considered in this chapter are radially symmetric about the origin. For this type of filter it suffices to specify a cross section extending as a function of distance from the origin along a radial line, as shown in Fig. 4.17(b). The complete filter transfer function can then be generated by rotating the cross section 360° about the origin. It should also be noted that specification of radially symmetric filters centered on the $N \times N$ frequency square is based on the assumption that the origin of the Fourier transform has been centered on the square, as discussed in Section 3.3.2.

For an ideal lowpass-filter cross section, the point of transition between $H(u, v) = 1$ and $H(u, v) = 0$ is often called the *cut-off frequency*. In the case of Fig. 4.17(b), for example, the cut-off frequency is D_0. As the cross section is, rotated about the origin, the point D_0 traces a circle and we obtain a locus of cut-off frequencies

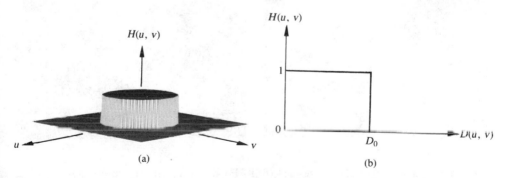

Figure 4.17   (a) Perspective plot of an ideal lowpass-filter transfer function. (b) Filter cross section.

all of which are a distance D_0 from the origin. As will be seen below, the cut-off–frequency concept is quite useful in specifying the characteristics of a given filter, and it also serves as a common base for comparing the behavior of different types of filters.

The sharp cut-off frequencies of an ideal lowpass filter cannot be realized with electronic components, although they can certainly be simulated in a computer. The effects of using these "nonphysical" filters on a digital image are discussed after the following example.

Example: The 256×256 image shown in Fig. 4.18(a) will be used to illustrate all the lowpass filters discussed in this section. The performance of these filters will be compared by using the same cut-off–frequency loci. One way to establish a set of standard loci is to compute circles that enclose various amounts of the total signal power P_T. This quantity is obtained by summing the power at each point (u, v) for $u, v = 0, 1, \ldots , N - 1$; that is,

$$P_T = \sum_{u=0}^{N-1} \sum_{v=0}^{N-1} P(u, v),$$

where $P(u, v)$ is given by Eq. (3.1-13). Assuming that the transform has been centered, a circle of radius r with origin at the center of the frequency square encloses β percent of the power, where

$$\beta = 100 \left[\sum_u \sum_v P(u, v)/P_T \right]$$

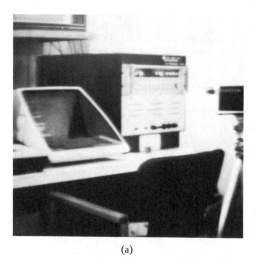
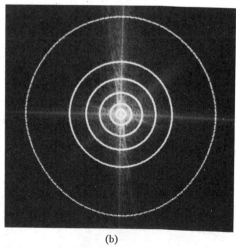

(a)	(b)

Figure 4.18   (a) A 256×256 image, and (b) its Fourier spectrum. The superimposed circles, which have radii equal to 5, 11, 22, 36, 53, and 98, enclose, respectively, 90, 95, 98, 99, 99.5, and 99.9 percent of the image power.

and the summation is taken over values of (u, v) which lie inside the circle or on its boundary.

Figure 4.18(b) shows the Fourier transform of Fig. 4.18(a). The superimposed circles, which have radii of 5, 11, 22, 36, 53, and 98, enclose β percent of the power for β = 90, 95, 98, 99, 99.5, and 99.9, respectively. It is noted that the power spectrum falls off rather rapidly, with 90% of the total power being enclosed by the relatively small radius of 5. Since we are dealing with a 256 $\times$ 256 image and the Fourier transform has been centered, a circle of radius $(\sqrt{2})(128)$ would enclose 100% of the power.

The results of applying ideal lowpass filters with cut-off frequencies at the above radii are shown in Fig. 4.19. Part (a) of this figure is, for all practical purposes, useless. The severe blurring in this image is a clear indication that most of the edge information in the picture is contained within the 10% power removed by the filter. As the filter radius was increased the degree of blurring was, of course, decreased. It is interesting to note, however, that all the filtered images are characterized by considerable "ringing." This phenomenon, which is explained below, is visible even in Fig. 4.19(f), where only 0.1% of the power was removed.   □

The blurring and ringing properties of the ILPF can be easily explained by resorting to the convolution theorem. Since the Fourier transforms of the original and blurred images are related in the frequency domain by the equation

$$G(u, v) = H(u, v)F(u, v),$$

it follows from this theorem that the following expression holds in the spatial domain:

$$g(x, y) = h(x, y)*f(x, y),$$

where $h(x, y)$ is the inverse Fourier transform of the filter transfer function $H(u, v)$.

The key to understanding blurring as a convolution process in the spatial domain lies in the nature of $h(x, y)$. For an ILPF, $h(x, y)$ has the general form shown in Fig. 4.20(a).[†] Suppose that $f(x, y)$ is a simple image composed of two bright pixels on a black background, as shown in Fig. 4.20(b). We may view the two bright points as approximations of two impulses whose strength depends on the brightness of these points. Then, the convolution of $h(x, y)$ and $f(x, y)$ is simply a process of "copying" $h(x, y)$ at the location of each impulse, as explained in Section 3.3.8. The result of this operation, which is shown in Fig. 4.20(c), explains how the two original points are blurred as a consequence of convolving $f(x, y)$ with the blurring function $h(x, y)$. These concepts are extended to more-complex images by considering each pixel as an impulse with a strength proportional to the gray level of the pixel.

[†] The reader can verify this by taking the inverse Fourier transform of Eq. (4.3-4).

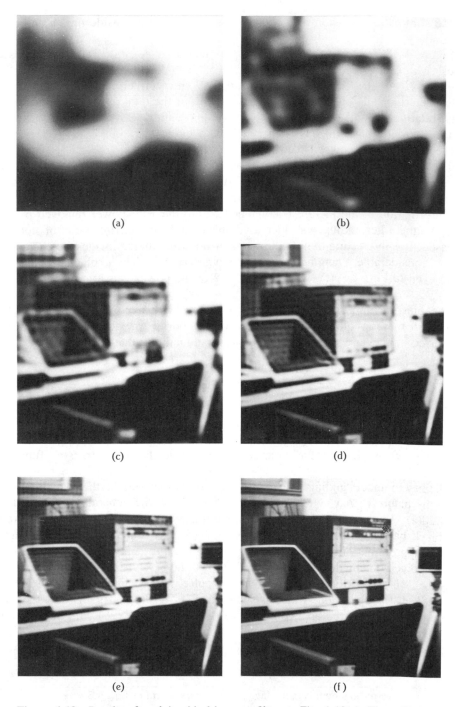

Figure 4.19 Results of applying ideal lowpass filters to Fig. 4.18(a). The radii shown in Fig. 4.18(b) were used.

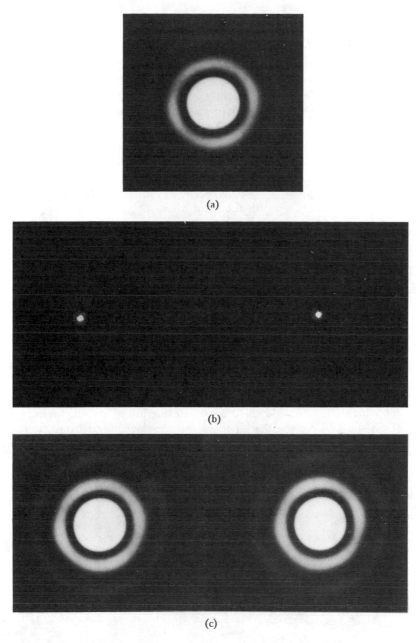

Figure 4.20 Illustration of the blurring process in the spatial domain. (a) Blurring function $h(x, y)$ for an ideal lowpass filter. (b) A simple image composed of two bright dots. (c) Convolution of $h(x, y)$ and $f(x, y)$.

The shape of $h(x, y)$ depends on the radius of the filter function in the frequency domain. By computing the inverse transform of $H(u, v)$ for an ILPF, it can be shown that the radii of the concentric rings in $h(x, y)$ are inversely proportional to the value of D_0 in Eq. (4.3-4). Thus severe filtering in the frequency domain (i.e., choice of a small D_0) produces a relatively small number of broad rings in the $N \times N$ region of $h(x, y)$ and, consequently, pronounced blurring in $g(x, y)$. As D_0 increases, the number of rings in a given region increases, thus producing more finely spaced rings and less blurring. This effect can be observed by comparing Figs. 4.19(d) and (e). If D_0 is outside the $N \times N$ domain of definition of $F(u, v)$, $h(x, y)$ becomes unity in its corresponding $N \times N$ spatial region and the convolution of $h(x, y)$ and $f(x, y)$ is simply $f(x, y)$. This situation, of course, corresponds to no filtering at all. The spatial domain effect of the filters discussed below can be explained in a similar manner as for the ideal filter.

Butterworth filter

The transfer function of the Butterworth lowpass filter (BLPF) of order n and with cut-off frequency locus at a distance D_0 from the origin is defined by the relation

$$H(u, v) = \frac{1}{1 + [D(u, v)/D_0]^{2n}}, \tag{4.3-6}$$

where $D(u, v)$ is given by Eq. (4.3-5). A perspective plot and cross section of the BLPF function are shown in Fig. 4.21.

Unlike the ILPF, the BLPF transfer function does not have a sharp discontinuity that establishes a clear cut-off between passed and filtered frequencies. For filters with smooth transfer functions it is customary to define a cut-off frequency locus at points for which $H(u, v)$ is down to a certain fraction of its maximum value. In the case of Eq. (4.3-6) we see that $H(u, v) = 0.5$ (down 50% from its maximum value of one) when $D(u, v) = D_0$. Another value commonly used is $1/\sqrt{2}$ of the

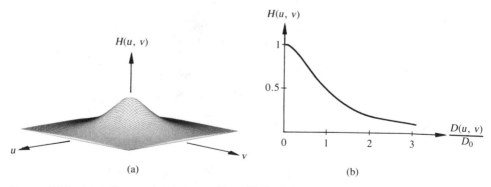

(a)   (b)

Figure 4.21   (a) A Butterworth lowpass filter. (b) Radial cross sections for $n = 1$.

maximum value of $H(u, v)$. For Eq. (4.3-6), the following simple modification yields the desired value when $D(u, v) = D_0$:

$$H(u, v) = \frac{1}{1 + [\sqrt{2} - 1][D(u, v)/D_0]^{2n}}$$

$$= \frac{1}{1 + 0.414[D(u, v)/D_0]^{2n}}.$$

(4.3-7)

Example: Figure 4.22 shows the results of applying BLPFs (Eq. 4.3-7) to Fig. 4.18(a), with $n = 1$ and D_0 equal to the first five radii shown in Fig. 4.18(b). Note that these images are considerably less blurred than the corresponding results obtained with ideal lowpass filters. The reason is that the "tail" in the BLPF passes a fairly high amount of high-frequency information, thus preserving more of the edge content in the picture. It is also of interest to note that no ringing is evident in any of the images processed with the BLPF, a fact attributed to the filter's smooth transition between low and high frequencies.   □

As indicated in Section 4.1, all the filtering results presented in this section were obtained by directly computing the FFT without extending the images to avoid wraparound error. As shown in Fig. 4.22(e), the error is certainly not objectionable since this image is essentially of the same quality as the original, in spite of the fact that convolution with a broad filter was carried out. The reason for this is that the spectrum of $f(x, y)$ falls off rapidly, with 90% of the signal power being contained inside a circle of radius 5. Therefore the amplitude of $F(u, v)$ is relatively small over a large portion of the frequency plane, and these small values attenuate the wraparound error caused by overlaps in the convolution periods. This behavior is typical in practice and often allows us to ignore the error incurred in discrete convolution when the periodic constraints imposed by Eqs. (3.3-33) and (3.3-34) are not satisfied.

Example: The lowpass filtering results given thus far have been with images of good quality in order to illustrate and compare the effect of the filters discussed in this section. Figure 4.23 shows two practical applications of lowpass filtering for image smoothing. The image shown in Fig. 4.23(a) was digitized with only 16 gray levels and, as a consequence, exhibits a considerable amount of false contouring. Figure 4.23(b) is the result of smoothing this image with a lowpass Butterworth filter of order 1. Similarly, Fig. 4.23(d) shows the effect of applying a BLPF to the noisy image of Fig. 4.23(c). It is noted from these examples that lowpass filtering is a cosmetic process that reduces spurious effects at the expense of image sharpness.   □

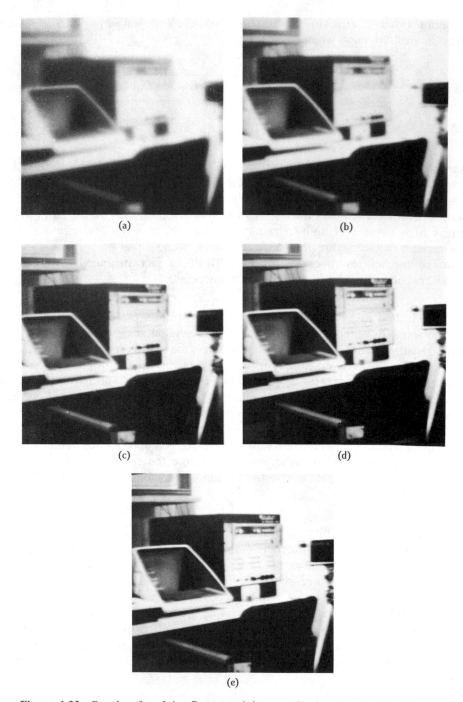

(a)

(b)

(c)

(d)

(e)

Figure 4.22   Results of applying Butterworth lowpass filters to Fig. 4.18(a). The first five radii shown in Fig. 4.18(b) were used.

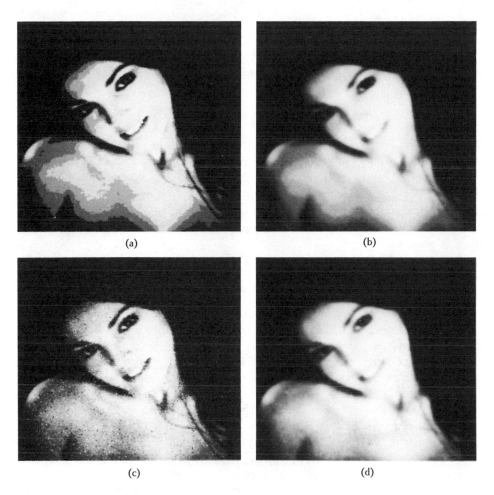

Figure 4.23   Two examples of image smoothing by lowpass filtering (see text).

4.3.4   Averaging of Multiple Images

Consider a noisy image $g(x, y)$ that is formed by the addition of noise $\eta(x, y)$ to an original image $f(x, y)$; that is,

$$g(x, y) = f(x, y) + \eta(x, y), \qquad (4.3\text{-}8)$$

where it is assumed that at every pair of coordinates (x, y) the noise is uncorrelated and has zero average value. The objective of the following procedure is to obtain a smoothed result by adding a given set of noisy images $\{g_i(x, y)\}$.

   If the noise satisfies the constraints just stated, it is a simple problem to show (e.g., see Papoulis [1965]) that if an image $\bar{g}(x, y)$ is formed by averaging M

different noisy images,

$$\bar{g}(x, y) = \frac{1}{M} \sum_{i=1}^{M} g_i(x, y)$$ (4.3-9)

then it follows that

$$E\{\bar{g}(x, y)\} = f(x, y)$$ (4.3-10)

and

$$\sigma^2_{\bar{g}(x, y)} = \frac{1}{M} \sigma^2_{\eta(x, y)},$$ (4.3-11)

where $E\{\bar{g}(x, y)\}$ is the expected value of $\bar{g}$, $\sigma^2_{\bar{g}(x, y)}$ and $\sigma^2_{\eta(x, y)}$ are the variances of $\bar{g}$ and η, all at coordinates (x, y). The standard deviation at any point in the average image is given by

$$\sigma_{\bar{g}(x, y)} = \frac{1}{\sqrt{M}} \sigma_{\eta(x, y)}.$$ (4.3-12)

Equations (4.3-11) and (4.3-12) indicate that as M increases, the variability of the pixel values decreases. Since $E\{\bar{g}(x, y)\} = f(x, y)$, this means that $\bar{g}(x, y)$ will approach $f(x, y)$ as the number of noisy images used in the averaging process increases. In practice, the principal difficulty in using this method lies in being able to register the images so that corresponding pixels line up correctly.

Example: As an illustration of the averaging method, consider the images shown in Fig. 4.24. Part (a) of this figure shows an original image, and part (b) is the same image, with each pixel corrupted by additive Gaussian noise with zero mean and standard deviation equal to 20. Since negative pixel values were not allowed, any $\bar{g}(x, y)$ that was negative as a result of adding noise to $f(x, y)$ was replaced by $|\bar{g}(x, y)|$. In this sense, the noise can only be considered approximately Gaussian. Registration was not a problem in this case because all noisy images were generated from the same source.

Figures 4.24(c) through (h) show the results of using $M = 2, 5, 10, 25, 50,$ and 100, respectively, in the averaging process given in Eq. (4.3-9). There is little discernible difference between the original noisy image and the sum of two samples. When $M = 5$, however, the reduction in noise is quite apparent. The same is true of the case where $M = 10$, although some noisy regions are still clearly visible. (Compare, for example, the edges of the robe sleeve and leg nearest the right side of Figs. 4.24a and e.) Averaging 25 copies (Fig. 4.24f) yielded an image that is almost of the same quality and definition as the original. A little noise is still visible in regions such as the sleeve and leg mentioned above, but it is difficult to tell the two images apart by casual observation. The results for $M = 50$ and $M = 100$ are, for all practical purposes, of the same quality as the original image. □

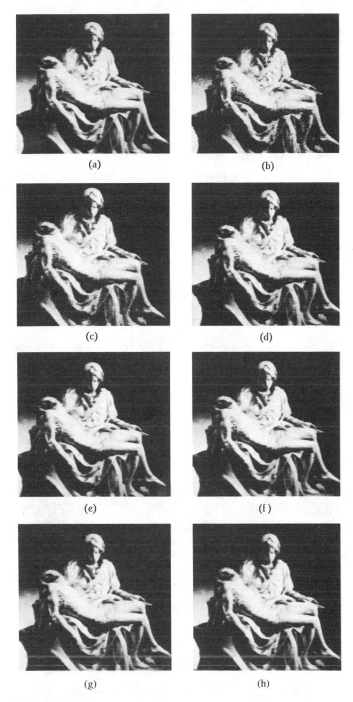

Figure 4.24 Smoothing by superposition of multiple images. (a) Original image. (b) Noisy image. (c) through (h) Results obtained by averaging 2, 5, 10, 25, 50, and 100 copies, respectively.

175

4.4   IMAGE SHARPENING

Sharpening techniques are useful primarily as enhancement tools for highlighting edges in an image. Following the same format as in Section 4.3, we present below sharpening methods in both the spatial and frequency domains.

4.4.1   Sharpening by Differentiation

It was noted in Section 4.3 that averaging pixels over a region tends to blur detail in an image. Since averaging is analogous to integration, it is natural to expect that differentiation will have the opposite effect and thus sharpen a given image.

The most commonly used method of differentiation in image processing applications is the *gradient*. Given a function $f(x, y)$, the gradient of f at coordinates (x, y) is defined as the *vector*

$$\mathbf{G}[f(x, y)] = \begin{bmatrix} \dfrac{\partial f}{\partial x} \\[2mm] \dfrac{\partial f}{\partial y} \end{bmatrix}. \tag{4.4-1}$$

Two important properties of the gradient are: (1) the vector $\mathbf{G}[f(x, y)]$ points in the direction of the maximum rate of increase of the function $f(x, y)$; and (2) the magnitude of $\mathbf{G}[f(x, y)]$, denoted by $G[f(x, y)]$, and given by

$$G[f(x, y)] = \text{mag}[\mathbf{G}] = [(\partial f/\partial x)^2 + (\partial f/\partial y)^2]^{1/2} \tag{4.4-2}$$

equals the maximum rate of increase of $f(x, y)$ per unit distance in the direction of $\mathbf{G}$.

Equation (4.4-2) is the basis for a number of approaches to image differentiation. It is noted that this expression is in the form of a two-dimensional derivative function and that it is always positive. In practice, the scalar function $G[f(x, y)]$ is commonly referred to as the gradient of f. This terminology will be used throughout the following discussion to avoid having to continually refer to $G[f(x, y)]$ as "the magnitude of the gradient." The reader should, however, keep in mind the basic difference between Eqs. (4.4-1) and (4.4-2).

For a digital image, the derivatives in Eq. (4.4-2) are approximated by differences. One typical approximation is given by the relation

$$\begin{aligned} G[f(x, y)] \cong \{&[f(x, y) - f(x + 1, y)]^2 \\ &+ [f(x, y) - f(x, y + 1)]^2\}^{1/2}. \end{aligned} \tag{4.4-3}$$

Similar results are obtained by using absolute values, as follows:

$$\begin{aligned} G[f(x, y)] \cong &|f(x, y) - f(x + 1, y)| \\ &+ |f(x, y) - f(x, y + 1)|. \end{aligned} \tag{4.4-4}$$

This formulation is more desirable for a computer implementation of the gradient. It is also easier to program in assembly language if speed of computation is an essential requirement.

The relationship between pixels in Eqs. (4.4-3) and (4.4-4) is shown in Fig. 4.25(a). For an $N \times N$ image, note that it is not possible to take the gradient for pixels in the last row ($x = N$) or the last column ($y = N$). If an $N \times N$ gradient image is desired, one procedure that can be followed for pixels in these regions is to duplicate the gradients obtained in the previous row when $x = N$ and the previous column when $y = N$.

The above arrangement for approximating the gradient is by no means unique. Another useful approximation, sometimes called the *Roberts gradient*, uses the cross-differences shown in Fig. 4.25(b). This approximation is given by the relation

$$G[f(x, y)] = \{[f(x, y) - f(x + 1, y + 1)]^2$$
$$+ [f(x + 1, y) - f(x, y + 1)]^2\}^{1/2} \qquad (4.4\text{-}5)$$

or, using absolute values,

$$G[f(x, y)] \cong |f(x, y) - f(x + 1, y + 1)|$$
$$+ |f(x + 1, y) - f(x, y + 1)|. \qquad (4.4\text{-}6)$$

Note that in all the approximations given above the value of the gradient is proportional to the difference in gray level between adjacent pixels. Thus, as expected, the gradient assumes relatively large values for prominent edges in an image, and small values in regions that are fairly smooth, being zero only in regions that have a constant gray level. These properties of the gradient are illustrated in Fig. 4.26. The digital image shown in Fig. 4.26(a) is composed of two levels. As shown in Fig. 4.26(b), the gradient operation (Eq. 4.4-4 was used) reduces all the constant white regions to zero (black), leaving only the points associated with abrupt changes in gray level (in this case the edge boundaries and the small spot on the upper-right part of the letter T).

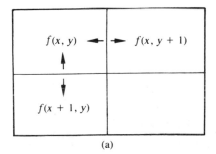

(a)

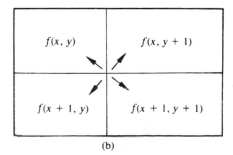

(b)

Figure 4.25 Two procedures for computing a two-dimensional, discrete gradient.

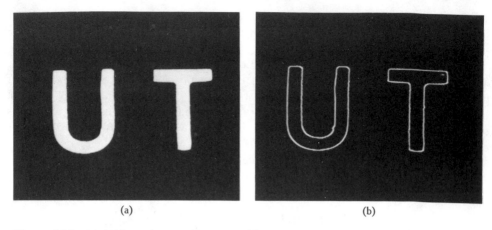

(a)   (b)

Figure 4.26   (a) A binary image. (b) Result of computing the gradient.

Once a method for approximating the gradient has been selected, there are numerous ways of using the results for generating a gradient image $g(x, y)$. The simplest approach is to let the value of g at coordinates (x, y) be equal to the gradient of f at that point, that is,

$$g(x, y) = G[f(x, y)]. \qquad (4.4\text{-}7)$$

The principal disadvantage of this method is that all smooth regions in $f(x, y)$ appear dark in $g(x, y)$ because of the relatively small values of the gradient in these regions. One solution to this problem is to form $g(x, y)$ as follows:

$$g(x, y) = \begin{cases} G[f(x, y] & \text{if } G[f(x, y)] \geq T \\ f(x, y) & \text{otherwise}, \end{cases} \qquad (4.4\text{-}8)$$

where T is a nonnegative threshold. By properly selecting T, it is possible to emphasize significant edges without destroying the characteristics of smooth backgrounds. A variation of this approach where edges are set to a specified gray level L_G is given by

$$g(x, y) = \begin{cases} L_G & \text{if } G[f(x, y)] \geq T \\ f(x, y) & \text{otherwise}. \end{cases} \qquad (4.4\text{-}9)$$

It is sometimes desirable to study the gray-level variation of edges without interference from the background. This can be accomplished by forming the gradient image as follows:

$$g(x, y) = \begin{cases} G[f(x, y)] & \text{if } G[f(x, y)] \geq T \\ L_B & \text{otherwise}, \end{cases} \qquad (4.4\text{-}10)$$

where L_B is a specified level for the background.

Finally, if only the location of edges is of interest, the relation

$$g(x, y) = \begin{cases} L_G & \text{if } G[f(x, y)] \geq T \\ L_B & \text{otherwise} \end{cases} \qquad (4.4\text{-}11)$$

gives a binary gradient picture where the edges and background are displayed in any two specified gray levels.

Example: The types of edge enhancement that can be obtained by using Eq. (4.4-4) and Eqs. (4.4-7) through (4.4-11) are illustrated in Fig. 4.27. Part (a) of the figure shows an original image of moderate complexity. Figure 4.27(b) is the result of using the gradient scheme given by Eq. (4.4-7). Note that a considerable amount of small segments appeared in the resulting image, with the strongest intensities taking place around the border of the aircraft. This is an expected result since the magnitude of the gradient is proportional to changes in gray levels and should be more prominent in regions of an image containing distinct edges.

Figure 4.27(c) was obtained by using Eq. (4.4-8) with $T = 25$, which is approximately 10% of the maximum gray-level value in the original image. The gradient values appear a dark shade of gray because they are displayed on the relatively light background of the image. The important points to note in connection with this figure is that only prominent edges are outlined as a result of using a threshold, and also that the background has not been completely obliterated.

Figure 4.27(d) is the result of using Eq. (4.4-9) with $T = 25$ and $L_G = 255$, the latter being the brightest possible level in the system used to display the results. It is noted that Figs. 4.27(c) and (d) are the same, with the exception that the gradient points exceeding the threshold are much more visible in the latter image.

Figure 4.27(e) was obtained by using Eq. (4.4-10) with the same threshold as above and a background level of $L_B = 0$, which is the darkest possible display level. The principal use of this particular approach is to examine the relative strength of gradient points that exceed the specified threshold. In this case, we see that the outline of the aircraft and the cloud near the bottom of the image are quite prominent in relation to other sections of the picture.

Finally, Fig. 4.27(f) was obtained by using Eq. (4.4-11) with $T = 25$, $L_G = 255$, and $L_B = 0$. This equation is useful for displaying only the gradient points above the specified threshold.

4.4.2 Highpass Filtering

It was shown in Section 4.3.3 that an image can be blurred by attenuating the high-frequency components of its Fourier transform. Since edges and other abrupt changes in gray levels are associated with high-frequency components, image sharpening can be achieved in the frequency domain by a *highpass filtering* process, which attenuates the low-frequency components without disturbing high-frequency information in the Fourier transform.

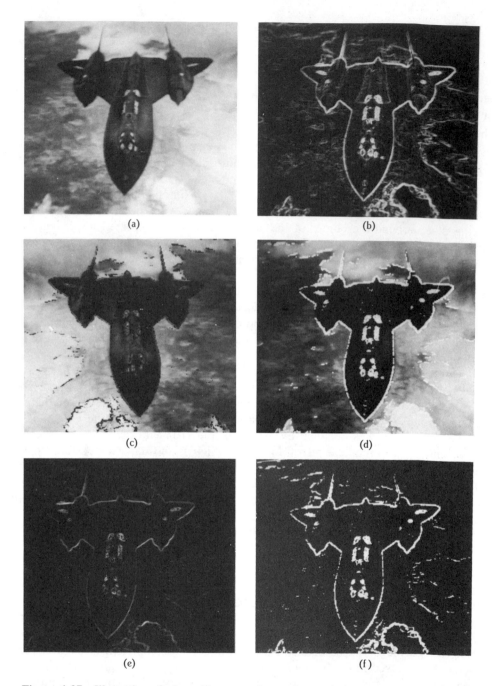

Figure 4.27   Illustration of edge enhancement by gradient techniques.

We consider below the high-frequency counterparts of the filters developed in Section 4.3.3. As before, we will only consider zero-phase-shift filters that are radially symmetric and can be completely specified by a cross section extending as a function of distance from the origin of the Fourier transform.

Ideal filter
A two-dimensional ideal highpass filter (IHPF) is one whose transfer function satisfies the relation

$$H(u, v) = \begin{cases} 0 & \text{if } D(u, v) \leq D_0 \\ 1 & \text{if } D(u, v) > D_0, \end{cases} \qquad (4.4\text{-}12)$$

where D_0 is the cut-off distance measured from the origin of the frequency plane, and $D(u, v)$ is given by Eq. (4.3-5). A perspective plot and cross section of the IHPF function are shown in Fig. 4.28. It is noted that this filter is just the opposite of the ideal lowpass filter discussed in Section 4.4.3 since it completely attenuates all frequencies inside a circle of radius D_0 while passing, without attenuation, all frequencies outside the circle. As in the case of the ideal lowpass filter, the IHPF is not physically realizable.

Butterworth filter
The transfer function of the Butterworth highpass filter (BHPF) of order n and with cut-off frequency locus at a distance D_0 from the origin is defined by the relation

$$H(u, v) = \frac{1}{1 + [D_0 /D(u, v)]^{2n}}, \qquad (4.4\text{-}13)$$

where $D(u, v)$ is given by Eq. (4.3-5). A perspective plot and cross section of the BHPF function are shown in Fig. 4.29.

Note that when $D(u, v) = D_0$, $H(u, v)$ is down to ½ of its maximum value. As in the case of the Butterworth lowpass filter, it is common practice to select

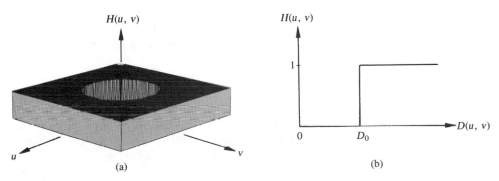

Figure 4.28 Perspective plot and radial cross section of ideal highpass filter.

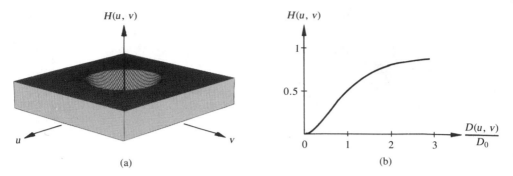

Figure 4.29   Perspective plot and radial cross section of Butterworth highpass filter for $n = 1$.

the cut-off frequency locus at points for which $H(u, v)$ is down to $1/\sqrt{2}$ of its maximum value. Equation (4.4-13) is easily modified to satisfy this constraint by using the following scaling:

$$H(u, v) = \frac{1}{1 + [\sqrt{2} - 1][D_0/D(u, v)]^{2n}}$$

$$= \frac{1}{1 + 0.414[D_0/D(u, v)]^{2n}}. \tag{4.4-14}$$

Example: Figure 4.30(a) shows a chest x-ray that was poorly developed, and Fig. 4.30(b) shows the image after it was processed with a highpass Butterworth filter of order 1. Only the edges are predominant in this image because the low-frequency components were severely attenuated, thus making different (but smooth) gray-level regions appear essentially the same.

A technique often used to alleviate this problem consists of adding a constant to a highpass filter transfer function in order to preserve the low-frequency components. This, of course, amplifies the high-frequency components to values that are higher than in the original transform. This technique, called *high-frequency emphasis*, is illustrated in Fig. 4.30(c). Note that the image in this case has a little better tonality, particularly in the lower-left part of the photograph.

Although high-frequency emphasis preserves the low-frequency components, the proportionally larger high-frequency terms tend to obscure the result, as shown by the small gain in quality from Fig. 4.30(b) to Fig. 4.30(c). A technique often used to compensate for this problem is to do some post-filtering processing to redistribute the gray levels. Histogram equalization is ideally suited for this because of its simplicity. Figure 4.30(d) shows the significant improvement that can be obtained by histogram-equalizing an image that has been processed by high-frequency emphasis. ☐

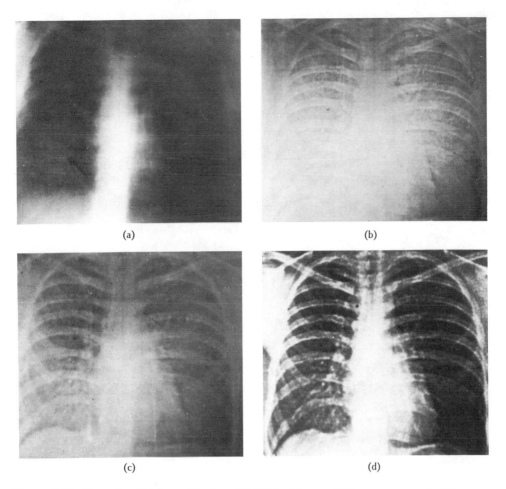

(a)

(b)

(c)

(d)

Figure 4.30 Example of highpass filtering. (a) Original image. (b) Image processed with a highpass Butterworth filter. (c) Result of high-frequency emphasis. (d) High-frequency emphasis and histogram equalization. (From Hall *et al.* [1971].)

4.5 ENHANCEMENT BASED ON AN IMAGE MODEL

The illumination–reflectance model introduced in Section 2.2 can be used as the basis for a frequency domain procedure that is useful for improving the appearance of an image by simultaneous brightness range compression and contrast enhancement. From the discussion in Section 2.2 we have that an image $f(x, y)$ can be expressed in terms of its illumination and reflectance components by means of the relation

$$f(x, y) = i(x, y)r(x, y). \tag{4.5-1}$$

Equation (4.5-1) cannot be used directly in order to operate separately on the frequency components of illumination and reflectance because the Fourier transform of the product of two functions is not separable; in other words,

$$\mathfrak{F}\{f(x, y)\} \neq \mathfrak{F}\{i(x, y)\}\mathfrak{F}\{r(x, y)\}$$

Suppose, however, that we let

$$\begin{aligned} z(x, y) &= \ln f(x, y) \\ &= \ln i(x, y) + \ln r(x, y). \end{aligned} \tag{4.5-2}$$

Then, it follows that

$$\begin{aligned} \mathfrak{F}\{z(x, y)\} &= \mathfrak{F}\{\ln f(x, y)\} \\ &= \mathfrak{F}\{\ln i(x, y)\} + \mathfrak{F}\{\ln r(x, y)\} \end{aligned} \tag{4.5-3}$$

or

$$Z(u, v) = I(u, v) + R(u, v), \tag{4.5-4}$$

where $I(u, v)$ and $R(u, v)$ are the Fourier transforms of $\ln i(x, y)$ and $\ln r(x, y)$, respectively.

If we process $Z(u, v)$ by means of a filter function $H(u, v)$, it follows from Eq. (4.1-2) that

$$\begin{aligned} S(u, v) &= H(u, v)Z(u, v) \\ &= H(u, v)I(u, v) + H(u, v)R(u, v), \end{aligned} \tag{4.5-5}$$

where $S(u, v)$ is the Fourier transform of the result. In the spatial domain, we have the relation

$$\begin{aligned} s(x, y) &= \mathfrak{F}^{-1}\{S(u, v)\} \\ &= \mathfrak{F}^{-1}\{H(u, v)I(u, v)\} + \mathfrak{F}^{-1}\{H(u, v)R(u, v)\}. \end{aligned} \tag{4.5-6}$$

By letting

$$i'(x, y) = \mathfrak{F}^{-1}\{H(u, v)I(u, v)\} \tag{4.5-7}$$

and

$$r'(x, y) = \mathfrak{F}^{-1}\{H(u, v)R(u, v)\}, \tag{4.5-8}$$

we can express Eq. (4.5-6) in the form

$$s(x, y) = i'(x, y) + r'(x, y). \tag{4.5-9}$$

Finally, since $z(x, y)$ was formed by taking the logarithm of the original image

$f(x, y)$, we now perform the inverse operation to obtain the desired enhanced image $g(x, y)$; that is,

$$
\begin{aligned}
g(x, y) &= \exp\{s(x, y)\} \\
&= \exp\{i'(x, y)\} \cdot \exp\{r'(x, y)\} \\
&= i_0(x, y)r_0(x, y),
\end{aligned} \tag{4.5-10}
$$

where

$$
i_0(x, y) = \exp\{i'(x, y)\} \tag{4.5-11}
$$

and

$$
r_0(x, y) = \exp\{r'(x, y)\} \tag{4.5-12}
$$

are the illumination and reflectance components of the output image.

The enhancement approach using the foregoing concepts is summarized in Fig. 4.31. This method is based on a special case of a class of systems known as *homomorphic systems*. In this particular application, the key to the approach is the fact that separation of the illumination and reflectance components is achieved in the form shown in Eq. (4.5-4). It is then possible for the *homomorphic filter function H(u, v)* to operate on these components separately, as indicated in Eq. (4.5-5).

The illumination component of an image is generally characterized by slow spatial variations. The reflectance component, on the other hand, tends to vary abruptly, particularly at the junctions of very dissimilar objects. These characteristics lead us to associate the low frequencies of the Fourier transform of the logarithm of an image with illumination, and the high frequencies with reflectance. Although this is a rough approximation, it can be used to advantage in image enhancement.

Illumination is directly responsible for the dynamic range achieved by the pixels in an image. Similarly, contrast is a function of the reflective nature of the objects in the image. A good deal of control can be gained over these components by using a homomorphic filter. This requires specification of a filter function $H(u, v)$ that will affect the low- and high-frequency components of the Fourier transform in different ways. A cross section of such a function is shown in Fig. 4.32. A complete specification of $H(u, v)$ is obtained by rotating the cross section $360°$ about the vertical axis. If the parameters γ_L and γ_H are chosen so that $\gamma_L < 1$ and $\gamma_H > 1$, the filter function shown in Fig. 4.32 will tend to decrease the low frequencies and amplify the high frequencies. The net result is simultaneous dynamic range compression and contrast enhancement.

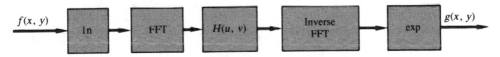

Figure 4.31   Homomorphic filtering approach for image enhancement.

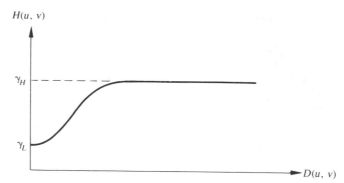

Figure 4.32   Cross section of a circularly symmetric filter function for use in homomorphic filtering. $D(u, v)$ is the distance from the origin.

Example: Figure 4.33 is typical of the results that can be obtained with the homomorphic filter function shown in Fig. 4.32. We note in the original image, Fig. 4.33(a), that the details inside the room are obscured by the glare from the outside walls. Figure 4.33(b) shows the result of processing this image by homomorphic filtering with $\gamma_L = 0.5$ and $\gamma_H = 2.0$ in the above filter function. A reduction of dynamic range in the brightness, together with an increase in contrast, brought out the details of objects inside the room and balanced the levels of the outside wall.   □

4.6   GENERATION OF SPATIAL MASKS FROM FREQUENCY-DOMAIN SPECIFICATIONS

As indicated in Section 4.1, speed and simplicity of implementation are important features of spatial masks for image processing. On the other hand, certain filtering functions (such as lowpass filtering) are more conveniently specified in the frequency domain. In this section we develop a method for generating spatial masks that approximate (in a least-square-error sense) a given frequency-domain filter.

As discussed in Section 4.1, the filtering process in the frequency domain is based on the equation

$$G(u, v) = H(u, v)F(u, v), \tag{4.6-1}$$

where $F(u, v)$ and $G(u, v)$ are the Fourier transforms of the input and output images, respectively, and $H(u, v)$ is the filter transfer function. From the convolution theorem (Section 3.3.8), we know that Eq. (4.6-1) can be implemented in the spatial domain by the expression

$$g(x, y) = \sum_{i=0}^{N-1} \sum_{k=0}^{N-1} h(x - i, y - k)f(i, k) \tag{4.6-2}$$

with $x = 0, 1, 2, \ldots, N - 1$ and $y = 0, 1, 2, \ldots, N - 1$. For simplicity in notation, it is assumed that we are working with square image arrays. Also, it is

(a)   (b)

Figure 4.33 (a) Original image. (b) Image processed by homomorphic filtering to achieve simultaneous dynamic range compression and contrast enhancement. (From Stockham [1972].)

understood that all functions have been properly extended, as discussed in Section 3.3.8, under Convolution.

In Eq. (4.6-2), h is the spatial representation of the filter (i.e., the inverse Fourier transform of $H(u, v)$), f is the input image, and g is the filtered image. We often refer to h as a *spatial convolution mask*. If this mask is of size $N \times N$, the result given in Eq. (4.6-2) is identical to taking the inverse Fourier transform of $G(u, v)$ in Eq. (4.6-1).

Since H is the Fourier transform of h, it follows from Eq. (3.2-9) that

$$H(u, v) = \frac{1}{N} \sum_{x=0}^{N-1} \sum_{y=0}^{N-1} h(x, y) \exp[-j2\pi(ux + vy)/N] \qquad (4.6\text{-}3)$$

for $u, v = 0, 1, 2, \ldots, N - 1$. Suppose, however, that we restrict $h(x, y)$ to be zero for values of $x > n$ and $y > n$, with $n < N$. This in effect creates an $n \times n$ convolution mask $\hat{h}$ with Fourier transform

$$\hat{H}(u, v) = \frac{1}{N} \sum_{x=0}^{n-1} \sum_{y=0}^{n-1} \hat{h}(x, y) \exp[-j2\pi(ux + vy)/N] \qquad (4.6\text{-}4)$$

for $u, v = 0, 1, 2, \ldots, N - 1$. The objective in the following discussion is to find the coefficients of $\hat{h}(x, y)$ so that the error quantity

$$e^2 = \sum_{u=0}^{N-1} \sum_{v=0}^{N-1} |\hat{H}(u, v) - H(u, v)|^2 \qquad (4.6\text{-}5)$$

is minimized, where $|\cdot|$ designates the complex magnitude.

Equation (4.6-4) can be expressed in the following matrix form:

$$\hat{\mathbf{H}} = \mathbf{C}\hat{\mathbf{h}}, \tag{4.6-6}$$

where $\hat{\mathbf{H}}$ is a column vector of order N^2 containing the terms for $\hat{H}(u, v)$ in some order, $\hat{\mathbf{h}}$ is a column vector of order n^2 containing the elements of $\hat{h}(x, y)$ in some order, and $\mathbf{C}$ is an $N^2 \times n^2$ matrix of exponential terms whose positions are determined by the ordering in $\hat{\mathbf{H}}$ and $\hat{\mathbf{h}}$. A simple procedure for generating the elements $\hat{\mathbf{H}}(i)$, $i = 0, 1, 2, \ldots, N^2 - 1$, of the vector $\hat{\mathbf{H}}$ from $\hat{H}(u, v)$ is as follows:

$$\hat{H}(u, v) \Rightarrow \hat{\mathbf{H}}(i) \tag{4.6-7}$$

for $i = uN + v$, with $u, v = 0, 1, 2, \ldots, N - 1$. It is noted that stepping through the rows of $\hat{H}(u, v)$ by letting $u = 0, v = 0, 1, 2, \ldots, N - 1; u = 1, v = 0, 1, 2, \ldots, N - 1$; and so on, corresponds to forming the first N elements of $\hat{\mathbf{H}}$ from the first row of $\hat{H}(u, v)$, the next N elements from the second row, and so forth. The elements of $\hat{\mathbf{h}}$, denoted by $\hat{h}(k)$, $k = 0, 1, 2, \ldots, n^2 - 1$, are similarly formed by letting

$$\hat{h}(x, y) \Rightarrow \hat{h}(k) \tag{4.6-8}$$

for $k = xn + y$, with $x, y = 0, 1, 2, \ldots, n - 1$. Finally, the corresponding elements of the matrix $\mathbf{C}$, denoted by $C(i, k)$, are generated from the exponential terms

$$\frac{1}{N} \exp[-j2\pi(ux + vy)/N] \Rightarrow C(i, k) \tag{4.6-9}$$

for $i = uN + v$ and $k = xn + y$, with $u, v = 0, 1, 2, \ldots, N - 1$, and $x, y = 0, 1, 2, \ldots, N - 1$.

Using matrix notation, Eq. (4.6-5) can be written in the form

$$\begin{aligned} e^2 &= (\hat{\mathbf{H}} - \mathbf{H})^*(\hat{\mathbf{H}} - \mathbf{H}) \\ &= \|\hat{\mathbf{H}} - \mathbf{H}\|^2 \\ &= \|\mathbf{C}\hat{\mathbf{h}} - \mathbf{H}\|^2, \end{aligned} \tag{4.6-10}$$

where $*$ is the conjugate transpose, $\| \cdot \|$ is the complex Euclidean norm, and $\mathbf{H}$ is a vector formed from $H(u, v)$ in the manner explained above. We find the minimum of e^2 with respect to $\hat{\mathbf{h}}$ by taking the partial derivative and equating it to the zero vector:

$$\frac{\partial e^2}{\partial \hat{\mathbf{h}}} = 2\mathbf{C}^*(\mathbf{C}\hat{\mathbf{h}} - \mathbf{H}) = \mathbf{0} \tag{4.6-11}$$

or

$$\begin{aligned} \hat{\mathbf{h}} &= (\mathbf{C}^*\mathbf{C})^{-1}\mathbf{C}^*\mathbf{H} \\ &= \mathbf{C}^{\#}\mathbf{H} \end{aligned} \tag{4.6-12}$$

where the matrix $\mathbf{C}^{\#} = (\mathbf{C}^*\mathbf{C})^{-1}\mathbf{C}^*$ is often called the *Moore–Penrose generalized inverse* (Noble [1969]).

Equation (4.6-12) yields the necessary minimum-error coefficients to construct an $n \times n$ convolution mask $\hat{h}(x, y)$ from a specified $N \times N$ filter function $H(u, v)$ in the frequency domain. In general, the elements of $\hat{h}(x, y)$ are complex quantities. However, it is easily shown that if the frequency-domain filter function is real and symmetric (like all the filters discussed in this chapter), then $\hat{h}(x, y)$ will also be real and symmetric.

Example: As an illustration of the method just developed, the test pattern shown in Fig. 4.34(a) was filtered using a Butterworth lowpass filter to produce the blurred image shown in Fig. 4.34(b). A 9×9 convolution mask was generated using Eq.

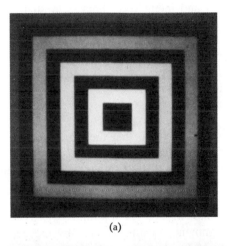

(a)

(b)

(c)

Figure 4.34   (a) Original image. (b) Blurred image obtained with a Butterworth lowpass filter of order 1 in the frequency domain. (c) Image blurred spatially by a 9×9 convolution mask obtained using Eq. (4.6-12). (From Meyer and Gonzalez [1983].)

(4.6-12) and applied to the original image. The result, shown in Fig. 4.34(c), is slightly less blurred than that obtained by using the complete filter in the frequency domain. This is expected since the spatial-domain process with $n < N$ is only an approximation in the least-square-error sense.   □

4.7   PSEUDO-COLOR IMAGE PROCESSING

Attention has been focused thus far on processing techniques for monochrome images. A relatively recent and potentially powerful area of digital image processing is the use of pseudo-color for image display and enhancement. The motivation for using color in image processing is provided by the fact that the human eye can discern thousands of color shades and intensities. This is in sharp contrast with the eye's relatively poor performance with gray levels where, as indicated in Section 2.1, only one to two dozen shades of gray are detectable at any one point in an image by the average observer. The reader needs only to turn off the color next time he views a TV set in order to verify the superior performance of the eye when interpreting color versus monochrome information.

The basic idea behind the use of pseudo-color should be carefully distinguished from techniques known as false-color processing. The latter are analogous to true-color photography, with the exception that they may deal with light bands that are outside the visible spectrum. Infrared photography is an example of this, where interest lies not in true color fidelity, but rather on information that is most evident in the infrared spectrum. In pseudo-color, the situation is fundamentally different in that processing starts out with a monochrome image. The objective is then to assign a color to each pixel based, for example, on its intensity. The range of techniques for color assignment are limited only by the capabilities of the display system and the ingenuity of the user. As will be seen in the following discussion, even some straightforward techniques for color coding can sometimes bring out information that is often difficult to detect and interpret in a monochrome image.

4.7.1   Color Fundamentals

Although the process followed by the human brain in perceiving color is a physiopsychological phenomenon that is not yet fully understood, the physical nature of color can be expressed on a formal basis supported by experimental and theoretical results.

In 1666, Sir Isaac Newton discovered that when a beam of sunlight is passed through a glass prism the emerging beam of light is not white, but consists instead of a continuous spectrum of colors ranging from violet at one end to red at the other. As shown in Plate I, the color spectrum may be divided into six broad regions: violet, blue, green, yellow, orange, and red. When viewed in full color (Plate II) no color in the spectrum ends abruptly, but rather we have a situation where each color blends smoothly into the next.

Basically, the colors we perceive in an object are determined by the nature of the light reflected from the object. As illustrated in Plate II, visible light is composed of a relatively narrow band of frequencies in the electromagnetic energy spectrum. A body that reflects light that is relatively balanced in all visible wavelengths appears white to the observer. On the other hand, a body that favors reflectance in a limited range of the visible spectrum will exhibit some shades of color. For example, green objects reflect light with wavelengths primarily in the 500 to 570 nm (10^{-9} m) range, while absorbing most of the energy at other wavelengths.

Due to the structure of the human eye, all colors are seen as variable combinations of the three so-called *primary colors* red (R), green (G), and blue (B). For the purpose of standardization, the CIE (Commission Internationale de l'Eclairage— the International Commission on Illumination) designated in 1931 the following specific wavelength values to the three primary colors: blue = 435.8 nm, green = 546.1 nm, and red = 700 nm. We note from Plate II, however, that no single color may be called red, green, or blue. Thus once we have settled on three specific color wavelengths for the purpose of standardization, one needs to realize that these three fixed RGB components acting alone cannot generate all spectrum colors. This is important because use of the word "primary" has been widely misinterpreted to mean that the three standard primaries, when mixed in various intensity proportions can produce all visible colors. This is not true, unless the wavelength is also allowed to vary.

The primary colors can be added to produce the *secondary* colors of light— magenta (red plus blue), cyan (green plus blue), and yellow (red plus green). Mixing the three primaries, or a secondary with its opposite primary color, in the right intensities produces white light. This is shown in Plate III(a), which also illustrates the three primary colors and their combinations to produce the secondary colors.

It is important to differentiate between the primary colors of light and the primary colors of pigments or colorants. In the latter, a primary color is defined as one that subtracts or absorbs a primary color of light and reflects or transmits the other two. Therefore the primary colors of pigments are magenta, cyan, and yellow, while the secondary colors are red, green, and blue. These colors are shown in Plate III(b). It is noted that a proper combination of the three pigment primaries, or a secondary with its opposite primary, produces black.

Color television reception is an example of the additive nature of light colors. The interior of many color TV tubes is composed of a large array of triangular dot patterns of electron-sensitive phosphor. When excited, each dot in a triad is capable of producing light in one of the primary colors. The intensity of the red-emitting phosphor dots is modulated by an electron gun inside the tube, which generates pulses corresponding to the "red energy" seen by the TV camera. The green and blue phosphor dots in each triad are modulated in the same manner. The effect, viewed on the television receiver, is that the three primary colors from each phosphor triad are "added" together and received by the color-sensitive cones in the eye, and a full-color image is perceived. Thirty successive image changes per second in all three colors complete the illusion of a continuous image display on the screen.

The characteristics generally used to distinguish one color from another are *brightness; hue,* and *saturation.* Brightness refers to intensity. Hue is an attribute associated with the dominant wavelength in a mixture of light waves. Thus hue represents dominant color as perceived by an observer; when we call an object red, orange, or yellow we are specifying its hue. Saturation refers to relative purity or the amount of white light mixed with a hue. The pure spectrum colors are fully saturated. Colors such as pink (red and white) and lavender (violet and white) are less saturated, with the degree of saturation being inversely proportional to the amount of white light added.

Hue and saturation taken together are called *chromaticity,* and therefore a color may be characterized by its brightness and chromaticity. The amounts of red, green, and blue needed to form any given color are called the *tristimulus* values and are denoted, respectively, by X, Y, and Z. A color is then specified by its *trichromatic coefficients,* defined as

$$x = \frac{X}{X + Y + Z} \qquad (4.7\text{-}1)$$

$$y = \frac{Y}{X + Y + Z} \qquad (4.7\text{-}2)$$

and

$$z = \frac{Z}{X + Y + Z}. \qquad (4.7\text{-}3)$$

It is evident from these equations that

$$x + y + z = 1. \qquad (4.7\text{-}4)$$

Given any wavelength of light in the visible spectrum, the tristimulus values needed to produce the color corresponding to that wavelength can be obtained directly from curves or tables that have been compiled from extensive experimental results (Walsh [1958], Kiver [1965]).

Another approach for specifying colors is the *chromaticity diagram* (Plate IV), which shows color composition as a function of x (red) and y (green). For any value of x and y, the corresponding value of z (blue) is obtained from Eq. (4.7-4) by noting that $z = 1 - (x + y)$. The point marked "Green" in Plate IV, for example, has approximately 62% green and 25% red content. It then follows from Eq. (4.7-4) that the composition of blue is approximately 13%.

The positions of the various spectrum colors, from violet at 380 nm to red at 780 nm, are indicated around the boundary of the tongue-shaped chromaticity diagram. These are the pure colors shown in the spectrum of Plate II. Any point not actually on the boundary but within the diagram represents some mixture of spectrum colors. The point of equal energy shown in Plate IV corresponds to equal fractions of the three primary colors; it represents the CIE standard for white light. Any point located on the boundary of the chromaticity chart is said to be completely saturated. As a point leaves the boundary and approaches the point of equal energy, more white light is added to the color and it becomes less saturated. The saturation at the point of equal energy is zero.

The chromaticity diagram is useful for color mixing because a straight line segment joining any two points in the diagram defines all the different color variations that can be obtained by combining these two colors additively. Consider, for example, a straight line drawn from the Red to the Green points shown in Plate IV. If there is more red light than green light, the exact point representing the new color will be on the line segment, but it will be closer to the red point than to the green point. Similarly, a line drawn from the point of equal energy to any point on the boundary of the chart will define all the shades of particular spectrum color.

Extension of the above procedure to three colors is straightforward. To determine the range of colors that can be obtained from any three given colors in the chromaticity diagram, we simply draw connecting lines to each of the three color points. The result is a triangle, and any color inside the triangle can be produced by various combinations of the three initial colors. It is noted that a triangle with vertices at any three *fixed* colors does not enclose the entire color region in Plate IV. This supports graphically the remark made earlier that not all colors can be obtained with three single primaries.

In the following discussion, the intensity of the three primary colors at coordinates (x, y) of an image will be denoted by $I_R(x, y)$, $I_G(x, y)$, and $I_B(x, y)$. Thus each pixel in a color image will be considered as an additive combination of these three intensity values at the coordinates of the pixel.

4.7.2 Density Slicing

The technique of *density* (or *intensity*) *slicing* and color coding is one of the simplest examples of pseudo-color image processing. If an image is viewed as a two-dimensional intensity function (see Section 1.2), the method can be interpreted as one of placing planes parallel to the coordinate plane of the image; each plane then "slices" the function in the area of intersection. Figure 4.35 shows a simple example of this where a plane at $f(x, y) = l_i$ is used to slice a function into two levels. The term "density slicing" arises from calling the gray levels densities, a terminology that is commonly associated with this particular method.

It is evident that if a different color is assigned to each side of the plane shown in Fig. 4.35, then any pixel whose gray level is above the plane will be coded with one color, while any pixel below the plane will be coded with the other. Levels that lie on the plane itself may be arbitrarily assigned one of the two colors. The result of this scheme would produce a two-color image whose relative appearance can be controlled by moving the slicing plane up and down the gray-level axis.

In general, the technique may be summarized as follows. Suppose that M planes are defined at levels $l_1, l_2, \ldots, l_M$, and let l_0 represent black $[f(x, y) = 0]$ and l_L represent white $[f(x, y) = L]$. Then, assuming that $0 < M < L$, the M planes

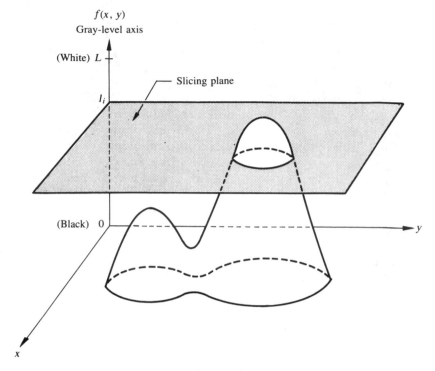

Figure 4.35 Geometrical interpretation of the density-slicing technique.

partition the gray scale into $M + 1$ regions and color assignments are made according to the relation:

$$f(x, y) = c_k \qquad \text{if } f(x, y) \in R_k, \tag{4.7-5}$$

where c_k is the color associated with the kth region R_k defined by the partitioning planes.

It is important to note that the idea of planes is useful primarily for a geometrical interpretation of the density-slicing technique. An alternative representation is shown in Fig. 4.36, which defines the same mapping as Fig. 4.35. According to the mapping function shown in Fig. 4.36, any input gray level is assigned one of two colors, depending on whether it is above or below the value of l_i. When more levels are used, the mapping function assumes a staircase form. This type of mapping is a special case of the approach discussed in the following section.

Example: An example of density slicing is shown in Plate V. Part (a) is a monochrome image of the Picker Thyroid Phantom (a radiation test pattern), and Plate V(b) is the result of density slicing this image into eight color regions. It is noted that

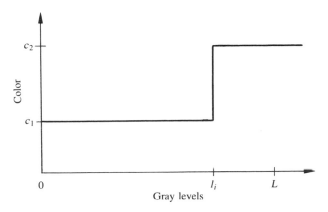

Figure 4.36 An alternate representation of the density-slicing method.

regions that appear of constant intensity in the monochrome image are really quite variable, as shown by the various colors in the sliced image. The left lobe, for instance, is a dull gray in the monochrome image, and it is difficult to pick out variations in intensity. By contrast, the color image clearly shows eight different regions of constant intensity, one for each of the colors used.   □

4.7.3 Gray-Level-to-Color Transformations

It is possible to specify other types of transformations that are more general and thus are capable of achieving a wider range of pseudo-color enhancement results than the simple density-slicing technique discussed in the previous section. An approach that is particularly attractive is shown in Fig. 4.37. Basically, the idea underlying this approach is to perform three independent transformations on the gray levels of any input pixel. The three results are then fed separately into the red, green, and blue guns of a color television monitor. This produces a composite image whose color content is modulated by the nature of the transformation function. It should be kept in mind that these are transformations on the gray-level values of an image and that they are not functions of position.

As indicated in the previous section, the method shown in Fig. 4.36 is a special case of the technique just described. The generation of colors in Fig. 4.36 is accomplished by piecewise linear functions of the gray levels. On the other hand, the method discussed in this section can be based on smooth, nonlinear functions that, as might be expected, gives the technique considerably more flexibility. This is demonstrated by the following example.

Example: Plate VI(a) shows a composite monochrome image consisting of two images of luggage obtained from an airport x-ray scanning system. The image on

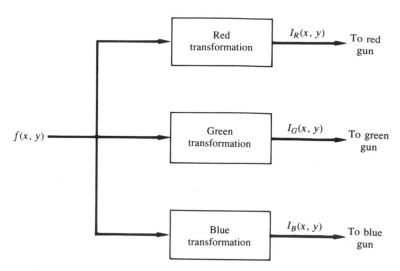

Figure 4.37   Functional block diagram for pseudo-color image processing.

the left contains ordinary articles. The image on the right contains the same articles, as well as a block of simulated plastic explosives. The purpose of this example is to illustrate the use of gray-level-to-color transformations for performing various degrees of enhancement.

The transformation functions used are shown in Fig. 4.38. These sinusoidal functions contain regions of relatively constant value around the peaks as well as regions that change rapidly near the valleys. By changing the phase and frequency of each sinusoid it is possible to emphasize (in color) ranges in the gray scale. For instance, if all three transformations have the same phase and frequency, the output image will be monochrome. A small change in the phase between the three transformations will produce little change in pixels whose gray levels correspond to peaks in the sinusoids, especially if the sinusoids have broad profiles (i.e., low frequencies). Pixels with gray-level values in the steep section of the sinusoids will be assigned a much stronger color content as a result of significant differences between the amplitudes of the three sinusoids caused by the phase displacement between them.

The image shown in Plate VI(b) was obtained with the transformation functions in Fig. 4.38(a), which shows the gray-level bands corresponding to the explosive, garment bag, and background, respectively. Note that the explosive and background have quite different gray levels, but they were both coded with approximately the same color as a result of the periodicity of the sine waves. The image shown in Plate VI(c) was obtained with the transformation functions in Fig. 4.38(b). In this case the explosive and garment bag intensity bands were mapped by very similar transformations and thus received essentially the same color assignments. Note that

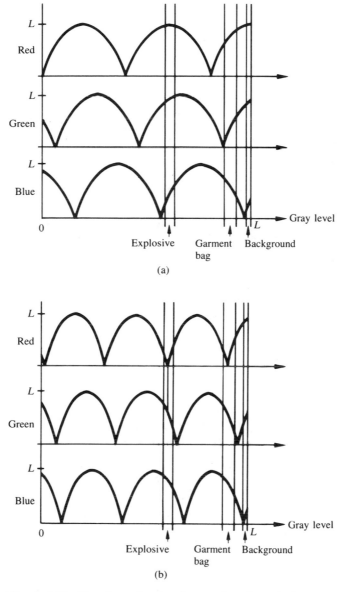

Figure 4.38 Transformation functions used to obtain the images in Plate VI (see text).

this allowed us to "see" through the explosives. The background mappings were about the same as those used for Plate VI(b), producing almost identical color assignments.   □

4.7.4 A Filtering Approach

Figure 4.39 shows a color-coding scheme that is based on frequency-domain operations. The idea depicted in this figure is the same as the basic filtering approach discussed earlier in this chapter, with the exception that the Fourier transform of an image is modified independently by three filter functions to produce three images that can be fed into the red, green, and blue inputs of a color monitor. Consider, for example, the sequence of steps followed in obtaining the image for the red channel. The Fourier transform of the input image is altered by using a specified filter function. The processed image is then obtained by using the inverse Fourier transform. This can then be followed by additional processing (such as histogram equalization) before the image is fed into the red input of the monitor. Similar comments apply to the other two paths in Fig. 4.39.

The objective of this color-processing technique is to color-code regions of an image based on frequency content. A typical filtering approach is to use lowpass, bandpass (or bandreject), and highpass filters to obtain three ranges of frequency components. We have already discussed lowpass and highpass filters. Bandreject and bandpass filters are an extension of these concepts.

A simple approach for generating filters that reject or attenuate frequencies about a circular neighborhood of a point (u_0, v_0) is to perform a translation of coordinates for the highpass filters discussed in Section 4.4.2. We illustrate the procedure for the ideal filter.

An ideal bandreject filter (IBRF), which suppresses all frequencies in a neighborhood of radius D_0 about a point (u_0, v_0), is given by the relation

$$H(u, v) = \begin{cases} 0 & \text{if } D(u, v) \leq D_0 \\ 1 & \text{if } D(u,v) > D_0, \end{cases} \tag{4.7-6}$$

where

$$D(u, v) = [(u - u_0)^2 + (v - v_0)^2]^{1/2} \tag{4.7-7}$$

Note that Eq. 4.7-6 is identical in form to Eq. (4.4-12), but the distance function $D(u, v)$ is computed about the point (u_0, v_0) instead of the origin.

Due to the symmetry of the Fourier transform, band rejection that is not about the origin must be carried out in symmetric *pairs* in order to obtain meaningful results. In the case of the ideal filter we modify Eq. (4.7-6) as follows:

$$H(u, v) = \begin{cases} 0 & \text{if } D_1(u, v) \leq D_0 \text{ or } D_2(u, v) \leq D_0 \\ 1 & \text{otherwise,} \end{cases} \tag{4.7-8}$$

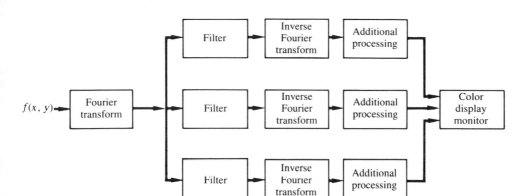

Figure 4.39 A filtering model for pseudo-color image enhancement.

where

$$D_1(u, v) = \{(u - u_0)^2 + (v - v_0)^2\}^{1/2} \tag{4.7-9}$$

and

$$D_2(u, v) = \{(u + u_0)^2 + (v + v_0)^2\}^{1/2} \tag{4.7-10}$$

The procedure can be extended in a similar manner to four or more regions. The Butterworth filter given in Section 4.4.2 can also be applied directly to band rejection by following the technique just described for the ideal filter. Figure 4.40 shows a perspective plot of a typical IBRF transfer function.

The filter discussed above is localized about some point off the origin of the Fourier transform. If it is desired to remove a band of frequencies centered about the origin, we can consider symmetric filters similar to the low and highpass filters discussed earlier. The procedure is illustrated for the ideal and Butterworth filters.

A radially symmetric ideal bandreject filter, which removes a band of frequencies about the origin, is given by the relation

$$H(u, v) = \begin{cases} 1 & \text{if } D(u, v) < D_0 - \dfrac{W}{2} \\[2ex] 0 & \text{if } D_0 - \dfrac{W}{2} \leq D(u, v) \leq D_0 + \dfrac{W}{2} \\[2ex] 1 & \text{if } D(u, v) > D_0 + \dfrac{W}{2}, \end{cases} \tag{4.7-11}$$

where W is the width of the band and D_0 is its radial center. As is the case with all radially symmetric filters, this filter can be completely specified by a cross section.

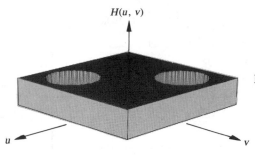

Figure 4.40   Ideal bandreject filter.

A radially symmetric Butterworth bandreject filter (BBRF) of order n has the transfer function

$$H(u, v) = \frac{1}{1 + \left[\dfrac{D(u, v)W}{D^2(u, v) - D_0^2} \right]^{2n}}, \tag{4.7-12}$$

where W is defined as the "width" of the band and D_0 is its center.

Bandpass filters pass frequencies in a specified band or region, while attenuating, or completely suppressing, all other frequencies. Therefore they are exactly the opposite of bandreject filters. It then follows that, if $H_R(u, v)$ is the transfer function of any of the bandreject filters just discussed, the corresponding bandpass function, $H(u, v)$ can be obtained simply by "flipping" $H_R(u, v)$; that is,

$$H(u, v) = -[H_R(u, v) - 1]. \tag{4.7-13}$$

Example: Plate VII(a) shows a monochrome image and Plates VII(b) and (c) are the results of using Butterworth filters. Plate VII(b) shows (in the red gun of a color monitor) the result of applying a highpass filter with the cut-off point at the circle enclosing 90% of the image energy (see Section 4.3.3). Plate VII(c) shows the highpass filtered image on the red gun, as well as a lowpass (blue gun) and bandpass (green gun) filtered version of Plate VII(a). The lowpass image was obtained with the cut-off point at the circle enclosing 98% of the image energy; the bandpass range was between the circles enclosing 20% and 95% of the energy. The principal enhancement resulting from this process was the increased visibility of the outer ring, which is almost invisible in the original image.   □

4.8   CONCLUDING REMARKS

The material presented in this chapter is representative of techniques commonly used in practice for digital image enhancement. It must be kept in mind, however, that this area of image processing is a dynamic field where reports of new techniques and applications are commonplace in the literature. For this reason, the topics included in this chapter were selected mostly for their value as fundamental material that would serve as a foundation for further study of this field.

REFERENCES

Additional reading for the material in Section 4.1 may be found in Gonzalez [1986]. Our discussion on histogram processing techniques is based on the papers by Hall *et al.* [1971], Hall [1974], Hummel [1974], Gonzalez and Fittes [1977], and Woods and Gonzalez [1981]. For further details on local enhancement see Ketcham [1976], Harris [1977], and Narendra and Fitch [1981].

The neighborhood averaging approach introduced in Section 4.3.1 is based on a similar discussion by Rosenfeld and Kak [1982]. For details on implementing median filters see Huang *et al.* [1979], Wolfe and Mannos [1979], and Chaudhuri [1983]. The lowpass-filtering concepts developed in Section 4.3.3 are based on a direct extension of one-dimensional filters where, instead of using a single variable, we used the distance from the origin of the Fourier transform in order to obtain circularly symmetric filter functions. This is also true of the other filters discussed in this chapter. For a discussion of one-dimensional filters see, for example, the books by Weinberg [1962] and by Budak [1974]. The method of smoothing by image averaging was first proposed by Kohler and Howell [1963].

Early references on image sharpening by differentiation are Goldmard and Hollywood [1951] and Kovasznay and Joseph [1953, 1955]. The Roberts gradient approach was proposed by Roberts [1965]. A survey of techniques used in this area a decade later is given by Davis [1975]. The articles by Prewitt [1970] and Frei and Chen [1977] are also of interest. More recent work in this field emphasizes computational speed, as exemplified by Lee [1983] and Chaudhuri [1983]. Our discussion on high-frequency emphasis is from Hall *et al.* [1971].

The material in Section 4.5 is based on a paper by Stockham [1972]; see also the book by Oppenheim and Schafer [1975]. The material in Section 4.6 is from Schutten and Vermeij [1980] and Meyer and Gonzalez [1983]. Basic material on color fundamendals may be found in the books by Walsh [1958] and by Kiver [1965]. The techniques discussed in Sections 4.6.2 through 4.6.4 are based on the papers by Smith [1963], Roth [1968], Billingsley *et al.* [1970], and Andrews *et al.* [1972]. Additional reading on pseudo-color image processing may be found in Green [1983].

PROBLEMS

4.1 Explain why the discrete histogram-equalization technique will not, in general, yield a flat histogram.

4.2 Suppose that a digital image is histogram-equalized. Show that a second pass of histogram equalization will produce exactly the same result as the first pass.

4.3 A given image has the gray level *PDF* $p_r(r)$ shown below. It is desired to transform the gray levels of this image so that they will have the specified $p_z(z)$ shown below. Assuming

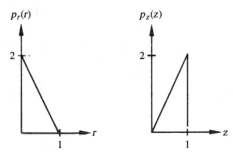

continuous quantities, find the transformation (in terms of r and z) that will accomplish this.

4.4 Propose a method for updating the local histogram for use in the local enhancement technique discussed in Section 4.2.4.

4.5 Consider the neighborhood-averaging expression given in Eq. (4.3-1), and suppose that $M = 4$, corresponding to forming an average of the four immediate neighbors of (x, y), but excluding (x, y) itself.
a) Find the equivalent filter $H(u, v)$ in the frequency domain.
b) Show that this is a lowpass filter.

4.6 a) Develop a procedure for computing the median of an $n \times n$ neighborhood.
b) Propose a technique for updating the median as the center of the neighborhood is moved from pixel to pixel.

4.7 Under what condition does the Butterworth lowpass filter given in Eq. (4.3-6) become an ideal lowpass filter?

4.8 In a given industrial application, it is desired to use x-ray imaging to inspect the inside of certain iron castings. The objective is to look for voids in the castings, which typically appear as small blobs in the image. However, high noise content often makes inspection difficult, so it is decided to use image averaging to reduce the noise and thus improve visible contrast. The goal is to keep averaging to a minimum in order to reduce the time the parts have to remain stationary during imaging. After numerous experiments, it is concluded that decreasing the gray-level variance by a factor of 10 is sufficient. If the imaging device can produce 30 frames/sec, how long would the castings have to remain stationary during imaging to achieve the desired decrease in variance? Assume that the noise is uncorrelated and has zero mean.

4.9 The basic approach used to compute the digital gradient (Section 4.4.1) involves taking differences of the form $f(x, y) - f(x + 1, y)$.
a) Obtain the filter transfer function, $H(u, v)$, for performing the equivalent process in the frequency domain.
b) Show that this is a highpass filter.

4.10 A popular procedure for image enhancement combines high-frequency emphasis and histogram equalization to achieve edge sharpening and contrast enhancement.
a) Prove whether or not it matters which process is applied first.
b) If the order does matter, give a rationale for using one or the other method first.

4.11 Suppose that we are given a set of images generated by an experiment dealing with the analysis of stellar events. Each image contains a set of bright, widely scattered dots corresponding to stars in a sparse section of the universe. The problem is that the stars are barely visible, due to superimposed illumination resulting from atmospheric dispersion. If we model these images as the product of a constant illumination component with a set of impulses, give an enhancement procedure based on homomorphic filtering designed to bring out the image components due to the stars themselves.

4.12 With reference to the discussion in Section 4.6, show that if $H(u, v)$ is real and symmetric, $h(x, y)$ must also be real and symmetric.

4.13 In an automatic assembly application, it is desired to color code three classes of parts to simplify detection. However, only a monochrome TV camera is available. Propose a technique for using this camera to detect the three different colors.

4.14 A skilled medical technician is charged with the job of inspecting a certain class of images generated by an electron microscope. In order to simplify the inspection task, the technician decides to use digital image enhancement and, to this end, examines a set of representative images and finds the following problems: (1) bright, isolated dots that are of no interest; (2) lack of sharpness; (3) not enough contrast in some images; and (4) shifts in the average gray-level value, when this value should be K to perform correctly certain intensity measurements. The technician wishes to correct these problems and then color in constant red all gray levels in the band between I_1 and I_2, while keeping normal tonality in the remaining gray levels. Propose a sequence of processing steps that the technician can follow to achieve the desired goal.

DIGITAL
IMAGE
PROCESSING

Plates I–VII

Plate I

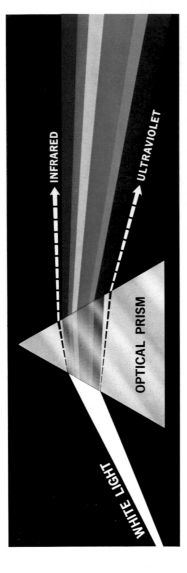

Plate I. Color spectrum seen by passing white light through a prism. (Courtesy of General Electric Co., Lamp Business Division.)

Plate II

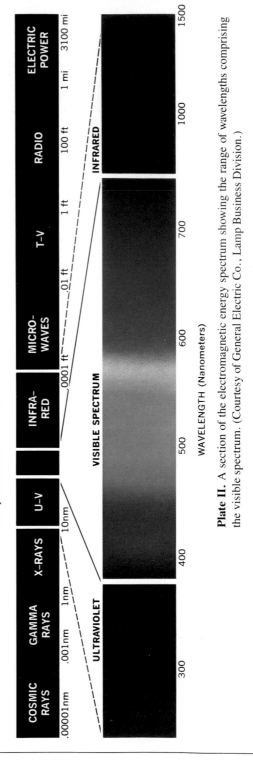

Plate II. A section of the electromagnetic energy spectrum showing the range of wavelengths comprising the visible spectrum. (Courtesy of General Electric Co., Lamp Business Division.)

Plate III

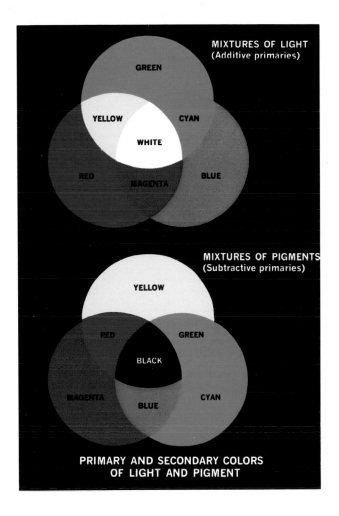

Plate III. Primary and secondary colors of light and pigments. (Courtesy of General Electric Co., Lamp Business Division.)

Plate IV

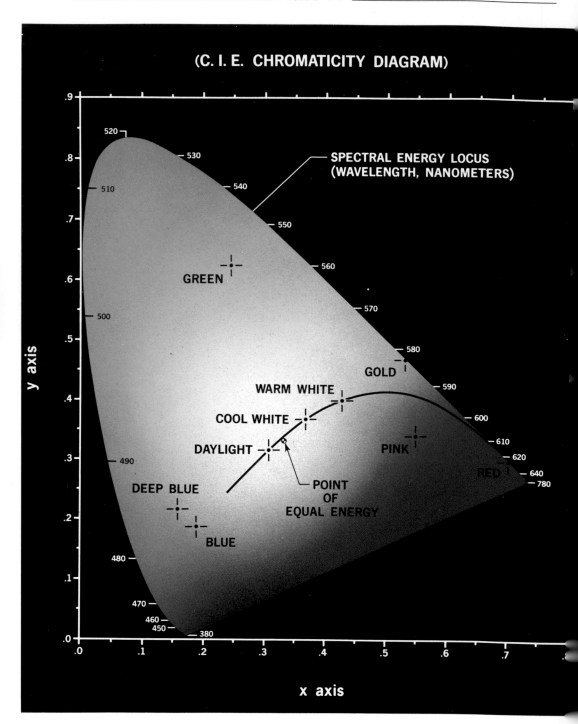

Plate IV. Chromaticity diagram. (Courtesy of General Electric Co., Lamp Business Division.)

Plate V

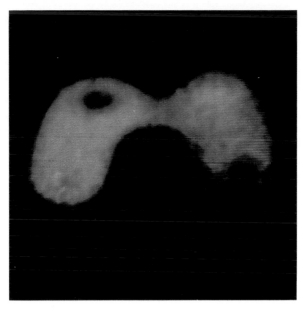

(a)

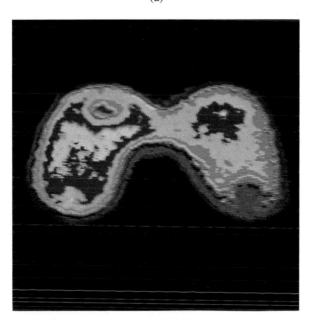

(b)

Plate V. (a) Monochrome image of the Picker Thyroid Phantom. (b) Result of density slicing into eight color regions. (Courtesy of Dr. J.L. Blankenship, Instrumentation and Controls Division, Oak Ridge National Laboratory.)

Plate VI

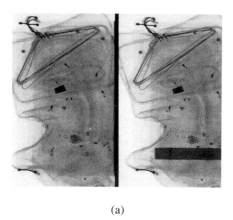

(a)

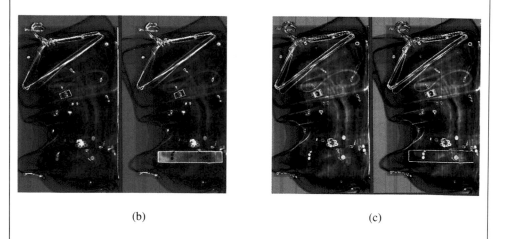

(b)   (c)

Plate VI. Pseudo-color enhancement by using the gray-level to color transformations in Fig. 4.38. Original image courtesy of Dr. Mike Hurwitz, Research and Development Center, Westinghouse Electric Corporation.

Plate VII

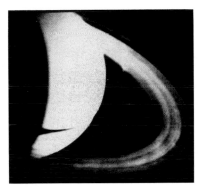

(a)

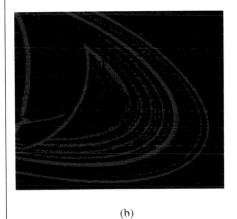

(b)

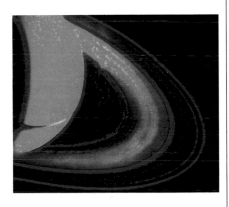

(c)

Plate VII. (a) Monochrome image. (b) Result of highpass Butterworth filter displayed on the red gun of a color monitor. (c) Composite image with the lowpass, bandpass, and highpass images displayed on the blue, green, and red guns, respectively.

CHAPTER 5

IMAGE RESTORATION

Things which we see are not by themselves what we see. . . . It remains completely unknown to us what the objects may be by themselves and apart from the receptivity of our senses. We know nothing but our manner of perceiving them. . . .

Immanuel Kant

As in image enhancement, the ultimate goal of restoration techniques is to improve a given image in some sense. For the purpose of differentiation, we consider restoration to be a process that attempts to reconstruct or recover an image that has been degraded by using some a priori knowledge of the degradation phenomenon. Thus restoration techniques are oriented toward modeling the degradation and applying the inverse process in order to recover the original image. This usually involves formulating a criterion of goodness that will yield some optimal estimate of the desired result. Enhancement techniques, on the other hand, are basically heuristic procedures which are designed to manipulate an image in order to take advantage of the psychophysical aspects of the human visual system. For example, contrast stretching is considered an enhancement technique because it is based primarily on the pleasing aspects it might present to the viewer, while removal of image blur by applying a deblurring function is considered a restoration problem.

Early techniques for digital image restoration were derived mostly from frequency-domain concepts. Attention is focused in this chapter, however, on a more modern, algebraic approach to the problem. This approach has the advantage that it allows the derivation of numerous restoration techniques starting from the same basic principles. Although a direct solution by algebraic methods generally involves the manipulation of large systems of simultaneous equations, it is shown in the following sections that, under certain conditions, it is possible to reduce computational complexity to the same level as that required by traditional frequency-domain restoration techniques.

The material developed in the following sections is strictly introductory. We consider only the restoration problem from the point where a degraded, *digital* image is given; thus topics dealing with sensor, digitizer, and display degradations are not considered in this chapter. These subjects, although of importance in the overall treatment of image-restoration applications, are outside the mainstream of our present discussion. The references cited at the end of the chapter provide a starting point to the voluminous literature on these and related topics.

5.1   DEGRADATION MODEL

As shown in Fig. 5.1, the degradation process will be modeled in this chapter as an operator (or system) H, which together with an additive noise term $\eta(x, y)$ operates on an input image $f(x, y)$ to produce a degraded image $g(x, y)$. The digital image-restoration problem may be viewed as that of obtaining an approximation to $f(x, y)$, given $g(x, y)$ and a knowledge of the degradation in the form of the operator H. It is assumed that our knowledge about $\eta(x, y)$ is limited to information of a statistical nature.

5.1.1   Some Definitions

The input–output relationship in Fig. 5.1 is given by the expression

$$g(x, y) = Hf(x, y) + \eta(x, y). \tag{5.1-1}$$

For the moment, let us assume that $\eta(x, y) = 0$ so that $g(x, y) = Hf(x, y)$. We define H to be *linear* if

$$H[k_1 f_1(x, y) + k_2 f_2(x, y)] = k_1 Hf_1(x, y) + k_2 Hf_2(x, y), \tag{5.1-2}$$

where k_1 and k_2 are constants and $f_1(x, y)$ and $f_2(x, y)$ are any two input images.
    If we let $k_1 = k_2 = 1$, Eq. (5.1-2) becomes

$$H[f_1(x, y) + f_2(x, y)] = Hf_1(x, y) + Hf_2(x, y), \tag{5.1-3}$$

which is called the property of *additivity;* this property simply says that, if H is a linear operator, the response to a sum of two inputs is equal to the sum of the two responses.

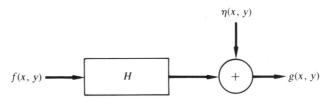

Figure 5.1   A model of the image degradation process.

With $f_2(x, y) = 0$, Eq. (5.1-2) becomes

$$H[k_1 f_1(x, y)] = k_1 H f_1(x, y).$$ (5.1-4)

This is called the property of *homogeneity,* which says that the response to a constant multiple of any input is equal to the response to that input multiplied by the same constant. Thus we see that a linear operator possesses both the property of additivity and the property of homogeneity.

An operator having the input–output relationship $g(x, y) = Hf(x, y)$ is said to be *position* (or *space*) *invariant* if

$$Hf(x - \alpha, y - \beta) = g(x - \alpha, y - \beta)$$ (5.1-5)

for any $f(x, y)$ and any α and β. This definition indicates that the response at any point in the image depends only on the value of the input at that point and not on the position of the point.

5.1.2 Degradation Model for Continuous Functions

From the definition of the impulse function given in Eq. (3.3-46), we can express $f(x, y)$ in the form

$$f(x, y) = \int\!\!\!\int_{-\infty}^{\infty} f(\alpha, \beta)\delta(x - \alpha, y - \beta) \, d\alpha d\beta.$$ (5.1-6)

Then, if $\eta(x, y) = 0$ in Eq. (5.1-1),

$$g(x, y) = Hf(x, y) = H \int\!\!\!\int_{-\infty}^{\infty} f(\alpha, \beta)\delta(x - \alpha, y - \beta) \, d\alpha d\beta.$$ (5.1-7)

If H is a linear operator, and we assume that the additivity property is valid for integrals, then

$$g(x, y) = \int\!\!\!\int_{-\infty}^{\infty} H[f(\alpha, \beta)\delta(x - \alpha, y - \beta)] \, d\alpha d\beta.$$ (5.1-8)

Since $f(\alpha, \beta)$ is independent of x and y, it follows from the homogeneity property that

$$g(x, y) = \int\!\!\!\int_{-\infty}^{\infty} f(\alpha, \beta)H\delta(x - \alpha, y - \beta) \, d\alpha d\beta.$$ (5.1-9)

The term

$$h(x, \alpha, y, \beta) = H\delta(x - \alpha, y - \beta)$$ (5.1-10)

is called the *impulse response* of H. In other words, if $\eta(x, y) = 0$ in Eq. (5.1-1), we see that $h(x, \alpha, y, \beta)$ is the response of H to an impulse at coordinates (α, β). In optics, the impulse becomes a point of light and $h(x, \alpha, y, \beta)$ is commonly referred to in this case as the *point spread function* (PSF).

Substitution of Eq. (5.1-10) into Eq. (5.1-9) yields the expression

$$g(x, y) = \int\int_{-\infty}^{\infty} f(\alpha, \beta)h(x, \alpha, y, \beta)\, d\alpha d\beta, \qquad (5.1\text{-}11)$$

which is called the *superposition* (or *Fredholm*) *integral of the first kind*. This expression is of fundamental importance in linear system theory. It states that if the response of H to an impulse is known, then the response to any input $f(\alpha, \beta)$ can be calculated by means of Eq. (5.1-11). In other words, a linear system H is completely characterized by its impulse response.

If H is position invariant, it follows from Eq. (5.1-5) that

$$H\delta(x - \alpha, y - \beta) = h(x - \alpha, y - \beta). \qquad (5.1\text{-}12)$$

Equation (5.1-11) reduces in this case to

$$g(x, y) = \int\int_{-\infty}^{\infty} f(\alpha, \beta)h(x - \alpha, y - \beta)\, d\alpha d\beta, \qquad (5.1\text{-}13)$$

which is recognized as the convolution integral defined in Eq. (3.3-30).

In the presence of additive noise the expression describing a linear degradation model becomes

$$g(x, y) = \int\int_{-\infty}^{\infty} f(\alpha, \beta)h(x, \alpha, y, \beta)\, d\alpha d\beta + \eta(x, y). \qquad (5.1\text{-}14)$$

If H is position invariant, this expression becomes

$$g(x, y) = \int\int_{-\infty}^{\infty} f(\alpha, \beta)h(x - \alpha, y - \beta)\, d\alpha d\beta + \eta(x, y). \qquad (5.1\text{-}15)$$

The noise, of course, is assumed in both cases to be independent of position in the image.

Many types of degradations can be approximated by linear, position-invariant processes. The advantage of this approach is that the extensive tools of linear system theory then become available for the solution of image-restoration problems. Nonlinear and space-variant techniques, although more general (and usually more accurate), introduce difficulties that often have no known solution or are very difficult to solve computationally. Attention is focused in this chapter on linear, space-invariant restoration techniques. As will be seen in the following discussion, however, even this simplification can result in computational problems that, if attacked directly, are beyond the capabilities of most present-day computers.

5.1.3 Discrete Formulation

The development of a discrete, space-invariant degradation model is simplified by starting with the one-dimensional case and temporarily neglecting the noise term. Suppose that two functions $f(x)$ and $h(x)$ are sampled uniformly to form arrays of dimension A and B, respectively. In this case, we interpret x as a discrete variable in the ranges $0, 1, 2, \ldots, A - 1$ for $f(x)$ and $0, 1, 2, \ldots, B - 1$ for $h(x)$.

The discrete convolution formulation given in Section 3.3.8 is based on the assumption that the sampled functions are periodic with a period M. Overlap in the individual periods of the resulting convolution is avoided by choosing $M \geqslant A + B - 1$ and extending the functions with zeros so that their length is equal to M. Letting $f_e(x)$ and $h_e(x)$ represent the extended functions, it follows from Eq. (3.3-29) that their convolution is given by

$$g_e(x) = \sum_{m=0}^{M-1} f_e(m)h_e(x - m) \qquad (5.1\text{-}16)$$

for $x = 0, 1, 2, \ldots, M - 1$. Since both $f_e(x)$ and $h_e(x)$ are assumed to have a period equal to $M, g_e(x)$ also has this period.

It is easily verified by direct matrix multiplication that Eq. (5.1-16) can be expressed in the form

$$\mathbf{g} = \mathbf{Hf}, \qquad (5.1\text{-}17)$$

where $\mathbf{f}$ and $\mathbf{g}$ are M-dimensional column vectors given by

$$\mathbf{f} = \begin{bmatrix} f_e(0) \\ f_e(1) \\ \cdot \\ \cdot \\ \cdot \\ f_e(M - 1) \end{bmatrix} \qquad (5.1\text{-}18)$$

and

$$\mathbf{g} = \begin{bmatrix} g_e(0) \\ g_e(1) \\ \cdot \\ \cdot \\ \cdot \\ g_e(M - 1) \end{bmatrix} \qquad (5.1\text{-}19)$$

H is the $M \times M$ matrix

$$\mathbf{H} = \begin{bmatrix} h_e(0) & h_e(-1) & h_e(-2) & \cdots & h_e(-M+1) \\ h_e(1) & h_e(0) & h_e(-1) & \cdots & h_e(-M+2) \\ h_e(2) & h_e(1) & h_e(0) & \cdots & h_e(-M+3) \\ & \vdots & & & \\ h_e(M-1) & h_e(M-2) & h_e(M-3) & \cdots & h_e(0) \end{bmatrix}$$ (5.1-20)

Because of the periodicity assumption on $h_e(x)$, we have that $h_e(x) = h_e(M + x)$. Using this property, Eq. (5.1-20) may be written in the form

$$\mathbf{H} = \begin{bmatrix} h_e(0) & h_e(M-1) & h_e(M-2) & \cdots & h_e(1) \\ h_e(1) & h_e(0) & h_e(M-1) & \cdots & h_e(2) \\ h_e(2) & h_e(1) & h_e(0) & \cdots & h_e(3) \\ & \vdots & & & \\ h_e(M-1) & h_e(M-2) & h_e(M-3) & \cdots & h_e(0) \end{bmatrix}$$ (5.1-21)

The structure of this matrix plays a fundamental role throughout the remainder of this chapter. From Eq. (5.1-21) we see that the rows of **H** are related by a *circular shift* to the right; that is, the right-most element in one row is equal to the left-most element in the row immediately below. The shift is called circular because an element shifted out of the right end of a row reappears at the left end. It is also noted in Eq. (5.1-21) that the circularity of **H** is complete in the sense that it extends from the last row back to the first row. A square matrix in which each row is a circular shift of the preceding row, and the first row is a circular shift of the last row, is called a *circulant matrix*. It is important to keep in mind that the circular behavior of **H** is a direct consequence of the assumed periodicity of $h_e(x)$.

Example: Suppose that $A = 4$ and $B = 3$. We may choose $M = 6$ and then append two zeros to the samples of $f(x)$ and three zeros to samples of $h(x)$. In this case **f** and **g** are 6-dimensional vectors and **H** is the 6×6 matrix

$$\mathbf{H} = \begin{bmatrix} h_e(0) & h_e(5) & h_e(4) & \cdots & h_e(1) \\ h_e(1) & h_e(0) & h_e(5) & \cdots & h_e(2) \\ h_e(2) & h_e(1) & h_e(0) & \cdots & h_e(3) \\ & \vdots & & & \\ h_e(5) & h_e(4) & h_e(3) & \cdots & h_e(0) \end{bmatrix}$$

However, since $h_e(x) = 0$ for $x = 3, 4, 5$, and $h_e(x) = h(x)$ for $x = 0, 1, 2$, we have

$$\mathbf{H} = \begin{bmatrix} h(0) & & & & h(2) & h(1) \\ h(1) & h(0) & & & & h(2) \\ h(2) & h(1) & h(0) & & & \\ & h(2) & h(1) & h(0) & & \\ & & h(2) & h(1) & h(0) & \\ & & & h(2) & h(1) & h(0) \end{bmatrix}$$

where all elements not indicated in the matrix are zero.   □

Extension of the foregoing discussion to a two-dimensional, discrete degradation model is straightforward. Given two digitized images $f(x, y)$ and $h(x, y)$ of sizes $A \times B$ and $C \times D$, respectively, we form extended images of size $M \times N$ by padding the above functions with zeros. As indicated in Section 3.3.8, one procedure for doing this is to let

$$f_e(x, y) = \begin{cases} f(x, y) & 0 \leq x \leq A - 1 \quad \text{and} \quad 0 \leq y \leq B - 1 \\ 0 & A \leq x \leq M - 1 \quad \text{or} \quad B \leq y \leq N - 1 \end{cases}$$

and

$$h_e(x, y) = \begin{cases} h(x, y) & 0 \leq x \leq C - 1 \quad \text{and} \quad 0 \leq y \leq D - 1 \\ 0 & C \leq x \leq M - 1 \quad \text{or} \quad D \leq y \leq N - 1. \end{cases}$$

If we treat the extended functions $f_e(x, y)$ and $h_e(x, y)$ as being periodic in two dimensions, with periods M and N in the x and y directions, respectively, it then follows from Eq. (3.3-35) that the convolution of these two functions is given by the relation

$$g_e(x, y) = \sum_{m=0}^{M-1} \sum_{n=0}^{N-1} f_e(m, n)h_e(x - m, y - n) \tag{5.1-22}$$

for $x = 0, 1, 2, \ldots, M - 1$ and $y = 0, 1, 2, \ldots, N - 1$. The convolution function $g_e(x, y)$ is periodic with the same period of $f_e(x, y)$ and $h_e(x, y)$. Overlap of the individual convolution periods is avoided by choosing $M \geq A + C - 1$ and $N \geq B + D - 1$. In order to complete the discrete degradation model we add an $M \times N$ extended discrete noise term $\eta_e(x, y)$ to Eq. (5.1-22) so that

$$g_e(x, y) = \sum_{m=0}^{M-1} \sum_{n=0}^{N-1} f_e(m, n)h_e(x - m, y - n) + \eta_e(x, y) \tag{5.1-23}$$

for $x = 0, 1, 2, \ldots, M - 1$ and $y = 0, 1, 2, \ldots, N - 1$.

Let **f**, **g**, and **n** represent MN-dimensional column vectors formed by stacking the rows of the $M \times N$ functions $f_e(x, y)$, $g_e(x, y)$, and $\eta_e(x, y)$. The first N elements of **f**, for example, are the elements in the first row of $f_e(x, y)$, the next N elements are from the second row, and so forth for all M rows of $f_e(x, y)$. Using this convention, Eq. (5.1-23) can be expressed in the following vector-matrix form:

$$\mathbf{g} = \mathbf{H}\mathbf{f} + \mathbf{n}, \tag{5.1-24}$$

where **f**, **g**, and **n** are of dimension $(MN) \times 1$ and **H** is of dimension $MN \times MN$. This matrix consists of M^2 partitions, each partition being of size $N \times N$ and ordered according to

$$\mathbf{H} = \begin{bmatrix} \mathbf{H}_0 & \mathbf{H}_{M-1} & \mathbf{H}_{M-2} & \cdots & \mathbf{H}_1 \\ \mathbf{H}_1 & \mathbf{H}_0 & \mathbf{H}_{M-1} & \cdots & \mathbf{H}_2 \\ \mathbf{H}_2 & \mathbf{H}_1 & \mathbf{H}_0 & \cdots & \mathbf{H}_3 \\ \cdot \\ \cdot \\ \cdot \\ \mathbf{H}_{M-1} & \mathbf{H}_{M-2} & \mathbf{H}_{M-3} & \cdots & \mathbf{H}_0 \end{bmatrix} \tag{5.1-25}$$

Each partition $\mathbf{H}_j$ is constructed from the jth row of the extended function $h_e(x, y)$, as follows:

$$\mathbf{H}_j = \begin{bmatrix} h_e(j, 0) & h_e(j, N-1) & h_e(j, N-2) & \cdots & h_e(j, 1) \\ h_e(j, 1) & h_e(j, 0) & h_e(j, N-1) & \cdots & h_e(j, 2) \\ h_e(j, 2) & h_e(j, 1) & h_e(j, 0) & \cdots & h_e(j, 3) \\ \cdot \\ \cdot \\ \cdot \\ h_e(j, N-1) & h_e(j, N-2) & h_e(j, N-3) & \cdots & h_e(j, 0) \end{bmatrix} \tag{5.1-26}$$

where, as in Eq. (5.1-21), use was made of the periodicity of $h_e(x, y)$. It is noted that $\mathbf{H}_j$ is a circulant matrix and that the blocks of **H** are also subscripted in a circular manner. For these reasons, the matrix **H** given in Eq. (5.1-25) is often called a *block-circulant* matrix.

Most of the discussion in the following sections is centered around the discrete degradation model given in Eq. (5.1-24). It is important to keep in mind that this expression was derived under the assumption of a linear, space-invariant degradation process. As indicated earlier, the objective is to estimate the ideal image $f(x, y)$, given $g(x, y)$, and a knowledge of $h(x, y)$ and $\eta(x, y)$. In terms of Eq. (5.1-24), this means that we are interested in estimating **f**, given **g** and some knowledge about **H** and **n**.

Although Eq. (5.1-24) seems deceptively simple, a direct solution of this expression to obtain the elements of **f** is a monumental processing task for images of practical size. If, for example, $M = N = 512$, we have that **H** is of size $262,144 \times$

262,144. Thus to obtain **f** directly would require the solution of a system of 262,144 simultaneous linear equations. Fortunately, the complexity of this problem can be reduced considerably by taking advantage of the circulant properties of **H**, as shown in the following section.

5.2 DIAGONALIZATION OF CIRCULANT AND BLOCK-CIRCULANT MATRICES

We show in this section that solutions that are computationally feasible may be obtained from the model given in Eq. (5.1-24) by diagonalizing the **H** matrix. In order to simplify the explanation we begin the discussion by considering circulant matrices; the procedure is then extended to block-circulant matrices.

5.2.1 Circulant Matrices

Consider an $M \times M$ circulant matrix **H** of the form

$$\mathbf{H} = \begin{bmatrix} h_e(0) & h_e(M-1) & h_e(M-2) & \cdots & h_e(1) \\ h_e(1) & h_e(0) & h_e(M-1) & \cdots & h_e(2) \\ h_e(2) & h_e(1) & h_e(0) & \cdots & h_e(3) \\ \vdots & & & & \\ h_e(M-1) & h_e(M-2) & h_e(M-3) & \cdots & h_e(0) \end{bmatrix} \quad (5.2\text{-}1)$$

Let us define a scalar function $\lambda(k)$ and a vector $\mathbf{w}(k)$ as follows:

$$\lambda(k) = h_e(0) + h_e(M-1) \exp\left[j\frac{2\pi}{M}k\right] + h_e(M-2)\exp\left[j\frac{2\pi}{M}2k\right]$$

$$+ \cdots + h_e(1)\exp\left[j\frac{2\pi}{M}(M-1)k\right], \quad (5.2\text{-}2)$$

where $j = \sqrt{-1}$, and

$$\mathbf{w}(k) = \begin{bmatrix} 1 \\ \exp\left[j\dfrac{2\pi}{M}k\right] \\ \exp\left[j\dfrac{2\pi}{M}2k\right] \\ \vdots \\ \exp\left[j\dfrac{2\pi}{M}(M-1)k\right] \end{bmatrix} \quad (5.2\text{-}3)$$

for $k = 0, 1, 2, \ldots, M - 1$. It can be shown by matrix multiplication that

$$\mathbf{H}\mathbf{w}(k) = \lambda(k)\mathbf{w}(k). \qquad (5.2\text{-}4)$$

This expression indicates that $\mathbf{w}(k)$ is an eigenvector of the circulant matrix $\mathbf{H}$ and $\lambda(k)$ is its corresponding eigenvalue.

Suppose that we form an $M \times M$ matrix $\mathbf{W}$ by using the M eigenvectors of $\mathbf{H}$ as columns; that is,

$$\mathbf{W} = [\mathbf{w}(0) \quad \mathbf{w}(1) \quad \mathbf{w}(2) \cdot \cdot \cdot \mathbf{w}(M - 1)]. \qquad (5.2\text{-}5)$$

The kith element of $\mathbf{W}$, denoted as $W(k, i)$ is given by

$$W(k, i) = \exp\left[j \frac{2\pi}{M} ki \right] \qquad (5.2\text{-}6)$$

for $k, i = 0, 1, 2, \ldots, M - 1$. Due to the orthogonality properties of the complex exponential, the inverse matrix, $\mathbf{W}^{-1}$, can be written by inspection; its kith element symbolized as $W^{-1}(k, i)$, is given by

$$W^{-1}(k, i) = \frac{1}{M} \exp\left[-j \frac{2\pi}{M} ki \right]. \qquad (5.2\text{-}7)$$

It can be verified by using Eqs. (5.2-6) and (5.2-7) that

$$\mathbf{W}\mathbf{W}^{-1} = \mathbf{W}^{-1}\mathbf{W} = \mathbf{I}, \qquad (5.2\text{-}8)$$

where $\mathbf{I}$ is the $M \times M$ identity matrix.

The importance of the existence of the inverse matrix $\mathbf{W}^{-1}$ is that it guarantees that the columns of $\mathbf{W}$ (i.e., the eigenvectors of $\mathbf{H}$) are *linearly independent*. It then follows from elementary matrix theory (Noble [1969]) that $\mathbf{H}$ may be expressed in the form

$$\mathbf{H} = \mathbf{W}\mathbf{D}\mathbf{W}^{-1} \qquad (5.2\text{-}9)$$

or, using Eq. (5.2-8),

$$\mathbf{D} = \mathbf{W}^{-1}\mathbf{H}\mathbf{W}, \qquad (5.2\text{-}10)$$

where $\mathbf{D}$ is a diagonal matrix whose elements $D(k, k)$ are the eigenvalues of $\mathbf{H}$; that is,

$$D(k, k) = \lambda(k). \qquad (5.2\text{-}11)$$

Equation (5.2-10) indicates that $\mathbf{H}$ is diagonalized by using $\mathbf{W}^{-1}$ and $\mathbf{W}$ in the order indicated.

5.2.2 Block-Circulant Matrices

The transformation matrix for diagonalizing block circulants is constructed as follows.

Let

$$w_M(i, m) = \exp\left[j \frac{2\pi}{M} im\right] \tag{5.2-12}$$

and

$$w_N(k, n) = \exp\left[j \frac{2\pi}{N} kn\right]. \tag{5.2-13}$$

Based on this notation, we define a matrix $\mathbf{W}$ that is of size $MN \times MN$, and contains M^2 partitions of size $N \times N$. The imth partition of $\mathbf{W}$ is defined as

$$\mathbf{W}(i, m) = w_M(i, m)\mathbf{W}_N \tag{5.2-14}$$

for $i, m = 0, 1, 2, \ldots, M - 1$. $\mathbf{W}_N$ is an $N \times N$ matrix with elements

$$W_N(k, n) = w_N(k, n) \tag{5.2-15}$$

for $k, n = 0, 1, 2, \ldots, N - 1$.

The inverse matrix $\mathbf{W}^{-1}$ is also of size $MN \times MN$ with M^2 partitions of size $N \times N$. The imth partition of $\mathbf{W}^{-1}$, symbolized as $\mathbf{W}^{-1}(i, m)$, is defined as

$$\mathbf{W}^{-1}(i, m) = \frac{1}{M} w_M^{-1}(i, m)\mathbf{W}_N^{-1}, \tag{5.2-16}$$

where $w_M^{-1}(i, m)$ is given by

$$w_M^{-1}(i, m) = \exp\left[-j \frac{2\pi}{M} im\right] \tag{5.2-17}$$

for $i, m = 0, 1, 2, \ldots, M - 1$. The matrix $\mathbf{W}_N^{-1}$ has elements

$$W_N^{-1}(k, n) = \frac{1}{N} w_N^{-1}(k, n), \tag{5.2-18}$$

where

$$w_N^{-1}(k, n) = \exp\left[-j \frac{2\pi}{N} kn\right] \tag{5.2-19}$$

for $k, n = 0, 1, 2, \ldots, N - 1$. It can be verified by direct substitution of the above elements of $\mathbf{W}$ and $\mathbf{W}^{-1}$ that

$$\mathbf{W}\mathbf{W}^{-1} - \mathbf{W}^{-1}\mathbf{W} = \mathbf{I}, \tag{5.2-20}$$

where $\mathbf{I}$ is the $MN \times MN$ identity matrix.

By making use of the results in the previous section it can be shown (Hunt [1973]) that if $\mathbf{H}$ is a block-circulant matrix, it can be written as

$$\mathbf{H} = \mathbf{W}\mathbf{D}\mathbf{W}^{-1} \tag{5.2-21}$$

or

$$D = W^{-1}HW, \tag{5.2-22}$$

where **D** is a diagonal matrix whose elements $D(k, k)$ are related to the discrete Fourier transform of the extended function $h_e(x, y)$ given in Section 5.1.3. It can also be shown that the transpose of **H**, denoted by **H'**, is given by

$$H' = WD^*W^{-1}, \tag{5.2-23}$$

where D^* is the complex conjugate of **D**.

5.2.3 Effects of Diagonalization on the Degradation Model

Since the matrix **H** in the discrete, one-dimensional model of Eq. (5.1-17) is circulant, it may be expressed in the form of Eq. (5.2-9). Equation (5.1-17) then becomes

$$g = WDW^{-1}f. \tag{5.2-24}$$

Rearranging this equation, we have

$$W^{-1}g = DW^{-1}f. \tag{5.2-25}$$

The product $W^{-1}f$ is an M-dimensional column vector. From Eq. (5.2-7) and the definition of **f** given in Section 5.1.3, we have that the kth element of the product $W^{-1}f$, which we denote by $F(k)$, is given by

$$F(k) = \frac{1}{M} \sum_{i=0}^{M-1} f_e(i) \exp\left[-j\frac{2\pi}{M} ki \right] \tag{5.2-26}$$

for $k = 0, 1, 2, \ldots, M - 1$. This expression is recognized as the discrete Fourier transform of the extended sequence $f_e(x)$. In other words, multiplication of **f** by W^{-1} yields a vector whose elements are the Fourier transforms of the elements of **f**. Similarly, $W^{-1}g$ yields the Fourier transform of the elements of **g**, denoted by $G(k)$, $k = 0, 1, 2, \ldots, M - 1$.

Next, we examine the matrix **D** in Eq. (5.2-25). From the discussion in Section 5.2.1 we know that the main-diagonal elements of **D** are the eigenvalues of the circulant matrix **H**. The eigenvalues are given in Eq. (5.2-2), which, using the fact that

$$\exp\left[j\frac{2\pi}{M} (M - i)k \right] = \exp\left[-j\frac{2\pi}{M} ik \right], \tag{5.2-27}$$

may be written in the form

$$\lambda(k) = h_e(0) + h_e(1) \exp\left[-j\frac{2\pi}{M} k \right] + h_e(2) \exp\left[-j\frac{2\pi}{M} 2k \right]$$
$$+ \cdots + h_e(M - 1) \exp\left[-j\frac{2\pi}{M} (M - 1)k \right]. \tag{5.2-28}$$

From Eqs. (5.2-11) and (5.2-28) we have

$$D(k, k) = \lambda(k) = \sum_{i=0}^{M-1} h_e(i) \exp\left[-j\frac{2\pi}{M}ki\right] \qquad (5.2\text{-}29)$$

for $k = 0, 1, 2, \ldots , M - 1$. The right side of this equation is recognized as $MH(k)$, where $H(k)$ is the discrete Fourier transform of the extended sequence $h_e(x)$. Thus

$$D(k, k) = MH(k). \qquad (5.2\text{-}30)$$

We can combine these transforms into one result. Since $\mathbf{D}$ is a diagonal matrix, the product of $\mathbf{D}$ with any vector multiplies each element of that vector by a single diagonal element of $\mathbf{D}$. Consequently, the matrix formulation given in Eq. (5.2-25) can be reduced to a term-by-term product of one-dimensional Fourier transform sequences. In other words,

$$G(k) = MH(k)F(k) \qquad (5.2\text{-}31)$$

for $k = 0, 1, 2, \ldots , M - 1$, where $G(k)$ are the elements of the vector $\mathbf{W}^{-1}\mathbf{g}$ and $MH(k)F(k)$ the elements of vector $\mathbf{DW}^{-1}\mathbf{f}$. The right side of Eq. (5.2-31) is recognized as the convolution of $f_e(x)$ and $h_e(x)$ in the frequency domain (see Section 3.3.8). From a computational point of view, this result implies considerable simplification because $G(k)$, $H(k)$, and $F(k)$ are M-sample discrete transforms, which can be obtained by using a fast Fourier transform algorithm.

A procedure similar to the above development yields equivalent results for the two-dimensional degradation model. Multiplying both sides of Eq. (5.1-24) by $\mathbf{W}^{-1}$, and using Eqs. (5.2-20) and (5.2-21), yields

$$\mathbf{W}^{-1}\mathbf{g} = \mathbf{DW}^{-1}\mathbf{f} + \mathbf{W}^{-1}\mathbf{n}, \qquad (5.2\text{-}32)$$

where $\mathbf{W}^{-1}$ is an $MN \times MN$ matrix whose elements are given in Eq. (5.2-16), $\mathbf{D}$ is an $MN \times MN$ diagonal matrix, $\mathbf{H}$ is the $MN \times MN$ block-circulant matrix defined in Eq. (5.1-25), and $\mathbf{f}$ and $\mathbf{g}$ are vectors of dimension MN formed by stacking the rows of the extended images $f_e(x, y)$ and $g_e(x, y)$.

The left side of Eq. (5.2-32) is a vector of dimension $MN \times 1$. Let us denote its elements by $G(0, 0)$, $G(0, 1)$, $\ldots$, $G(0, N - 1)$; $G(1, 0)$, $G(1, 1)$, $\ldots$, $G(1, N - 1)$; $\ldots$; $G(M - 1, 0)$, $G(M - 1, 1)$, $\ldots$, $G(M - 1, N - 1)$. It can be shown (Hunt [1973]) that

$$G(u, v) = \frac{1}{MN} \sum_{x=0}^{M-1} \sum_{y=0}^{N-1} g_e(x, y) \exp[-j2\pi(ux/M + vy/N)] \qquad (5.2\text{-}33)$$

for $u = 0, 1, 2, \ldots , M - 1$, and $v = 0, 1, 2, \ldots , N - 1$. This expression is recognized as the two-dimensional Fourier transform of $g_e(x, y)$. In other words, the elements of $\mathbf{W}^{-1}\mathbf{g}$ correspond to the stacked rows of the Fourier transform matrix with elements $G(u, v)$, for $u = 0, 1, 2, \ldots , M - 1$, and $v = 0, 1, 2,$

. . . , $N - 1$. Similarly, we have that the vectors $\mathbf{W}^{-1}\mathbf{f}$ and $\mathbf{W}^{-1}\mathbf{n}$ are MN-dimensional and contain elements $F(u, v)$ and $N(u, v)$, where

$$F(u, v) = \frac{1}{MN} \sum_{x=0}^{M-1} \sum_{y=0}^{N-1} f_e(x, y) \exp[-j2\pi(ux/M + vy/N)] \qquad (5.2\text{-}34)$$

and

$$N(u, v) = \frac{1}{MN} \sum_{x=0}^{M-1} \sum_{y=0}^{N-1} \eta_e(x, y) \exp[-j2\pi(ux/M + vy/N)] \qquad (5.2\text{-}35)$$

for $u = 0, 1, 2, \ldots, M - 1$ and $v = 0, 1, 2, \ldots, N - 1$.

Finally, we have that the elements of the diagonal matrix $\mathbf{D}$ are related to the Fourier transform of the extended impulse response function $h_e(x, y)$; that is,

$$H(u, v) = \frac{1}{MN} \sum_{x=0}^{M-1} \sum_{y=0}^{N-1} h_e(x, y) \exp[-j2\pi(ux/M + vy/N)] \qquad (5.2\text{-}36)$$

for $u = 0, 1, 2, \ldots, M - 1$, and $v = 0, 1, 2, \ldots, N - 1$. The MN diagonal elements of $\mathbf{D}$ are formed as follows. The first N elements are $H(0, 0)$, $H(0, 1), \ldots, H(0, N - 1)$; the next, $H(1, 0), H(1, 1), \ldots, H(1, N - 1)$; and so forth, with the last N diagonal elements being $H(M - 1, 0), H(M - 1, 1), \ldots, H(M - 1, N - 1)$. The off-diagonal elements are, of course, zero. The entire matrix formed from the above elements is then multiplied by MN to obtain $\mathbf{D}$. A more concise way of expressing this construction is the following:

$$D(k, i) = \begin{cases} MNH\left(\left[\dfrac{k}{N}\right], k \bmod N\right) & \text{if } i = k \\ 0 & \text{if } i \neq k, \end{cases} \qquad (5.2\text{-}37)$$

where $[p]$ is used to denote the greatest integer not exceeding p, and $k \bmod N$ is the remainder obtained by dividing k by N.

By using Eqs. (5.2-33) through (5.2-36) it is not difficult to show that the individual elements of Eq. (5.2-32) are related by the expression

$$G(u, v) = MNH(u, v)F(u, v) + N(u, v) \qquad (5.2\text{-}38)$$

for $u = 0, 1, 2, \ldots, M - 1$, and $v = 0, 1, 2, \ldots, N - 1$.

Since the term MN is simply a scale factor, it will be convenient for notational purposes to absorb it in $H(u, v)$. With this assumption, Eqs. (5.2-37) and (5.2-38) may be expressed as

$$D(k, i) = \begin{cases} H\left(\left[\dfrac{k}{N}\right], k \bmod N\right) & \text{if } i = k \\ 0 & \text{if } i \neq k \end{cases} \qquad (5.2\text{-}39)$$

for k, $i = 0, 1, 2, \ldots, MN - 1$, and

$$G(u, v) = H(u, v)F(u, v) + N(u, v) \tag{5.2-40}$$

for $u = 0, 1, 2, \ldots, M - 1$, and $v = 0, 1, 2, \ldots, N - 1$, where it is understood that $H(u, v)$ is now scaled by the factor MN.

The significance of Eq. (5.2-38) or (5.2-40) is that the large system of equations implicit in the model given in Eq. (5.1-24) can be reduced to computation of a few discrete Fourier transforms of size $M \times N$. For $M = N = 512$, for example, this is a simple problem if we use an FFT algorithm. As mentioned earlier, however, the problem becomes almost an infeasible computational task if approached directly from the model given in Eq. (5.1-24).

The model given in Eq. (5.1-24) will be used in the following sections as the basis for deriving several image-restoration approaches. The results, given in matrix form, will then be simplified by using the concepts derived in this section. The reader should keep in mind that the simplifications achieved above are the result of assuming that (1) the degradation is a linear, space-invariant process, and (2) all images are treated as extended, periodic functions.

Before leaving this section, it is important to note that Eq. (5.2-40) could have been written directly from Eq. (5.1-15) via the convolution theorem. However, our objective was to show that the same result could be achieved by a matrix formulation. In so doing, we established a number of important matrix properties that are used in the following section to develop a unified approach to restoration.

5.3 ALGEBRAIC APPROACH TO RESTORATION

As indicated in Section 5.1.3, the objective of image restoration is to estimate an original image $\mathbf{f}$, given a degraded image $\mathbf{g}$ and some knowledge or assumption about $\mathbf{H}$ and $\mathbf{n}$. By assuming that these quantities are related according to the model given in Eq. (5.1-24), it is possible to formulate a class of image-restoration problems in a unified linear algebraic framework.

Central to the algebraic approach is the concept of seeking an estimate of $\mathbf{f}$, denoted by $\hat{\mathbf{f}}$, which minimizes a predefined criterion of performance. Because of their simplicity, we focus attention in this chapter on least-squares criterion functions. As will be seen in the following sections, this choice has the added advantage of yielding a central approach for the derivation of several well-known restoration methods. These methods are the result of considering either an unconstrained or a constrained approach to the least-squares restoration problem.

5.3.1 Unconstrained Restoration

From Eq. (5.1-24), the noise term in the degradation model is given by

$$\mathbf{n} = \mathbf{g} - \mathbf{H}\mathbf{f}. \tag{5.3-1}$$

In the absence of any knowledge about $\mathbf{n}$, a meaningful criterion function is to seek an $\hat{\mathbf{f}}$ such that $\mathbf{H}\hat{\mathbf{f}}$ approximates $\mathbf{g}$ in a least-squares sense by assuming that the norm of the noise term is as small as possible. In other words, we wish to find an $\hat{\mathbf{f}}$ such that

$$\|\mathbf{n}\|^2 = \|\mathbf{g} - \mathbf{H}\hat{\mathbf{f}}\|^2 \tag{5.3-2}$$

is minimum, where, by definition, $\|\mathbf{n}\|^2 = \mathbf{n}'\mathbf{n}$, and $\|\mathbf{g} - \mathbf{H}\hat{\mathbf{f}}\|^2 = (\mathbf{g} - \mathbf{H}\hat{\mathbf{f}})'$ $(\mathbf{g} - \mathbf{H}\hat{\mathbf{f}})$ are the squared norms of $\mathbf{n}$ and $(\mathbf{g} - \mathbf{H}\hat{\mathbf{f}})$, respectively. From Eq. (5.3-2), we may equivalently view this problem as one of minimizing the criterion function

$$J(\hat{\mathbf{f}}) = \|\mathbf{g} - \mathbf{H}\hat{\mathbf{f}}\|^2 \tag{5.3-3}$$

with respect to $\hat{\mathbf{f}}$. Aside from the requirement that it minimize Eq. (5.3-3), $\hat{\mathbf{f}}$ is not constrained in any other way.

Minimization of Eq. (5.3-3) is straightforward. We simply differentiate J with respect to $\hat{\mathbf{f}}$, and set the result equal to the zero vector; that is,

$$\frac{\partial J(\hat{\mathbf{f}})}{\partial \hat{\mathbf{f}}} = 0 = -2\mathbf{H}'(\mathbf{g} - \mathbf{H}\hat{\mathbf{f}}). \tag{5.3-4}$$

Solving Eq. (5.3-4) for $\hat{\mathbf{f}}$ yields

$$\hat{\mathbf{f}} = (\mathbf{H}'\mathbf{H})^{-1}\mathbf{H}'\mathbf{g}. \tag{5.3-5}$$

By letting $M = N$ so that $\mathbf{H}$ is a square matrix, and assuming that $\mathbf{H}^{-1}$ exists, Eq. (5.3-5) reduces to

$$\begin{aligned}\hat{\mathbf{f}} &= \mathbf{H}^{-1}(\mathbf{H}')^{-1}\mathbf{H}'\mathbf{g} \\ &= \mathbf{H}^{-1}\mathbf{g}.\end{aligned} \tag{5.3-6}$$

5.3.2 Constrained Restoration

Let $\mathbf{Q}$ be a linear operator on $\mathbf{f}$. ·In this section, we consider the least-squares restoration problem as one of minimizing functions of the form $\|\mathbf{Q}\hat{\mathbf{f}}\|^2$, subject to the constraint $\|\mathbf{g} - \mathbf{H}\hat{\mathbf{f}}\|^2 = \|\mathbf{n}\|^2$. This approach introduces considerable flexibility in the restoration process because it yields different solutions for different choices of $\mathbf{Q}$. It is noted that the constraint imposed on a solution is consistent with the model of Eq. (5.1-24).

The addition of an equality constraint in the minimization problem can be handled without difficulty by using the method of *Lagrange multipliers* (Elsgolc [1961]). The procedure is to express the constraint in the form $\alpha(\|\mathbf{g} - \mathbf{H}\hat{\mathbf{f}}\|^2 - \|\mathbf{n}\|^2)$ and then append it to the function $\|\mathbf{Q}\hat{\mathbf{f}}\|^2$. In other words, we seek an $\hat{\mathbf{f}}$ that minimizes the criterion function

$$J(\hat{\mathbf{f}}) = \|\mathbf{Q}\hat{\mathbf{f}}\|^2 + \alpha(\|\mathbf{g} - \mathbf{H}\hat{\mathbf{f}}\|^2 - \|\mathbf{n}\|^2), \tag{5.3-7}$$

where α is a constant called the *Lagrange multiplier*. Once the constraint has been appended, minimization is carried out in the usual way.

Differentiating Eq. (5.3-7) with respect to $\hat{\mathbf{f}}$ and setting the result equal to the zero vector yields

$$\frac{\partial J(\hat{\mathbf{f}})}{\partial \hat{\mathbf{f}}} = 0 = 2\mathbf{Q}'\mathbf{Q}\hat{\mathbf{f}} - 2\alpha\,\mathbf{H}'(\mathbf{g} - \mathbf{H}\hat{\mathbf{f}}). \qquad (5.3\text{-}8)$$

The solution is obtained by solving Eq. (5.3-8) for $\hat{\mathbf{f}}$; that is,

$$\hat{\mathbf{f}} = (\mathbf{H}'\mathbf{H} + \gamma\mathbf{Q}'\mathbf{Q})^{-1}\mathbf{H}'\mathbf{g}, \qquad (5.3\text{-}9)$$

where $\gamma = 1/\alpha$. This quantity must be adjusted so that the constraint is satisfied, a problem considered later in this chapter. Equations (5.3-6) and (5.3-9) are the basis for all the restoration procedures discussed in the following sections. It is shown in Section 5.4, for example, that Eq. (5.3-6) leads to the traditional inverse-filter restoration method. Similarly, the general formulation given in Eq. (5.3-9) can be used to derive results such as the classical Wiener filter, as well as other restoration techniques, simply by selecting an appropriate transformation matrix $\mathbf{Q}$ and using the simplifications derived in Section 5.2.

5.4 INVERSE FILTERING

5.4.1 Formulation

We begin the derivation of image-restoration techniques by considering the unconstrained result given in Eq. (5.3-6), which, assuming that $M = N$ and using Eq. (5.2-21), may be expressed in the form

$$\begin{aligned}\hat{\mathbf{f}} &= \mathbf{H}^{-1}\mathbf{g} \\ &= (\mathbf{W}\mathbf{D}\mathbf{W}^{-1})^{-1}\mathbf{g} \qquad (5.4\text{-}1) \\ &= \mathbf{W}\mathbf{D}^{-1}\mathbf{W}^{-1}\mathbf{g}.\end{aligned}$$

Premultiplying both sides of Eq. (5.4-1) by $\mathbf{W}^{-1}$ yields

$$\mathbf{W}^{-1}\hat{\mathbf{f}} = \mathbf{D}^{-1}\mathbf{W}^{-1}\mathbf{g}. \qquad (5.4\text{-}2)$$

It then follows from the discussion in Section 5.2.3 that the elements composing Eq. (5.4-2) may be written in the form

$$\hat{F}(u, v) = \frac{G(u, v)}{H(u, v)} \qquad (5.4\text{-}3)$$

for $u, v = 0, 1, 2, \ldots, N - 1$. According to Eq. (5.2-39), $H(u, v)$ is assumed to be scaled by N^2 and use has been made of the fact that $\mathbf{D}$ is a diagonal matrix, thus allowing a straightforward procedure for obtaining $\mathbf{D}^{-1}$.

The image-restoration approach given by Eq. (5.4-3) is commonly referred to as the *inverse filter* method. This terminology arises from considering $H(u, v)$ as a "filter" function that multiplies $F(u, v)$ to produce the transform of the degraded image $g_e(x, y)$. The division of $G(u, v)$ by $H(u, v)$ indicated in Eq. (5.4-3) then constitutes an inverse filtering operation in this context. The restored image is, of course, obtained by using the relation

$$\hat{f}(x, y) = \mathfrak{F}^{-1}[\hat{F}(u, v)]$$
$$= \mathfrak{F}^{-1}[G(u, v)/H(u, v)] \qquad (5.4\text{-}4)$$

for $x, y = 0, 1, 2, \ldots, N - 1$. This procedure is normally implemented by means of an FFT algorithm.

Equation (5.4-4) points out that computational difficulties will be encountered in the restoration process if $H(u, v)$ vanishes or becomes very small in any region of interest in the uv plane. If the zeros of $H(u, v)$ are located at a few known points in the uv plane, they can generally be neglected when computing $\hat{F}(u, v)$ without noticeably affecting the restored result.

A more serious difficulty arises in the presence of noise. Substitution of Eq. (5.2-40) into Eq. (5.4-3) yields

$$\hat{F}(u, v) = F(u, v) + \frac{N(u, v)}{H(u, v)}. \qquad (5.4\text{-}5)$$

This expression clearly indicates that if $H(u, v)$ is zero or becomes very small, the term $N(u, v)/H(u, v)$ could dominate the restoration result $\mathfrak{F}^{-1}[\hat{F}(u, v)]$. In practice one often finds that $H(u, v)$ drops off rapidly as a function of distance from the origin of the uv plane. The noise term, on the other hand, usually falls off at a much slower rate. In situations like this, reasonable results can often be obtained by carrying out the restoration in a limited neighborhood about the origin in order to avoid small values of $H(u, v)$. An example of this approach is given below.

Example: Figure 5.2(a) shows a point image $f(x, y)$ and Fig. 5.2(b) is a degraded image $g(x, y)$ obtained by blurring $f(x, y)$. If we consider the point source to be an

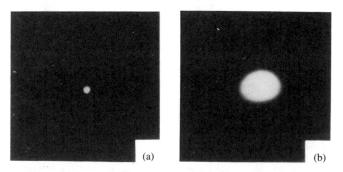

(a)   (b)

Figure 5.2   Blurring of a point source to obtain $H(u, v)$.

approximation to a unit impulse function, then it follows that

$$G(u, v) = H(u, v)F(u, v)$$
$$\approx H(u, v),$$

since $\mathscr{F}[\delta(x - x_0, y - y_0)] = 1$. This expression indicates that the transfer function $H(u, v)$ can be approximated by the Fourier transform of the degraded image. The procedure of blurring a known function to obtain an approximation to $H(u, v)$ is a useful one in practice because it can often be used in a trial-and-error mode to restore images for which the blurring function $H(u, v)$ is not known a priori.

The result of applying the same blurring function as above to the ideal image shown in Fig. 5.3(a) is shown in Fig. 5.3(b). The restored image shown in Fig. 5.3(c) was obtained by using Eq. (5.4-4) for values of u and v near enough to the origin of the uv plane to avoid excessively small values of $H(u, v)$. The result of

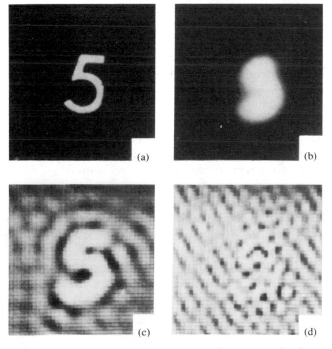

Figure 5.3 Example of image restoration by inverse filtering.
(a) Original image $f(x, y)$. (b) Degraded (blurred) image $g(x, y)$.
(c) Result of restoration by considering a neighborhood about
the origin of the uv plane that does not include excessively
small values of $H(u, v)$. (d) Result of using a larger neighborhood
in which this condition does not hold. (From McGlamery [1967].)

carrying out the restoration for a larger neighborhood is shown in Fig. 5.3(d). These results clearly point out the difficulties introduced by a vanishing function $H(u, v)$.

□

Before leaving this section, it is of interest to note that if $H(u, v)$, $G(u, v)$, and $N(u, v)$ are all known, an exact inverse filtering expression can be obtained directly from Eq. (5.2-40); that is,

$$F(u, v) = \frac{G(u, v)}{H(u, v)} - \frac{N(u, v)}{H(u, v)}. \tag{5.4-6}$$

The problem with this formulation, of course, is that the noise is seldom known well enough to allow computation of $N(u, v)$.

5.4.2 Removal of Blur Caused by Uniform Linear Motion

There are practical applications in which $H(u, v)$ can be obtained analytically, but the solution has zero values in the frequency range of interest. An example of the difficulties caused by a vanishing $H(u, v)$ was given in the previous section. In the following discussion we consider the problem of restoring an image that has been blurred by uniform linear motion. We have singled out this problem because of its practical implications, and also because it lends itself well to an analytical formulation. Solution of the uniform-blurring case also demonstrates how zeros of $H(u, v)$ can be handled computationally. These considerations are important because they often arise in practice in other contexts of image restoration by inverse filtering.

Suppose that an image $f(x, y)$ undergoes planar motion, and let $x_0(t)$ and $y_0(t)$ be the time-varying components of motion in the x and y directions, respectively. The total exposure at any point of the recording medium (e.g., film) is obtained in this case by integrating the instantaneous exposure over the time interval during which the shutter is open. To isolate the effect of image motion, it is assumed that shutter opening and closing takes place instantaneously, and that the optical imaging process is perfect. Then, if T is the duration of the exposure, we have

$$g(x, y) = \int_0^T f[x - x_0(t), y - y_0(t)]\, dt, \tag{5.4-7}$$

where $g(x, y)$ is the blurred image.

From Eq. (3.1-9), the Fourier transform of Eq. (5.4-7) is given by

$$G(u, v) = \int\!\!\!\int_{-\infty}^{\infty} g(x, y) \exp[-j2\pi(ux + vy)]\, dx\, dy$$

$$= \int\!\!\!\int_{-\infty}^{\infty} \left[\int_0^T f[x - x_0(t), y - y_0(t)]\, dt \right] \exp[-j2\pi(ux + vy)]\, dx\, dy. \tag{5.4-8}$$

If we assume that the order of integration can be reversed, then Eq. (5.4-8) can be expressed in the form

$$G(u, v) = \int_0^T \left[\int\!\!\int_{-\infty}^{\infty} f[x - x_0(t), y - y_0(t)] \exp[-j2\pi(ux + vy)] \, dxdy \right] dt. \quad (5.4-9)$$

The term inside the outer brackets is recognized as the Fourier transform of the displaced function $f[x - x_0(t), y - y_0(t)]$. By using Eq. (3.3-7b) we then have the relation

$$G(u, v) = \int_0^T F(u, v) \exp[-j2\pi(ux_0(t) + vy_0(t))] \, dt$$

$$= F(u, v) \int_0^T \exp[-j2\pi(ux_0(t) + vy_0(t))] \, dt, \quad (5.4-10)$$

where the last step follows from the fact that $F(u, v)$ is independent of t.
    By defining

$$H(u, v) = \int_0^T \exp[-j2\pi(ux_0(t) + vy_0(t))] \, dt, \quad (5.4-11)$$

Eq. (5.4-10) may be expressed in the familiar form

$$G(u, v) = H(u, v)F(u, v). \quad (5.4-12)$$

If the nature of the motion variables $x_0(t)$ and $y_0(t)$ is known, the transfer function $H(u, v)$ can be obtained directly from Eq. (5.4-11). As an illustration, suppose that the image in question undergoes uniform linear motion in the x direction only, at a rate given by $x_0(t) = at/T$. When $t = T$, we see that the image has been displaced by a total distance a. With $y_0(t) = 0$, Eq. (5.4-11) yields

$$H(u, v) = \int_0^T \exp[-j2\pi ux_0(t)] \, dt$$

$$= \int_0^T \exp[-j2\pi uat/T] \, dt \quad (5.4-13)$$

$$= \frac{T}{\pi ua} \sin(\pi ua) \, e^{-j\pi ua}.$$

It is evident that H vanishes at values of u given by $u = n/a$, where n is an integer.
    When $f(x, y)$ is zero (or known) outside an interval $0 \leqslant x \leqslant L$, it is possible to avoid the problem presented by Eq. (5.4-13) and reconstruct the image completely

from a knowledge of $g(x, y)$ in this interval. Since y is time invariant, let us suppress this variable temporarily and write Eq. (5.4-7) as

$$g(x) = \int_0^T f[x - x_0(t)] \, dt$$

$$= \int_0^T f(x - at/T) \, dt \qquad 0 \leq x \leq L. \tag{5.4-14}$$

Substitution $\tau = x - at/T$ in this expression and ignoring a scale factor yields

$$g(x) = \int_{x-a}^x f(\tau) \, d\tau \qquad 0 \leq x \leq L. \tag{5.4-15}$$

Then, by differentiation,

$$g'(x) = f(x) - f(x - a) \qquad 0 \leq x \leq L \tag{5.4-16}$$

or

$$f(x) = g'(x) + f(x - a) \qquad 0 \leq x \leq L. \tag{5.4-17}$$

It will be convenient in the following development to assume that $L = Ka$, where K is an integer. Then the variable x may be expressed in the form

$$x = z + ma, \tag{5.4-18}$$

where z assumes values in the interval $[0, a]$ and m is the integral part of (x/a). For example, if $a = 2$ and $x = 3.5$, then $m = 1$ (the integral part of 3.5/2), and $z = 1.5$. Clearly, $z + ma = 3.5$, as required. Note also that, for $L = Ka$, the index m can assume any of the integer values $0, 1, \ldots, K - 1$. For instance, when $x = L$, we have that $z = a$ and $m = K - 1$.

Substitution of Eq. (5.4-18) into Eq. (5.4-17) yields the expression

$$f(z + ma) = g'(z + ma) + f[z + (m - 1)a]. \tag{5.4-19}$$

Next, let us denote by $\phi(z)$ the portion of the scene that moves into the range $0 \leq z < a$ during exposure; that is,

$$\phi(z) = f(z - a) \qquad 0 \leq z < a. \tag{5.4-20}$$

Equation (5.4-19) can be solved recursively in terms of $\phi(z)$. Thus for $m = 0$, we have

$$\begin{aligned} f(z) &= g'(z) + f(z - a) \\ &= g'(z) + \phi(z). \end{aligned} \tag{5.4-21}$$

For $m = 1$, Eq. (5.4-19) becomes

$$f(z + a) = g'(z + a) + f(z). \tag{5.4-22}$$

Substitution of Eq. (5.4-21) into Eq. (5.4-22) yields

$$f(z + a) = g'(z + a) + g'(z) + \phi(z). \qquad (5.4\text{-}23)$$

In the next step we let $m = 2$. This results in the expression

$$f(z + 2a) = g'(z + 2a) + f(z + a) \qquad (5.4\text{-}24)$$

or, substituting Eq. (5.4-23) for $f(z + a)$,

$$f(z + 2a) = g'(z + 2a) + g'(z + a) + g'(z) + \phi(z). \qquad (5.4\text{-}25)$$

It is evident that continuing with this procedure will yield the result

$$f(z + ma) = \sum_{k=0}^{m} g'(z + ka) + \phi(z). \qquad (5.4\text{-}26)$$

However, since $x = z + ma$, Eq. (5.4-26) may be expressed in the form

$$f(x) = \sum_{k=0}^{m} g'(x - ka) + \phi(x - ma) \qquad 0 \leqslant x \leqslant L. \qquad (5.4\text{-}27)$$

Since $g(x)$ is known, the problem is reduced to that of estimating $\phi(x)$.

One way to estimate this function directly from the blurred image is as follows. First we note that, as x varies from 0 to L, m ranges from 0 to $K - 1$. Since the argument of ϕ is $(x - ma)$, which is always in the range $0 \leqslant x - ma < a$, it follows that ϕ is repeated K times during the evaluation of $f(x)$ for $0 \leqslant x \leqslant L$. Next, we define

$$\tilde{f}(x) = \sum_{j=0}^{m} g'(x - ja) \qquad (5.4\text{-}28)$$

and rewrite Eq. (5.4-27) as

$$\phi(x - ma) = f(x) - \tilde{f}(x). \qquad (5.4\text{-}29)$$

If we evaluate the left and right sides of Eq. (5.4-29) for $ka \leqslant x < (k + 1)a$, and add the results for $k = 0, 1, \ldots, K - 1$, we obtain

$$K\phi(x) = \sum_{k=0}^{K-1} f(x + ka) - \sum_{k=0}^{K-1} \tilde{f}(x + ka) \qquad 0 \leqslant x < a, \qquad (5.4\text{-}30)$$

where $m - 0$, since $0 \leqslant x < a$. Dividing through by K yields

$$\phi(x) = \frac{1}{K} \sum_{k=0}^{K-1} f(x + ka) - \frac{1}{K} \sum_{k=0}^{K-1} \tilde{f}(x + ka). \qquad (5.4\text{-}31)$$

The first sum on the right side of this expression is, of course, unknown. However, it is evident that for large values of K it approaches the average value of f. Thus, this sum may be taken as a constant A and we have the approximation

$$\phi(x) \approx A - \frac{1}{K} \sum_{k=0}^{K-1} \tilde{f}(x + ka) \qquad 0 \leq x < a \tag{5.4-32}$$

or

$$\phi(x - ma) \approx A - \frac{1}{K} \sum_{k=0}^{K-1} \tilde{f}[x + ka - ma] \qquad 0 \leq x \leq L. \tag{5.4-33}$$

Substitution of Eq. (5.4-28) for $\tilde{f}$ yields†

$$\phi(x - ma) \approx A - \frac{1}{K} \sum_{k=0}^{K-1} \sum_{j=0}^{k} g'(x + ka - ma - ja)$$

$$\approx A - \frac{1}{K} \sum_{k=0}^{K-1} \sum_{j=0}^{k} g'(x - ma + (k - j)a). \tag{5.4-34}$$

From Eq. (5.4-29) we then have the final result

$$f(x) \approx A - \frac{1}{K} \sum_{k=0}^{K-1} \sum_{j=0}^{k} g'(x - ma + (k - j)a) + \sum_{j=0}^{m} g'(x - ja) \tag{5.4-35}$$

for $0 \leq x \leq L$. Reintroducing the suppressed variable y yields

$$f(x, y) \approx A - \frac{1}{K} \sum_{k=0}^{K-1} \sum_{j=0}^{k} g'(x - ma + (k - j)a, y) + \sum_{j=0}^{m} g'(x - ja, y)$$

$$\tag{5.4-36}$$

for $0 \leq x, y \leq L$. As before, it is assumed that $f(x, y)$ is a square image. Interchanging x and y in the right side of Eq. (5.4-36) would give the reconstruction of an image that moves only in the y direction during exposure. The above concepts can also be used to derive a deblurring expression that takes into account simultaneous uniform motion in both directions.

Example: The image shown in Fig. 5.4(a) was blurred by uniform linear motion in one direction during exposure, with the total distance traveled being approximately equal to one-eighth the width of the photograph. Figure 5.4(b) is the deblurred result obtained by using Eq. (5.4-36) with x and y interchanged since motion is in the y direction. It is noted that the error in the approximation given by this equation is certainly not objectionable. ☐

---

† Note that the limit on the second summation is k instead of m. If we had started from Eq. (5.4-18) with $x + ka - ma$ instead of x, the limit in the summation of Eq. (5.4-28) would have been k, since, from Eq. (5.4-18), $x + (ka - ma) = z + ma + (ka - ma) = z + ka$.

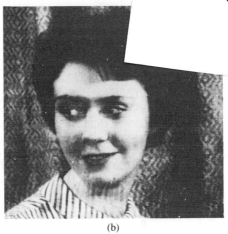

(a)   (b)

Figure 5.4   (a) Image blurred by uniform linear motion. (b) Image restored by using Eq. (5.4-36). (From Sondhi [1972].)

5.5   LEAST-MEAN-SQUARE (WIENER) FILTER

Let $\mathbf{R_f}$ and $\mathbf{R_n}$ be the correlation matrices of $\mathbf{f}$ and $\mathbf{n}$, defined respectively by the equations

$$\mathbf{R_f} = E\{\mathbf{ff'}\} \tag{5.5-1}$$

and

$$\mathbf{R_n} = E\{\mathbf{nn'}\}, \tag{5.5-2}$$

where $E\{\cdot\}$ denotes the expected value operation. The ijth element of $\mathbf{R_f}$ is given by $E\{f_i f_j\}$, which is the correlation between the ith and the jth elements of $\mathbf{f}$. Similarly, the ijth element of $\mathbf{R_n}$ gives the correlation between the two corresponding elements in $\mathbf{n}$. Since the elements of $\mathbf{f}$ and $\mathbf{n}$ are real, $E\{f_i f_j\} = E\{f_j f_i\}$, and $E\{n_i n_j\} = E\{n_j n_i\}$, it follows that $\mathbf{R_f}$ and $\mathbf{R_n}$ are real symmetric matrices. For most image functions the correlation between pixels (i.e., elements of $\mathbf{f}$ or $\mathbf{n}$) does not extend beyond a distance of 20 to 30 points in the image (see Section 6.4), so a typical correlation matrix will have a band of nonzero elements about the main diagonal and zeros in the right-upper and left-lower corner regions. Assuming that the correlation between any two pixels is a function of the distance between the pixels and not their position, it can be shown (Andrews and Hunt [1977]) that $\mathbf{R_f}$ and $\mathbf{R_n}$ can be made to approximate block-circulant matrices and therefore can be diagonalized by the matrix $\mathbf{W}$ using the procedure described in Section 5.2.2. Using $\mathbf{A}$ and $\mathbf{B}$ to denote matrices, we then have

$$\mathbf{R_f} = \mathbf{WAW}^{-1} \tag{5.5-3}$$

and

$$\mathbf{R_n} = \mathbf{WBW}^{-1}. \tag{5.5-4}$$

Just as the elements of the diagonal matrix $\mathbf{D}$ in the relation $\mathbf{H} = \mathbf{HDW}^{-1}$ were shown to correspond to the Fourier transform of the block elements of $\mathbf{H}$, it can be shown that the elements of $\mathbf{A}$ and $\mathbf{B}$ are the transforms of the correlation elements in $\mathbf{R_f}$ and $\mathbf{R_n}$, respectively. As indicated in Problem 3.3, the Fourier transform of these correlations is called the power spectrum (or *spectral density*) of $f_e(x, y)$ and $\eta_e(x, y)$, respectively, and will be denoted in the following discussion by $S_f(u, v)$ and $S_\eta(u, v)$.

By defining

$$\mathbf{Q'Q} = \mathbf{R_f}^{-1}\mathbf{R_n} \tag{5.5-5}$$

and substituting this expression in Eq. (5.3-9) we obtain

$$\hat{\mathbf{f}} = (\mathbf{H'H} + \gamma \mathbf{R_f}^{-1}\mathbf{R_n})^{-1}\mathbf{H'g}. \tag{5.5-6}$$

Using Eqs. (5.2-21), (5.2-23), (5.5-3), and (5.5-4) yields

$$\hat{\mathbf{f}} = (\mathbf{WD^*DW}^{-1} + \gamma \mathbf{WA}^{-1}\mathbf{BW}^{-1})^{-1}\mathbf{WD^*W}^{-1}\mathbf{g}. \tag{5.5-7}$$

After multiplying both sides by $\mathbf{W}^{-1}$ and some matrix manipulations this equation reduces to the form

$$\mathbf{W}^{-1}\hat{\mathbf{f}} = (\mathbf{D^*D} + \gamma \mathbf{A}^{-1}\mathbf{B})^{-1}\mathbf{D^*W}^{-1}\mathbf{g}. \tag{5.5-8}$$

Keeping in mind the meaning of the elements of $\mathbf{A}$ and $\mathbf{B}$, recognizing that the matrices inside the parentheses are diagonal, and making use of the concepts developed in Section 5.2.3, allows us to write the elements of Eq. (5.5-8) in the form

$$
\begin{aligned}
\hat{F}(u, v) &= \left[\frac{H^*(u, v)}{|H(u, v)|^2 + \gamma[S_\eta(u, v)/S_f(u, v)]} \right] G(u, v) \\
&= \left[\frac{1}{H(u, v)} \frac{|H(u, v)|^2}{|H(u, v)|^2 + \gamma[S_\eta(u, v)/S_f(u, v)]} \right] G(u, v)
\end{aligned}
\tag{5.5-9}
$$

for $u, v = 0, 1, 2, \ldots, N - 1$, where $|H(u, v)|^2 = H^*(u, v)H(u, v)$ and we have assumed that $M = N$.

When $\gamma = 1$, the term inside the outer brackets in Eq. (5.5-9) reduces to the so-called *Wiener filter*. If γ is variable we refer to this expression as the *parametric Wiener filter*. In the absence of noise, $S_\eta(u, v) = 0$ and either form of the Wiener filter reduces to the ideal inverse filter discussed in the previous section. It is important to note that, by setting $\gamma = 1$, we can no longer say in general that the use of Eq. (5.5-9) yields an optimal solution in the sense defined in Section 5.3.2 because, as pointed out in that section, γ must be adjusted to satisfy the constraint $\|\mathbf{g} - \mathbf{H}\hat{\mathbf{f}}\|^2 = \|\mathbf{n}\|^2$. It can be shown, however, that the solution obtained with

$\gamma = 1$ is optimal in the sense that it minimizes the quantity $E\{[f(x, y) - \hat{f}(x, y)]^2\}$. Clearly, this is a statistical criterion in which f and $\hat{f}$ are treated as random variables.

When $S_\eta(u, v)$ and $S_f(u, v)$ are not known (a problem often encountered in practice) it is sometimes useful to approximate Eq. (5.5-9) by the relation

$$\hat{F}(u, v) \approx \left[\frac{1}{H(u, v)} \frac{|H(u, v)|^2}{|H(u, v)|^2 + K}\right] G(u, v), \qquad (5.5\text{-}10)$$

where K is a constant. An example of results obtained with this equation is given below. The problem of selecting the optimal γ for image restoration is discussed in some detail in the following section.

Example: The first column in Fig. 5.5 shows three pictures of a domino corrupted by linear motion (at $-45°$ with respect to the horizontal) and noise whose variance at any point in the image was proportional to the brightness of the point. The three images were generated by varying the constant of proportionality so that the ratios of maximum brightness to noise amplitude were 1, 10, and 100, respectively, as shown on the left side of Fig. 5.5. The Fourier spectra of the degraded images are shown in Fig. 5.5(b).

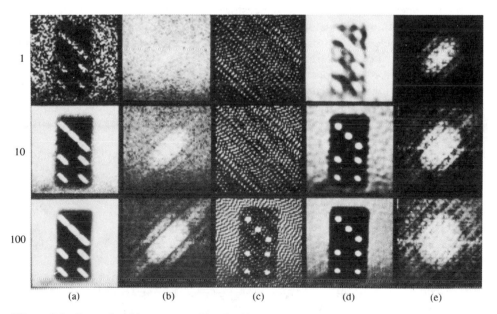

(a)   (b)   (c)   (d)   (e)

Figure 5.5 Example of image restoration by inverse and Wiener filters. (a) Degraded images, and (b) their Fourier spectra. (c) Images restored by inverse filtering. (d) Images restored by Wiener filtering. (e) Fourier spectra of images in (d). (From Harris [1968].)

Since the effects of uniform linear motion can be expressed analytically, an equation describing $H(u, v)$ can be obtained without difficulty, as shown in Section 5.4.2. Figure 5.5(c) was obtained by direct inverse filtering following the procedure described in Section 5.4.1. The results are dominated by noise, but as shown in the third image, the inverse filter was successful in removing the degradation (i.e., blur) due to motion. By contrast, Fig. 5.5(d) shows the results obtained using Eq. (5.5-10) with $K = 2\sigma^2$, where σ^2 is the noise variance. The improvements over the direct inverse filtering approach are obvious, particularly for the third image. The Fourier spectra of the restored images are shown in Fig. 5.5(e).   □

5.6 CONSTRAINED LEAST-SQUARES RESTORATION

The least-mean-square approach derived in the previous section is a statistical procedure, since the criterion for optimality is based on the correlation matrices of the image and noise functions. This implies that the results obtained by using a Wiener filter are optimal in an average sense. The restoration procedure developed in this section, on the other hand, is optimal for *each* given image and only requires knowledge of the noise mean and variance. In the course of the following development we also consider the problem of adjusting γ so that the constraint leading to Eq. (5.3-9) is satisfied.

As indicated in Section 5.3.2, the restoration solution obtained by using Eq. (5.3-9) depends on the choice of the matrix $\mathbf{Q}$. Due to ill-conditioning, this equation will sometimes yield solutions that are obscured by large oscillating values. Therefore it is of interest to investigate the feasibility of choosing $\mathbf{Q}$ such that these adverse effects are minimized. One possibility, suggested by Phillips [1962], is to formulate a criterion of optimality based on a measure of smoothness such as, for example, minimizing some function of the second derivative. In order to see how this criterion can be expressed in a form that is compatible with Eq. (5.3-9), let us first consider the one-dimensional case.

Given a discrete function $f(x)$, $x = 0, 1, 2, \ldots$, we may approximate its second derivative at a point x by the expression

$$\frac{\partial^2 f(x)}{\partial x^2} \approx f(x + 1) - 2f(x) + f(x - 1). \tag{5.6-1}$$

A criterion based on this expression, then, might be to minimize $[\partial^2 f/\partial x^2]^2$ over x; that is,

$$\text{minimize} \left\{ \sum_x [f(x + 1) - 2f(x) + f(x - 1)]^2 \right\} \tag{5.6-2}$$

or, in matrix notation,

$$\text{minimize } \{\mathbf{f}'\mathbf{C}'\mathbf{C}\mathbf{f}\}, \tag{5.6-3}$$

where

$$
\mathbf{C} =
\begin{bmatrix}
1 & & & & & & & \\
-2 & 1 & & & & & & \\
1 & -2 & 1 & & & & & \\
 & 1 & -2 & & 1 & & & \\
 & & & \cdot & & & & \\
 & & & & \cdot & & & \\
 & & & & & \cdot & & \\
 & & & & 1 & -2 & 1 & \\
 & & & & & 1 & -2 & \\
 & & & & & & 1 &
\end{bmatrix}
\tag{5.6-4}
$$

is a smoothing matrix, and $\mathbf{f}$ is a vector whose elements are the samples of $f(x)$.

In the two-dimensional case we consider a direct extension of Eq. (5.6-1). In this case the criterion is to

$$
\text{minimize} \left[\frac{\partial^2 f(x,\,y)}{\partial x^2} + \frac{\partial^2 f(x,\,y)}{\partial y^2}\right]^2,
\tag{5.6-5}
$$

where the derivative function is approximated by the expression

$$
\begin{aligned}
\frac{\partial^2 f}{\partial x^2} + \frac{\partial^2 f}{\partial y^2} &\approx f(x+1,\,y) - 2f(x,\,y) + f(x-1,\,y) \\
&\quad + f(x,\,y+1) - 2f(x,\,y) + f(x,\,y-1) \\
&\approx f(x+1,\,y) + f(x-1,\,y) + f(x,\,y+1) + f(x,\,y-1) \\
&\quad - 4f(x,\,y).
\end{aligned}
\tag{5.6-6}
$$

The derivative function given in Eq. (5.6-5) is recognized as the Laplacian operator discussed in Section 3.3.7.

Equation (5.6-6) can be implemented directly in a computer. However, the same operation can be carried out by convolving $f(x,\,y)$ with the operator

$$
p(x,\,y) =
\begin{bmatrix}
0 & 1 & 0 \\
1 & -4 & 1 \\
0 & 1 & 0
\end{bmatrix}
\tag{5.6-7}
$$

As indicated in Section 5.1.3, wraparound error in the discrete convolution process is avoided by extending $f(x,\,y)$ and $p(x,\,y)$. We have already considered the formation of $f_e(x,\,y)$. We form $p_e(x,\,y)$ in the same manner, that is,

$$
p_e(x,\,y) =
\begin{cases}
p(x,\,y) & 0 \leqslant x \leqslant 2 \quad \text{and} \quad 0 \leqslant y \leqslant 2 \\
0 & 3 \leqslant x \leqslant M - 1 \quad \text{or} \quad 3 \leqslant y \leqslant N - 1.
\end{cases}
$$

If $f(x, y)$ is of size $A \times B$, we choose $M \geq A + 3 - 1$ and $N \geq B + 3 - 1$, since $p(x, y)$ is of size 3×3.

The convolution of the extended functions is then

$$g_e(x, y) = \sum_{m=0}^{M-1} \sum_{n=0}^{N-1} f_e(m, n) p_e(x - m, y - n), \qquad (5.6\text{-}8)$$

which agrees with Eq. (5.1-23).

Following an argument similar to the one given in Section 5.1.3 we may express the above smoothness criterion in matrix form. First we construct a block-circulant matrix of the form

$$\mathbf{C} = \begin{bmatrix} \mathbf{C}_0 & \mathbf{C}_{M-1} & \mathbf{C}_{M-2} & \cdots & \mathbf{C}_1 \\ \mathbf{C}_1 & \mathbf{C}_0 & \mathbf{C}_{M-1} & \cdots & \mathbf{C}_2 \\ \mathbf{C}_2 & \mathbf{C}_1 & \mathbf{C}_0 & \cdots & \mathbf{C}_3 \\ \cdot & & & & \\ \cdot & & & & \\ \cdot & & & & \\ \mathbf{C}_{M-1} & \mathbf{C}_{M-2} & \mathbf{C}_{M-3} & \cdots & \mathbf{C}_0 \end{bmatrix} \qquad (5.6\text{-}9)$$

where each submatrix $\mathbf{C}_j$ is an $N \times N$ circulant constructed from the jth row of $p_e(x, y)$; that is,

$$\mathbf{C}_j = \begin{bmatrix} p_e(j, 0) & p_e(j, N-1) & \cdots & p_e(j, 1) \\ p_e(j, 1) & p_e(j, 0) & \cdots & p_e(j, 2) \\ \cdot & & & \\ \cdot & & & \\ \cdot & & & \\ p_e(j, N-1) & p_e(j, N-2) & \cdots & p_e(j, 0) \end{bmatrix} \qquad (5.6\text{-}10)$$

Since $\mathbf{C}$ is block circulant, it is diagonalized by the matrix $\mathbf{W}$ defined in Section 5.2.2. In other words,

$$\mathbf{E} = \mathbf{W}^{-1} \mathbf{C} \mathbf{W}, \qquad (5.6\text{-}11)$$

where $\mathbf{E}$ is a diagonal matrix whose elements are given by

$$E(k, i) = \begin{cases} P\left(\left[\dfrac{k}{N} \right], k \bmod N \right) & \text{if } i = k \\ 0 & \text{if } i \neq k, \end{cases} \qquad (5.6\text{-}12)$$

as in Eq. (5.2-29). In this case $P(u, v)$ is the two-dimensional Fourier transform of $p_e(x, y)$. As indicated in connection with Eqs. (5.2-37) and (5.2-39), it is assumed that Eq. (5.6-12) has been scaled by the factor MN.

Since the convolution operation described above is equivalent to implementing Eq. (5.6-6), we may express the smoothness criterion of Eq. (5.6-5) in the same form as Eq. (5.6-3); that is,

$$\text{minimize } \{\mathbf{f}'\mathbf{C}'\mathbf{C}\mathbf{f}\}, \tag{5.6-13}$$

where $\mathbf{f}$ is an MN-dimensional vector and $\mathbf{C}$ is of size $MN \times MN$. By letting $\mathbf{Q} = \mathbf{C}$, this criterion may be expressed in the form

$$\text{minimize } \|\mathbf{Q}\mathbf{f}\|^2, \tag{5.6-14}$$

which is in the same form as that used in Section 5.3.2. In fact, if we require that the constraint $\|\mathbf{g} - \mathbf{H}\hat{\mathbf{f}}\|^2 = \|\mathbf{n}\|^2$ be satisfied, the optimal solution is given by Eq. (5.3-9) with $\mathbf{Q} = \mathbf{C}$; that is,

$$\hat{\mathbf{f}} = (\mathbf{H}'\mathbf{H} + \gamma\mathbf{C}'\mathbf{C})^{-1}\mathbf{H}'\mathbf{g}. \tag{5.6-15}$$

By using Eqs. (5.2-21), (5.2-23), and (5.6-11), Eq. (5.6-15) may be expressed in the form

$$\hat{\mathbf{f}} = (\mathbf{W}\mathbf{D}^*\mathbf{D}\mathbf{W}^{-1} + \gamma\mathbf{W}\mathbf{E}^*\mathbf{E}\mathbf{W}^{-1})^{-1}\mathbf{W}\mathbf{D}^*\mathbf{W}^{-1}\mathbf{g}. \tag{5.6-16}$$

After multiplying both sides by $\mathbf{W}^{-1}$ and some matrix manipulations, this equation reduces to

$$\mathbf{W}^{-1}\hat{\mathbf{f}} = (\mathbf{D}^*\mathbf{D} + \gamma\mathbf{E}^*\mathbf{E})^{-1}\mathbf{D}^*\mathbf{W}^{-1}\mathbf{g}. \tag{5.6-17}$$

By keeping in mind that the elements inside the parentheses are diagonal, and making use of the concepts developed in Section 5.2.3, we can express the elements of Eq. (5.6-17) in the form

$$\hat{F}(u, v) = \left[\frac{H^*(u, v)}{|H(u, v)|^2 + \gamma|P(u, v)|^2}\right]G(u, v) \tag{5.6-18}$$

for $u, v = 0, 1, 2, \ldots, N - 1$, where $|H(u, v)|^2 = H^*(u, v)H(u, v)$, and we have assumed that $M = N$. Note that Eq. (5.6-18) resembles the parametric Wiener filter derived in the previous section. The principal difference between Eqs. (5.5-9) and (5.6-18) is that the latter does not require explicit knowledge of statistical parameters other than an estimate of the noise mean and variance, as will be seen below.

The general formulation given in Eq. (5.3-9) requires that γ be adjusted to satisfy the constraint $\|\mathbf{g} - \mathbf{H}\mathbf{f}\|^2 = \|\mathbf{N}\|^2$. Thus the solution given in Eq. (5.6-18) can be optimal only when γ satisfies this condition. An iterative procedure for estimating this parameter is as follows.

Define a residual vector $\mathbf{r}$ as

$$\mathbf{r} = \mathbf{g} - \mathbf{H}\hat{\mathbf{f}}. \tag{5.6-19}$$

Substituting Eq. (5.6-15) for $\hat{\mathbf{f}}$ yields

$$\mathbf{r} = \mathbf{g} - \mathbf{H}(\mathbf{H}'\mathbf{H} + \gamma\mathbf{C}'\mathbf{C})^{-1}\mathbf{H}'\mathbf{g}. \tag{5.6-20}$$

This expression indicates that $\mathbf{r}$ is a function of γ. In fact, it can be shown (Hunt [1973]) that

$$\phi(\gamma) = \mathbf{r}'\mathbf{r}$$
$$= \|\mathbf{r}\|^2 \qquad (5.6\text{-}21)$$

is a monotonically increasing function of γ. What we wish to do is adjust γ so that

$$\|\mathbf{r}\|^2 = \|\mathbf{n}\|^2 \pm a, \qquad (5.6\text{-}22)$$

where a is an accuracy factor. Clearly, if $\|\mathbf{r}\|^2 = \|\mathbf{n}\|^2$ the constraint $\|\mathbf{g} - \mathbf{H}\hat{\mathbf{f}}\|^2 = \|\mathbf{n}\|^2$ will be strictly satisfied, in view of Eq. (5.6-19).

Since $\phi(\gamma)$ is monotonic, finding a γ that satisfies Eq. (5.6-17) is not a difficult problem. One simple approach is to

(1) Specify an initial value of γ.
(2) Compute $\hat{\mathbf{f}}$ and $\|\mathbf{r}\|^2$.
(3) Stop if Eq. (5.6-22) is satisfied; otherwise return to Step 2 after increasing γ if $\|\mathbf{r}\|^2 < \|\mathbf{n}\|^2 - a$ or decreasing γ if $\|\mathbf{r}\|^2 > \|\mathbf{n}\|^2 + a$.

Other procedures such as a Newton–Raphson algorithm can be used to improve speed of convergence.

Implementation of the above concepts requires some knowledge about $\|\mathbf{n}\|^2$. The variance of $\eta_e(x, y)$ is given by

$$\sigma_\eta^2 = E\{[\eta_e(x, y) - \bar{\eta}_e]^2\}$$
$$= E\{\eta_e^2(x, y)\} - \bar{\eta}_e^2, \qquad (5.6\text{-}23)$$

where

$$\bar{\eta}_e = \frac{1}{(M - 1)(N - 1)} \sum_x \sum_y \eta_e(x, y) \qquad (5.6\text{-}24)$$

is the mean value of $\eta_e(x, y)$. If we approximate the expected value of $\eta_e^2(x, y)$ by a sample average, Eq. (5.6-23) becomes

$$\sigma_\eta^2 = \frac{1}{(M - 1)(N - 1)} \sum_x \sum_y \eta_e^2(x, y) - \bar{\eta}_e^2. \qquad (5.6\text{-}25)$$

The summation term simply indicates squaring and adding all values in the array $\eta_e(x, y)$, $x = 0, 1, 2, \ldots, M - 1$, and $y = 0, 1, 2, \ldots, N - 1$. This we recognize simply as the product $\mathbf{n}'\mathbf{n}$, which, by definition, is equal to $\|\mathbf{n}\|^2$. Thus Eq. (5.6-23) reduces to

$$\sigma_\eta^2 = \frac{\|\mathbf{n}\|^2}{(M - 1)(N - 1)} - \bar{\eta}_e^2 \qquad (5.6\text{-}26)$$

or

$$\|\mathbf{n}\|^2 = (M - 1)(N - 1)[\sigma_\eta^2 + \bar{\eta}_e^2]. \qquad (5.6\text{-}27)$$

The importance of this equation is that it allows us to establish a value for the constraint in terms of the noise mean and variance, quantities that, if not known, can often be approximated or measured in practice.

The constrained least-squares restoration procedure can be summarized as follows:

Step 1. Choose an initial value of γ, and obtain an estimate of $\|\mathbf{n}\|^2$ using Eq. (5.6-27).

Step 2. Compute $\hat{F}(u, v)$ using Eq. (5.6-18). Obtain $\hat{\mathbf{f}}$ by taking the inverse Fourier transform of $\hat{F}(u, v)$.

Step 3. Form the residual vector $\mathbf{r}$ according to Eq. (5.6-19), and compute $\phi(\gamma) = \|\mathbf{r}\|^2$.

Step 4. Increment or decrement γ.
(a) $\phi(\gamma) > \|\mathbf{n}\|^2 - a$. Increment γ according to the algorithm given above or other appropriate method (such as a Newton–Raphson procedure).
(b) $\phi(\gamma) > \|\mathbf{n}\|^2 + a$. Decrement γ according to an appropriate algorithm.

Step 5. Return to Step 2 and continue unless Step 6 is true.

Step 6. $\phi(\gamma) = \|\mathbf{n}\|^2 \pm a$, where a determines the accuracy with which the constraint is satisfied. Stop the estimation procedure, with $\hat{\mathbf{f}}$ for the present value of γ being the restored image.

Example: Figure 5.6(b) was obtained by convolving the Gaussian-shaped point-spread function

$$h(x, y) = \exp\left[- \left(\frac{x^2 + y^2}{2400} \right)^2 \right],$$

with the original image shown in Fig. 5.6(a), and adding noise drawn from a uniform distribution in the interval [0, 0.5]. Figure 5.6(c) is the result of using the above algorithm with $\gamma = 0$ (inverse filter). The ill-conditioned nature of the solution is evident by the dominance of the noise on the restored image. Figure 5.6(d) was obtained by allowing the algorithm to seek a γ that would satisfy the constraint. The variance and mean of the uniform density in the interval [0, 0.5] were used to estimate $\|\mathbf{n}\|^2$ and the accuracy factor a was chosen so that $a = 0.025\|\mathbf{n}\|^2$. The improvement of the constrained solution over direct inverse filtering is quite visible. $\square$

5.7   INTERACTIVE RESTORATION

Thus far, attention has been focused on a strictly analytical approach to restoration. In many applications, it is practical to take advantage of human intuition, coupled

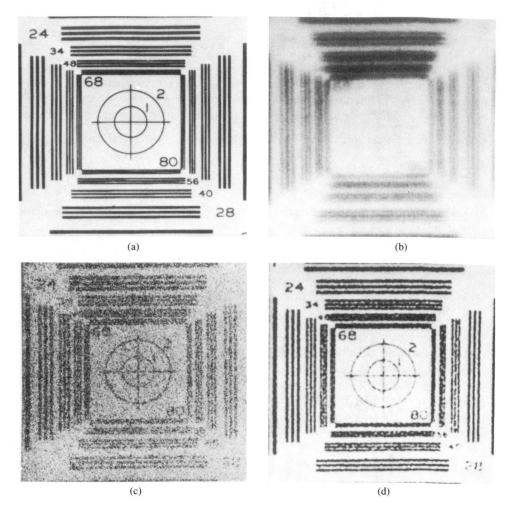

Figure 5.6 (a) Original image. (b) Image blurred and corrupted by additive noise. (c) Image restored by inverse filtering. (d) Image restored by the method of constrained least squares. (From Hunt [1973].)

with the versatility of a digital computer, to restore images in an interactive mode. In this case, the observer has control over the restoration process and, by "tuning" the available parameters, is able to obtain a final result that may be quite adequate for a specific purpose. We give below two examples of this approach.

One of the simplest cases of image corruption that lends itself well to interactive restoration is the occurrence of a two-dimensional sinusoidal interference pattern (often called *coherent noise*) superimposed on an image. Let $\eta(x, y)$ denote a sinusoidal interference pattern of amplitude A and two-dimensional frequency components (u_0, v_0); that is,

$$\eta(x, y) = A \sin(u_0 x + v_0 y). \tag{5.7-1}$$

It can be shown by direct substitution of Eq. (5.7-1) into Eq. (3.1-9) that the Fourier transform of $\eta(x, y)$ is given by the relation

$$N(u, v) = \frac{-jA}{2} [\delta(u - u_0/2\pi, v - v_0/2\pi) - \delta(u + u_0/2\pi, v + v_0/2\pi)]. \tag{5.7-2}$$

In other words, the Fourier transform of a two-dimensional sine function is a pair of impulses of strength $-A/2$ and $A/2$ located, respectively, at coordinates ($u_0/2\pi$, $v_0/2\pi$) and ($-u_0/2\pi$, $-v_0/2\pi$) of the frequency plane. It is also noted that the transform has only imaginary components in this case.

Since the only degradation being considered is additive noise, we have from Eq. (5.2-40) that

$$G(u, v) = F(u, v) + N(u, v). \tag{5.7-3}$$

A display of the magnitude of $G(u, v)$ will contain the magnitude of the sum of $F(u, v)$ and $N(u, v)$. If A is large enough, the two impulses of $N(u, v)$ will usually appear as bright dots on the display, especially if they are located relatively far from the origin so that the contribution of the components of $F(u, v)$ is small.

If $\eta(x, y)$ were completely known, the original image could, of course, be recovered by subtracting the interference from $g(x, y)$. Since this is seldom the case, a useful approach is to identify visually the location of impulse components in the frequency domain and use a bandreject filter (see Section 4.7.4) at these locations.

Example: The image shown in Fig. 5.7(a) was corrupted by a sinusoidal pattern of the form shown in Eq. (5.7-1). The Fourier spectrum of this image, shown in Fig. 5.7(b), clearly exhibits a pair of symmetric impulses due to the sinusoidal interference. Figure 5.7(c) was obtained by manually placing (from a computer console) two bandreject filters of radius 1 at the location of the impulses and then taking the inverse Fourier transform of the result. For all practical purposes, the restored image is seen to be free of interference.   □

The presence of a single, clearly defined interference pattern such as the one just illustrated seldom occurs in practice. A notable example is found in images that have been derived from electro-optical scanners, such as those commonly used in space missions. A common problem of these sensors is interference caused by coupling and amplification of low-level signals in the electronic circuitry. The result is that images reconstructed from the scanner output tend to contain a pronounced, two-dimensional periodic structure superimposed on the scene data.

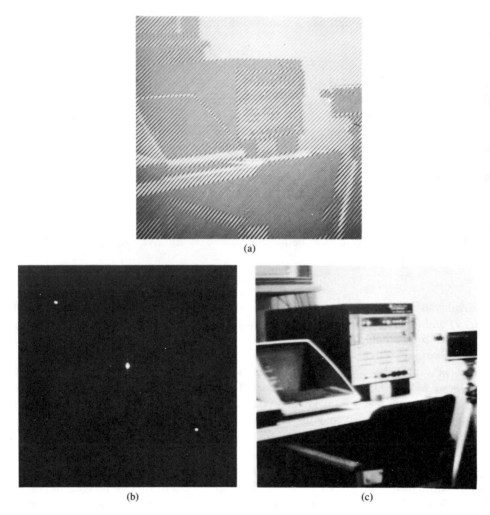

(a)

(b)   (c)

Figure 5.7 Example of sinusoidal interference removal. (a) Corrupted image. (b) Fourier spectrum showing impulses due to sinusoidal pattern. (c) Image restored by using a band-reject filter with a radius of one.

An example of this type of periodic image degradation is shown in Fig. 5.8(a), which is a picture of the Martian terrain taken by the *Mariner 6* spacecraft. The interference pattern is quite similar to the one shown in Fig. 5.7(a), but the former pattern is considerably more subtle and , consequently, harder to detect in the frequency plane.

Figure 5.8(b) shows the Fourier spectrum of the image in question. The starlike components were caused by the interference, and it is noted that several pairs of components are present, indicating that the pattern was composed of more than

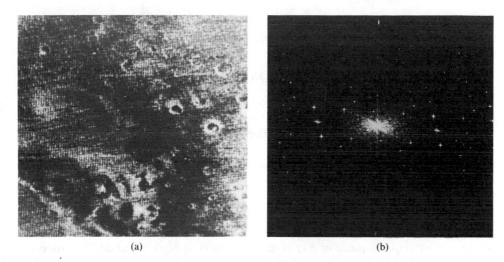

Figure 5.8 (a) Picture of the Martian terrain taken by *Mariner 6*. (b) Fourier spectrum. Note the periodic interference in the image and the corresponding spikes in the spectrum. (Courtesy of NASA, Jet Propulsion Laboratory.)

just one sinusoidal component. When several interference components are present, the method discussed above is not always acceptable because it may remove too much image information in the filtering process. In addition, these components generally are not single-frequency bursts. Instead, they tend to have broad skirts that carry information about the interference pattern. These skirts are not always easily detectable from the normal transform background.

A procedure that has found acceptance in processing space-related scenes consists of first isolating the principal contributions of the interference pattern and then subtracting a variable, weighted portion of the pattern from the corrupted image. Although the procedure is developed below in the context of a specific application, the basic approach is quite general and can be applied to other enhancement tasks where multiple periodic interference is a problem.

The first step is to extract the principal frequency components of the interference pattern. This can be done by placing a bandpass filter $H(u, v)$ at the location of each spike (see Section 4.7.4). If $H(u, v)$ is constructed to pass only components associated with the interference pattern, it follows that the Fourier transform of the pattern is given by the relation

$$P(u, v) - H(u, v)G(u, v), \qquad (5.7\text{-}4)$$

where $G(u, v)$ is the Fourier transform of the corrupted image $g(x, y)$ and, for $N \times N$ digitization, u and v assume values in the range $0, 1, \ldots, N - 1$.

It is important to note that the formation of $H(u, v)$ requires a large degree of judgment as to what is or is not an interference spike. For this reason, the bandpass filter is generally constructed interactively by observing the spectrum of $G(u, v)$ on a display. Once a particular filter has been selected, the corresponding pattern in the spatial domain is obtained from the expression

$$p(x, y) = \mathcal{F}^{-1}\{H(u, v)G(u, v)\}. \tag{5.7-5}$$

Since the corrupted image is formed by the addition of $f(x, y)$ and the interference, and if $p(x, y)$ were completely known, it would be a simple matter to subtract the pattern from $g(x, y)$ to obtain $f(x, y)$. The problem, of course, is that the above filtering procedure usually yields only an approximation of the true pattern. In order to minimize the effects of components not present in the estimate of $p(x, y)$, we instead subtract from $g(x, y)$ a weighted portion of $p(x, y)$ to obtain an estimate of $f(x, y)$; that is,

$$\hat{f}(x, y) = g(x, y) - w(x, y)p(x, y), \tag{5.7-6}$$

where $\hat{f}(x, y)$ is the estimate of $f(x, y)$ and $w(x, y)$ is to be determined. The function $w(x, y)$ is called a *weighting* or *modulation* function, and the objective of the procedure is to select this function so that the result is optimized in some meaningful way. One approach is to select $w(x, y)$ so that the variance of $\hat{f}(x, y)$ is minimized over a specified neighborhood of every point (x, y).

Consider a neighborhood of size $(2X + 1)$ by $(2Y + 1)$ about a point (x, y). The "local" variance of $\hat{f}(x, y)$ at coordinates (x, y) is given by

$$\sigma^2(x, y) = \frac{1}{(2X + 1)(2Y + 1)} \sum_{m=-X}^{X} \sum_{n=-Y}^{Y} \{\hat{f}(x + m, y + n) - \overline{\hat{f}}(x, y)\}^2, \tag{5.7-7}$$

where $\overline{\hat{f}}(x, y)$ is the average value of $\hat{f}(x, y)$ in the neighborhood; that is,

$$\overline{\hat{f}}(x, y) = \frac{1}{(2X + 1)(2Y + 1)} \sum_{m=-X}^{X} \sum_{n=-Y}^{Y} \hat{f}(x + m, y + n). \tag{5.7-8}$$

Points on or near the edge of the image can be treated by considering partial neighborhoods.

Substitution of Eq. (5.7-6) into Eq. (5.7-7) yields

$$\sigma^2(x, y) = \frac{1}{(2X + 1)(2Y + 1)} \sum_{m=-X}^{X} \sum_{n=-Y}^{Y} \{[g(x + m, y + n)$$
$$- w(x + m, y + n)p(x + m, y + n)] - [\overline{g}(x, y) - \overline{w(x, y)p(x, y)}]\}^2. \tag{5.7-9}$$

By assuming that $w(x, y)$ remains essentially constant over the neighborhood, we obtain the approximations

$$w(x + m, y + n) = w(x, y) \tag{5.7-10}$$

for $-X \leq m \leq X$ and $-Y \leq n \leq Y$; also

$$\overline{w(x, y)p(x, y)} = w(x, y)\overline{p}(x, y) \tag{5.7-11}$$

in the neighborhood. With these approximations, Eq. (5.7-9) becomes

$$\sigma^2(x, y) = \frac{1}{(2X + 1)(2Y + 1)} \sum_{m=-X}^{X} \sum_{n=-Y}^{Y} \{[g(x + m, y + n)$$
$$- w(x, y)p(x + m, y + n)] - [\bar{g}(x, y) - w(x, y)\bar{p}(x, y)]\}^2.$$

$$(5.7\text{-}12)$$

To minimize $\sigma^2(x, y)$ we solve

$$\frac{\partial \sigma^2(x, y)}{\partial w(x, y)} - 0 \tag{5.7-13}$$

for $w(x, y)$. The result is

$$w(x, y) = \frac{\overline{g(x, y)p(x, y)} - \bar{g}(x, y)\bar{p}(x, y)}{\overline{p^2(x, y)} - \bar{p}^2(x, y)}. \tag{5.7-14}$$

To obtain the restored image $\hat{f}(x, y)$ we compute $w(x, y)$ from Eq. (5.7-14) and then make use of Eq. (5.7-6). It is important to note that, since $w(x, y)$ is assumed to be constant in a neighborhood, it is not necessary to compute this function for every value of x and y in the image. Instead, $w(x, y)$ is computed for *one* point in each nonoverlapping neighborhood (preferably the center point) and then used to process all the image points contained in that neighborhood.

Example: Figures 5.9 through 5.11 show the result of applying the above technique to the image shown in Fig. 5.8(a). In this case $N = 512$ and a neighborhood with $X = Y = 15$ was selected. Figure 5.9 is the Fourier spectrum of the corrupted image, but the origin was not shifted to the center of the frequency plane. Figure 5.10(a) shows the spectrum of $P(u, v)$, where only the noise spikes are present, and Fig. 5.10(b) is the interference pattern $p(x, y)$ obtained by taking the inverse Fourier transform of $P(u, v)$. Note the similarity between this pattern and the structure of the noise present in Fig. 5.8(a). Finally, Fig. 5.11 shows the processed image obtained by using Eq. (5.7-6). The periodic interference has, for all practical purposes, been removed, leaving only spotty noise that is not periodic. This noise can be processed by other methods such as neighborhood averaging or lowpass filtering. □

5.8 RESTORATION IN THE SPATIAL DOMAIN

Once a suitable frequency-domain restoration filter has been obtained by any of the methods discussed in the previous sections, it is often desirable to implement the solution in the spatial domain via a convolution mask in order to expedite processing (see Section 4.1). As indicated in Section 4.6 the coefficients of a convolution mask can be obtained directly from a given filter function via Eq. (4.6-12). Although the discussion in Section 4.6 deals with enhancement, the concepts developed in that section are equally applicable to restoration; the difference lies in the

Figure 5.9 Fourier spectrum (without shifting) of the image shown in Fig. 5.8(a). (Courtesy of NASA, Jet Propulsion Laboratory.)

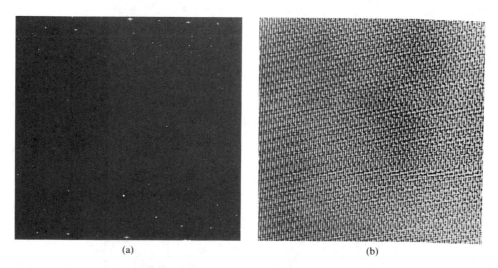

(a)   (b)

Figure 5.10 (a) Fourier spectrum of $P(u, v)$. (b) Corresponding interference pattern $p(x, y)$. (Courtesy of NASA, Jet Propulsion Laboratory.)

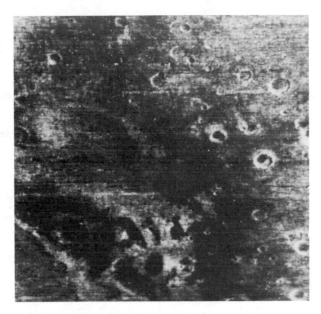

Figure 5.11 Processed image. (Courtesy of NASA, Jet Propulsion Laboratory.)

nature of the filter. The use of these concepts for image restoration are illustrated by the following example.

Example: Figure 5.12(a) shows an infrared image of a set of military targets in a field. The image is corrupted by nearly periodic scanner interference, visible as a "ripple" effect in the vertical direction. Because of its periodic nature, the interference produces bursts of concentrated energy in the vertical axis of the Fourier spectrum of the image, as shown in Fig. 5.13(a).

A simple approach for reducing the effect of the interference is to use a notch filter, $H(u, v)$, which attenuates the values of the Fourier transform in the vertical axis and multiplies all other values of the transform by 1, in a manner analogous to the procedure discussed in Section 5.7. Such a filter is shown in Fig. 5.13(b) superimposed on the spectrum, where the dark bands are the attenuated regions.

The result of using the notch filter and taking the inverse Fourier transform is shown in Fig. 5.12(b). Note that, for all practical purposes, the interference was eliminated from the image. The image shown in Fig. 5.12(c) was obtained by applying a 9 × 9 convolution mask (see Section 4.1) to the original, corrupted image. The coefficients of this mask were generated from the notch filter using Eq. (4.6-12). Since this small mask is only an approximation of the Fourier filtering process, some vertical lines are still visible in the processed image. A second pass of the mask further reduced the interference (at the cost of some noticeable blurring), as shown in Fig. 5.12(d). □

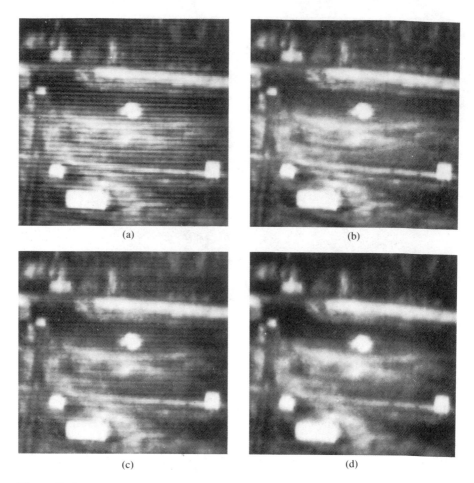

Figure 5.12   (a) Infrared image showing interference. (b) Image restored using a notch filter in the frequency domain. (c) Image restored using a 9 × 9 convolution mask. (d) Result of applying the mask a second time. (From Meyer and Gonzalez [1983].)

5.9   GEOMETRIC TRANSFORMATIONS

We conclude this chapter with an introductory discussion on the use of geometric transformations for image restoration. Unlike the techniques discussed thus far, geometric transformations generally modify the spatial relationships between pixels in an image. For this reason, geometric transformations are often called *rubber-sheet transformations* since they can be viewed as the process of "printing" an image on a sheet of rubber and then stretching this sheet according to some predefined set of rules.

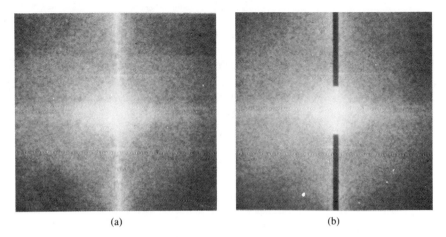

(a)   (b)

Figure 5.13 (a) Fourier spectrum of the image in Fig. 5.12(a). (b) Notch filter superimposed on the spectrum. (From Meyer and Gonzalez [1983].)

In terms of digital image processing, a geometric transformation consists of two basic operations: (1) a *spatial transformation*, which defines the "rearrangement" of pixels on the image plane, and (2) a *gray-level interpolation*, which deals with the assignment of gray levels to pixels in the spatially transformed image. The fundamental ideas underlying these concepts, and their use in the context of image restoration, are discussed in the following sections.

5.9.1 Spatial Transformations

Suppose that an image f with pixel coordinates (x, y) undergoes geometric distortion to produce an image g with coordinates $(\hat{x}, \hat{y})$. This transformation may be expressed as

$$\hat{x} = r(x, y) \tag{5.9-1}$$

and

$$\hat{y} = s(x, y), \tag{5.9-2}$$

where $r(x, y)$ and $s(x, y)$ represent the spatial transformations that produced the geometrically distorted image $g(\hat{x}, \hat{y})$. For example, if $r(x, y) = x/2$ and $s(x, y) = y/2$, the "distortion" is simply a shrinking of the size of $f(x, y)$ by one half in both spatial directions.

If $r(x, y)$ and $s(x, y)$ were known analytically it might be possible in principle to recover $f(x, y)$ from the distorted image $g(\hat{x}, \hat{y})$ by applying the transformations in reverse. In practice, however, it is generally not possible to formulate analytically a single set of functions $r(x, y)$ and $s(x, y)$ that describe the geometric distortion process over the entire image plane. The method used most frequently to overcome this difficulty is to formulate the spatial relocation of pixels through the use of *tiepoints,* which are a subset of pixels whose location in the input (distorted) and output (corrected) images is known precisely.

Consider Fig. 5.14, which shows quadrilateral regions in a distorted and corresponding corrected image. The vertices of the quadrilaterals are corresponding tiepoints. Suppose that the geometric distortion process within the quadrilateral regions is modeled by a pair of bilinear equations so that

$$r(x, y) = c_1 x + c_2 y + c_3 xy + c_4 \tag{5.9-3}$$

and

$$s(x, y) = c_5 x + c_6 y + c_7 xy + c_8. \tag{5.9-4}$$

Then, from Eqs. (5.9-1) and (5.9-2), it follows that

$$\hat{x} = c_1 x + c_2 y + c_3 xy + c_4 \tag{5.9-5}$$

$$\hat{y} = c_5 x + c_6 y + c_7 xy + c_8. \tag{5.9-6}$$

Since there are a total of eight known tiepoints, these equations can be easily solved for the eight coefficients c_i, $i = 1, 2, \ldots, 8$. Once the coefficients are known, they constitute the model used to transform *all* pixels within the quadrilateral region characterized by the tiepoints used to obtain the coefficients. In general, enough tiepoints are needed to generate a set of quadrilaterals that cover the entire image, with each quadrilateral having its own set of coefficients. The generation of tiepoints is discussed in the following section.

The procedure used to generate the corrected image is straightforward. For example, to generate $f(0, 0)$, we substitute $(x, y) = (0, 0)$ into Eqs. (5.9-5) and (5.9-6) and obtain a pair of coordinates $(\hat{x}, \hat{y})$ from those equations. Then, we let $f(0, 0) = g(\hat{x}, \hat{y})$, where $\hat{x}$ and $\hat{y}$ are the coordinate values just obtained. Next, we substitute $(x, y) = (0, 1)$ into Eqs. (5.9-5) and (5.9-6), obtain another pair of values $(\hat{x}, \hat{y})$, and let $f(0, 1) = g(\hat{x}, \hat{y})$ for those coordinate values. The procedure

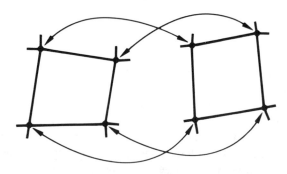

Figure 5.14   Corresponding tiepoints in two image segments.

is continued pixel by pixel until an array whose size does not exceed the size of image g has been obtained. It can be shown that a column (rather than a row) scan would yield identical results. Also, it is important to bear in mind that a bookkeeping procedure is needed to keep track of which quadrilaterals apply at a given pixel location in order to use the proper coefficients.

5.9.2 Gray-Level Interpolation

The above method steps through integer values of the coordinates (x, y) to yield the corrected image $f(x, y)$. However, depending on the coefficients c_i, Eqs. (5.9-5) and (5.9-6) can yield non-integer values for $\hat{x}$ and $\hat{y}$. Since the distorted image g is digital, its pixel values are defined only at integer coordinates. Thus using non-integer values for $\hat{x}$ and $\hat{y}$ causes a mapping into locations of g for which no gray levels are defined. It then becomes necessary to infer what the gray-level values at those locations should be, based only on the pixel values at integer-coordinate locations. The technique used to accomplish this is called *gray-level interpolation*.

The simplest scheme for gray-level interpolation is based on a nearest-neighbor approach. This method, also called *zero-order interpolation*, is illustrated in Fig. 5.15. This figure shows (1) the mapping of integer coordinates (x, y) into fractional coordinates $(\hat{x}, \hat{y})$ by means of Eqs. (5.9-5) and (5.9-6), (2) the selection of the closest integer-coordinate neighbor to $(\hat{x}, \hat{y})$, and (3) the assignment of the gray level of this nearest neighbor to the pixel located at (x, y).

Although nearest-neighbor interpolation is certainly simple to implement, this method often has the drawback of producing undesirable artifacts, such as distortion of straight edges in images of fine resolution. Smoother results can be obtained by using more-sophisticated techniques such as *cubic convolution interpolation* (Bernstein [1976]), which fits a surface of the $(\sin x)/x$ type through a much larger number of neighbors (e.g., 16) in order to obtain a smooth estimate of the gray level at any desired point. However, this technique is costly from a computational point of view, and a reasonable compromise is to use a *bilinear interpolation* approach that uses the gray levels of the four nearest neighbors. In other words, the idea is that

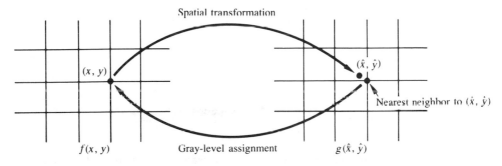

Figure 5.15 Gray-level interpolation based on the nearest-neighbor concept.

we know the gray level of each of the four integral nearest neighbors of a nonintegral pair of coordinates $(\hat{x}, \hat{y})$. The gray-level value of $(\hat{x}, \hat{y})$, denoted by $v(\hat{x}, \hat{y})$, can then be interpolated from the values of its neighbors by using the relationship

$$v(\hat{x}, \hat{y}) = a\hat{x} + b\hat{y} + c\hat{x}\hat{y} + d, \tag{5.9-7}$$

where the four coefficients are easily determined from the four equations in four unknowns that can be written using the four known neighbors of $(\hat{x}, \hat{y})$. Once these coefficients have been determined, we compute $v(\hat{x}, \hat{y})$ and assign this value to the location in $f(x, y)$, which yielded the spatial mapping into location $(\hat{x}, \hat{y})$. This procedure is easily visualized with the aid of Fig. 5.15. The exception is that, instead of using the gray-level value of the nearest neighbor to $(\hat{x}, \hat{y})$, we actually interpolate a value at location $(\hat{x}, \hat{y})$ and use this value for the gray-level assignment at (x, y).

Example: The methods developed in this and the previous section can be illustrated by applying these techniques to the problem of correcting an image that has been distorted geometrically. The image in question is shown in Fig. 5.16(a). This image exhibits the "barrel" distortion found in many vidicon-based imaging cameras. The rectilinear grid in Fig. 5.16(a) is severely distorted, particularly near the edges of the image. Note also that the distortion is not uniform, and that the degree of distortion increased nonlinearly as a function of distance from the center of the image.

As indicated in Section 5.9.1, the use of Eqs. (5.9-5) and (5.9-6) requires knowledge of tiepoints in both the distorted and corrected images. In this particular case, tiepoints are the *reseau marks* visible in Fig. 5.16(a) as the small dark dots

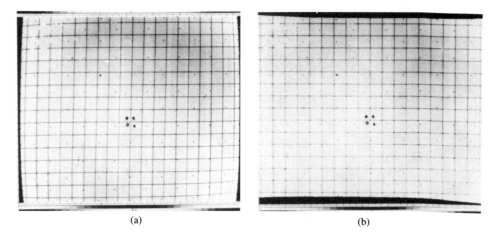

(a)   (b)

Figure 5.16   (a) Distorted image. (b) Image after geometric correction. (From O'Handley and Green [1972].)

scattered throughout the image. (Reseau marks are small metallic squares embedded directly on the surface of the imaging tube.) Since the locations of these marks are known precisely, they serve as ideal tiepoints. The result of using Eqs. (5.9-5) and (5.9-6) for spatial mappings and Eq. (5.9-7) for gray-level interpolation is shown in Fig. 5.16(b). Note the significant degree of geometric correction achieved by using these equations.   □

The preceding example is one of the many possible uses of geometric transformations for image restoration. Another important application is *image registration,* where we wish to find correspondence between two images. The procedure for image registration is the same as the method just illustrated for geometric correction, but the emphasis is on transformimg an image so that it will correspond with another image of the same scene, but viewed perhaps from another perspective. Other applications of the techniques discussed in this section include rectification of display distortions, map projections, and cartographic projections. The books by Castleman [1979] and Green [1983] have numerous examples of these applications.

Before leaving this section, we mention that establishing corresponding tiepoints in two images can in many cases be a rather difficult task. Not every situation is characterized by the availability of controlled artifacts such as reseau marks. When marks are not known a priori, tiepoints are usually established by using correlation techniques (see Chapter 8) to find corresponding features in two images. However, correlation measures are affected by factors such as noise and image rotation and thus generally yield less-precise spatial correspondences between tiepoints.

5.10   CONCLUDING REMARKS

The principal concepts developed in this chapter are a formulation of the image-restoration problem in the framework of linear algebra, and the subsequent simplification of algebraic solutions based on the properties of circulant and block-circulant matrices.

The image-restoration techniques derived in the previous sections are all based on a least-squares criterion of optimality. The reader is reminded that the use of the word "optimal" in this context refers strictly to a mathematical concept, and not to optimal response of the human visual system. In fact, our present lack of knowledge about visual perception precludes a general formulation of the image-restoration problem that takes into account observer preferences and capabilities. In view of these limitations, the advantage of the procedure followed in this chapter is the development of a basic approach from which a set of previously known (but not unified) results can be derived. Thus the power of the algebraic approach is evident in the simplicity by which methods such as the Wiener and constrained least-squares filters can be obtained starting from the same basic principles.

The key points leading to the results in the first eight sections of this chapter are based on the assumption of linear, space-invariant degradations. This assumption leads immediately to the convolution integral, whose discrete formulation can be expressed in terms of the basic degradation model given in Eq. (5.1-24). The assumed periodicity of the input functions further simplified the problem by producing circulant and block-circulant matrices. In terms of implementation, these matrices allow all the derived restoration techniques to be carried out in the frequency domain by means of a two-dimensional FFT algorithm, thus greatly reducing the computational complexity posed by the original matrix formulation of the degradation process.

The material in Section 5.8 provides a convenient way to implement in the spatial domain an approximation of the results in Sections 5.2 through 5.7. Finally, the discussion in Section 5.9 gives an introduction to the problem of restoring images that have been distorted geometrically.

REFERENCES

The definitions given in Section 5.1 were adapted from Schwarz and Friedland [1965], and a background for most of the basic matrix operations used in this chapter can be found in Deutsch [1965], Noble [1969], and Bellman [1970]. The development of the discrete degradation model in terms of circulant and block-circulant matrices is based on two papers by Hunt [1971, 1973]. These papers and the book by Bellman [1970] also consider the diagonalization properties discussed in Section 5.2. Additional information on the material of Section 5.3, as well as the algebraic derivation of the various restoration techniques used in this chapter, may be found in Andrews and Hunt [1977]. That book, devoted entirely to the topic of image restoration, treats in detail other restoration techniques in addition to the ones developed here.

The inverse filtering approach has been considered by numerous investigators. References for the material in Section 5.4 are McGlamery [1967], Sondhi [1972], Cutrona and Hall [1968], and Slepian [1967]. Additional references on the least-squares restoration approach discussed in Section 5.5 are Helstrom [1967], Slepian [1967], Harris [1968], Rino [1969], Horner [1969], and Rosenfeld and Kak [1982]. It is of interest to compare the classical derivations in these references with the algebraic approach given in Section 5.5. The material in Section 5.6 is based on a paper by Hunt [1973]. Some other references related to the topics discussed in Sections 5.1 through 5.7 are Slepian and Pollak [1961], Phillips [1962], Twomey [1963], Shack [1964], Lohman and Paris [1965], Harris [1966], Meuller and Reynolds [1967], Blackman [1968], Huang [1968], Rushforth and Harris [1968], MacAdam [1970], Falconer [1970], Som [1971], Frieden [1972, 1974], Habibi [1972], Sawchuck [1972], Robbins and Huang [1972], Andrews [1974], Jain and Angel [1974], and Anderson and Netravaly [1976].

The material in Section 5.8 is from Meyer and Gonzalez [1983]. Additional reading for the topics in Section 5.9 may be found in O'Handley and Green [1972], Bernstein [1976], Castleman [1979], and Green [1983].

PROBLEMS

5.1 Consider a linear, position-invariant image-degradation system with impulse response $h(x - \alpha, y - \beta) = e^{[(x-\alpha)^2 + (y-\beta)^2]}$. Suppose that the input to the system is an image consisting of a line of infinitesimal width located at $x = a$, and modeled by $f(x, y) = \delta(x - a)$. Assuming no noise, what is the output image $g(x, y)$?

5.2 Show the validity of Eq. (5.2-8).

5.3 Derive an equation analogous to Eq. (5.4-13), but for arbitrary uniform velocity in both the x and y directions.

5.4 Consider the problem of image blurring caused by uniform acceleration in the x direction. If the image is at rest at time $t = 0$ and accelerates with a uniform acceleration $x_0(t) = at^2/2$ for a time T, find the transfer function $H(u, v)$.

5.5 Suppose that an image is blurred by a process that can be modeled as a Butterworth lowpass filter of order 1. In the absence of noise, what is the equation of the Wiener filter you would use to restore this image?

5.6 a) Show how Eq. (5.5-8) follows from Eq. (5.5-7).
b) Show how Eq. (5.5-9) follows from Eq. (5.5-8).

5.7 Assuming that the model in Fig. 5.1 is linear and position-invariant, show that the power spectrum of the output is given by $|G(u, v)|^2 = |H(u, v)|^2 |F(u, v)|^2 + |N(u, v)|^2$. Refer to Eq. (5.2-40).

5.8 Cannon [1974] suggested a restoration filter $R(u, v)$ satisfying the condition $|\hat{F}(u, v)|^2 = |R(u, v)|^2 |G(u, v)|^2$ and based on the premise of forcing the power spectrum of the restored image, $|\hat{F}(u, v)|^2$, to equal the power spectrum of the original image, $|F(u, v)|^2$.
a) Find $R(u, v)$ in terms of $|F(u, v)|^2$, $|H(u, v)|^2$, and $|N(u, v)|^2$. (*Hint:* Refer to Fig. 5.1, Eq. (5.2-40), and Problem 5.7.)
b) Use your result in (a) to state a result in the form of Eq. (5.5-9).

5.9 Start with Eq. (5.7-12) and derive Eq. (5.7-14).

5.10 Suppose that, instead of using quadrilaterals, we were to use triangular regions in Section 5.9 to establish a spatial transformation and gray-level interpolation. What would be the equations analogous to Eqs. (5.9-5), (5.9-6), and (5.9-7) if triangular regions were used?

CHAPTER 6

IMAGE ENCODING

But if I'm content with a little,
Enough is as good as a feast.
Isaac Bickerstaffe

As discussed in Section 2.3, digital representations of images usually require a very large number of bits. In many applications, it is important to consider techniques for representing an image, or the information contained in the image, with fewer bits. In the terminology of information theory this is referred to as *source encoding*.

Applications of source encoding in the field of image processing generally fall into one of three categories: (1) image data compression, (2) image transmission, and (3) feature extraction. The methods discussed in this chapter are applicable to any of these three categories. It is important to note, however, that these techniques are very much problem-oriented. In other words, while the final objective of encoding is data reduction, the choice of one encoding technique over another is dictated by the problem at hand. For example, data compression applications are motivated by the need to reduce storage requirements. In this particular problem, it is usually important to employ encoding techniques that allow perfect reconstruction (by means of a *decoder*) of the data from their coded form. Encoder–decoder pairs that incur zero error are referred to as *information preserving.*

In image-transmission applications, such as the transmission of space-probe pictures for human interpretation, interest lies in techniques that achieve maximum reduction in the quantity of data to be transmitted, subject to the constraint that a reasonable amount of fidelity be preserved. In this case, emphasis is placed on reducing the amount of data that must be transmitted and the encoding technique need not be information-preserving, as long as the resulting images are acceptable for visual or machine analysis.

Feature-extraction applications are used primarily for pattern recognition by computer. In this case, the most important consideration is the choice of encoding techniques that will reduce the data subject to the constraint that enough information be preserved to allow a machine to differentiate between items of interest in an image. Consider, for example, the problem of classifying by machine different types of agricultural crops in a satellite image. Two types of features are important in this case: those that differentiate between vegetation and nonvegetation; and those that can be used to differentiate between types of vegetation. Other features, such as those related to the difference between a road and a river, need not be taken into account in selecting an encoding procedure for this particular problem.

6.1 FIDELITY CRITERIA

6.1.1 Objective Fidelity Criteria

In some image-transmission systems some errors in the reconstructed image can be tolerated. In this case a fidelity criterion can be used as a measure of system quality. Examples of objective fidelity criteria are the root-mean-square (rms) error between the input image and output image, and the rms signal-to-noise ratio of the output image. Suppose that the input image consists of the $N \times N$ array of pixels $f(x, y)$, $x, y = 0, 1, \ldots, N - 1$. As discussed in Section 2.3, each pixel is an m-bit binary word corresponding to one of the 2^m possible gray-level values. The encoder reduces the data bulk from $N \times N \times m$ bits to a fewer number of bits. The decoder processes these bits to reconstruct the output picture consisting of the $N \times N$ array of picture elements $g(x, y)$, $x, y = 0, 1, \ldots, N - 1$, where each pixel is also an m-bit binary word corresponding to one of 2^m possible gray-level values.

For any value of x and y in the range $0, 1, \ldots, N - 1$, the error between an input pixel and the corresponding output pixel is

$$e(x, y) = g(x, y) - f(x, y). \tag{6.1-1}$$

The squared error averaged over the image array is

$$\overline{e^2} = \frac{1}{N^2} \sum_{x=0}^{N-1} \sum_{y=0}^{N-1} e^2(x, y)$$

$$= \frac{1}{N^2} \sum_{x=0}^{N-1} \sum_{y=0}^{N-1} [g(x, y) - f(x, y)]^2 \tag{6.1-2}$$

and the rms error is defined as

$$e_{\text{rms}} = [\overline{e^2}]^{1/2}. \tag{6.1-3}$$

We can also consider the difference between the output and input images to be "noise," so that each output signal (pixel) consists of an input signal (the corresponding input pixel) plus noise (the error); that is,

$$g(x, y) = f(x, y) + e(x, y). \tag{6.1-4}$$

The *mean-square signal-to-noise ratio* of the output image is defined as the average of $g^2(x, y)$ divided by the average of $e^2(x, y)$ over the image array. In other words,

$$(SNR)_{ms} = \sum_{x=0}^{N-1}\sum_{y=0}^{N-1} g^2(x, y) \Big/ \sum_{x=0}^{N-1}\sum_{y=0}^{N-1} e^2(x, y). \tag{6.1-5}$$

The rms value of (SNR) is then given by

$$(SNR)_{rms} = \left[\sum_{x=0}^{N-1}\sum_{y=0}^{N-1} g^2(x, y) \Big/ \sum_{x=0}^{N-1}\sum_{y=0}^{N-1} [g(x, y) - f(x, y)]^2 \right]^{1/2}, \tag{6.1-6}$$

where the variable term in the denominator is the noise expressed in terms of the input and output images.

An alternate definition of signal-to-noise ratio is the square root of the peak value of $g(x, y)$ squared (assuming the minimum value is zero) and the rms noise; that is,

$$(SNR)_p = \{[\text{peak value of } g(x, y)]^2/e_{rms}\}^{1/2}, \tag{6.1-7}$$

where e_{rms} is given by Eq. (6.1-3). The peak value of $g(x, y)$ is the total dynamic range of the output image. Hence, $(SNR)_{rms}$ and $(SNR)_p$ differ by a scale constant equal to the ratio of maximum signal level to the average signal level.

6.1.2 Subjective Fidelity Criteria

When the output images are to be viewed by people, as in the case of broadcast television, it is more appropriate to use a subjective fidelity criterion corresponding to how good the images look to human observers. The human visual system has peculiar characteristics so that two pictures having the same amount of rms error may appear to have drastically different visual qualities. As indicated in Section 2.1, an important characteristic of the human visual system is its logarithmic sensitivity to light intensity so that errors in dark areas of an image are much more noticeable than errors in light areas. The human visual system is also sensitive to abrupt spatial changes in gray level so that errors on or near the edges are more bothersome than errors in background texture. The subjective quality of an image can be evaluated by showing the image to a number of observers and averaging their evaluations. One possibility is to use an absolute scale such as the one used by Panel 6 of the Television Allocations Study Organization (Frendendall and Behrend [1960]):

(1) *Excellent*—An image of extremely high quality, as good as you could desire.

(2) *Fine*—An image of high quality, providing enjoyable viewing. Interference is not objectionable.

(3) *Passable*—An image of acceptable quality. Interference is not objectionable.

(4) *Marginal*—An image of poor quality; you wish you could improve it. Interference is somewhat objectionable.

(5) *Inferior*—A very poor image, but you could watch it. Objectionable interference is definitely present.

(6) *Unusable*—An image so bad that you could not watch it.

Another possibility is to use the pair-comparison method, where observers are shown images two at a time and asked to express a preference. Both methods have advantages and disadvantages. By averaging the results of many observers (20 observers are usually adequate) the first method results in an absolute number between 1 and 6 for each image but some observers may allow the scale to drift during the course of looking at a sequence of images. The second method avoids this difficulty but yields only a rank ordering of the images.

6.2 THE ENCODING PROCESS

Encoders can be modeled as a sequence of three operations, as illustrated in Fig. 6.1, where images are expressed in vector form (see Section 3.6). The mapping operation maps the input data from the pixel domain into another domain where the quantizer and coder can be used more efficiently in the sense that fewer bits are required to code the mapped data than would be required to code the original input data. The quantizer rounds off each mapped datum to one of a smaller number of possible values so that fewer code words with fewer bits are required. The coder assigns a code word to each quantizer output.

6.2.1 The Mapping

The mapping operation maps the input set of numbers (pixels) into another set of numbers. The basic procedure is best explained by means of some simple examples.

In *run-length* encoding, the sequence of image elements along a scan line (row) $x_1, x_2, \ldots, x_N$ is mapped into a sequence of pairs $(g_1, l_1), (g_2, l_2), \ldots, (g_k, l_k)$,

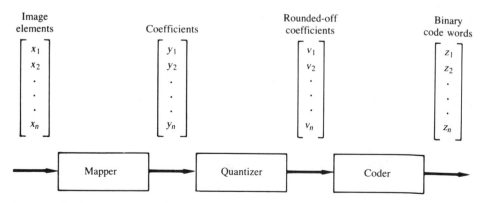

Figure 6.1 An encoder model.

where g_i denotes the gray level and l_i the run length of the ith run, as illustrated in Fig. 6.2. For pictures such as weather maps, significantly fewer bits may be required to encode the run-length sequence than the image element sequence. This mapping is *reversible* because the sequence of image elements can be reconstructed from the sequence of runs.

Another mapping of utility in image encoding is the linear transformation

$$\begin{bmatrix} y_1 \\ y_2 \\ \cdot \\ \cdot \\ \cdot \\ y_n \end{bmatrix} = \begin{bmatrix} a_{11} & a_{12} & \cdots & a_{1n} \\ a_{21} & a_{22} & \cdots & a_{2n} \\ \cdot & & \cdot & \cdot \\ \cdot & & \cdot & \cdot \\ \cdot & & \cdot & \cdot \\ a_{n1} & a_{n2} & \cdots & a_{nn} \end{bmatrix} \begin{bmatrix} x_1 \\ x_2 \\ \cdot \\ \cdot \\ \cdot \\ x_n \end{bmatrix} \tag{6.2-1}$$

or

$$\mathbf{y} = \mathbf{Ax}. \tag{6.2-2}$$

This transformation may or may not be reversible, depending on the choice of $\mathbf{A}$. In this case the vector of pixels $\mathbf{x}$ is transformed into a vector of coefficients $\mathbf{y}$. For some sets of vectors $\mathbf{x}$ and some transformations $\mathbf{A}$, fewer bits are required to

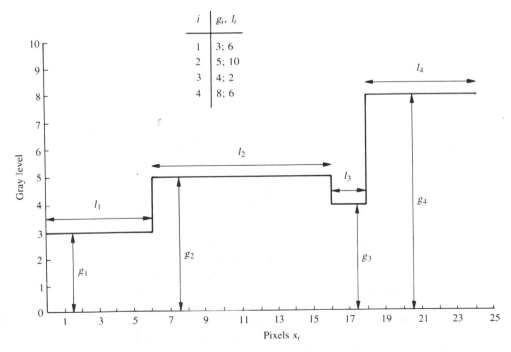

Figure 6.2 Example of run-length mapping.

encode the n coefficients of **y** than the n pixels of **x**. In particular, if the elements $x_1, x_2, \ldots, x_n$ are highly correlated and the transformation matrix **A** is chosen such that the coefficients $y_1, y_2, \ldots, y_n$ are less correlated, then the y_is can be individually coded more efficiently than the x_is.

A *difference mapping* is obtained if we use the matrix

$$\mathbf{A} = \begin{bmatrix} 1 & 0 & 0 & 0 & 0 & 0 \\ 1 & -1 & 0 & 0 & 0 & 0 \\ 0 & 1 & -1 & 0 & 0 & 0 \\ 0 & 0 & 1 & -1 & 0 & 0 \\ 0 & 0 & 0 & 1 & -1 & 0 \\ 0 & 0 & 0 & 0 & 1 & -1 \end{bmatrix} \qquad (6.2\text{-}3)$$

in Eq. (6.2-2). The first element of **y** is $y_1 = x_1$. However, all subsequent coefficients are given by $y_i = x_{i-1} - x_i$. If the gray levels of adjacent pixels are similar, then the differences $y_i = x_{i-1} - x_i$, will, on the average, be smaller than the gray levels so that it should require fewer bits to code them. This mapping is also reversible.

The above examples are typical of mapping procedures used in image encoding. Some additional techniques are developed later in this chapter in the context of specific encoding applications.

6.2.2 The Quantizer

Consider the number of possible values for each of the coefficients y_i resulting from the linear transformation given by Eq. (6.2-1). Each coefficient is a linear combination of n pixels; that is,

$$y_i = a_{i1}x_1 + a_{i2}x_2 + \cdots + a_{in}x_n. \qquad (6.2\text{-}4)$$

If each element x_j in the sum can have any of 2^m different values then each $a_{ij}x_j$ term can also have any of 2^m different values. The sum of n such terms could have any of $(2^m)^n = 2^{mn}$ different values. Consequently, a natural binary representation would require mn-bit code words to assign a unique word to each of the possible 2^{mn} values of y_i. Since only m-bit words would be required to code any x_j, and our objective is to use fewer bits to code the y_i, we must round off the y_i to a fewer number of allowed levels.

A quantizer is a device whose output can have only a limited number of possible values. Each input is forced to one of the allowable output values. One way to accomplish this is to divide the input range into a number of bins, as illustrated in Fig. 6.3. If an input falls into the kth bin, then the output is the value w_k associated with that bin. One possibility is to make w_k correspond to the center of the kth bin so that each input is rounded off to the center of the bin into which it falls. A *uniform quantizer* is one in which all bin widths are equal. *Nonuniform quantizers* allow different bins to have different widths.

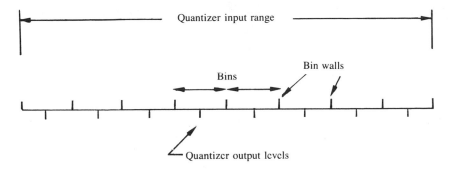

Figure 6.3   Input–output relationship.

The quantizer operation is nonreversible because, given the output value, we cannot in general determine the input value. Let y represent any input value from the vector **y** shown in Fig. 6.1, and let v be the corresponding output of the quantizer. The quantization error is the difference between the quantizer output and input; that is,

$$e_q = v - y. \tag{6.2-5}$$

Clearly, the minimum error is zero, which happens only when the input equals one of the allowed output values. The maximum error for a uniform quantizer of bin width Δ is half the bin width; that is, $e_{qmax} = \Delta/2$.

The rms error is the square root of the mean-square error averaged over all possible values of the input y. If y is equally likely to be any value within the bin, then the mean-square error is

$$e_q^2 = \int_{v-\Delta/2}^{v+\Delta/2} (v - y)^2 \, dy. \tag{6.2-6}$$

If all the quantizer bins have the same width Δ and if for each bin the input values y are equally likely to be any value within that bin, then the error e_{qrms} is the same for all bins so that the quantizer rms error is given by the square root of Eq. (6.2-6), even for the inputs y that are more likely to fall in some bins than others.

If the rms value of the input y is given by

$$y_{rms} = \sqrt{\int y^2 \, dy} \tag{6.2-7}$$

then the signal-to-quantization distortion (signal-to-quantization noise) ratio is given by

$$Q_{SNR} = y_{rms}/e_{qrms}. \tag{6.2-8}$$

If all values of y within the bins are not equally likely then the squared error $(v - y)^2$ must be weighted by the probability density function $p(y)$:

$$e_q^2 = \int_{v-\Delta/2}^{v+\Delta/2} (v - y)^2 p(y)\, dy \qquad\qquad (6.2\text{-}9)$$

and the total quantization error is a weighted average of these terms. In other words, the error term for each bin must be weighted by the probability

$$\int_{v-\Delta/2}^{v+\Delta/2} p(y)\, dy$$

that y fell in that bin.

For some mappings, greater efficiency can be achieved by using a different quantizer and/or coder for each of the different coefficients produced by the mapping. For example, the linear transformation defined by Eq. (6.2-1) results in coefficients of unequal variances. Since the dynamic ranges of the coefficients can differ greatly, we can use more quantizer bins and therefore more bits to code the coefficients with the larger variances and fewer quantizer bins and fewer bits to code the coefficients with the smaller variances. The quantizers could be uniform or nonuniform, and the codes could be of equal length or unequal length. This concept is discussed in greater detail in Section 6.4.2.

6.2.3 The Coder

The inputs to the coder are the n elements of the vector $\mathbf{v}$ in Fig. 6.1. Suppose that each element v_i can assume one of M values (levels) $w_1, w_2, \ldots, w_M$. For each input v_i, the coder outputs a binary word whose value depends on the value w_k of the input. The coder input–output relationship is one-to-one in that a unique code word c_k is assigned to each possible input value w_k. Hence, the process is reversible because given a code word c_k we know w_k. The coder does not introduce any error into the encoding process. If the coder must handle M possible input values, then designing the coder amounts to choosing M unique binary code words and assigning one of them to each input.

An *equal-length code* is a set of code words each of which has the same number of bits, along with a rule for assigning code words to quantizer output levels. One example of an equal-length code is the natural binary code. One possible assignment rule for the natural code is to order the code words according to their binary value. For example, suppose that there are eight possible coder input values (quantizer output levels) ordered $w_1, w_2, \ldots, w_8$; then the natural code is $c_1 = 000$, $c_2 = 001, \ldots, c_8 = 111$, as illustrated in Table 6.1. There are 8! possible assignments of the eight code words to the eight inputs. The *reflected binary* or *Gray code*, also illustrated in Table 6.1, has the property that any two adjacent code words in the set differ in only one bit position.

Table 6.1   Some Typical Codes

Input	Natural Code	Gray Code	B_1-Code	B_2-Code	S_2-Code
w_1	000	111	C0	C00	00
w_2	001	110	C1	C01	01
w_3	010	100	C0C0	C10	10
w_4	011	101	C0C1	C11	1100
w_5	100	001	C1C0	C00C00	1101
w_6	101	000	C1C1	C00C01	1110
w_7	110	010	C0C0C0	C00C10	111100
w_8	111	011	C0C0C1	C00C11	111101

A *uniquely decodable code* is a code with the property that a sequence of code words can be decoded in only one way. The code $c_1 = 0$, $c_2 = 1$, $c_3 = 01$, $c_4 = 10$ is not unique because the sequence of bits 0011 could be decoded as $c_1c_1c_2c_2$ or as $c_1c_3c_2$. All the codes presented in Table 6.1 are uniquely decodable.

An *instantaneous code* is one that can be decoded instantaneously. That is, if we look at the sequence of incoming bits one at a time, we know the value of the input when we come to the end of a code word. We do not have to look ahead at any future incoming bits in order to decode the bit stream. All of the codes in Table 6.1 are instantaneous except for the B-codes, which require that we look one bit ahead to decode. The B-codes are discussed below.

We would like to design the coder to use as few bits as possible. Since there are 2^M unique equal-length code words of length $b = \log_2 M$ bits, the b-bit natural code can handle up to 2^M possible input levels and the number of bits output for each input is b. This is an optimal code only when all input levels w_1, w_2, . . . , w_M are equally likely. When some input levels occur more often than others, greater efficiency can be achieved by using an unequal-length code and assigning the shortest code words to the most likely inputs and longer code words to the least likely inputs.

Given the coder input probabilities, it is of interest to determine the minimum number of bits required to code these inputs and generate a code that would achieve this minimum. In order to reach this objective we must first understand the concept of entropy.

Entropy
Suppose we have a set of M random variables $\alpha_1, \alpha_2, . . . , \alpha_M$ with probabilities $p_1 = p(\alpha_1)$, $p_2 = p(\alpha_2)$, . . . , $p_M = p(\alpha_M)$. Then the entropy in bits is defined as

$$H = - \sum_{k=1}^{M} p_k \log_2 p_k. \qquad (6.2\text{-}10)$$

Suppose there are $M = 8$ random variables and that they are equally likely; that is, $p_1 = p_2 = \cdots = p_8 = 1/8$. Then the entropy is

$$H = -\sum_{k=1}^{8} \frac{1}{8} \log_2 \frac{1}{8}$$
$$= 3.$$

On the other hand, if $p_1 = 1$, $p_2 = p_3 = \cdots = p_8 = 0$, then the entropy is

$$H = 0.$$

In general, the entropy for M random variables can range from 0 to $\log_2 M$.

Entropy is a measure of the degree of randomness of the set of random variables. The least random case is when one of the random variables has probability 1 so that the outcome is known in advance and $H = 0$. The most random case is when all events are equally likely. In this case $p_1 = p_2 = \cdots = p_M = 1/M$ and $H = \log_2 M$. This concept is similar to the entropy concept in thermodynamics.

In our coding applications, entropy represents the amount of information associated with the set of coder input values and gives a lower bound on the average number of bits required to code those inputs. If the set of coder input levels is w_1, w_2, . . . , w_M with probabilities p_1, p_2, . . . , p_M, then we are guaranteed that it is not possible to code them using less than

$$H = -\sum_{k=1}^{M} p_k \log_2 p_k$$

bits on the average. Therefore the entropy concept provides a performance criterion against which we can measure any particular code. That is, if we design a code with code words $c_1, c_2, \ldots, c_M$ with word lengths $\beta_1, \beta_2, \ldots, \beta_M$, the average number of bits required by the coder is

$$R = \sum_{k=1}^{M} \beta_k p_k. \tag{6.2-11}$$

If R is close to H the coder is near optimum; if it is significantly different from H it is not.

The entropy defined in Eq. (6.2-10) is the first-order entropy. It takes into account only the relative probabilities of the M possible input values w_1, w_2, . . . , w_M. If successive inputs are independent, then the first-order entropy is also a bound on the average number of bits per input required to code a sequence of inputs. If successive inputs are not independent then the entropy associated with a sequence of inputs is less per input than for an individual input. The second-order entropy is defined as

$$H_2 = -\sum_{i=1}^{M} \sum_{j=1}^{M} p(w_i, w_j) \log_2 p(w_i, w_j), \tag{6.2-12}$$

where $p(w_i, w_j)$ is the joint probability density function of the two random variables w_i and w_j. It represents a lower bound on the number of bits required to code a sequence of inputs if we code them two at a time (e.g., we input two successive quantizer levels and output a single code word). Similarly, we can define a third-order entropy

$$H_3 = -\sum_{i=1}^{M} \sum_{j=1}^{M} \sum_{k=1}^{M} p(w_i, w_j, w_k) \log_2 p(w_i, w_j, w_k), \qquad (6.2\text{-}13)$$

which is a bound on the number of bits required to code the inputs three at a time. It can be shown that $H_1 \geqslant H_2 \geqslant \cdots$. We do not pursue these higher-order entropies for two reasons. First, the amount of computation required to obtain higher-order probabilities is prohibitive in practice and second, the purpose of the mapping operation in the encoder is to transform the input picture elements that are usually highly dependent into a set of coefficients that are much less dependent so that they can be efficiently coded one at a time.

Huffman code

A *compact code* is one with an average word length less than or equal to the average length of all other uniquely decodable codes for the same set of input probabilities; that is, it is a minimum-length code. Given a set of input probabilities we can generate a compact code using an algorithm due to Huffman [1952]. A Huffman code can be constructed by first ordering the input probabilities according to their magnitudes, as illustrated in Fig. 6.4 for six input values. The two smallest probabilities are combined by addition to form a new set of probabilities. The new set of probabilities, which has one fewer probability than the original set, is again ordered according to magnitude. Equal probabilities can be ordered in any way (e.g., the 0.1 obtained by combining input probabilities 0.06 and 0.04 could be placed in any three of the bottom step 1 entries). When we get down to two probabilities we stop, as in step 4. Code words are generated by starting at the last step and

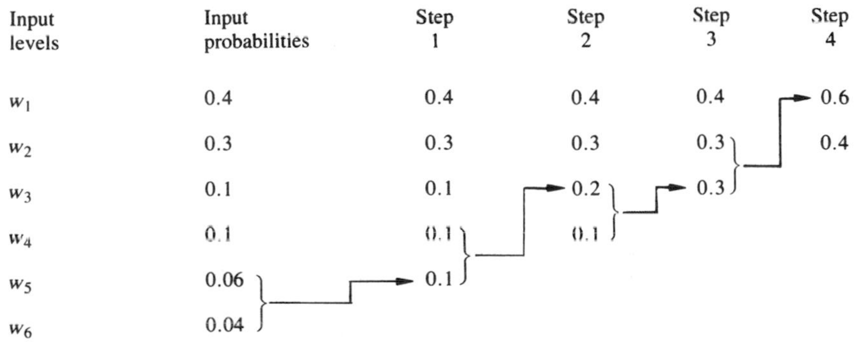

Input levels	Input probabilities	Step 1	Step 2	Step 3	Step 4
w_1	0.4	0.4	0.4	0.4	0.6
w_2	0.3	0.3	0.3	0.3	0.4
w_3	0.1	0.1	0.2	0.3	
w_4	0.1	0.1	0.1		
w_5	0.06	0.1			
w_6	0.04				

Figure 6.4 Construction of a Huffman code.

working backward. We start by assigning 0 to one of the last two combined probabilities, and 1 to the other, as illustrated in Fig. 6.5, where we have placed a 0 to the left of the 0.6 in step 4 and a 1 to the left of the 0.4. We now proceed backward to step 3, decomposing probabilities and generating code words as we go. For example, the 0.6 in step 4 is decomposed back into the two 0.3 probabilities in step 3. The 0 associated with the 0.6 remains the first bit of each of its decomposed code words and the 1 associated with 0.4 remains the first bit of the 0.4 in step 3. A second bit, a 0 and 1, respectively, is appended to each of the code words associated with their reconstructed probabilities to obtain the code words in step 3. The same procedure is repeated to go back to step 2, and again to step 1, and finally to the input probabilities, at which point we have a code word assigned to each input level w_i. It can be proved that the procedure outlined above generates a compact code.

For the input probabilities listed in Fig. 6.4 the entropy is

$$H = (-0.4)\log(0.4) - (0.3)\log(0.3) - (0.1)\log(0.1) - (0.1)\log(0.1)$$
$$- (0.06)\log(0.06) - (0.04)\log(0.04)$$
$$= 2.14 \text{ bits.}$$

The average word length of the Huffman code for this example is

$$R = 1(0.4) + 2(0.3) + 3(0.1) + 4(0.1) + 5(0.06) + 5(0.04)$$
$$= 2.20 \text{ bits.}$$

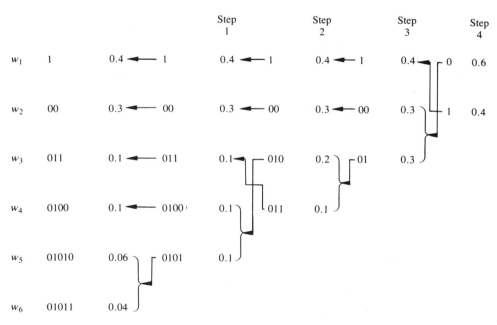

Figure 6.5   Construction of Huffman code words.

B-codes

In some applications the probabilities of the coder inputs obey a power law. is, the probabilities of the M coder inputs are of the form

$$p_k = k^{-\gamma} \qquad\qquad (6.2\text{-}14)$$

for $k = 1, 2, \ldots, M$, and some positive constant γ. For example, the distribution of run lengths for many types of graphics (e.g., typewritten text) is approximately exponential. The B-codes are nearly optimal for data that obey Eq. (6.2-14).

The B_1-code is presented in Table 6.1. Half of the bits in each code word are "continuation" bits labeled C and the other half are "information" bits. The information bits use a natural code that increases in length, as illustrated in Table 6.1. The continuation bit is, of course, either 0 or 1, but it can be determined by either of two rules: for 2-level data where each pixel is white or black, the continuation bit can be set equal to the gray level, say, $C = 0$ for black and $C = 1$ for white. The other possibility is to let it alternate with each code word since its only purpose is to signify how long a code word is. For example, the sequence of code words for the sequence of inputs w_1, w_8, w_5 could be $\underline{00}$ $\underline{10}$ $\underline{10}$ $\underline{11}$ $\underline{01}$ $\underline{00}$ or $\underline{10}$ $\underline{00}$ $\underline{00}$ $\underline{01}$ $\underline{11}$ $\underline{10}$, where we have underlined the continuation bits. A change in the continuation bits signifies the start of a new code word. Note that the code is not instantaneous because the decoder must look ahead to the next continuation bit in order to determine whether or not the present code word has ended.

Implementation of the B_1-code is much simpler than for the Huffman code. For example, in coding run lengths the coder for the information bits is simply an up-counter that counts up by one for each new datum until the end of the run is reached. At the end of each run the counter is reset to zero and the continuation bit is flipped. Similarly, decoding can be accomplished by presetting a down-counter with information bits and letting it count down until the continuation bit changes state. Higher-order B-codes can also be constructed. A B_n-code uses n information bits for each continuation bit, as illustrated in Table 6.1 for $n = 2$.

For the set of input probabilities listed in Fig. 6.4 the average length of the B_1-code is

$$R = 2(0.4) + 2(0.3) + 4(0.1) + 4(0.1) + 4(0.06) + 4(0.04)$$
$$= 2.6$$

and the average length of the B_2-code is

$$R = 3(0.4) + 3(0.3) + 3(0.1) + 3(0.1) + 6(0.06) + 6(0.04)$$
$$= 3.3.$$

Shift codes

Another unequal-length code that is easy to implement and is reasonably efficient for inputs with monotonically decreasing probabilities is the S_n code. For example, the S_2-code uses 2-bit code words so that we have a total of four distinct 2-bit code words c_1, c_2, c_3, and c_4. Three of these code words c_1, c_2, c_3 are assigned to the first three input values w_1, w_2, w_3 and the remaining code word is used to signify that the input is outside this range. When this event occurs the first three code words are shifted by 3 and assigned to the inputs w_4, w_5, w_6. If the input is still outside this range the shift code word is used again and the three code words are shifted to w_7, w_8, w_9, and so on. As an example, suppose that an input falls on the range w_1 to w_3, say w_2; then the coder outputs code word c_2. Suppose the input is w_5; then the coder outputs code word c_4 (to indicate shift) followed by code word c_2. For input w_9 the shift code word c_4 is used twice, followed by code word c_3. This code is illustrated in Table 6.1, where $c_1 = 00$, $c_2 = 01$, $c_3 = 10$, and $c_4 = 11$.

For the set of input probabilities listed in Fig. 6.4 the average length of the S_3 code is

$$R = 2(0.4) + 2(0.3) + 2(0.1) + 4(0.1) + 4(0.06) + 4(0.04)$$
$$= 2.4.$$

These results are summarized in Table 6.2, along with the results for the previous examples.

The general encoding process described in Sections 6.2.1 through 6.2.3 is illustrated in the context of image processing in Sections 6.3 and 6.4, where several examples of error-free encoding and encoding relative to a fidelity criterion are given. Although these techniques are developed in the context of specific applications to clarify the presentation, the approaches shown are quite general and can be applied to a much larger class of problems than those considered in the following discussion.

Table 6.2

Inputs	Probabilities	Huffman Code	B_1-Code	B_2-Code	S_2-Code	Natural Code
w_1	0.4	1	C0	C00	00	000
w_2	0.3	00	C1	C01	01	001
w_3	0.1	011	C0C0	C10	10	010
w_4	0.1	0100	C0C1	C11	1100	011
w_5	0.06	01010	C1C0	C00C00	1101	100
w_6	0.04	01011	C1C1	C00C01	1110	101
Entropy	2.14					
Average Code Word Length		2.2	2.6	3.3	2.4	3.0

6.3 ERROR-FREE ENCODING

As indicated in the beginning of this chapter, it is of interest in some applications to compress the amount of data in an image, subject to the constraint that the encoding process be reversible in the sense that an exact replica of the original image must be reconstructible from its encoded form. In this section we consider three examples of error-free encoding.

6.3.1 Example 1. Differential Encoding for Storage of LANDSAT Imagery

One frame of LANDSAT† imagery consists of four digital images. Each image is of the same scene, but taken through a different spectral window. Two of the spectral windows are in the visible region of the spectrum (corresponding more or less to the green and red regions of the visible spectrum) and two are in the infrared region. An example of a LANDSAT frame is presented in Fig. 6.6. The white line sloping down to the right in the bottom two pictures is an interstate highway; the small white puffs in the top parts of the bottom two pictures are clouds. Figure 6.7 is another LANDSAT image of the same location but taken on a different day. These scenes are 100 × 100 nautical miles. Each image is represented by a 2340 × 3234 array of pixels. Each pixel is a 7-bit binary word corresponding to one of 128 gray levels, with 0 corresponding to black and 127 corresponding to white.

LANDSAT images are stored on magnetic tape. The number of bits required to store one frame is $(2340)(3234)(7)(4) = 211,000,000$. LANDSAT collects 30 frames per day so that the number of bits to be archived is 6,000,000,000 per day or approximately 2.2×10^{11} bits per year. If the data bulk (number of bits) could be reduced by a factor of 2, the number of data tapes (and the number of warehouses required to store them) could be reduced by the same factor. In order to avoid the possibility of destroying information that may be useful to future users of the data, the data must be stored in a format that allows exact reconstruction of the original digital images.

The histograms of the pixel gray-level values for each of the four images presented in Fig. 6.6 are shown in Fig. 6.8. It is noted that most of the 128 gray-level values occur infrequently. For three of the images most gray levels fall in the range 16 to 48. One of the images is "lighter" with most of the levels between 48 and 64. Other LANDSAT images have other characteristics. For example, the polar ice caps are lighter and the ocean is darker.

Let us look at the differences in the gray levels of adjacent picture elements down each scan line. That is, if the picture elements from left to right along the

---

† LANDSAT is an abbreviation for *Land Satellite*, a name given by NASA to satellites designed to monitor the surface of the Earth.

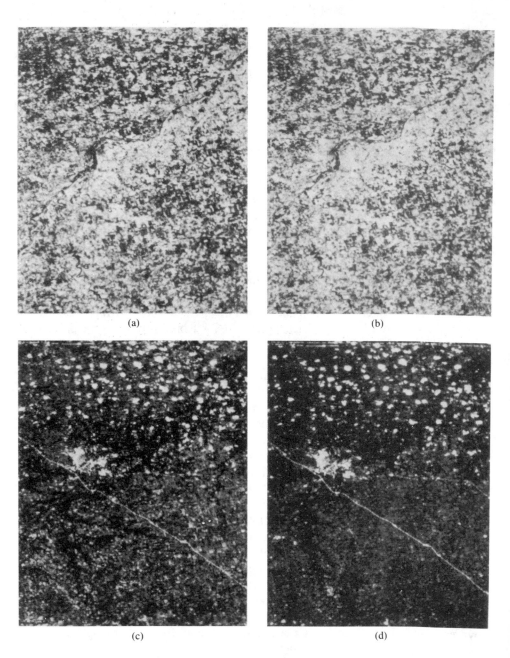

(a)   (b)

(c)   (d)

Figure 6.6   A LANDSAT frame.

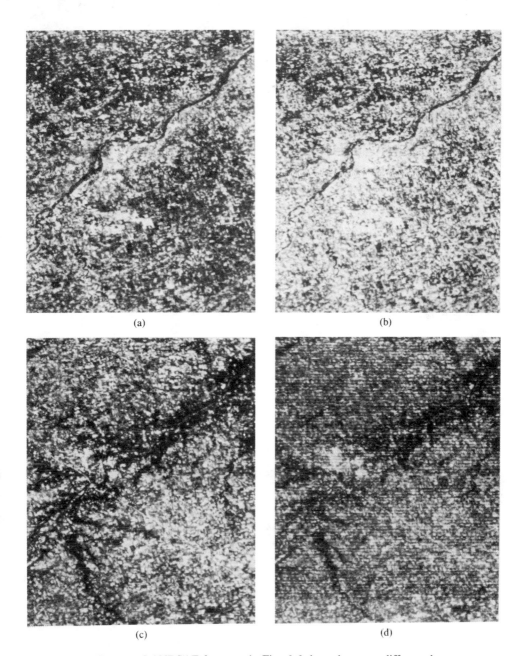

(a)   (b)

(c)   (d)

Figure 6.7   The same LANDSAT frame as in Fig. 6.6, but taken on a different day.

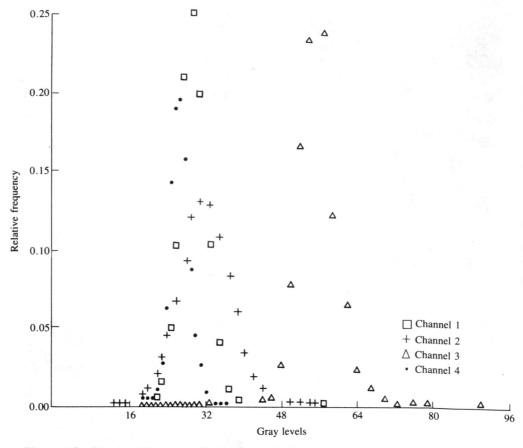

Figure 6.8 Gray-level histograms for the images in Fig. 6.6.

jth row (scan line) are given by $x_1, x_2, \ldots, x_{3234}$, then we can map this set of 3234 integers into the new set of 3234 integers $x_1, x_2 - x_1, x_3 - x_2, \ldots,$ $x_{3234} - x_{3233}$. This is the difference mapping defined by Eq. (6.2-3).

Each of the original image elements x_i is one of the integers $0, 1, \ldots, 127$. Therefore each difference $x_i - x_{i-1}$ is an integer with a value between -127 and 127. To assign a unique equal-length binary code word to each picture element x_i requires 7-bit code words. To assign a unique equal-length binary code word to each picture-element difference $x_i - x_{i-1}$ requires 8-bit code words, assuming that the quantizer outputs a separate value for each of the above 255 differences.

The histograms of the differences $x_i - x_{i-1}$ for each of the four images of Fig. 6.6 are shown in Fig. 6.9. It is noted that all four histograms are peaked about 0 (including the channel 3 image whose gray-level histogram was different from those of channels 1, 2, and 4). Most of the differences fall in the range -8 to $+8$. The

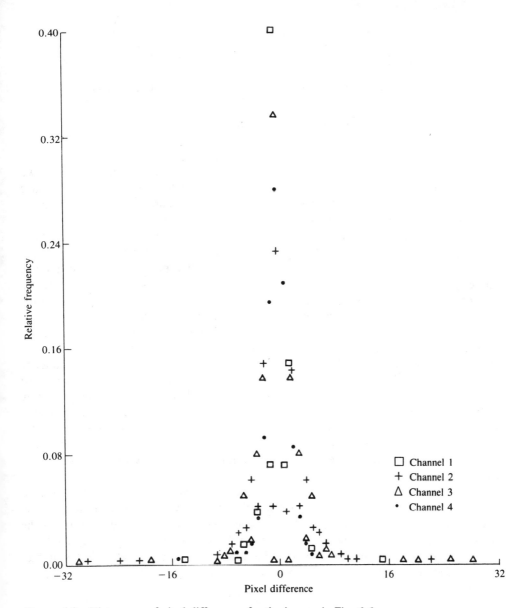

Figure 6.9 Histograms of pixel differences for the images in Fig. 6.6

difference operation has mapped the input set of pixel values into a different set of numbers having much more structure (less randomness).

Suppose that we construct a code consisting of the 16 code words $c_1, c_2, \ldots, c_{16}$. We could, for example, use the natural code so that $c_1 = 0000$, $c_2 = 0001$, $\ldots, c_{16} = 1111$. Let us assign 14 of these 16 code words to the 14 differences

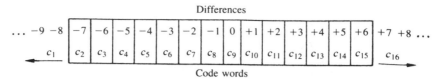

Figure 6.10   Illustration of code-word assignments.

$-7, -6, \ldots, -1, 0, +1, \ldots, +6$, as illustrated in Fig. 6.10. Of the two remaining code words, c_1 and c_{16}, we use c_{16} to indicate that the pixel difference was greater than $+6$ and c_1 to indicate that it was less than -7. This is a double-sided version of the shift code discussed in the previous section.

Any pixel difference from -127 to $+127$ can then be coded by one or more of the 16 code words if we use the following rule: If the difference $\Delta_i = x_i - x_{i-1}$ falls in the range -7 to $+6$ use the code word corresponding to the difference value. For example, -7 would be coded as c_2, -6 as c_3, etc. If the difference Δ_i is more than $+6$ we first use the shift-up code word c_{16} and shift all code words up by 14 units so that they are now assigned to the differences $+7, +8, \ldots, +20$ as illustrated in Fig. 6.11. Any difference Δ_i falling in the range $+7, \ldots, +20$ is coded by using the shift-up code word c_{16} followed by the code word corresponding to the difference. For example, $+8$ could be coded by using the sequence of two code words c_{16}, c_3. If the difference is greater than $+20$ we use the shift code word again and shift the code words up by another 14 units so that they now span the range $+21, +22, \ldots, +34$. The difference $+22$ would be coded by using the sequence of three code words c_{16}, c_{16}, c_3. For differences greater than $+34$ the procedure is repeated. The shift-up code word is used again and again until the difference Δ_i falls in the range spanned by the 14 code words $c_2, \ldots, c_{15}$.

For a difference less than -7 we use the same procedure, except that instead of using the shift-up code word c_{16} we use the shift-down code word c_1 to shift the code words down by 14 units. Each difference less than -7 is coded by using the shift-down code word c_1 one or more times followed by one of the code words $c_2, \ldots, c_{15}$ indicating the range in which the difference value is located. For example, -23 would be coded with the sequence c_1, c_1, c_{14}.

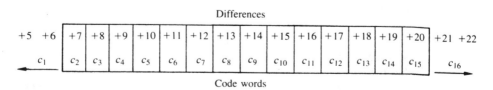

Figure 6.11   Illustration of code-word assignments after shifting.

Any difference value from -127 to $+127$ can be coded by using a sequence of one or more of the 16 code words $c_1, \ldots, c_{15}$. If we use the natural code $c_1 = 000$, $c_2 = 0001, \ldots, c_{16} = 1111$ then most differences can be coded with 4 bits because most fall in the range -7 to $+6$. Occasionally, two 4-bit code words requiring a total of 8 bits are required. On rarer occasions 12 or more bits are necessary. On the average, about 4.3 bits per picture element are required for the images in Figs. 6.6 and 6.7.

The relative frequency of using each of the 16 code words for the four images of Fig. 6.6 is presented in Fig. 6.12. The code words corresponding to differences near 0 are used more often than those corresponding to differences further from 0. Consequently, an unequal-length code would be more efficient than an equal-length code such as the natural code used above. The code shown in Fig. 6.13 has been found to be efficient for a large number of LANDSAT frames. The average number of bits per pixel averaged over all four channels for several different LANDSAT frames was about 3.5 bits per picture element, as illustrated in Table 6.3. This corresponds to a compression ratio of 2 relative to the 7-bit input picture elements. Table 6.3 also shows the average number of bits required by the Huffman code for the data of Fig. 6.6. It requires a fraction of a bit per picture element less than the code of Fig. 6.13.

The number of code words required to encode a LANDSAT frame using either of the codes discussed in the preceding paragraphs (equal length or unequal length) depends on the characteristics of the data, since the number of times the shift words are used is strongly dependent upon variations in a scene. The equal-length code has the advantage that all code words are 4-bit words and can be written on magnetic tape two per 8-bit byte, although the record length is different for different frames of data. The unequal length code has the disadvantage that it must be written as a sequence of words ranging from 2 to 7 bits in length.

6.3.2 Example 2. Contour Encoding

A digital image may be viewed as a function of two variables. The variables are the spatial coordinates and the value of the function at each coordinate is the gray level of the image at that point. Since there are a finite number of discrete levels of gray, we can visualize the function as a number of plateaus (or steps) with the plateau height equal to the gray level. Dark values correspond to low plateaus and light values correspond to high plateaus. A large area of picture elements with the same gray level would produce a large plateau. A single pixel surrounded by pixels having different gray levels would make a small plateau. Knowledge of the height, location, and shape of all the plateaus is equivalent to knowledge of the image.

The contour-encoding algorithm presented in this section reduces an image to a list of contours or plateaus. Each contour is uniquely determined by specifying (1) its gray level; (2) the location (row and column) of one pixel on its boundary, called the *initial point* (IP); and (3) a sequence of directionals that give the direction of travel as we trace around the outer extremity of the contour. The algorithm

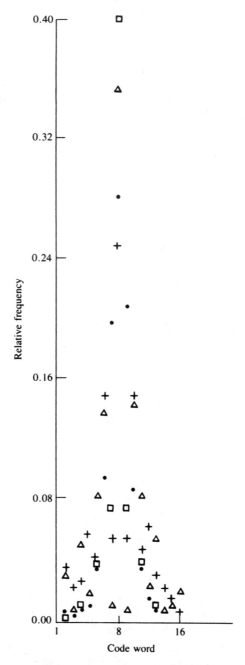

Figure 6.12 Relative frequencies of using each code word.

Table 6.3   Average Number of Bits Per Pixel Required to Code Some LANDSAT Frames

	Channel 1	Channel 2	Channel 3	Channel 4
Shift code	3.0865	3.8466	3.5894	3.3685
Huffman code	2.7517	3.5893	3.2900	2.8101

consists of two subalgorithms—an IP algorithm for locating new initial points (new contours) and a T algorithm for tracing contours after they are located. The subalgo-- rithms are used sequentially. The IP algorithm is used to locate the first initial point on the first contour and then the T algorithm is used to trace it; the IP algorithm is then used to locate the second initial point on the second contour, and the T algorithm is used to trace it; and so on. The IP algorithm locates all contours; none are located twice. The T algorithm traces the outer boundary of the largest connected set of elements having the same value as the initial point; it always terminates back at the initial point. For each contour, the algorithm outputs the value (gray level) and location of the initial point and the direction of travel around the boundary. All elements enclosed by the contour and having the same value as the contour are neglected.

c_1	1010
c_2	111 1111
c_3	11 1110
c_4	1 1110
c_5	1101
c_6	100
c_7	1100
c_8	00
c_9	0110
c_{10}	0111
c_{11}	0100
c_{12}	0101
c_{13}	1 1100
c_{14}	1 1101
c_{15}	111 1110
c_{16}	1101

Figure 6.13   A code that is nearly as efficient as the Huffman code.

The T algorithm

The T algorithm employs the classical rule for finding the way out of a maze–always turn left. As illustrated in Fig. 6.14, tracing a contour implies defining the direction of travel between adjacent elements such that no element outside the contour and adjacent to it has the same gray level as the elements on the countour. The rule for deciding the direction of travel out of each element is given relative to the direction of entry into that element by the *left-most-looking* (LML) rule.

LML rule. Look at the element to the left (relative to the direction of entry); if this element has the same value, move to it; if not, look at the element straight ahead; if this element has the same value, move to it; if not, look to the right; if this element has the same value, move to it; if not, look back; if this element has the same value, move to it; if not, none of the adjacent elements have the same value so that the contour consists of only one point.

The contour shown in Fig. 6.14 was traced by repeated applications of this rule, starting at the indicated IP. The direction of travel into the *first* IP is always assumed to be from the left side of the page, so that the "left relative to the direction of the entry into the IP" is "up." However, we cannot move up above the IP, so we look straight ahead. This element does have the same value as the IP and so we move to it and again apply the LML rule. It is noted that the procedure terminates back at the IP. Figure 6.15 illustrates the four contours generated by four applications of the T algorithm, each starting at the IP shown in the figure.

The T algorithm also assigns one of four indicators to each element of the two-dimensional array. These indicators are required by the IP algorithm described in the next section. Hence, when the two-dimensional array is stored in memory, two extra bits must be allocated to each element in order to store the appropriate

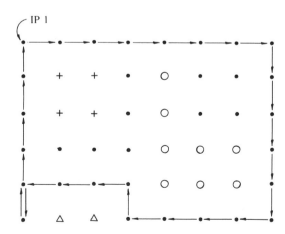

Figure 6.14 Contour No. 1 for an array with four gray levels.

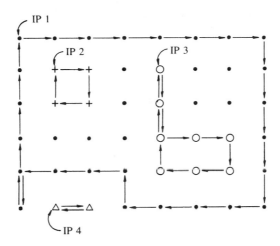

Figure 6.15   Four IPs and corresponding contours.

indicator. We denote the four indicators by D, A, R, and I. When the two-dimensional data array is read into memory, each element is assigned the indicator I. As the T algorithm moves from element to element tracing out a contour it also replaces the indicator for each element on the contour with either a D, A, or R indicator according to the *indicator assignment* (IA) rule.

IA rule. The indicator assigned to each contour element depends on the direction of travel into that element and the direction of travel out of that element, as indicated in Fig. 6.16. Some elements are passed through twice. When we pass through an element for the second time (this can be determined by checking its indicator—if it is not I we are passing it for the second time) we first determine an indicator for this pass from Fig. 6.16, but then use Fig. 6.17 to determine the indicator finally assigned to the element. (No elements are passed through more than twice.) The only exception to this rule is an IP, which always retains the indicator I.

	Direction of travel out of element	
	↑ or →	↓ or ←
↑ or ←	A	R
↓ or →	R	D

Direction of travel into element

Figure 6.16   Indicators for all possible combinations of directions of travel into and out of a pixel.

Indicator assigned on (first pass, second pass)	(D, A)	(D, R)	(A, R)
	(A, D)	(R, D)	(R, A)
	(R, R)	(D, D)	(A, A)
Final indicator assignment	R	D	A

Figure 6.17   Final assignments for each pair of indicators determined on the first pass and the second pass.

As an example, we again consider the contour illustrated in Fig. 6.14. At each element, the T algorithm applies the LML rule to determine the next direction of travel and then applies the IA rule to update the indicator for that element. The indicator stored in memory for each element on the contour shown in Fig. 6.15 is labeled next to that element in Fig. 6.18. At this point all elements not on the contour still have indicator I. However, as contours 2, 3, and 4 are traced out, all elements on these contours (except the IPs) will be assigned an A, R, or D indicator. The IPs and all elements not lying on the contour retain the indicator I.

The IP algorithm

The IP algorithm employs a systematic search procedure for determining initial points. The search for IPs starts with the element in the upper left-hand corner (the first-row, first-column element) and proceeds to the right across the first row until the end of the row is reached. Then the second row is searched from left to right,

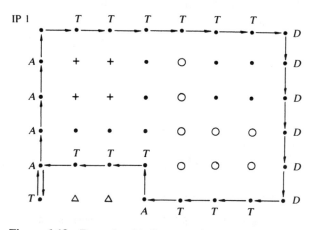

Figure 6.18   Example of indicator assignment.

then the third row, and so on, until we reach the element in the lov
corner of the data array. At this point all IPs have been located and
terminates. Hence, each element in the two-dimensional data array is tested to detei-
mine whether or not it is an IP.

As we move from element to element across each row in the data searching
for IPs we must simultaneously compile a *comparison point list* (CPL).

Rule for construction of CPL. As we start across each row the list is empty. As
we move across the row we check the indicator on each element we encounter. If
the indicator is *A* (for add) we add the value of that element (its gray level) to the
bottom of the list; if the indicator is *D* (for drop) we delete the *last* entry on the
list; if the indicator is *I* or *R* the list is left unchanged.

At the end of a row the comparison point list will be empty because, for each
row, the number of deletions is equal to the number of additions.

We are now ready to specify the test to be made on each element to determine
whether or not it is an IP.

IP rule. The element under test is an IP if it meets both of the following requirements:
(1) its indicator is *I,* and (2) its value (gray level) is not equal to the value of the
last entry in the CPL.

The 3-level, 14×13 array shown in Fig. 6.19 summarizes the concepts just
discussed. In this case, the contour-tracing algorithm reduced the image to a representation requiring eight contours.

Encoding approach

Sequential applications of the IP and T algorithms constitute the mapping section
of the encoding process illustrated in Fig. 6.1. The algorithm is initialized at the
first-row, first-column element. This element is always an IP, say IP #1. Then we
employ the T algorithm to trace out the first contour and simultaneously set the
element indicators. After arriving back at IP #1 we recall the IP algorithm to
search for a new IP. When a new IP, say #2, is encountered we again call on the
T algorithm to trace this contour and simultaneously set the appropriate element
indicators. Then the IP algorithm is used to search for IP #3, and so on. Each
resulting contour consists of (1) its gray level, (2) the row number of its IP, (3)
the column number of its IP, and (4) the sequence of directionals (directions of
travel) around its perimeter.

One possibility for coding the contours is to use the natural code for the gray
levels and the rows and columns of the initial points, and *Freeman's chain code*
(Freeman [1961]) for the directionals. This chain code, illustrated in Fig. 6.20,
uses the code word 00 to indicate up, 01 to the right, 10 down, and 11 to the left.
For example, the sequence of directions for the third contour of Fig. 6.15 is 10,
10, 01, 01, 10, 11, 11, 00, 00, and 00. Figure 6.21(a) lists the codes used to code
the contour number, the contour gray level, the row and column of the initial point,

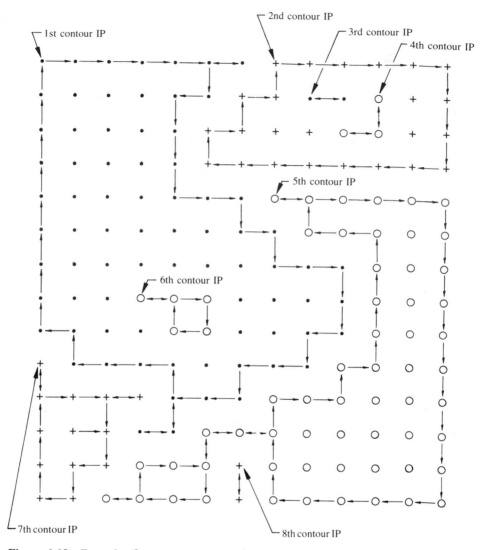

Figure 6.19 Example of contour-tracer operation.

and the directionals, respectively. Figure 6.21(b) shows the output of the coder using these codes to code the four contours of Fig. 6.15.

It is important for decoding purposes to know when the end of each set of directionals is reached and a new contour is to be started. This can be accomplished with no additional bits because all contours (sequences of directions) must terminate back at the starting point. We need only keep track of the number of right–left directionals and the number of up–down directionals. When they are both 0 we are

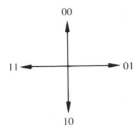

Figure 6.20 Binary coding of directionals.

Contour #	Code word	Gray level	Code word	Row or column	Code word	Direction of travel	Code word
1	00	•	00	1	000	↑	00
2	01	+	01	2	001	→	01
3	10	○	10	3	010	↓	10
4	11	△	11	4	011	←	11
				5	100		
				6	101		
				7	110		
				8	111		

(a)

Contour #	Value of IP	Row of IP	Column of IP	Direction to first element after IP	Direction to second element after IP	etc.						
00	00	000	000	01	01	01	01	...	(44 more bits)	...		
01	01	001	001	01	10	11	00					
10	10	001	100	10	10	01	01	10	11	11	00	00	00
11	11	101	011	01	11							

(b)

Figure 6.21 (a) A set of codes for the contour number, gray level, row, column, and direction of travel. (b) Coder output for the example in Fig. 6.15.

back at the IP and the next datum must correspond to a new contour. This rule works for all contours of length 2 or more. For contours of length 1 (single points) we use the binary pair 11; this is an impossible first directional because the pixel could not be an IP if it has the same gray level as the pixel to its left.

More-sophisticated codes can be used to code the contour with fewer bits. For example, since successive gray levels are usually highly correlated, the entropy of the gray-level differences is usually significantly less than the entropy of the gray levels, and therefore it is possible to code the differences with fewer bits than the number required to code the gray levels directly. The same is true for the row and column numbers for the initial points. Coding the differences between the row numbers of successive contours will require fewer bits than coding the sequence of row numbers when, on the average, these are naming new IPs on each row, as is the case for many image types. A similar statement holds for the column numbers.

As indicated above, a straightforward way to code the directionals is to use Freeman's chain code. Clearly, all possible sequences of directionals are not equally likely. Indeed, most sequences are impossible, due to the constraint that the contour must terminate back at the initial point. However, it is difficult to take this structure into account. For example, the Huffman coding technique would require a different Huffman code for each different sequence length (e.g., one code for sequences of length 0, another code for sequences of length 2, etc.). Furthermore, just enumerating the possible sequences, much less determining their probabilities, gets out of hand as the sequence length increases.

The number of bits required to code a particular image depends not only on the set of codes used, but also on the number of contours, which in turn depends on the amount of detail in the image and the number of gray levels. In Fig. 6.22(d) we present some results for the three images shown in Figs. 6.22(a) through (c). The set of codes used was

> *Gray levels:* the gray-level differences between successive gray levels were coded using a Huffman code.
>
> *Row numbers of IPs:* the differences between successive row numbers (run lengths) were coded using the natural code.
>
> *Column numbers of IPs:* the differences between successive column numbers were coded using a Huffman code.
>
> *Directionals:* the directionals were coded using Freeman's chain-code.

All Huffman codes were based on the statistics of the gray-level differences averaged over the three images in Fig. 6.22. It is noted that the efficiency of the contour depends on the amount of detail in the images and also on the number of quantization levels for the pixels. In other words, for images having a large number of small contours the method is not very efficient. For images that have a few number of larger contours the efficiency is improved.

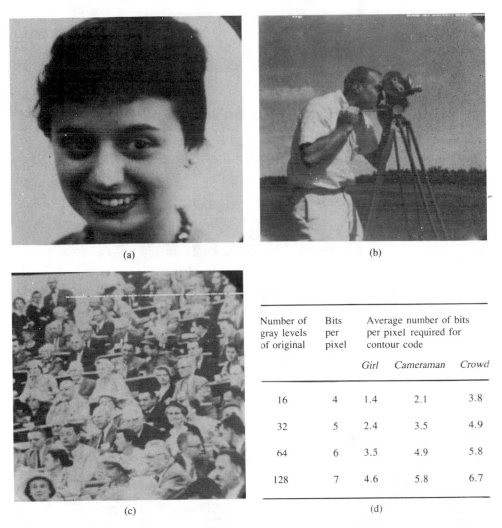

Number of gray levels of original	Bits per pixel	Average number of bits per pixel required for contour code		
		Girl	*Cameraman*	*Crowd*
16	4	1.4	2.1	3.8
32	5	2.4	3.5	4.9
64	6	3.5	4.9	5.8
128	7	4.6	5.8	6.7

(a)   (b)   (c)   (d)

Figure 6.22 (a) Girl. (b) Cameraman. (c) Crowd. (d) Contour-coding results.

These facts are further demonstrated by experiments conducted with the binary images shown in Fig. 6.23. Gattis and Wintz [1971] used a procedure similar to the one just described to encode the contours of these images. The average number of bits needed to code the contours of the drawing, printed text, and fingerprint were 0.15, 0.15, and 0.50, respectively. As expected, the average number of bits was proportional to the complexity of the image.

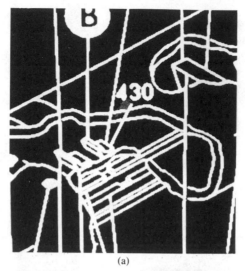

(a)

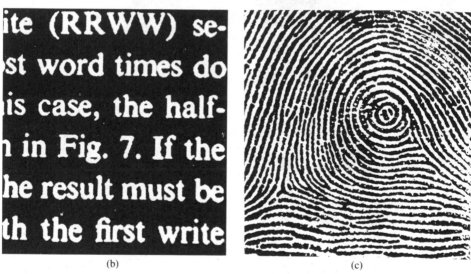

(b)   (c)

Figure 6.23   Contour-coding results. (a) Section of aircraft drawing, 0.15 bits per pixel.
(b) Sample of printed text, 0.15 bits per pixel. (c) Section of fingerprint, 0.50 bits per pixel.

Reconstruction mapping

The reconstruction of an image from its contour code is straightforward, given an
understanding of the mapping strategy. It employs the basic rules employed by the
T algorithm and the IP algorithm. The reconstruction algorithm reconstructs each
element in the data array starting with the first-column, first-row element. Since

this element is IP #1 its value is known. Furthermore, the elements in the data array corresponding to contour #1 can be reconstructed along with their indicators by using the system output and the IA rule. After reconstructing this contour and arriving back at IP #1 we move, element by element, across the first row, then the second row, etc. As we move across each row we also compile a CPL according to the CPL rule. Each element encountered is either an IP, an element on a contour already reconstructed, or an element not belonging to a contour. The reconstruction rule is

(1) If the element is an IP, reconstruct the contour and set the indicators.

(2) If the element indicator is not I, it has already been reconstructed. Hence, move to the next element.

(3) If the element is not an IP, and its indicator is I, its value is the last entry on the CPL.

6.3.3 Example 3. Run-Length Encoding for Flood Maps

River flood control in the United States is the responsibility of the U.S. Army Corps of Engineers (USACE). This agency monitors stream and reservoir water levels, precipitation, etc., in order to predict possible flooding conditions and to minimize flood damage by opening or closing flood gates, and raising or lowering reservoir levels. Collecting this input data over a total watershed such as the Mississippi River Valley is a major problem.

An infrared image from a LANDSAT frame that includes a part of the Ohio River is presented in Fig. 6.24(a). Water appears dark because it absorbs electromagnetic radiation in the infrared band. For this reason it is relatively easy to classify each resolution element† as either "water" or "not water" with high accuracy, using multispectral signature-analysis techniques. The output of such a classification algorithm is presented in image form in Fig. 6.24(b), where all resolution elements classified as water are assigned a dark gray level and all nonwater resolution elements are assigned a light gray level. This image was collected at a time when the river level was near normal. A LANDSAT image of the same region, but taken at a time when the river was flooded, is shown in Fig. 6.24(c). The classification results are presented in Fig. 6.24(d). Similarly, Fig. 6.25 shows a reservoir at its normal and flooded stages along with the classification results. Processed images such as those presented in Figs. 6.24(b) and (d) and Figs. 6.25(b) and (d) are of value to the USACE, provided they can be delivered within hours. The problem is to transmit them at a reasonable cost to the USACE computer from the receiving station, which may be hundreds of miles away.

---

† In earth-resources applications, pixels are sometimes called "resolution elements."

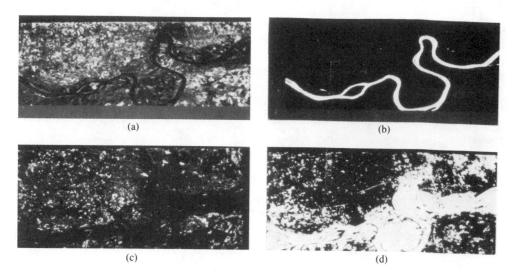

Figure 6.24   Two parts of a LANDSAT frame (a, c) and corresponding classification maps (b, d).

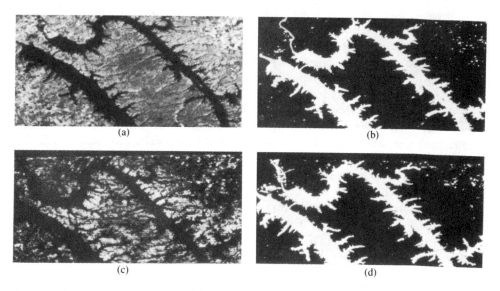

Figure 6.25   Same areas as in Fig. 6.24, but under flooded conditions.

One-dimensional run-length encoding (RLC)

A scan line of pixels consists of a sequence of integers (gray levels) $x_1, x_2, \ldots ,$ x_N. In run-length encoding we map this sequence of integers into a sequence of integer pairs (g_k, l_k), where g_k denotes gray levels and l_k denotes run lengths. The run length is the number of juxtaposed picture elements having the same gray level.

As illustrated in Fig. 6.3, we start at the leftmost pixel and set g_1 equal to x_1 and l_1 equal to the length of the run of pixels with gray-level g_1. At the first gray-level transition we set g_2 equal to the gray-level value of the second run and l_2 equal to the length of this run. This procedure is repeated until we come to the end of the scan line, at which point we repeat the procedure for the next scan line. The number of runs can vary from 1 (every pixel on the scan line has the same gray level) to N (no two adjacent pixels have the same value). The corresponding run lengths l_k can vary from N to 1. To accommodate the longest possible run the natural code would require $\log_2 N$ bits. If most run lengths are significantly shorter than N, this code is not very efficient because many of the code words are not used or are used infrequently. Assuming that the quantizer outputs a unique value for each mapped pair (g_k, l_k), the next problem is to choose a code for the run lengths and gray levels.

The run-length statistics for the classification results of Figs. 6.24 and 6.25 are shown in Fig. 6.26. Note that the run lengths are reasonably close to a power law and, as discussed above, the B_1-code is a good approximation to the optimal Huffman code for 2-level data satisfying this condition. Since the continuation bit can be used to code the gray levels in the case of binary data, we will assume that $C = 0$ is used for dark runs and $C = 1$ for light runs.

The B_1-code for various run lengths is shown in the last column of Table 6.4 (the center column is discussed in the next section). The data compression ratios relative to the 1 bit per pixel that would be required for straightforward coding of each element are presented in the first column of Table 6.5 for each of the classified pictures of Figs. 6.24 and 6.25. The second and third columns are discussed in the next section.

The run-length coding scheme described in the preceding paragraphs takes into account the data structure down each scan line, but not the structure between scan lines. Stated another way, it takes into account correlations between horizontal-resolution elements but not correlations between vertical-resolution elements.

Two-dimensional run-length encoding (PDQ and DDC)

A two-dimensional run-length encoding technique called a *predictive differential quantizer* (PDQ) is illustrated in Fig. 6.27. The PDQ mapping approach is to map the array of resolution elements into the sequence of integer pairs Δ' and Δ'', where Δ' is the difference between the starting points of runs on successive lines, and Δ'' is the difference between the run lengths on successive lines together with "new start" and "merge" indicators used to denote the start and the end of each dark area. PDQ mapping is similar to the contour algorithm described in Section 6.3.2, except that it simultaneously traces out the front and back contour edges rather than first going down the back side and then up the front side. It has the advantage that only two lines of pixels need to be stored, whereas the contour algorithm requires that the complete picture be stored. On the other hand, the PDQ approach results in more "new starts" than the contour algorithm, as illustrated in Fig. 6.27,

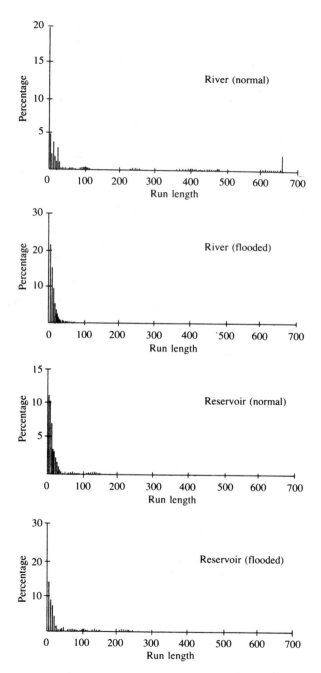

Figure 6.26 Run-length statistics for the classification results in Figs. 6.24 and 6.25.

Table 6.4   B$_1$ Code. $C = 0$ for Dark Runs; $C = 1$ for Light Runs in Run-length Coding. $C = 0$ for Δ'; $C = 1$ for Δ'' or Δ''' in PDQ and DDC coding.

Run Length	Δ', Δ'', Δ'''	Code Word
1	0	C0
2	+1	C1
3	−1	C0C0
4	+2	C0C1
5	−2	C1C0
6	+3	C1C1
7	−3	C0C0C0
8	+4	C0C0C1
9	−4	C0C1C0
10	+5	C0C1C1
11	−5	C1C0C0
12	+6	C1C0C1
13	−6	C1C1C0
14	+7	C1C1C1
15	−7	C0C0C0C0
16	+8	C0C0C0C1
.	.	.
.	.	.
.	.	.

Table 6.5   Data Compression Ratios Relative to 1 Bit per Pixel Required by the Original Digital Picture

	RLC	PDQ	DDC
River, normal	9.6	13.0	14.7
River, flooded	2.9	1.2	1.4
Reservoir, normal	6.7	5.3	6.2
Reservoir, flooded	6.3	4.5	5.6

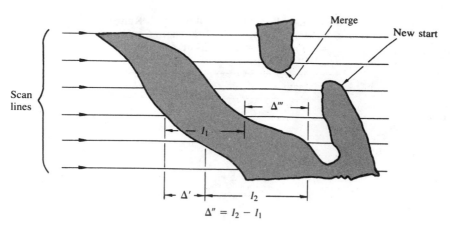

Figure 6.27   Illustration of the PDQ algorithm.

where, by the contour algorithm, the black area labeled "new start" would have been included in the same contour as the black area to the left.

Assuming that the quantizer outputs a different value for each output from the mapper, the remaining problem is to code the mapper outputs Δ', Δ'', *start*, and *merge*. The histograms for the quantities Δ' and Δ'' for the classified images of Figs. 6.24 and 6.25 are shown in Figs. 6.28 through 6.31. Using the B_1-code for Δ' and Δ'' (see Table 6.4) and also for the column numbers of the new starts and merges resulted in the data compression ratios shown in the second column of Table 6.5. The B_1-code is not efficient for coding the "new start" and "merge" column numbers, which are approximately uniformly distributed, but these occur infrequently relative to the Δ' and Δ'' (many Δ' and Δ'' are coded, on the average, for each "new start" and "merge") and it is convenient to use only one code for all four mapper outputs.

Another possibility is to code Δ' and Δ''' (the changes in the front and back edges of the dark areas) rather than Δ' and Δ''. This is called double delta coding (DDC). The histograms for Δ''' are also presented in Figs. 6.28 through 6.31. Using the B_1-code again we obtain the compression ratios listed in Table 6.5 under DDC. From these results we conclude that when there are a few large black areas, two-dimensional run-length coding is more efficient. For many small black areas one-dimensional run-length coding is more efficient.

6.4   IMAGE ENCODING RELATIVE TO A FIDELITY CRITERION

In many applications some error in the reconstructed image can be tolerated. In this section we present some examples of this case.

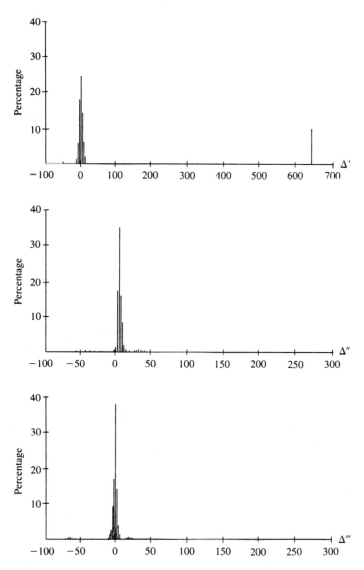

Figure 6.28   Difference histograms for Fig. 6.24(b).

6.4.1   Example 1. Differential Pulse Code Modulation (DPCM)

Values of adjacent pixels are highly correlated for most images. The autocorrelation function for the picture of the cameraman in Fig. 6.32(a) is shown in Fig. 6.32(b). If pixel x_{i-1} is a certain gray level, then the adjacent pixel x_i along the scan line is

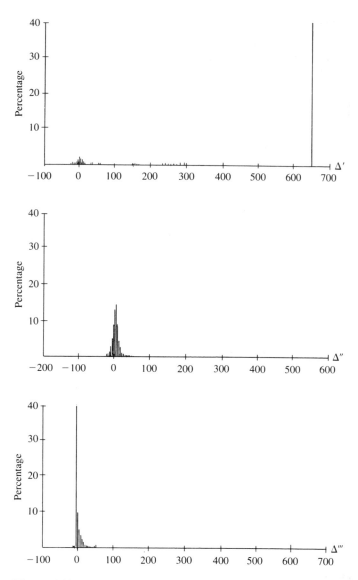

Figure 6.29   Difference histograms for Fig. 6.24(d).

likely to have a similar value. This is further illustrated by the histogram of pixel differences $x_i - x_{i-1}$ presented in Fig. 6.32(c). Whereas the pixel values range over 256 different gray levels in the image, most adjacent pixel differences are in a range of about 20 gray-level values. Differential pulse code modulation (DPCM) makes use of this property in the following manner. We observe a pixel x_{i-1} and based on this observed value we predict the value of the next pixel x_i. Let $\hat{x}_i$ be the predicted value of x_i, and let us subtract this value from the actual value x_i to

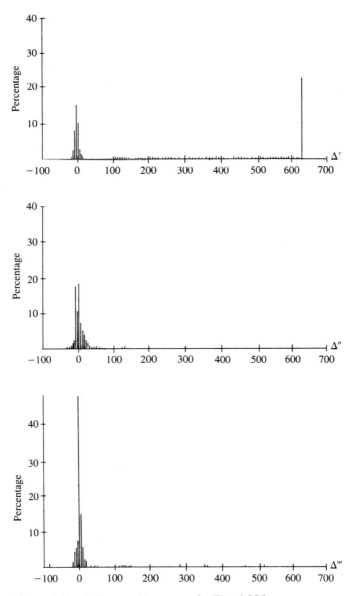

Figure 6.30   Difference histograms for Fig. 6.25(b).

obtain the difference $d_i = x_i - \hat{x}_i$. Assuming that the estimates are reasonably accurate, the difference $x_i - \hat{x}_i$ will, on the average, be significantly smaller in magnitude than the magnitude of the pixel x_i. Consequently, fewer quantization bins and fewer bits are required to code the sequence of differences than would be required to code the sequence of picture elements.

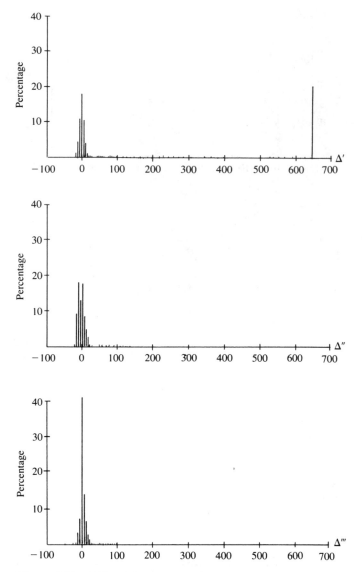

Figure 6.31   Difference histograms for Fig. 6.25(d).

The problem is to estimate x_i given that we know x_{i-1}. The linear estimator that results in the least-mean-square estimation error, $E\{(x_i - \hat{x}_i)^2\}$, is given by

$$\hat{x}_i = \rho x_{i-1} + (1 - \rho)m,\qquad(6.4\text{-}1)$$

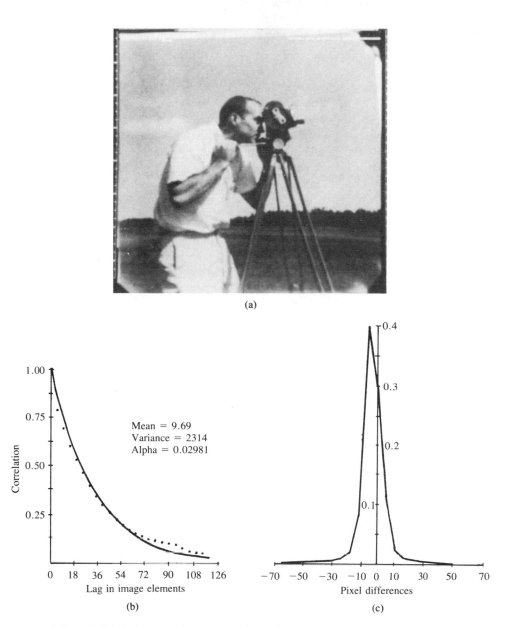

Figure 6.32 (a) Original image. (b) Autocorrelation function. (c) Histogram of pixel differences.

where m is the mean (average) gray level and ρ is the normalized correlation between the adjacent picture elements; that is,

$$\rho = \frac{E\{x_i x_{i-1}\}}{E\{x_i^2\}}. \tag{6.4-2}$$

The estimate $\hat{x}_i$ in Eq. (6.4-1) can be interpreted as a weighted average of the preceding pixel x_{i-1} and the mean of x_i. The weights depend on the correlation coefficient ρ. When the pixel values are highly correlated ρ approaches 1 and $1 - \rho$ approaches 0, in which case the estimate is based primarily on the value of x_{i-1}. When the pixel values are not very correlated the opposite condition holds and the estimate is based primarily on the mean value. For properly sampled images, ρ typically lies between 0.85 and 0.95.

It is easy to show that the variance of the difference

$$d_i = x_i - \hat{x}_i \tag{6.4-3}$$

is given by

$$\sigma_{d_i}^2 = (1 - \rho^2)\sigma_{x_i}^2, \tag{6.4-4}$$

where $\sigma_{x_i}^2$ is the variance of x_i. It can also be shown that the d_is are uncorrelated; that is, the mapping from the x_i to the d_i produces uncorrelated coefficients. Note that, if $\rho = 1$, this mapping is identical to the difference mapping defined by the transformation given in Eq. (6.2-3). Stated another way, the difference mapping defined by Eq. (6.2-3) corresponds to saying that $\hat{x}_i$ is the same as x_{i-1}.

The remaining problems are to quantize and code the differences d_i. A system block diagram for a typical DPCM encoder–decoder pair is shown in Fig. 6.33. The predictors in the encoder and decoders are identical. Both simply delay the input by an amount of time equal to the time between samples (the inverse of the

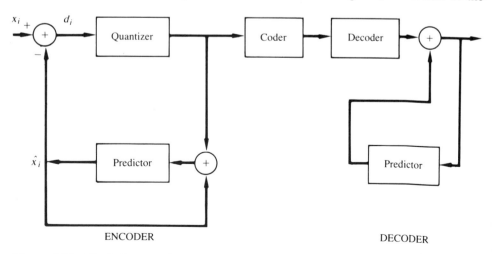

ENCODER   DECODER

Figure 6.33   Block diagram of DPCM system.

sampling rate) and scale this delayed input by a constant α. This factor is called the *prediction coefficient* and is chosen in accordance with Eq. (6.4.2); that is, the optimal value for the prediction coefficient α is the correlation coefficient ρ.

As indicated above, the mapping in this case consists of forming the difference given in Eq. (6.4-3). Without the quantizer in the loop, the estimates given by the encoder predictor would be based on the exact differences d_i. In addition, the decoding process would be simply the inverse mapping. With the quantizer in the loop, the estimates are based on the *quantized* differences, and the decoding process is no longer exact. Suppose, for example, that the quantizer can have only eight output levels spaced uniformly. The decoder would incur relatively little error on slowly varying (small differences) scan lines. On rapidly changing scan lines, however, the difference between adjacent pixels would become large and the decoder would not be able to follow the input because the largest difference out of the quantizer corresponds to a step of $+4$ or -4 quantizer bin widths. This inability to follow rapid gray-level variations is called *slope overload,* and it results in a smearing (blurring) of sharp edges in the reconstructed image. The encoder can be made to respond more rapidly to a rapidly changing input by increasing the bin width, but this occurs at the expense of increased error when the signal is slowly varying. This error is called *granular noise* because smooth sections of the reconstructed image appear "grainy." Consequently, the quantizer bin width is chosen to provide the best compromise between these two sources of error. Both slope overload and granular noise can be reduced by increasing the number of quantization levels at the expense of more bits to code the increased number of levels.

Some examples of DPCM coded–decoded pictures are presented in Fig. 6.34(a) through (c). The prediction coefficient was set equal to the correlation coefficient in all three cases. The differences were quantized with an exponential quantizer matched to the difference statistics of the image, and the natural code was used to code the quantizer output. At 3 bits per pixel very little distortion is noticeable. At 2 bits per pixel we observe both smeared gray-level edges and granular noise in the background (sky). At 1 bit per pixel severe distortions are evident. DPCM with a 1-bit quantizer is called *delta modulation.*

In many applications the bits out of the encoder are transmitted over a digital data transmission system (called a channel) to the decoder. Such channels are not usually perfect in the sense that errors occur; that is, a bit may be put into the channel a 1, but come out as 0. The effect of channel bit errors on the 3-bit image of Fig. 6.34(a) is illustrated in Fig. 6.34(d). It can be shown that with a prediction coefficient of α the duration of the error streak is proportional to $1/(1 - \alpha^2)$. For $\alpha = 1$, the errors persist until some corrective action is taken, as illustrated in Fig. 6.35(a), where we reinitialized at the start of each scan line; that is, the output of the predictor was set equal to the mean gray level for the first pixel of each scan line so that an error in the previous line would not persist past the end of that line. One way to counter this effect is to replace each scan line containing an error with the previous scan line. The image in Fig. 6.35(b) was obtained by applying this line-replacement method to the image of Fig. 6.35(a).

(a)

(b)

(c)

(d)

Figure 6.34 Example of DPCM coding of Fig. 6.32(a) and then decoding the result. (a) 3 bits/pixel. (b) 2 bits/pixel. (c) 1 bit/pixel. (d) Effect of channel error with 3 bits/pixel and a signal-to-noise ratio of 13.7.

6.4.2   Example 2. Transform Encoding

Image transforms such as the ones discussed in Chapter 3 are often used as the mapping function in the encoding procedure described in Fig. 6.1. An encoding method that employs this type of mapping is appropriately referred to as a *transform-encoding* technique.

In transform encoding we first subdivide a given $N \times N$ image into a number of subarrays. For one-dimensional encoding the subarrays are of size $1 \times n$ with

(a)   (b)

Figure 6.35   Illustration of (a) line initialization, and (b) line replacement. In both cases α was 1, the signal-to-noise ratio was 19.5, and 3 bits/pixel were used.

$n < N$, and each "subimage" may be interpreted as an n-dimensional vector. In two-dimensional encoding the subimages are usually $n \times n$ square arrays of pixels, with $n < N$. After dividing the image into subimages we code each subimage as a unit, independently of all other subimages. In *nonadaptive transform encoding* we use the same encoder for all subimages. In *adaptive transform encoding* we can choose the one that works best in some sense for the particular subimage content.

The purpose of the transform mapping is to reduce the correlation between pixels. The motivation behind this approach is to improve encoding efficiency by processing the transformed coefficients independently of each other. To illustrate this point we present a simplified example using a hypothetical 3-bit (8 gray-level) image. Consider a one-dimensional transform encoder with $n = 2$ so that the image is first subdivided into 1×2 arrays, where the two pixels in each 1×2 array are adjacent. In other words, the first array consists of the first and second pixels on the first scan line; the second array consists of the third and fourth pixels on the first scan line, and so on. Let the vector $\mathbf{x} = (x_1, x_2)'$ represent two adjacent picture elements, and let us make a scatter plot of the gray-level value of x_1 against the gray-level value of x_2, as illustrated in Fig. 6.36(a). Since each pixel has any of 8 gray levels there are 64 possible combinations of x_1 and x_2. However, all combinations are not equally likely. It is unlikely that x_1 will have a high value and x_2 a low value, and vice versa. Since adjacent pixels are more likely to have nearly the same gray level the most likely combinations are the ones in the vicinity of $x_1 = x_2$, this is, those in the shaded area of Fig. 6.36(a).

Now suppose we rotate the coordinate system, as illustrated in Fig. 6.36(b). In the new coordinate system the more likely values are not in the vicinity of $y_1 =$

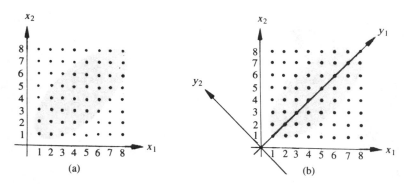

Figure 6.36 (a) Correlated pixels. (b) New coordinate system (y_1, y_2) for eliminating correlation.

y_2 but are lined up with the y_1 axis. Hence, the variables y_1 and y_2 are "more independent" than were x_1 and x_2; that is, y_2 is likely to be small independently of the value of y_1. Rotating the coordinate system also rearranged the variances. The total is the same, $\sigma_{y_1}^2 + \sigma_{y_2}^2 = \sigma_{x_1}^2 + \sigma_{x_2}^2$, but whereas both initial elements had the same variance ($\sigma_{x_1}^2 = \sigma_{x_2}^2$) more of the variance is now in the first component of the transformed space ($\sigma_{y_1}^2 > \sigma_{y_2}^2$). Finally, we note that given the coefficients y_1 and y_2 we can perform the inverse rotation to obtain the pixels x_1 and x_2.

The same procedure can be used for an $n \times n$ array of pixels, each of which is quantized to one of 2^K gray levels. In this case an n^2-dimensional coordinate system is required with each coordinate labeled with the values 1, 2, . . . , 2^K. Each of the $2^{n^2 K}$ points corresponds to one of the $2^{n^2 K}$ possible $n \times n$ subimages.

One-dimensional transformations
Rotating the n-dimensional coordinate system of the n pixels corresponds to arranging the pixels into the n vector, $\mathbf{x} = (x_1, x_2, \ldots , x_n)'$, and performing the linear transformation

$$\mathbf{y} = \mathbf{Ax}, \tag{6.4-5}$$

where $\mathbf{A}$ is an $n \times n$ unitary matrix, with elements a_{ki} k, $i = 1, 2, \ldots , n$, that determines the rotation, and $\mathbf{y} = (y_1, y_2, \ldots , y_n)'$ is an n vector. Since for unitary matrices $\mathbf{A}^{-1} = \mathbf{A}'$, the inverse rotation is accomplished by the inverse transformation

$$\mathbf{x} = \mathbf{A}'\mathbf{y}, \tag{6.4-6}$$

where $\mathbf{A}'$ is the transpose of $\mathbf{A}$.

According to Eq. (6.4-5), each coefficient y_k is a linear combination of all pixels; that is,

$$y_k = \sum_{i=1}^{n} a_{ki} x_i \tag{6.4-7}$$

for $k = 1, 2, \ldots , n$.

Similarly, Eq. (6.4-6) gives each pixel as a linear combination of all the coefficients:

$$x_i = \sum_{k-1}^{n} b_{ik} y_k \tag{6.4-8}$$

for $i = 1, 2, \ldots, n$.

With a slight change in notation, we see that Eqs. (6.4-7) and (6.4-8) are identical in form to the general transform relations given in Eqs. (3.5-1) and (3.5-2), with a_{ki} and b_{ki} being the forward and inverse transformation kernels, respectively.

For our purpose the best transformation would be one that results in statistically independent variables y. This transformation cannot be determined for two reasons. First, it evidently depends on very detailed statistics (the joint probability density function of the n pixels), which have not been deduced from basic physical laws and which cannot be measured. Second, even if the joint density function of the n pixels were known, the problem of determining a reversible transformation that results in independent coefficients is unsolved. The closest we can get with linear transformations to a transformation that produces independent coefficients is the one that produces uncorrelated coefficients. The resulting coefficients are uncorrelated but not necessarily statistically independent.

As indicated in Section 3.6, the transformation matrix **A** that produces uncorrelated coefficients is one whose rows are formed by the eigenvectors of the covariance matrix of the original pixel vectors. In this case, the samples used to obtain the covariance matrix would be all the n-dimensional vectors into which the given $N \times N$ image was decomposed. Equation (3.6-5) provides a convenient method for estimating the covariance matrix of a finite number of vector samples.

Two-dimensional transformations

For two-dimensional transformations the $n \times n$ array of pixels is arranged in the form of an $n \times n$ matrix **X** with elements x_{ij}, $i,j = 1, 2, \ldots, n$, and then transformed into an $n \times n$ matrix **Y** with elements y_{kl}, $k,l = 1, 2, \ldots, n$.

The general form of the transformation that maps the elements of **X** into the elements of **Y** is given by the relation

$$y_{kl} = \sum_{i=1}^{n} \sum_{j=1}^{n} x_{ij} a_{ijkl} \tag{6.4-9}$$

for $k,l = 1, 2, \ldots, n$. With a change in notation, we see that Eq. (6.4-9) is identical in form to Eq. (3.5-3), with a_{ijkl} being the forward transformation kernel.

The inverse transformation gives each original pixel as a linear combination of the coefficients; that is,

$$x_{ij} = \sum_{k=1}^{n} \sum_{l=1}^{n} y_{kl} b_{ijkl} \tag{6.4-10}$$

for $i,j = 1, 2, \ldots, n$, where b_{ijkl} is the inverse transformation kernel.

As indicated in Section 3.5, numerous types of transformations can be expressed in the form of Eqs. (6.4-9) and (6.4-10), depending on the choice of the kernel. The Fourier, Hadamard, and Hotelling transforms are the most popular for transform coding applications. The Fourier and Hadamard transforms fit directly in the format of Eqs. (6.4-9) and (6.4-10). When using the Hotelling transform, however, care must be exercised in interpreting the notation in these equations. The reason for this is best illustrated by a simple example.

Consider the problem of transforming a 2×2 subimage array

$$\mathbf{X} = \begin{bmatrix} x_{11} & x_{12} \\ x_{21} & x_{22} \end{bmatrix}$$

Expansion of Eq. (6.4-9) yields

$$y_{11} = x_{11}a_{1111} + x_{12}a_{1211} + x_{21}a_{2111} + x_{22}a_{2211}$$

$$y_{12} = x_{11}a_{1112} + x_{12}a_{1212} + x_{21}a_{2112} + x_{22}a_{2212}$$

$$y_{21} = x_{11}a_{1121} + x_{12}a_{1221} + x_{21}a_{2121} + x_{22}a_{2221}$$

$$y_{22} = x_{11}a_{1122} + x_{12}a_{1222} + x_{21}a_{2122} + x_{22}a_{2222}$$

Computation of the kernel values for, say, the Fourier or Hadamard transform is straightforward. From Section 3.5 we have, for example, that the Fourier kernel is given by

$$a_{ijkl} = \frac{1}{N} \exp[-j2\pi(ik + jl)/N]$$

with $N = 2$ in this case.

Interpretation of the kernel values for the Hotelling transform is different because, as indicated in Section 3.6 and again in Section 6.4.2, this transform is expressed in the *vector* form $\mathbf{y} = \mathbf{A}\mathbf{x}$. For a two-dimensional problem, the 2×2 subimage $\mathbf{X}$ can be expressed in vector form, as follows:

$$\mathbf{x} = \begin{bmatrix} x_{11} \\ x_{12} \\ x_{21} \\ x_{22} \end{bmatrix}$$

The transformation matrix $\mathbf{A}$ is formed from the eigenvectors of the covariance matrix of all the xs extracted from a given image. Suppose that $\mathbf{A}$ has the form

$$\mathbf{A} = \begin{bmatrix} e_{11} & e_{12} & e_{13} & e_{14} \\ e_{21} & e_{22} & e_{23} & e_{24} \\ e_{31} & e_{32} & e_{33} & e_{34} \\ e_{41} & e_{42} & e_{43} & e_{44} \end{bmatrix}$$

where e_{ij} is the jth component of the ith eigenvector. The transformed subimage **Y**, if expressed in vector form, is

$$\mathbf{y} = \begin{bmatrix} y_{11} \\ y_{12} \\ y_{21} \\ y_{22} \end{bmatrix}$$

Since $\mathbf{y} = \mathbf{Ax}$, we have

$$y_{11} = x_{11}e_{11} + x_{12}e_{12} + x_{21}e_{13} + x_{22}e_{14}$$

$$y_{12} = x_{11}e_{21} + x_{12}e_{22} + x_{21}e_{23} + x_{22}e_{24}$$

$$y_{21} = x_{11}e_{31} + x_{12}e_{32} + x_{21}e_{33} + x_{22}e_{34}$$

$$y_{22} = x_{11}e_{41} + x_{12}e_{42} + x_{21}e_{43} + x_{22}e_{44}$$

Thus we see that the *form* of this expansion is identical to the one obtained from Eq. (6.4-9), since each y_{kl} is given as a linear combination of all the x_{ij}, for $i,j = 1, 2, \ldots , n$. Note, however, that the elements of **A** do not follow the same notation used for the kernels in Eq. (6.4-9). In other words, the Hotelling transform can be used in a two-dimensional formulation, as long as the elements in the transformation are interpreted properly. Similar comments hold for the inverse transformation.

Basis images
Another interpretation of Eq. (6.4-10) is possible. Let us write that equation in the form

$$\mathbf{X} = \sum_{k=1}^{n} \sum_{l=1}^{n} y_{kl}\mathbf{B}_{kl} \tag{6.4-11}$$

and interpret this as a series expansion of the $n \times n$ subimage **X** into n^2 $n \times n$ *basis images*:

$$\mathbf{B}_{kl} = \begin{bmatrix} b_{kl11} & b_{kl12} & \cdots & b_{kl1n} \\ b_{kl21} & b_{kl22} & \cdots & b_{kl2n} \\ \cdot & \cdot & \cdot & \cdot \\ \cdot & \cdot & \cdot & \cdot \\ \cdot & \cdot & \cdot & \cdot \\ b_{kln1} & b_{kln2} & \cdots & b_{klnn} \end{bmatrix} \tag{6.4-12}$$

with the y_{kl} for $k,l = 1, 2, \ldots , n$, being the coefficients (weights) of the expansion. Hence, Eq. (6.4-11) gives the image **X** as a weighted sum of the basis images $\mathbf{B}_{kl}$. The coefficients of the expansion are given by Eq. (6.4-9), which may be written in the form

$$\mathbf{y} = \mathbf{A}_{kl}\mathbf{X}, \tag{6.4-13}$$

where $\mathbf{A}_{kl}$ is formed in the same manner as $\mathbf{B}_{kl}$, except that the forward kernel is used.

Figure 6.37(a) shows the Hadamard basis images for $N = 256$ and $n = 16$. Since the inverse Hadamard kernel b_{ijkl} depends only on the values of i, j, k, and l, all $N \times N$ images that are subdivided into $n \times n$ subimages have the same set of Hadamard basis images $\mathbf{B}_{kl}$. Computation of $\mathbf{B}_{kl}$ for the Hotelling transformation, on the other hand, depends on the inverse of the transformation matrix $\mathbf{A}$. In other words, the b_{ijkl} in Eq. (6.4-10) depends in this case on the values of $\mathbf{A}^{-1}$ in the same manner shown above for the forward transform. Since the entries in $\mathbf{A}^{-1}$ in turn depend on the covariance matrix of the subimages, the $\mathbf{B}_{kl}$ for the Hotelling transform are different for different images. The case shown in Fig. 6.37(b), for example, corresponds to the picture of the cameraman in Fig. 6.32(a), with $n = 16$.

We have already noted that if a set of subimages is transformed such that the coefficients y_{kl} are "more independent" than the original pixels x_{ij}, then the variances of the coefficients are in general not equal. Therefore we can index the basis images such that the terms in Eq. (6.4-11) are ordered according to the variances of the coefficients. In this manner, successive terms contribute proportionally less and less, on the average, to the total. Indeed, for some choices of basis images the coefficients become insignificant after the first, say, η terms so that an approximate representation for the original image can be obtained by truncating the series after the first η terms; that is,

$$\mathbf{X} = \sum_{k=1}^{n} \sum_{l=1}^{n} y_{kl}\mathbf{B}_{kl} \approx \sum_{k=1}^{\eta} \sum_{l=1}^{\eta} y_{kl}\mathbf{B}_{kl} = \hat{\mathbf{X}}. \qquad (6.4-14)$$

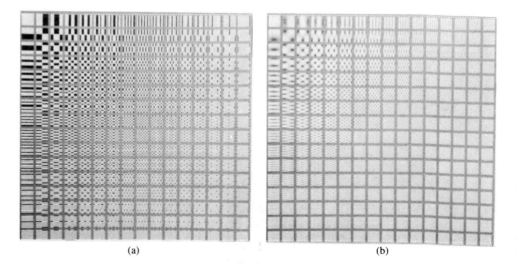

(a)   (b)

Figure 6.37   (a) Hadamard basis images. (b) Hotelling basis images.

The mean-square approximation error between the original $\mathbf{X}$ and the approximate image $\hat{\mathbf{X}}$ is given by

$$
\begin{aligned}
e_{\text{ms}} &= E\{\|\mathbf{X} - \hat{\mathbf{X}}\|^2\} \\
&= E\left\{\left\|\sum_{k=1}^{n}\sum_{l=1}^{n} y_{kl}\mathbf{B}_{kl} - \sum_{k=1}^{\eta}\sum_{l=1}^{\eta} y_{kl}\mathbf{B}_{kl}\right\|^2\right\} \\
&= E\left\{\left\|\sum_{k=\eta+1}^{n}\sum_{l=\eta+1}^{n} y_{kl}\mathbf{B}_{kl}\right\|^2\right\} \\
&= \sum_{k=\eta+1}^{n}\sum_{l=\eta+1}^{n} \sigma_{y_{kl}}^2,
\end{aligned}
\tag{6.4-15}
$$

where $\|\mathbf{X} - \hat{\mathbf{X}}\|$ is the norm of the matrix difference $(\mathbf{X} - \hat{\mathbf{X}})$, and the last step follows because the basis images are orthonormal. Equation (6.4-15) states that the mean-square approximation error is given by the sum of variances of the discarded coefficients.

We now pose the following problem: What set of basis images minimizes the mean square error by packing the most variance into the first η coefficients? The solution to this problem is the same as the solution to the seemingly unrelated problem of determining the set of basis images that produce uncorrelated coefficients. The Hotelling transformation: (a) produces uncorrelated coefficients; (b) minimizes the mean-square approximation error; and (c) packs the maximum amount of variance into the first η coordinates (for any η).

The cameraman picture was divided into 16×16 subimages and each subimage was expanded in a Hotelling, Fourier, and Hadamard series expansion. The sample variances of the coefficients are presented in Fig. 6.38(a). It is noted from Fig.

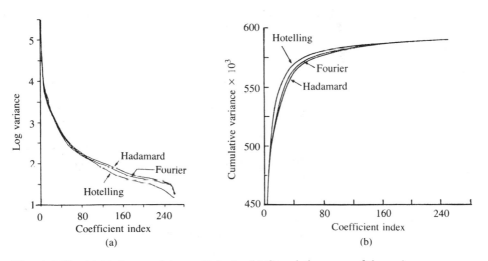

Figure 6.38   (a) Variances of the coefficients. (b) Cumulative sums of the variances.

6.38(b) that all three transformations are approximately equally efficient in packing the variances into lower-order coefficients.

Some approximations to the cameraman picture using the Hotelling, Hadamard, and Fourier transforms are presented in Figs. 6.39 and 6.40. These pictures were obtained by dividing the image into 16×16 subimages, representing each subimage with its expansion in terms of the 16×16 basis images, and truncating the expansion

(b)   (c)

Figure 6.39   Reconstructed images obtained by retaining the first 128 of the $n^2 = 256$ terms in Eq. (6.4-15) for each of the 256 16×16 subimages of the original 256×256 cameraman picture. (a) Hotelling transform: $e_{ms} = 0.34\%$. (b) Fourier transform: $e_{ms} = 0.45\%$. (c) Hadamard transform: $e_{ms} = 0.49\%$.

(a)

(b)

(c)

Figure 6.40 Reconstructed images obtained by retaining the first 64 of the $n^2 = 256$ terms in Eq. (6.4-15) for each of the 256 16 × 16 subimages of the original cameraman picture. (a) Hotelling transform: $e_{ms} = 0.34\%$. (b) Fourier transform: $e_{ms} = 0.45\%$. (c) Hadamard transform: $e_{ms} = 0.49\%$.

after η terms. As shown in Fig. 6.38, half of the terms ($\eta = 128$) can be discarded with no visible degradation in image quality, although some mean-square error is incurred. Truncating the expansion after 64 terms (Fig. 6.40) results in a visible blurring or lowpass filtering effect. This phenomenon can be explained by considering the basis images shown in Fig. 6.37. Note in those images that increasing index corresponds to increasing frequency content (i.e., the complexity of the basis images increases as a function of increasing index). Hence, truncating the expansion at η terms corresponds to discarding all image energy at frequencies higher than those corresponding to the first η basis images. Also note that for small η the subimage edges are visible. Figure 6.41 shows the error between the reconstructed image of Fig. 6.39(b) and the original cameraman image. It is evident that the largest errors occur in the high-detail (high-frequency) parts of the image and at the edges of the basis images.

Quantizing the coefficients

In our discussion of image encoding thus far, we have assumed that the quantizer is capable of assigning a unique value to each output from the mapper. This is not an unreasonable assumption for the methods discussed earlier in this chapter because we were dealing with a manageable number of distinct mapper outputs. In difference mapping, for example, the number of distinct differences out of the mapper is on the same order as the number of levels in the image. In transform mapping, on the other hand, the number of distinct output values may be infinite. For instance, each component y_{kl} out of the Hotelling transform is a linear combination of all the pixels in the input subarray. Although the input pixels may range only over L gray levels, the linear combination that produces y_{kl} is formed by weighting each pixel with an eigenvector component. Since these components depend on the covariance matrix of the input subarray, it is not difficult to see that each y_{kl} can, in theory, assume an infinite number of different values. In practice, the number is finite

Figure 6.41   Error between Fig. 6.39(b) and the original cameraman picture.

because of computer limitations, but even so, the range of values obtainable in a typical computer is so large that it becomes necessary to use a quantization strategy for the mapper outputs.

As illustrated in Fig. 6.38, the variance of the output coefficients vary widely. Therefore it would be inefficient to use the same quantizer for all coefficients. In other words, if the quantizer output levels are adjusted to span the range of the coefficients with the largest variance, then the coefficients with much smaller variances would fall in a much smaller range, with the result that most of the quantizer levels would not be used. This effect can be reduced by first scaling each coefficient by the inverse of its standard deviation to form the normalized coefficients $y_{kl} = y_{kl}/\sigma_{kl}$, all of which have unit variance and can be efficiently quantized with the same quantizer.

Using the same quantizer for each normalized coefficient y_{kl} and the natural or gray code to assign equal-length code words to all quantizer output levels results in each coefficient requiring the same number of bits. Since the coefficients with the larger variances generally contribute significantly more to the reconstructed image than the coefficients with the smaller variances, the total distortion due to quantizing the coefficients may be lessened by allotting more quantization levels and/or bits to the coefficients with the larger variances and proportionally fewer to the coefficients with the smaller variances. Also, since each coefficient corresponds to a particular frequency band, and the sensitivity of the human visual system to distortion is dependent on the frequency of the distortions, better subjective quality may be obtained in some cases by allotting more quantization levels and/or bits to those coefficients corresponding to the frequencies to which the eye is most sensitive in a given image.

Another quantization strategy is to choose the quantized levels so that they minimize the total quantizer mean-square error. For an $n \times n$ array this error is defined as

$$e_q^2 = E\left\{ \sum_{k=1}^{n} \sum_{l=1}^{n} (y_{kl} - \hat{y}_{kl})^2 \right\}, \tag{6.4-16}$$

where $\hat{y}_{kl}$ is the quantized value of y_{kl}. Equation (6.4-16) depends on the joint probability density function of y_{kl} and $\hat{y}_{kl}$. Since each coefficient is a linear combination of n^2 pixels, the central limit theorem indicates that the distributions of the y_{kl}s tend toward a Gaussian density since some of the pixels are more or less independent. Indeed, histograms for the coefficients for various transformations have been constructed and found to be roughly "bell-shaped." This effect becomes more pronounced with array size.

Panter and Dite [1951] and Max [1960] investigated quantization strategies that minimize the mean-square error of a *single* coefficient. They found that if the probability density function of y_{kl} is uniform, then a quantizer with uniformly spaced output levels is optimal. For other distributions the mean-square error can be decreased by using a nonuniform quantizer with the spacing between output levels decreased in regions of high probability and increased in regions of low probability. For a Gaussian distribution the nonuniform quantizer can be 20 to 30% more efficient than the uniform quantizer.

Quantization strategies for minimizing the *total* mean-square error were investigated by Huang and Schultheiss [1963], who determined the optimal allocation of a total of M bits to the n^2 coefficients when using a natural code for each coefficient. That is, all of the code words for each coefficient have the same length, but different coefficients have a different number of quantization levels and therefore require a natural code of a different length. They found that the number of bits m_{kl} used to code coefficient y_{kl} should be proportional to $\log \sigma_{kl}^2$. They give an algorithm for computing the m_{kl}, $k,l = 1, 2, \ldots, n$, such that Eq. (6.4-16) is minimized for a given M and the set of variances σ_{kl}^2 $k,l = 1, 2, \ldots, n$. This technique, called *block quantization,* is significantly more efficient than using the same number of bits $m_{kl} = M/n^2$ for all coefficients. Its disadvantage lies in the implementation problems inherent in handling binary words of unequal lengths.

Block quantization simply means using a different quantizer for each coefficient. Each quantizer can have a different number of quantization bins and a different spacing between the bins. The two images shown in Fig. 6.42 were obtained by subdividing the cameraman picture into 16×16 subimages. Each subimage was expanded into a set of Fourier basis images and the expansion truncated at $\eta = 128$ terms. The 128 retained coefficients y_{kl} were quantized using the two basic approaches discussed above. The results shown in Fig. 6.42(a) were obtained by normalizing the coefficients (i.e., $y_{kl} = y_{kl}/\sigma_{kl}$) and using a 16-level, uniform quantizer. The Fourier expansion was then formed with the resulting coefficients to yield the reconstructed image. The same procedure was used to obtain the image in Fig. 6.42(b), except that the number of levels used to quantize the 128 coefficients was made proportional to the quantity $\log \sigma_{kl}^2$. The two results are of approximately equal subjective quality, although the error [computed by averaging $(y_{kl} - \hat{y}_{kl})^2$ over all subimages] is much larger for Fig. 6.42(a). The *spatial* error between the original and Fig. 6.42(b) is shown in Fig. 6.42(c).

Figure 6.43(a) shows the results of an identical experiment except that four quantization levels were used for each of the normalized coefficients. Figure 6.43(b) shows the results of using the same total number of bits but with the block quantization algorithm. The latter technique makes much more efficient use of the bits and this results in a picture of significantly better subjective quality and less mean-square error.

Coding considerations

Coding performance for a transform encoder depends primarily on (1) the transformation, (2) the quantization strategy, (3) the subpicture size, and (4) the subpicture shape.

Transformation. The best transformation from both a mean-square-error and subjective-quality viewpoint is the Hotelling transformation, but it is closely followed by

(a)

(b)   (c)

Figure 6.42 Reconstructed images obtained by quantizing the 128 coefficients of Fig. 6.39(b) using an average of 2 bits/pixel (4 bits per retained coefficient). (a) All 128 normalized coefficients quantized to 16 levels: error = 2.09%. (b) The 128 coefficients block quantized: error = 0.78%. (c) Magnitude of spatial error between Figs. 6.39(b) and 6.42(c).

the Fourier and Hadamard transformations. Each is separated by 0.1 or 0.2 bits per pixel for $n = 8$ or 16. For $n = 4$ the performances are essentially the same.

Quantization strategy. Both mean-square error and subjective quality are quite sensitive to the efficiency with which bits are used to code the coefficients. The simplest strategy is to form the normalized coefficients $y_{kl} = y_{kl}/\sigma_{kl}$ and use the same quantizer

(a)   (b)

Figure 6.43   Reconstructed images obtained by quantizing the 128 coefficients of Fig. 6.39(b) using an average of 1 bit/pixel (2 bits per retained coefficient). (a) All 128 coefficients quantized to 4 levels: error = 8.68%. (b) The coefficients block quantized: error = 2.21%.

(number of bits) for each coefficient. If η coefficients are retained and m bits used to code each coefficient then a total of $m\eta/n^2$ bits per pixel are required. For good-quality reproductions, approximately half the coefficients should be retained, in which case 7 bits per coefficient must be used. Hence, $m\eta/n^2 \approx m(n^2/2)/n^2 = m/2 = 3.5$ bits per pixel are required. If the normalized coefficients are quantized with the same 7- or 8-bit quantizer, but only the $m_{kl} \sim \log\sigma_{ykl}^2$ most-significant bits retained (block quantization), the same quality pictures can be obtained with a savings of about 1 bit per pixel. Sometimes a further 0.1 bit per pixel can be saved by choosing the bit assignments to give the best subjective quality. A further saving of 0.2 to 0.3 bit per pixel can be achieved by quantizing the coefficients with the same quantizer and using a Huffman code to assign code words of unequal lengths to the quantizer output levels.

Subpicture size. Mean-square-error performance should improve with increasing n since the number of correlations taken into account increases with n. However, most images contain significant correlations between pixels for only about 20 adjacent pixels, although this number is strongly dependent on the amount of detail in the picture. Hence, a point of diminishing returns is reached and $n > 16$ is not warranted. Even a smaller n, say $n = 8$, does not significantly increase the error.

This argument does not appear to apply when subjective quality is the criterion of goodness. The subjective quality appears to be essentially independent of n for $n \geq 4$. Since the number of computations per pixel is proportional to n, 4×4 is a reasonable choice for subpicture size.

Subpicture shape. Transforming two-dimensional $n \times n$ arrays of pixels yields better performance than one-dimensional arrays of pixels but the gain is surprisingly small—about 0.2 bits per pixel. However, a larger n is required for one-dimensional arrays. For example, if two-dimensional arrays of size 4×4 are reasonable, one-dimensional arrays of 1×16 pixels are required to obtain comparable results.

Effect of bit errors in the coefficients

Since the decoder reconstructs pixels from linear combinations of the coefficients, an error in a coefficient leads to errors in all the pixels reconstructed from it. If the complete image is transformed as a unit, (i.e., $n = N$) then one or more errors in the coefficients results in some error in all the reconstructed pixels. If the $N \times N$ image is first divided into $n \times n$ subimages and each subimage coded independently, then only the subimages with errors are affected.

The images presented in Fig. 6.44 were obtained by starting with the image of Fig. 6.42(b) and making random bit errors in the coefficients at error rates of one error per 1000 and 100 bits, respectively. The structure of the blocks containing errors can be explained by recalling that each resulting subimage is a weighted sum of basis images. Hence, changing the value of a coefficient results in the corresponding basis image receiving the wrong weight in the reconstruction process.

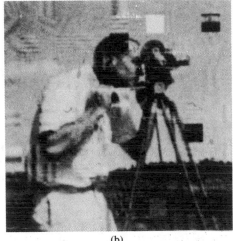

(a) (b)

Figure 6.44 Reconstructed pictures obtained after dividing the picture into 16×16 subpictures, expanding each subpicture into a Fourier series expansion and retaining the first 128 terms, block quantizing the coefficients using 2 bits/pixel, and making: (a) bit error rate $= 10^{-3}$; (b) bit error rate $= 10^{-2}$.

Adaptive transform encoding

Transform encoders can be made to adapt to local image structure by allowing a number of modes of operation and, for each subimage, choosing the mode that is most efficient for that subimage. Bookkeeping information that indicates which mode was used must be coded along with the subimage pixels. In general, increasing the number of modes decreases the number of bits required to code the subimage pixels, but increases the number of bits required to code the bookkeeping information.

Since the Hotelling transformation is matched to the subimage statistics, one might be tempted to use different transformations for subimages with different statistics. However, if we segregate the cameraman subimages with different statistics into different groups and compute the Hotelling transformation matrix for each group, we would find them strikingly similar. Hence, using different transformations for different subimages is not generally warranted. On the other hand, once the transformation is chosen (whether Hotelling, Fourier, Hadamard, or other) significant encoding efficiency can be achieved by adapting to the coefficients generated for each subpicture. There are a number of schemes for accomplishing this, but most are variations of the following three methods.

Method 1. Compute all n^2 coefficients (ordered according to their variances) and determine the smallest η for which the quantity

$$\sum_{k=1}^{\eta} \sum_{l=1}^{\eta} |y_{kl}|^2 \bigg/ \sum_{k=1}^{n} \sum_{l=1}^{n} |y_{kl}|^2$$

exceeds a predetermined threshold, (e.g., 0.99). Code the first η coefficients and code the number η. Making the threshold dependent on the average subimage brightness improves the subjective quality of the image due to the properties of the human visual system discussed in Section 2.1.3.

Method 2. Compute all n^2 coefficients and retain all that exceed a predetermined threshold. Code the retained coefficients and code which coefficients are retained using, for example, a run-length code. As in Method 1 the threshold can depend on the average brightness.

Method 3. A pattern-recognition algorithm (see Tou and Gonzalez [1974]) is first used to classify each subimage into one of three types, according to the gray level and the amount of detail in the subpicture. The three types of subimages are (1) high detail, (2) low detail and darker than average, and (3) low detail and brighter than average. The Hotelling transformation is used to map the subimage array into a set of coefficients. A different block quantizer and the Huffman code are used to complete the encoding of each of the three types of images. For the high-detail subimages, twice as many coefficients are retained as for the two low-detail types. Of the two low-detail types, a finer quantizer is used for the dark images, since the human visual system is more sensitive to errors in dark regions.

The results shown in Fig. 6.45 were obtained by adaptive transform encoding using Method 3. Figures 6.45(a) and (b) were encoded using an average of 0.59

Figure 6.45 Illustration of adaptive transform encoding performance. (a) Original image. (b) Decoded image at 0.89 bit/pixel. (c) Original image. (d) Decoded image at 0.86 bit/pixel.

and 1.13 bits per pixel, respectively. For the original 64-level image of Fig. 6.45(c), the encoded image shown in Fig. 6.45(d) was obtained using 0.86 bit per pixel. These results indicate that adaptive transform coding can yield reasonably good quality pictures at rates below 1 bit per pixel.

6.4.3   Example 3. Hybrid Encoding for RPV TV

Remotely piloted vehicles (RPVs) are small aircraft that operate without a pilot. In certain military applications RPVs are more effective than piloted aircraft because they are smaller and therefore provide less radar cross section and present less of a target. They are also less expensive because pilot support equipment is not required. A television camera inside the RPV looks ahead and transmits a continuous image to the "pilot" who observes a TV monitor some distance away. The pilot flies the RPV by remote control signals. A squadron of 20 RPVs would require 20 simultaneous TV transmissions. Significant data compression is required to reliably transmit this number of TV channels over long distances with low-power, inexpensive transmitters, and antennas that operate in a hostile (jamming) environment. A typical specification calls for a transmission bit rate of less than 0.5 Mbit per second. This corresponds to a data compression ratio of approximately 60 to 1.

One possibility is to transmit only every 10th frame; that is, transmit 3 frames per second rather than the 30 frames per second generated by the TV camera. This is about the minimum number of frames per second required by the pilot to maintain adequate control of the RPV due to the picture "jumping" because of RPV attitude fluctuations. (If RPV attitude information is also transmitted and used to keep the picture "centered" on the monitor, then frame rates of less than 1 frame per second can be tolerated.) A frame rate reduction from 30 frames per second to 3 frames per second yields a compression ratio of 10 to 1.

The remaining problem is to achieve a 6-to-1 compression by encoding each transmitted frame, which allows us about 1 bit per pixel, assuming that the original TV picture is digitized using 6 bits. The encoder must, of course, satisfy rather severe weight, volume, and power requirements along with reasonable cost, say, 2 lb, 25 in^3, and 10 watts. These specifications can be met with hybrid encoding techniques.

Hybrid encoding, due to Habibi [1974], combines the concepts of transform encoding and DPCM into a system that achieves essentially the same performance as two-dimensional transform encoding, but it is easier to implement. Hybrid encoding uses one-dimensional transform encoding in the horizontal direction and DPCM in the vertical direction.

Each scan line is first subdivided into sub-blocks containing n pixels each. Each of the resulting $1 \times n$ arrays is processed using a transformation such as, for example, the Hotelling, Hadamard, or Discrete Cosine transform. The purpose of the transformation is to reduce the correlation (i.e., redundancy) in the horizontal direction. Successive scan lines are also highly correlated in most images. Thus since the pixels in a $1 \times n$ subarray are correlated with the pixels in the corresponding subarray in the next line, we also expect the coefficients produced by the transformation to be correlated. This correlation between coefficients in the vertical direction can be diminished by differencing the coefficients using DPCM. Since the coefficients generally have different variances, it follows that the differences between coefficients will also have different variances. In order to efficiently code the coefficient differences we can use the block quantization method mentioned in the previous section.

As an illustration of hybrid encoding, consider the image shown in Fig. 6.46(a). This image was encoded using the Discrete Cosine transformation (with $n = 32$)

(a)   (b)

(c)   (d)

Figure 6.46   (a) Original image. (b) through (d) Decoded images using 2, 1, and 1/2 bits per pixel, respectively.

in the horizontal direction and DPCM in the vertical direction. The differences were processed using the block quantization bit assignments shown in Table 6.6. The decoded images for 2, 1 and 1/2 bits per pixel are presented in Figs. 6.46(b) through (d). The 2-bit image has only a very small degradation relative to the original. The 1-bit image has more degradation. The 1/2-bit image not only has very noticeable degradation, but the edges of the 1×32 blocks are also apparent.

Table 6.6   Bit Allocation for Coefficient Differences

Coefficient Differences	2 Bits	1 Bit	1/2 Bit
1	4	3	3
2	4	3	2
3	3	2	2
4	3	2	1
5	3	2	1
6	3	2	1
7	3	2	1
8	3	2	1
9	3	2	1
10	3	2	1
11	3	2	1
12	2	1	1
13	2	1	0
14	2	1	0
15	2	1	0
16	2	1	0
17	2	1	0
18	2	1	0
19	2	1	0
20	1	0	0
21	1	0	0
22	1	0	0
23	1	0	0
24	1	0	0
25	1	0	0
26	1	0	0
27	1	0	0
28	1	0	0
29	1	0	0
30	1	0	0
31	1	0	0
32	1	0	0

The same experiment was performed on the image presented in Fig. 6.47(a). The decoded images are presented in Figs. 6.47(b) through (d) for 2 bits, 1 bit, and 1/2 bit, respectively. Careful observation of these images leads to the same conclusion as for the images shown in Fig. 6.46.

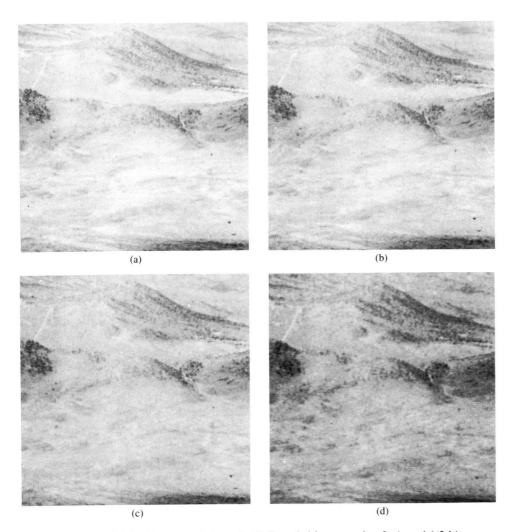

Figure 6.47 (a) Original image. (b) through (d) Decoded images using 2, 1, and 1/2 bits per pixel, respectively.

6.5   USE OF THE MAPPER OUTPUTS AS FEATURES

The encoding problem discussed in the previous sections deals with data compaction, subject to the constraint that a reconstructed image be either the same as, or a reasonable facsimile of, the original. In some applications, such as pattern recognition by machine, interest also lies in data compaction, but the constraint is one of preserving only enough information to allow an image, or parts of an image, to be classified into one of several categories or pattern classes. Without a human operator in the loop, reconstruction of the original image is no longer an essential requirement. The problem of reducing the representation of an image to a small number of components carrying enough discriminating information is referred to as *feature extraction*.

Many of the mapping techniques used in the encoding process described in Fig. 6.1 are also often used for feature extraction. In other words, in this type of application we are generally not interested in quantizing or coding techniques. Instead, the mapper outputs are used as features that are input directly into a pattern-recognition device. Of the methods normally associated with an encoder mapping operation, the Hotelling transform is one of the most often used for feature extraction. In this section we illustrate uses of this transform for extracting feature information from multispectral imagery.

Satellite and airborne multispectral sensors provide data in the form of several images of the same area of the Earth's surface, but taken through different spectral windows or bands. The number of spectral bands varies, but typically ranges from 4, as with the NASA LANDSAT, to 20 or more for many aircraft-borne sensors. The spectral bands typically exhibit high interband correlations so that a significant amount of redundancy exists between the spectral images. These correlations, coupled with the large quantities of data, lead to the consideration of efficient methods of information extraction for user-analysis purposes.

An example of some aircraft multispectral imagery is presented in Fig. 6.48. These data were taken by a 6-band multispectral scanner flown over Tippecanoe County, Indiana, at a mean altitude of 3000 feet. The six images shown in Fig. 6.48 correspond to the six bands in the scanner. These images, which are 384 by 239 pixels and represent an area of approximately 0.9 by 0.7 mi, are typical of multispectral data taken over agricultural terrain. The scanner bands used are listed in Table 6.7. By comparing Fig. 6.48 with the bands in this table we see that vegetation, which is dark in the visible bands (1, 2, 3), appears bright in the infrared bands (4, 5). By contrast, the roof tops and roads appear light in the visible bands and dark in the infrared bands.

Suppose that the six digital images presented in Fig. 6.48 are stacked one behind the other as illustrated in Fig. 6.49. We can then form one 6-element column vector $\mathbf{x} = (x_1, x_2, \ldots, x_6)'$ for each ground pixel. In other words, the elements of this vector correspond to the same point on the ground, but give the gray level in each of the six different bands. If we were to compute the average value for each x_i and the correlation between every pair of elements x_i and x_j over the entire

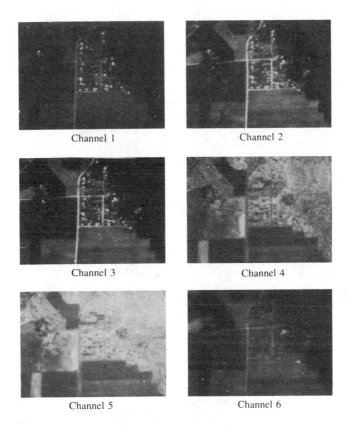

Figure 6.48 Six spectral images from an airborne scanner. (Courtesy of the Laboratory for Applications of Remote Sensing, Purdue University.)

Table 6.7   Channel Number and Wavelengths

Channel	Wavelength Band (μm)
1	0.40–0.44
2	0.62–0.66
3	0.66–0.72
4	0.80–1.00
5	1.00–1.40
6	2.00–2.60

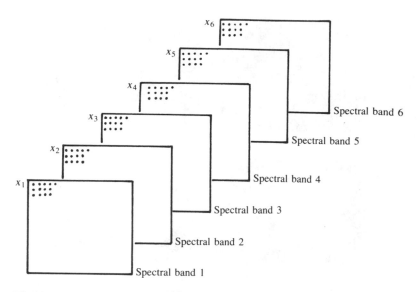

Figure 6.49 Obtaining six corresponding elements to form a pixel vector.

image, we would in general find that the elements have different means and are highly correlated. As indicated in Section 3.6, the components can be normalized about their means and their correlation eliminated by use of the Hotelling transformation

$$y = A(x - m_x),$$ (6.5-1)

where m_x is the mean vector population and the rows of A are formed from the normalized eigenvectors of the covariance matrix C_x. In the present application there were 384×239 vectors x available for computing the mean vector and covariance matrix. The eigenvalues of C_x are listed in Table 6.8.

The transformation given in Eq. (6.5-1) was applied to the images in Fig. 6.48. The results are shown in Fig. 6.50. These images are referred to as the *principal-component images* because, as indicated in Section 3.6, the Hotelling transform picks out the orthogonal components with the largest variance. The energy-packing property of this principal-component transformation manifests itself as a significant increase in contrast (variance) in the first images, with monotonically

Table 6.8   Eigenvalues of the Covariance Matrix of the Images Shown in Fig. 6.48

λ_1	λ_2	λ_3	λ_4	λ_5	λ_6
3210	931.4	118.5	83.88	64.00	13.40

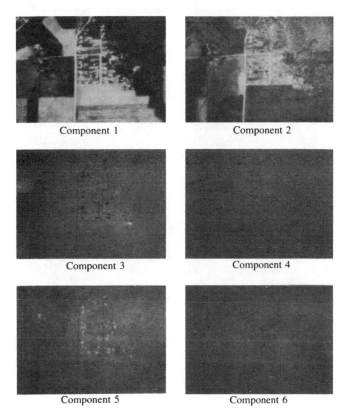

Component 1   Component 2

Component 3   Component 4

Component 5   Component 6

Figure 6.50 Six principal-component images computed from
the data in Fig. 6.48. (Courtesy of the Laboratory for Applications
of Remote Sensing, Purdue University.)

decreasing contrast as their variance decreases. In fact, as indicated by the values
in Table 6.8, 97% of the variance is contained in the first three images.

In some pattern-recognition applications the problem is to classify each ground
resolution element into one of several classes, based on its multispectral representation
x. Interest in automatic pattern-recognition techniques is motivated by the large
quantities of data generated by the scanner as it moves along the flight path. Since
the amount of computation is dependent on the dimensionality of **x**, the usual procedure
is to choose a subset of the elements of this vector for processing by the pattern-
recognition machine. The problem of selecting a priori the best subset is generally
difficult, and is usually based on the combination of (1) statistical interclass distance
measures (resulting from an exhaustive search of all possible combinations of the
spectral bands) to form a subset of given dimension, and (2) an intuitive selection
based on known characteristics of the areas in question.

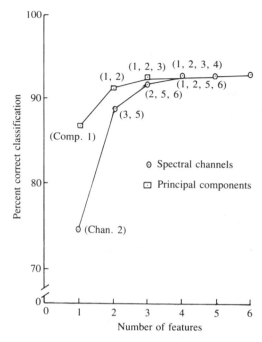

Figure 6.51 Classification accuracy versus number of features using the spectral bands and the principal components.

Computer classification results using the best subset of the original spectral channel vector **x** and using a subset of the principal components vector **y** are presented in Fig. 6.51. A Gaussian maximum-likelihood decision rule (Tou and Gonzalez [1974]) was used to classify selected areas of the data set into one of six classes (various types of vegetation, roads, etc.). The sixth class was a null class into which all points having classification-error probabilities greater than a specified threshold were placed. All points in this null class were considered errors and were used as such in computing classification accuracy.

The abscissa in Fig. 6.51 is the number of features (spectral channels or principal components) used in the classification. For each number m of features, an exhaustive search was conducted to determine the m-member set of features giving the highest percentage of correct classification results. The features used are listed in Table 6.9. This table and Fig. 6.51 point out the feature-selection advantages inherent in the principal components. For each value of m, the first m principal components are the best selection. In addition, for small values of m, the principal components contain more class-separability information than any group of m original spectral channels.

Table 6.9 Principal Components and Corresponding Spectral Channels

n	Principal Components	Spectral Channels
1	1	2
2	1,2	3,5
3	1,2,3	2,5,6
4	1,2,3,4	1,2,5,6
5	1,2,3,4,5	1,2,3,5,6
6	1,2,3,4,5,6	1,2,3,4,5,6

Table 6.10 Channel Numbers and Corresponding Wavelengths

Channel	Wavelength Band (μm)
1	0.47–0.61
2	0.68–0.89
3	0.59–0.71

Table 6.11 Eigenvalues of the Images Shown in Fig. 6.52

λ_1	λ_2	λ_3
1689	512.5	158.0

Results similar to the above have also been obtained with satellite multispectral data. The channels and corresponding sample images from the *Apollo* 9-S065 experiment over Imperial Valley, California, are shown in Table 6.10 and Fig. 6.52, respectively. For this particular data set, **x** was a three-dimensional vector. The transformation into principal components was carried out as in the preceding example. The eigenvalues are listed in Table 6.11 and the principal-component images are shown in Fig. 6.53. In this case the first two eigenvalues represented approximately 93% of the total data variance.

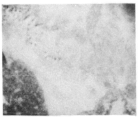  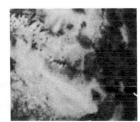

Channel 1   Channel 2   Channel 3

Figure 6.52 Three spectral images from a satellite scanner.

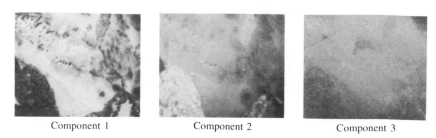

Component 1   Component 2   Component 3

Figure 6.53   Three principal-component images corresponding to the data in Fig. 6.52.

6.6 CONCLUDING REMARKS

The success of any encoding technique is ultimately dependent on how well it matches the structure (i.e., departure from randomness) in a given image. The ideal approach in designing an efficient encoder is first to determine the structure of the data and then choose a method that best fits that structure. Since structural properties inherent in pictorial data are not well understood, however, the design and implementation of an image encoder often involves a certain amount of experimentation. The concepts introduced in this chapter are representative of available techniques that have been found of practical value in image-processing applications.

In some applications, such as encoding images that exhibit regularity (rivers, man-made objects, etc.), the structural properties of interest often manifest themselves in the form of boundaries. Encoding strategies that take this type of structure into account include the contour-encoding approach developed in Section 6.3.2. In other applications, such as encoding satellite imagery, the structure is not so obvious and a typical approach is to let the statistical information in the image dictate the choice of encoding technique. The Hotelling transformation is an example of this approach.

When encoded images are to be used ultimately for human viewing and interpretation, one must take into account the effects produced by the encoding approach on the visual system. The sensitivity of the human visual system to errors in a reconstructed image depends on such factors as the frequency spectrum of the error, the gray-level content, and the amount of detail in the image. Hence, it is possible to increase the efficiency of an encoder by allowing distortions that minimize degradations in subjective quality. Transform encoding is an example where some aspects of both statistical and psychovisual properties are taken into account. Transform encoders perform a sequence of two operations, the first of which is based on statistical considerations and the second on psychovisual considerations. The first operation is a linear transformation whose objective is to reduce the statistical dependence of the pixels. The second operation is to quantize individually and code each of the resulting coefficients. The number of bits required to code the coefficients depends on the number of quantizer levels, which is dictated by the sensitivity of the visual system to the subjective effect of the quantizer error.

REFERENCES

The book by Abramson [1963] contains an excellent introduction to information theory and source encoding. Two special issues of *Proceedings of the IEEE* [1967, 1972] are also of interest as general references.

The paper by Frendendall and Behrend [1960] deals with procedures for evaluating subjective image quality (Section 6.1). Additional reading for Section 6.2 are Abramson [1963], Wintz [1972], Huffman [1952], Meyer, Rosdolsky and Huang [1973], Max [1961], Panter [1951], Schreiber [1967], and Huang [1977].

Section 6.3.1 is based on the report by Duan and Wintz [1974]. References for the contour-encoding algorithm developed in Section 6.3.2 are Graham [1967] and Wilkins and Wintz [1970]. For additional references for Section 6.3.3 see Chen and Wintz [1976].

Additional reading for the material in Section 6.4.1 may be found in Huang [1965] and Essman and Wintz [1973]. Section 6.4.2 is based on the work of Habibi (see Habibi and Wintz [1971]). Additional reading for Section 6.4.3 may be found in the paper by Habibi [1974]. A book by Clarke [1985] dealing with transform coding is excellent additional reading for the material in Section 6.4.

For references on the Hotelling transform (Section 6.5) see the Reference section at the end of Chapter 3. The examples given in Section 6.5 are based on the paper by Ready and Wintz [1973].

Other references related to the material in this chapter are Huang [1966], Schreiber [1967], Huang and Schulthesis [1963], Stevens [1951], Gattis and Wintz [1971], Schreiber [1956], Proctor and Wintz [1971], Tasto and Wintz [1971, 1972], Wood [1969], Gish and Pierce [1968], Sakrison and Algazi [1971], Habibi [1971], Wilkins and Wintz [1970], and Kramer and Mathews [1956].

Some survey articles of interest are Netravali and Limb [1980], Jain [1981], *IEEE Transaction on Communications* [1981] (special issue on picture communication systems), *Proceedings of the IEEE* [1980] (special issue on the encoding of graphics), and *Proceedings of the IEEE* [1985] (special issue on visual communication systems).

PROBLEMS

6.1 With reference to the discussion in Section 6.2, let y denote the input to a quantizer such that y is a random variable with a uniform probability density function $p(y)$ defined over the range of values $0 \leq y \leq A$. Assign a unique m-bit code word to each possible quantizer output so that the number of bins is 2^m. Denote the $2^m + 1$ bin walls by $B_0 = 0$, B_1, B_2, . . . , $B_{2^m} = A$, and the 2^m quantizer outputs by b_1, b_2, . . . , b_{2^m}. Based on this problem set-up, do the following:

a) Compute the mean-square quantization error e_q^2 as a function of A and m.

b) Compute the maximum squared quantization error.

c) Determine how many bits are required to guarantee that the mean-square error as a percentage of the average signal energy (y_{rms}^2) is less than 0.1%.

d) Repeat (c) using the maximum-square error.

6.2 Assume eight coder inputs w_i, $i = 1, 2, \ldots, 8$, with probabilities 0.6, 0.2, 0.08, 0.06, 0.02, 0.02, 0.01, and 0.01, respectively.
  a) Construct the Gray code for these inputs and compute the average word length.
  b) Construct the Huffman code and obtain the average word length.
  c) Compute the entropy.

6.3 Using the inputs listed in Problem 6.2, construct the following codes and obtain the average word length in each case: (a) B_1-code, (b) B_2-code, and (c) S_2-code.

6.4 Assume 16 possible coder inputs w_k, $k = 1, 2, \ldots, 16$, with probabilities given by the triangles in Fig. 6.12. Read the probabilities from this figure, making sure they sum to 1. Then, obtain the following codes and their respective average word lengths: (a) natural code, (b) B_1-code, (c) B_2-code, and (d) S_2-code.

6.5 The picture shown in Fig. 6.14 could be encoded using the natural code for each pixel. How many bits are required for the natural code? Refer to Fig. 6.21 and compute the number of bits required by the contour code for this picture.

6.6 Refer to the picture in Fig. 6.19. How many bits are required to code this picture using the natural code for each pixel? Construct a set of codes as in Fig. 6.21(a) for this picture. List the coder outputs for the first few directionals, as in Fig. 6.21(b), and calculate the total number of bits required.

6.7 Suppose that we observe a sequence of random variables $x_1, x_2, \ldots$. We wish to predict the value of the next (as-yet unknown) random variable x_i given knowledge of the values of the preceding random variables $x_1, x_2, \ldots, x_{i-1}$. The first-order linear predictor $\hat{x}_i$ for x_i is given by $\hat{x}_i = \alpha x_{i-1} + \beta$, where α and β are constants to be determined. Assume that all the random variables x_i have the same mean $m = E\{x_i\}$ and the same variance $\sigma^2 = E\{(x_i - m)^2\}$, and that successive pairs of random variables x_i, x_{i-1} have the same correlation coefficient $\rho = E\{x_i x_{i-1}\}/E\{x_i^2\}$. Finding the optimal linear predictor corresponds to finding α and β such that the mean-square prediction error $E\{(\hat{x}_i - x_i)^2\}$ is minimized.
  a) Show that the optimal linear predictor is given by Eq. (6.4-1).
  b) Show that this estimator is unbiased in the sense that $E\{\hat{x}_i\} = E\{x_i\}$.
  c) Show that the resulting minimum mean-square error is given by Eq. (6.4-4).

6.8 Mapper and quantizer errors are orthogonal and therefore additive. Refer to the encoder defined in Fig. 6.1 and neglect the coder box that introduces no error. Assume the input to be a random vector $\mathbf{x}$ with energy $E\{\|\mathbf{x}\|^2\} = \sum_{i=1}^{n} x_i^2$. Let the mapper be a linear orthonormal transformation, such as the Fourier transform, so that the output random vector $\mathbf{y}$ has energy $E\{\|\mathbf{y}\|^2\} = \sum_{i=1}^{n} y_i^2 = \sum_{i=1}^{n} x_i^2$. Suppose that the mapper output is truncated after m terms with $m < n$ so that only the first m terms $y_1, y_2, \ldots, y_m$ are passed to the quantizer. The higher-order terms are discarded. Define the mean-square mapper error as $e_m^2 = E\{\|\mathbf{y} - \mathbf{x}\|^2\}$, the mean-square quantizer error as $e_q^2 = E\{\|\mathbf{v} - \mathbf{y}\|^2\}$, where $\mathbf{v}$ is output of the quantizer, and the total mean-square error as $e_T^2 = E\{\|\mathbf{v} - \mathbf{x}\|^2\}$.
  a) Show that $e_m^2 = \sum_{i=m+1}^{n} y_i^2$; that is, the mapper error is equal to the discarded energy.
  b) Show that, since the mapper and quantizer errors are uncorrelated, the total square error is $e_T^2 = e_m^2 + e_q^2$.

CHAPTER 7

IMAGE SEGMENTATION

The whole is equal to the sum of its parts.
Euclid

The whole is greater than the sum of its parts.
Max Wertheimer

Segmentation is the process that subdivides an image into its constituent parts or objects. Segmentation is one of the most important elements in automated image analysis because it is at this step that objects or other entities of interest are extracted from an image for subsequent processing, such as description and recognition.

Segmentation algorithms generally are based on one of two basic properties of gray-level values: discontinuity and similarity. In the first category, we partition an image based on abrupt changes in gray level. The principal areas of interest within this category are the detection of isolated points, and the detection of lines and edges in an image. The principal approaches in the second category are based on thresholding, region growing, and region splitting and merging. The concept of segmenting an image based on discontinuity or similarity of the gray-level values of its pixels is applicable to both static and dynamic (time-varying) images. In the latter case, however, motion can often be used as a powerful cue to improve the performance of segmentation algorithms.

7.1 THE DETECTION OF DISCONTINUITIES

In this section we present a number of techniques for detecting points, lines, and edges in an image. The methods generally used to detect these properties are based on small spatial masks, as discussed in Section 4.1.1. In what follows, we express the right side of Eq. (4.1-3) in vector form. This notation, although completely equivalent in meaning, is more suitable for the purposes of the present discussion.

w_1	w_2	w_3
w_4	w_5	w_6
w_7	w_8	w_9

Figure 7.1   A general
3×3 mask.

Let $w_1, w_2, \ldots, w_9$ represent the coefficients of the 3×3 mask shown in Fig. 7.1, and let $x_1, x_2, \ldots, x_9$ represent the gray levels of the pixels under the mask (see Fig. 7.5a) when the mask is in an arbitrary position in the image (see Fig. 4.1). The coefficients and corresponding gray levels can be expressed as column vectors; that is,

$$\mathbf{w} = \begin{bmatrix} w_1 \\ w_2 \\ \cdot \\ \cdot \\ \cdot \\ w_9 \end{bmatrix} \tag{7.1-1}$$

and

$$\mathbf{x} = \begin{bmatrix} x_1 \\ x_2 \\ \cdot \\ \cdot \\ \cdot \\ x_9 \end{bmatrix} \tag{7.1-2}$$

Then, the right side of Eq. (4.1-3) can be expressed as the inner product of $\mathbf{w}$ and $\mathbf{x}$:

$$\mathbf{w}'\mathbf{x} = w_1x_1 + w_2x_2 + \cdots + w_9x_9, \tag{7.1-3}$$

where the prime (') indicates vector transposition. Clearly, Eqs. (7.1-3) and (4.1-3) are identical. Also observe that the notation $\mathbf{w}'\mathbf{x}$ is perfectly general and applies to masks of arbitrary size. For example, for an $n \times n$ mask, we would work witn n^2-dimensional vectors. The notation given in Eq. (7.1-3) will be used throughout this section.

7.1.1   Point Detection

The problem of detecting and then segmenting isolated points in an image applies in noise removal and particle analysis. Although point detection was already addressed briefly in Section 4.1.1 as an illustration of spatial-mask processing, we consider this problem here from a slightly different notational viewpoint and as part of a more general framework in the detection of gray-level discontinuities.

−1	−1	−1
−1	8	−1
−1	−1	−1

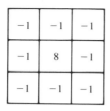

Figure 7.2 A mask used for detecting isolated points different from a constant background.

The basic mask used for detecting isolated points in an image is shown in Fig. 7.2. With reference to the discussion in Section 4.1.1, the center of this mask is moved from pixel to pixel in an image. At each mask location we compute the sum of products given by Eq. (7.1-3), using the coefficients in the mask of Fig. 7.2; that is, we compute the vector product

$$\mathbf{w}'\mathbf{x} = -x_1 - x_2 - x_3 - x_4 + 8x_5 - x_6 - x_7 - x_8 - x_9. \tag{7.1-4}$$

In an area of constant gray level the result of this operation would be 0. On the other hand, if the mask is centered at an isolated point (x_5), whose intensity is greater than the background, then the result would be greater than 0.

In practice, when one is interested only in strong responses, we say that an isolated point whose intensity is significantly different from the background has been detected if

$$|\mathbf{w}'\mathbf{x}| > T, \tag{7.1-5}$$

where T is a nonnegative threshold. The value of T establishes the relative gray level of what we are willing to call a significant point or particle in an image.

7.1.2 Line Detection

Point detection is a fairly straightforward procedure. The next level of complexity involves the detection of lines in an image. Consider the masks shown in Fig. 7.3. If the first mask were moved around an image, it would respond more strongly to lines (one pixel thick) oriented horizontally. With constant background, the maximum response would result when the line passed through the middle row of the mask. The reader can easily verify this by sketching a simple array of 1s with a line of a

−1	−1	−1
2	2	2
−1	−1	−1

−1	−1	2
−1	2	−1
2	−1	−1

−1	2	−1
−1	2	−1
−1	2	−1

2	−1	−1
−1	2	1
−1	−1	2

Figure 7.3 Line masks.

different gray level (say, 5s) running horizontally through the array. A similar experiment would reveal that the second mask in Fig. 7.3 responds best to lines oriented at 45°; the third mask to vertical lines; and the fourth mask to lines in the $-45°$ direction. These directions can also be established by noting that the preferred direction of each mask is weighted with a larger coefficient (i.e., 2) than other possible directions.

Let $\mathbf{w}_1$, $\mathbf{w}_2$, $\mathbf{w}_3$, and $\mathbf{w}_4$ be nine-dimensional vectors formed from the entries of the four masks shown in Fig. 7.3. As discussed above for the point mask, the individual responses of the line masks at any point in the image are given by $\mathbf{w}_i' \mathbf{x}$ for $i = 1, 2, 3, 4$. As before, $\mathbf{x}$ is the vector formed from the nine image pixels inside the mask area. Given a particular $\mathbf{x}$, suppose we wish to determine the closest match between the region in question and one of the four line masks. We say that $\mathbf{x}$ is closest to the ith mask if the response of this mask is the largest; in other words, if

$$\mathbf{w}_i' \mathbf{x} > \mathbf{w}_j' \mathbf{x} \qquad (7.1\text{-}6)$$

for all values of j, excluding $j = i$. If, for example, $\mathbf{w}_1' \mathbf{x}$ were greater than $\mathbf{w}_j' \mathbf{x}$, $j = 2, 3, 4$, we would conclude that the region represented by $\mathbf{x}$ is characterized by a horizontal line since this is the feature to which the first mask is most responsive.

7.1.3 Edge Detection

Although point and line detection certainly are elements of any discussion on segmentation, edge detection is by far the most common approach for detecting meaningful discontinuities in gray level. The reason for this is that isolated points and thin lines are not frequent occurrences in most applications of practical interest.

Basic formulation

We define an edge as the boundary between two regions with relatively distinct gray-level properties. In the following discussion, it is assumed that the regions in question are sufficiently homogeneous so that the transition between two regions can be determined on the basis of gray-level discontinuities alone. When this assumption is not valid, the segmentation techniques discussed in Sections 7.3 or 7.4 are generally more applicable than edge detection.

Basically, the idea underlying most edge-detection techniques is the computation of a local derivative operator. This concept can be easily illustrated with the aid of Fig. 7.4. Part (a) of this figure shows an image of a simple light object on a dark background, the gray-level profile along a horizontal scan line of the image, and the first and second derivatives of the profile. Note from the profile that an edge (transition from dark to light) is modeled as a ramp, rather than as an abrupt change of gray level. This model is representative of the fact that edges in digital images are generally slightly blurred as a result of sampling.

The first derivative of an edge modeled in this manner is 0 in all regions of constant gray level, and assumes a constant value during a gray-level transition. The second derivative, on the other hand, is 0 in all locations, except at the onset

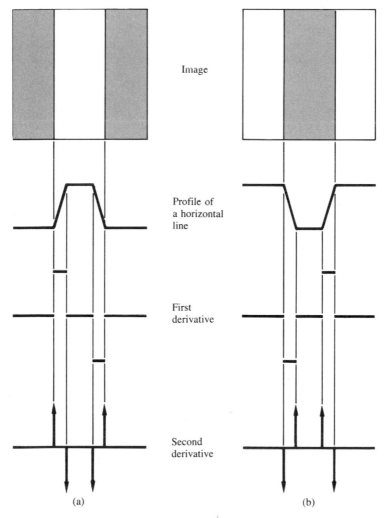

Figure 7.4 Elements of edge detection by derivative operators. (a) Light object on a dark background. (b) Dark object on a light background. (From Fu, Gonzalez, and Lee [1987].)

and termination of a gray-level transition. Based on these remarks and the concepts illustrated in Fig. 7.4, it is evident that the magnitude of the first derivative can be used to detect the presence of an edge, while the sign of the second derivative can be used to determine whether an edge pixel lies on the dark (background) or light (object) side of an edge. The sign of the second derivative in Fig. 7.4(a), for example, is positive for pixels lying on the dark side of both the leading and trailing edges of the object, while the sign is negative for pixels on the light side of these edges. Similar comments apply to the case of a dark object on a light background, as shown in Fig. 7.4(b). It is of interest to note that an identical interpretation regarding the sign of the second derivative is true for this case.

Although the discussion thus far has been limited to a one-dimensional horizontal profile, a similar argument applies to an edge of any orientation in an image. We simply define a profile perpendicular to the edge direction at any given point and interpret the results as in the preceding discussion. As will be shown in the following two sections, the first derivative at any point in an image can be obtained by using the magnitude of the gradient at that point, while the second derivative is given by the Laplacian.

Gradient operators

The concept of using the gradient for image differentiation was briefly introduced in Section 4.4.1. In the present discussion, we expand the ideas introduced in that section and develop a vector representation consistent with the notation being carried out in this section.

As indicated in Section 4.4.1, the gradient of an image $f(x, y)$ at location (x, y) is defined as the two-dimensional vector

$$\mathbf{G}[f(x, y)] = \begin{bmatrix} G_x \\ G_y \end{bmatrix} = \begin{bmatrix} \dfrac{\partial f}{\partial x} \\ \dfrac{\partial f}{\partial y} \end{bmatrix} \tag{7.1-7}$$

It is well known from vector analysis that the vector $\mathbf{G}$ points in the direction of maximum rate of change of f at location (x, y). For edge detection, we are interested in the magnitude of this vector, generally referred to simply as the *gradient* and denoted by $G[f(x, y)]$, where

$$G[f(x, y)] = [G_x^2 + G_y^2]^{1/2} \tag{7.1-8}$$

This quantity is equal to the maximum rate of increase of $f(x, y)$ per unit distance in the direction of $\mathbf{G}$.

It is common practice to approximate the gradient by absolute values:

$$G[f(x, y)] \approx |G_x| + |G_y|. \tag{7.1-9}$$

This approximation is considerably easier to implement, particularly when dedicated hardware is being employed.

The *direction* of the gradient vector is also an important quantity. Letting $\alpha(x, y)$ represent the direction angle of $\mathbf{G}$ at location (x, y), it follows from vector analysis that

$$\alpha(x, y) = \tan^{-1}(G_y/G_x), \tag{7.1-10}$$

where the angle is measured with respect to the x axis. As discussed in Section

7.2.1, Eq. (7.1-10) is a useful tool for linking edge points that have been detected by using the gradient.

Note from Eq. (7.1-7) that computation of the gradient is based on obtaining the partial derivatives $\partial f/\partial x$ and $\partial f/\partial y$ at every pixel location. There are a number of ways to do this. One approach is to use first-order differences in a 2×2 region, as was done in Eqs. (4.4-3) through (4.4-6). A slightly more complicated approach involving pixels in a 3×3 neighborhood about point (x, y) can be formulated as follows. Consider the subimage area shown in Fig. 7.5(a), where x_5 represents the gray level at location (x, y) and the other x_i represents the gray levels of the 8-neighbors of (x, y). We define the component of the gradient vector in the x direction as

$$G_x = (x_7 + 2x_8 + x_9) - (x_1 + 2x_2 + x_3) \tag{7.1-11}$$

and in the y direction as

$$G_y = (x_3 + 2x_6 + x_9) - (x_1 + 2x_4 + x_7). \tag{7.1-12}$$

Using a 3×3 area in the computation of the gradient has the advantage of increased smoothing over 2×2 operators, tending to make the derivative operations less sensitive to noise. Weighting the pixels closest to the center by 2 also produces additional smoothing (see Problem 7.2). It is possible to base gradient computations over larger neighborhoods (Kirsch [1971]), but 3×3 neighborhoods are by far

x_1	x_2	x_3
x_4	x_5	x_6
x_7	x_8	x_9

(a)

-1	-2	-1
0	0	0
1	2	1

(b)

-1	0	1
-2	0	2
-1	0	1

(c)

Figure 7.5   (a) 3×3 image region. (b) Mask used to compute G_x at center point of the 3×3 region. (c) Mask used to compute G_y at that point. These masks are often referred to as the *Sobel operators*.

the most popular because of advantages in computational speed and modest hardware requirements.

It follows from the discussion in the previous two sections that G_x, as given in Eq. (7.1-11), can be computed by using the mask shown in Fig. 7.5(b). Similarly, G_y can be computed by using the mask shown in Fig. 7.5(c). These two masks are commonly referred to as the *Sobel operators*. The responses of these two operators at any point (x, y) are combined using Eq. (7.1-8) or (7.1-9) to obtain the gradient at that point. Convolving these masks with an image $f(x, y)$ yields the gradient at all points in the image, the result often being referred to as a *gradient image*. There are numerous ways to generate a gradient image based on the use of thresholds, as discussed in Section 4.4.1.

Example: Figure 7.6(a) shows an original image and Fig. 7.6(b) is the result of computing G_x with the mask shown in Fig. 7.5(b). Note the strength of the response of horizontal edges, such as the river bank in the background, and the lack of response of vertical edges, such as those in the extended arm. Figure 7.6(c) showed the opposite result when G_y was computed using the mask in Fig. 7.5(c). The gradient image obtained by combining these two results via Eq. (7.1-8) is shown in Fig. 7.6(d).   ☐

It is important to note that Eqs. (7.1-11) and (7.1-12) are special cases of the general formulation given in Eq. (7.1-3). Thus if $\mathbf{x}$ is a vector containing the pixel values shown in Fig. 7.5(a), we have

$$G_x = \mathbf{w}_1'\mathbf{x} \qquad\qquad (7.1\text{-}13)$$

and

$$G_y = \mathbf{w}_2'\mathbf{x}, \qquad\qquad (7.1\text{-}14)$$

where $\mathbf{w}_1$ and $\mathbf{w}_2$ are the vectors containing the coefficients of the masks shown in Figs. 7.5(b) and (c), respectively. The formulations given in Eqs. (7.1-8) and (7.1-9) then become

$$G[f(x, y)] = [(\mathbf{w}_1'\mathbf{x})^2 + (\mathbf{w}_2'\mathbf{x})^2]^{1/2} \qquad\qquad (7.1\text{-}15)$$

and

$$G[f(x, y)] \approx |\mathbf{w}_1'\mathbf{x}| + |\mathbf{w}_2'\mathbf{x}|, \qquad\qquad (7.1\text{-}16)$$

which are, of course, completely equivalent to those equations.

Laplacian operator

The Laplacian is a second-order derivative operator defined as

$$L[f(x, y)] = \partial^2 f/\partial x^2 + \partial^2 f/\partial y^2. \qquad\qquad (7.1\text{-}17)$$

(a)

(b)

(c)

(d)

Figure 7.6 (a) Original image. (b) Result of applying the mask in Fig. 7.5(b) to obtain G_x. (c) Result of using the mask in Fig. 7.5(c) to obtain G_y. (d) Complete gradient image obtained by using Eq. (7.1-8).

0	1	0
1	−4	1
0	1	0

Figure 7.7   Mask used to compute the Laplacian.

With reference to Fig. 7.5(a), we define the digital Laplacian at point (x, y) with gray level x_5 as

$$L[f(x, y)] = x_2 + x_4 + x_6 + x_8 - 4x_5. \tag{7.1-18}$$

This operation can be implemented by convolving the mask shown in Fig. 7.7 with an image $f(x, y)$. If a vector $\mathbf{w}$ is formed from the coefficients of this mask we can express the Laplacian in vector form:

$$L[f(x, y)] = \mathbf{w}'\mathbf{x}, \tag{7.1-19}$$

where $\mathbf{x}$ has the same meaning as in the previous sections. Note that the Laplacian is 0 in constant areas and on the ramp section of an edge, as expected of a second-order derivative.

Although, as indicated in Section 7.1.3, the Laplacian responds to transitions in intensity, it is seldom used by itself for edge detection. The reason is that, being a second-derivative operator, the Laplacian is typically unacceptably sensitive to noise. Thus this operator is usually delegated to the secondary role of serving as a detector for establishing whether a given pixel is on the dark or light side of an edge. The usefulness of this property is demonstrated in Section 7.3.5.

7.1.4   Combined Detection

The vector formulation for the detection of points, lines, and edges has the important advantage that it can be used to detect combinations of these features using a technique developed by Frei and Chen [1977]. In order to see how this can be accomplished, let us consider two hypothetical masks with only three components. In this case, we would have two vectors, $\mathbf{w}_1$ and $\mathbf{w}_2$, which are three-dimensional. Assuming that $\mathbf{w}_1$ and $\mathbf{w}_2$ are orthogonal and normalized so that they have unit magnitude, we have that the terms $\mathbf{w}_1'\mathbf{x}$ and $\mathbf{w}_2'\mathbf{x}$ are equal to the projections of $\mathbf{x}$ onto the vectors $\mathbf{w}_1$ and $\mathbf{w}_2$, respectively. This follows from the fact that, for $\mathbf{w}_1$,

$$\mathbf{w}_1'\mathbf{x} = \|\mathbf{w}_1\| \, \|\mathbf{x}\| \cos \theta, \tag{7.1-20}$$

where θ is the angle between the two vectors. Since $\|\mathbf{w}_1\| = 1$,

$$\|\mathbf{x}\| \cos \theta = \mathbf{w}_1'\mathbf{x}, \tag{7.1-21}$$

which is the projection of $\mathbf{x}$ onto $\mathbf{w}_1$ (see Fig. 7.8). Similar comments hold for $\mathbf{w}_2$.

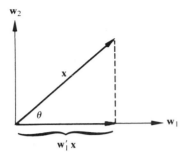

Figure 7.8 Projection of **x** onto unit vector $\mathbf{w}_1$.

Now suppose that we have three orthogonal vectors of unit magnitude, $\mathbf{w}_1$, $\mathbf{w}_2$, $\mathbf{w}_3$, corresponding to three, 3-point masks. The products $\mathbf{w}_1'\mathbf{x}$, $\mathbf{w}_2'\mathbf{x}$, and $\mathbf{w}_3'\mathbf{x}$ represent the projections of **x** onto the vectors $\mathbf{w}_1$, $\mathbf{w}_2$, and $\mathbf{w}_3$. According to our earlier discussion, these products also represent the *individual* responses of the three masks. Suppose that masks 1 and 2 are for lines and mask 3 is for points. It is reasonable to ask: Is the region represented by **x** more like a line or more like a point? Since there are two masks representing lines and we are interested only in the line properties of **x**, and not on what type of line is present, we could answer the question by projecting **x** onto the subspace of $\mathbf{w}_1$ and $\mathbf{w}_2$ (which in this case is a plane) and also onto $\mathbf{w}_3$. The angle between **x** and each of these two projections would tell us whether **x** is closer to the line or the point subspace. This can be seen from the geometrical arrangement shown in Fig. 7.9. The magnitude of the

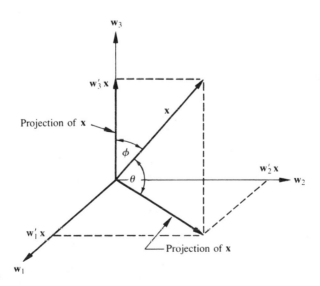

Figure 7.9 Projections of **x** onto subspace (plane) determined by $\mathbf{w}_1$ and $\mathbf{w}_2$, and onto subspace $\mathbf{w}_3$.

projection of $\mathbf{x}$ onto the plane determined by $\mathbf{w}_1$ and $\mathbf{w}_2$ is given by the quantity $[(\mathbf{w}_1'\mathbf{x})^2 + (\mathbf{w}_2'\mathbf{x})^2]^{1/2}$, while the magnitude (i.e., norm) of $\mathbf{x}$ is

$$\|\mathbf{x}\| = [(\mathbf{w}_1'\mathbf{x})^2 + (\mathbf{w}_2'\mathbf{x})^2 + (\mathbf{w}_3'\mathbf{x})^2]^{1/2}. \tag{7.1-22}$$

The angle between $\mathbf{x}$ and its projection is then

$$\begin{aligned}
\theta &= \cos^{-1}\left\{ \frac{[(\mathbf{w}_1'\mathbf{x})^2 + (\mathbf{w}_2'\mathbf{x})^2]^{1/2}}{[(\mathbf{w}_1'\mathbf{x})^2 + (\mathbf{w}_2'\mathbf{x})^2 + (\mathbf{w}_3'\mathbf{x})^2]^{1/2}} \right\} \\
&= \cos^{-1}\left\{ \frac{\left[\sum_{i=1}^{2} (\mathbf{w}_i'\mathbf{x})^2 \right]^{1/2}}{\left[\sum_{j=1}^{3} (\mathbf{w}_j'\mathbf{x})^2 \right]^{1/2}} \right\} \\
&= \cos^{-1}\left\{ \frac{1}{\|\mathbf{x}\|} \left[\sum_{i=1}^{2} (\mathbf{w}_i'\mathbf{x})^2 \right]^{1/2} \right\},
\end{aligned} \tag{7.1-23}$$

where the last step follows from Eq. (7.1-22). A similar development would yield the angle of projection onto the $\mathbf{w}_3$ subspace:

$$\begin{aligned}
\phi &= \cos^{-1}\left\{ \frac{1}{\|\mathbf{x}\|} \left[\sum_{i=3}^{3} (\mathbf{w}_i'\mathbf{x})^2 \right]^{1/2} \right\} \\
&= \cos^{-1}\left\{ \frac{1}{\|\mathbf{x}\|} |\mathbf{w}_3'\mathbf{x}| \right\}.
\end{aligned} \tag{7.1-24}$$

Thus if $\theta < \phi$, we say that the region represented by $\mathbf{x}$ is closer to the characteristics of a line than of a point.

If we now consider 3×3 masks, the problem becomes nine-dimensional, but the above concepts are still valid. We need, however, 9 nine-dimensional orthogonal vectors to form a complete basis. The masks shown in Fig. 7.10 (proposed by Frei and Chen [1977]) satisfy this condition. The first four masks are suitable for detecting edges; the second set of four masks represents templates suitable for line detection; and the last mask (added to complete the bases) is proportional to the average of the pixels in the region at which the mask is located in an image.

Given a 3×3 region represented by $\mathbf{x}$, and assuming that the vectors $\mathbf{w}_i$, $i = 1, 2, \ldots, 9$, have been normalized, we have from the above discussion that

$$p_e = \left[\sum_{i=1}^{4} (\mathbf{w}_i'\mathbf{x})^2 \right]^{1/2} \tag{7.1-25}$$

$$p_l = \left[\sum_{i=5}^{8} (\mathbf{w}_i'\mathbf{x})^2 \right]^{1/2} \tag{7.1-26}$$

and

$$p_a = |\mathbf{w}_9'\mathbf{x}|, \tag{7.1-27}$$

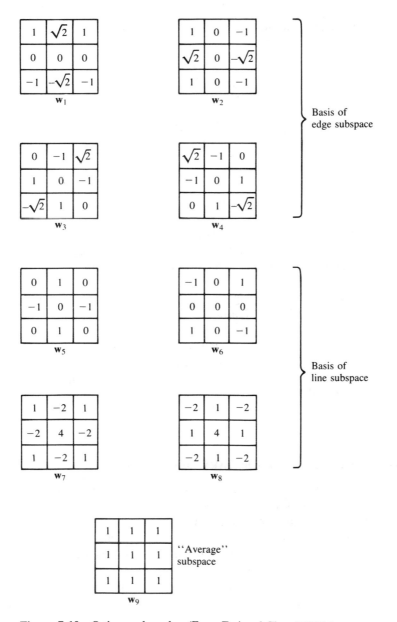

Figure 7.10 Orthogonal masks. (From Frei and Chen [1977].)

where p_e, p_l, and p_a are the magnitudes of the projections of **x** onto the edge, line, and average subspaces, respectively.

Similarly, we have that

$$\theta_e = \cos^{-1}\left\{\frac{1}{\|\mathbf{x}\|}\left[\sum_{i=1}^{4}(\mathbf{w}_i'\mathbf{x})^2\right]^{1/2}\right\} \tag{7.1-28}$$

$$\theta_l = \cos^{-1}\left\{\frac{1}{\|\mathbf{x}\|}\left[\sum_{i=5}^{8}(\mathbf{w}_i'\mathbf{x})^2\right]^{1/2}\right\} \tag{7.1-29}$$

and

$$\theta_a = \cos^{-1}\left\{\frac{1}{\|\mathbf{x}\|}\left|\mathbf{w}_9'\mathbf{x}\right|\right\}, \tag{7.1-30}$$

where θ_e, θ_l and θ_a are the angles between **x** and its projections onto the edge, line, and average subspaces, respectively. These concepts are, of course, directly extendable to other bases and dimensions, as long as the basis vectors are orthogonal.

Example: The image shown in Fig. 7.11(a) is a 256 × 256 aerial photograph of the site of a football stadium. Figures 7.11(b) through (j) are the magnitudes of the projections along the individual basis vectors obtained by using each of the masks in Fig. 7.10 and, for each position of the ith mask, computing a pixel value equal to $|\mathbf{w}_i'\mathbf{x}|$. Figure 7.11(k) shows the magnitude of the projections onto the edge subspace [Eq. (7.1-25)], and Fig. 7.11(l) was formed from the magnitudes of the projections onto the line subspace [Eq. (7.1-26)]. In this example, the best results were obtained with the edge subspace projections, thus indicating a strong edge content in the original image. □

7.2   EDGE LINKING AND BOUNDARY DETECTION

The techniques discussed in the previous section detect intensity discontinuities. Ideally, these techniques should yield only pixels lying on the boundary between objects and the background. In practice, this set of pixels seldom characterizes a boundary completely because of noise, breaks in the boundary due to nonuniform illumination, and other effects that introduce spurious intensity discontinuities. Thus edge-detection algorithms are typically followed by linking and other boundary-detection procedures designed to assemble edge pixels into a meaningful set of object boundaries. In the following sections we consider several techniques suited for this purpose.

7.2.1   Local Analysis

One of the simplest approaches for linking edge points is to analyze the characteristics of pixels in a small neighborhood (e.g., 3 × 3 or 5 × 5) about every point (x, y) in an image that has undergone an edge-detection process. All points that are similar (as defined below) are linked, thus forming a boundary of pixels that share some common properties.

The two principal properties used for establishing similarity of edge pixels in this kind of analysis are (1) the strength of the response of the gradient operator used to produce the edge pixel, and (2) the direction of the gradient. The first property is given by the value of $G[f(x, y)]$, as defined in Eq. (7.1-8) or (7.1-9). Thus we say that an edge pixel with coordinates (x', y') and in the predefined neighborhood of (x, y), is similar in magnitude to the pixel at (x, y) if

$$|G[f(x, y)] - G[f(x', y')]| \leq T, \qquad (7.2\text{-}1)$$

where T is a threshold.

The direction of the gradient vector is given by Eq. (7.1-10). Then, we say that an edge pixel at (x', y') in the predefined neighborhood of (x, y) has an angle similar to the pixel at (x, y) if

$$|\alpha(x, y) - \alpha(x', y')| < A, \qquad (7.2\text{-}2)$$

where A is an angle threshold. Note that the direction of the edge at (x, y) is, in reality, perpendicular to the direction of the gradient vector at that point. However, for the purpose of comparing directions, Eq. (7.2-2) yields equivalent results.

Based on the foregoing concepts, we link a point in the predefined neighborhood of (x, y) to the pixel at (x, y) if both the magnitude and direction criteria are satisfied. This process is repeated for every location in the image, keeping a record of linked points as the center of the neighborhood is moved from pixel to pixel. A simple bookkeeping procedure is to assign a different gray level to each set of linked edge pixels.

Example: As an illustration of the foregoing procedure, consider Fig. 7.12(a), which shows an image of the rear of a vehicle. The objective is to find rectangles whose sizes makes them suitable candidates for license plates. The formation of these rectangles can be accomplished by detecting strong horizontal and vertical edges. Figures 7.12(b) and (c) show the horizontal and vertical components of the Sobel operators discussed in the previous section. Finally, Fig. 7.12(d) shows the results of linking all points that simultaneously had a gradient value greater than 25 and whose gradient directions did not differ by more than 15°. The horizontal lines were formed by sequentially applying these criteria to every row of Fig. 7.12(c), while a sequential column scan of Fig. 7.12(b) yielded the vertical lines. Further processing consisted of linking edge segments separated by small breaks and deleting isolated short segments. □

7.2.2 Global Analysis via the Hough Transform

In this section we consider the linking of points by determining whether or not they lie on a curve of specified shape. Unlike the local-analysis method discussed in the previous section, we now consider the relation between pixels on a global

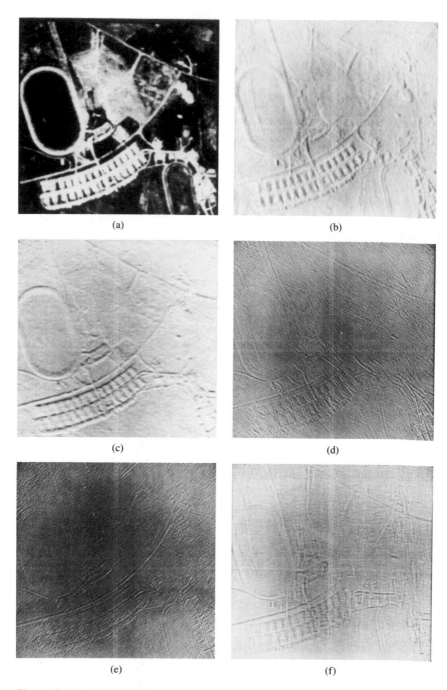

Figure 7.11 (a) Original image. (b) through (f) Projections onto w_1, w_2, w_3, w_4, and w_5 subspaces, respectively. (From Hall and Frei [1976].)

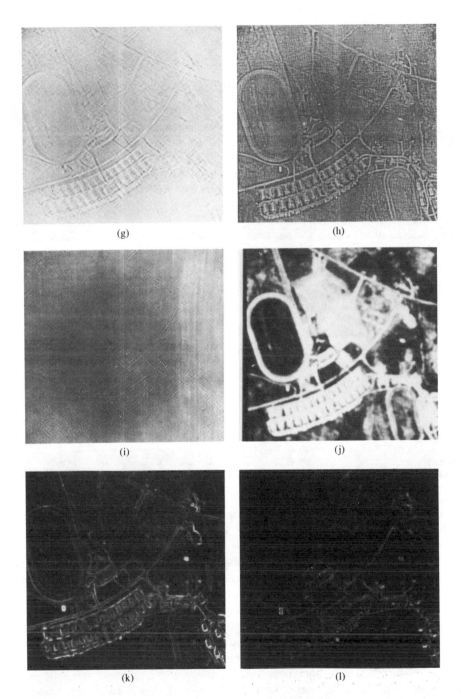

Figure 7.11   (Continued.) (g) through (j) Projections onto w_6, w_7, w_8, and w_9 subspaces. (k) Magnitude of projection onto edge subspace. (l) Magnitude of projection onto line subspace. (From Hall and Frei [1976].)

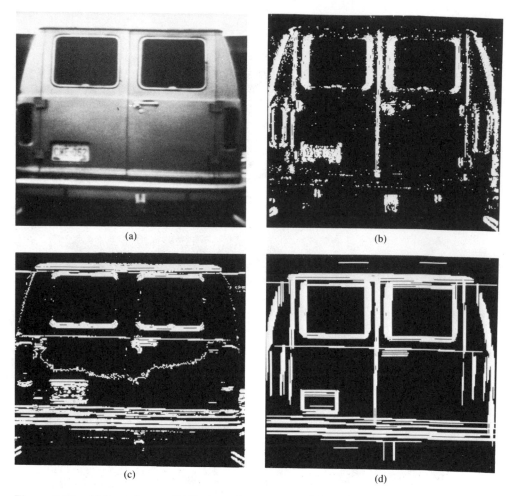

Figure 7.12 (a) Input image. (b) Horizontal component of the gradient. (c) Vertical component of the gradient. (d) Result of edge linking. (Courtesy of Perceptics Corporation.)

basis by using the Hough transform introduced in Section 3.7. The approach consists of (1) computing the gradient of an image, (2) specifying subdivisions in the $\rho\theta$ plane (Fig. 3.32), (3) examining the counts of the accumulator cells for high pixel concentrations, and (4) examining the relation (principally for continuity) between pixels in a chosen cell. The concept of continuity in this case is usually based on computing the distance between pixels found to be disconnected as we traverse the set of pixels corresponding to a given accumulator cell. A gap at any point is said to be significant if the distance between that point and its closest neighbor exceeds a given threshold. (See Section 2.4 for a discussion of connectivity, neighborhoods, and distance measures.)

Example: As an illustration of the concepts just discussed consider Fig. 7.13(a), which shows an aerial infrared image containing two hangars and a runway. Figure 7.13(b) is a thresholded gradient image obtained using the Sobel operators introduced in Section 7.1.3 (note the small gaps in the borders of the runway). Figure 7.13(c) is the linear Hough transform of the gradient image, and Fig. 7.13(d) shows (in white) the set of pixels linked according to the criteria that (1) they belonged to one of the three accumulator cells with the highest count, and (2) there were no gaps longer than five pixels. Note the disappearance of the gaps as a result of linking.   □

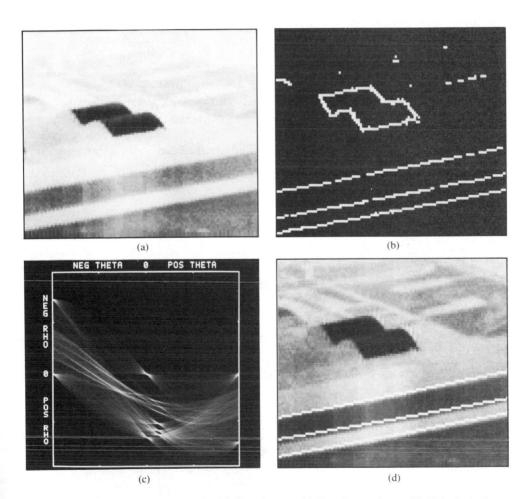

Figure 7.13   (a) Infrared image. (b) Gradient image. (c) Hough transform. (d) Linked pixels satisfying two criteria (see text). (Courtesy of D. R. Cate, Texas Instruments, Inc.)

7.2.3   Global Analysis via Graph-Theoretic Techniques

The method discussed in the previous section is based on having a set of edge points obtained typically through a gradient operation. Since the gradient is a derivative, it is seldom suitable as a preprocessing step in situations characterized by high noise content. In this section we discuss a global approach based on representing edge segments in the form of a graph structure and searching the graph for low-cost paths that correspond to significant edges. As will be seen, this representation provides a rugged approach that performs well in the presence of noise. As might be expected, the procedure is considerably more complicated and requires more processing time than the methods discussed thus far.

We begin the development with some basic definitions. A *graph* $G = (N, A)$ is a finite, nonempty set of nodes N, together with a set A of unordered pairs of distinct elements of N. Each pair (n_i, n_j) of A is called an *arc*. A graph in which the arcs are directed is called a *directed graph*. If an arc is directed from node n_i to node n_j, then n_j is said to be a *successor* of its *parent* node n_i. The process of identifying the successors of a node is called *expansion* of the node. In each graph we will define levels, such that level 0 consists of a single node, called the *start* node, and the nodes in the last level are called *goal* nodes. A *cost* $c(n_i, n_j)$ can be associated with every arc (n_i, n_j). A sequence of nodes $n_1, n_2, \ldots, n_k$ with each node n_i being a successor of node n_{i-1} is called a *path* from n_1 to n_k, and the cost of the path is given by

$$c = \sum_{i=2}^{k} c(n_{i-1}, n_i) \tag{7.2-3}$$

Finally, we define an *edge element* as the boundary between two pixels p and q, such that p and q are 4-neighbors, as illustrated in Fig. 7.14. In this context, an *edge* is a sequence of edge elements.

In order to illustrate how the foregoing concepts apply to edge detection, consider the 3×3 image shown in Fig. 7.15, where the outer numbers are pixel coordinates and the numbers in parentheses represent intensity. With each edge element defined by pixels p and q we associate the cost

$$c(p, q) = H - [f(p) - f(q)], \tag{7.2-4}$$

where H is the highest-intensity value in the image (7 in this example), $f(p)$ is the

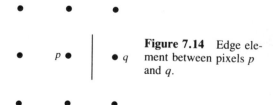

Figure 7.14   Edge element between pixels p and q.

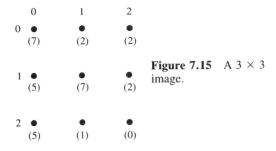

Figure 7.15 A 3 × 3 image.

intensity value of p, and $f(q)$ is the intensity value of q. As indicated above, p and q are 4-neighbors.

The graph for this problem is shown in Fig. 7.16. Each node in this graph corresponds to an edge element, and an arc exists between two nodes if the two corresponding edge elements taken in succession can be part of an edge. The cost of each edge element, computed using Eq. (7.2-4), is shown by the arc leading into it, and goal nodes are shown as shaded rectangles. Each path between the start node and a goal node is a possible edge. For simplicity, it has been assumed that the edge starts in the top row and terminates in the last row, so that the first element of an edge can be only $[(0, 0), (0, 1)]$ or $[(0, 1), (0, 2)]$ and the last

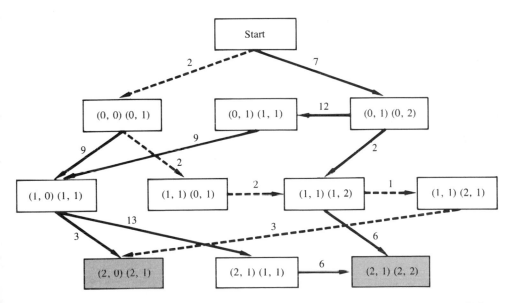

Figure 7.16 Graph used for finding an edge in the image of Fig. 7.7. The pair $(a, b)(c, d)$ in each box refers to points p and q, respectively. Note that p is assumed to be to the right of the path as the image is traversed from top to bottom. The dashed lines indicate the minimum-cost path. (Adapted from Martelli [1972].)

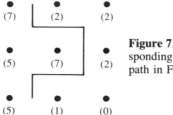

Figure 7.17 Edge corresponding to minimum-cost path in Fig. 7.16.

element $[(2, 0), (2, 1)]$ or $[(2, 1), (2, 2)]$. The minimum-cost path, computed using Eq. (7.2-3), is shown as a dashed line, and the corresponding edge is shown in Fig. 7.17.

In general, the problem of finding a minimum-cost path is not trivial from a computational point of view. Typically, the approach is to sacrifice optimality for the sake of speed, and the algorithm discussed below is representative of a class of procedures that use heuristics in order to reduce the search effort. Let $r(n)$ be an estimate of the cost of a minimum-cost path from the start node s to a goal node, where the path is constrained to go through n. This cost can be expressed as the estimate of the cost of a minimum-cost path from s to n plus an estimate of the cost of that path from n to a goal node; that is,

$$r(n) = g(n) + h(n). \tag{7.2-5}$$

Here, $g(n)$ can be chosen as the lowest-cost path from s to n found so far, and $h(n)$ is obtained by using any available heuristic information (e.g., expanding only certain nodes based on previous costs in getting to that node). An algorithm that uses $r(n)$ as the basis for performing a graph search is as follows:

Step 1: Mark the start node OPEN and set $g(s) = 0$.

Step 2: If no node is OPEN exit with failure; otherwise continue.

Step 3: Mark CLOSED the OPEN node n whose estimate $r(n)$ computed from Eq. (7.2-5) is smallest. (Ties for minimum r values are resolved arbitrarily, but always in favor of a goal node.)

Step 4: If n is a goal node, exit with the solution path obtained by tracing back through the pointers; otherwise continue.

Step 5: Expand node n, generating all of its successors. (If there are no successors go to Step 2.)

Step 6: If a successor n_i is not marked, set

$$r(n_i) = g(n) + c(n, n_i),$$

mark it OPEN, and direct pointers from it back to n.

Step 7: If a successor n_i is marked CLOSED or OPEN, update its value by letting

$$g'(n_i) = \min[g(n_i), g(n) + c(n, n_i)].$$

Mark OPEN those CLOSED successors whose g' values were thus lowered and redirect to n the pointers from all nodes whose g' values were lowered. Go to Step 2.

In general, this algorithm is not guaranteed to find a minimum-cost path; its advantage is speed via the use of heuristics. It can be shown, however, that if $h(n)$ is a lower bound on the cost of the minimal-cost path from node n to a goal node, then the procedure will indeed find an optimal path to a goal (Hart, Nilsson, and Raphael [1968]). If no heuristic information is available (i.e., $h \equiv 0$) then the procedure reduces to the *uniform-cost algorithm* of Dijkstra [1959].

Example: Figure 7.18 shows a typical result obtainable with this procedure. Figure 7.18(a) shows a noisy image and Fig. 7.18(b) is the result of edge segmentation by searching the corresponding graph for low-cost paths. Heuristics were brought into play by not expanding those nodes whose cost exceeded a given threshold. ☐

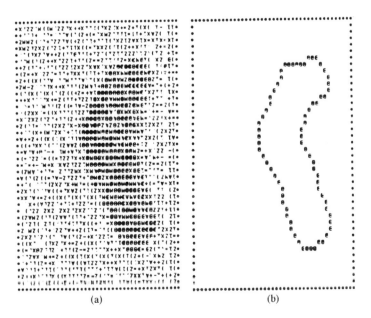

(a)   (b)

Figure 7.18 (a) Noisy image. (b) Result of edge detection by using the heuristic graph search. (From Martelli [1976].)

7.3   THRESHOLDING

Thresholding is one of the most important approaches to image segmentation. In this section, we develop a number of techniques for thresholding and discuss the merits and limitations of these methods.

7.3.1   Foundation

Suppose that the gray-level histogram shown in Fig. 7.19(a) corresponds to an image, $f(x, y)$, composed of light objects on a dark background, such that object and background pixels have gray levels grouped into two dominant modes. One obvious way to extract the objects from the background is to select a threshold T that separates these modes. Then, any point (x, y) for which $f(x, y) > T$ is called an object point; otherwise, the point is called a background point. A slightly more general case of this approach is shown in Fig. 7.19(b). In this case the image histogram is characterized by three dominant modes (for example, two types of light objects on a dark background). Here, we can use the same basic approach and classify a point (x, y) as belonging to one object class if $T_1 < f(x, y) \leq T_2$, to the other object class if $f(x, y) > T_2$, and to the background if $f(x, y) \leq T_1$. This type of *multilevel thresholding* is generally less reliable than its single-threshold counterpart because of the difficulty in establishing multiple thresholds that effectively isolate regions of interest, especially when the number of corresponding histogram modes is large. Typically, problems of this nature, if handled by thresholding, are best addressed by a single, variable threshold, as discussed later in this section.

Based on the foregoing concepts, we may view thresholding as an operation that involves tests against a function T of the form

$$T = T[x, y, p(x, y), f(x, y)], \tag{7.3-1}$$

where $f(x, y)$ is the gray level of point (x, y), and $p(x, y)$ denotes some local

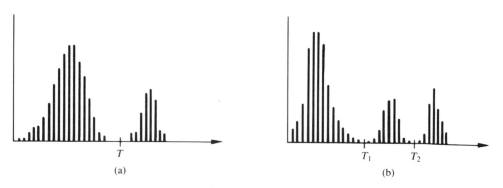

Figure 7.19   Gray-level histograms that can be partitioned by (a) a single threshold, and (b) multiple thresholds.

property of this point—for example, the average gray level of a neighborhood centered at (x, y). We create a thresholded image $g(x, y)$ by defining

$$g(x, y) = \begin{cases} 1 & \text{if } f(x, y) > T \\ 0 & \text{if } f(x, y) \leqslant T \end{cases} \qquad (7.3\text{-}2)$$

Thus in examining $g(x, y)$, we find that pixels labeled 1 (or any other convenient intensity level) correspond to objects, while pixels labeled 0 correspond to the background.

When T depends only on $f(x, y)$, the threshold is called *global*. (Figure 7.19a shows an example of such a threshold.) If T depends on both $f(x, y)$ and $p(x, y)$, then the threshold is called *local*. If, in addition, T depends on the spatial coordinates x and y, it is called a *dynamic threshold*.

7.3.2 The Role of Illumination

With reference to the discussion in Section 2.2, we may view the formation of an image $f(x, y)$ as the product of a reflectance component $r(x, y)$ and an illumination component $i(x, y)$. The purpose of this section is to discuss briefly the effect of illumination on image segmentation.

As an introduction to this problem, consider the computer-generated reflectance function shown in Fig. 7.20(a). The histogram of this function, shown in Fig. 7.20(b), is clearly bimodal and could easily be segmented by placing a single threshold in the histogram valley. Suppose that we multiply the reflectance function in Fig. 7.20(a) by the illumination function shown in Fig. 7.20(c) to yield the image $f(x, y)$ shown in Fig. 7.20(d). The histogram of this image is shown in Fig. 7.20(e). Note that the original valley was virtually eliminated, making segmentation by a single threshold an impossible task. Although we never really have the reflectance function by itself to work with, this simple example illustrates that the nature of objects and background could be such that they are easily separable, while the image resulting from poor (in this case nonuniform) illumination could be quite difficult to segment.

The reason for the histogram in Fig. 7.20(e) being so corrupted can be explained with the aid of the discussion in Section 4.5. Taking the natural logarithm of $f(x, y) = i(x, y) r(x, y)$ yields the sum $z(x, y) = \ln f(x, y) = \ln i(x, y) + \ln r(x, y) = i'(x, y) + r'(x, y)$. We know from probability theory (Papoulis [1965]) that if $i'(x, y)$ and $r'(x, y)$ are independent random variables, the histogram of $z(x, y)$ is given by the convolution of the histograms of $i'(x, y)$ and $r'(x, y)$. If $i(x, y)$ were constant, $i'(x, y)$ would be constant also, and its histogram would be a simple spike (like an impulse). The convolution of this impulse-like function with the histogram of $r'(x, y)$ would leave the basic shape of this histogram virtually unchanged (see Fig. 3.15). On the other hand, if $i'(x, y)$ had a broader histogram (resulting, from nonuniform illumination), the convolution process would smear the histogram of $r'(x, y)$, yielding a histogram for $z(x, y)$ whose shape could be quite different from the

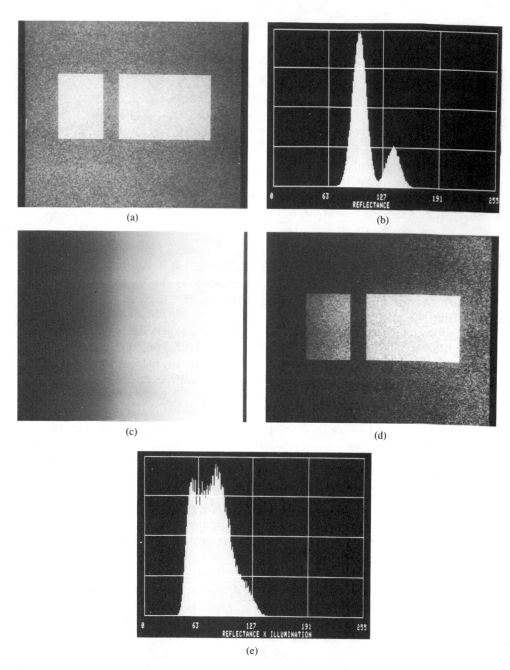

Figure 7.20   (a) Computer-generated reflectance function. (b) Histogram of reflectance function. (c) Computer-generated illumination function. (d) Image produced by the product of the illumination and reflectance functions. (e) Histogram of image.

shape of the histogram of $r'(x, y)$. The degree of distortion depends on the broadness of the histogram of $i'(x, y)$, which in turn depends on the nonuniformity of the illumination function.

In the preceding discussion we have dealt with the logarithm of $f(x, y)$ instead of dealing with the image function directly, but the essence of the problem is clearly explained by using the logarithm to separate the illumination and reflectance components. This allowed us to view histogram formation as a convolution process, thus explaining why a clear valley in the histogram of the reflectance function could be virtually eliminated by improper illumination.

When access to the illumination source is available, a solution frequently used in practice to compensate for nonuniformity is to project the illumination pattern onto a constant, white reflective surface. This yields an image $g(x, y) = ki(x, y)$, where k is a constant that depends on the surface and $i(x, y)$ is the illumination pattern. Then, for any image $f(x, y) = i(x, y) r(x, y)$ obtained with the same illumination function, we simply divide $f(x, y)$ by $g(x, y)$, yielding a normalized function $h(x, y) = f(x, y)/g(x, y) = r(x, y)/k$. Thus if $r(x, y)$ can be segmented by using a single threshold T, then $h(x, y)$ can also be segmented by using a single threshold of value T/k. Note that this method works well only if the illumination pattern produced by $i(x, y)$ does not change from image to image. Typically, the normalization of $f(x, y)$ by $g(x, y)$ is carried out using an ALU (Arithmetic-Logic Unit) processor, as discussed in Section 2.4.4.

7.3.3 A Global Thresholding Technique

A simple approach that is often useful for segmenting an image consists of dividing the gray scale into bands and using thresholds to determine regions or to obtain boundary points.

As an introduction to this technique, suppose that the gray levels in a given image $f(x, y)$ have the histogram shown in Fig. 7.21(a). Based on the discussion in Section 4.2, we conclude from the histogram that a large number of pixels in $f(x, y)$ are dark, with the remaining pixels being distributed fairly even in the remaining portion of the gray scale. This histogram behavior is characteristic of images consisting of gray objects supcrimposed on a dark background. To outline

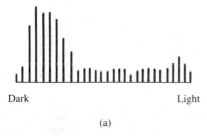

Dark   Light

(a)

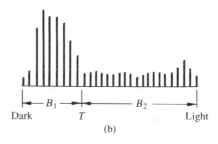

Dark   T   Light

(b)

Figure 7.21 Histogram thresholding.

358   **Image Segmentation**

the boundary between objects and the background, we divide the histogram into two bands separated by a threshold T, as shown in Fig. 7.21(b). The goal is to select T so that band B_1 contains, as closely as possible, levels associated with the background, while B_2 contains the levels of the objects. As the image is scanned, a change in gray level from one band to the other denotes the presence of a boundary. In order to detect boundaries in both the horizontal and vertical directions, two passes through $f(x, y)$ are required. Once B_1 and B_2 have been selected, the procedure is as follows:

Pass 1. For each row in $f(x, y)$ (i.e., $x = 0, 1, . . . , N - 1$), create a corresponding row in an intermediate image $g_1(x, y)$ using the following relation for $y = 1, 2, . . . , N - 1$:

$$g_1(x, y) = \begin{cases} L_E & \text{if the levels of } f(x, y) \text{ and } f(x, y - 1) \\ & \text{are in different bands of the gray scale,} \\ L_B & \text{otherwise,} \end{cases} \quad (7.3\text{-}3)$$

where L_E and L_B are specified edge and background levels, respectively.

Pass 2. For each column in $f(x, y)$ (i.e., $y = 0, 1, . . . , N - 1$), create a corresponding column in an intermediate image $g_2(x, y)$ using the following relation for $x = 1, 2, . . . , N - 1$:

$$g_2(x, y) = \begin{cases} L_E & \text{if the levels of } f(x, y) \text{ and } f(x - 1, y) \\ & \text{are in different bands of the gray scale,} \\ L_B & \text{otherwise.} \end{cases} \quad (7.3\text{-}4)$$

The desired image, consisting of the points on the boundary of objects different (as defined by T) from the background, is obtained by using the following relation for $x, y = 0, 1, . . . , N - 1$:

$$g(x, y) = \begin{cases} L_E & \text{if either } g_1(x, y) \text{ or } g_2(x, y) \\ & \text{is equal to } L_E, \\ L_B & \text{otherwise.} \end{cases} \quad (7.3\text{-}5)$$

Example: The gray-level thresholding technique just described is illustrated in Fig. 7.22. The original image, Fig. 7.22(a), is a 256-level picture of the Sombrero (Spanish for hat) Nebula. The histogram of this image, shown in Fig. 7.22(b), contains two prominent peaks, one in the dark, and one in the light portion of the gray scale. The first peak corresponds to the background, the second to the light tones in the image itself. Figure 7.22(c) was obtained using Eqs. (7.3-3) through (7.3-5) with $B_1 = B_2$ (i.e., $T = 128$), $L_E = 0$, and $L_B = 255$. Figure 7.22(d) was formed by superimposing the edges on Fig. 7.22(a). □

The above procedure is easily generalized to more gray-level bands. In fact, since the relations in Eqs. (7.3-3) and (7.3-4) are based only on a change in gray-level band from one pixel to the next, the basic technique for establishing boundary

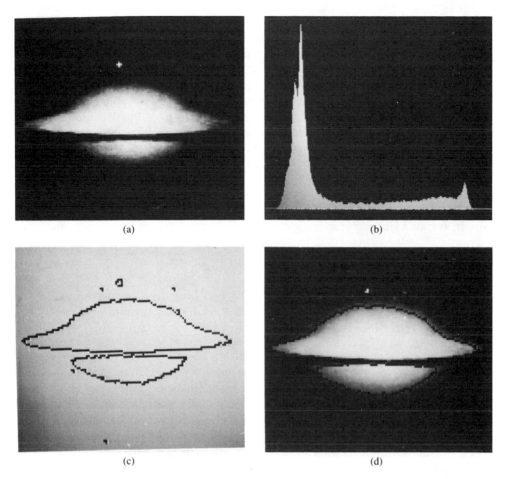

(a)

(b)

(c)

(d)

Figure 7.22 Edge extraction by gray-level thresholding. (a) Picture of Sombrero Nebula. (b) Histogram. (c) Edge image obtained with $T = 128$. (d) Edges superimposed on original.

points would be the same if more than two bands were considered. One possible extension would be to code the edge points with different gray levels, depending on the band in which the change took place.

By thresholding more gray-level bands, it is possible to increase the power of the edge-extraction technique. The problem, of course, is where to place the thresholds. One approach is to specify the number and location of the thresholds by trial and error. This method is satisfactory if the number of different images to be processed is small. In situations where automatic setting of the thresholds (as in machine-perception applications) is required, the problem becomes one of characterizing a given histogram in some invariant manner. This problem is discussed next.

7.3.4   Optimal Thresholding

Suppose it is known a priori that an image contains only two principal brightness regions. The histogram of such a picture may be considered as an estimate of the brightness probability density function, $p(x)$. This overall density function would be the sum or mixture of two unimodal densities, one for the light and one for the dark regions in the image. Furthermore, the mixture parameters would be proportional to the areas of the picture of each brightness. If the form of the densities is known or assumed, then it is possible to determine an optimal threshold (in terms of minimum error) for segmenting the image into the two brightness regions.

Suppose that an image contains two values combined with additive Gaussian noise. The mixture probability density function is given by

$$p(x) = P_1 p_1(x) + P_2 p_2(x), \tag{7.3-6}$$

which, for the Gaussian case, is

$$p(x) = \frac{P_1}{\sqrt{2\pi}\,\sigma_1} \exp\left[-\frac{(x-\mu_1)^2}{2\sigma_1^2}\right] + \frac{P_2}{\sqrt{2\pi}\,\sigma_2} \exp\left[-\frac{(x-\mu_2)^2}{2\sigma_2^2}\right], \tag{7.3-7}$$

where μ_1 and μ_2 are the mean values of the two brightness levels, σ_1 and σ_2 are the standard deviations about the means, and P_1 and P_2 are the a priori probabilities of the two levels. Since the constraint

$$P_1 + P_2 = 1 \tag{7.3-8}$$

must be satisfied, the mixture density has five unknown parameters. If all the parameters are known, the optimal threshold is easily determined.

Suppose that the dark regions correspond to the background and the bright regions correspond to objects. In this case $\mu_1 < \mu_2$ and we may define a threshold T so that all pixels with a gray level below T are considered background points and all pixels with a level above T are considered object points. The probability of (erroneously) classifying an object point as a background point is

$$E_1(T) = \int_{-\infty}^{T} p_2(x)\, dx. \tag{7.3-9}$$

Similarly, the probability of classifying a background point as an object point is

$$E_2(T) = \int_{T}^{\infty} p_1(x)\, dx. \tag{7.3-10}$$

Therefore the overall probability of error is given by

$$E(T) = P_2 E_1(T) + P_1 E_2(T). \tag{7.3-11}$$

To find the threshold value for which this error is minimal, we may differentiate $E(T)$ with respect to T (using Liebnitz's rule) and equate the result to 0. The result is

$$P_1 p_1(T) = P_2 p_2(T). \tag{7.3-12}$$

Applying this result to the Gaussian density gives, after taking logarithms and simplifying, a quadratic equation,

$$AT^2 + BT + C = 0, \qquad (7.3\text{-}13)$$

where

$$A = \sigma_1^2 - \sigma_2^2$$
$$B = 2(\mu_1\sigma_2^2 - \mu_2\sigma_1^2) \qquad (7.3\text{-}14)$$
$$C = \sigma_1^2\mu_2^2 - \sigma_2^2\mu_1^2 + 2\sigma_1^2\sigma_2^2 \ln(\sigma_2 P_1/\sigma_1 P_2).$$

The possibility of two solutions indicates that it may require two threshold values to obtain the optimal solution.

If the variances are equal, $\sigma^2 = \sigma_1^2 = \sigma_2^2$, a single threshold is sufficient:

$$T = \frac{\mu_1 + \mu_2}{2} + \frac{\sigma^2}{\mu_1 - \mu_2} \ln\left(\frac{P_2}{P_1}\right). \qquad (7.3\text{-}15)$$

If the prior probabilities are equal, $P_1 = P_2$, the optimal threshold is just the average of the means. The same is true if $\sigma = 0$. The determination of the optimal threshold may be accomplished easily for other unimodal densities of known form, such as the Raleigh and log-normal densities.

To estimate the parameters from a histogram of an image one may use a maximum likelihood or minimum mean-square error approach. For example, the mean-square error between the mixture density $p(x)$ and the experimental histogram $h(x_i)$ is

$$M = \frac{1}{N} \sum_{i=1}^{N} [p(x_i) - h(x_i)]^2, \qquad (7.3\text{-}16)$$

where an N-point histogram is assumed.

In general, it is not a simple matter to determine analytically parameters that minimize this mean-square error. Even for the Gaussian case, the straightforward computation of equating the partial derivatives to 0 leads to a set of simultaneous transcendental equations that usually can be solved only by numerical procedures. Since the gradient is easily computed, a conjugate gradient or Newton's method for simultaneous nonlinear equations may be used to minimize M. With either of these iterative methods, starting values must be specified. Assuming the a priori probabilities to be equal may be sufficient. Starting values for the means and variances may be determined by detecting modes in the histogram or simply by dividing the histogram into two parts about its mean value, and computing means and variances of the two parts to be used as starting values.

Example: As an illustration of optimal threshold selection we consider in the following discussion an approach developed by Chow and Kaneko [1972] for outlining boundaries of the left ventricle in cardioangiograms (i.e., x-ray pictures of a heart, which has been injected with a dye).

Before thresholding, the images were first preprocessed by (1) taking the logarithm of every pixel to invert the exponential effects caused by radioactive absorption, (2) subtracting two images that were obtained before and after the dye agent was applied in order to remove the spinal column present in both images, and (3) averaging several angiograms to remove noise (see Section 4.3.4). Figure 7.23 shows a cardioangiogram before and after preprocessing (the regions marked A and B and explained below).

In order to compute the optimal thresholds, each preprocessed image was subdivided into 7 × 7 regions (the original images were of size 256 × 256) with 50% overlap. Each of the 49 resulting regions contained 64 × 64 pixels. Figures 7.24(a) and 7.24(b) are the histograms of the regions marked A and B in Fig. 7.23(b). Note that the histogram for region A is very clearly bimodal, indicating the presence of a boundary. The histogram for region B, on the other hand, is unimodal, indicating the absence of two markedly distinct regions.

After all 49 histograms were computed, a test of bimodality was performed to reject the unimodal histograms. The remaining histograms were then fitted by bimodal Gaussian density curves (see Eq. 7.3-7) using a conjugate gradient hill-climbing method to minimize the error function given in Eq. (7.3-16). The ×s and ⊙s in Fig. 7.24(a) are two fits to the histogram shown in black dots. The optimal thresholds were then obtained by using Eqs. (7.3-13) and (7.3-14).

At this stage of the process only the regions with bimodal histograms were assigned thresholds. The thresholds for the remaining regions were obtained by interpolating these thresholds. After this was done, a second interpolation was carried out in a point-by-point manner using neighboring threshold values so that, at the

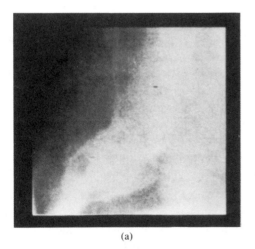
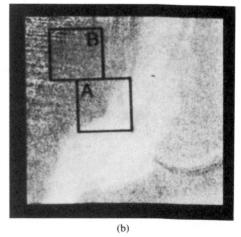

(a)   (b)

Figure 7.23   A cardioangiogram before and after processing. (From Chow and Kaneko [1972].)

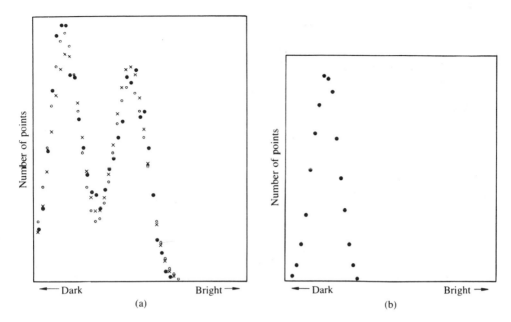

Figure 7.24 Histograms (black dots) of regions A and B in Fig. 7.23(b). (From Chow and Kaneko [1972].)

end of the procedure, every point in the image was assigned a threshold. Finally, a binary decision was carried out for each pixel using the rule

$$f(x, y) = \begin{cases} 1 & \text{if } f(x, y) \geq T_{xy} \\ 0 & \text{otherwise}, \end{cases}$$

where T_{xy} was the threshold computed at location (x, y) in the image. Boundaries were then obtained by taking the gradient of the binary picture. The results are shown in Fig. 7.25, in which the boundary was superimposed on the original image. Note that these are dynamic thresholds since they depend on the spatial coordinates (x, y). □

7.3.5 Threshold Selection Based on Boundary Characteristics

One of the most important aspects in selecting a threshold is the capability of reliably identifying the mode peaks in a given histogram. This is particularly important for automatic threshold selection in situations where image characteristics can change over a broad range of intensity distributions. Based on the discussion in the last three sections, it is intuitively evident that the chances of selecting a "good" threshold should be considerably enhanced if the histogram peaks are tall, narrow, symmetric, and separated by deep valleys.

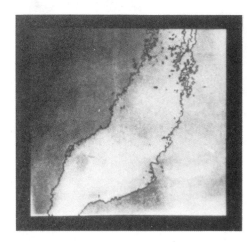

Figure 7.25 Cardioangiogram showing super-imposed boundaries. (From Chow and Kaneko [1972].)

One approach for improving the shape of histograms is to consider only those pixels that lie on or near the boundary between objects and the background. One immediate and obvious improvement is that this makes histograms less dependent on the relative size between objects and the background. For instance, the intensity histogram of an image composed of a large, nearly constant background area and one small object would be dominated by a large peak, due to the concentration of background pixels. If, on the other hand, only the pixels on or near the boundary between the object and the background were used, the resulting histogram would have peaks of approximately the same height. In addition, the probability that a given pixel lies on an object is usually equal to the probability that it lies on the background, thus improving the symmetry of the histogram peaks. Finally, as will be seen below, using pixels that satisfy some simple measures based on gradient and Laplacian operators has a tendency to deepen the valley between histogram peaks.

The principal problem with the foregoing comments is that they implicitly assume that the boundary between objects and background is known. This information is clearly not available during segmentation since finding a division between objects and background is the ultimate goal of the procedures discussed in this section. However, we know from the material in Section 7.1.3 that an indication of whether a pixel is on an edge may be obtained by computing its gradient. In addition, use of the Laplacian can yield information regarding whether a given pixel lies on the dark (e.g., background) or light (object) side of an edge. Since, as discussed above, the Laplacian is 0 on the interior of an ideal ramp edge, we may expect in practice that the valleys of histograms formed from the pixels selected by a gradient/Laplacian criterion to be sparsely populated. This property produces the highly desirable deep valleys mentioned above.

The gradient $G[f(x, y)]$ at any point in an image is given by Eq. (7.1-8) or (7.1-9). Similarly, the Laplacian $L[f(x, y)]$ is given by Eq. (7.1-17). We may use these two quantities to form a three-level image, as follows:

$$s(x, y) = \begin{cases} 0 & \text{if } G[f(x, y)] < T, \\ + & \text{if } G[f(x, y)] \geq T \text{ and } L[f(x, y)] \geq 0, \\ - & \text{if } G[f(x, y)] \geq T \text{ and } L[f(x, y)] < 0, \end{cases} \qquad (7.3\text{-}17)$$

where the symbols 0, +, and − represent any three distinct gray levels, and T is a threshold. Assuming a dark object on a light background, and with reference to Fig. 7.4(b), the use of Eq. (7.3-17) produces an image $s(x, y)$ in which all pixels that are not on an edge (as determined by $G[f(x, y)]$ being less than T) are labeled 0, all pixels on the dark side of an edge are labeled +, and all pixels on the light side of an edge are labeled −. The symbols + and − in Eq. (7.3-17) are reversed for a light object on a dark background. Figure 7.26 shows the labeling produced by Eq. (7.3-17) for an image of a dark, underlined stroke written on a light background.

The information obtained by using the procedure just discussed can be used to generate a segmented, binary image in which 1s correspond to objects of interest and 0s correspond to the background. First we note that the transition (along a horizontal or vertical scan line) from a light background to a dark object must be characterized by the occurrence of a − followed by a + in $s(x, y)$. The interior of the object is composed of pixels that are labeled either 0 or +. Finally, the transition from the object back to the background is characterized by the occurrence of a +

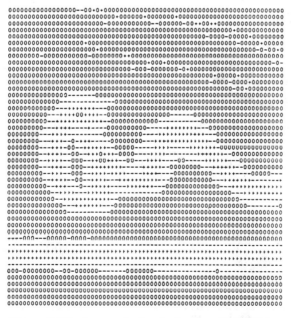

Figure 7.26 Image of a handwritten stroke coded by using Eq. (7.2-24). (From White and Rohrer [1983].)

followed by a $-$. Thus we have that a horizontal or vertical scan line containing a section of an object has the following structure:

$$(\cdots)(-, +)(0 \text{ or } +)(+, -)(\cdots),$$

where $(\cdots)$ represents any combinaticn of $+$, $-$, and 0. The innermost parentheses contain object points and are labeled 1. All other pixels along the same scan line are labeled 0, with the exception of any other sequence of (0 or $+$) bounded by $(-, +)$ and $(+, -)$.

Example: As an illustration of the concepts discussed in this section, consider Fig. 7.27(a), which shows an image of an ordinary scenic bank check. Figure 7.28 shows the histogram as a function of gradient values for pixels with gradients greater than 5. Note that this histogram has the properties discussed earlier. That is, it has two dominant modes that are symmetric, nearly of the same height, and are separated by a distinct valley. Finally, Fig. 7.27(b) shows the segmented image obtained by using Eq. (7.3-17) with T at or near the midpoint of the valley. The result was made binary by using the sequence analysis discussed above. Note that, although T is a constant threshold, its value was applied locally since the segmented image was generated via Eq. (7.3-17), which involves local gradient and Laplacian computations. ☐

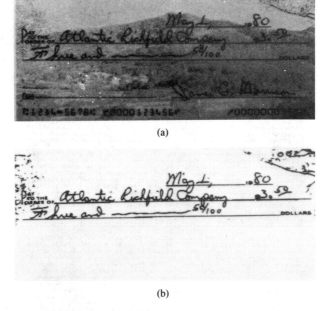

(a)

(b)

Figure 7.27   (a) Original image. (b) Segmented image. (From White and Rohrer [1983].)

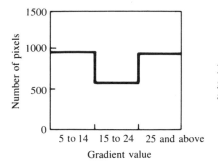

Figure 7.28   Histogram of pixels with gradients greater than 5. (From White and Rohrer [1983].)

7.3.6   Thresholds Based on Several Variables

Thus far we have been concerned with thresholding a single intensity variable. In some cases, a sensor might make available more than one variable to characterize each pixel in an image. A notable example is color photography, where red (R), green (G), and blue (B) components are used to form a composite color image (see Section 4.7). In this case, each pixel is characterized by three values and it becomes possible to construct a three-dimensional histogram. The basic procedure is the same as that used for one variable. For example, given three 16-level images corresponding to the RGB components, we form a $16 \times 16 \times 16$ grid (cube) and insert in each cell of the cube the number of pixels whose RGB components have intensities corresponding to the coordinates defining the location of that particular cell. Each entry can then be divided by the total number of pixels in the image to form a normalized histogram.

The concept of thresholding now becomes one of finding clusters of points in three-dimensional space. Suppose, for example, that we find K significant clusters of points in the histogram. The image can be segmented by assigning one intensity to pixels whose RGB components are closer to one cluster and another intensity to the other pixels in the image. This concept is easily extendable to more components and certainly to more clusters. The principal difficulty is that cluster seeking becomes an increasingly complex task as the number of variables is increased. The reader interested in pursuing techniques for cluster seeking can consult, for example, the book by Tou and Gonzalez [1974].

Example: As an illustration of the multivariable histogram approach, consider the images shown in Fig. 7.29. Figure 7.29(a) is a monochrome picture of a color photograph. The original color image was composed of three 16-level RGB images. For our purposes, it is sufficient to point out that the scarf was a vivid red and that the hair and facial colors were light and different in spectral characteristics from the window and other background features.

Figure 7.29(b) was obtained by thresholding about one of the histogram clusters. It is important to note that the window, which in the monochrome picture is close

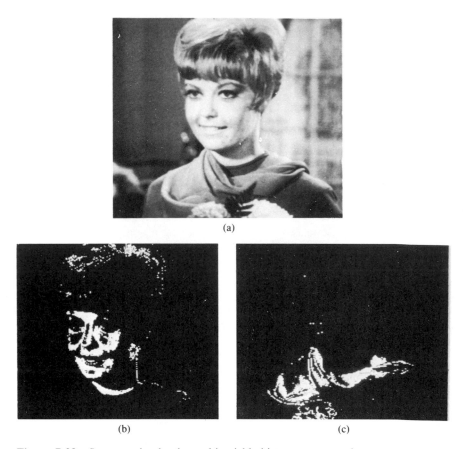

(a)

(b)   (c)

Figure 7.29   Segmentation by the multivariable histogram approach.

in intensity to the hair, does not appear in the segmented image because of our use of multispectral characteristics to separate these two regions. Figure 7.29(c) was obtained by thresholding about a cluster close to the red axis. In this case only the scarf and part of a flower (which was also red) appeared in the segmented result. The threshold used to obtain both results was a distance of one cell. Thus any pixel whose components were outside the cell enclosing the center of the cluster in question was classified as background (black). Pixels whose components placed them inside the cell were coded white.   ☐

7.4   REGION-ORIENTED SEGMENTATION

The objective of segmentation is to partition an image into regions. In Sections 7.1 and 7.2 we approached this problem by finding boundaries between regions based on intensity discontinuities, while in Section 7.3 segmentation was accomplished via thresholds based on the distribution of pixel properties, such as intensity or color. In this section we discuss segmentation techniques that are based on finding the regions directly.

7.4.1 Basic Formulation

Let R represent the entire image region. We may view segmentation as a process that partitions R into n subregions, $R_1, R_2, \ldots, R_n$, such that

(a) $\bigcup_{i=1}^{n} R_i = R,$

(b) R_i is a connected region, $i = 1, 2, \ldots, n,$

(c) $R_i \cap R_j = \phi$ for all i and j, $i \neq j,$

(d) $P(R_i) = \text{TRUE}$ for $i = 1, 2, \ldots, n,$

(e) $P(R_i \cup R_j) = \text{FALSE}$ for $i \neq j,$

where $P(R_i)$ is a logical predicate defined over the points in set R_i, and ϕ is the null set.

Condition (a) indicates that the segmentation must be complete; that is, every pixel must be in a region. The second condition requires that points in a region must be connected (see Section 2.4.2 regarding connectivity). Condition (c) indicates that the regions must be disjoint. Condition (d) deals with the properties that must be satisfied by the pixels in a segmented region. One simple example is $P(R_i) = \text{TRUE}$ if all pixels in R_i have the same intensity. Finally, condition (e) indicates that regions R_i and R_j are different in the sense of predicate P. The use of these conditions in segmentation algorithms is discussed in the following sections.

7.4.2 Region Growing by Pixel Aggregation

As implied by its name, region growing is a procedure that groups pixels or subregions into larger regions. The simplest of these approaches is *pixel aggregation,* where we start with a set of "seed" points and from these grow regions by appending to each seed point those neighboring pixels that have similar properties (e.g., gray level, texture, color). As a simple illustration of this procedure consider Fig. 7.30(a), where the numbers inside the cells represent gray-level values. Let the points with coordinates (3, 2) and (3, 4) be used as seeds. Using two starting points will result in a segmentation consisting of, at most, two regions: R_1 associated with seed (3, 2) and R_2 associated with seed (3, 4). The property P that we will use to include a pixel in either region is that the absolute difference between the gray level of that pixel and the gray level of the seed be less than a threshold T. Any pixel that satisfies this property simultaneously for both seeds is assigned to region R_1. The result obtained using $T = 3$ is shown in Fig. 7.30(b). In this case, the segmentation consists of two regions, where the points in R_1 are denoted by *a*s and the points in R_2 by *b*s. Note that any starting point in either of these two resulting regions would have yielded the same result. If, on the other hand, we had chosen $T = 8$, a single region would have resulted, as shown in Fig. 7.30(c).

	1	2	3	4	5
1	0	0	5	6	7
2	1	1	5	8	7
3	0	1	6	7	7
4	2	0	7	6	6
5	0	1	5	6	5

(a)

a	a	b	b	b
a	a	b	b	b
a	a	b	b	b
a	a	b	b	b
a	a	b	b	b

(b)

a	a	a	a	a
a	a	a	a	a
a	a	a	a	a
a	a	a	a	a
a	a	a	a	a

(c)

Figure 7.30 Example of region growing using known starting points. (a) Original image array. (b) Segmentation result using an absolute difference of less than 3 between intensity levels. (c) Result using an absolute difference less than 8.

The preceding example, although simple in nature, points out some important problems in region growing. Two immediate problems are the selection of initial seeds that properly represent regions of interest, and the selection of suitable properties for including points in the various regions during the growing process. Selecting a set of one or more starting points can often be based on the nature of the problem. For example, in military applications of infrared imaging, targets of interest are hotter (and thus appear brighter) than the background. Choosing the brightest pixels is then a natural starting point for a region-growing algorithm. When a priori information is not available one may proceed, by computing at every pixel, the same set of properties that will ultimately be used to assign pixels to regions during the growing process. If the result of this computation shows clusters of values, then the pixels whose properties place them near the centroid of these clusters can be used as seeds. For instance, in the example given above, a gray-level histogram would show that points with intensity of 1 and 7 are the most predominant.

The selection of similarity criteria is dependent not only on the problem under consideration, but also on the type of image data available. For example, the analysis of land-use satellite imagery is heavily dependent on the use of color. This problem would be significantly more difficult to handle by using monochrome images alone. Unfortunately, the availability of multispectral and other complementary image data is the exception rather than the rule in image processing. Typically, region analysis must be carried out using a set of descriptors based on intensity and spatial properties (e.g., moments, texture) of a single image source. A discussion of descriptors useful for region characterization is given in Section 8.3.

It is important to note that descriptors alone can yield misleading results if connectivity or adjacency information is not used in the region-growing process. An illustration of this is easily visualized by considering a random arrangement of pixels with only three distinct intensity values. Grouping pixels with the same intensity to form a "region" without paying attention to connectivity would yield a segmentation result that is meaningless in the context of this discussion.

Another important problem in region growing is the formulation of a stopping rule. Basically, we stop growing a region when no more pixels satisfy the criteria for inclusion in that region. We mentioned above criteria such as intensity, texture, and color, that are local in nature and do not take into account the "history" of region growth. Additional criteria that increase the power of a region-growing algorithm incorporate the concept of size, likeness between a candidate pixel and the pixels grown thus far (e.g., a comparison of the intensity of a candidate and the average intensity of the region), and the shape of a given region being grown. The use of these types of descriptors is based on the assumption that a model of expected results is at least partially available.

Example: Figure 7.31(a) is a picture of a section of a map containing a single seed point (shown as a white dot). The criteria used for region growth were (1) that the absolute difference in gray level between the seed and a candidate point

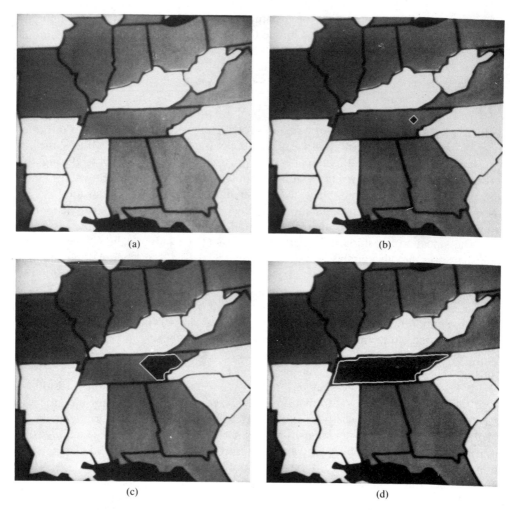

Figure 7.31   (a) Original image showing seed point. (b) Early stage of region growth. (c) Intermediate stage of growth. (d) Final region.

not exceed 10% of the difference between the minimum and maximum gray levels in the entire image (255 in this case), and (2) that any pixel added to the region be 8-connected to at least one pixel previously included in the region.

Figure 7.31(b) shows a region in the early stages of growth. The order in which pixels were considered was such that pixels with the same D_4 distance from the seed point were considered first. Increasing the value of this distance to expand growth resulted in a diamond-shaped region (see Section 2.4.3). Figure 7.31(c) shows the region in an intermediate stage of growth. Note how the diamond shape has been distorted as a result of hitting a boundary established by pixels that failed to satisfy the gray-level criterion. Finally, Fig. 7.31(d) shows the complete region grown by this technique. It is worth noting that, although other pixels in neighboring regions satisfied the gray-level criterion, growth stopped because these pixels did not satisfy the connectivity criterion due to the separation caused by the dark border around the grown region.   ☐

7.4.3 Region Splitting and Merging

The procedure discussed in the previous section grows regions starting from a given set of seed points. An alternative is initially to subdivide an image into a set of arbitrary, disjointed regions and then merge and/or split the regions in an attempt to satisfy the conditions stated in Section 7.4.1. A split and merge algorithm that iteratively works toward satisfying these constraints may be explained as follows.

Let R represent the entire image region and select a predicate P as discussed in Section 7.4.1 Assuming a square image, one approach for segmenting R is to subdivide it successively into smaller and smaller quadrant regions such that, for any region R_i, $P(R_i)$ = TRUE. That is, if $P(R)$ = FALSE, we divide the image into quadrants. If P is FALSE for any quadrant, we subdivide that quadrant into subquadrants, and so on. This particular splitting technique has a convenient representation in the form of a so-called *quadtree* (i.e., a tree in which each node has exactly four descendants). A simple illustration is shown in Fig. 7.32. Note that the root of the tree corresponds to the entire image and that each node corresponds to a subdivision. In this case, only R_4 was subdivided further.

If we used only splitting, it is likely that the final partition would contain adjacent regions with identical properties. This may be remedied by allowing merging, as well as splitting. In order to satisfy the constraints of Section 7.4.1, we merge only adjacent regions whose combined pixels satisfy the predicate P; that is, we merge two adjacent regions R_i and R_k only if $P(R_i \cup R_k)$ = TRUE.

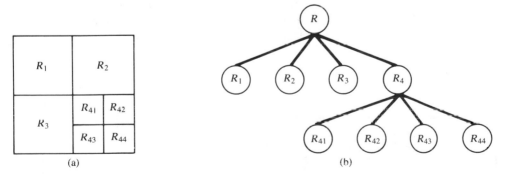

(a)   (b)

Figure 7.32 (a) Partitioned image. (b) Corresponding quadtree.

The preceding discussion may be summarized by the following procedure in which, at any step, we:

(1) Split into four disjointed quadrants any region R_i where $P(R_i) = $ FALSE.

(2) Merge any adjacent regions R_j and R_k for which $P(R_j \cup R_k) = $ TRUE.

(3) Stop when no further merging or splitting is possible.

A number of variations on this basic theme are possible (Horowitz and Pavlidis [1974]). For example, one possibility is initially to split the image into a set of square blocks. Further splitting is carried out as above, but merging is initially limited to groups of four blocks that are descendants in the quadtree representation and that satisfy the predicate P. When no further mergings of this type are possible, the procedure is terminated by one final merging of regions satisfying Step 2 above. At this point, the regions that are merged may be of different sizes. The principal advantage of this approach is that it uses the same quadtree for splitting and merging, until the final merging step.

Example: An illustration of the split-and-merge algorithm discussed above is shown in Fig. 7.33. The image under consideration consists of a single object and background. For simplicity, we assume that both the object and background have constant gray levels and that $P(R_i) = $ TRUE if all pixels in R_i have the same intensity. Then, for the entire image region R, it follows that $P(R) = $ FALSE, so the image is split as shown in Fig. 7.33(a). In the next step, only the top left region satisfies the predicate so it is not unchanged, while the other three quadrant regions are split into sub-quadrants, as shown in Fig. 7.33(b). At this point several regions can be merged, with the exception of the two subquadrants that include the lower part of the object; these do not satisfy the predicate and must be split further. The results of the split-and-merge operation are shown in Fig. 7.33(c). At this point all regions satisfy P, and merging the appropriate regions from the last split operation yields the final, segmented result shown in Fig. 7.33(d).

A more practical example is shown in Fig. 7.34. In this case $P(R_i) = $ TRUE if at least 80% of the pixels in R_i have the property $|z_j - m_i| \leq 2\sigma_i$, where z_j is the gray level of the jth pixel in R_i, m_i is the mean gray level of that region, and σ_i is the standard deviation of the gray levels in R_i. If $P(R_i) = $ TRUE under this condition,

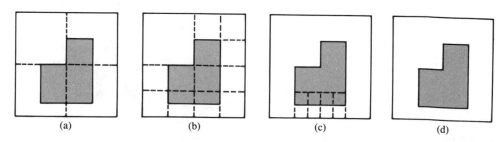

(a)	(b)	(c)	(d)

Figure 7.33   Example of split-and-merge algorithm. (From Fu, Gonzalez, and Lee [1987].)

Figure 7.34   (a) Original image. (b) Result of split-and-merge procedure. (c) Result of thresholding Fig. 7.34(b).

then the value of all the pixels in R_i were set equal to m_i. The result of applying this technique to the image in Fig. 7.34(a) is shown in Fig. 7.34(b). Note the "block" effect in some corners of the image and near the leaf due to shading. The image shown in Fig. 7.34(c) was obtained by thresholding Fig. 7.34(b) with a threshold placed midway between the two principal peaks of the histogram. The light-shade blocks (and the stem of the leaf) were eliminated by thresholding.   ⊔

7.5   THE USE OF MOTION IN SEGMENTATION

Motion is a powerful cue used by humans and other animals to extract objects of interest from a background of irrelevant detail. In imaging applications, motion arises from a relative displacement between the sensing system and the scene being viewed, such as in robotic applications, autonomous navigation, and dynamic scene analysis. In the following sections we consider the use of motion in segmentation from both a spatial and frequency-domain viewpoint.

7.5.1 Spatial Techniques

Basic approach

One of the simplest approaches for detecting changes between two image frames $f(x, y, t_i)$ and $f(x, y, t_j)$ taken at times t_i and t_j, respectively, is to compare the two images on a pixel-by-pixel basis. One procedure for doing this is to form a *difference image*.

Suppose that we have a reference image containing only stationary components. If we compare this image against a subsequent image having the same environment but including a moving object, the difference of the two images will cancel the stationary components, leaving only nonzero entries that correspond to the nonstationary image components.

A difference image between two images taken at times t_i and t_j may be defined as

$$d_{ij}(x, y) = \begin{cases} 1 & \text{if } |f(x, y, t_i) - f(x, y, t_j)| > \theta, \\ 0 & \text{otherwise}, \end{cases} \qquad (7.5\text{-}1)$$

where θ is a threshold. Note that $d_{ij}(x, y)$ has a 1 at spatial coordinates (x, y) only if the gray-level difference between the two images is appreciably different at those coordinates, as determined by the threshold θ.

In dynamic image analysis, all pixels in $d_{ij}(x, y)$ with value 1 are considered the result of object motion. This approach is applicable only if the two images are registered and the illumination is relatively constant within the bounds established by θ. In practice, 1-valued entries in $d_{ij}(x, y)$ often arise as a result of noise. Typically, these will be isolated points in the difference image and a simple approach for their removal is to form 4- or 8-connected regions of 1s in $d_{ij}(x, y)$ and then ignore any region that has less than a predetermined number of entries. This may result in ignoring small and/or slow-moving objects, but it enhances the chances that the remaining entries in the difference image are truly due to motion.

The foregoing concepts are illustrated in Fig. 7.35. Figure 7.35(a) shows a reference-image frame taken at time t_i and containing a single object of constant intensity that is moving with uniform velocity over a background surface, also of constant intensity. Figure 7.35(b) shows a current frame taken at time t_j, and Fig. 7.35(c) shows the difference image computed using Eq. (7.5-1) with a threshold larger than the constant background intensity. Note that two disjoint regions were generated by the differencing process: one region is the result of the leading edge and the other of the trailing edge of the moving object.

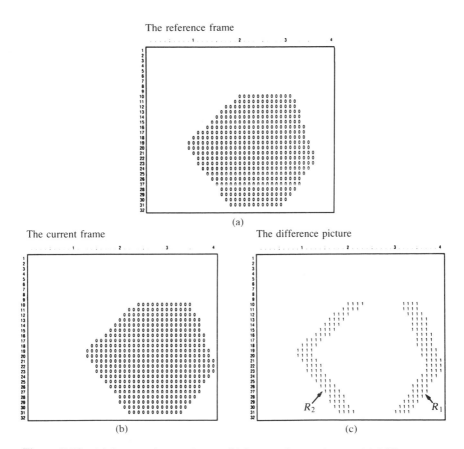

Figure 7.35 (a) Image taken at time t_i. (b) Image taken at time t_j. (c) Difference image. (From Jain [1981].)

Accumulative differences

As indicated in the previous section, a difference image will often contain isolated entries that are due to noise. Although the number of these entries can be reduced or completely eliminated by a thresholded connectivity analysis, this filtering process can also remove small or slow-moving objects. The approach discussed in this section addresses this problem by considering changes at a pixel location on several frames, thus introducing a "memory" into the process. The basic idea is to ignore changes that occur only sporadically over a frame sequence and can therefore be attributed to random noise.

Consider a sequence of image frames $f(x, y, t_1)$, $f(x, y, t_2)$, . . . , $f(x, y, t_n)$, and let $f(x, y, t_1)$ be the *reference image*. An accumulative difference image is formed by comparing this reference image with every subsequent image in the sequence. A counter for each pixel location in the accumulative image is incremented every time there is a difference at that pixel location between the reference and an image in the sequence. Thus when the kth frame is being compared with the reference, the entry in a given pixel of the accumulative image gives the number of times the gray level at that position was different from the corresponding pixel value in the reference image. Differences are established, for example, by use of Eq. (7.5-1).

The foregoing concepts are illustrated in Fig. 7.36. Parts (a) through (e) of this figure show a rectangular object (denoted by 0s) that is moving to the right with a constant velocity of 1 pixel per frame. The images shown represent instants of time corresponding to one-pixel displacements. Figure 7.36(a) is the reference-image frame, Figs. 7.36(b) through (d) are frames 2, 3, and 4 in the sequence,

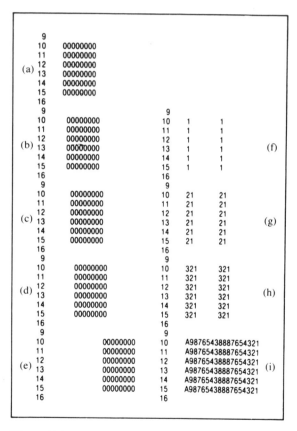

Figure 7.36 (a) Reference-image frame. (b)–(e) Frames 2, 3, 4, and 11. (f)–(i) Accumulative difference images for frames 2, 3, 4, and 11 (the numbers 9–16 on the border are line references only and are not related to this discussion). (From Jain [1981].)

and Fig. 7.36(e) is the 11th frame. Figures 7.36(f) through (i) are the corresponding accumulative images, which may be explained as follows. In Fig. 7.36(f), the left column of 1s is due to differences between the object in Fig. 7.36(a) and the background in 7.36(b). The right column of 1s is caused by differences between the background in the reference image and the leading edge of the moving object. By the time of the fourth frame (Fig. 7.36d), the first nonzero column of the accumulative difference image shows three counts, indicating three total differences between that column in the reference image and the corresponding column in the subsequent frames. Finally, Fig. 7.36(a) shows a total of 10 (represented by "A" in hexadecimal) changes at that location. The other entries in that figure are explained in a similar manner.

It is often useful to consider three types of accumulative difference images: absolute (AADI), positive (PADI) and negative (NADI). The latter two quantities are obtained by using Eq. (7.5-1) without the absolute value, and using the reference frame instead of $f(x, y, t_i)$. Assuming that the gray levels of an object are numerically greater than the background, if the difference is positive, it is compared against a positive threshold; if it is negative, the difference is compared against a negative threshold. This definition is reversed if the gray levels of the object are less than the background.

Example: Figures 7.37(a) through (c) show the AADI, PADI, and NADI for a 20×20 pixel object whose intensity is greater than the background and which is moving with constant velocity in a southeasterly direction. It is important to note that the spatial growth of the PADI stops when the object is displaced from its original position. In other words, when an object whose gray levels are greater than the background is completely displaced from its position in the reference image there will be no new entries generated in the positive accumulative difference image. Thus when its growth stops, the PADI gives the initial location of the object in the reference frame. As will be seen in the next section, this property can be used to advantage in creating a reference from a dynamic sequence of images. It is also noted in Fig. 7.37 that the AADI contains the regions of both the PADI and the NADI, and that the entries in these images give an indication of the speed and direction of the object movement. The images in Fig. 7.37 are shown in intensity-coded form in Fig. 7.38.   □

Establishing a reference image
A key to the success of the techniques discussed in the previous two sections is having a reference image against which subsequent comparisons can be made. As indicated above, the difference between two images in a dynamic imaging problem has the tendency to cancel all stationary components, leaving only image elements that correspond to noise and to the moving objects. The noise problem can be handled by the filtering approach mentioned earlier, or by forming an accumulative difference image, as discussed in the previous section.

Figure 7.37 (a) Absolute, (b) positive, and (c) negative accumulative difference images for a 20 × 20 pixel object with intensity greater than the background and moving in a southeasterly direction. (From Jain [1983].)

```
9999999999999999999
9999999999999999999
9999999999999999999
99888888888888888888811
99888888888888888888811
99888888888888888888811
998877777777777777772211
998877777777777777772211
998877777777777777772211
99887766666666666666332211
99887766666666666666332211
99887766666666666666332211
99887766555555555554332211
99887766555555555554332211
99887766555555555554332211
998877665544444444445544332211
998877665544444444445544332211
998877665544444444445544332211
99887766554433333333665544332211
99887766554433333333665544332211
  1122334455666666666665544332211
  112233445566777777776655442332211
  112233445566777777776655442332211
  1122334455666666666665544332211
  112233445566777777776655442332211
  112233445566777777776655442332211
    1122334455666666666665544332211
    112233445566777777776655442332211
    112233445566777777776655442332211
    1122334455666666666665544332211
    1122334455666666666665544332211
    1122334455666666666665544332211
      11223344555555555555544332211
      11223344555555555555544332211
      11223344555555555555544332211
        11223344444444444444444332211
        11223344444444444444444332211
        11223344444444444444444332211
          112233333333333333333332211
          112233333333333333333332211
          112233333333333333333332211
            1122222222222222222222211
            1122222222222222222222211
            1122222222222222222222211
              11111111111111111111
              11111111111111111111
              11111111111111111111
```
(a)

```
9999999999999999999
9999999999999999999
9999999999999999999
99888888888888888888
99888888888888888888
99888888888888888888
99887777777777777777
99887777777777777777
99887777777777777777
99887766666666666666
99887766666666666666
99887766666666666666
99887766555555555555
99887766555555555555
99887766555555555555
99887766554444444444
99887766554444444444
99887766554444444444
99887766554433333333
99887766554433333333
```
(b)

```
                          11
                          11
                          11
                        2211
                        2211
                        2211
                      332211
                      332211
                      332211
                    44332211
                    44332211
                    44332211
                  5544332211
                  5544332211
                  5544332211
                665544332211
                665544332211
112233445566666666666655442332211
112233445566777777776655442332211
112233445566777777776655442332211
1122334455666666666665544332211
112233445566777777776655442332211
112233445566777777776655442332211
1122334455666666666665544332211
112233445566777777776655442332211
112233445566777777776655442332211
  1122334455666666666665544332211
  1122334455666666666665544332211
  1122334455666666666665544332211
    11223344555555555555544332211
    11223344555555555555544332211
    11223344555555555555544332211
      11223344444444444444444332211
      11223344444444444444444332211
      11223344444444444444444332211
        112233333333333333333332211
        112233333333333333333332211
        112233333333333333333332211
          1122222222222222222222211
          1122222222222222222222211
          1122222222222222222222211
            11111111111111111111
            11111111111111111111
            11111111111111111111
```
(c)

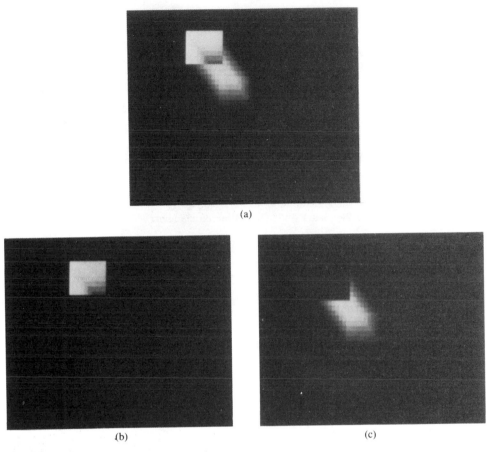

Figure 7.38   Intensity-coded accumulative difference images for Fig. 7.37. (a) AADI, (b) PADI, and (c) NADI. (From Jain [1983].)

In practice, it is not always possible to obtain a reference image with only stationary elements and it becomes necessary to build a reference from a set of images containing one or more moving objects. This is particularly true in situations describing busy scenes or in cases where frequent updating is required. One procedure for generating a reference image is as follows. Suppose that we consider the first image in a sequence to be the reference image. When a nonstationary component has moved completely out of its position in the reference frame, the corresponding background in the present frame can be duplicated in the location originally occupied by the object in the reference frame. When all moving objects have moved completely out of their original positions, a reference image containing only stationary components will have been created. Object displacement can be established by monitoring the growth of the PADI, as discussed in the previous section.

(a)   (b)

Figure 7.39   Two image frames of a traffic scene. There are two principal moving objects: a white car in the middle of the picture and a pedestrian on the lower left. (From Jain [1981].)

Example: An illustration of the approach discussed above is shown in Figs. 7.39 and 7.40. Figure 7.39 shows two image frames of a traffic intersection. The first image is considered the reference, and the second depicts the same scene some time later. The principal moving features are the automobile moving from left to right, and a pedestrian crossing the street in the bottom left of the picture. Removal of the moving automobile is shown in Fig. 7.40(a); the pedestrian is removed in Fig. 7.40(b).

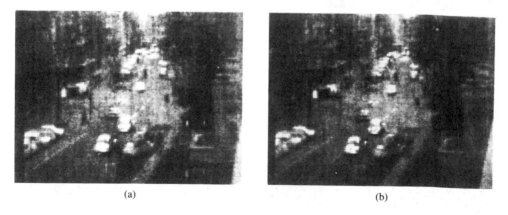

(a)   (b)

Figure 7.40   (a) Image with automobile removed and background restored. (b) Image with pedestrian removed and background restored. The latter image can be used as a reference. (From Jain [1981].)

7.5.2 Frequency-Domain Techniques

The techniques discussed in the previous section deal with image motion using spatial methods. In this section we consider the problem of determining motion estimates via a Fourier transform formulation.

Consider a sequence $f(x, y, t)$, $t = 0, 1, \ldots, T - 1$, of T digital image frames of size $M \times N$ generated by a stationary camera. We begin the development by assuming that all frames have a homogeneous background of zero intensity. The exception is a single, one-pixel object of unit intensity that is moving with constant velocity. Suppose that for frame one ($t = 0$) we project the image plane onto the x axis; that is, we sum the pixel intensities across the columns. This operation yields a one-dimensional array with M entries that are 0, except at the location where the object is projected. If we multiply the components of the array by $\exp[j2\pi k_1 x \Delta t]$, $x = 0, 1, \ldots, M - 1$, and the object is at coordinates (x', y') at that instant of time, then the result of the sum is equal to $\exp[j2\pi k_1 x' \Delta t]$. In this notation k_1 is a positive integer and Δt is the time interval between frames.

Suppose that in frame two ($t = 1$) the object has moved to coordinates ($x' + 1$, y'), that is, it has moved one pixel parallel to the x axis; then, repeating the above procedure would yield the sum $\exp[j2\pi k_1(x' + 1)\Delta t]$. If the object continues to move one pixel location per frame, then at any integer instant of time we have the result $\exp[j2\pi k_1(x' + t)\Delta t]$, which, using Euler's formula, may be expressed as

$$\exp[j2\pi k_1(x' + t)\Delta t] = \cos[2\pi k_1(x' + t)\Delta t] + j \sin[2\pi k_1(x' + t)\Delta t]$$
$$t = 0, 1, \ldots, T - 1. \tag{7.5-2}$$

In other words, the procedure outlined above yields a complex sinusoid with frequency k_1. If the object were moving v_1 pixels (in the x direction) between frames, then the sinusoid would have frequency $v_1 k_1$. Since t varies between 0 and $T - 1$ in integer increments, if we restrict k_1 to have integer values then the discrete Fourier transform of the complex sinusoid would have two peaks, one located at frequency $v_1 k_1$ and the other at $T - v_1 k_1$. This latter peak is due to symmetry foldover, as discussed in Section 3.3.3, and may be ignored. Thus a peak search in the Fourier spectrum would yield $v_1 k_1$. Division of this quantity by k_1 yields v_1, which is the velocity component in the x direction since the frame rate is assumed to be known. A similar discussion using projections onto the y axis would yield v_2, the component of velocity in the y direction.

It is of interest to note that a sequence of frames in which no motion takes place would yield identical exponential terms whose Fourier transform would consist of a single peak at a frequency of 0 (i.e., a single DC term). Therefore since the operations discussed thus far are linear, the general case involving one or more moving objects in an arbitrary static background would have a Fourier transform with a peak at DC corresponding to static image components, and peaks at locations proportional to the velocities of the objects.

The foregoing concepts may be summarized using the following relations. For a sequence of T digital images of size $M \times N$, the sum of the weighted projections onto the x axis at any integer instant of time is given by

$$g_x(t, k_1) = \sum_{x=0}^{M-1} \sum_{y=0}^{N-1} f(x, y, t)e^{j2\pi k_1 x \Delta t} \qquad t = 0, 1, \ldots, T-1 \qquad (7.5\text{-}3)$$

Similarly, the sum of the projections onto the y axis is given by

$$g_y(t, k_2) = \sum_{y=0}^{N-1} \sum_{x=0}^{M-1} f(x, y, t)e^{j2\pi k_2 y \Delta t} \qquad t = 0, 1, \ldots, T-1, \qquad (7.5\text{-}4)$$

where k_1 and k_2 are positive integers.

The one-dimensional Fourier transforms of Eqs. (7.5-3) and (7.5-4), respectively, are given by

$$G_x(u_1, k_1) = \frac{1}{T} \sum_{t=0}^{T-1} g_x(t, k_1)e^{-j2\pi u_1 t/T} \qquad u_1 = 0, 1, \ldots, T-1 \qquad (7.5\text{-}5)$$

and

$$G_y(u_2, k_2) = \frac{1}{T} \sum_{t=0}^{T-1} g_y(t, k_2)e^{-j2\pi u_2 t/T} \qquad u_2 = 0, 1, \ldots, T-1. \qquad (7.5\text{-}6)$$

In practice, computation of these transforms is carried out using a fast Fourier transform algorithm, as discussed in Section 3.4.

Based on the above discussion, the frequency–velocity relationship is given by

$$u_1 = k_1 v_1 \qquad (7.5\text{-}7)$$

and

$$u_2 = k_2 v_2. \qquad (7.5\text{-}8)$$

It is also important to note that in this formulation the unit of velocity is in pixels per total frame time. For example, $v_1 = 10$ is interpreted as a motion of 10 pixels in T frames. Assuming that frames are taken uniformly, the actual physical speed would depend on the frame rate and the distance between pixels. Thus if $v_1 = 10$, $T = 30$, the frame rate is two images per second, and the distance between pixels is 0.5 m, the actual physical speed in the x direction would be

$$v_1 = (10 \text{ pixels})(0.5 \text{ m/pixel})(2 \text{ frames/sec})/(30 \text{ frames})$$
$$= 1/3 \text{ m/sec}.$$

The sign of the x component of the velocity is obtained by computing

$$S_{1x} = \frac{d^2 \text{Re}[g_x(t, k_1)]}{dt^2} \bigg|_{t=n} \qquad (7.5\text{-}9)$$

and

$$S_{2x} = \frac{d^2\text{Im}[g_x(t, k_2)]}{dt^2} \bigg|_{t = n} \tag{7.5-10}$$

Since $g_x(t, k_1)$ is sinusoidal, it can be shown that S_{1x} and S_{2x} will have the same sign at an arbitrary point in time n if the velocity component v_1 is positive. Conversely, opposite signs in S_{1x} and S_{2x} indicate a negative component. If either S_{1x} or S_{2x} is zero, we consider the next closest point in time, $t = n \pm \Delta t$. Similar comments apply to computing the sign of v_2.

Example: The effectiveness of the approach just derived is illustrated in Figs. 7.41 through 7.44. Figure 7.41 shows one of a 32-frame sequence of LANDSAT images generated by adding white noise to a reference image. The sequence contains a superimposed target moving at 0.5 pixel per frame in the x direction and 1 pixel per frame in the y direction. The target, shown circled in Fig. 7.42, has a Gaussian intensity distribution spread over a small (9-pixel) area and is not easily discernible by eye. The results of computing Eqs. (7.5-5) and (7.5-6) with $k_1 = 6$ and $k_2 = 4$ are shown in Figs. 7.43 and 7.44, respectively. The peak at $u_1 = 3$ in Fig. 7.43 yields $v_1 = 0.5$ from Eq. (7.5-7). Similarly, the peak at $u_2 = 4$ in Fig. 7.44 yields $v_y = 1.0$ from Eq. (7.5-8). $\square$

Figure 7.41 LANDSAT frame. (From Cowart, Snyder, and Ruedger [1983].)

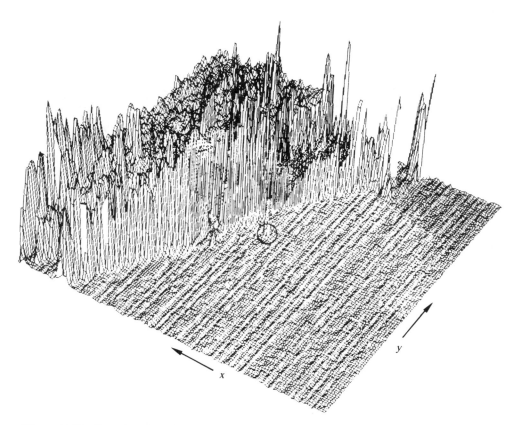

Figure 7.42   Intensity plot of Fig. 7.41 with target circled. (From Rajala, Riddle, and Snyder [1983].)

Guidelines for the selection of k_1 and k_2 can be explained with the aid of Figs. 7.43 and 7.44 in the above example. For instance, suppose that instead of using $k_2 = 4$ we had used $k_2 = 15$. In this case the peaks in Fig. 7.44 would now be at $u_2 = 15$ and 17 since $v_2 = 1.0$. This would be a seriously aliased result which, as discussed in Section 3.3.9, is caused by undersampling (too few frames in the present discussion since the range of u is determined by T). Keeping in mind that $u = kv$, one possibility is to select k as the integer closest to $k = u_{max}/v_{max}$, where u_{max} is the aliasing frequency limitation established by T, and v_{max} is the maximum expected object velocity.

7.6   CONCLUDING REMARKS

Image segmentation is an essential preliminary step in most automatic pictorial pattern-recognition and scene-analysis problems. As indicated by the range of examples presented in the previous sections, the choice of one segmentation technique

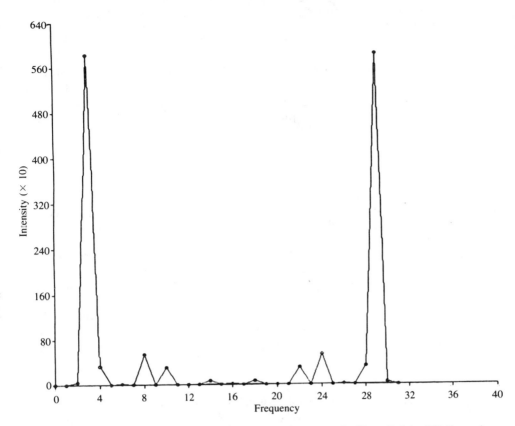

Figure 7.43 Spectrum of Eq. (7.5-5) showing a peak at $u_1 = 3$. (From Rajala, Riddle, and Snyder [1983].)

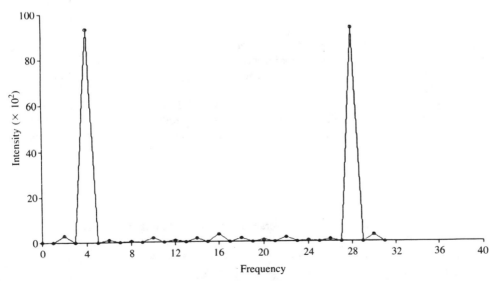

Figure 7.44 Spectrum of Eq. (7.5-6) showing a peak at $u_2 = 4$. (From Rajala, Riddle, and Snyder [1983].)

over another is dictated mostly by the peculiar characteristics of the problem being considered. The methods discussed in this chapter, although far from exhaustive, are representative of techniques commonly used in practice. The references cited below can be used as the basis for further study of this topic.

REFERENCES

Work dealing with the use of masks to detect gray-level discontinuities has received considerable attention in the literature. Mask structures that complement the ones discussed in Section 7.1 may be found in the papers by Roberts [1965], Prewitt [1970], Kirsch [1971], and Robinson [1976]. A review article by Fram and Deutsch [1975] contains several masks and an evaluation of their performance. The vector formulation used for simultaneous detection of discontinuities is based on a paper by Frei and Chen [1977]. Additional general reading on the fundamentals of mask detection and their use in image processing can be found in the books by Marr [1982], Rosenfeld and Kak [1982] and Fu, Gonzalez, and Lee [1987]. The latter two books also provide additional details on the material in Sections 7.2.1 and 7.2.2. The material in Section 7.2.3 is based on two papers by Martelli [1972, 1976]. Another interesting approach based on a minimum-cost search is given by Ramer [1975]. Additional reading on graph-searching techniques may be found in Nilsson [1971, 1980]. Edge following can also be approached from the viewpoint of dynamic programming. For further details on this topic see Ballard and Brown [1982].

Thresholding is one of the earliest techniques developed for segmenting digital images. Some typical early references on this topic are the papers by Doyle [1962], Narasimhan and Fornago [1963], and Rosenfeld et al. [1965]. The optimal thresholding technique developed in Section 7.3.4 is due to Chow and Kaneko [1972]. The method presented in Section 7.3.5 is based on a paper by White and Rohrer [1983]. A survey paper by Weska [1978] is also of interest.

Early references on region-oriented segmentation are Muerle and Allen [1968] and Brice and Fennema [1970]. The review papers by Zucker [1976] and Fu and Mui [1981] establish some unifying concepts and discuss the merits of various segmentation techniques. The concept of a quadtree discussed in Section 7.4.3 was introduced by Klinger [1972, 1976], who called this approach *regular decomposition*. More-recent developments in this area are exemplified by the discussions in Ballard and Brown [1982], and by results such as those presented by Grosky and Jain [1983] and Mark and Abel [1985].

The material in Section 7.5.1 is based on two papers by Jain [1981, 1983]. The discussion in Section 7.5.2 is based on a technique developed by Rajala, Riddle, and Snyder [1983]. Other references of interest in dynamic image analysis are Aggarwal and Badler [1980], Thompson and Barnard [1981], Webb and Aggarwal [1981], Yachida [1983], and Adiv [1985].

PROBLEMS

7.1 A binary image is known to contain straight lines oriented horizontally, vertically, at 45° and at −45°. Give a set of 3 × 3 masks that can be used to detect one-pixel-long breaks in these lines. Assume that the gray level of the lines is 1, and that the gray level of the background is 0.

7.2 The results obtained by a single pass through an image of some two-dimensional masks can also be achieved by two passes using one-dimensional masks. For example, the result of using a 3 × 3 smoothing mask with coefficients 1/9 can also be obtained by first passing through an image the mask [1 1 1]. The result of this pass is then followed by a pass of the mask $\begin{bmatrix} 1 \\ 1 \\ 1 \end{bmatrix}$. The final result is then scaled by 1/9. Show that the Sobel masks (Fig. 7.5) can be implemented by one pass of a *differencing* mask of the form [−1 0 1] (or its vertical counterpart) followed by a *smoothing* mask of the form [1 2 1] (or its vertical counterpart).

7.3 Specify the direction of the line(s) that causes the strongest response in each of the line masks shown in Fig. 7.10. Assume that all lines are one pixel thick.

7.4 Show that the digital Laplacian given in Eq. (7.1 18) is proportional (by the factor −1/4) to subtracting from $f(x, y)$ an average of the 4-neighbors of (x, y). (The process of subtracting a blurred version of $f(x, y)$ from itself is called *unsharp masking*.)

7.5 Propose a technique for detecting gaps of length ranging between 1 and L pixels in line segments of a gradient image. Assume that the background is constant, that all lines have been coded with the same intensity level, and that the lines are one pixel thick. Base your technique on 8-neighbor connectivity analysis (Section 2.4), rather than attempting to construct masks for detecting the gaps.

7.6 a) Superimpose on Fig. 7.15 all the possible edges given by the graph in Fig. 7.16.
 b) Compute the cost of the minimum-cost path.

7.7 Find the edge corresponding to the minimum-cost path in the subimage shown below, where the numbers in parentheses indicate intensity. Assume that the edge starts on the first column and ends in the last column.

	0	1	2
0	.	.	.
	(2)	(1)	(0)
1	.	.	.
	(1)	(1)	(7)
2	.	.	.
	(6)	(8)	(2)

7.8 Suppose that an image is composed of small, nonoverlapping blobs of mean gray level $m_1 = 150$ and variance $\sigma_1^2 = 400$ scattered on a background of mean $m_2 = 25$ and variance $\sigma_2^2 = 625$. It is known that all the blobs occupy approximately 20% of the image area. Propose a technique, based on thresholding, for segmenting the blobs out of the image.

7.9 Suppose that an image has the following intensity distributions, where $p_1(z)$ corresponds to the intensity of objects and $p_2(z)$ corresponds to the intensity of the background. Assuming that $P_1 = P_2$, find the optimal threshold between object and background pixels.

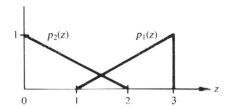

7.10 Start with Eq. (7.3-12) and derive Eqs. (7.3-13) and (7.3-14).

7.11 Derive Eq. (7.3-15) starting from Eqs. (7.3-13) and (7.3-14).

7.12 Consider the image in Problem 7.8 and propose a segmentation scheme based on region growing.

7.13 Segment the image shown below using the split-and-merge procedure discussed in Section 7.4.3. Let $P(R_i)$ = TRUE if all pixels in R_i have the same intensity. Show the quadtree corresponding to your segmentation.

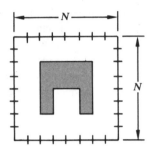

7.14 It is desired to determine the speed of a bullet in flight by high-speed imaging techniques. The method of choice involves the use of a flash that exposes the imaging surface of a TV camera for T sec. The bullet is 2.5 cm long, 1 cm wide, and it is known that its range of speed is 750 ± 250 m/sec. The camera optics are such that they produce an image in which the bullet occupies 10% of the horizontal resolution of a 256 × 256 digital image.

a) Determine the minimum value of T that will guarantee that the blur due to motion does not exceed 1 pixel.

b) Determine the minimum number of frames per second that would have to be taken in order to guarantee that at least two complete images of the bullet are obtained during its path through the field of view of the camera.

c) Propose a segmentation procedure for automatically extracting the bullet from a sequence of frames.

d) Propose a method for automatically determining the speed of the bullet.

CHAPTER 8

REPRESENTATION AND DESCRIPTION

Well, but reflect; have we not several times
acknowledged that names rightly given are the
likenesses and images of the things which they
name?

Socrates

After an image has been segmented into regions by methods such as those discussed in Chapter 7, it is usually of interest to represent and describe the resulting aggregate of segmented pixels in a form suitable for further computer processing. Basically, we have two choices for representing a region: (1) we can represent the region based on its external characteristics (i.e., its boundary), or (2) we may choose to represent it in terms of its internal characteristics (i.e., the pixels comprising the region). Choosing a representation scheme, however, is only part of the task of making the data useful to a computer. The next task is to *describe* the region based on the chosen representation. For example, we may elect to represent a region by its boundary, and to describe the boundary by features such as its length, the orientation of the straight line joining the extreme points, and the number of concavities in the boundary.

Generally, an external representation is chosen when the primary focus is on shape characteristics (also called morphological features), while an internal representation is selected when one is interested in reflectivity properties, such as color and texture. In either case, it is important that the features selected as descriptors be as insensitive as possible to such variations as changes in size, translation, and rotation. For the most part, the descriptors discussed in this chapter satisfy one or more of these properties.

8.1 REPRESENTATION SCHEMES

The segmentation techniques discussed in Chapter 7 yield "raw" data in the form of pixels along a boundary, or pixels contained in a region. Although these data are sometimes used directly to obtain descriptors (e.g., in determining the texture of a region), it is a standard practice to use schemes that compact the data into representations that are considerably more useful in the computation of descriptors. A number of representation approaches are discussed in this section.

8.1.1 Chain Codes

Chain codes are used to represent a boundary by a connected sequence of straight line segments of specified length and direction. Typically, this representation is based on the 4- or 8-connectivity of the segments, where the direction of each segment is coded using a numbering scheme such as the one shown in Fig. 8.1.

Since digital images are usually acquired and processed in a grid format with equal spacing in the x and y directions, one could generate a chain code by following a boundary in, say, a clockwise direction and assigning a direction to the segments connecting every pair of pixels. This is generally unacceptable for two principal reasons: first, the resulting chain of codes will usually be quite long and second, any small disturbances along the boundary due to noise or imperfect segmentation will cause changes in the code that may not necessarily be related to the shape of the boundary.

An approach frequently used to circumvent the problems just discussed is to "resample" the boundary by selecting a larger grid spacing, as illustrated in Fig. 8.2(a). Then, as the boundary is traversed, we assign a boundary point to each node of the large grid, depending on the proximity of the original boundary to that node, as shown in Fig. 8.2(b). The resampled boundary obtained in this way can then be represented by a 4- or 8-code, as shown in Figs. 8.2(c) and (d), respectively,

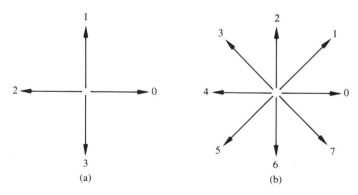

(a)   (b)

Figure 8.1   Directions for (a) 4-directional chain code, and (b) 8-directional chain code.

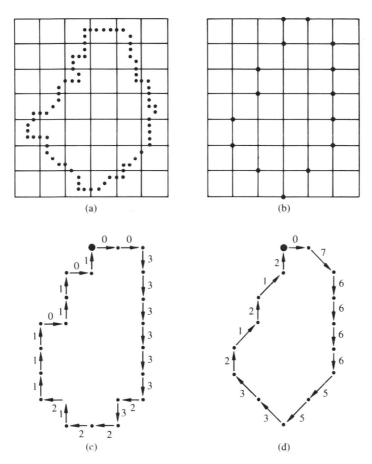

Figure 8.2 (a) Digital boundary with resampling grid superimposed. (b) Result of resampling. (c) 4-directional chain code. (d) 8-directional chain code.

where the starting point is at the dot and the boundary in Fig. 8.2(c) was obtained by following the shortest allowable external 4-path in the grid of Fig. 8.2(b). The boundary representation in Fig. 8.2(c) is the chain code 0033 . . . 01, and in Fig. 8.2(d) it is the code 076 . . . 12. As might be expected, the accuracy of the resulting code representation depends on the spacing of the sampling grid.

It is important to note that the chain code of a given boundary depends on the starting point. It is possible, however, to normalize the code by a straightforward procedure: Given a chain code generated by starting in an arbitrary position, we treat it as a circular sequence of direction numbers and redefine the starting point so that the resulting sequence of numbers forms an integer of minimum magnitude. We can also normalize for rotation by using the first difference of the chain code, instead of the code itself. The difference is computed simply by counting (in a counterclockwise manner) the number of directions that separate two adjacent elements of the code. For instance, the first difference of the 4-direction chain code 10103322 is 3133030. If we treat the code as a circular sequence, then the first element of the difference is computed using the transition between the last and first components of the chain. In this example the result is 33133030. Size normalization can be achieved by altering the size of the resampling grid.

The preceding normalizations are exact only if the boundaries themselves are invariant to rotation and scale change. In practice, this is seldom the case. For instance, the same object digitized in two different orientations will in general have different boundary shapes, with the degree of dissimilarity being proportional to image resolution. This effect can be reduced by selecting chain elements that are large in proportion to the distance between pixels in the digitized image or by orienting the resampling grid along the principal axes of the object to be coded, as discussed in Section 8.2.2.

8.1.2   Polygonal Approximations

A digital boundary can be approximated with arbitrary accuracy by a polygon. For a closed curve, the approximation is exact when the number of segments in the polygon is equal to the number of points in the boundary so that each pair of adjacent points defines a segment in the polygon. In practice, the goal of a polygonal approximation is to capture the "essence" of the boundary shape with the fewest possible polygonal segments. Although this problem is in general not trivial and can very quickly turn into a time-consuming iterative search, there are a number of polygonal-approximation techniques whose modest complexity and processing requirements make them well-suited for image-processing applications. Several of these techniques are presented in this section.

We begin the discussion with a method proposed by Sklansky, Chazin, and Hansen [1972] for finding minimum-perimeter polygons. The procedure is best explained by means of an example. Suppose that we enclose a given boundary by a set of concatenated cells, as shown in Fig. 8.3(a). We can visualize this enclosure as consisting of two walls corresponding to the outside and inside boundaries of the strip of cells, and we can think of the object boundary as a rubber band contained within the walls. If we now allow the rubber band to shrink, it will take the shape shown in Fig. 8.3(b), thus producing a polygon of minimum perimeter that fits in the geometry established by the cell strip. If the cells are chosen so that each cell encompasses only one point on the boundary, then the error in each cell between the original boundary and the rubber-band approximation would be at most $\sqrt{2}d$, where d is the distance between pixels. This error can be reduced by half by forcing each cell to be centered on its corresponding pixel.

Merging techniques based on error or other criteria have been applied to the problem of polygonal approximation. One approach is to merge points along a boundary until the least-square-error line fit of the points merged thus far exceeds

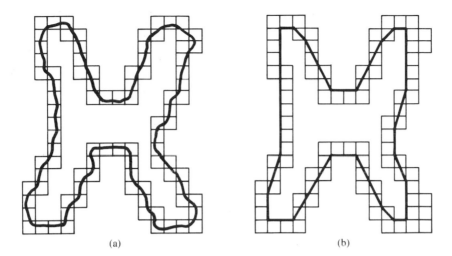

Figure 8.3   (a) Object boundary enclosed by cells. (b) Minimum-perimeter polygon.

a preset threshold. When this occurs, the parameters of the line are stored, the error is set to 0, and the procedure is repeated, merging new points along the boundary until the error again exceeds the threshold. At the end of the procedure the intersections of adjacent line segments form the vertices of the polygon. One of the principal difficulties with this method is that vertices generally do not correspond to inflections (such as corners) in the boundary because a new line is not started until the error threshold is exceeded. If, for instance, a long straight line were being tracked and it turned a corner, a number (depending on the threshold) of points past the corner would be absorbed before the threshold was exceeded. It is possible, however, to use splitting along with merging to alleviate this difficulty, as mentioned at the end of this section.

One approach to boundary segment *splitting* is to successively subdivide a segment into two parts until a given criterion is satisfied. For instance, we might require that the maximum perpendicular distance from a boundary segment to the line joining its two end points not exceed a preset threshold. If it does, the furthest point becomes a vertex, thus subdividing the initial segment into two subsegments. This approach has the advantage that it "seeks" prominent inflection points. For a closed boundary, the best starting points are usually the two furthest points in the boundary. As an example, Fig. 8.4(a) shows an object boundary, and Fig. 8.4(b) shows a subdivision of this boundary (solid line) about its furthest points. The point marked c has the largest perpendicular distance from the top segment to line ab. Similarly, point d has the largest distance in the bottom segment. Figure 8.4(c) shows the result of using the splitting procedure with a threshold equal to 0.25 times the length of line ab. Since no point in the new boundary segments has a perpendicular distance (to

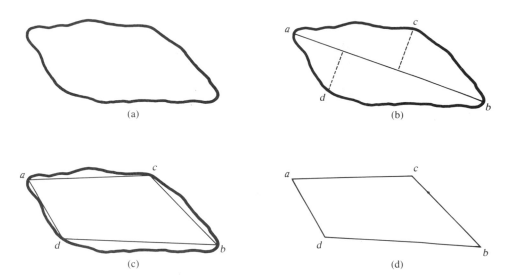

Figure 8.4   (a) Original boundary. (b) Boundary divided into segments based on distance computations. (c) Joining of vertices. (d) Resulting polygon.

its corresponding straight line segment) that exceeds this threshold, the procedure terminates with the polygon shown in Fig. 8.4(d).

Before leaving this section, we point out that a considerable amount of work has been done in the development of techniques that combine merging and splitting. A comprehensive discussion of these methods is given by Pavlidis [1977].

8.1.3   Signatures

A signature is a one-dimensional functional representation of a boundary. There are a number of ways to generate signatures. One of the simplest is to plot the distance from the centroid to the boundary as a function of angle, as illustrated in Fig. 8.5. Regardless of how a signature is generated, however, the basic idea is to reduce the boundary representation to a one-dimensional function, which presumably is easier to describe than the original two-dimensional boundary.

Signatures generated by the approach just described are obviously dependent on size and starting point. Size normalization can be achieved simply by normalizing the $r(\theta)$ curve to, say, unit maximum value. The starting-point problem can be solved by first obtaining the chain code of the boundary and then using the approach discussed in Section 8.1.1.

Distance versus angle is, of course, not the only way to generate a signature. We could, for example, traverse the boundary and plot the angle between a line tangent to the boundary and a reference line as a function of position along the boundary (Ambler *et al.* [1975]). The resulting signature, although quite different from the $r(\theta)$ curve, would carry information about basic shape characteristics. For

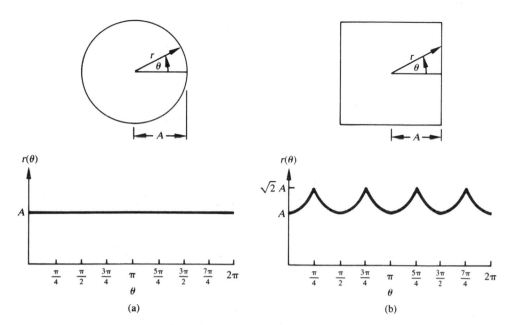

Figure 8.5   Two simple boundary shapes and their corresponding distance-versus-angle signatures. In (a) $r(\theta)$ is constant, while in (b) $r(\theta) = A \sec \theta$. (From Fu, Gonzalez, and Lee [1987].)

instance, horizontal segments in the curve would correspond to straight lines along the boundary since the tangent angle would be constant there. A variation of this approach is to use the so-called *slope density function* as a signature (Nahin [1974]). This function is simply a histogram of tangent-angle values. Since a histogram is a measure of concentration of values, the slope density function would respond strongly to sections of the boundary with constant tangent angles (straight or nearly straight segments) and have deep valleys in sections producing rapidly varying angles (corners or other sharp inflections).

8.1.4   Boundary Segments

It is often useful to decompose a boundary into segments in order to reduce its complexity and thus simplify the description process. This approach is particularly attractive when the boundary contains one or more significant concavities that carry shape information. This allows the use of the convex hull of the region enclosed by the boundary as a tool for a robust decomposition of the boundary.

The *convex hull H* of an arbitrary set S is the smallest convex set containing S. The set difference $H - S$ is called the *convex deficiency D* of the set S. In order to see how these concepts might be used to partition a boundary into meaningful segments, consider Fig. 8.6(a), which shows an object (set S) and its convex deficiency (shaded regions). The region boundary can be partitioned by following the contour

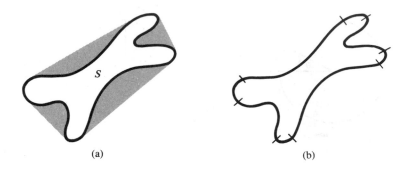

Figure 8.6   (a) A region (S) and its convex deficiency (shaded). (b) Partitioned boundary.

of S and marking the points at which a transition is made into or out of a component of the convex deficiency. The result in this case is shown in Fig. 8.6(b). Note that in principle this scheme is independent of region size and orientation.

In practice, digital boundaries tend to be irregular as a result of digitization, noise, and variations in segmentation. These effects usually result in a convex deficiency that has small, meaningless components scattered randomly throughout the boundary. Rather than attempt to sort out these irregularities by post-processing, it is common practice to smooth a boundary prior to partitioning. There are a number of ways to do this. One approach is to traverse the boundary and replace the coordinates of each pixel by the average coordinates of m of its neighbors along the boundary. This works for small irregularities, but it is time consuming and difficult to control in the sense that large values of m can result in excessive smoothing, while small values of m might not be sufficient in some segments of the boundary. A more-rugged technique is to use a polygonal approximation, as discussed in Section 8.1.2, prior to finding the convex deficiency of a given region. Regardless of the method used for smoothing, most digital boundaries of interest are simple polygons (i.e., polygons without self intersection). An algorithm for finding the convex hull of such polygons is given by Graham and Yao [1983].

Before leaving this section, we point out that the concepts of a convex hull and its deficiency are equally useful for describing an entire region, as well as just its boundary. For example, one might describe a region based on its area and the area of its convex deficiency, the number of components in the convex deficiency, the relative location of these components, and so on.

8.1.5   The Skeleton of a Region

An important approach for representing the structural shape of a plane region is to reduce it to a graph. This is often accomplished by obtaining the *skeleton* of the region via a thinning (also called *skeletonizing*) algorithm. Thinning procedures

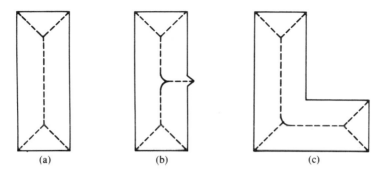

Figure 8.7 Medial axes of three simple regions.

play a central role in a broad range of problems in image processing, ranging from automated inspection of printed circuit boards to counting of asbestos fibers in air filters.

The skeleton of a region may be defined via the medial axis transformation (MAT) proposed by Blum [1967]. The MAT of a region R with border B is as follows. For each point p in R, we find its closest neighbor in B. If p has more than one such neighbor, then it is said to belong to the *medial axis* (skeleton) of R. It is important to note that the concept of "closest" depends on the definition of a distance (see Section 2.4.3) and therefore the results of a MAT operation will be influenced by the choice of a given distance measure. Some examples using the Euclidean distance are shown in Fig. 8.7.

Although the MAT of a region yields an intuitively pleasing skeleton, a direct implementation of the above definition is typically prohibitive from a computational viewpoint because it potentially involves calculating the distance from every interior point to every point on the boundary of a region. A number of algorithms have been proposed for improving computational efficiency while at the same time attempting to produce a medial axis representation of a given region. Typically, these are thinning algorithms that iteratively delete edge points of a region subject to the constraints that the deletion of these points (1) does not remove end points, (2) does not break connectedness, and (3) does not cause excessive erosion of the region. Although some attempts have been made to use skeletons in gray-scale images (Dyer and Rosenfeld [1979], Salari and Siy [1984]) this type of representation is usually associated with binary data.

In this section we present an algorithm developed by Zhang and Suen [1984] for thinning binary regions. In the following discussion it is assumed that region points have value 1 and background points have value 0. The method consists of successive passes of two basic steps applied to the contour points of the given region, where a *contour point* is any pixel with value 1 and having at least one 8-neighbor valued 0. With reference to the 8-neighborhood definition shown in Fig.

8.8, the first step flags a contour point p for deletion if the following conditions are satisfied:

(a) $2 \leqslant N(p_1) \leqslant 6$,

(b) $S(p_1) = 1$,

(c) $p_2 \cdot p_4 \cdot p_6 = 0$,

(d) $p_4 \cdot p_6 \cdot p_8 = 0$,

$$(8.1\text{-}1)$$

where $N(p_1)$ is the number of nonzero neighbors of p_1; that is,

$$N(p_1) = p_2 + p_3 + \cdots + p_8 + p_9 \tag{8.1-2}$$

and $S(p_1)$ is the number of 0-1 transitions in the ordered sequence of $p_2, p_3, \ldots,$ p_8, p_9. For example, $N(p_1) = 4$ and $S(p_1) = 3$ in Fig. 8.9.

In the second step, conditions (a) and (b) remain the same, but conditions (c) and (d) are changed to

(c′) $p_2 \cdot p_4 \cdot p_8 = 0$,

(d′) $p_2 \cdot p_6 \cdot p_8 = 0$.

$$(8.1\text{-}3)$$

Step 1 is applied to every border pixel in the binary region under consideration. If one or more of the conditions (a) through (d) are violated, the value of the point in question is not changed. If all conditions are satisfied the point is flagged for deletion. It is important to note, however, that the point is not deleted until all border points have been processed. This prevents changing the structure of the data during execution of the algorithm. After Step 1 has been applied to all border points, those that were flagged are deleted (i.e., changed to 0). Then, Step 2 is applied to the resulting data in exactly the same manner as Step 1.

Based on the foregoing comments, note that one iteration of the thinning algorithm consists of (1) applying Step 1 to flag border points for deletion; (2) deleting the flagged points; (3) applying Step 2 to flag the remaining border points for deletion; and (4) deleting the flagged points. This basic procedure is applied iteratively until no further points are deleted, at which time the algorithm terminates, yielding the skeleton of the region.

Condition (a) is violated when contour point p_1 has only one or seven 8-neighbors valued 1. Having only one such neighbor implies that p_1 is the end point of a skeleton stroke and obviously should not be deleted. If p_1 had seven such neighbors and it was deleted, this would cause erosion into the region. Condition (b) is violated

p_9	p_2	p_3
p_8	p_1	p_4
p_7	p_6	p_5

Figure 8.8 Neighborhood arrangement used by the thinning algorithm.

0	0	1
1	p_1	0
1	0	1

Figure 8.9 Illustration of conditions (a) and (b) in Eq. (8.1-1). In this case $N(p_1) = 4$ and $S(p_1) = 3$.

when it is applied to points on a stroke one pixel thick. Thus this condition prevents disconnection of segments of a skeleton during the thinning operation. Conditions (c) and (d) are satisfied simultaneously by the following minimum set of values: $p_4 = 0$, or p_6, or ($p_2 = 0$ and $p_8 = 0$). Thus with reference to the neighborhood arrangement in Fig. 8.8, a point that satisfies these conditions, as well as conditions (a) and (b), is an east or south boundary point, or a northwest corner point in the boundary. In either case, p_1 is not part of the skeleton and should be removed. Similarly, conditions (c′) and (d′) are satisfied simultaneously by the following minimum set of values: $p_2 = 0$, or $p_8 = 0$, or ($p_4 = 0$ and $p_6 = 0$). These correspond to north or west boundary points, or a southeast corner point. Note that northeast corner points have $p_2 = 0$ and $p_4 = 0$ and thus satisfy conditions (c) and (d), as well as (c′) and (d′). This is also true for southwest corner points, which have $p_6 = 0$ and $p_8 = 0$.

Example: Figure 8.10(a) shows the result of applying Step 1 of the thinning algorithm to the boundary of a simple region. The dots indicate the points flagged and subsequently removed at the end of Step 1. Figure 8.10(b) shows the results obtained with Step 2, and Fig. 8.10(c) is the skeleton obtained after several iterations through

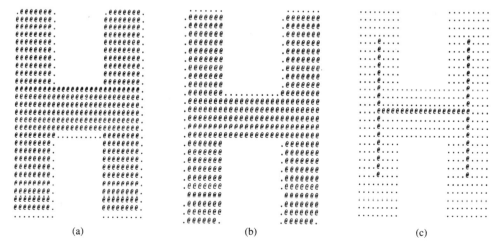

(a) (b) (c)

Figure 8.10 (a) Result of Step 1 of the thinning algorithm during the first iteration through a region. (b) Result of Step 2. (c) Final result. (From Zhang and Suen [1984].)

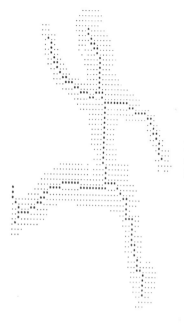

Figure 8.11   Another example of thinning. (From Zhang and Suen [1984].)

these two steps. The skeleton of a region with less-regular properties is shown in Fig. 8.11.   □

8.2   BOUNDARY DESCRIPTORS

8.2.1   Some Simple Descriptors

The *length* of a contour is one of its simplest descriptors. A rough approximation of the length may be obtained simply by counting the number of pixels along the contour. For a chain-coded curve with unit spacing in both directions, the length is given exactly by the number of vertical and horizontal components plus $\sqrt{2}$ times the number of diagonal components.

The *diameter* of a boundary B is defined as

$$\text{Diam } (B) = \max_{i,j} [D(p_i, p_j)], \qquad (8.2\text{-}1)$$

where D is a distance measure (see Section 2.4.3) and p_i and p_j are points on the boundary. The value of the diameter and the orientation of a line connecting the two extreme points that comprise the diameter (this line is called the *major axis* of the boundary) are useful descriptors of a boundary. Algorithms for computing the diameter may be found in Shamos [1978], in Fischler [1980], and in Toussaint [1982].

Curvature is defined as the rate of change of slope. In general, it is difficult to obtain reliable measures of curvature at a point in a digital boundary because these boundaries tend to be locally "ragged." However, it is sometimes useful to use the difference between the slopes of adjacent boundary segments (which have been represented as straight lines) as a descriptor of curvature at the point of intersection of the segments. For example, the vertices of boundaries such as those shown in Figs. 8.3(b) and 8.4(d) lend themselves well to curvature descriptions. As the boundary is traversed in the clockwise direction, we say that a vertex point p is part of a *convex* segment if the change in slope at p is nonnegative; otherwise, we say that p belongs to a segment that is *concave*. One can further refine the description of curvature at a point by using ranges in the change of slope. For instance, we could say that p is part of a nearly straight segment if the change is less than $10°$ or that p is a *corner* point if the change exceeds $90°$. Note, however, that these descriptors must be used with care because their interpretation is strongly dependent on the length of the individual segments relative to the overall length of the boundary.

8.2.2 Shape Numbers

With reference to Section 8.1.1, a chain-coded boundary has several first differences, depending on the starting point. The *shape number* of such a boundary, based on the 4-directional code of Fig. 8.1(a), is defined as the first difference of smallest magnitude. The *order* n of a shape number is defined as the number of digits in its representation. It is noted that n is even for a closed boundary, and that its value limits the number of possible different shapes. Figure 8.12 shows all the shapes of order 4, 6, and 8, along with their chain-code representations, first differences, and corresponding shape numbers. Note that the first differences were computed by treating the chain codes as a circular sequence in the manner discussed in Section 8.1.1.

Although, as indicated at the end of Section 8.1.1, the first difference of a chain code is independent of rotation, in general the coded boundary will depend on the orientation of the grid. One way to normalize the grid orientation follows.

As indicated in the previous section, the *major axis* of a boundary is the straight line segment joining the two points furthest away from each other. The *minor axis* is perpendicular to the major axis and of such length that a box could be formed that just encloses the boundary. The ratio of the major to the minor axis is called the *eccentricity* of the boundary, and the rectangle just described is called the *basic rectangle*. In most cases a unique shape number will be obtained by aligning the chain-code grid with the sides of the basic rectangle. Freeman and Shapira [1975] give a procedure for finding the basic rectangle directly from a closed, chain-coded curve.

In practice, given a desired shape order, we find the rectangle of order n whose eccentricity best approximates that of the basic rectangle, and use this new rectangle to establish the grid size. For example, if $n = 12$, all the rectangles of order 12 (i.e., those whose perimeter length is 12) are 2×4, 3×3, and 1×5. If the eccentricity of the 2×4 rectangle best matches the eccentricity of the basic rectangle for a given boundary, we establish a 2×4 grid centered on the basic rectangle

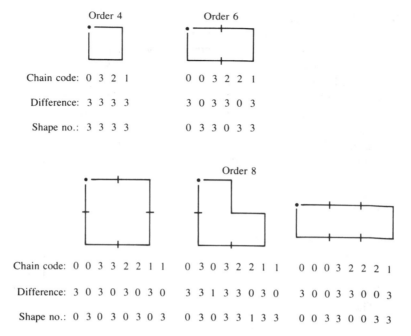

Figure 8.12 All shapes of order 4, 6, and 8. The directions are from Fig. 8.1(a), and the dot indicates the starting point.

and use the procedure outlined in Section 8.1.1 to obtain the chain code. The shape number follows from the first difference of this code, as indicated above. Although the order of the resulting shape number will usually be equal to n because of the way the grid spacing was selected, boundaries with depressions comparable to this spacing will sometimes yield shape numbers of order greater than n. In this case, we specify a rectangle of order lower than n and repeat the procedure until the resulting shape number is of order n.

Example: Suppose that we specify $n = 18$ for the boundary shown in Fig. 8.13(a). In order to obtain a shape number of this order we follow the steps discussed above. First we find the basic rectangle, as shown in Fig. 8.13(b). The closest rectangle of order 18 is a 3×6 rectangle, so we subdivide the basic rectangle as shown in Fig. 8.13(c), where it is noted that the chain-code directions are aligned with the resulting grid. Finally, we obtain the chain code and use its first difference to compute the shape number, as shown in Fig. 8.13(d). ☐

8.2.3 Fourier Descriptors

In this section we show that the discrete Fourier transform (DFT) can be used as the basis for describing the shape of a boundary on a quantitative basis. Suppose that M points on the boundary of a region are available. We may view the region

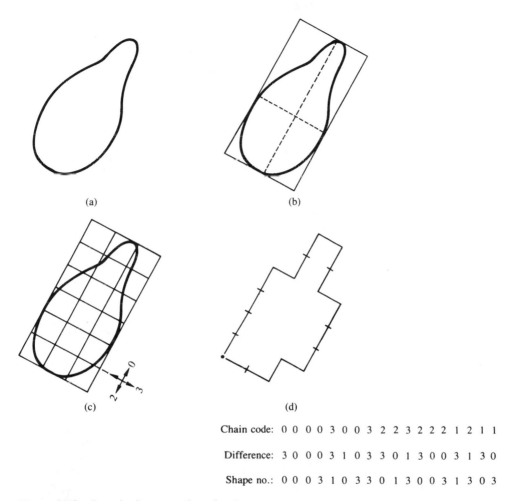

Chain code: 0 0 0 0 3 0 0 3 2 2 3 2 2 2 1 2 1 1

Difference: 3 0 0 0 3 1 0 3 3 0 1 3 0 0 3 1 3 0

Shape no.: 0 0 0 3 1 0 3 3 0 1 3 0 0 3 1 3 0 3

Figure 8.13 Steps in the generation of a shape number.

as being in the complex plane, with the ordinate being the imaginary axis and the abscissa being the real axis, as shown in Fig. 8.14. The x–y coordinates of each point in the contour to be analyzed become complex numbers $x + jy$. Starting at an arbitrary point on the contour, and tracing once around it, yields a sequence of complex numbers. The DFT of this sequence will be referred to in the following discussion as the Fourier Descriptor (FD) of the contour.

Since the DFT is a reversible linear transformation, there is no information gained or lost by this process. However, certain simple manipulations of this frequency-domain representation of shape can eliminate dependency on position, size, and orientation. Given an arbitrary FD, several successive steps can normalize it

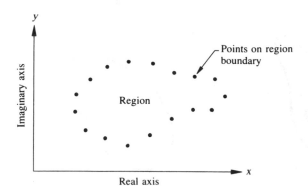

Figure 8.14   Representation of a region boundary in the complex plane.

so that it can be matched to a test set of FDs regardless of its original size, position, and orientation.

Normalization

The frequency-domain operations that affect the size, orientation, and starting point of the contour follow directly from properties of the DFT (see Section 3.3). To change the size of the contour, the components of the FD are simply multiplied by a constant. Due to linearity, the inverse transform will have its coordinates multiplied by the same constant.

To rotate the contour in the spatial domain simply requires multiplying each coordinate by $\exp(j\theta)$, where θ is the angle of rotation. Again, by linearity, the constant $\exp(j\theta)$ has the same effect when the frequency-domain coefficients are multiplied by it.

To see how the contour starting point can be moved in the frequency domain, recall the periodicity property of the DFT. The finite sequence of numbers in the spatial domain actually represents one cycle of a periodic function. The DFT coefficients are actually coefficients of the Fourier series representation of this periodic function. Remembering these facts, it is easy to see that shifting the starting point of the contour in the spatial domain corresponds to multiplying the kth frequency coefficient in the frequency domain by $\exp(jkT)$, where T is the fraction of a period through which the starting point is shifted. (As T goes from 0 to 2π, the starting point traverses the whole contour once.)

Given the FD of an arbitrary contour, the normalization procedure requires performing the normalization operations such that the contour has a standard size, orientation, and starting point. A standard size is easily defined by requiring the Fourier component $F(1)$ to have unity magnitude. If the contour is a simple closed figure, and it is traced in the counterclockwise direction, this coefficient will be the largest.

The orientation and starting-point operations affect only the phases of the FD coefficients. Since there are two allowable operations, the definition of standard position and orientation must involve the phases of at least two coefficients. Let us denote the FD array of length M by $\{F(-M/2 + 1), \ldots, F(-1), F(0), F(1), \ldots, F(M/2)\}$. One obvious coefficient to use is $F(1)$, already normalized to have unity magnitude. If we start by requiring the phase of $F(1)$ to be some value, say 0, it can be shown that if the kth coefficient is also required to have zero phase, there are $(k - 1)$ possible starting-point/orientation combinations that satisfy these restrictions.

The obvious procedure is to require $F(1)$ and $F(2)$ to have phases equal to some specified value, thereby achieving a unique standard normalization. This sounds like a solution to the problem, but while $F(1)$ is guaranteed to have unity magnitude after normalizing the FD for size, there is no such guarantee for $F(2)$. A consistent solution to this problem can be obtained by selecting a nonzero coefficient to use for normalization, and then using a third coefficient to resolve the ambiguity that may be caused by the multiple normalization effect.

Practical considerations

The practical implementation of this procedure requires paying attention to a few details not mentioned above. Theoretically, the procedure involves an exact representation of a contour sampled at uniform spacing. While nonuniform spacing can result in a frequency-domain representation that converges faster, there are some serious difficulties involved in attempting to define a standard sampling strategy using nonuniform spacing.

Remembering that the FFT algorithm requires an input array whose length is an integer power of 2, it is clear that the length of an arbitrary chain representation must be adjusted before the FFT can be used. A procedure for doing this is to compute the perimeter of the contour, divide it by the desired length (desired power of 2), and starting at one point, trace around the contour saving the coordinates of appropriately spaced points. The desired power of 2 might be the smallest power of 2 larger than the length of the chain.

Practically, the input to the shape-analysis algorithm will be a contour taken from a sampled picture. The perimeter of this contour will be an approximation of the actual perimeter of the contour. While it can be argued that, for high enough sampling density in the original picture, the chain is an arbitrarily good approximation of the contour, this argument breaks down if one considers the density of points around the approximate contour versus the exact contour.

Consider an isosceles right triangle oriented so that the legs line up with the x and y axes, with the hypotenuse at 45°. The "length" of the contour, if an ordinary 4-neighbor chain is used, will be four times the length of one leg; the hypotenuse will be as long as both legs combined. Obviously, the density of points on the hypotenuse will depart from the proper value by a factor of $\sqrt{2}$. This error will cause the normalized Fourier descriptors (NFDs) of simple figures such as triangles to differ substantially, and render the algorithm virtually useless. One solution to this problem is to use an 8-neighbor chain code, in which the four diagonal neighbors of a point can also be the next points in the chain. In the example just considered, this eliminates the point density error.

Other practical considerations involve the normalization process. While, theoretically, any nonzero coefficient can be used with $F(1)$ to define standard orientation and starting point as outlined above, practical contours show the effects of noise and quantization error. This noise perturbs the phases of the FD coefficients so that the coefficients of lower amplitude can be substantially affected. It can be shown that the mean-square error in the frequency domain corresponds to the point-by-point mean-square error in the spatial domain. It follows from this result that slight shifts in orientation and/or starting point due to noise can have drastic effects on the classification of shapes made using this criterion. One way to minimize this effect is to choose the largest-magnitude coefficients as normalization coefficients. $F(1)$ is already the largest, so the second largest is chosen to accompany $F(1)$. Generally a third coefficient will be required to decide which of the allowable normalizations is optimal, as explained above. This coefficient can be chosen to be the largest remaining coefficient suitable for resolving the ambiguity.

The normalization procedure tends to reduce the proportion of the information contained in the phase, as compared to that contained in the magnitudes. Also, it can be shown that if the contour under analysis has bilateral symmetry, the resulting NFD will have phases equal to either the normalization phase (phase to which the normalization coefficients are constrained), or that value plus 180°. In view of these results, classification using only the magnitudes of the NFD seems like a reasonable procedure. In this case, the normalization procedure consists of simply dividing each coefficient by the magnitude of $F(1)$.

Example: As an illustration of the above approach for shape description, consider the aircraft silhouettes shown in Fig. 8.15. These silhouettes were obtained by (1) computing the NFDs of the boundary (512 points were used), (2) retaining the 32 lowest-frequency components while setting the rest equal to 0, and (3) taking the inverse Fourier transform of the modified 512-array to obtain an approximation of the original data. As shown in Fig. 8.15, the results, although a bit distorted, retained the basic features of the different aircraft. Therefore the information present in the lowest 32 components was sufficient to differentiate between the shapes of these aircraft.   □

8.2.4 Moments

The shape of boundary segments (and of signatures) can be described quantitatively by using moments. In order to see how this can be accomplished, consider Fig. 8.16(a), which shows the segment of a boundary, and Fig. 8.16(b), which shows the segment represented as a one-dimensional function $g(r)$ of an arbitrary variable

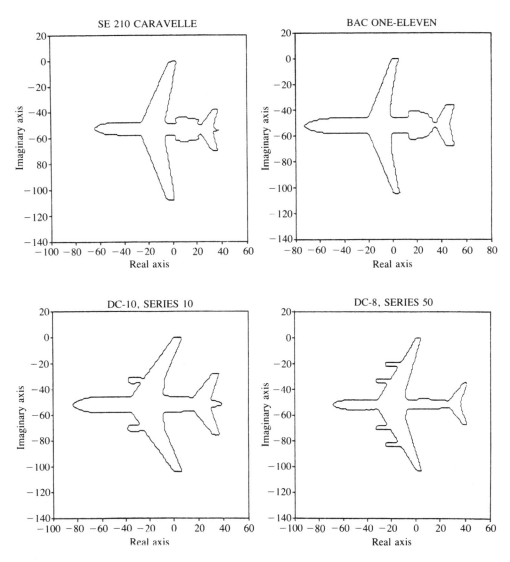

Figure 8.15   Shapes obtained by using Fourier descriptors. (Courtesy of T. Wallace, Electrical Engineering Department, Purdue University.)

r. Suppose that we treat the amplitude of *g* as a random variable *a* and form an amplitude histogram $p(a_i)$, $i = 1, 2, \ldots, K$, where K is the number of discrete amplitude increments. Then, the *n*th moment of *a* about its mean is

$$\mu_n(a) = \sum_{i=1}^{K} (a_i - m)^n p(a_i), \tag{8.2-2}$$

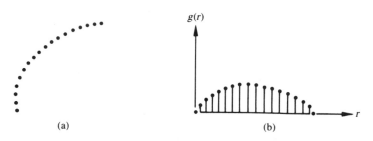

$g(r)$

(a)   (b)

Figure 8.16   (a) Boundary segment. (b) Representation as a one-dimensional function.

where

$$m = \sum_{i=1}^{K} a_i p(a_i). \qquad (8.2\text{-}3)$$

The quantity m is recognized as the mean or average value of a and μ_2 as its variance. Generally, only the first few moments are required to differentiate between signatures of clearly distinct shapes.

An alternative approach is to normalize $g(r)$ to unit area and treat it as a histogram. In this case, r becomes the random variable and the moments are given by

$$\mu_n(r) = \sum_{i=1}^{L} (r_i - m)^n g(r_i), \qquad (8.2\text{-}4)$$

where

$$m = \sum_{i=1}^{L} r_i g(r_i). \qquad (8.2\text{-}5)$$

In this notation, L is the number of points on the boundary, and $\mu_n(r)$ is directly related to the shape of $g(r)$. For example, the second moment $\mu_2(r)$ would measure the spread of the curve about the mean value of r and the third moment $\mu_3(r)$ would measure its symmetry with reference to the mean. Naturally, it is possible to use both moment representations simultaneously to describe a given boundary segment or signature.

Before leaving this section we point out that, basically, what has been accomplished here is to reduce the description task to that of describing one-dimensional functions. Although moments are by far the most popular method, they are not the only descriptors that could be used for this purpose. For instance, we could also compute the one-dimensional discrete Fourier transform given in Eq. (3.2-2), obtain its spectrum, and use the first k components of the spectrum to describe $g(r)$. The advantage of moments over other techniques one could use is that the former descriptors are straightforward to implement and also carry a "physical" interpretation of boundary shape. The insensitivity of this approach to rotation is clear from Fig. 8.16. Size normalization, if desired, can be achieved by scaling the range of r.

8.3 REGIONAL DESCRIPTORS

8.3.1 Some Simple Descriptors

The *area* of a region is defined as the number of pixels contained within its boundary. The *perimeter* of a region is the length of its boundary. Although area and perimeter are sometimes used as descriptors, they are applicable primarily in situations in which the size of the objects of interest is invariant. A more frequent use of these two descriptors is in establishing a measure of *compactness* of a region, defined as (perimeter)^2/area. It is of interest to note that compactness is a dimensionless quantity (and thus is insensitive to scale changes) and that it is minimal for a disk-shaped region. With the exception of errors introduced by rotation of a digital region, compactness is also insensitive to orientation.

The *principal axes* of a region are the eigenvectors of the covariance matrix obtained by using the pixels within the region as random variables. The computation of this matrix was already discussed in Section 3.6.1. The two eigenvectors of the covariance matrix point in the directions of maximal region spread, subject to the constraint that they be orthogonal. A measure of the degree of spread is given by the corresponding eigenvalues. Thus the principal spread and direction of a region can be described by the largest eigenvalue and its corresponding eigenvector. This type of description is insensitive to rotation, but does depend on scale changes if one uses eigenvalues as a measure of spread. One approach used frequently to compensate for this difficulty is to use the *ratio* of the large to the small eigenvalue as a descriptor.

Other simple measures used as region descriptors include the mean and median of the gray levels, the minimum and maximum gray-level values, and the number of pixels with values above and below the mean.

8.3.2 Topological Descriptors

Topological properties are useful for global descriptions of regions in the image plane. Simply defined, topology is the study of properties of a figure that are unaffected by any deformation, as long as there is no tearing or joining of the figure. (These are sometimes called *rubber-sheet* distortions.) Consider, for example, Fig. 8.17. If we define as a topological descriptor the number of holes in the region, it is evident that this property will not be affected by a stretching or rotation transformation. In general, however, the number of holes will change if we tear or fold the region. Note that, since stretching affects distance, topological properties do not depend on any notion of distance or any properties implicitly based on the concept of a distance measure.

Another topological property useful for region description is the number of connected components. A connected component of a set is a subset of maximal

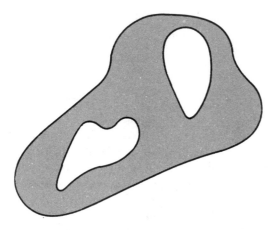

Figure 8.17   A region with two holes.

size such that any two of its points can be joined by a connected curve lying entirely within the subset. Figure 8.18 shows a region with three connected components.

The number of holes H and connected components C in a figure can be used to define the *Euler number E* as follows:

$$E = C - H. \tag{8.3-1}$$

The Euler number is also a topological property. The regions shown in Fig. 8.19, for example, have Euler numbers equal to 0 and -1, respectively, since the "A" has one connected component and one hole and the "B" one connected component but two holes.

Regions represented by straight line segments (referred to as *polygonal networks*) have a particularly simple interpretation in terms of the Euler number. A polygonal

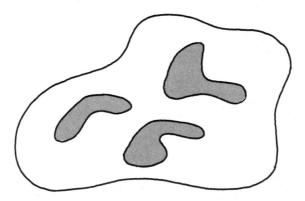

Figure 8.18   A region with three connected components.

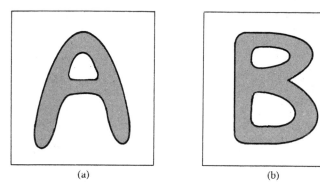

(a)   (b)

Figure 8.19   Regions with Euler number equal to 0 and -1, respectively.

network is shown in Fig. 8.20. It is often important to classify interior regions of such a network into faces and holes. If we denote the number of vertices by W, the number of edges by Q, and the number of faces by F, we have the following relationship, called the *Euler formula*:

$$W - Q + F = C - H, \tag{8.3-2}$$

which, in view of Eq. (8.3-1), is related to the Euler number:

$$W - Q + F = C - H = E. \tag{8.3-4}$$

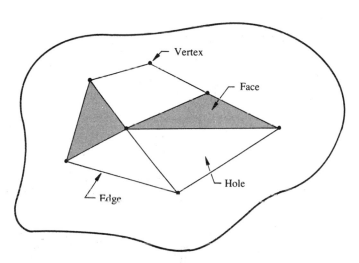

Figure 8.20   A region containing a polygonal network.

The network shown in Fig. 8.20 has 7 vertices, 11 edges, 2 faces, 1 connected region, and 3 holes; thus,

$$7 - 11 + 2 = 1 - 3 = -2.$$

Although topological concepts are rather general, they provide an additional feature that is often useful in characterizing regions in a scene.

8.3.3 Texture

An important approach to region description is to quantify its *texture* content. Although no formal definition of texture exists, we intuitively view this descriptor as providing a measure of properties such as smoothness, coarseness, and regularity (some examples are shown in Fig. 8.21). The three principal approaches used in image processing to describe the texture of a region are statistical, structural, and spectral. Statistical approaches yield characterizations of textures as smooth, coarse, grainy, and so on. Structural techniques, on the other hand, deal with the arrangement of image primitives, such as the description of texture based on regularly spaced parallel lines. Spectral techniques are based on properties of the Fourier spectrum and are used primarily to detect global periodicity in an image by identifying high-energy, narrow peaks in the spectrum (see Sections 5.7 and 5.8).

Statistical approaches
One of the simplest approaches for describing texture is to use moments of the gray-level histogram of an image or region. Let z be a random variable denoting discrete image intensity, and let $p(z_i)$, $i = 1, 2, \ldots, L$ be the corresponding histogram, where L is the number of distinct intensity levels. As indicated in Section 8.2.4, the nth moment of z about the mean is defined as

$$\mu_n(z) = \sum_{i=1}^{L} (z_i - m)^n p(z_i),$$

(8.3-5)

where m is the mean value of z (i.e., the average image intensity):

$$m = \sum_{i=1}^{L} z_i\, p(z_i).$$

(8.3-6)

Note from Eq. (8.3-5) that $\mu_0 = 1$ and $\mu_1 = 0$. The second moment (also called the *variance* and denoted by $\sigma^2(z)$) is of particular importance in texture description. It is a measure of gray-level contrast that can be used to establish descriptors of relative smoothness. For example, the measure

$$R = 1 - \frac{1}{1 + \sigma^2(z)}$$

(8.3-7)

is 0 for areas of constant intensity ($\sigma^2(z) = 0$ if all z_is have the same value) and approaches 1 for large values of $\sigma^2(z)$. The third moment is a measure of the skewness of the histogram while the fourth moment is a measure of its relative

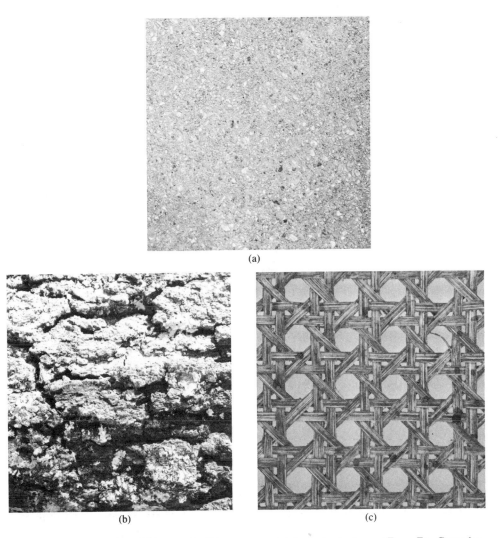

Figure 8.21 Examples of (a) smooth, (b) coarse, and (c) regular textures. (From Fu, Gonzalez, and Lee [1987].)

flatness. The fifth and higher moments are not so easily related to histogram shape, but they do provide further quantitative discrimination of texture content.

Measures of texture computed using only histograms suffer from the limitation that they carry no information regarding the relative position of pixels with respect to each other. One way to bring this type of information into the texture-analysis process is to consider not only the distribution of intensities, but also the positions of pixels with equal or nearly equal intensity values.

Let P be a position operator and let $\mathbf{A}$ be a $k \times k$ matrix whose element a_{ij} is the number of times that points with gray level z_i occur (in the position specified by P) relative to points with gray level z_j, with $1 \leq i, j \leq k$. For instance, consider an image with three gray levels, $z_1 = 0$, $z_2 = 1$, and $z_3 = 2$, as follows:

$$
\begin{matrix}
0 & 0 & 0 & 1 & 2 \\
1 & 1 & 0 & 1 & 1 \\
2 & 2 & 1 & 0 & 0 \\
1 & 1 & 0 & 2 & 0 \\
0 & 0 & 1 & 0 & 1
\end{matrix}
$$

If we define the position operator P as "one pixel to the right and one pixel below," then we obtain the following 3×3 matrix $\mathbf{A}$:

$$
\mathbf{A} = \begin{bmatrix} 4 & 2 & 1 \\ 2 & 3 & 2 \\ 0 & 2 & 0 \end{bmatrix}
$$

where, for example, a_{11} (top left) is the number of times that a point with level $z_1 = 0$ appears one pixel location below and to the right of a pixel with the same gray level, while a_{13} (top right) is the number of times that a point with level $z_1 = 0$ appears one pixel location below and to the right of a point with gray level $z_3 = 2$. It is important to note that the size of $\mathbf{A}$ is determined strictly by the number of distinct gray levels in the input image. Thus application of the concepts discussed in this section usually requires that intensities be requantized into a few gray-level bands in order to keep the size of $\mathbf{A}$ manageable.

Let n be the total number of point pairs in the image that satisfy P (in the above example, $n = 16$). If we define a matrix $\mathbf{C}$ formed by dividing every element of $\mathbf{A}$ by n, then c_{ij} is an estimate of the joint probability that a pair of points satisfying P will have values (z_i, z_j). The matrix $\mathbf{C}$ is called a *gray-level co-occurrence matrix*. Since $\mathbf{C}$ depends on P, it is possible to detect the presence of given texture patterns by choosing an appropriate position operator. For instance, the operator used in the above example is sensitive to bands of constant intensity running at $-45°$. (Note that the highest value in $\mathbf{A}$ was $a_{11} = 4$, partially due to a streak of points with intensity 0 and running at $-45°$.) In a more general situation, the problem is to analyze a given $\mathbf{C}$ matrix in order to categorize the texture of the region over which $\mathbf{C}$ was computed. A set of descriptors proposed by Haralick [1979] include

(1) Maximum probability

$$
\max_{i,j}(c_{ij})
$$

(2) Element-difference moment of order k,

$$
\sum_i \sum_j (i - j)^k c_{ij}
$$

(3) Inverse element-difference moment of order k,

$$\sum_i \sum_j c_{ij}/(i-j)^k \quad i \neq j$$

(4) Entropy

$$-\sum_i \sum_j c_{ij} \log c_{ij}$$

(5) Uniformity

$$\sum_i \sum_j c_{ij}^2$$

The basic idea is to characterize the "content" of $\mathbf{C}$ via these descriptors. For example, the first property gives an indication of the strongest response to P (as in the above example). The second descriptor has a relatively low value when the high values of $\mathbf{C}$ are near the main diagonal since the differences $(i - j)$ are smaller there. The third descriptor has the opposite effect. The fourth descriptor is a measure of randomness, achieving its highest value when all elements of $\mathbf{C}$ are equal. Conversely, the fifth descriptor is lowest when the c_{ij}s are all equal.

One approach for using these descriptors is to "teach" a system representative descriptor values for a set of different textures. The texture of an unknown region is then subsequently determined by how closely its descriptors match those stored in the system memory. Matching is discussed in more detail in Section 8.5.

Structural approaches
As mentioned at the beginning of this section, a second major category of texture description is based on structural concepts. Suppose that we have a rule of the form $S \rightarrow aS$, which indicates that the symbol S may be rewritten as aS (e.g., three applications of this rule would yield the string $aaaS$). If we let a represent a circle (Fig. 8.22a) and assign the meaning of "circles to the right" to a string of the form aaa . . . , then the rule $S \rightarrow aS$ allows us to generate a texture pattern of the form shown in Fig. 8.22(b).

Suppose next that we add some new rules to this scheme: $S \rightarrow bA$, $A \rightarrow cA$, $A \rightarrow c$, $A \rightarrow bS$, $S \rightarrow a$, such that the presence of a b means "circle down" and the presence of a c means "circle to the left." We can now generate a string of the form $aaabccbaa$ that corresponds to a 3×3 matrix of circles. Larger texture patterns, such as the one shown in Fig. 8.22(c) can easily be generated in the same way. (Note, however, that these rules can also generate structures that are not rectangular.)

The basic idea in the foregoing discussion is that a simple "texture primitive" can be used to form more-complex texture patterns by means of some rules that limit the number of possible arrangements of the primitive(s). These concepts lie at the heart of relational descriptions, a topic that will be treated in considerably more detail in Section 8.4.

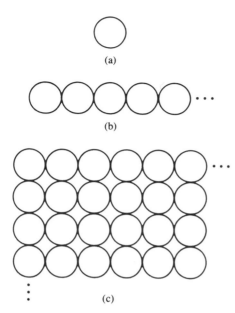

(a)

(b)

(c)

Figure 8.22 (a) Texture primitive. (b) Pattern generated by the rule $S \rightarrow aS$. (c) Two-dimensional texture pattern generated by this plus other rules.

Spectral approaches

As indicated in Sections 5.7 and 5.8, the Fourier spectrum is ideally suited for describing the directionality of periodic or almost periodic two-dimensional patterns in an image. These global texture patterns, while being easily distinguishable as concentrations of high-energy bursts in the spectrum, are generally quite difficult to detect using spatial methods because of the local nature of these techniques.

In the present discussion we consider three features of the Fourier spectrum that are useful for texture description: (1) prominent peaks in the spectrum give the principal direction of the texture patterns; (2) the location of the peaks in the frequency plane gives the fundamental spatial period of the patterns; and (3) by eliminating any periodic components via filtering we are left with nonperiodic image elements, which can then be described by statistical techniques. The reader is reminded that the spectrum of a real image is symmetric about the origin, so only half of the frequency plane needs to be considered. Thus, for the purpose of analysis, every periodic pattern is associated with only one peak in the spectrum, rather than two.

The detection and interpretation of the spectrum features just mentioned is often simplified by expressing the spectrum in polar coordinates to yield a function $S(r, \theta)$, where S is the spectrum function and r and θ are the variables in this coordinate system. Then, in each direction θ, one can consider $S(r, \theta)$ as a one-dimensional function $S_\theta(r)$. Similarly, for each frequency r, $S_r(\theta)$ is a one-dimensional function. Analyzing $S_\theta(r)$ for a fixed value of θ yields the behavior of the spectrum (e.g., the presence of peaks) along a radial direction from the origin, while analyzing $S_r(\theta)$ for a fixed value of r yields the behavior along a circle centered at the origin.

A more global description is obtained by integrating (summing for discrete variables) these functions, as follows:

$$S(r) = \sum_{\theta=0}^{\pi} S_\theta(r) \tag{8.3-8}$$

and

$$S(\theta) = \sum_{r=1}^{R} S_r(\theta), \tag{8.3-9}$$

where R is the radius of a circle centered at the origin. For an $N \times N$ spectrum, R is typically chosen as $N/2$.

The results of Eqs. (8.3-8) and (8.3-9) constitute a pair of values $[S(r), S(\theta)]$ for each pair of coordinates (r, θ). By varying these coordinates, we can generate two one-dimensional functions, $S(r)$ and $S(\theta)$, that constitute a spectral-energy description of texture for an entire image or region under consideration. Furthermore, we can compute descriptors of these functions themselves in order to characterize their behavior in a quantitative manner. Typical descriptors one might use for this purpose are the location of the highest value, the mean and variance of both the amplitude and axial variations (see Section 8.2.4), and the distance between the mean and the highest value of the function.

Example: Figure 8.23 is an illustration of the use of Eqs. (8.3-8) and (8.3-9) for global texture description. Figure 8.23(a) shows an image with periodic texture and Fig. 8.23(b) is its spectrum. Figures 8.23(c) and (d) are plots of $S(r)$ and $S(\theta)$, respectively. The plot of $S(r)$ has a typical structure showing high energy content near the origin with progressively lower values for high frequencies. The plot of $S(\theta)$ shows prominent peaks at intervals of 45°, which clearly correspond to this type of periodicity in the texture content of the image.

As an illustration of how the plot of $S(\theta)$ could be used in this case to differentiate between two texture patterns, Fig. 8.23(e) shows another image whose texture pattern is predominantly in the horizontal and vertical directions. The plot of $S(\theta)$ for the spectrum of this image is shown in Fig. 8.23(f). As expected, this plot shows high peaks at 90° intervals. It would be a simple matter to discriminate between the two texture patterns by analyzing their corresponding $S(\theta)$ waveforms. □

8.3.4 Moments

Given a two-dimensional continuous function $f(x, y)$ we define the moment of order $(p + q)$ by the relation

$$m_{pq} = \int_{-\infty}^{\infty} \int_{-\infty}^{\infty} x^p y^q f(x, y)\, dx dy \tag{8.3-10}$$

for $p, q = 0, 1, 2, \ldots$.

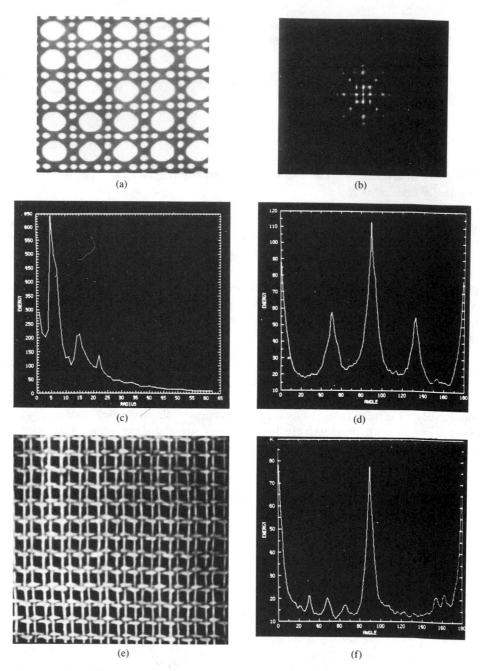

Figure 8.23   (a) Image showing periodic texture. (b) Spectrum. (c) Plot of $S(r)$. (d) Plot of $S(\theta)$. (e) Another image with a different type of periodic texture. (f) Plot of $S(\theta)$. (Courtesy of D. Brzakovic, University of Tennessee.)

A uniqueness theorem (Papoulis [1965]) states that if $f(x, y)$ is piecewise continuous and has nonzero values only in a finite part of the x–y plane, then moments of all orders exist and the moment sequence (m_{pq}) is uniquely determined by $f(x, y)$. Conversely (m_{pq}) uniquely determines $f(x, y)$. The *central moments* can be expressed as

$$\mu_{pq} = \int_{-\infty}^{\infty} \int_{-\infty}^{\infty} (x - \bar{x})^p (y - \bar{y})^q f(x, y) \, dx dy, \qquad (8.3\text{-}11)$$

where

$$\bar{x} = \frac{m_{10}}{m_{00}}, \qquad \bar{y} = \frac{m_{01}}{m_{00}}.$$

For a digital image, Eq. (8.3-11) becomes

$$\mu_{pq} = \sum_x \sum_y (x - \bar{x})^p (y - \bar{y})^q f(x, y). \qquad (8.3\text{-}12)$$

The central moments of order 3 are as follows:

$$\mu_{10} = \sum_x \sum_y (x - \bar{x})^1 (y - \bar{y})^0 f(x, y)$$

$$= m_{10} - \frac{m_{10}}{m_{00}} (m_{00})$$

$$= 0$$

$$\mu_{11} = \sum_x \sum_y (x - \bar{x})^1 (y - \bar{y})^1 f(x, y)$$

$$= m_{11} - \frac{m_{10} m_{01}}{m_{00}}$$

$$\mu_{20} = \sum_x \sum_y (x - \bar{x})^2 (y - \bar{y})^0 f(x, y)$$

$$= m_{20} - \frac{2m_{10}^2}{m_{00}} + \frac{m_{10}^2}{m_{00}} = m_{20} - \frac{m_{10}^2}{m_{00}}$$

$$\mu_{02} = \sum_x \sum_y (x - \bar{x})^0 (y - \bar{y})^2 f(x, y)$$

$$= m_{02} - \frac{m_{01}^2}{m_{00}}$$

$$\mu_{30} = \sum_x \sum_y (x - \bar{x})^{13} (y - \bar{y})^0 f(x, y)$$

$$= m_{30} - 3\bar{x} m_{20} + 2m_{10} \bar{x}^2$$

$$\mu_{12} = \sum_x \sum_y (x - \bar{x})^1 (y - \bar{y})^2 f(x, y)$$
$$= m_{12} - 2\bar{y}m_{11} - \bar{x}m_{02} + 2\bar{y}^2 m_{10}$$

$$\mu_{21} = \sum_x \sum_y (x - \bar{x})^2 (y - \bar{y})^1 f(x, y)$$
$$= m_{21} - 2\bar{x}m_{11} - \bar{y}m_{20} + 2\bar{x}^2 m_{01}$$

$$\mu_{03} = \sum_x \sum_y (x - \bar{x})^0 (y - \bar{y})^3 f(x, y)$$
$$= m_{03} - 3\bar{y}m_{02} + 2\bar{y}^2 m_{01}$$

In summary,

$$\mu_{00} = m_{00}, \qquad\qquad \mu_{11} = m_{11} - \bar{y}m_{10}$$
$$\mu_{10} = 0, \qquad\qquad \mu_{30} = m_{30} - 3\bar{x}m_{20} + 2m_{10}\bar{x}^2$$
$$\mu_{01} = 0, \qquad\qquad \mu_{12} = m_{12} - 2\bar{y}m_{11} - \bar{x}m_{02} + 2\bar{y}^2 m_{10}$$
$$\mu_{20} = m_{20} - \bar{x}m_{10}, \qquad \mu_{21} = m_{21} - 2\bar{x}m_{11} - \bar{y}m_{20} + 2\bar{x}^2 m_{01}$$
$$\mu_{02} = m_{02} - \bar{y}m_{01}, \qquad \mu_{03} = m_{03} - 3\bar{y}m_{02} + 2\bar{y}^2 m_{01}$$

The *normalized central moments*, denoted by η_{pq}, are defined as

$$\eta_{pq} = \frac{\mu_{pq}}{\mu_{00}^\gamma}, \tag{8.3-13}$$

where

$$\gamma = \frac{p + q}{2} + 1 \tag{8.3-14}$$

for $p + q = 2, 3, \ldots$.

From the second and third moments, a set of seven *invariant moments* can be derived.† They are given by

$$\phi_1 = \eta_{20} + \eta_{02} \tag{8.3-15}$$
$$\phi_2 = (\eta_{20} - \eta_{02})^2 + 4\eta_{11}^2 \tag{8.3-16}$$
$$\phi_3 = (\eta_{30} - 3\eta_{12})^2 + (3\eta_{21} - \eta_{03})^2 \tag{8.3-17}$$
$$\phi_4 = (\eta_{30} + \eta_{12})^2 + (\eta_{21} + \eta_{03})^2 \tag{8.3-18}$$

---

† Derivation of these results involves concepts that are beyond the scope of the present discussion. The interested reader should consult the book by Bell [1965] and the paper by Hu [1962] for a detailed discussion.

$$\phi_5 = (\eta_{30} - 3\eta_{12})(\eta_{30} + \eta_{12})[(\eta_{30} + \eta_{12})^2 - 3(\eta_{21} + \eta_{03})^2]$$
$$+ (3\eta_{21} - \eta_{03})(\eta_{21} + \eta_{03})[3(\eta_{30} + \eta_{12})^2 - (\eta_{21} + \eta_{03})^2] \qquad (8.3\text{-}19)$$

$$\phi_6 = (\eta_{20} - \eta_{02})[(\eta_{30} + \eta_{12})^2 - (\eta_{21} + \eta_{03})^2]$$
$$+ 4\eta_{11}(\eta_{30} + \eta_{12})(\eta_{21} + \eta_{03}) \qquad (8.3\text{-}20)$$

$$\phi_7 = (3\eta_{21} - \eta_{30})(\eta_{30} + \eta_{12})[(\eta_{30} + \eta_{12})^2 - 3(\eta_{21} + \eta_{03})^2]$$
$$+ (3\eta_{12} - \eta_{30})(\eta_{21} + \eta_{03})[3(\eta_{30} + \eta_{12})^2 - (\eta_{21} + \eta_{03})^2] \qquad (8.3\text{-}21)$$

This set of moments has been shown to be invariant to translation, rotation, and scale change (Hu [1962]).

Example: The image shown in Fig. 8.24(a) was reduced to half size in Fig. 8.24(b), mirror-imaged in Fig. 8.24(c), and rotated by 2° and 45°, as shown in Figs. 8.24(d) and (e). The seven moment invariants given in Eqs. (8.3-15) through (8.3-21) were then computed for each of these images, and the logarithm of the results taken to reduce the dynamic range. As shown in Table 8.1, the results for Figs. 8.24(b) through (e) are in reasonable agreement with the invariants computed for the original image. The major cause of error can be attributed to the digital nature of the data.

$\square$

8.4 DESCRIPTIONS OF SIMILARITY

Measures of similarity may be established at various levels of complexity in an image, ranging from the trivial case of comparing two pixels to the highly complex problem of determining in some meaningful way how similar two or more scenes are.

8.4.1 Distance Measures

Some of the techniques discussed previously can be used as the basis of comparison between two image regions. Consider, for example, the moment descriptors introduced in Section 8.3.4. Suppose that the moments for two regions are arranged in the form of two vectors, $\mathbf{x}_1$ and $\mathbf{x}_2$. The distance between $\mathbf{x}_1$ and $\mathbf{x}_2$, given by

$$D(\mathbf{x}_1, \mathbf{x}_2) = \|\mathbf{x}_1 - \mathbf{x}_2\|$$
$$= \sqrt{(\mathbf{x}_1 - \mathbf{x}_2)'(\mathbf{x}_1 - \mathbf{x}_2)}, \qquad (8.4\text{-}1)$$

where the prime (') indicates vector transposition, may be used as a measure of similarity between these two descriptors. This becomes a particularly attractive approach if we are interested in comparing a given descriptor of unknown origin with two or more descriptors whose characteristics have been previously established. If the known descriptors are denoted by $\mathbf{x}_1, \mathbf{x}_2, \ldots, \mathbf{x}_L$ and the unknown descriptor by $\mathbf{x}$, then we say that $\mathbf{x}$ is more similar to the ith descriptor if $\mathbf{x}$ is closer to $\mathbf{x}_i$ than to any other vector; that is, if

$$D(\mathbf{x}, \mathbf{x}_i) < D(\mathbf{x}, \mathbf{x}_j) \qquad (8.4\text{-}2)$$

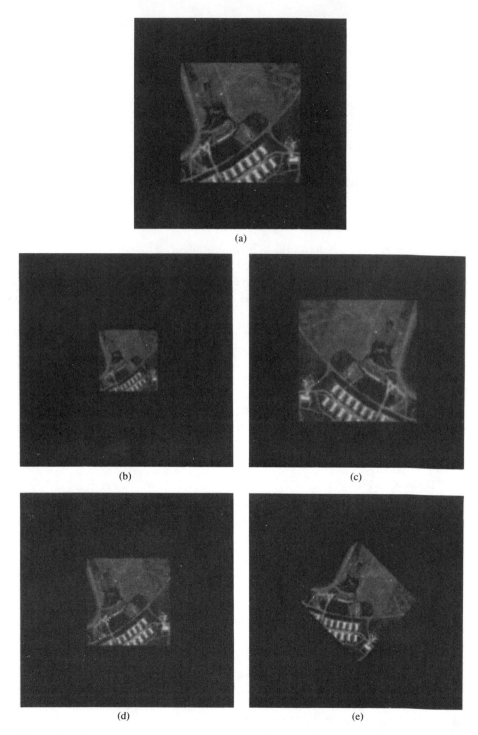

Figure 8.24 Images used to demonstrate properties of moment invariants.

Table 8.1 Moment Invariants for the Images in Figs. 7.23(a) through (e)

Invariant (Log)	Original	Half Size	Mirrored	Rotated 2°	Rotated 45°
ϕ_1	6.249	6.226	6.919	6.253	6.318
ϕ_2	17.180	16.954	19.955	17.270	16.803
ϕ_3	22.655	23.531	26.689	22.836	19.724
ϕ_4	22.919	24.236	26.901	23.130	20.437
ϕ_5	45.749	48.349	53.724	46.136	40.525
ϕ_6	31.830	32.916	37.134	32.068	29.315
ϕ_7	45.589	48.343	53.590	46.017	40.470

for $j = 1, 2, \ldots, L, j \neq i$. This approach can be used with a variety of descriptors, as long as they can be expressed meaningfully in vector form.

8.4.2 Correlation

Given a digital image $f(x, y)$ of size $M \times N$, suppose that we wish to determine if it contains a region similar to some region $w(x, y)$ of size $J \times K$, where $J < M$ and $K < N$. One of the methods most often used for the solution of this problem is to perform a correlation between $w(x, y)$ and $f(x, y)$.

In its simplest form, the correlation between these two real functions is given by

$$R(m, n) = \sum_x \sum_y f(x, y)w(x - m, y - n), \tag{8.4-3}$$

where $m = 0, 1, 2, \ldots, M - 1, n = 0, 1, 2, \ldots, N - 1$, and the summation is taken over the image region where $w(x, y)$ is defined. The procedure is illustrated in Fig. 8.25; for any value of (m, n) inside $f(x, y)$ we apply Eq. (8.4-3) to obtain one value of R. As m and n are varied, $w(x, y)$ moves around the image area and we obtain the function $R(m, n)$. The maximum value of $R(m, n)$ then indicates the position where $w(x, y)$ best matched $f(x, y)$. Note that accuracy will be lost for values of m and n near the edges of $f(x, y)$, with the amount of error being proportional to the size of $w(x, y)$.

Example: Figure 8.26 illustrates the concepts just discussed. Figure 8.26(a) is $f(x, y)$, Fig. 8.26(b) is $w(x, y)$, and Fig. 8.26(c) is $R(m, n)$ displayed as an intensity function. Note the higher intensity of $R(m, n)$ in the position where the best match between $f(x, y)$ and $w(x, y)$ was found. □

The correlation function given in Eq. (8.4-3), although simple in nature, has the drawback that it is sensitive to scale changes in the amplitude of $f(x, y)$ and

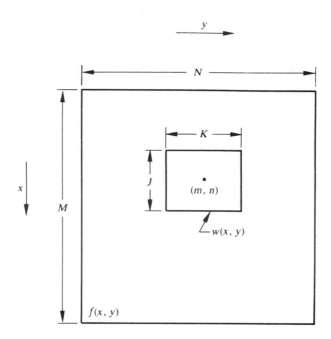

Figure 8.25 Arrangement for obtaining the correlation of
$f(x, y)$ and $w(x, y)$ at a given point (m, n).

$w(x, y)$. A method frequently used to overcome this difficulty is to perform matching
via the *correlation coefficient*, defined as

$$r(m, n) = \frac{\sum_x \sum_y [f(x, y) - \bar{f}(x, y)][w(x - m, y - n) - \bar{w}]}{\left[\sum_x \sum_y [f(x, y) - \bar{f}(x, y)]^2 \sum_x \sum_y [w(x - m, y - n) - \bar{w}]^2\right]^{1/2}} \qquad (8.4\text{-}4)$$

where $m = 0, 1, 2, \ldots, M - 1$, $n = 0, 1, 2, \ldots, N - 1$, $\bar{w}$ is the average
intensity of the mask (this value is computed only once), $\bar{f}(x, y)$ is the average
value of $f(x, y)$ in the region coincident with $w(x, y)$, and the summations are
taken over the coordinates common to both f and w. It is not difficult to show that
$r(m, n)$ is scaled to the range from -1 to 1, independent of scale changes in the
amplitude of $f(x, y)$ and $w(x, y)$.

   As mentioned in Section 3.3.8, correlation can also be carried out in the frequency
domain via an FFT algorithm. If the functions are of the same size, this approach
can be more efficient than a direct implementation of correlation in the spatial
domain. In implementing Eq. (8.4-3), however, it is important to note that $w(x, y)$
is usually of much smaller dimension than $f(x, y)$. A trade-off estimate performed
by Campbell [1969] indicates that if the number of nonzero terms in $w(x, y)$ is less

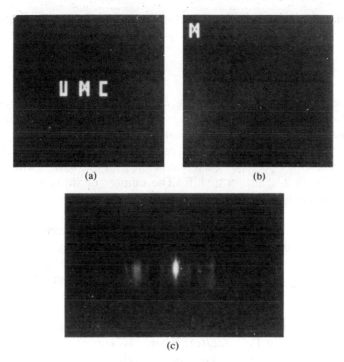

Figure 8.26   Example of correlation. Note the brightness of
$R(m, n)$ at the position where the two letters match. (From Hall
et al. [1971].)

than 132, then a direct implementation of Eq. (8.4-3) is more efficient than using
the FFT approach. This figure, of course, depends on the machine and algorithms
used, but it gives an indication of approximate image size when one should begin
to consider the frequency domain as an alternative. Equation (8.4-4) is considerably
more difficult to implement using the FFT and is usually computed directly in the
spatial domain.

8.4.3   Boundary Matching

Suppose that two object contours C_1 and C_2 are coded into strings $a_1a_2 \ldots a_n$
and $b_1b_2 \ldots b_m$, respectively. Let A represent the number of matches between
the two strings, where we say that a match has occurred in the jth position if $a_j = b_j$. The number of symbols that do not match up is given by

$$B = \max(|C_1|, |C_2|) - A, \tag{8.4-5}$$

where $|C|$ is the length (number of symbols) of string C. It can be shown that $B = 0$ if and only if C_1 and C_2 are identical.

A simple measure of similarity between strings C_1 and C_2 is defined as the ratio

$$R = A/B$$
$$= A/[\max(|C_1|, |C_2|) - A].$$

(8.4-6)

Based on the above comment regarding B, R is infinite for a perfect match and zero when none of the symbols in C_1 and C_2 match (i.e., $A = 0$ in this case). Since the matching is done on a symbol-by-symbol basis, the starting point on each boundary when creating the string representation is important. Alternatively, we can start at arbitrary points on each boundary, shift one string (with wraparound), and compute Eq. (8.4-6) for each shift. The number of shifts required to perform all necessary comparisons is $\max(|C_1|, |C_2|)$.

Example: Figures 8.27(a) and (b) show a sample boundary from each of two classes of objects. The boundaries were approximated by a polygonal fit (Figs. 8.27c and d) and then strings were formed by computing the interior angle between the polygonal segments as the polygon was traversed in a clockwise direction. Angles were coded into one of eight possible symbols corresponding to 45° increments, $s_1:0 < \theta \leq 45°$, $s_2:45° < \theta \leq 90°$, . . . , $s_8:315° \leq \theta \leq 0°$.

The results of computing the measure R for five samples of object 1 against themselves are shown in Fig. 8.27(e), where the entries correspond to values of $R = A/B$ and, for example, the notation 1.c refers to the third string for object class 1. Figure 8.27(f) shows the results for the strings of the second object class. Finally, Fig. 8.27(g) is a tabulation of R values obtained by comparing strings of one class against the other. The important thing to note is that all values of R in this last table are considerably smaller than any entry in the preceding two tables, indicating that the R measure achieved a high degree of discrimination between the two classes of objects. For instance, if string 1.a had been an unknown, the smallest value in comparing it with the other strings of class 1 would have been 4.67. By contrast, the largest value in a comparison against class 2 would have been 1.24. Thus classification of this string into class 1 based on the maximum value of R would have been a simple, unambiguous matter. □

8.5 RELATIONAL DESCRIPTIONS

The description approaches discussed in the previous three sections generally apply to individual boundaries and regions of interest in an image. The next level of complexity in the description process is to organize these components in a way that exploits any structural relationships that may exist between them. Although a unified body of theory dealing with techniques for relating components of an image has yet to be developed, the idea of using techniques based on grammatical concepts is emerging as a promising approach to the structural-description problem.

As an introduction to this concept, consider the simple staircase structure shown in Fig. 8.28(a). Assuming that this structure has been segmented out of an image,

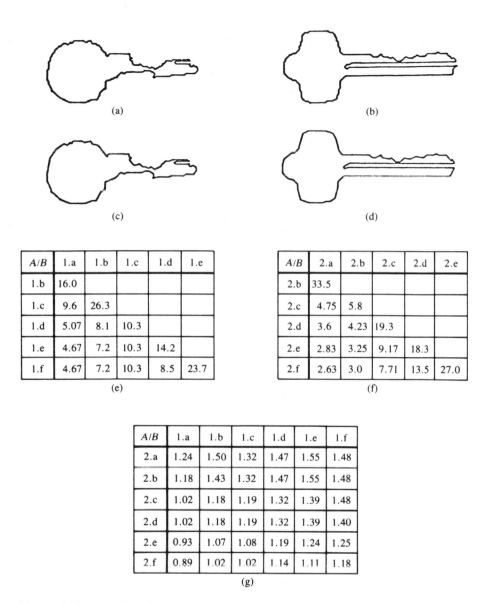

A/B	1.a	1.b	1.c	1.d	1.e
1.b	16.0				
1.c	9.6	26.3			
1.d	5.07	8.1	10.3		
1.e	4.67	7.2	10.3	14.2	
1.f	4.67	7.2	10.3	8.5	23.7

(e)

A/B	2.a	2.b	2.c	2.d	2.e
2.b	33.5				
2.c	4.75	5.8			
2.d	3.6	4.23	19.3		
2.e	2.83	3.25	9.17	18.3	
2.f	2.63	3.0	7.71	13.5	27.0

(f)

A/B	1.a	1.b	1.c	1.d	1.e	1.f
2.a	1.24	1.50	1.32	1.47	1.55	1.48
2.b	1.18	1.43	1.32	1.47	1.55	1.48
2.c	1.02	1.18	1.19	1.32	1.39	1.48
2.d	1.02	1.18	1.19	1.32	1.39	1.40
2.e	0.93	1.07	1.08	1.19	1.24	1.25
2.f	0.89	1.02	1.02	1.14	1.11	1.18

(g)

Figure 8.27 (a) and (b) Sample boundaries of two different object classes, (c) and (d) their corresponding polygonal approximations, and (e) through (g) tabulations of $R = A/B$ (Adapted from Sze and Yang [1981].)

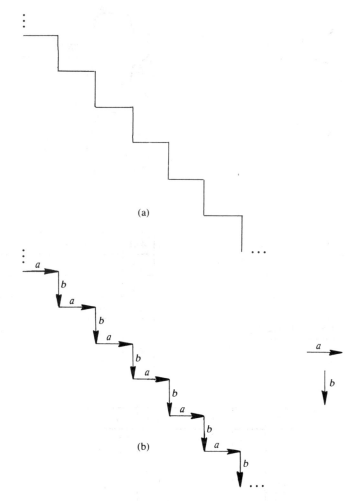

Figure 8.28   (a) A simple staircase structure. (b) Coded structure.

let us suppose that we wish to describe it in some formal way. By defining the two *primitive elements* a and b shown, we may code Fig. 8.28(a) in the form shown in Fig. 8.28(b). The most-obvious property of the coded structure is the repetitiveness of the elements a and b. Therefore a simple description approach would be to formulate a recursive relationship involving these primitive elements. One possibility is to use the following *rewriting rules*:

(1) $S \rightarrow aA$,

(2) $A \rightarrow bS$,

(3) $A \rightarrow b$,

where S and A are variables and the elements a and b are constants corresponding to the primitives defined above. The first rule indicates that S can be replaced by primitive a and variable A. This variable, in turn, can be replaced by b and S or by b alone. If we replace A by bS, this takes us back to the first rule and the procedure can be repeated. If A is replaced by b, the procedure terminates because no variables are left in the expression. Figure 8.29 illustrates some sample derivations of these rules, where the numbers below the structures represent the order in which rules 1, 2, and 3 were applied. Note that the relationship between a and b is preserved by the fact that these rules force an a to be always followed by a b.

In the following discussion it is assumed that all derivations start with a special symbol S (called the *starting symbol*). Based on this convention, the first element in the structures generated by the above rules is always an a and the last element a b. Other variations of starting and ending elements are easily incorporated by adding more rules. The key point of this illustration, however, is that three simple rewriting rules can be used to generate (or describe) an infinite number of "similar" structures. As shown in the following sections, this approach also enjoys the advantage of having a solid theoretical foundation.

8.5.1 String Grammars and Languages

The coded structure illustrated in Fig. 8.28 is composed of connected strings of symbols. In this section we introduce some concepts from formal language theory for handling such strings. This field deals with the study of mathematical models used for the generation, translation, or other processes involving strings of an artificial language.

The origin of formal language theory may be traced to the mid-1950s with the development by Noam Chomsky of mathematical models of grammars related to his work in natural languages. One of the original goals of the work of linguists working in this area was to develop computational grammars capable of describing natural languages such as English. The hope was that, if this could be done, it would be a relatively simple matter to "teach" computers to interpret natural languages for the purposes of translation and problem solving. Although it is generally agreed that these expectations have been unrealized thus far, spin-offs of research in this

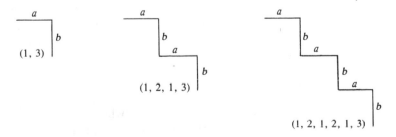

Figure 8.29 Sample derivations for the rules $S \rightarrow aA$, $A \rightarrow bS$, $A \rightarrow b$.

area have had significant impact on other fields such as compiler design, computer languages, automata theory, and, more recently, pattern recognition and image processing.

We begin the development with some basic definitions.

An *alphabet V* is any finite set of symbols.

A *sentence, string,* or *word* over an alphabet V is any string of finite length composed of symbols from the alphabet. For example, given the alphabet $V = \{0, 1\}$, the following are valid sentences: $\{0, 1, 00, 01, 10, 11, 000, 001, \ldots\}$.

The sentence with no symbols is called the *empty sentence,* which we shall denote by λ. For an alphabet V, we will use V^* to denote the set of all sentences composed by symbols from V, including the empty sentence. The symbol V^+ will denote the set of sentences $V^* - \lambda$. For example, given the alphabet $V = \{a, b\}$, we have $V^* = \{\lambda, a, b, aa, ab, ba, \ldots\}$ and $V^* = \{a, b, aa, ab, ba, \ldots\}$.

A *language* is any set (not necessarily finite) of sentences over an alphabet.

As is true in natural languages, a serious study of formal language theory must be focused on grammars and their properties. We define a *formal string grammar* (or simply *grammar*) as the four-tuple $G = (N, \Sigma, P, S)$, where N is a set of *nonterminals* (variables); Σ is a set of terminals (constants); P is a set of productions or rewriting rules; and S is the *start* or *root* symbol. It is assumed that S belongs to the set N, and that N and Σ are disjoint sets. The alphabet V is the union of N and Σ. 🖋

The *language* generated by G, denoted by $L(G)$, is the set of strings that satisfy two conditions: (1) each string is composed only of terminals (i.e., each string is a *terminal* sentence), and (2) each string can be derived from S by suitable applications of productions from the set P.

The following notation will be used throughout this section. Nonterminals will be denoted by capital letters: $S, A, B, C, \ldots$. Lowercase letters at the beginning of the alphabet will be used for terminals: $a, b, c, \ldots$. Strings of terminals will be denoted by lowercase letters toward the end of the alphabet: $v, w, x, \ldots$. Strings of mixed terminals and nonterminals will be represented by lowercase Greek letters: $\alpha, \beta, \gamma, \delta, \ldots$.

The set P of productions consists of expressions of the form $\alpha \rightarrow \beta$, where α is a string in V^+ and β is a string in V^*. In other words, the symbol $\rightarrow$ indicates replacement of the string α by the string β. The symbol $\underset{}{\overset{}{\Rightarrow}}$ will be used to indicate operations of the form $\gamma\alpha\delta \underset{G}{\overset{}{\Rightarrow}} \gamma\beta\delta$ in the grammar G; that is, $\underset{G}{\overset{}{\Rightarrow}}$ indicates the replacement of α by β by means of the production $\alpha \rightarrow \beta$, γ and δ being left unchanged. It is customary to drop the G and simply use the symbol $\Rightarrow$ when it is clear which grammar is being considered.

Example: Consider the grammar $G = (N, \Sigma, P, S)$, where $N = \{S\}$, $\Sigma = \{a, b\}$ and $P = \{S \rightarrow aSb, S \rightarrow ab\}$. If the first production is applied $m - 1$ times, we obtain

$$S \Rightarrow aSb \Rightarrow aaSbb \Rightarrow a^3Sb^3 \Rightarrow \cdots a^{m-1}Sb^{m-1}.$$

Applying now the second production results in the string

$$a^{m-1}Sb^{m-1} \Rightarrow a^m b^m.$$

The language generated by this grammar is seen to consist solely of strings of this type, where the length of a particular string depends on m. We may express $L(G)$ in the form $L(G) = \{a^m b^m | m \geqslant 1\}$. Note that the simple grammar of this example is capable of producing a language with an infinite number of strings. $\Box$

Types of phrase structure grammars
Grammars of the form described above, in which the productions have the general form $\alpha \rightarrow \beta$, are called *phrase structure grammars*. It is common practice to categorize these grammars based on the type of restrictions placed on the productions.

A grammar in which the general form of productions $\alpha \rightarrow \beta$ (α in V^+ and β in V^*) is allowed is called an *unrestricted grammar*.

A *context-sensitive grammar* has productions of the form $\alpha_1 A \alpha_2 \rightarrow \alpha_1 \beta \alpha_2$, where α_1 and α_2 are in V^*, β is in V^+, and A is in N. This grammar allows replacement of the nonterminal A by the string β only when A appears in the context $\alpha_1 A \alpha_2$ of strings α_1 and α_2.

A *context-free grammar* has productions of the form $A \rightarrow \beta$, where A is in N and β is in V^+. The name "context free" arises from the fact that the variable A may be replaced by a string β regardless of the context in which A appears.

Finally, a *regular grammar* is one with productions of the form $A \rightarrow aB$ or $A \rightarrow a$, where A and B are variables in N and a is a terminal in Σ. Alternative valid productions are $A \rightarrow Ba$ and $A \rightarrow a$. However, once one of the two types has been chosen, the other set must be excluded.

These grammars are sometimes called *type* 0, 1, 2, and 3 *grammars*, respectively. It is interesting to note that all regular grammars are context free, all context-free grammars are context sensitive, and all context-sensitive grammars are unrestricted.

Although unrestricted grammars are considerably more powerful than the other three types, their generality presents some serious difficulties from both a theoretical and a practical point of view. To a large extent, this is also true of context-sensitive grammars. For these reasons, most of the work dealing with the use of grammatical concepts for image description and pattern recognition has been limited to context-free and regular grammars.

Example: The grammar given in the previous example is context free because its productions are of the form $S \rightarrow \beta_1$, and $S \rightarrow \beta_2$, with S being a single nonterminal and $\beta_1 = aSb$, $\beta_2 = ab$ being strings in V^+. It is interesting to note that the language generated by this context-free grammar, $L(G) = \{a^m b^m \mid m \geqslant 1\}$, cannot be generated by a regular grammar. In other words, the types of productions allowed under the definition of a regular grammar are not capable of generating *only* strings of the form $a^m b^m$. For instance, the regular grammar $G = (N, \Sigma, P, S)$, with $N = \{S\}$, $\Sigma = \{a, b\}$, $P = \{S \rightarrow aS, S \rightarrow bS, S \rightarrow a, S \rightarrow b\}$, can generate the strings $a^m b^m$, but it is also capable of generating other types of strings such as a^m and b^m. $\Box$

Use of positional operators

Since strings are one-dimensional structures, it is necessary when applying them to image description to establish an appropriate method for reducing two-dimensional positional relations to one-dimensional form.

Most applications of string grammars to image description are based on the idea of extracting connected line segments from the objects of interest. One approach is to follow the contour of an object and code the result with segments of specified direction and/or length. This procedure is illustrated in Fig. 8.30.

Another, somewhat more general, approach is to describe sections of an image (such as small homogeneous regions) by directed line segments, which can be joined in other ways besides head-to-tail connections. This approach is illustrated in Fig. 8.31(a); Fig. 8.31(b) shows some typical operations that can be defined on the extracted line segments.

The two approaches just described, although not exhaustive, are typical of procedures used for reducing two-dimensional information to string form. The following examples should further clarify these concepts.

Example: An interesting illustration of image description by boundary tracking is the grammar proposed by Ledley [1964, 1965] to characterize submedian and telocentric chromosomes. This grammar utilizes the primitive elements shown in Fig. 8.32(a), which are detected as a chromosome boundary is tracked in a clockwise direction. Typical submedian and telocentric chromosome shapes are shown in Fig. 8.32(b), along with the string representation obtained by tracking the boundary of each chromosome. The complete grammar is given by $G = (N, \Sigma, P, S)$, where $\Sigma = \{a, b, c, d, e\}$, $N = \{S, T, A, B, C, D, E, F\}$, and

$P:$

1) $S \rightarrow C \cdot C$	7) $E \rightarrow F \cdot c$	13) $B \rightarrow B \cdot b$
2) $T \rightarrow A \cdot C$	8) $D \rightarrow c \cdot F$	14) $B \rightarrow b$
3) $C \rightarrow B \cdot C$	9) $A \rightarrow b \cdot A$	15) $B \rightarrow d$
4) $C \rightarrow C \cdot B$	10) $A \rightarrow A \cdot b$	16) $F \rightarrow b \cdot F$
5) $C \rightarrow F \cdot D$	11) $A \rightarrow e$	17) $F \rightarrow F \cdot b$
6) $C \rightarrow E \cdot F$	12) $B \rightarrow b \cdot B$	18) $F \rightarrow a$

The operator "$\cdot$" is used to describe simple connectivity of the terms in a production as the boundary is tracked in a clockwise direction.   □

The above grammar is in reality a combination of two grammars with starting symbols S and T, respectively. Thus starting with S allows generation of structures that correspond to submedian chromosomes. Similarly, starting with T produces structures that correspond to telocentric chromosomes.

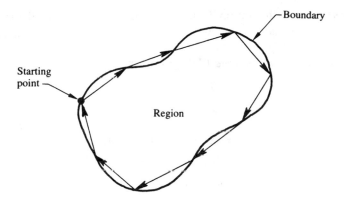

Figure 8.30 Coding a region boundary with directed line segments.

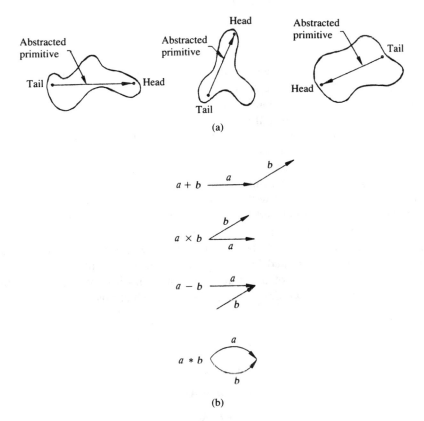

Figure 8.31 (a) Abstraction of regions by directed line segments. (b) Some operations involving the abstracted primitives.

Example: As a second illustration, let us discuss in some detail the Picture Description Language (PDL) proposed by Shaw [1970] for describing objects using operators of the form shown in Fig. 8.31(b).

Consider the following simple PDL grammar:

$$G = (N, \Sigma, P, S)$$

with

$$N = \{S, A_1, A_2, A_3, A_4, A_5\}$$
$$\Sigma = \{a\nearrow, b\searrow, c\rightarrow, d\downarrow\}$$

$$P: \quad S \rightarrow d + A_1$$
$$A_1 \rightarrow c + A_2$$
$$A_2 \rightarrow \sim d*A_3$$
$$A_3 \rightarrow a + A_4$$
$$A_4 \rightarrow b*A_5$$
$$A_5 \rightarrow c,$$

where $(\sim d)$ indicates the primitive d with its direction reversed, and a, b, c, and d are elements whose directions are shown in the set Σ.

Application of the first production yields a primitive d followed by a variable A_1 not yet defined. All we know at this point is that the tail of the structure represented by A_1 will be connected to the head of d because this primitive is followed by the $+$ operator. The variable A_1 resolves into $d + A_2$, where A_2 is not yet defined. Similarly, A_2 resolves into $\sim d*A_3$. The results of applying the first three productions are shown in Figs. 8.33(a), (b), and (c). From the definition of the operator $*$ we know that when A_3 is resolved it will be connected to the composite structure shown in Fig. 8.33(c) in a tail-to-tail and head-to-head manner. The final result obtained by applying all the productions is shown in Fig. 8.33(f).

The PDL grammar described above can generate only one structure. However, the scope of structures generated by this grammar can be extended by introducing recursiveness—the capability of a variable to replace itself—into the productions. For example, suppose that we define the following productions:

$$S \rightarrow d + A_1$$
$$A_1 \rightarrow c + A_1$$
$$A_1 \rightarrow \sim d*A_2$$
$$A_2 \rightarrow a + A_2$$
$$A_2 \rightarrow b*A_2$$
$$A_2 \rightarrow c$$

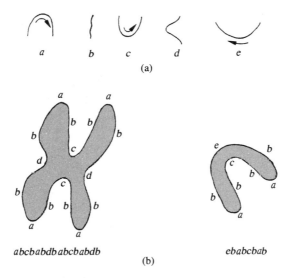

Figure 8.32 (a) Primitives of a chromosome grammar. (b) Submedian and telocentric chromosomes.
(From Ledley [1964].)

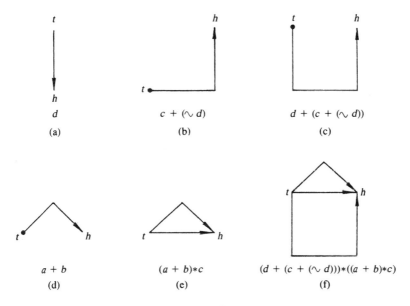

Figure 8.33 Steps in the construction of a PDL structure. Note the heads
and tails of composite structures.

If these productions were applied in the order shown, they would produce Fig. 8.33(f). However, this new set of productions allows, for instance, the application of the first production followed by the third, completely omitting the second production. If the remaining productions were applied in order, we would obtain a triangular structure. Furthermore, these productions allow the generation of infinite structures by repeated substitutions of a variable by itself. The variety of structures generated by the above grammar can be increased further by letting A_1 and A_2 equal S. This substitution would yield the maximum capability of this grammar. $\square$

8.5.2 Higher-Dimensional Grammars

The types of string grammars discussed in the previous section are best suited for applications where the connectivity of primitives can be expressed in a head-to-tail or other continuous manner. In this section we consider a more general approach to the grammatical description problem by allowing a higher level of primitive description capability. The grammars required to handle this added capability are, as should be expected, more complex and more difficult to analyze on a formal basis. As an illustration of these concepts, we consider below two typical generalizations of string grammars.

Tree grammars

A *tree T* is a finite set of one or more nodes such that

(1) there is a unique node designated the root; and

(2) the remaining nodes are partitioned into m disjointed sets $T_1, \ldots, T_m$, each of which in turn is a tree called a *subtree* of T.

The *tree frontier* is the set of nodes at the bottom of the tree (the *leaves*), taken in order from left to right. For example, the tree shown below has root $\$$ and frontier xy.

Generally, two types of information in a tree are important, namely: (1) information about a node stored as a set of words describing the node, and (2) information relating a node to its neighbors stored as a set of pointers to those neighbors. As used in image description, the first type of information identifies a pattern primitive, while the second type defines the physical relationship of the primitive to other substructures.

Example: The structure shown in Fig. 8.34(a) can be represented by a tree by using the relationship "inside of." Thus denoting the root of the tree by the symbol

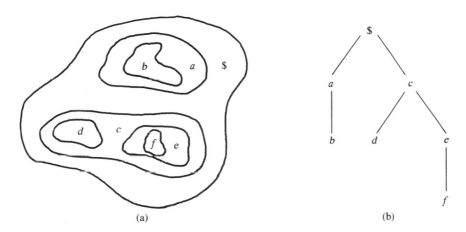

Figure 8.34   (a) A simple composite region. (b) Tree representation obtained by using the relationship "inside of."

$, we see from Fig. 8.34(a) that the first level of complexity involves a and c inside $. This produces two branches emanating from the root, as shown in Fig. 8.34(b). The next level involves b inside a and d and e inside c. Finally, we complete the tree by noting that f is inside e.   □

A *tree grammar* is defined as the five-tuple $G = (N, \Sigma, P, r, S)$, where N and Σ are, as before, sets of nonterminals and terminals, respectively; S is the start symbol, which can, in general, be a tree; P is a set of productions of the form $\Omega \to \Psi$, where Ω and Ψ are trees; and r is a *ranking function* that denotes the number of direct descendants of a node whose label is a terminal in the grammar.

The form of production $\Omega \to \Psi$ is analogous to that given for unrestricted string grammars and, as such, is usually too general to be of much practical use. A type of production that has found wide acceptance in the study of tree systems is an *expansive* production, which is of the form,

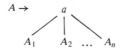

where $A, A_1, A_2, \ldots, A_n$ are nonterminals, and a is a terminal. A tree grammar that has only productions of this form is called an *expansive tree grammar*.

Example: As an illustration of a tree grammar, consider the circuit structure shown in Fig. 8.35(a). The tree representation shown in Fig. 8.35(b) was obtained by defining the root at the left-most node and using the relationship "connected to."

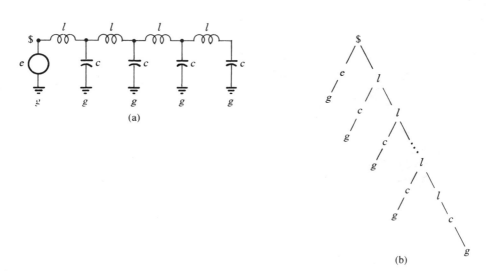

(a)

(b)

Figure 8.35   Tree representation of a connected figure.

A tree grammar that generates only trees of this form is given by $G = (N, \Sigma, P, r, S)$, where $N = \{S, A\}$, $\Sigma = \{e, g, l, c, \$\}$, and P is the following set of productions:

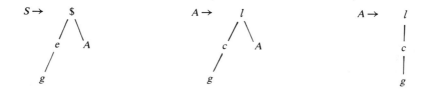

The ranking functions in this case are $r(e) = 1$, $r(g) = 0$, $r(l) = \{2, 1\}$, $r(c) = 1$, $r(\$) = 2$. Note that only three simple productions can generate an infinite number of structures by the recursiveness defined on A.

An expansive tree grammar that generates the same structures is given by $G = (N, \Sigma, P, r, S)$, where $N = \{S, A_1, A_2, A_3, A_4, A_5\}$, $\Sigma = \{e, g, l, c, \$\}$, and the set P consists of the following productions:

$$A_3 \rightarrow c \qquad\qquad A_5 \rightarrow g \qquad\qquad A_2 \rightarrow l$$

$$A_5 \qquad\qquad\qquad\qquad\qquad\qquad\qquad A_3$$

The ranking functions are $r(e) = 1$, $r(g) = 0$, $r(l) = \{1, 2\}$, $r(c) = 1$, $r(\$) = 2$.

$\square$

Web grammars

As illustrated in Fig. 8.36, webs are undirected graph structures whose nodes are labeled. When used for image description, webs allow representations at a level considerably more abstract than that afforded by string or tree formalisms.

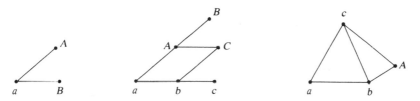

Figure 8.36 Some simple webs.

In a conventional phrase-structure string grammar rewriting rules of the form $\alpha \rightarrow \beta$ are used to replace one string by another. Such a rule is completely specified by specifying strings α and β; any string $\gamma\alpha\delta$ that contains α as a substring can immediately be rewritten as $\gamma\beta\delta$. Similarly, the productions of expansive tree grammars are interpreted without difficulty. The definition of rewriting rules involving webs, however, is much more complicated. Thus if we want to replace a subweb α of the web ω by another subweb β, it is necessary to specify how to *embed* β in ω in place of α. As will be seen below this can be done by using embedding rules. An important point, however, is that the definition of an embedding rule must not depend on the "host web" ω because we want to be able to replace α by β in any web containing α as a subweb.

Let V be a set of labels and N_α and N_β the set of nodes of webs α and β, respectively. Based on the above concepts we define a *web rewriting rule* as a triplet (α, β, ϕ), where ϕ is a function from $N_\beta \times N_\alpha^\dagger$ into 2^V (the set of subsets of labels). This function specifies the embedding of β in place of α; that is, it specifies how to join to nodes of β to the neighbors of each node of the *removed* subweb α. Since ϕ is a function from the set of ordered pairs $N_\beta \times N_\alpha$, its argument is of the form (n, m), for n in N_β, and m in N_α. The values of $\phi(n,m)$ specify the allowed connections of n to the neighbors of m. For example, $\phi(B, A) = \{C, D\}$ means "join node B (in β) to the neighbors of node A (in α) whose labels are

---

† The symbol $\times$ is used in this context to denote the cartesian product of the sets N_β and N_α (i.e., the set of ordered pairs (n, m) such that n is an element of N_β and m is an element of N_α).

either C or D." We will omit the embedding specification and instead use the term "normal" to denote situations in which there is no ambiguity in a rewriting rule.

A *web grammar* is defined as a four-tuple $G = (N, \Sigma, P, S)$ where N is the nonterminal vocabulary, Σ is the terminal vocabulary, P is a set of web productions, and S is the starting symbol. As usual, S is in N, and the vocabulary V is the union of N and Σ.

Example: Consider the web grammar $G = (N, \Sigma, P, S)$, where

$$N = \{S\},$$

$$\Sigma = \{a, b, c\}, \text{ and}$$

$$P \text{ is the following set of triplets}$$

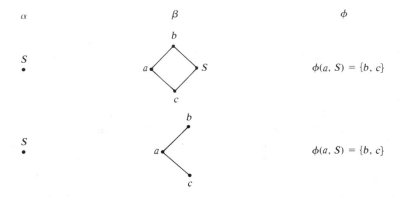

The embedding specified by ϕ indicates that α ($\alpha = S$ in this case) can be rewritten as β by connecting node a of β to the neighbors of S labeled b and c. Note that the rule does not apply in this case to the first execution of a production because the generation starts with a single point web without neighbors. In situations like this, it will be implicitly understood that ϕ is null for the first application of the production, and that the embedding rule describes replacements during the course of a derivation in which the subweb to be rewritten is embedded in a host web.

It is easily verified that this web grammar produces structures of the form

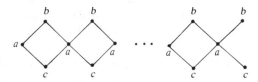

The above definition of a web grammar is analogous to that of an unrestricted string grammar and, as such, is too broad to be of much practical use. As in the case of string grammars, however, it is possible to define restricted types of web grammars by limiting the generality of the productions.

We shall call a web rewriting rule (α, β, ϕ) *context sensitive* if there exists a nonterminal point A of α such that $(\alpha - A)$ is a subweb of β. In this case the rule rewrites only a single point of α, regardless of how complex α is. If α contains a single point, we will call (α, β, ϕ) a *context-free* rule. Note that this is a special case of a context-sensitive rule since $(\alpha - A)$ is empty when α contains a single point. By representing strings as webs (e.g., the string $aAbc \ . \ . \ .$ may be expressed as the web $\overset{a}{\bullet} \to \overset{A}{\bullet} \to \overset{b}{\bullet} \to \overset{c}{\bullet} \to \ . \ . \ .$) it is easily shown that the above rewriting rules are analogous to context-sensitive and context-free string productions, as defined in Section 8.5.1.

If the terminal vocabulary of a web grammar consists of a single symbol, every point of every web generated by the grammar will have the same label. In this case we can ignore the labels and identify the webs by their underlying graphs. This special type of web grammar is sometimes referred to as a *graph grammar*.

Example: Consider the context-sensitive graph grammar $G = (N, \Sigma, P, S)$, where

$$N = \{A, B, C, S\}$$

$$\Sigma = \{a\}, \text{ and}$$

P is the following set of triplets:

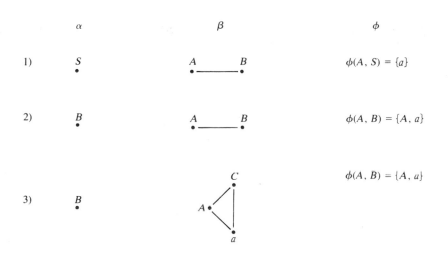

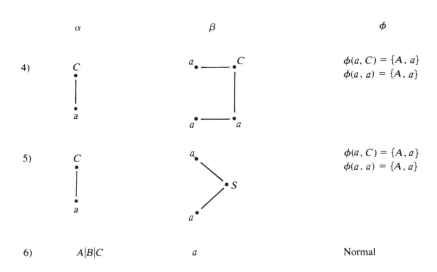

	α	β	φ
4)	C〔 a	a —— C 〔 a —— a	$\phi(a, C) = \{A, a\}$ $\phi(a, a) = \{A, a\}$
5)	C〔 a	a⟩S a	$\phi(a, C) = \{A, a\}$ $\phi(a, a) = \{A, a\}$
6)	$A\|B\|C$	a	Normal

This grammar generates graph structures that consist of an arbitrary number of series and parallel sections. The parallel segments are separated by at least one series element, and all structures begin and end with at least one such element. Two simple derivations are as follows:

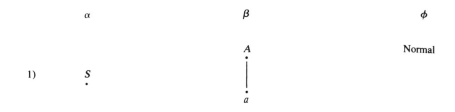

As in the previous example, the single terminal a has been omitted from the final patterns. ☐

Example: The following context-sensitive web grammar generates some simple geometrical figures: $G = (N, \Sigma, P, S)$, where

$$N = \{S, A, B\}$$
$$\Sigma = \{a, b, c\}, \text{ and}$$

P is the following set of triplets:

	α	β	φ
			Normal
1)	S	A 〔 a	

	α	β	ϕ

2) A
    •
    ⋮
    •
    a

    b •——• A
    | |
    a •——• a

    $\phi(b, A) = \{b, a\}$
    $\phi(a, a) = \text{Normal}$

3) b •———• A

    b •——• A
    | |
    b • • a

    $\psi(a, A) = \{b, a\}$
    $\phi(b, b) = \text{Normal}$

4) A
    •
    ⋮
    •
    a

    b •——• b
    | |
    a •——• B

    $\phi(b, A) = \{b, a\}$
    $\phi(a, a) = \text{Normal}$

5) a •———• B

    a •——• b
    | |
    a •——• B

    $\phi(b, B) = \{b, a\}$
    $\phi(a, a) = \text{Normal}$

6) b
    •
    ⋮
    •
    B

    b •——• A
    | |
    a •——• a

    $\phi(a, B) = \{b, a\}$
    $\phi(b, b) = \text{Normal}$

7) A

    b

    Normal

8) B

    a

    Normal

As an example, consider the following derivation:

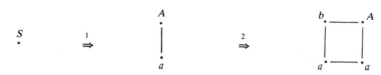

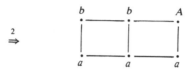

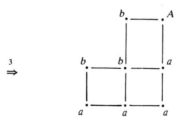

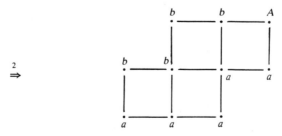

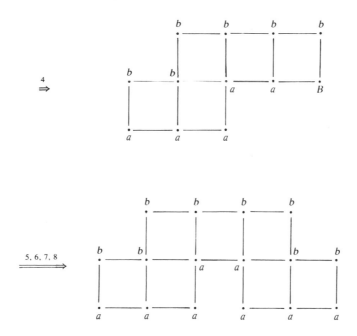

Note that the upper edge of the structure is labeled with bs and the lower edge with as. The structures generated by this grammar, all of which share this property, consist of the set of geometrical structures that can be drawn by stacking squares to the right, above, or below the previously drawn square. Also note that a transition upward or downward can be made only from a square that was drawn to the right. ☐

8.6 CONCLUDING REMARKS

The representation and description of objects or regions that have been segmented out of an image are early steps in the operation of most automated image-analysis systems. As indicated by the range of description techniques covered in this chapter, the choice of one description method over another is dictated by the problem under consideration. The objective is to choose descriptors that "capture" essential differences between objects, or classes of objects, while maintaining as much independence as possible to changes in factors such as location, size, and orientation.

Although we have concluded our treatment of digital image processing by discussing representation and description, the reader should bear in mind that, as mentioned above, these are preliminary processes in automated image analysis. Methods for performing this type of analysis are beyond the scope of this book, being topics of books dedicated to this subject matter. As an introduction to this area, the reader is referred to the representative books by Duda and Hart [1973], Tou and Gonzalez

[1974], Gonzalez and Thomason [1978], Ballard and Brown [1982], Fu [1982], Horn [1986] and Fu, Gonzalez, and Lee [1987].

REFERENCES

The chain-code representation discussed in Section 8.1.1 was first proposed by Freeman [1961, 1974]. Further reading on polygonal approximations may be found in the paper by Sklansky *et al.* [1972] and in the book by Pavlidis [1977]. References for our discussion on signatures are Ambler *et al.* [1975], Nahim [1974], and Ballard and Brown [1982]. The skeletonizing algorithm discussed in Section 8.1.5 is from Zhang and Suen [1984]. Some useful additional comments on the properties and implementation of this algorithm may be found in a paper by Lu and Wang [1986].

For additional reading on the material in Section 8.2.1 see Rosenfeld and Kak [1982]. The discussion on shape numbers is based on the work of Bribiesca and Guzman [1980] and Bribiesca [1981]. The material in Section 8.2.3 was contributed by T. Wallace (Electrical Engineering Department, Purdue University). See also the papers by Brill [1968], Zahn and Roskies [1972], and Persoon and Fu [1977]. The material in Section 8.2.4 is based on elementary probability theory.

Additional details on the material in Sections 8.3.1 and 8.3.2 may be found in Duda and Hart [1973] and in Ballard and Brown [1982]. Texture descriptors have received a great deal of attention in the past few years. For further reading on the statistical aspects of texture see Haralick *et al.* [1973], Bajcsy and Lieberman [1976], Haralick [1979], and Cross and Jain [1983]. On structural texture, see Lu and Fu [1978], and Tomita *et al.* [1982]. Our discussion on spectral techniques for texture analysis is based on an early paper by Bajcsy [1973]. The moment-invariant approach discussed in Section 8.3.4 is due to Hu [1962]. Additional reading on this topic may be found in Bell [1965] and Wong and Hall [1978].

The material in Section 8.4.1 is based on a similar discussion by Tou and Gonzalez [1974]. For additional details on correlation see Horowitz [1957], Harris [1964], Anuta [1969], Pratt [1974], and Rosenfeld and Kak [1982]. The boundary matching approach discussed in Section 8.4.3 is from Sze and Yang [1981]. Additional details on the material in Section 8.5 may be found in the books by Gonzalez and Thomason [1978], and by Fu [1982].

PROBLEMS

8.1 a) Show that redefining the starting point of a chain code so that the resulting sequence of numbers forms an integer of minimum magnitude makes the code independent of where one initially starts on the boundary.

    b) Find the normalized starting point of the code 11076765543322.

8.2 a) Show that the first difference of a chain code normalizes it to rotation, as explained in Section 8.1.1.

    b) Compute the first difference of the code 0101030303323232212111.

8.3 a) Show that the rubber-band polygonal approximation approach discussed in Section 8.1.2 yields a polygon with minimum perimeter.

    b) Show that if each cell corresponds to a pixel on the boundary, then the maximum possible error in that cell is $\sqrt{2}d$, where d is the grid distance between pixels.

8.4 **a)** Discuss the effect on the resulting polygon if the error threshold is set to zero in the merging method discussed in Section 8.1.2.

b) What would be the effect on the splitting method?

8.5 (a) Plot the signature of a square boundary using the tangent angle method discussed in Section 8.1.3. (b) Repeat for the slope density function. Assume that the square is aligned with the x and y axes, and let the x axis be the reference line. Start at the corner closest to the origin.

8.6 Find the medial axis of (a) a circle, (b) a square, and (c) an equilateral triangle.

8.7 (a) For each of the figures shown below, discuss the action taken at point p by Step 1 of the thinning algorithm presented in Section 8.1.5. (b) Repeat for Step 2. Assume that $p = 1$ in all cases.

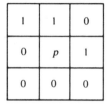

8.8 **a)** What is the order of the shape number for the figure shown below?

b) Obtain the shape number.

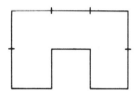

8.9 The procedure discussed in Section 8.2.3 for using Fourier descriptors consists of expressing the coordinates of a contour as complex numbers, taking the DFT of these numbers, and keeping only a few components of the DFT as descriptors of the boundary shape. The inverse DFT is then an approximation to the original contour. What class of contour shapes would have a DFT consisting of real numbers and how would the axis system in Fig. 8.14 have to be set up to obtain these real numbers?

8.10 Give the fewest number of moment descriptors needed to differentiate between the signatures of the figures shown in Fig. 8.5.

8.11 Find the Euler number of the characters 0, 1, 8, 9, and X.

8.12 It is desired to design an image processing system for detecting imperfections on the inside of certain solid plastic wafers. The wafers are examined by means of a low-energy x-ray imaging system, which yields images of 512 × 512 resolution with 8 bits per pixel. In the absence of imperfections, the images appear "bland," having a mean gray level of 100 with a noise variance of 400. The imperfections appear as bloblike regions in which the pixels have excursions in intensity of 50 gray levels or more about a mean of 100. A wafer is considered defective if such a region occupies an area exceeding 20×20 pixels in size. Propose an approach for solving this problem utilizing texture analysis.

8.13 Obtain the gray-level co-occurrence matrix of a 5×5 image composed of a checkerboard of alternating 1s and 0s if (a) the position operator P is defined as "one pixel to the right," and (b) "two pixels to the right." Assume that the top, left pixel has value 0.

8.14 Consider a checkerboard image composed of alternating black and white squares, each of size $m \times m$. Give a position operator that would yield a diagonal co-occurrence matrix.

8.15 An alternative to Eq. (8.4-2) is to use a function of the form $d_k(\mathbf{x}) = \mathbf{x}'\mathbf{x}_k - \frac{1}{2} \mathbf{x}_k'\mathbf{x}_k$. Then, we say that $\mathbf{x}$ is more similar to $\mathbf{x}_i$ if $d_i(\mathbf{x}) > d_j(\mathbf{x})$, $j = 1, 2, \ldots, L, j \neq i$. Show that performing decisions in this way is equivalent to implementing Eq. (8.4-2).

8.16 Show that the correlation coefficient given in Eq. (8.4-4) has values in the range $[-1, 1]$. (*Hint:* Express $r(m, n)$ in vector form.)

8.17 Show that $B = \max(|C_1|, |C_2|) - A$ in Eq. (8.4-5) is zero if and only if C_1 and C_2 are identical strings.

8.18 Give an expansive tree grammar for generating images consisting of alternating 1s and 0s in both spatial directions (i.e., a checkerboard pattern). Assume that the top, left element is a 1, and that all images terminate with a 1 as the bottom, left element.

IMAGE
DISPLAY
SUBROUTINES

This appendix contains two FORTRAN subroutines used for displaying image data of size 64 × 64 on a single sheet of line-printer paper. As discussed in Appendix B, the images included in that appendix are coded with the characters 0 through 9 and A through V to represent 32 gray levels. Once these characters have been read into an array denoted by AR, they have to be converted to an integer array, called IA, whose values range from 0 through 31. This conversion is accomplished by Subroutine CONVRT(AR), which is listed below. Note that the only parameter passed to this subroutine is the character array AR, which must be set up as CHARACTER*1 AR(64, 64) in the calling program. The output of this subroutine is integer array IA, which resides as COMMON IA(64, 64), INTEGER*2 IA, in all programs.

```
      SUBROUTINE CONVRT(AR)
C
C
C         THIS SUBROUTINE CONVERTS CHARACTER DATA RANGING FROM 0
C    TO 9 AND A TO V STORED IN ARRAY "AR" TO INTEGER DATA RANGING
C    FROM 0 TO 31, REPRESENTING THE SHADES OF GRAY.  THE INTEGER
C    DATA IS STORED IN ARRAY "IA".
C
C    MAJOR VARIABLES:
C
C         IA    ---     INTEGER ARRAY CONTAINING VALUES RANGING FROM
C                       0 TO 31 REPRESENTING THE SHADES OF GRAY.
```

```
C          AR   ---      CHARACTER ARRAY CONTAINING VALUES RANGING
C                        FROM 0 THROUGH 9 AND A THROUGH V WHICH
C                        CORRESPOND TO THE THIRTY-TWO GRAY LEVELS.
C
C          SUBPROGRAMS CALLED:      NONE
C
C          WRITTEN BY:
C                            NABEEL W. H. SUFI
C                        ELECTRICAL ENGINEERING DEPT.,
C                      UNIVERSITY OF TENNESSEE, KNOXVILLE
C
           COMMON IA(64,64)
           INTEGER*2 IA
           INTEGER I, J
           CHARACTER*1 AR(64,64)
C
C    LOOP THROUGH EACH ELEMENT OF 64*64 ARRAY
C
           DO 20 I=1,64
             DO 40 J= 1,64
C
C    CHECK IF THE CHARACTER IS BETWEEN 0 AND 9
C
               IF ((AR(I,J).GE. '0').AND.(AR(I,J).LE. '9')) THEN
                  IA(I,J)=ICHAR(AR(I,J)(AR(I,J)) -ICHAR('0')
C
C    IF CHARACTER IS NOT BETWEEN 0 AND 9 THEN
C    IT MUST BE BETWEEN A AND V BY DEFAULT
C
               ELSE
                  IA(I,J)=ICHAR(AR(I,J))-ICHAR('A')+10
               ENDIF
  40         CONTINUE
  20       CONTINUE
C
           RETURN
           END
```

The subroutine actually used to display images on a line printer is subroutine DSP, which converts the integer values in array IA to gray levels by overstriking characters on a line printer, as discussed below. Subroutine DSP is called as follows:

CALL DSP(NX,NY,LAW,IL,IH,NEG,LG)

The arguments are:

NX—Number of rows of IA to be printed; maximum NX is 64.
NY—Number of columns of IA to be printed; maximum NY is 64. If NX = NY = 64 a full page is output.
LAW—Gray-level scale translation variable.
LAW = 1: linear scale,
LAW = 2: square-root scale,

LAW = 3: logarithmic scale,
LAW = 4: "absorption" scale.
IL—minimum gray level in IA, calculated in the calling program.
IH—maximum gray level in IA, calculated in the calling program.
NEG—a value equal to 1 gives the normal image; a value equal to 0 gives
the negative of the image.
LG—logical unit number for the line printer.

The characters used in the program to obtain the 32 gray levels are shown in Fig.
A.1. The characters in a column, when over-printed, produce the gray level indicated.

```
MMMMMMHHHHHXHXOZWMNOS=I*++=:-.-
WWWWWW###*++----        =   -    -
####OO+-
OOO
+
```

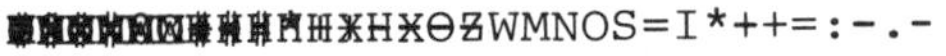

■■■■■■■■###■#XHXOZWMNOS=I*++=:-.-   Gray levels

Figure A.1 Over-print characters used to obtain 32 gray
levels. The 32nd character is a blank.

```
      SUBROUTINE DSP(NX,NY,LAW,IL,IH,NEG,LG)
C
C     **LINE PRINTER IMAGE OUTPUT SUBROUTINE**
C
C     ADAPTED BY B. A. FITTES, ELECTRICAL ENG.
C     DEPT., UNIVERSITY OF TENNESSEE, FROM
C     A PROGRAM WRITTEN BY J. L. BLANKENSHIP,
C     INSTRUMENTATION AND CONTROLS DIV., OAK
C     RIDGE NATIONAL LABORATORY, OAK RIDGE,
C     TN.  THE OVERPRINT METHOD USED IS FROM
C     "CONSIDERATIONS FOR EFFICIENT PICTURE
C     OUTPUT VIA LINE PRINTER," BY P. HENDERSON
C     AND S. TANIMOTO, REPORT NO. 153, 1974,
C     COMPUTER SCIENCE LAB., ELEC. ENG. DEPT.,
C     PRINCETON UNIVERSITY.
      COMMON IA(64,64)
      INTEGER*2 IA
      INTEGER*2 IB(64,64),LEV(32),BLANK(5)
```

```
        LOGICAL*1 LINE(128,5),GRAY(32,5)
C       SPECIFY GRAY-LEVEL CHARACTERS
        DATA GRAY /6*'M',5*'H','X','H','X','O',
      1 'Z','W','M','N','O','S','=','I','*','+',
      2 '+','=',':','-','.','-',' ',6*'W',3*'#',
      3 '*','+','+',4*'-',5*' ','=',' ',' ',' ','-',
      4 3*' ','-',3*' ',4*'#','O','O','+','-',
      5 24*' ','O','O','O',29*' ','+',31*' '/
        GN=32.0
        FL=IL
        FH=IH
        IF ((FH-FL).GT.0.0) GO TO 100
        T=FL
        FL=FH
        FH=T
  100   RANGE=(FH-FL+1)/GN
        AA=(SQRT(FH)-SQRT(FL))/GN
        EE=(FH-FL)/ALOG(GN+1.0)
        T=AMAX1(FL,1.0)
        SS=-(1.0/GN)*ALOG(FH/T)
C
C
C       A VECTOR LEV IS COMPUTED NEXT.   THIS
C       VECTOR IS A SET OF BREAK POINTS USED TO
C       DETERMINE THE SCALED VALUE OF IA(I,J).
C       THE MATRIX IB IS THE RESULT OF SCALING
C       IA.   IB(I,J)=K IF IA(I,J) IS LESS THAN
C       LEV(K+1) BUT GREATER THAN OR EQUAL TO
C       LEV(K).
C
        DO 160 I=1,32
        GO TO (110,120,130,140),LAW
  110   FLEV=FL+(I-1)*RANGE+0.5
        GO TO 150
  120   FLEV=(SQRT(FL)+(I-1)*AA)**2+0.5
        GO TO 150
  130   FLEV=FL+EE*ALOG(FLOAT(I))+0.5
        GO TO 150
  140   FLEV=FH*EXP(SS*(GN-I))+0.5
  150   LEV(I)=FLEV
  160   CONTINUE
        IF (NX.GT.64) NX=64
        IF (NY.GT.64) NY=64
        DO 180 I=1,NX
        DO 180 J=1,NY
        KLT=1
        DO 170 K=1,32
```

```
          IF (IA(I,J).GE.LEV(K)) KLT=K
   170 CONTINUE
          IB(1,J)=KLT
   180 CONTINUE
C
C
C         ONCE IB HAS BEEN COMPUTED, THE PICTURE CAN
C         BE PRINTED.   EACH POINT IN THE PICTURE CAN
C         CONSIST OF UP TO FIVE CHARACTERS OVERPRINTED
C         ON ONE ANOTHER.   SINCE THERE ARE 32 POSSIBLE
C         GRAY LEVELS, THERE IS A 32X5 MATRIX, GRAY,
C         THAT CONTAINS ALL OF THE COMBINATIONS.  SINCE
C         EACH ELEMENT OF IB IS AN INTEGER BETWEEN
C         1 AND 32, IT CAN BE USED AS AN INDEX ON
C         GRAY TO OBTAIN THE CORRECT COMBINATION.
C         THE OUTPUT BUFFER, LINE, IS A 128X5 MATRIX.
C         EACH POINT IS OUTPUT TWICE HORIZONTALLY AND
C         ONCE VERTICALLY TO ATTEMPT TO COMPENSATE
C         FOR THE SPACING OF THE PRINTER.  HENCE, THE
C         FULL OUTPUT BUFFER REPRESENTS ONE ROW OF IB.
C         AS THE ROW IS GENERATED THERE IS A VECTOR,
C         BLANK, THAT INDICATES WHETHER OR NOT ANY
C         NON-BLANK CHARACTERS ARE PRESENT IN THE
C         BUFFER.  IF THERE ARE NOT ANY, THAT ROW IS
C         NOT PRINTED.   THIS SPEEDS UP THE PRINTING
C         PROCESS.
C
          WRITE(LG,1)
          IX=NX
          IY=2*NY
          DO 210 I=1,IX
          DO 190 J=1,5
          BLANK(J)=0
   190 CONTINUE
          DO 200 K=2,IY,2
          J=K/2
          NG=IB(I,J)
          IF (NEG.EQ.0) NG=33-NG
          DO 200 L=1,5
          LINE(K-1,L)=GRAY(NG,L)
          LINE(K,L)=GRAY(NG,L)
          IF (NG.NE.32) BLANK(L)=1
   200 CONTINUE
          WRITE (LG,2)
          DO 210 L=1,5
          IF (BLANK(L).EQ.0) GO TO 210
          WRITE (LG,3) (LINE(M,L), M=1,IY)
   210 CONTINUE
     1 FORMAT (1H1)
     2 FORMAT (1H )
     3 FORMAT (1H+,3X,128A1)
          RETURN
          END
```

CODED
IMAGES

The following 64 × 64, 32-level images can be used as test data for many of the image-processing concepts developed in the text. Along with each image is shown a coded array that contains an alphanumeric character for each pixel in the image. The range of these characters is from 0 through 9 and A through V, which corresponds to 32 gray levels. The first step after reading the coded image into a computer is to convert the alphanumeric characters into numerical levels in the range 0 to 31 using the routine given in Appendix A. The resulting numerical array can be used in its original form or it can be corrupted by, for example, adding noise to each pixel. This flexibility allows generation of a variety of input data that can be used to illustrate the effects of image-processing algorithms. The results before and after processing can be displayed on a standard line printer by using the subroutine DSP given in Appendix. A. When using this routine, the gray-tone images may look slightly different from the ones shown in the following pages, depending on the type of line printer used.

Figure B.1 Mona Lisa.

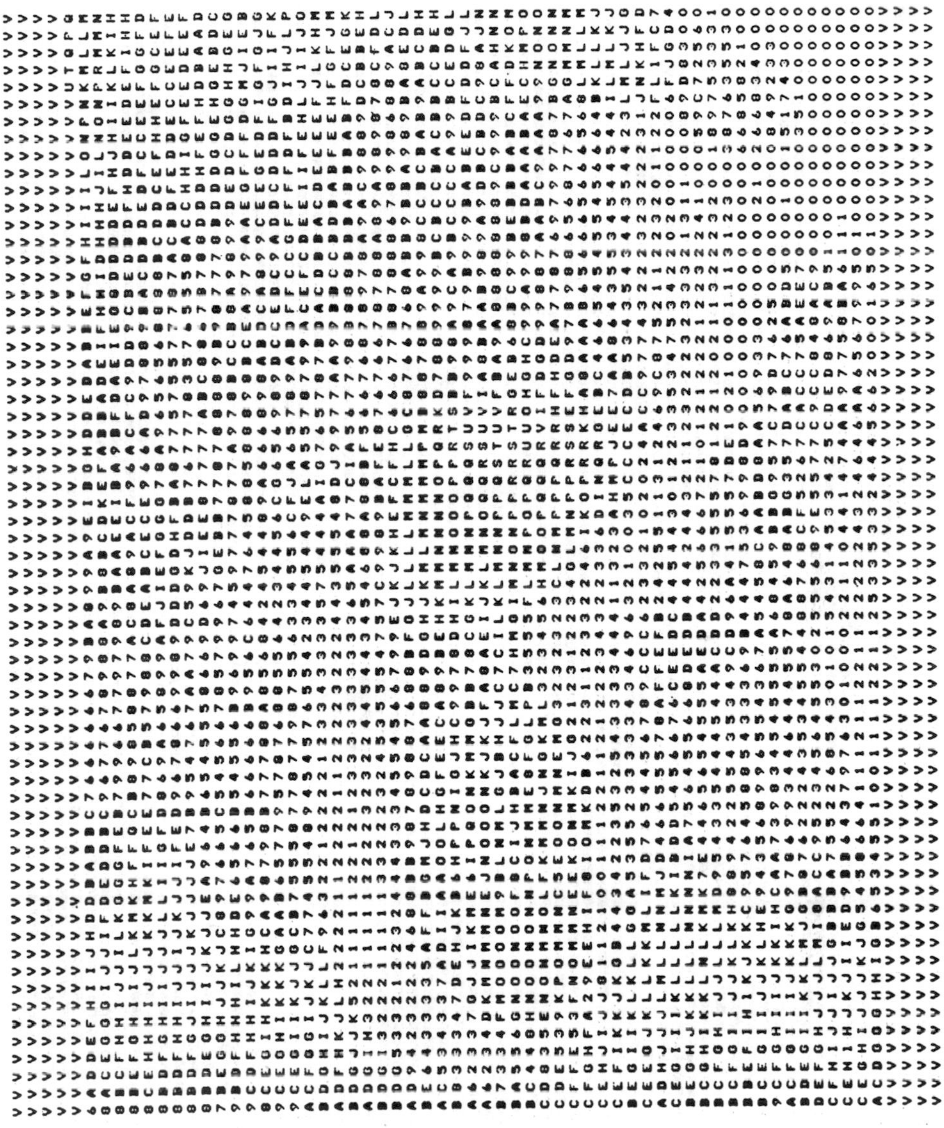

Figure B.2 Coded Mona Lisa.

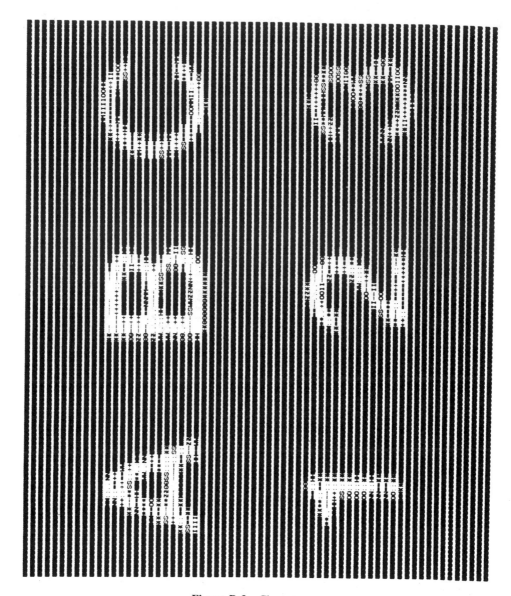

Figure B.3   Characters.

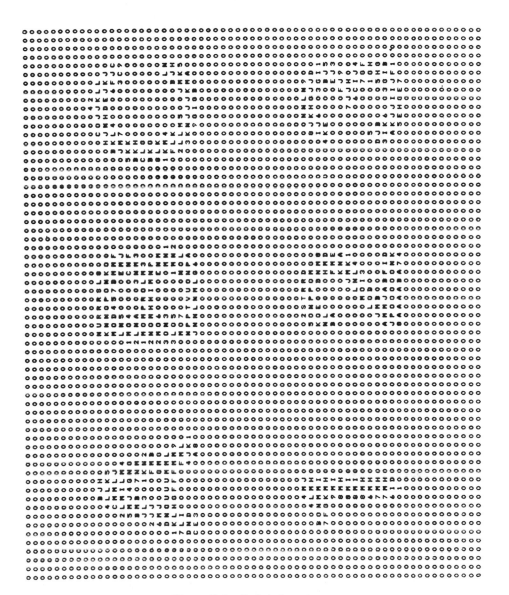

Figure B.4   Coded characters.

Figure B.5   Jet.

Figure B.6   Coded jet.

Figure B.7   Lincoln.

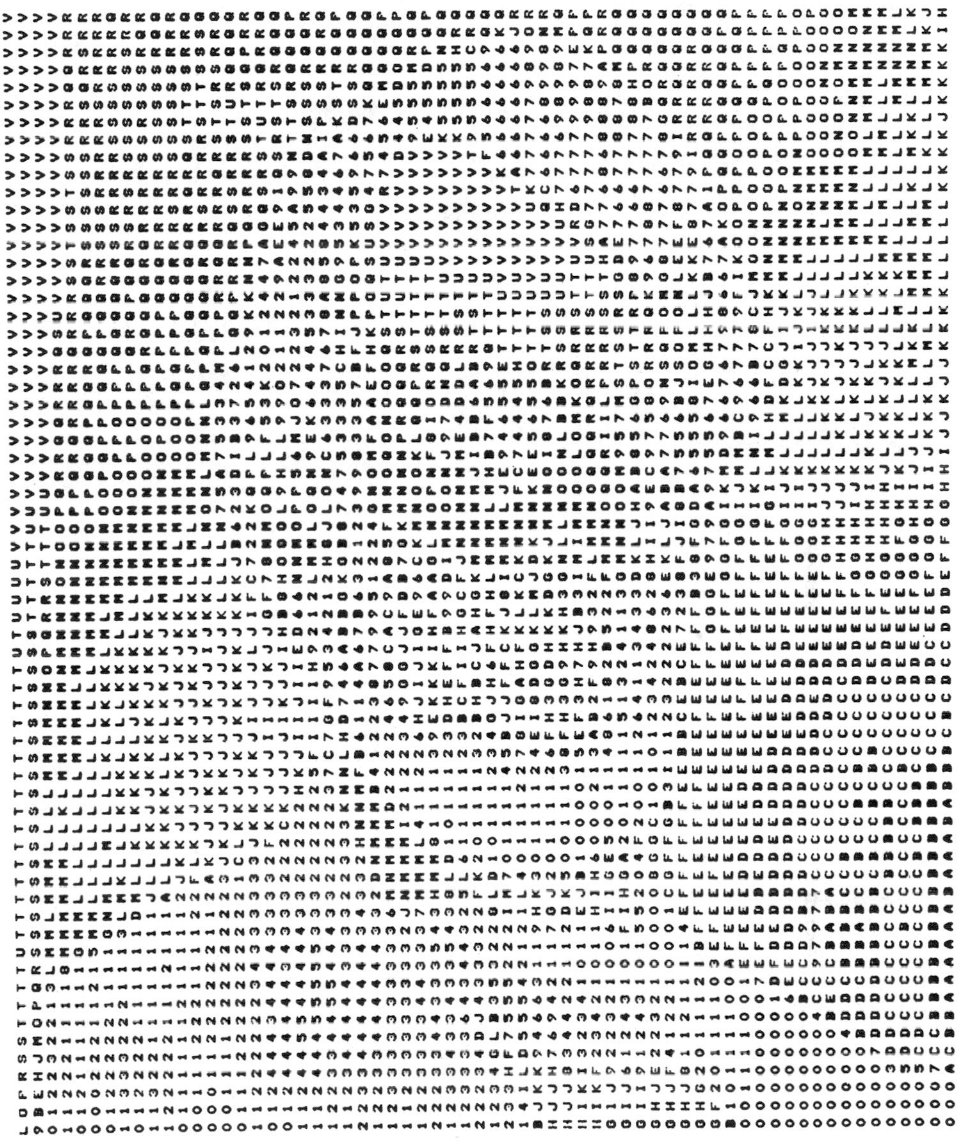

Figure B.8 Coded Lincoln.

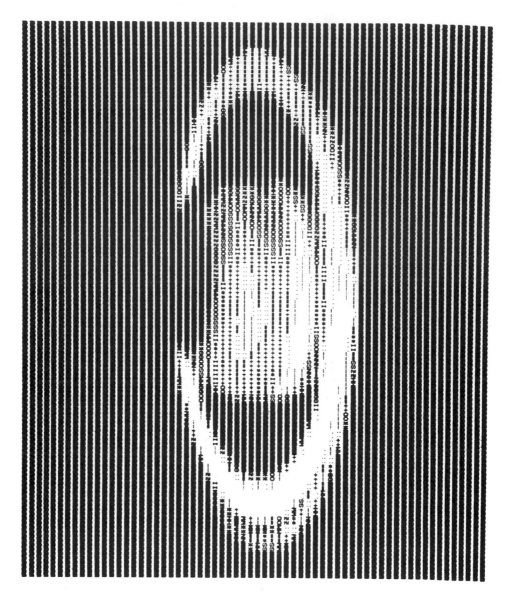

Figure B.9   Saturn.

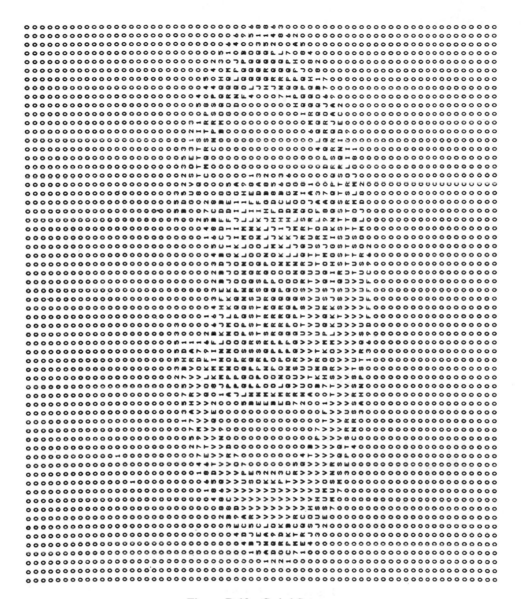

Figure B.10 Coded Saturn.

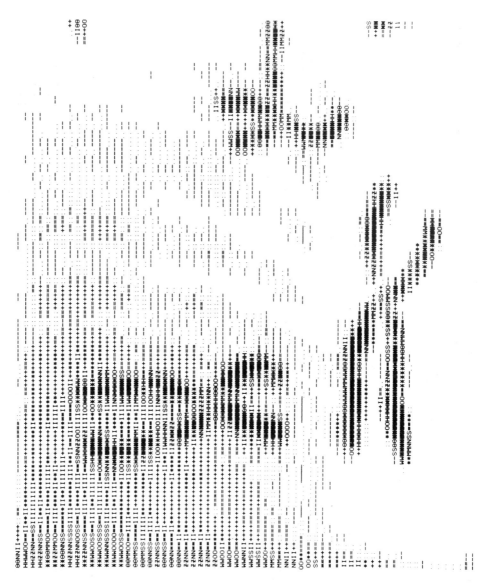

Figure B.11   Chromosomes.

Figure B.12 Coded chromosomes.

Figure B.13 Fingerprint.

Figure B.14 Coded fingerprint.

Figure B.15   Statue of Liberty.

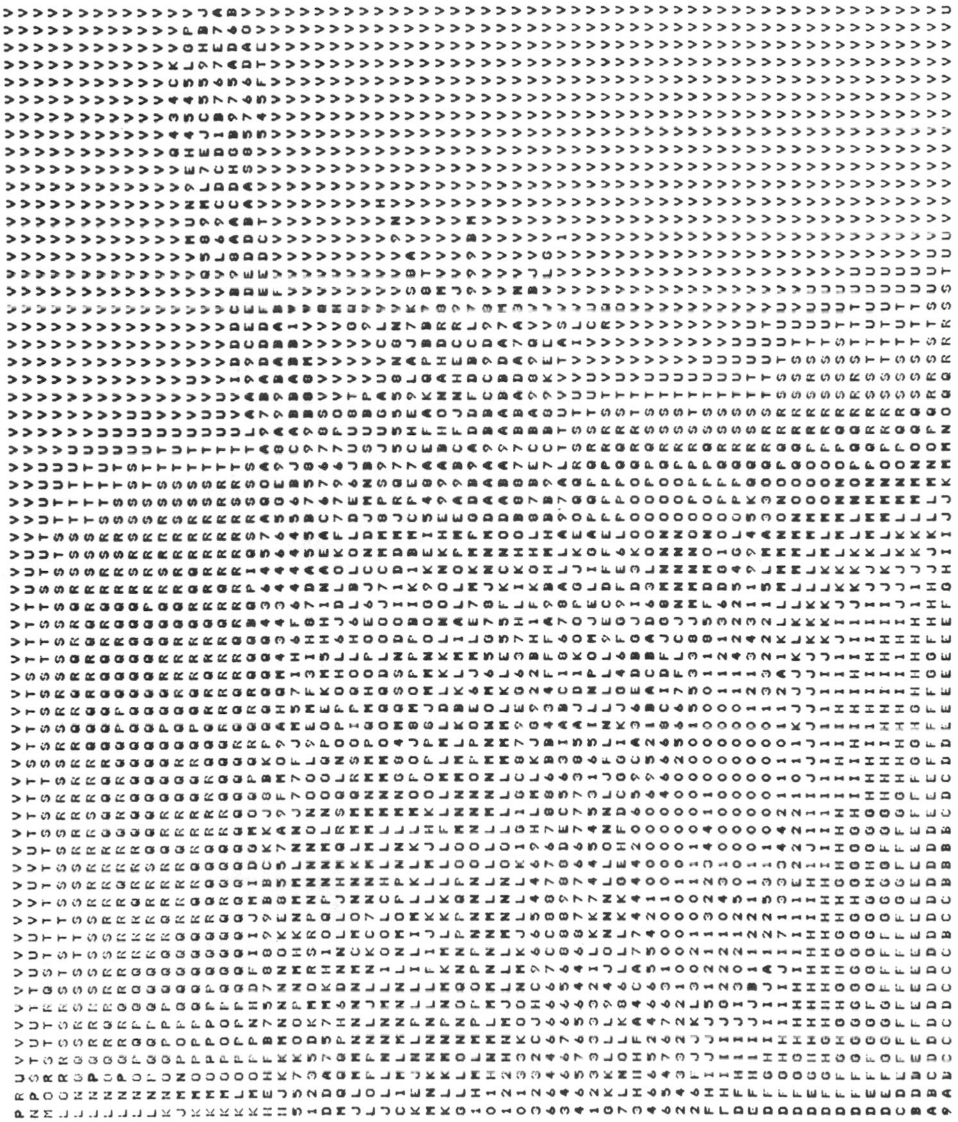

Figure B.16   Coded Statue of Liberty.

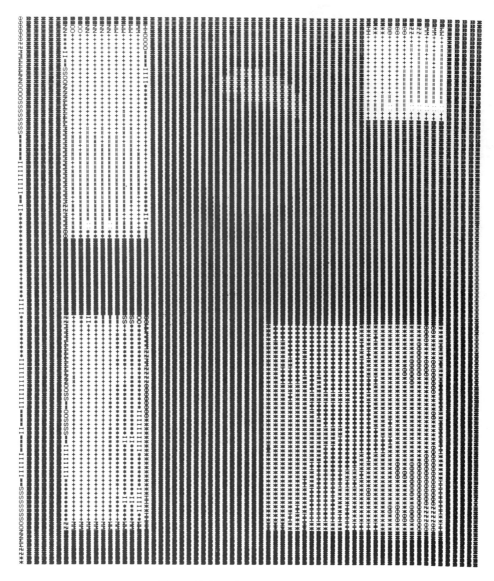

Figure B.17 Geometrical figures.

Figure B.18 Coded geometrical figures.

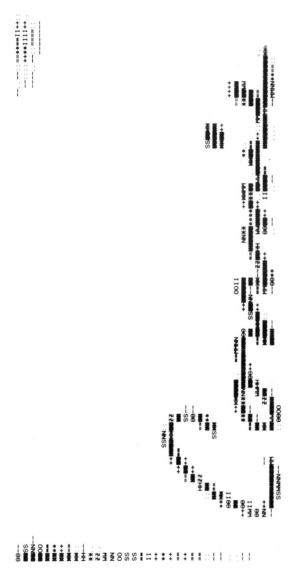

Figure B.19   Word.

Figure B.20   Coded word.

Figure B.21   Boy.

Figure B.22 Coded boy.

Figure B.23   Biplane.

Figure B.24 Coded biplane.

BIBLIOGRAPHY

Abramson, A. [1963]. *Information Theory and Coding,* McGraw-Hill, New York.

Adiv, G. [1985]. "Determining Three-Dimensional Motion and Structure from Optical Flow Generated by Several Moving Objects." *IEEE Trans. Pattern Anal. Mach. Intell.,* vol. PAMI-7, no. 4, pp. 384–401.

Aggarwal, J.K. and Badler, N.I., eds. [1980]. "Motion and Time-Varying Imagery." *IEEE Trans. Pattern Anal. Mach. Intell.,* Special Issue, vol. PAMI-2, no. 6, pp. 493–588.

Ahmed, N., Natarajan, T., and Rao, K.R. [1974]. "Discrete Cosine Transforms." *IEEE Trans. Comp.,* vol. C-23, pp. 90–93.

Ahmed, N. and Rao, K.R. [1975]. *Orthogonal Transforms for Digital Signal Processing,* Springer-Verlag, New York.

Ambler, A.P., *et al.* [1975]. "A Versatile System for Computer Controlled Assembly." *Artificial Intell.,* vol. 6, no. 2, pp. 129–156.

Anderson, G.L., and Netravaly, A.N. [1976]. "Image Restoration Based on a Subjective Criterion." *IEEE Trans. Syst. Man. Cyb.,* vol. SMC-6, no. 12, pp. 845–853.

Andrews, H.C. [1970]. *Computer Techniques in Image Processing,* Academic Press, New York.

Andrews, H.C., Tescher, A.G., and Kruger, R.P. [1972]. "Image Processing by Digital Computer." *IEEE Spectrum,* vol. 9, no. 7, pp. 20–32.

Andrews, H.C. [1974]. "Digital Image Restoration: A Survey." *Computer J.,* vol. 7, no. 5, pp. 36–45.

Andrews, H.C. and Hunt B.R. [1977]. *Digital Image Restoration,* Prentice-Hall, Englewood Cliffs, N.J.

Anuta, P.F. [1969]. "Digital Registration of Multispectral Video Imagery." *Soc. Photo-Optical Instrum. Engs.,* vol. 7, pp. 168–175.

Bajcsy, R. [1973]. "Computer Description of Textured Surfaces." *Proc. 1973 Int. Conf. Artificial Intell.,* Stanford, Calif. pp. 572–579.

Bajcsy, R. and Lieberman, L. [1976]. "Texture Gradient as a Depth Cue." *Comput. Graph. Image Proc.,* vol. 5, no. 1, pp. 52–67.

Ballard, D.H. [1981]. "Generalizing the Hough Transform to Detect Arbitrary Shapes." *Pattern Recognition*, vol. 13, no. 2, pp. 111–122.

Ballard, D.H. and Brown, C.M. [1982]. *Computer Vision*, Prentice-Hall, Englewood Cliffs, N.J.

Baumert, L.D., Golomb, S.W., and Hall, M., Jr. [1962]. "Discovery of a Hadamard Matrix of Order 92." *Bull. Am. Math. Soc.*, vol. 68, pp. 237–238.

Bell, E.T. [1965]. *Men of Mathematics*, Simon and Schuster, New York.

Bellman, R. [1970]. *Introduction to Matrix Analysis*, 2nd ed., McGraw-Hill, New York.

Bernstein, R. [1976]. "Digital Image Processing of Earth Observation Sensor Data." *IBM J. Res. Dev.*, vol. 20, no. 1, pp. 40–56.

Biberman, L.M. [1973]. "Image Quality." in *Perception of Displayed Information*, Biberman, L.M. ed., Plenum Press, New York.

Billingsley, F.C., Goetz, A.F.H., and Lindsley, J.N. [1970]. "Color Differentiation by Computer Image Processing." *Photo. Sci. Eng.*, vol. 14, no. 1, pp. 28–35.

Blackman, E.S. [1968]. "Effects of Noise on the Determination of Photographic System Modulation Transfer Function." *Photogr. Sci. Eng.*, vol. 12, pp. 244–250.

Blackman, R.B. and Tukey, J.W. [1958]. *The Measurement of Power Spectra*, Dover Publications, New York.

Blum, H. [1967]. "A Transformation for Extracting New Descriptors of Shape." in *Models for the Perception of Speech and Visual Form*, Wathen-Dunn, W., ed., MIT Press, Cambridge, Mass.

Brice, C.R. and Fennema, C.L. [1970]. "Scene Analysis Using Regions." *Artificial Intelligence*, vol. 1, pp. 205–226.

Bribiesca, E. [1981]. "Arithmetic Operations Among Shapes Using Shape Numbers." *Pattern Recog.*, vol. 13, no. 2, pp. 123–138.

Bribiesca, E. and Guzman, A. [1980]. "How to Describe Pure Form and How to Measure Differences in Shape Using Shape Numbers." *Pattern Recog.*, vol. 12, no. 2, pp. 101–112.

Brigham, E.O. [1974]. *The Fast Fourier Transform*, Prentice-Hall, Englewood Cliffs, N.J.

Brill, E.L. [1968]. "Character Recognition Via Fourier Descriptors." WESCON, Paper 25/3, Los Angeles, Calif.

Brown, J.L., Jr. [1960]. "Mean-Square Truncation Error in Series Expansions of Random Functions." *J. SIAM*, vol. 8, pp. 18–32.

Budak, A. [1974]. *Passive and Active Network Analysis and Synthesis*, Houghton Mifflin, Boston.

Campbell, J.D. [1969]. "Edge Structure and the Representation of Pictures." Ph.D. dissertation, Dept. of Elec. Eng., University of Missouri, Columbia.

Cannon, T.M. [1974]. "Digital Image Deblurring by Non-Linear Homomorphic Filtering." Ph.D. Thesis, University of Utah.

Carlson, A.B. [1968]. *Communication Systems*, McGraw-Hill, New York.

Castleman, K.R. [1979]. *Digital Image Processing*, Prentice-Hall, Englewood Cliffs, N.J.

Chaudhuri, B.B. [1983]. "A Note on Fast Algorithms for Spatial Domain Techniques in Image Processing." *IEEE Trans. Syst. Man Cyb.*, vol. SMC-13, no. 6, pp. 1166–1169.

Chen, P.H. and Wintz, P.A. [1976]. "Data Compression for Satellite Images." TR-EE-76-9, School of Electrical Engineering, Purdue University, West Lafayette, Ind.

Chow, C.K. and Kaneko, T. [1972]. "Automatic Boundary Detection of the Left Ventricle from Cineangiograms." *Comp. and Biomed. Res.*, vol. 5, pp. 388–410.

Clark, R.J. [1985]. *Transform Coding of Images*, Academic Press, New York.

Cochran, W.T., Cooley, J.W., et al. [1967]. "*What is the Fast Fourier Transform?*" *IEEE Trans. Audio and Electroacoustics*, vol. AU-15, no. 2, pp. 45–55.

Cooley, J.W. and Tukey, J.W. [1965]. "An Algorithm for the Machine Calculation of Complex Fourier Series." *Math. of Comput.*, vol. 19, pp. 297–301.

Cooley, J.W., Lewis, P.A.W., and Welch, P.D. [1967a]. "Historical Notes on the Fast Fourier Transform." *IEEE Trans. Audio and Electroacoustics*, vol. AU-15, no. 2, pp. 76–79.

Cooley, J.W., Lewis, P.A.W., and Welch, P.D. [1967b]. "Application of the Fast Fourier Transform to Computation of Fourier Integrals." *IEEE Trans. Audio and Electroacoustics,* vol. AU-15, no. 2, pp. 79–84.

Cooley, J.W., Lewis, P.A.W., and Welch, P.D. [1969]. "The Fast Fourier Transform and its Applications." *IEEE Trans. Educ.,* vol. E-12, no. 1, pp. 27–34.

Cornsweet, T.N. [1970]. *Visual Perception,* Academic Press, New York.

Cowart, A.E., Snyder, W.E., and Ruedger, W.H. [1983]. "The Detection of Unresolved Targets Using the Hough Transform." *Comput. Vision Graph Image Proc.,* vol. 21, pp. 222–238.

Cross, G.R. and Jain, A.K. [1983]. "Markov Random Field Texture Models." *IEEE Trans. Pattern Anal. Mach. Intell.,* vol. PAMI-5, no. 1, pp. 25–39.

Cutrona, L.J., Leith, E.N., and Palermo, C.J. [1960]. "Optical Data Processing and Filtering Systems." *IRE Trans. Info. Theory,* vol. IT-6, no. 3, pp. 386–400.

Cutrona, L.J. and Hall, W.D. [1968]. "Some Considerations in Post-Facto Blur Removal." In *Evaluation of Motion-Degraded Images,* NASA Publ. SP-193, pp. 139–148.

Danielson, G.C. and Lanczos, C. [1942]. "Some Improvements in Practical Fourier Analysis and Their Application to X-Ray Scattering from Liquids." *J. Franklin Institute,* vol. 233, pp. 365–380 and 435–452.

Davenport, W.B. and Root, W.L. [1958]. *An Introduction to the Theory of Random Signals and Noise,* McGraw-Hill, New York.

Davis, L.S. [1975]. "A Survey of Edge Detection Techniques." *Comput. Graphics Image Proc.,* vol. 4, pp. 248–270.

Davis, L.S. [1982]. "Hierarchical Generalized Hough Transforms and Line-Segment Based Generalized Hough Transforms." *Pattern Recog.,* vol. 15, no. 4, pp. 277–285.

Davis, P.J. [1979]. *Circulant Matrices,* Wiley, New York.

Deutsch, R. [1965]. *Estimation Theory,* Prentice-Hall, Englewood Cliffs, N.J.

Digital Image Processing [1974]. Special issue of *Computer,* vol. 7, no. 5.

Digital Picture Processing [1972]. Special issue of the *Proceedings of the IEEE,* vol. 60, no. 7.

Dijkstra, E. [1959]. "Note on Two Problems in Connection with Graphs." *Numerische Mathematik,* vol. 1, pp. 269–271.

Doyle W. [1962]. "Operations Useful for Similarity-Invariant Pattern Recognition." *J. ACM,* vol. 9, pp. 259–267.

Duan, J.R. and Wintz, P.A. [1974]. "Information Preserving Coding for Multispectral Scanner Data." TR-EE-74-15, School of Electrical Engineering, Purdue University, W. Lafayette, Ind.

Duda, R.O. and Hart, P.E. [1972]. "Use of the Hough Transformation to Detect Lines and Curves in Pictures." *Comm. ACM,* vol. 15, no. 1, pp. 11–15.

Duda, R.O. and Hart, P.E. [1973]. *Pattern Classification and Scene Analysis,* Wiley, New York.

Dudani, S.A. and Luk, A. [1977]. "Locating Straight-Edge Segments on Outdoor Scenes." *Proc. Conf. Pattern Recog. Image Proc.* vol. 2, pp. 367–380.

Dyer, C.R. [1983]. "Gauge Inspection Using Hough Transforms." *IEEE Trans. Pattern Anal. Machine Intell.,* vol. PAMI-5, no. 6, pp. 621–623.

Dyer, C.R. and Rosenfeld, A. [1979]. "Thinning Algorithms for Grayscale Pictures." *IEEE Trans. Pattern Anal. Machine Intell.,* vol. PAMI-1, no. 1, pp. 88–89.

Elias, P. [1952]. "Fourier Treatment of Optical Processes." *J. Opt. Soc. Am.,* vol. 42, no. 2, pp. 127–134.

Elsgolc, L.E. [1962]. *Calculus of Variations,* Addison-Wesley, Reading, Mass.

Essman, J. and Wintz, P.A. [1973]. "The Effects of Channel Errors in DPCM Systems and Comparison with PCM Systems." *IEEE Trans. on Comm.,* vol. 21, no. 8, pp. 867–877.

Evans, R.M. [1959]. *An Introduction to Color,* Wiley, New York.

Falconer, D.G. [1970]. "Image Enhancement and Film Grain Noise." *Opt. Acta,* vol. 17, pp. 693–705.

Falconer, D.G. [1977]. "Target Tracking with the Hough Transform." *Proc. Asilomar Conf. Circ. Syst. Comput.,* vol. 11, pp. 249–252.

Fine, N.J. [1949]. "On the Walsh Functions." *Trans. Am. Math. Soc.,* vol. 65, pp. 373–414.

Fine, N.J. [1950]. "The Generalized Walsh Functions." *Trans. Am. Math. Soc.*, vol. 69, pp. 66–77.

Fischler, M.A. [1980]. "Fast Algorithms for Two Maximal Distance Problems with Applications to Image Analysis." *Pattern Recog.*, vol. 12, pp. 35–40.

Fram, J.R. and Deutsch, E.S. [1975]. "On the Quantitative Evaluation of Edge Detection Schemes and Their Comparison with Human Performance." *IEEE Trans. Computers*, vol. C-24, no. 6, pp. 616–628.

Frendendall, G.L. and Behrend, W.L. [1960]. "Picture Quality—Procedures for Evaluating Subjective Effects of Interference." *Proc. IRE*, vol. 48, pp. 1030–1034.

Freeman, H. [1961]. "On the Encoding of Arbitrary Geometric Configurations." *IEEE Trans. Elec. Computers*, vol. EC-10, pp. 260–268.

Freeman, H. [1974]. "Computer Processing of Line Drawings." *Comput. Surveys*, vol. 6, pp. 57–97.

Freeman, H. and Shapira, R. [1975]. "Determining the Minimum-Area Encasing Rectangle for an Arbitrary Closed Curve." *Comm. ACM*, vol. 18, no. 7, pp. 409–413.

Frei, W. and Chen, C.C. [1977]. "Fast Boundary Detection: A Generalization and a New Algorithm." *IEEE Trans. Computers*, vol. C-26, no. 10, pp. 988–998.

Frieden, B.R. [1972]. "Restoring with Maximum Likelihood and Maximum Entropy." *J. Opt. Soc. Am.*, vol. 62, pp. 511–518.

Frieden, B.R. [1974]. "Image Restoration by Discrete Deconvolution of Minimal Length." *J. Opt. Soc. Am.*, vol. 64, pp. 682–686.

Fu, K.S. [1974]. *Syntactic Methods in Pattern Recognition*, Academic Press, New York.

Fu, K.S. and Rosenfeld A. [1976]. "Pattern Recognition and Image Processing." *IEEE Trans. Computers*, vol. C-25, no. 12, pp. 1336–1346.

Fu, K.S. [1982]. *Syntactic Pattern Recognition and Applications*, Prentice-Hall, Englewood Cliffs, N.J.

Fu, K.S., Gonzalez, R.C., and Lee, C.S.G. [1987]. *Robotics: Control, Sensing, Vision, and Intelligence*, McGraw-Hill, New York.

Fu, K.S. and Mui, J.K. [1981]. "A Survey of Image Segmentation." *Pattern Recog.*, vol. 13, no. 1, pp. 3–16.

Gattis, J. and Wintz. P.A. [1971]. "Automated Techniques for Data Analysis and Transmission." TR-EE-71-37, School of Electrical Engineering, Purdue University, West Lafayette, Ind.

Gaven, J.V., Jr., Tavitian, J., and Harabedian, A. [1970]. "The Informative Value of Sampled Images as a Function of the Number of Gray Levels Used in Encoding the Images." *Phot. Sci. Eng.*, vol. 14, no. 1, pp. 16–20.

Gentleman, W.M. and Sande, G. [1966]. "Fast Fourier Transform for Fun and Profit." *Fall Joint Computer Conf.*, vol. 29, pp. 563–578, Spartan, Washington, D.C.

Gentleman, W.M. [1968]. "Matrix Multiplication and Fast Fourier Transformations." *Bell System Tech. J.*, vol. 47, pp. 1099–1103.

Gish, H. and Pierce, J.N. [1968]. "Asymptotically Efficient Quantizer." *IEEE Trans. Info. Theory*, vol. IT-14, pp. 676–683.

Goldmark, P.C. and Hollywood, J.M. [1951]. "A New Technique for Improving the Sharpness of Television Pictures," *Proc. IRE*, vol. 39, pp. 1314–1322.

Golomb, S.W. and Baumert, L.D. [1963]. "The Search for Hadamard Matrices." *Am. Math. Monthly*, vol. 70, pp. 27–31.

Gonzalez, R.C. [1972]. "Syntactic Pattern Recognition—Introduction and Survey." *Proc. Natl. Elec. Conf.*, vol. 27, pp. 27–31.

Gonzalez, R.C. [1985]. "Computer Vision." *Yearbook of Science and Technology*, McGraw-Hill, New York, pp. 128–132.

Gonzalez, R.C. [1985]. "Industrial Computer Vision." In *Advances in Information Systems Science*, Tou, J.T., ed., Plenum, New York, pp. 345–385.

Gonzalez, R.C. [1986]. "Image Enhancement and Restoration." In *Handbook of Pattern Recogni-*

tion and Image Processing, Young, T.Y. and Fu, K.S., eds., Academic Press, New York, pp. 191–213.

Gonzalez, R.C. and Fittes, B.A. [1975]. "Gray-Level Transformations for Interactive Image Enhancement." *Proc. Second Conf. Remotely Manned Syst.,* pp. 17–19.

Gonzalez, R.C., Edwards, J.J., and Thomason, M.G. [1976]. "An Algorithm for the Inference of Tree Grammars." *Int. J. Comput. Info. Sci.,* vol. 5, no. 2, pp. 145–163.

Gonzalez, R.C. and Fittes, B.A. [1977]. "Gray-Level Transformations for Interactive Image Enhancement." *Mechanism and Machine Theory,* vol. 12, pp. 111–122.

Gonzalez, R.C. and Thomason, M.G. [1978]. *Syntactic Pattern Recognition: An Introduction.* Addison-Wesley, Reading, Mass.

Gonzalez, R.C., Barrero, A., and Thomason, M.G. [1978]. "A Measure of Scene Content." *Proc. Pattern Recog. Image Proc. Conf.,* vol. 1, pp. 385–389.

Gonzalez, R.C. and Safabakhsh, R. [1982]. "Computer Vision Techniques for Industrial Applications." *Computer,* vol. 15, no. 12, pp. 17–32.

Gonzalez, R.C., Woods, R.E., and Swain, W.T. [1986]. "Digital Image Processing: An Introduction." *Digital Design,* vol. 16, no. 4, pp. 15–20.

Good, I.J. [1958]. "The Interaction Algorithm and Practical Fourier Analysis." *J. R. Stat. Soc. (Lond.),* vol. B20, pp. 361–367; *Addendum,* vol. 22, 1960, pp. 372–375.

Goodman, J.W. [1968]. *Introduction to Fourier Optics,* McGraw-Hill, New York.

Graham, C.H., ed. [1965]. *Vision and Visual Perception,* Wiley, New York.

Graham, D.N. [1967]. "Image Transmission by Two-Dimensional Contour Coding." *Proc. IEEE,* vol. 55, pp. 336–346.

Graham, R.L. and Yao, F.F. [1983]. "Finding the Convex Hull of a Simple Polygon." *J. Algorithms,* vol. 4, pp. 324–331.

Green, W.B. [1983]. *Digital Image Processing—A Systems Approach,* Van Nostrand Reinhold, New York.

Grosky, W.I. and Jain, R. [1983]. "Optimal Quadtrees for Image Segments." *IEEE Trans. Pattern Anal. Machine Intell.,* vol. PAMI-5, no. 1, pp. 77–83.

Habibi, A. [1971]. "Comparison of *N*th Order DPCM Encoder with Linear Transformations and Block Quantization Techniques." *IEEE Trans. Commun. Tech.,* vol. COM-19, no. 6.

Habibi, A. [1972]. "Two-Dimensional Bayesian Estimate of Images." *Proc. IEEE,* vol. 60, pp. 878–883.

Habibi, A. and Wintz, P.A. [1971]. "Image Coding by Linear Transformations and Block Quantization." *IEEE Trans. Comm. Tech.,* vol. COM-19, pp. 50–62.

Habibi, A. and Wintz. P.A. [1974]. "Hybrid Coding of Pictorial Data." *IEEE Trans. Comm. Tech.,* vol. COM-22, no. 5, pp. 614–624.

Hadamard, J. [1893]. "Resolution d'une Question Relative aux Determinants." *Bull. Sci. Math.,* Ser. 2, vol. 17, Part I, pp. 240–246.

Hall, E.L. [1972]. "Automated Computer Diagnosis Applied to Lung Cancer." *Proc. 1972 Int. Conf. on Cybernetics Soc.,* New Orleans, La.

Hall, E.L. [1974]. "Almost Uniform Distributions for Computer Image Enhancement." *IEEE Trans. Computers,* vol. C-23, no. 2, pp. 207–208.

Hall, E.L. [1979]. *Computer Image Processing and Recognition,* Academic Press, New York.

Hall, E.L. *et al.* [1971]. "A Survey of Preprocessing and Feature Extraction Techniques for Radiographic Images." *IEEE Trans. Comput.,* vol. C-20, no. 9, pp. 1032–1044.

Hall, E.L. and Frei, W. [1976]. "Invariant Features for Quantitative Scene Analysis." Final Report, Contract F 08606-72-C-0008, Image Processing Institute, University of Southern California.

Hammond, J.L. and Johnson, R.S. [1962]. "Orthogonal Square-Wave Functions." *J. Franklin Inst.,* vol. 273, pp. 211–225.

Harmuth, H.F. [1968]. "A Generalized Concept of Frequency and Some Applications." *IEEE Trans. Info. Theory,* vol. IT-14, no. 3, pp. 375–382.

Haralick, R.M. [1979]. "Statistical and Structural Approaches to Texture." *Proc. 4th Int. Joint Conf. Pattern Recog.*, pp. 45–60.

Haralick, R.M., Shanmugan, R., and Dinstein, I. [1973]. "Textural Features for Image Classification." *IEEE Trans Syst. Man Cyb.*, vol. SMC-3, no. 6, pp. 610–621.

Harris, J.L. [1964]. "Resolving Power and Decision Theory." *J. Opt. Soc. Am.*, vol. 54, pp. 606–611.

Harris, J.L. [1966]. "Image Evaluation and Restoration." *J. Opt. Soc. Am.*, vol. 56, pp. 569–574.

Harris, J.L. [1968]. "Potential and Limitations of Techniques for Processing Linear Motion-Degraded Images." In *Eval. Motion Degraded Images*, NASA Publ. SP-193, pp. 131–138.

Hart, P.E., Nilsson, N.J., and Raphael, B. [1968]. "A Formal Basis for the Heuristic Determination of Minimum-Cost Paths." *IEEE Trans. Syst. Man Cyb*, vol. SMC-4, pp. 100–107.

Hecht, E. and Zajac, A. [1975]. *Optics*, Addison-Wesley, Reading, Mass.

Helstrom, C.W. [1967]. "Image Restoration by the Method of Least Squares." *J. Opt. Soc. Am.*, vol. 57, no. 3, pp. 297–303.

Henderson, K.W. [1964]. "Some Notes on the Walsh Functions." *IEEE Trans. Electronic Computers*, vol. EC-13, no. 1, pp. 50–52.

Horn, B.K.P. [1986]. *Robot Vision*, McGraw-Hill, New York.

Horner, J.L. [1969]. "Optical Spatial Filtering with the Least-Mean-Square-Error Filter." *J. Opt. Soc. Am.*, vol. 59, pp. 553–558.

Horowitz, M. [1957]. "Efficient Use of a Picture Correlator." *J. Opt. Soc. Am.*, vol. 47, p. 327.

Horowitz, S.L. and Pavlidis, T. [1974]. "Picture Segmentation by a Directed Split-and-Merge Procedure." *Proc. 2nd Int. Joint Conf. Pattern Recog.*, pp. 424–433.

Hotelling, H. [1933]. "Analysis of a Complex of Statistical Variables into Principal Components." *J. Educ. Psychol.*, vol. 24, pp. 417–441 and 498–520.

Hough, P.V.C. [1962]. "Methods and Means for Recognizing Complex Patterns." U.S. Patent 3,069,654.

Hu, M.K. [1962]. "Visual Pattern Recognition by Moment Invariants." *IRE Trans. Info. Theory*, vol. IT-8, pp. 179–187.

Huang, T.S. [1965]. "PCM Picture Transmission." *IEEE Spectrum*, vol. 2, no. 12, pp. 57–63.

Huang, T.S. [1966]. "Digital Picture Coding." *Proc. Natl. Electron. Conf.*, pp. 793–797.

Huang, T.S. [1968]. "Digital Computer Analysis of Linear Shift-Variant Systems." in *Evaluation of Motion-Degraded Images*, NASA Publ. SP-193, pp. 83–87.

Huang, T.S., ed. [1975]. *Picture Processing and Digital Filtering*, Springer, New York.

Huang, T.S., Yang, G.T., and Tang, G. Y. [1979]. "A Fast Two-Dimensional Median Filtering Algorithm." *IEEE Trans. Acoust., Speech, Sig. Proc.*, vol. ASSP-27, pp. 13–18.

Huang, Y. and Schultheiss, P.M. [1963]. "Block Quantization of Correlated Gaussian Random Variables." *IEEE Trans. Commun. Syst.*, vol. CS-11, pp. 289–296.

Huffman, D.A. [1952]. "A Method for the Construction of Minimum Redundancy Codes." *Proc. IRE*, vol. 40, no. 10, pp. 1098–1101.

Hummel, R.A. [1974]. "Histogram Modification Techniques." Technical Report TR-329, F-44620-72C-0062, Computer Science Center, University of Maryland, College Park, Md.

Hunt, B.R. [1971]. "A Matrix Theory Proof of the Discrete Convolution Theorem." *IEEE Trans. Audio and Electroacoust.*, vol. AU-19, no. 4, pp. 285–288.

Hunt, B.R. [1973]. "The Application of Constrained Least Squares Estimation to Image Restoration by Digital Computer." *IEEE Trans. Comput., vol. C-22, no. 9, pp. 805–812.*

IEEE Trans. Circuits and Syst. [1975]. Special issue on digital filtering and image processing, vol. CAS-2, pp. 161–304.

IEEE Trans. Computers [1972]. Special issue on two-dimensional signal processing, vol. C-21, no. 7.

IEEE Trans. Commun. [1981]. Special issue on picture communication systems, vol. COM-29, no. 12.

IES Lighting Handbook [1972]. Illuminating Engineering Society Press, New York.

Jain, A.K. [1975]. "A Fast Karhunen-Loève Transform for a Class of Random Processes." *IEEE Trans. Commun.*, vol. COM-24, pp. 1023–1029.

Jain, A.K. [1981]. "Image Data Compression: A Review." *Proc. IEEE*, vol. 69, pp. 349–389.

Jain, A.K. and Angel, E. [1974]. "Image Restoration, Modeling, and Reduction of Dimensionality." *IEEE Trans. Computers*, vol. C-23, pp. 470–476.

Jain, R. [1981]. "Dynamic Scene Analysis Using Pixel-Based Processes." *Computer*, vol. 14, no. 8, pp. 12–18.

Jain, R. [1983]. "Segmentation of Frame Sequences Obtained by a Moving Observer." Report GMR-4247, General Motors Research Laboratories, Warren, Mich.

Kahaner, D.K. [1970]. "Matrix Description of the Fast Fourier Transform." *IEEE Trans. Audio Electroacoustics*, vol. AU-18, no. 4, pp. 442–450.

Karhunen, K. [1947]. "Über Lineare Methoden in der Wahrscheinlichkeitsrechnung." *Ann. Acad. Sci. Fennicae*, Ser. A137. (Translated by I. Selin in "On Linear Methods in Probability Theory." T-131, 1960, The RAND Corp., Santa Monica, Calif.)

Ketcham, D.J. [1976]. "Real-Time Image Enhancement Techniques." *Proc. Soc. Photo-Optical Instrum. Eng.* vol. 74, pp. 120–125.

Kimme, C., Ballard, D.H., and Sklansky, J. [1975]. "Finding Circles by an Array of Accumulators." *Comm. ACM*, vol. 18, no. 2, pp. 120–122.

Kirsch, R. [1971]. "Computer Determination of the Constituent Structure of Biological Images." *Comput. Biomed. Res.*, vol. 4, pp. 315–328.

Kiver, M.S. [1955]. *Color Television Fundamentals*, McGraw-Hill, New York.

Klinger, A. [1972]. "Patterns and Search Statistics." In *Optimizing Methods in Statistics*, Rustagi, J.S., ed., Academic Press, New York, pp. 303–339.

Klinger, A. [1976]. "Experiments in Picture Representation Using Regular Decomposition." *Comput. Graphics Image Proc.*, vol. 5, pp. 68–105.

Kodak Plates and Films for Scientific Photography [1973]. Publication no. P-315, Eastman Kodak Co., Rochester, N.Y.

Kohler, R.J. and Howell, H.K. [1963]. "Photographic Image Enhancement by Superposition of Multiple Images." *Photogr. Sci. Eng.*, vol. 7, no. 4, pp. 241–245.

Koschman, A. [1954]. "On the Filtering of Nonstationary Time Series." *Proc. 1954 Natl. Electron. Conf.*, p. 126.

Kramer, H.P. and Mathews, M.V. [1956]. "A Linear Coding for Transmitting a Set of Correlated Variables." *IRE Trans. Info. Theory*, vol. IT-2, pp. 41–46.

Kovasznay, L.S.G. and Joseph, H.M. [1953]. "Processing of Two-Dimensional Patterns by Scanning Techniques." *Science*, vol. 118, pp. 475–477.

Kovasznay, L.S.G. and Joseph, H.M. [1955]. "Image Processing." *Proc. IRE*, vol. 43, pp. 560–570.

Kushnir, M., Abe, K., and Matsumoto, K. [1985]. "Recognition of Handprinted Hebrew Characters Using Features Selected in the Hough Transform Space." *Pattern Recog.*, vol. 18, no. 2, pp. 103–114.

Lawley, D.N. and Maxwell, A.E. [1963]. *Factor Analysis as a Statistical Method*, Butterworth, London.

Ledley, R.S. [1964]. "High-Speed Automatic Analysis of Biomedical Pictures." *Science*, vol 146, no. 3461, pp. 216–223.

Ledley, R.S., *et al.* [1965]. "FIDAC: Film Input to Digital Automatic Computer and Associated Syntax-Directed Pattern Recognition Programming System." In *Optical and Electro-Optical Information Processing Systems*, Tippet, J., Beckowitz, D., Clapp, L., Koester, C., and Vanderburgh, A., Jr., eds., MIT Press, Cambridge, Mass., Chapter 33.

Lee, C.C. [1983]. "Elimination of Redundant Operations for a Fast Sobel Operator." *IEEE Trans. Syst. Man Cybern.*, vol. SMC-13, no. 3, pp. 242–245.

Legault, R.R. [1973]. "The Aliasing Problems in Two-Dimensional Sampled Imagery." In *Perception of Displayed Information*, Biberman, L.M., ed., Plenum Press, New York.

Lipkin, B.S. and Rosenfeld, A., eds. [1970]. *Picture Processing and Psychopictorics*, Academic Press, New York.

Loève, M. [1948]. "Fonctions Aléatoires de Second Ordre." in P. Lévy, *Processus Stochastiques et Mouvement Brownien*, Hermann, Paris, France.

Lohman, A.W. and Paris, D.P. [1965]. "Space-Variant Image Formation." *J. Opt. Soc. Am.*, vol. 55, pp. 1007–1013.

Lu, H.E. and Wang, P.S.P. [1986]. "A Comment on 'A Fast Parallel Algorithm for Thinning Digital Patterns.'" *Comm. ACM*, vol. 29, no. 3, pp. 239–242.

Lu, S.Y. and Fu, K.S. [1978]. "A Syntactic Approach to Texture Analysis." *Comput. Graph. Image Proc.*, vol. 7, no. 3, pp. 303–330.

MacAdam, D.P. [1970]. "Digital Image Restoration by Constrained Deconvolution." *J. Opt. Soc. Am.*, vol. 60, pp. 1617–1627.

Mark, D.M. and Abel, D.J. [1985]. "Linear Quadtrees from Vector Representations of Polygons." *IEEE Trans. Pattern Anal. Machine Intell.*, vol. PAMI-7, no. 3, pp. 344–349.

Marr, D. [1982]. *Vision*, Freeman, San Francisco, Calif.

Martelli, A. [1972]. "Edge Detection Using Heuristic Search Methods." *Comput. Graphics Image Proc.*, vol. 1, pp. 169–182.

Martelli, A. [1976]. "An Application of Heuristic Search Methods to Edge and Contour Detection." *Comm. ACM*, vol. 19, no. 2, pp. 73–83.

Max, J. [1960]. "Quantizing for Minimum Distortion." *IRE Trans. Info. Theory*, vol. IT-6, pp. 7–12.

McFarlane, M.D. [1972]. "Digital Pictures Fifty Years Ago." *Proc. IEEE*, vol. 60, no. 7, pp. 768–770.

McGlamery, B.L. [1967]. "Restoration of Turbulence-Degraded Images." *J. Opt. Soc. Am.*, vol. 57, no. 3, pp. 293–297.

Mees, C.E.K. and James, T.H. [1966]. *The Theory of the Photographic Process*, Macmillan, New York.

Merlin, P.M. and Farber, D.J. [1975]. "A Parallel Mechanism for Detecting Curves in Pictures." *IEEE Trans. Comput.*, vol. C-24, no. 1, pp. 96–98.

Meyer, E.R. and Gonzalez, R.C. [1983]. "Spatial Techniques for Digital Image Enhancement and Restoration." *Proc. First South Afr. Symp. Digital Image Proc.*, Univ. of Natal, Durban, South Africa, pp. 137–182.

Meyer, H., Rosdolsky, H.G., and Huang, T.S. [1973]. "Optimum Run Length Codes." *IEEE Trans. Comm.*, vol. COM-22, no. 6, pp. 826–835.

Moon, P. [1961]. *The Scientific Basis of Illuminating Engineering*, Dover, New York.

Mueller, P.F. and Reynolds, G.O. [1967]. "Image Restoration by Removal of Random Media Degradations." *J. Opt. Soc. Am.*, vol. 57, pp. 1338–1344.

Muerle, J.L. and Allen, D.C. [1968]. "Experimental Evaluation of Techniques for Automatic Segmentation of Objects in a Complex Scene." In *Pictorial Pattern Recognition*, (G.C. Cheng et al., eds.), Thompson Book Co., Washington, D.C.

Nahim, P.J. [1974]. "The Theory of Measurement of a Silhouette Description for Image Processing and Recognition." *Pattern Recog.*, vol. 6, no. 2, pp. 85–95.

Narasimhan, R. and Fornango, J.P. [1963]. "Some Further Experiments in the Parallel Processing of Pictures." *IEEE Trans. Elec. Computers*, vol. EC-12, pp. 748–750.

Narendra, P.M. and Fitch, R.C. [1981]. "Real-Time Adaptive Contrast Enhancement." *IEEE Trans. Pattern Anal. Mach. Intell.*, vol. PAMI-3, no. 6, pp. 655–661.

Nelson, C.N. [1971]. "Prediction of Densities in Fine Detail in Photographic Images." *Photogr. Sci. Eng.*, vol. 15, pp. 82–97.

Netravali, A.N. and Limb, J.O. [1980]. "Picture Coding: A Review." *Proc. IEEE*, vol. 68, no. 7, pp. 366–406.

Nilsson, N.J. [1971]. *Problem Solving Methods in Artificial Intelligence*, McGraw-Hill, New York.

Nilsson, N.J. [1980]. *Principles of Artificial Intelligence*, Tioga Pub., Palo Alto, Calif.

Noble, B. [1969]. *Applied Linear Algebra*, Prentice-Hall, Englewood Cliffs, N.J.

O'Gorman, F. and Clowes, M.B. [1976]. "Finding Picture Edges Through Collinearity of Feature Points." *IEEE Trans. Comput.*, vol. C-25, no. 4, pp. 449–454.

O'Handley, D.A. and Green, W.B. [1972]. "Recent Developments in Digital Image Processing at the Image Processing Laboratory of the Jet Propulsion Laboratory." *Proc. IEEE*, vol. 60, no. 7, pp. 821–828.

Ohlander, R.B. [1975]. "Analysis of Natural Scenes." Ph.D. dissertation, Dept. of Computer Science, Carnegie-Mellon Univ., Pittsburgh, Penn.

O'Neill, E.L. [1956]. "Spatial Filtering in Optics." *IRE Trans. Info. Theory*, vol. IT-2, no. 2, pp. 56–65.

Oppenheim, A.V., Schafer, R.W., and Stockham, T.G., Jr. [1968]. "Nonlinear Filtering of Multiplied and Convolved Signals." *Proc. IEEE*, vol. 56, no. 8, pp. 1264–1291.

Oppenheim, A.V. and Schafer, R.W. [1975]. *Digital Signal Processing*, Prentice-Hall, Englewood Cliffs, N.J.

Panter, P.F. and Dite, W. [1951]. "Quantization Distortion in Pulse Code Modulation with Nonuniform Spacing of Levels." *Proc. IRE*, vol. 39, pp. 44–48.

Papoulis, A. [1962]. *The Fourier Integral and Its Applications*, McGraw-Hill, New York.

Papoulis, A. [1965]. *Probability, Random Variables, and Stochastic Processes*, McGraw-Hill, New York.

Papoulis, A. [1968]. *Systems and Transforms with Applications in Optics*, McGraw-Hill, New York.

Pattern Recognition [1970]. Special issue on pattern recognition in photogrammetry, vol. 2, no. 4.

Pavlidis, T. [1972]. "Segmentation of Pictures and Maps Through Functional Approximation." *Comp. Graph. Image Proc.*, vol. 1, pp. 360–372.

Pavlidis, T. [1977]. *Structural Pattern Recognition*, Springer-Verlag, New York.

Pearson, D.E. [1975]. *Transmission and Display of Pictorial Information*, Wiley (Halsted Press), New York.

Perrin, F.H. [1960]. "Methods of Appraising Photographic Systems." *J. SMPTE*, vol. 49, pp. 151–156 and 239–249.

Persoon, E. and Fu, K.S. [1977]. "Shape Discrimination Using Fourier Descriptors." *IEEE Trans. Systems Man Cyb.*, vol. SMC-7, no. 2, pp. 170–179.

Phillips, D.L. [1962]. "A Technique for the Numerical Solution of Certain Integral Equations of the First Kind." *J. Assoc. Comp. Mach.*, vol. 9, pp. 84–97.

Pratt, W.K. [1971]. "Spatial Transform Coding of Color Images." *IEEE Trans. Comm. Tech.*, vol. COM-19, no. 6, pp. 980–991.

Pratt, W.K. [1974]. "Correlation Techniques of Image Registration." *IEEE Trans. Aerospace and Elec. Syst.*, vol. AES-10, no. 3, pp. 353–358.

Pratt, W.K. [1978]. *Digital Image Processing*, Wiley, New York.

Prewitt, J.M.S. [1970]. "Object Enhancement and Extraction." in *Picture Processing and Psychopictorics*, Lipkin, B.S. and Rosenfeld, A., eds., Academic Press, New York.

Price, K.E. [1976]. "Change Detection and Analysis in Multispectral Images." Dept. of Computer Science, Carnegie-Mellon Univ., Pittsburgh, Penn.

Proc. IEEE [1967]. Special issue on redundancy reduction, vol. 55, no. 3.

Proc. IEEE [1972]. Special issue on digital picture processing, vol. 60, no. 7.

Proc. IEEE [1980]. Special issue on the encoding of graphics, vol. 68, no. 7.

Proc. IEEE [1985]. Special issue on visual communication systems, vol. 73, no. 2.

Proctor, C.W. and Wintz, P.A. [1971]. "Picture Bandwidth Reduction for Noisy Channels." TR-EE 71-30, School of Electrical Engineering, Purdue University, West Lafayette, Ind.

Rajala, S.A., Riddle, A.N., and Snyder, W.E. [1983]. "Application of the One-Dimensional Fourier Transform for Tracking Moving Objects in Noisy Environments." *Comput. Vis. Graph. Image Proc.*, vol. 21, pp. 280–293.

Ramer, U. [1975]. "Extraction of Line Structures from Photographs of Curved Objects." *Comput. Graphics Image Proc.*, vol. 4, pp. 81–103.

Ready, P.J. and Wintz, P.A. [1973]. "Information Extraction, SNR Improvement, and Data Compression in Multispectral Imagery." *IEEE Trans. Comm.*, vol. COM-21, no. 10, pp. 1123–1131.

Rino, C.L. [1969]. "Bandlimited Image Restoration by Linear Mean-Square Estimation." *J. Opt. Soc. Am.*, vol. 59, pp. 547–553.

Riseman, E.A. and Arbib, M.A. [1977]. "Computational Techniques in Visual Systems. Part II: Segmenting Static Scenes." IEEE Computer Society Repository, R77–87.

Robbins, G.M. and Huang, T.S. [1972]. "Inverse Filtering for Linear Shift-Variant Imaging Systems." *Proc. IEEE*, vol. 60, pp. 862–872.

Roberts, L.G. [1965]. "Machine Perception of Three-Dimensional Solids." In *Optical and Electro-Optical Information Processing*, Tippet, J.T., ed., MIT Press, Cambridge, Mass.

Robinson, G.S. [1976]. "Detection and Coding of Edges Using Directional Masks." University of Southern Cal., Image Processing Institute, Report no. 660.

Rosenfeld, A. [1969]. *Picture Processing by Computer*, Academic Press, New York.

Rosenfeld, A. [1972]. "Picture Processing." *Comput. Graph. Image Proc.*, vol. 1, pp. 394–416.

Rosenfeld, A. [1973]. "Progress in Picture Processing: 1969–71," *Comput. Surv.*, vol. 5, pp. 81–108.

Rosenfeld, A. [1974]. "Picture Processing: 1973," *Comput. Graph. Image Proc.*, vol. 3, pp. 178–194.

Rosenfeld, A. *et al.* [1965]. "Automatic Cloud Interpretation," *Photogrammetr. Eng.*, vol. 31, pp. 991–1002.

Rosenfeld, A. and Kak, A.C. [1982]. *Digital Picture Processing*, 2nd ed., Academic Press, New York.

Roth, W. [1968]. "Full Color and Three-Dimensional Effects in Radiographic Displays." *Investigative Radiol.*, vol. 3, pp. 56–60.

Rudnick, P. [1966]. "Note on the Calculation of Fourier Series." *Math. Comput.*, vol. 20, pp. 429–430.

Runge, C. [1903]. *Zeit. für Math. and Physik*, vol. 48, p. 433.

Runge, C. [1905]. *Zeit. für Math. and Physik*, vol. 53, p. 117.

Runge, C. and König, H. [1924]. "Die Grundlehren der Mathematischen Wissenschaften." *Vorlesungen über Numerisches Rechnen*, vol. 11, Julius Springer, Berlin, Germany.

Rushforth, C.K. and Harris, R.W. [1968]. "Restoration, Resolution, and Noise." *J. Opt. Soc. Am.*, vol. 58, pp. 539–545.

Sakrison, D.J. and Algazi, V.R. [1971]. "Comparison of Line-by-Line and Two-Dimensional Encoding of Random Images." *IEEE Trans. Info. Theory*, vol. IT-17, no. 4, pp. 386–398.

Salari, E. and Siy, P. [1984]. "The Ridge-Seeking Method for Obtaining the Skeleton of Digital Images." *IEEE Trans. Syst. Man Cyb.*, vol. SMC-14, no. 3, pp. 524–528.

Sawchuk, A.A. [1972]. "Space-Variant Image Motion Degradation and Restoration." *Proc. IEEE*, vol. 60, pp. 854–861.

Schreiber, W.F. [1956]. "The Measurement of Third Order Probability Distributions of Television Signals." *IRE Trans. Info. Theory*, vol. IT-2, pp. 94–105.

Schreiber, W.F. [1967]. "Picture Coding." *Proc. IEEE*, (Special issue on Redundancy Reduction), vol. 55, pp. 320–330.

Schutten, R.W. and Vermeij, G.F. [1980]. "The Approximation of Image Blur Restoration Filters by Finite Impulse Responses." *IEEE Trans. Pattern Anal. Mach. Intell.*, vol. PAMI-2, no. 2, pp. 176–180.

Schwartz, J.W. and Barker, R.C. [1966]. "Bit-Plane Encoding: A Technique for Source Encoding." *IEEE Trans. Aerosp. Elec. Systems*, vol. AES-2, no. 4, pp. 385–392.

Schwarz, R.E. and Friedland, B. [1965]. *Linear Systems*, McGraw-Hill, New York.

Scoville, F.W. [1965]. "The Subjective Effect of Brightness and Spatial Quantization." *Q. Rep.*, no. 78, MIT Research Laboratory of Electronics.

Seidman, J. [1972]. "Some Practical Applications of Digital Filtering in Image Processing." *Proc. Conf. Comput. Image Proc. Recog.*, University of Missouri, Columbia, vol. 2, pp. 9–1–1 through 9–1–16.

Selin, I. [1965]. *Detection Theory*, Princeton University Press, Princeton, N.J.

Shack, R.V. [1964]. "The Influence of Image Motion and Shutter Operation on the Photographic Transfer Function." *Appl. Opt.*, vol. 3, pp. 1171–1181.

Shamos, M.I. [1978]. "Computational Geometry." Ph.D. Thesis, Yale University, New Haven, Conn.

Shanks, J.L. [1969]. "Computation of the Fast Walsh-Fourier Transform." *IEEE Trans. Comput.*, vol. C-18, no. 5, pp. 457–459.

Shaw, A.C. [1970]. "Parsing of Graph-Representable Pictures." *J. ACM*, vol. 17, no. 3, pp. 453–481.

Sheppard, J.J., Jr. [1968]. *Human Color Perception*, Elsevier, New York.

Sheppard, J.J., Jr., Stratton, R.H., and Gazley, C., Jr. [1969]. "Pseudocolor as a Means of Image Enhancement." *Am. J. Optom. Arch. Am. Acad. Optom.*, vol. 46, pp. 735–754.

Sklansky, J., Chazin, R.L., and Hansen, B.J. [1972]. "Minimum-Perimeter Polygons of Digitized Silhouettes." *IEEE Trans. Comput.*, vol. C-21, no. 3, pp. 260–268.

Slepian, D. [1967a]. "Linear Least-Squares Filtering of Distorted Images." *J. Opt. Soc. Am.*, vol. 57, pp. 918–922.

Slepian, D. [1967b]. "Restoration of Photographs Blurred by Image Motion." *BSTJ*, vol. 46, pp. 2353–2362.

Slepian, D. and Pollak, H.O. [1961]. "Prolate Spheroidal Wave Functions, Fourier Analysis, and Uncertainty–I." *Bell Sys. Tech. J.*, vol. 40, pp. 43–64.

Smith, S.L. [1963]. "Color Coding and Visual Separability in Information Displays." *J. Appl. Psychol.*, vol. 47, pp. 358–364.

Snider, H.L. [1973]. "Image Quality and Observer Performance." In *Perception of Displayed Information*, Biberman, L.M., ed., Plenum Press, New York.

Som, S.C. [1971]. "Analysis of the Effect of Linear Smear." *J. Opt. Soc. Am.*, vol. 61, pp. 859–864.

Sondhi, M.M. [1972]. "Image Restoration: The Removal of Spatially Invariant Degradations." *Proc. IEEE*, vol. 60, no. 7, pp. 842–853.

Stevens, S.S. [1951]. *Handbook of Experimental Psychology*, Wiley, New York.

Stockham, T.G., Jr. [1972]. "Image Processing in the Context of a Visual Model." *Proc. IEEE*, vol. 60, no. 7, pp. 828–842.

Stumpff, K. [1939]. *Tafeln und Aufgaben zur Harmonischen Analyse und Periodogrammrechnung*, Julius Springer, Berlin, Germany.

Sze, T.W. and Yang, Y.H. [1981]. "A Simple Contour Matching Algorithm." *IEEE Trans. Pattern Anal. Mach. Intell.*, vol. PAMI-3, no. 6, pp. 676–678.

Tasto, M. and Wintz, P.A. [1971]. "Image Coding by Adaptive Block Quantization." *IEEE Trans. Comm. Tech.*, vol. COM-19, pp. 957–972.

Tasto, M. and Wintz, P.A. [1972]. "A Bound on the Rate-Distortion Function and Application to Images." *IEEE Trans. Info. Theory*, vol. IT-18, pp. 150–159.

Thomas, J.B. [1969]. *Statistical Communication Theory*, Wiley, New York.

Thomas, L.H. [1963]. "Using a Computer to Solve Problems in Physics." *Application of Digital Computers*, Ginn, Boston, Mass.

Thomason, M.G. and Gonzalez, R.C. [1975]. "Syntactic Recognition of Imperfectly Specified Patterns." *IEEE Trans. Comput.*, vol. C-24, no. 1, pp. 93–96.

Thompson, W.B. and Barnard, S.T. [1981]. "Lower-Level Estimation and Interpretation of Visual Motion." *Computer*, vol. 14, no. 8, pp. 20–28.

Titchmarsh, E.C. [1948]. *Introduction to the Theory of Fourier Integrals*, Oxford Univ. Press, New York.

Tomita, F., Shirai, Y., and Tsuji, S. [1982]. "Description of Texture by a Structural Analysis." *IEEE Trans. Pattern Anal. Mach. Intell.*, vol. PAMI-4, no. 2, pp. 183–191.

Toriwaki, J.I., Kato, N., and Fukumura, T. [1979]. "Parallel Local Operations for a New Distance Transformation of a Line Pattern and Their Applications." *IEEE Trans. System, Man, Cyb.*, vol. SMC-9, no. 10, pp. 628–643.

Tou, J.T. and Gonzalez, R.C. [1974]. *Pattern Recognition Principles*, Addison-Wesley, Reading, Mass.

Toussaint, G.T. [1982]. "Computational Geometric Problems in Pattern Recognition." In *Pattern Recognition Theory and Applications*, Kittler, J., Fu, K.S., and Pau, L.F., eds., Reidel, New York, pp. 73–91.

Twomey, S. [1963]. "On the Numerical Solution of Fredholm Integral Equations of the First Kind by the Inversion of the Linear System Produced by Quadrature." *J. Assoc. Comput. Mach.*, vol. 10, pp. 97–101.

VanderBrug, G.J. and Rosenfeld, A. [1977]. "Two-Stage Template Matchings." *IEEE Trans. Comput.*, vol. C-26, no. 4, pp. 384–394.

Van Valkenburg, M.E. [1955]. *Network Analysis*, Prentice-Hall, Englewood Cliffs, N.J.

Walsh, J.W.T. [1958]. *Photometry*, Dover, New York.

Walsh, J.L. [1923]. "A Closed Set of Normal Orthogonal Functions." *Am. J. Math.*, vol. 45, no. 1, pp. 5–24.

Webb, J.A. and Aggarwal, J.K. [1981]. "Visually Interpreting the Motion of Objects in Space." *Computer*, vol. 14, no. 8, pp. 40–49.

Wechsler, W. and Sklansky, J. [1977]. "Automatic Detection of Ribs in Chest Radiographs." *Pattern Recog.*, vol. 9, no. 1, pp. 21–28.

Weinberg, L. [1962]. *Network Analysis and Synthesis*, McGraw-Hill, New York.

Weska, J.S. [1978]. "A Survey of Theshold Selection Techniques." *Comput. Graphics Image Proc.*, vol. 7, pp. 259–265.

Whelchel, J.E., Jr. and Guinn, D.F. [1968]. "The Fast Fourier-Hadamard Transform and its Use in Signal Representation and Classification." *Eascon 1968 Convention Record*, pp. 561–573.

White, J.M. and Rohrer, G.D. [1983]. "Image Thresholding for Optical Character Recognition and Other Applications Requiring Character Image Extraction." *IBM J. Res. Devel.*, vol. 27, no. 4, pp. 400–411.

Wilkins, L.C. and Wintz, P.A. [1970]. "Studies on Data Compression, Part I: Picture Coding by Contours, Part II: Error Analysis of Run-Length Codes." TR-EE 70–17, School of Electrical Engineering, Purdue University, Lafayette, Ind.

Williamson, J. [1944]. "Hadamard's Determinant Theorem and the Sum of Four Squares." *Duke Math. J.*, vol. 11, pp. 65–81.

Wintz, P.A. [1972]. "Transform Picture Coding." *Proc. IEEE*, vol. 60, no. 7, pp. 809–820.

Wolfe, G.J. and Mannos, J.L. [1979]. "Fast Median Filter Implementation." *Proc. Soc. Photo-Optical Inst. Eng.*, vol. 207, pp. 154–160.

Wong, R.Y. and Hall, E.L. [1978]. "Scene Matching with Invariant Moments." *Comput. Graph. Image Proc.*, vol. 8, pp. 16–24.

Wood, R.C. [1969]. "On Optimum Quantization." *IEEE Trans. Info. Theory*, vol. IT-15, pp. 248–252.

Woods, R.E. and Gonzalez, R.C. [1981]. "Real-Time Digital Image Enhancement." *Proc. IEEE*, vol. 69, no. 5, pp. 643–654.

Yachida, M. [1983]. "Determining Velocity Maps by Spatio-Temporal Neighborhoods from Image Sequences." *Comput. Vis. Graph. Image Proc.*, vol. 21, no. 2, pp. 262–279.

Yates, F. [1937]. "The Design and Analysis of Factorial Experiments." Commonwealth Agricultural Bureaux, Farnam Royal, Burks, England.

Zahn, C.T. and Roskies, R.Z. [1972]. "Fourier Descriptors for Plane Closed Curves." *IEEE Trans. Comput.*, vol. C-21, no. 3, pp. 269–281.

Zhang, T.Y. and Suen, C.Y. [1984]. "A Fast Parallel Algorithm for Thinning Digital Patterns." *Comm. ACM*, vol. 27, no. 3, pp. 236–239.

Zucker, S.W. [1976]. "Region Growing: Childhood and Adolescence." *Comput. Graphics Image Proc.*, vol. 5, pp. 382–399.

INDEX

ADDISON-WESLEY ▲ THE SIGN
AND COMPUTER ENGINEERING
OF EXCELLENCE IN ELECTRIC
ADDISON-WESLEY ▲ THE SIGN
AND COMPUTER ENGINEERING
OF EXCELLENCE IN ELECTRIC
ADDISON-WESLEY ▲ THE SIGN
AND COMPUTER ENGINEERING
OF EXCELLENCE IN ELECTRIC
ADDISON-WESLEY ▲ THE SIGN
AND COMPUTER ENGINEERING
OF EXCELLENCE IN ELECTRIC

ADDISON-WESLEY ▲ THE SIGN
AND COMPUTER ENGINEERING
OF EXCELLENCE IN ELECTRIC
ADDISON-WESLEY ▲ THE SIGN
AND COMPUTER ENGINEERING
OF EXCELLENCE IN ELECTRIC
ADDISON-WESLEY ▲ THE SIGN
AND COMPUTER ENGINEERING
OF EXCELLENCE IN ELECTRIC
ADDISON-WESLEY ▲ THE SIGN
AND COMPUTER ENGINEERING
OF EXCELLENCE IN ELECTRIC